TEN SHORT NOVELS

TEN SHORT NOVELS

with General Introduction and Prefaces

by THOMAS L. ASHTON

University of Massachusetts, Amherst

D. C. HEATH AND COMPANY

Lexington, Massachusetts   Toronto

CONTENTS

Thomas Mann

Franz Kafka

Saul Bellow

Alexander Solzhenitsyn

Carson McCullers

Yukio Mishima

GENERAL INTRODUCTION: THE SHORT NOVEL

Invitation should be the purpose of a General Introduction—invitation and nothing more. Readers are cordially invited to use and enjoy the ten critical prefaces and short novels that follow this introduction. If you are certain that you wish to do so immediately, these opening remarks are not meant to stand in your way. What follows is no more than an explanation for this particular collection intended to serve as a rationale for its invitation. Both the critical prefaces and the ten excellent short novels made available here can certainly stand on their own. But they also stand together very well, for both the prefaces and their respective novels proceed to a goal. The collection as a whole incorporates a design that intends to make that goal attainable. The invitation extended by this General Introduction is twofold: read the collection, and, if you wish, read about its intentional design to learn about the goal served by the choices guiding both its commentary and its selected novels. Take a look at the book, and take a look at why the book has been shaped as such. For understanding this book is precisely this book's goal. Its design wants you to find satisfaction in your own understanding of ten short novels, satisfaction both in putting your understanding to work and in being pleased with your results. For if you understand this book, it will have served its ultimate purpose of making all our reading more understandable, and so more valuable as well.

READING

Reading about reading has to come before reading about the short novel, just as reading about the short novel comes before reading about ten short novels. But we all know how to read—so why read about it? Our certainty is the result of a change that takes place between high school and college: reading, writing, and arithmetic become literature, freshman composition, and mathematics. Math and composition are only advanced arithmetic and writing, but reading suddenly becomes not a process but that strange thing literature. In effect this change tells us that we can read well enough to understand whatever literature is shoved at us, and more mistakenly that there is no advanced reading because once you know how to read you know how to read whatever it is you are reading. The assumption is that growth in overall understanding is all that is necessary for the understanding of difficult reading, for reading ability itself doesn't grow beyond a point long passed. But how, we may ask, can our understanding have grown when our reading ability has remained constant? And the answer is that if you can understand therefore you can read and if you can read you can understand, for the question is a chicken-and-egg one whose circular reasoning fails to understand why we read in the first place. As children we read for two kinds of wonder: the wonder of discovery, and the wonder of mastery. Reading makes new worlds available to us, and our ability to master that process guarantees that there will always be new worlds available—in reading, discovery and mastery are perfectly united. But we lose sight of that union as we mature, for both new worlds and mastery come to be taken for granted. Life becomes more important and reading less wonderful and its mastery accomplished. The paradox is that the wonder of fiction is inseparable from our ability to master it, so that it can be made to reveal life's greatest wonder if we understand how it is made. That understanding requires a difficult admission, for if we begin to read seeking new worlds, we soon learn that realizing those worlds depends on our willingness to accept new responsibilities. Those very responsibilities often make us wish to preserve the worlds of fiction as they were at first—unspoiled fantasies. But doing just that we keep them from continuing to demand greater mastery as the price of continuing wonder. Reading becomes just another responsibility, and not wanting that responsibility we lean on the assumption that reading ability does not go beyond wherever we allow it to stop growing. The choice then is the evasion of responsibility or the reward of ever maturing wonder. For if we accept our reading responsibilities, the first thing that we come to understand is that reading is a dialogue with another human mind, a mind that wishes to share an experience with us, not without purpose, but for the cause of understanding on both parts. That mutual understanding requests that both reader and writer participate in an act of communication—the writer by making literature's fundamental choice, the decision of what to say and what not to say; and the reader by measuring what is said against the reality he knows, to isolate the writer's choices. To know the inherent choices of a fiction is to decide whether or not we want them for our own, and that decision represents our own acknowledgment that communication has occurred, and that our knowledge has been increased by it whether or not we agree or disagree. That final decision is fully our own, and understanding its responsibilities is the aim of advanced reading and its reward—the wonder of both discovery and mastery that is contained within ourselves—and fostering just that wonder is the intention of both the short novels and the critical prefaces of this collection.

READING THE SHORT NOVEL

Some fictions are longer than others. The long ones are called novels, the short ones are called short stories, and the ones in between are called short novels, novellas, novelettes, or equivalent terms in French and German. Distinctions of the short novel by length amount to no more than that, even when they are accompanied by reminders that short stories concentrate on a single incident, and that novels have a large cast of characters, both plots and sub-plots, and often contain both short stories and short novels within them. All this amounts to saying that a short novel is an economical novel, or a developed short story that goes beyond a single incident, and saying only that much ducks the question of the value of the short novel, the value of the middle way—assuming that the reader has the time for the longer novel, or for several short stories. To avoid the question of the value of the short novel is to refuse the responsibility of explaining its answer: fictions are as long as they need to be. Short stories make a single point, novels make an entire world, for that world is their point, but short novels are their point in themselves. They are long enough to build a fictional universe without asking that it be taken for granted (as in the short story), and short enough to direct that universe at a single thematic objective. That is their value for the study of literature, for in the short novel the operations of theme are manifest in every moment of the fictional universe. The writer's difficulty in the short novel is very much to our advantage. His problem is the construction of a fictional reality that is of significance to us, yet one which is also significant to himself. The larger the fictional vehicle, the easier the task—for more significance can be assigned to either party without taking from the other. But the short novel demands a shared reality that is significant in all its respects to both reader and writer. In this way, the short novel robs both writer and reader of the false belief in perspective that allows them to step back from the fictional world. This theft is to our advantage, for the loss of perspective means that the dialogue of reading the short novel will be one of equal compromises. That equality is the measure of a fiction's honesty. The value of the short novel is in the understanding that it is the most honest fiction because it has to be. The experience offered to us when we read the short novel, and particularly in a collection, first teaches us how a fictional reality may be made to exceed itself with symbol, myth, tragedy, epic, and aesthetic—and so we learn the forms of literature as we learn its fundamental technique, the making of one person's world another's. At the same time we are taught that actual reality may exceed itself when our individual understanding of it has been enlarged and our sense of humanity deepened. The literary lesson and the lesson about life are united by the short novel's inherent honesty, and that is why short novels alone, and none of them excerpts from larger novels, are here collected.

READING TEN SHORT NOVELS

The authors represented in this collection require no justification: four are winners of the Nobel Prize for Literature (William Faulkner, Thomas Mann, Saul Bellow, and Alexander Solzhenitsyn). Richard Wright remains the single most important black writer of the twentieth century; Yukio Mishima was and is the most important novelist of postwar Japan, nor can the significance of modern Japanese fiction be undervalued by any Western reader; in *The Ballad of the Sad Café*, Carson McCullers has given us, as others have noted, the most perfect contemporary American short novel. Of Dostoevsky, Conrad, and Kafka, it suffices to say that Dostoevsky is the father of modern literature, Conrad the father of the modern novel, and Kafka the father of the idea we call "modern." When the works of these authors appear here in translation, every effort has been made to provide the best translation in print. The success of the modern translations, as Magarshack's of Dostoevsky, or Weatherby's of Mishima, is well known, and where an older translation has never been equaled, becoming a classic in itself as with the Muirs' translation of Kafka, or Lowe-Porter's translation of Mann, that translation has been preferred here, rather than a modern translation made for the sake of newness alone.

The choices of the individual short novels and of their arrangement are interdependent, not independent. What was chosen was chosen not only for itself, but for its contribution to a design that intends to make each successive short novel necessary to increased understanding of the short novel to follow. Rather than earliest or easiest, basic comes first—what comes first is what has to come first. We begin with Conrad's *Youth* because in *Youth* Conrad himself discovered the meaning of the short novel. Proceeding from Conrad to Faulkner to Richard Wright, our progress is generally chronological, and that progress is enriched by available contrast and parallelism that deepen our understanding: the youth of *Youth* with the young convict of *Old Man*, the flood of *Old Man* with the flood of *Down by the Riverside*, most of all, the movement from first manhood to natural man to tragic man. Our first three short novels put three men in three boats to share backgrounds of realism, of adventure, and of nature as the maker of that adventure. That much modern novel, English and American, is necessary for Dostoevsky's *Notes from the Underground*— the earliest of the ten short novels, their center, and the necessary introduction to the European short novels that follow, which preserve a realistic context but emphasize structure to a greater degree. Conrad, Faulkner, and Wright raise difficult questions that help to explain the equally difficult answers provided by Dostoevsky, Mann, and Kafka. These first six short novels, as a group, could serve as the nucleus of a semester's course in the modern novel, and the four that follow could equally serve as the nucleus of a semester's course in the contemporary novel. Taken as a whole, the collection intends to study the novel from Dostoevsky to the present. Because Dostoevsky is the father of modern literature, he can be studied through his sons and their brothers: Conrad, Faulkner, Wright, and Mann and Kafka. Bellow, Solzhenitsyn, McCullers, and Mishima are contemporary sons and daughters of the moderns, and Dostoevsky's grandchildren, and we shall find that writers as disparate as Mishima and McCullers acknowledge that fact directly. And just as the modern authors may be contrasted to illustrate symbolic, mythic, tragic, fantastic, and aesthetic modes of fiction, so too their children not only contrast one another, but also teach us the meaning of contemporary fiction, by coming to understand its relationship with modern fiction—the relationship, for example of Bellow's death of a salesman with Kafka's, or of Solzhenitsyn's convict with Faulkner's, and with Dostoevsky's as well. Mishima returns us to Conrad, and as well provides a fitting conclusion to the struggles that precede *The Sound of Waves*— a gift whose simplicity, beauty, and innocence are our reward and the reward that contemporary life promises.

The critical prefaces of this collection serve four purposes, but those purposes are not intended to exclude the reader's own purpose. In no sense do they represent a final word, only a first that hopes to serve the purpose of the reader's own criticism. To that end they incorporate a continuing dialogue that emphasizes the relationship of a short novel to the novels before and after, as well as relevant biographical information and discussions of aspects of literature most readily available in their subject short novels—McCullers tells us about the fiction we call Gothic, Faulkner about mythic, Solzhenitsyn about epic. Finally each preface addresses its particular short novel directly, with an essay that must always be incomplete, but complete enough to encourage the reader's essay, be it written or not, for that essay is the only last word ever expected by fiction. A Glossary of Critical Concepts follows last, and is intended to facilitate understanding of terminology employed in the critical prefaces by serving as a cross-reference guide to those discussions as well as a convenient reference point for the understanding of any one short novel.

THOMAS ASHTON
*University of Massachusetts,
Amherst, 1978*

Joseph Conrad

YOUTH: A NARRATIVE

Preface

Youth is a story about growing up that could only be told by the coming of age of Conrad's talent and of the modern short novel as well. Because *Youth* is a turning point for writer, reader, and fiction itself, it is a necessary first choice for *Ten Short Novels*, revealing the operation of the fundamentals of literature at work in the selections that follow. By studying Conrad's solutions to the problems of writing *Youth*, we learn to read the greater and lesser works that follow in its wake.

Joseph Conrad (1857–1924) wrote *Youth: A Narrative* in the spring of 1898— the penultimate year of the nineteenth century. In the summer of the same year he was to begin his masterpiece *Lord Jim*, and *Youth* may be understood as a preface to that novel, a reminder in Conrad's words, that "the region of early youth must be left behind." Before Conrad himself could leave that literary region behind and enter the world of his major novels, he worked on the short fiction that followed the publication of two earlier novels. These stories were published in *Tales of Unrest* (1898)—the year of the composition of *Youth: A Narrative*. That a narrative should be differentiated from a tale is the point of Conrad's telling us in *Youth* that its hero Marlow "told the story, or rather the chronicle, of a voyage." The difference is the difference between the short story and the short novel, and Conrad, now writing for *Blackwood's Magazine* (*Maga*), was soon to produce his most memorable short novel *Heart of Darkness*. *Youth* thus comes at a turning point in Conrad's work in the short form, a point between *Tales of Unrest* and the 1902 volume, *Youth: A Narrative and Two Other Stories*, the other stories being *Heart of Darkness* and *The End of the Tether*. The turning point is marked in *Youth* by the first appearance in Conrad's fiction of the narrator Marlow, whom Conrad calls a "casual acquaintance," and who is a friend indeed in Conrad's fiction, solving the problems both of form and content heralded by the earlier *Nigger of the Narcissus*. In *Youth*, Conrad was to take hold of his own experience, the experience of his own twenty years in the merchant marine, and particularly the experience of his youthful voyage made at age twenty-four on the *Palestine*, renamed the *Judea* in *Youth*, and present that experience in a manner and style that would elevate its realism to the symbolic, and prove of lasting significance for twentieth-century fiction.

The young Marlow lugs a set of Byron's works aboard the *Judea*, but ignoring that Romantic literary legacy, he reads Carlyle's *Sartor Resartus* and Burnaby's *Ride to Khiva*, two likely choices for the library of the *Palestine* in the autum of 1881. Marlow likes Burnaby better than Carlyle, preferring its real-life adventure story of a 300-mile trek across central Asia made in the winter of 1875–76 to the moral dogmatism of Carlyle's philosophy. But Marlow's preference is Conrad's problem: how to turn his own maritime adventures into meaningful literature? how, with the novel in 1900 poised between the aestheticism to dominate the fiction to come of James Joyce and the Romantic realism to follow in the work of D. H. Lawrence, was Conrad to create a fiction of moral realism? how to make the introduction to *Lord Jim* the forerunner as well of *Heart of Darkness*? *Youth* is the victory that solves these problems.

Conrad writes that "*Youth* is a feat of memory. It is a record of experience; but that experience, in its facts, in its inwardness and in its outward coloring, begins and ends in myself." By contrast, "*Heart of Darkness* is experience too; but it is experience pushed a little beyond the actual." The two short novels solve the same problem with opposite techniques, but the problem is the same—*reality*—"that is for the readers to determine," writes Conrad. *Heart of Darkness* may be unreal, but the experience of *Youth* may also be unreal by being too private, too personal. One man's experience is as good and as worthless as another's—unless the reader participates in that experience, making it his own as well. Participation is Marlow's purpose. Marlow is no simple *persona* for Conrad speaking through him; in Conrad's words he is *not* "a clever screen, a mere device, a *personator*." Instead Marlow is "a most discreet, understanding man." Being discreet he keeps Conrad from being too private; being understanding he keeps Conrad that way too: "For all his assertiveness in matters of opinion, he is not an intrusive person." *Youth* is first of all a dialogue, a conversation between Marlow and his companions, who represent society, and one of whom passes Marlow's narrative on to us. Secondly *Youth* is a dialogue between Marlow and Conrad—between young Conrad as the Marlow of the tale and old Conrad as Marlow the teller. In this way Conrad makes private experience public—real for his readers—for we all know the dialogue that is the continuous conversation between ourselves of yesterday and of today. Conrad calls Marlow a man "of some vanity"; himself he calls "a man who has no very notable illusions about himself." The interaction of vanity and humility is of course all in one head, but the split makes that one head both Conrad's and his reader's, who together must work out Conrad's conflicted experience: "I follow the instincts of vain-glory and humility natural to all mankind. For it can hardly be denied that it is not their own deserts that men are most proud of, but rather of their prodigious luck, of their marvellous fortune." By this we may understand just why *Youth* is a *feat* of memory—a lucky feat for the young Marlow, and also for the man about to write *Lord Jim*. In *Youth* Marlow undergoes initiation, as Conrad the novelist comes of age precisely by recounting his own youthful voyage as Marlow's: "I don't think that either of us would care much to survive the other," Conrad puts it.

Marlow's feat, the feat of youth, is the feat of immortality. The voyage of the *Judea* is the journey to the knowledge of inevitable death. The pillar of fire that heralds the ship's end points to no promised land, only to loss of name, creed and soul: "*Judea*, London. Do or Die." The name is Biblical, the creed English, and their addition makes a soul into whose secret young Marlow is initiated: "the feeling that I could last forever, outlast the sea, the earth, and all men" is "the deceitful feeling that lures us on to joys, to perils, to love, to vain effort—to death." The nature of events is as complex as the ever changing sea, and the do or die attitude of youth is diehard. Maturity means learning that doing and dying are matters of luck, and that luck is not within us but without us in the very nature of reality. Captain Beard hires young Marlow as second mate because he "will do." He "does" by surviving spontaneous combustion and explosion—death and the bursting of the illusion of immortality—for we are the coal which the *Judea* carries and which destroys her, fossil fuel whose energy comes from organic decay. In this way the voyage that seemed "ordered for the illustration of life, that might stand for a symbol of existence," teaches its message. Not that the mate Mahon, "pronounced Mann," had never got on because "there was something wrong with his luck"—but with our luck! "The beautiful sunny winter weather . . . has more charm than in the summertime, because it is unexpected, and crisp, and you know it won't, it can't last long. It's like a windfall, like a godsend, like an unexpected piece of luck"—this is the knowledge of Marlow the teller, not Marlow the mate, who must learn: "In two days it blew a gale . . . it blew day after day: it blew with spite, without interval, without mercy, without rest. The world was nothing but an immensity of great foaming waves rushing at us, under a sky low enough to touch with the hand and dirty like a smoked ceiling." And man can do nothing: "You fight, work, sweat, nearly kill yourself, sometimes do kill yourself trying to accomplish something—and you can't" because the gale is a fire and the fire's explosion leaves the deck "a wilderness of smashed timber, lying crosswise like trees in a wood after a hurricane." All bad weather, all nature, all reality is one, and beyond Man, who hasn't got a thing to do with it—but if he knew only that, he wouldn't get anywhere. Youth's cruelty is its necessary blindness: "Oh, the glamour of youth! Oh, the fire of it, more dazzling than the flames of the burning ship, throwing a magic light on the wide earth, leaping audaciously to the sky, presently to be quenched by time, more cruel, more pitiless, more bitter than the sea—and like the flames on the burning ship surrounded by an impenetrable night." Without the blinding light of youth we should never see at all. We need it to see in the dark until we can see through the dark, as young Marlow does, finally understanding by the light of "a funeral pile kindled in the night" that "a magnificent death had come like a grace, like a gift, like a reward to that old ship at the end of her laborious days." Because he possesses a new perspective, because labor has borne understanding, Marlow is rewarded with a final vision of the East, now more than the land of mystery and romance: "I saw it looking at me." The men of the East "stared without a murmur," the men of the *Judea* sleep as though dead—the old skipper "looked as though he would never wake," Mahon "as though he had been shot where he sat." In the midst of this frozen scene Marlow sees the East as it sees him—each for what it really is and in that more than what it really is: "mysterious, resplendent and sombre, living and unchanged, full of danger and promise." Youth has become hope.

Conrad

YOUTH: A NARRATIVE

This could have occurred nowhere but in England, where men and sea interpenetrate, so to speak—the sea entering into the life of most men, and the men knowing something or everything about the sea, in the way of amusement, of travel, or of breadwinning.

We were sitting round a mahogany table that reflected the bottle, the claret glasses, and our faces as we leaned on our elbows. There was a director of companies, an accountant, a lawyer, Marlow, and myself. The director had been a *Conway* boy, the accountant had served four years at sea, the lawyer—a fine crusted Tory, High Churchman, the best of old fellows, the soul of honour—had been chief officer in the P. & O. service in the good old days when mail boats were square-rigged at least on two masts, and used to come down the China Sea before a fair monsoon with stunsails set alow and aloft. We all began life in the merchant service. Between the five of us there was the strong bond of the sea, and also the fellowship of the craft, which no amount of enthusiasm for yachting, cruising, and so on can give, since one is only the amusement of life and the other is life itself.

Marlow (at least I think that is how he spelt his name) told the story, or rather the chronicle, of a voyage:

"Yes, I have seen a little of the Eastern seas; but what I remember best is my first voyage there. You fellows know there are those voyages that seem ordered for the illustration of life, that might stand for a symbol of existence. You fight, work, sweat, nearly kill yourself, sometimes do kill yourself, trying to accomplish something—and you can't. Not from any fault of yours. You simply can do nothing, neither great nor little—not a thing in the world—not even marry an old maid, or get a wretched 600-ton cargo of coal to its port of destination.

"It was altogether a memorable affair. It was my first voyage to the East, and my first voyage as second mate; it was also my skipper's first command. You'll admit it was time. He was sixty if a day; a little man, with a broad, not very straight back, with bowed shoulders and one leg more bandy than the other, he had a queer twisted-about appearance you see so often in men who work in the fields. He had a nutcracker face—chin and nose trying to come together over a sunken mouth—and it was framed in iron-grey fluffy hair, that looked like a chin strap of cotton wool sprinkled with coal dust. And he had blue eyes in that old face of his, which were amazingly like a boy's, with that candid expression some quite common men preserve to the end of their days by a rare internal gift of simplicity of heart and rectitude of soul. What induced him to accept me was a wonder. I had come out of a crack Australian clipper, where I had been third officer, and he seemed to have a prejudice against crack clippers as aristocratic and high-toned. He said to me, 'You know, in this ship you will have to work.' I said I had to work in every ship I had ever been in. 'Ah, but this is different, and you gentlemen out of them big ships; . . . but there! I dare say you will do. Join tomorrow.'

"I joined tomorrow. It was twenty-two years ago; and I was just twenty. How time passes! It was one of the happiest days of my life. Fancy! Second mate for the first time—a really responsible officer! I wouldn't have thrown up my new billet for a fortune. The mate looked me over carefully. He was also an old chap, but of another stamp. He had a Roman nose, a snow-white, long beard, and his name was Mahon, but he insisted that it should be pronounced Mann. He was well connected; yet there was something wrong with his luck, and he had never got on.

"As to the captain, he had been for years in coasters, then in the Mediterranean, and last in the West Indian trade. He had never been round the Capes. He could just write a kind of sketchy hand, and didn't care for writing at all. Both were thorough good seamen of course, and between those two old chaps I felt like a small boy between two grandfathers.

"The ship also was old. Her name was the *Judea*. Queer name, isn't it? She belonged to a man Wilmer, Wilcox—some name like that; but he has been bankrupt and dead these twenty years or more, and his name don't matter. She had been laid up in Shadwell basin for ever so long. You may imagine her state. She was all rust, dust, grime—soot aloft, dirt on deck. To me it was like coming out of a palace into a ruined cottage. She was about 400 tons, had a primitive windlass, wooden latches to the doors, not a bit of brass about her, and a big square stern. There was on it, below her name in big letters, a lot of scrollwork, with the gilt off, and some sort of a coat of arms, with the motto 'Do or Die' underneath. I remember it took my fancy immensely. There was a touch of romance in it, something that made me love the old thing—something that appealed to my youth!

"We left London in ballast—sand ballast—to load a cargo of coal in a northern port for Bankok. Bankok! I thrilled. I had been six years at sea, but had only seen Melbourne and Sydney, very good places, charming places in their way—but Bankok!

"We worked out of the Thames under canvas, with a North Sea pilot on board. His name was Jermyn, and he dodged all day long about the galley drying his handkerchief before the stove. Apparently he never slept. He was a dismal man, with a perpetual tear sparkling at the end of his nose, who either had been in trouble, or was in trouble, or expected to be in trouble—couldn't be happy unless something went wrong. He mistrusted my youth, my common sense, and my seamanship, and made a point of showing it in a hundred little ways. I dare say he was right. It seems to me I knew very little then, and I know not much more now; but I cherish a hate for that Jermyn to this day.

"We were a week working up as far as Yarmouth Roads, and then we got in a gale—the famous October gale of twenty-two years ago. It was wind, lightning, sleet, snow, and a terrific sea. We were flying light, and you may imagine how bad it was when I tell you we had smashed bulwarks and a flooded deck. On the second night she shifted her ballast into the lee bow, and by that time we had been blown off somewhere on the Dogger Bank. There was nothing for it but go below with shovels and try to right her, and there we were in that vast hold, gloomy like a cavern, the tallow dips stuck and flickering on the beams, the gale howling above, the ship tossing about like mad on her side; there we all were, Jermyn, the captain, everyone, hardly able to keep our feet, engaged on that gravedigger's work, and trying to toss shovelfuls of wet sand up to windward. At every tumble of the ship you could see vaguely in the dim light men falling down with a great flourish of shovels. One of the ship's boys (we had two), impressed by the weirdness of the scene, wept as if his heart would break. We could hear him blubbering somewhere in the shadows.

"On the third day the gale died out, and by and by a north-country tug picked us up. We took sixteen days in all to get from London to Tyne! When we got into dock we had lost our turn for loading, and they hauled us off to a tier where we remained for a month. Mrs. Beard (the captain's name was Beard) came from Colchester to see the old man. She lived on board. The crew of runners had left, and there remained only the officers, one boy, and the steward, a mulatto who answered to the name of Abraham. Mrs. Beard was an old woman, with a face all wrinkled and ruddy like a winter apple, and the figure of a young girl. She caught sight of me once, sewing on a button, and insisted on having my shirts to repair. This was something different from the captains' wives I had known on board crack clippers. When I brought her the shirts, she said: 'And the socks? They want mending, I am sure, and John's—Captain Beard's—things are all in order now. I would be glad of something to do.' Bless the old woman. She overhauled my outfit for me, and meantime I read for the first time *Sartor Resartus* and Burnaby's *Ride to Khiva*. I didn't understand much of the first then; but I remember I preferred the soldier to the philosopher at the time; a preference which life has only confirmed. One was a man, and the other was either more—or less. However, they are both dead and Mrs. Beard is dead, and

youth, strength, genius, thoughts, achievements, simple hearts—all die. . . .
No matter.

"They loaded us at last. We shipped a crew. Eight able seamen and two boys.
We hauled off one evening to the buoys at the dock gates, ready to go out, and
with a fair prospect of beginning the voyage next day. Mrs. Beard was to start
for home by a late train. When the ship was fast we went to tea. We sat rather
silent through the meal—Mahon, the old couple, and I. I finished first, and
slipped away for a smoke, my cabin being in a deckhouse just against the poop.
It was high water, blowing fresh with a drizzle; the double dock gates were
opened, and the steam colliers were going in and out in the darkness with their
lights burning bright, a great plashing of propellers, rattling of winches, and a
lot of hailing on the pierheads. I watched the procession of headlights gliding high and of green lights gliding low in the night, when suddenly a red gleam
flashed at me, vanished, came into view again, and remained. The fore
end of a steamer loomed up close. I shouted down the cabin, 'Come up,
quick!' and then heard a startled voice saying afar in the dark, 'Stop
her, sir.' A bell jingled. Another voice cried warning, 'We are going right into
that barque, sir.' The answer to this was a gruff 'All right,' and the next thing
was a heavy crash as the steamer struck a glancing blow with a bluff of her bow
about our forerigging. There was a moment of confusion, yelling, and running
about. Steam roared. Then somebody was heard saying, 'All clear, sir.' . . . 'Are
you all right?' asked the gruff voice. I had jumped forward to see the damage,
and hailed back, 'I think so.' 'Easy astern,' said the gruff voice. A bell jingled.
'What steamer is that?' screamed Mahon. By that time she was no more to us
than a bulky shadow manoeuvring a little way off. They shouted at us some
name—a woman's name. Miranda or Melissa—or some such thing. 'This means
another month in this beastly hole,' said Mahon to me, as we peered with lamps
about the splintered bulwarks and broken braces. 'But where's the captain?'

"We had not heard or seen anything of him all that time. We went aft to
look. A doleful voice arose hailing somewhere in the middle of the dock, '*Judea*
ahoy!' . . . How the devil did he get there? . . . 'Hallo!' we shouted. 'I am adrift
in our boat without oars,' he cried. A belated water-man offered his services,
and Mahon struck a bargain with him for half a crown to tow our skipper alongside; but it was Mrs. Beard that came up the ladder first. They had been floating
about the dock in that mizzly cold rain for nearly an hour. I was never so surprised in my life.

"It appears that when he heard my shout 'Come up' he understood at once
what was the matter, caught up his wife, ran on deck, and across, and down
into our boat, which was fast to the ladder. Not bad for a sixty-year-old. Just
imagine that old fellow saving heroically in his arms that old woman—the
woman of his life. He set her down on a thwart, and was ready to climb back
on board when the painter came adrift somehow, and away they went together.
Of course in the confusion, we did not hear him shouting. He looked abashed.
She said cheerfully, 'I suppose it does not matter my losing the train now?'
'No, Jenny—you go below and get warm,' he growled. Then to us: 'A sailor

has no business with a wife—I say. There I was, out of the ship. Well, no harm done this time. Let's go and look at what that fool of a steamer smashed.'

"It wasn't much, but it delayed us three weeks. At the end of that time, the captain being engaged with his agents, I carried Mrs. Beard's bag to the railway station and put her all comfy into a third-class carriage. She lowered the window to say, 'You are a good young man. If you see John—Captain Beard—without his muffler at night, just remind him from me to keep his throat well wrapped up.' 'Certainly, Mrs. Beard,' I said. 'You are a good young man; I noticed how attentive you are to John—to Captain—' The train pulled out suddenly; I took my cap off to the old woman: I never saw her again. . . . Pass the bottle.

"We went to sea next day. When we made that start for Bankok we had been already three months out of London. We had expected to be a fortnight or so—at the outside.

"It was January, and the weather was beautiful—the beautiful sunny winter weather that has more charm than in the summertime, because it is unexpected, and crisp, and you know it won't, it can't last long. It's like a windfall, like a godsend, like an unexpected piece of luck.

"It lasted all down the North Sea, all down Channel; and it lasted till we were three hundred miles or so to the westward of the Lizards; then the wind went round to the sou'west and began to pipe up. In two days it blew a gale. The *Judea*, hove to, wallowed on the Atlantic like an old candle box. It blew day after day: it blew with spite, without interval, without mercy, without rest. The world was nothing but an immensity of great foaming waves rushing at us, under a sky low enough to touch with the hand and dirty like a smoked ceiling. In the stormy space surrounding us there was as much flying spray as air. Day after day and night after night there was nothing round the ship but the howl of the wind, the tumult of the sea, the noise of water pouring over her deck. There was no rest for her and no rest for us. She tossed, she pitched, she stood on her head, she sat on her tail, she rolled, she groaned, and we had to hold on while on deck and cling to our bunks when below, in a constant effort of body and worry of mind.

"One night Mahon spoke through the small window of my berth. It opened right into my very bed, and I was lying there sleepless, in my boots, feeling as though I had not slept for years, and could not if I tried. He said excitedly:

" 'You got the sounding rod in here, Marlow? I can't get the pumps to suck. By God! it's no child's play.'

"I gave him the sounding rod and lay down again, trying to think of various things—but I thought only of the pumps. When I came on deck they were still at it, and my watch relieved at the pumps. By the light of the lantern brought on deck to examine the sounding rod I caught a glimpse of their weary, serious faces. We pumped all the four hours. We pumped all night, all day, all the week—watch and watch. She was working herself loose, and leaked badly—not enough to drown us at once, but enough to kill us with the work at the pumps. And while we pumped the ship was going from us piecemeal: the bulwarks went, the stanchions were torn out, the ventilators smashed, the cabin door burst in. There was not a dry spot in the ship. She was being gutted bit by bit. The longboat changed, as if by magic, into matchwood where she stood in her gripes. I had lashed her myself, and was rather proud of my handiwork, which had withstood so long the malice of the sea. And we pumped. And there was no break in the weather. The sea was white like a sheet of foam, like a cauldron of boiling milk; there was not a break in the clouds, no—not the size of a man's hand—no, not for so much as ten seconds. There was for us no sky, there were for us no stars, no sun, no universe—nothing but angry clouds and an infuriated sea. We pumped watch and watch, for dear life; and it seemed to last for months, for years, for all eternity, as though we had been dead and gone to a hell for sailors. We forgot the day of the week, the name of the month, what year it was, and whether we had ever been ashore. The sails blew away, she lay broadside on under a weather cloth, the ocean poured over her, and we did not care. We turned those handles, and had the eyes of idiots. As soon as we had crawled on deck I used to take a round turn with a rope about the men, the pumps, and the mainmast, and we turned, we turned incessantly, with the water to our waists, to our necks, over our heads. It was all one. We had forgotten how it felt to be dry.

"And there was somewhere in me the thought: By Jove! this is the deuce of an adventure—something you read about; and it is my first voyage as second mate—and I am only twenty—and here I am lasting it out as well as any of these men, and keeping my chaps up to the mark. I was pleased. I would not have given up the experience for worlds. I had moments of exultation. Whenever the old dismantled craft pitched heavily with her counter high in the air, she seemed to me to throw up, like an appeal, like a defiance, like a cry to the clouds without mercy, the words written on her stern: 'Judea, London. Do or Die.'

"O youth! The strength of it, the faith of it, the imagination of it! To me she was not an old rattletrap carting about the world a lot of coal for a freight—to me she was the endeavour, the test, the trial of life. I think of her with pleasure, with affection, with regret—as you would think of someone dead you have loved. I shall never forget her. . . . Pass the bottle.

"One night when tied to the mast, as I explained, we were pumping on, deafened with the wind, and without spirit enough in us to wish ourselves dead, a heavy sea crashed aboard and swept clean over us. As soon as I got my breath I shouted, as in duty bound, 'Keep on, boys!' when suddenly I felt something hard floating on deck strike the calf of my leg. I made a grab at it and missed. It was so dark we could not see each other's faces within a foot—you understand.

"After that thump the ship kept quiet for a while, and the thing, whatever it was, struck my leg again. This time I caught it—and it was a saucepan. At first, being stupid with fatigue and thinking of nothing but the pumps, I did not understand what I had in my hand. Suddenly it dawned upon me, and I shouted, 'Boys, the house on deck is gone. Leave this, and let's look for the cook.'

"There was a deckhouse forward, which contained the galley, the cook's berth, and the quarters of the crew. As we had expected for days to see it swept away, the hands had been ordered to sleep in the cabin—the only safe place in the ship. The steward, Abraham, however, persisted in clinging to his berth, stupidly, like a mule—from sheer fright I believe, like an animal that won't leave a stable falling in an earthquake. So we went to look for him. It was chancing death, since once out of our lashings we were as exposed as if on a raft. But we went. The house was shattered as if a shell had exploded inside. Most of it had gone overboard—stove, men's quarters, and their property, all was gone; but two posts, holding a portion of the bulkhead to which Abraham's bunk was attached, remained as if by a miracle. We groped in the ruins and came upon this, and there he was, sitting in his bunk, surrounded by foam and wreckage, jabbering cheerfully to himself. He was out of his mind; completely and forever mad, with this sudden shock coming upon the fag end of his endurance. We snatched him up, lugged him aft, and pitched him headfirst down the cabin companion. You understand there was no time to carry him down with infinite precautions and wait to see how he got on. Those below would pick him up at the bottom of the stairs all right. We were in a hurry to go back to the pumps. That business could not wait. A bad leak is an inhuman thing.

"One would think that the sole purpose of that fiendish gale had been to make a lunatic of that poor devil of a mulatto. It eased before morning, and next day the sky cleared, and as the sea went down the leak took up. When it came to bending a fresh set of sails the crew demanded to put back—and really there was nothing else to do. Boats gone, decks swept clean, cabin gutted, men without a stitch but what they stood in, stores spoiled, ship strained. We put her head for home, and—would you believe it? The wind came east right in our teeth. It blew fresh, it blew continuously. We had to beat up every inch of the way, but she did not leak so badly, the water keeping comparatively smooth. Two hours' pumping in every four is no joke—but it kept her afloat as far as Falmouth.

"The good people there live on casualties of the sea, and no doubt were glad to see us. A hungry crowd of shipwrights sharpened their chisels at the sight of that carcass of a ship. And, by Jove! they had pretty pickings off us before they were done. I fancy the owner was already in a tight place. There were delays. Then it was decided to take part of the cargo out and caulk her topsides. This was done, the repairs finished, cargo reshipped; a new crew came on board, and we went out—for Bankok. At the end of a week we were back again. The crew said they weren't going to Bankok—a hundred and fifty days' passage—in a something hooker that wanted pumping eight hours out of the twenty-four; and the nautical papers inserted again the little paragraph: '*Judea*. Barque. Tyne to Bankok; coals; put back to Falmouth leaky and with crew refusing duty.'

"There were more delays—more tinkering. The owner came down for a day, and said she was as right as a little fiddle. Poor old Captain Beard looked like the ghost of a Geordie skipper—through the worry and humiliation of it. Remember he was sixty, and it was his first command. Mahon said it was a foolish business, and would end badly. I loved the ship more than ever, and wanted awfully to get to Bankok. To Bankok! Magic name, blessed name. Mesopotamia wasn't a patch on it. Remember I was twenty, and it was my first second-mate's billet, and the East was waiting for me.

"We went out and anchored in the outer roads with a fresh crew—the third. She leaked worse than ever. It was as if those confounded shipwrights had actually made a hole in her. This time we did not even go outside. The crew simply refused to man the windlass.

"They towed us back to the inner harbour, and we became a fixture, a feature, an institution of the place. People pointed us out to visitors as 'That 'ere barque that's going to Bankok—has been here six months—put back three times.' On holidays the small boys pulling about in boats would hail, 'Judea, ahoy!' and if a head showed above the rail shouted, 'Where you bound to?—Bankok?' and jeered. We were only three on board. The poor old skipper mooned in the cabin. Mahon undertook the cooking, and unexpectedly developed all a Frenchman's genius for preparing nice little messes. I looked languidly after the rigging. We became citizens of Falmouth. Every shopkeeper knew us. At the barber's or tobacconist's they asked familiarly, 'Do you think you will ever get to Bankok?' Meantime the owner, the underwriters, and the charterers squabbled amongst themselves in London, and our pay went on. . . . Pass the bottle.

"It was horrid. Morally it was worse than pumping for life. It seemed as though we had been forgotten by the world, belonged to nobody, would get nowhere; it seemed that, as if bewitched, we would have to live forever and ever in that inner harbour, a derision and a byword to generations of longshore loafers and dishonest boatmen. I obtained three months' pay and a five days' leave, and made a rush for London. It took me a day to get there and pretty well another to come back—but three months' pay went all the same. I don't know what I did with it. I went to a music hall, I believe, lunched, dined, and supped in a swell place in Regent Street, and was back in time, with nothing but a complete set of Byron's works and a new railway rug to show for three months' work. The boatman who pulled me off to the ship said: 'Hallo! I thought you had left the old thing. *She* will never get to Bankok.' 'That's all *you* know about it,' I said scornfully—but I didn't like that prophecy at all.

"Suddenly a man, some kind of agent to somebody, appeared with full powers. He had grog blossoms all over his face, an indomitable energy, and was a jolly soul. We leaped into life again. A hulk came alongside, took our cargo, and then we went into dry dock to get our copper stripped. No wonder she leaked. The poor thing, strained beyond endurance by the gale, had, as if in disgust, spat out all the oakum of her lower seams. She was recaulked, new coppered, and made as tight as a bottle. We went back to the hulk and reshipped our cargo.

"Then, on a fine moonlight night, all the rats left the ship.

"We had been infested with them. They had destroyed our sails, consumed more stores than the crew, affably shared our beds and our dangers, and now, when the ship was made seaworthy, concluded to clear out. I called Mahon to enjoy the spectacle. Rat after rat appeared on our rail, took a last look over his shoulder, and leaped with a hollow thud into the empty hulk. We tried to count them, but soon lost the tale. Mahon said: 'Well, well! don't talk to me about the intelligence of rats. They ought to have left before, when we had that narrow squeak from foundering. There you have the proof how silly is the superstition about them. They leave a good ship for an old rotten hulk, where there is nothing to eat, too, the fools! . . . I don't believe they know what is safe or what is good for them, any more than you or I.'

"And after some more talk, we agreed that the wisdom of rats had been grossly overrated, being in fact no greater than that of men.

"The story of the ship was known, by this, all up the Channel from Land's End to the Forelands, and we could get no crew on the south coast. They sent us one all complete from Liverpool, and we left once more—for Bankok.

"We had fair breezes, smooth water right into the tropics, and the old *Judea* lumbered along in the sunshine. When she went eight knots everything cracked aloft, and we tied our caps to our heads; but mostly she strolled on at the rate of three miles an hour. What could you expect? She was tired—that old ship. Her youth was where mine is—where yours is—you fellows who listen to this yarn; and what friend would throw your years and your weariness in your face? We didn't grumble at her. To us aft, at least, it seemed as though we had been born in her, reared in her, had lived in her for ages, had never known any other ship. I would just as soon have abused the old village church at home for not being a cathedral.

"And for me there was also my youth to make me patient. There was all the East before me, and all life, and the thought that I had been tried in that ship and had come out pretty well. And I thought of men of old who, centuries ago, went that road in ships that sailed no better, to the land of palms, and spices, and yellow sands, and of brown nations ruled by kings more cruel than Nero the Roman, and more splendid than Solomon the Jew. The old bark lumbered on, heavy with her age and the burden of her cargo, while I lived the life of youth in ignorance and hope. She lumbered on through an interminable procession of days; and the fresh gilding flashed back at the setting sun, seemed to cry out over the darkening sea the words painted on her stern, '*Judea*, London, Do or Die.'

"Then we entered the Indian Ocean and steered northerly for Java Head. The winds were light. Weeks slipped by. She crawled on, do or die, and people at home began to think of posting us as overdue.

"One Saturday evening, I being off duty, the men asked me to give them an extra bucket of water or so—for washing clothes. As I did not wish to screw on the fresh-water pump so late, I went forward whistling, and with a key in my hand to unlock the forepeak scuttle, intending to serve the water out of a spare tank we kept there.

"The smell down below was as unexpected as it was frightful. One would have thought hundreds of paraffin lamps had been flaring and smoking in that hole for days. I was glad to get out. The man with me coughed and said, 'Funny smell, sir.' I answered negligently, 'It's good for the health they say,' and walked aft.

"The first thing I did was to put my head down the square of the midship ventilator. As I lifted the lid a visible breath, something like a thin fog, a puff of faint haze, rose from the opening. The ascending air was hot, and had a heavy, sooty, paraffiny smell. I gave one sniff, and put down the lid gently. It was no use choking myself. The cargo was on fire.

"Next day she began to smoke in earnest. You see it was to be expected, for though the coal was of a safe kind, that cargo had been so handled, so broken up with handling, that it looked more like smithy coal than anything else. Then it had been wetted—more than once. It rained all the time we were taking it back from the hulk, and now with this long passage it got heated, and there was another case of spontaneous combustion.

"The captain called us into the cabin. He had a chart spread on the table, and looked unhappy. He said, 'The coast of West Australia is near, but I mean to proceed to our destination. It is the hurricane month, too; but we will just keep her head for Bankok, and fight the fire. No more putting back anywhere, if we all get roasted. We will try first to stifle this 'ere damned combustion by want of air.'

"We tried. We battened down everything, and still she smoked. The smoke kept coming out through imperceptible crevices; it forced itself through bulk-heads and covers; it oozed here and there and everywhere in slender threads, in an invisible film, in an incomprehensible manner. It made its way into the cabin, into the forecastle; it poisoned the sheltered places on the deck, it could be sniffed as high as the mainyard. It was clear that if the smoke came out the air came in. This was disheartening. This combustion refused to be stifled.

"We resolved to try water, and took the hatches off. Enormous volumes of smoke, whitish, yellowish, thick, greasy, misty, choking, ascended as high as the trucks. All hands cleared out aft. Then the poisonous cloud blew away, and we went back to work in a smoke that was no thicker now than that of an ordinary factory chimney.

"We rigged the force-pump, got the hose along, and by and by it burst. Well, it was as old as the ship—a prehistoric hose, and past repair. Then we pumped with the feeble head pump, drew water with buckets, and in this way managed in time to pour lots of Indian Ocean into the main hatch. The bright stream flashed in sunshine, fell into a layer of white crawling smoke, and vanished on the black surface of coal. Steam ascended mingling with the smoke. We poured salt water as into a barrel without a bottom. It was our fate to pump in that ship, to pump out of her, to pump into her; and after keeping water out of her to save ourselves from being drowned, we frantically poured water into her to save ourselves from being burnt.

"And she crawled on, do or die, in the serene weather. The sky was a miracle of purity, a miracle of azure. The sea was polished, was blue, was pellucid, was sparkling like a precious stone, extending on all sides, all round to the horizon—as if the whole terrestrial globe had been one jewel, one colossal sapphire, a single gem fashioned into a planet. And on the lustre of the great calm waters the *Judea* glided imperceptibly, enveloped in languid and unclean vapours, in a lazy cloud that drifted to leeward, light and slow; a pestiferous cloud defiling the splendour of sea and sky.

"All this time of course we saw no fire. The cargo smouldered at the bottom somewhere. Once Mahon, as we were working side by side, said to me with a queer smile: 'Now, if she only would spring a tidy leak—like that time when we first left the Channel—it would put a stopper on this fire. Wouldn't it?' I remarked irrelevantly, 'Do you remember the rats?'

"We fought the fire and sailed the ship too as carefully as though nothing had been the matter. The steward cooked and attended on us. Of the other twelve men, eight worked while four rested. Everyone took his turn, captain included. There was equality, and if not exactly fraternity, then a deal of good feeling. Sometimes a man, as he dashed a bucketful of water down the hatchway, would yell out, 'Hurrah for Bankok!' and the rest laughed. But generally we were taciturn and serious—and thirsty. Oh! how thirsty! And we had to be careful with the water. Strict allowance. The ship smoked, the sun blazed. . . . Pass the bottle.

"We tried everything. We even made an attempt to dig down to the fire. No good, of course. No man could remain more than a minute below. Mahon, who went first, fainted there, and the man who went to fetch him out did likewise. We lugged them out on deck. Then I leaped down to show how easily it could be done. They had learned wisdom by that time, and contented themselves by fishing for me with a chain-hook tied to a broom-handle, I believe. I did not offer to go and fetch up my shovel, which was left down below.

"Things began to look bad. We put the longboat into the water. The second boat was ready to swing out. We had also another, a 14-foot thing, on davits aft, where it was quite safe.

"Then, behold, the smoke suddenly decreased. We redoubled our efforts to flood the bottom of the ship. In two days there was no smoke at all. Everybody was on the broad grin. This was on a Friday. On Saturday no work, but sailing the ship of course, was done. The men washed their clothes and their faces for the first time in a fortnight, and had a special dinner given them. They spoke of spontaneous combustion with contempt, and implied *they* were the boys to put out combustions. Somehow we all felt as though we each had inherited a large fortune. But a beastly smell of burning hung about the ship. Captain Beard had hollow eyes and sunken cheeks. I had never noticed so much before how twisted and bowed he was. He and Mahon prowled soberly about hatches and ventilators, sniffing. It struck me suddenly poor Mahon was a very, very old chap. As to me, I was as pleased and proud as though I had helped to win a great naval battle. O! Youth!

"The night was fine. In the morning a homeward bound ship passed us hull down—the first we had seen for months; but we were nearing the land at last, Java Head being about 190 miles off, and nearly due north.

"Next day it was my watch on deck from eight to twelve. At breakfast the captain observed, 'It's wonderful how that smell hangs about the cabin.' About ten, the mate being on the poop, I stepped down on the main deck for a moment. The carpenter's bench stood abaft the mainmast: I leaned against it sucking at my pipe, and the carpenter, a young chap, came to talk to me. He remarked, 'I think we have done very well, haven't we?' and then I perceived with annoyance the fool was trying to tilt the bench. I said curtly, 'Don't, Chips,' and immediately became aware of a queer sensation, of an absurd delusion— I seemed somehow to be in the air. I heard all round me like a pent-up breath released—as if a thousand giants simultaneously had said Phoo!—and felt a dull concussion which made my ribs ache suddenly. No doubt about it—I was in the air, and my body was describing a short parabola. But short as it was, I had the time to think several thoughts in, as far as I can remember, the following order: 'This can't be the carpenter—What is it?—Some accident—Submarine volcano? Coals, gas!—By Jove! We are being blown up—Everybody's dead—I am falling into the after hatch—I see fire in it.'

"The coal dust suspended in the air of the hold had glowed dull red at the moment of the explosion. In the twinkling of an eye, in an infinitesimal fraction of a second since the first tilt of the bench, I was sprawling full length on the cargo. I picked myself up and scrambled out. It was quick like a rebound. The deck was a wilderness of smashed timber, lying crosswise like trees in a wood after a hurricane; an immense curtain of soiled rags waved gently before me— it was the mainsail blown to strips. I thought, The masts will be toppling over directly; and to get out of the way bolted on all fours towards the poop ladder. The first person I saw was Mahon, with eyes like saucers, his mouth open, and the long white hair standing straight on end round his head like a silver halo. He was just about to go down when the sight of the main deck stirring, heaving up, and changing into splinters before his eyes, petrified him on the top step. I stared at him in unbelief, and he stared at me with a queer kind of shocked curiosity. I did not know that I had no hair, no eyebrows, no eyelashes, that my young moustache was burnt off, that my face was black, one cheek laid open, my nose cut, and my chin bleeding. I had lost my cap, one of my slippers, and my shirt was torn to rags. Of all this I was not aware. I was amazed to see the ship still afloat, the poop deck whole—and, most of all, to see anybody alive. Also the peace of the sky and the serenity of the sea were distinctly surprising. I suppose I expected to see them convulsed with horror. . . . Pass the bottle.

"There was a voice hailing the ship from somewhere—in the air, in the sky— I couldn't tell. Presently I saw the captain—and he was mad. He asked me eagerly, 'Where's the cabin table?' and to hear such a question was a frightful shock. I had just been blown up, you understand, and vibrated with that experience—I wasn't quite sure whether I was alive. Mahon began to stamp with both feet and yelled at him, 'Good God! don't you see the deck's blown out of her?' I found my voice, and stammered out as if conscious of some gross neglect of duty, 'I don't know where the cabin table is.' It was like an absurd dream.

"Do you know what he wanted next? Well, he wanted to trim the yards. Very placidly, and as if lost in thought, he insisted on having the foreyard squared. 'I don't know if there's anybody alive,' said Mahon, almost tearfully. 'Surely,' he said, gently, 'there will be enough left to square the foreyard.'

"The old chap, it seems, was in his own berth winding up the chronometers, when the shock sent him spinning. Immediately it occurred to him—as he said afterwards—that the ship had struck something, and he ran out into the cabin. There, he saw, the cabin table had vanished somewhere. The deck being blown up, it had fallen down into the lazarette of course. Where we had our breakfast that morning he saw only a great hole in the floor. This appeared to him so awfully mysterious, and impressed him so immensely, that what he saw and heard after he got on deck were mere trifles in comparison. And, mark, he noticed directly the wheel deserted and his barque off her course—and his only thought was to get that miserable, stripped, undecked, smouldering shell of a ship back again with her head pointing at her port of destination. Bankok! That's what he was after. I tell you this quiet, bowed, bandy-legged, almost deformed little man was immense in the singleness of his idea and in his placid ignorance of our agitation. He motioned us forward with a commanding gesture, and went to take the wheel himself.

"Yes; that was the first thing we did—trim the yards of that wreck! No one was killed, or even disabled, but everyone was more or less hurt. You should have seen them! Some were in rags, with black faces, like coal-heavers, like sweeps, and had bullet heads that seemed closely cropped, but were in fact singed to the skin. Others, of the watch below, awakened by being shot out from their collapsing bunks, shivered incessantly, and kept on groaning even as we went about our work. But they all worked. That crew of Liverpool hard cases had in them the right stuff. It's my experience they always have. It is the sea that gives it—the vastness, the loneliness surrounding their dark stolid souls. Ah! Well! we stumbled, we crept, we fell, we barked our shins on the wreckage, we hauled. The masts stood, but we did not know how much they might be charred down below. It was nearly calm, but a long swell ran from the west and made her roll. They might go at any moment. We looked at them with apprehension. One could not foresee which way they would fall.

"Then we retreated aft and looked about us. The deck was a tangle of planks on edge, of planks on end, of splinters, of ruined woodwork. The masts rose from that chaos like big trees above a matted undergrowth. The interstices of that mass of wreckage were full of something whitish, sluggish, stirring—of something that was like a greasy fog. The smoke of the invisible fire was coming up again, was trailing, like a poisonous thick mist in some valley choked with deadwood. Already lazy wisps were beginning to curl upwards amongst the mass of splinters. Here and there a piece of timber, stuck upright, resembled a post. Half of a fife rail had been shot through the foresail, and the sky made a patch of glorious blue in the ignobly soiled canvas. A portion of several boards holding together had fallen across the rail, and one end protruded overboard, like a gangway leading upon nothing, like a gangway leading over the deep sea, leading to death—as if inviting us to walk the plank at once and be done with our ridiculous troubles. And still the air, the sky—a ghost, something invisible was hailing the ship.

"Someone had the sense to look over, and there was the helmsman, who had impulsively jumped overboard, anxious to come back. He yelled and swam lustily like a merman, keeping up with the ship. We threw him a rope, and presently he stood amongst us streaming with water and very crestfallen. The captain had surrendered the wheel, and apart, elbow on rail and chin in hand, gazed at the sea wistfully. We asked ourselves, What next? I thought, Now, this is something like. This is great. I wonder what will happen. O youth!

"Suddenly Mahon sighted a steamer far astern. Captain Beard said, 'We may do something with her yet.' We hoisted two flags, which said in the international language of the sea, 'On fire. Want immediate assistance.' The steamer grew bigger rapidly, and by and by spoke with two flags on her foremast, 'I am coming to your assistance.'

"In half an hour she was abreast, to windward, within hail, and rolling slightly, with her engines stopped. We lost our composure, and yelled all together with excitement, 'We've been blown up'. A man in a white helmet, on the bridge cried, 'Yes! All right! All right!' and he nodded his head, and smiled, and made soothing motions with his hand as though at a lot of frightened children. One of the boats dropped in the water, and walked towards us upon the sea with her long oars. Four Calashes pulled a swinging stroke. This was my first sight of Malay seamen. I've known them since, but what stuck me then was their unconcern; they came alongside, and even the bowman standing up and holding up to our main chains with the boathook did not deign to lift his head for a glance. I thought people who had been blown up deserved more attention.

"A little man, dry like a chip and agile like a monkey, clambered up. It was the mate of the steamer. He gave one look, and cried, 'O boys—you had better quit.'

"We were silent. He talked apart with the captain for a time—seemed to argue with him. Then they went away together to the steamer.

"When our skipper came back we learned that the steamer was the *Somerville*, Captain Nash, from West Australia to Singapore via Batavia with mails, and that the agreement was she should tow us to Anjer or Batavia, if possible, where we could extinguish the fire by scuttling, and then proceed on our voyage —to Bankok! The old man seemed excited. 'We will do it yet,' he said to Mahon, fiercely. He shook his fist at the sky. Nobody else said a word.

"At noon the steamer began to tow. She went ahead slim and high, and what was left of the *Judea* followed at the end of seventy fathom of tow-rope—followed her swiftly like a cloud of smoke with mastheads protruding above. We went aloft to furl the sails. We coughed on the yards, and were careful about the bunts. Do you see the lot of us there, putting a neat furl on the sails of that ship doomed to arrive nowhere? There was not a man who didn't think that at any moment the masts would topple over. From aloft we could not see the ship for smoke, and they worked carefully, passing the gaskets with even turns. 'Harbour furl—aloft there!' cried Mahon from below.

"You understand this? I don't think one of those chaps expected to get down in the usual way. When we did I heard them saying to each other, 'Well, I thought we would come down overboard, in a lump—sticks and all—blame me if I didn't.' 'That's what I was thinking to myself,' would answer wearily another battered and bandaged scarecrow. And, mind, these were men without the drilled-in habit of obedience. To an onlooker they would be a lot of profane scallywags without a redeeming point. What made them do it—what made them obey me when I, thinking consciously how fine it was, made them drop the bunt of the foresail twice to try and do it better? What? They had no professional reputation—no examples, no praise. It wasn't a sense of duty; they all knew well enough how to shirk, and laze, and dodge—when they had a mind to it—and mostly they had. Was it the two pounds ten a month that sent them there? They didn't think their pay half good enough. No; it was something in them, something inborn and subtle and everlasting. I don't say positively that the crew of a French or German merchantman wouldn't have done it, but I doubt whether it would have been done in the same way. There was a completeness in it, something solid like a principle, and masterful like an instinct—a disclosure of something secret—of that hidden something, that gift of good or evil that makes racial difference, that shapes the fate of nations.

"It was that night at ten that, for the first time since we had been fighting it, we saw the fire. The speed of the towing had fanned the smouldering destruction. A blue gleam appeared forward, shining below the wreck of the deck. It wavered in patches, it seemed to stir and creep like the light of a glow-worm. I saw it first, and told Mahon. 'Then the game's up,' he said. 'We had better stop this towing, or she will burst out suddenly fore and aft before we can clear out.' We set up a yell; rang bells to attract their attention; they towed on. At last Mahon and I had to crawl forward and cut the rope with an axe. There was no time to cast off the lashings. Red tongues could be seen licking the wilderness of splinters under our feet as we made our way back to the poop.

"Of course they very soon found out in the steamer that the rope was gone. She gave a loud blast of her whistle, her lights were seen sweeping in a wide circle, she came up ranging close alongside, and stopped. We were all in a tight group on the poop looking at her. Every man had saved a little bundle or a bag. Suddenly a conical flame with a twisted top shot up forward and threw upon the black sea a circle of light, with the two vessels side by side and heaving gently in its centre. Captain Beard had been sitting on the gratings still and mute for hours, but now he rose slowly and advanced in front of us, to the mizzen shrouds. Captain Nash hailed: 'Come along! Look sharp. I have mailbags on board. I will take you and your boats to Singapore.'

" 'Thank you! No!' said our skipper. 'We must see the last of the ship.'

" 'I can't stand by any longer,' shouted the other. 'Mails—you know.'

" 'Aye! aye! We are all right.'

" 'Very well! I'll report you in Singapore. . . . Good-bye!'

"He waved his hand. Our men dropped their bundles quietly. The steamer moved ahead, and passing out of the circle of light, vanished at once from our sight, dazzled by the fire which burned fiercely. And then I knew that I would see the East first as commander of a small boat. I thought it fine; and the fidelity to the old ship was fine. We should see the last of her. Oh, the glamour of youth! Oh, the fire of it, more dazzling than the flames of the burning ship, throwing a magic light on the wide earth, leaping audaciously to the sky, presently to be quenched by time, more cruel, more pitiless, more bitter than the sea—and like the flames on the burning ship surrounded by an impenetrable night.

"The old man warned us in his gentle and inflexible way that it was part of our duty to save for the underwriters as much as we could of the ship's gear. Accordingly we went to work aft, while she blazed forward to give us plenty of light. We lugged out a lot of rubbish. What didn't we save? An old barometer fixed with an absurd quantity of screws nearly cost me my life: a sudden rush of smoke came upon me, and I just got away in time. There were various stores, bolts of canvas, coils of rope; the poop looked like a marine bazaar, and the boats were lumbered to the gunwales. One would have thought the old man wanted to take as much as he could of his first command with him. He was very, very quiet, but off his balance evidently. Would you believe it? He wanted to take a length of old stream cable and a kedge anchor with him in the longboat. We said, 'Aye, aye, sir,' deferentially, and on the quiet let the things slip overboard. The heavy medicine chest went that way, two bags of green coffee, tins of paint—fancy, paint!—a whole lot of things. Then I was ordered with two hands into the boats to make a stowage and get them ready against the time it would be proper for us to leave the ship.

"We put everything straight, stepped the longboat's mast for our skipper, who was to take charge of her, and I was not sorry to sit down for a moment. My face felt raw, every limb ached as if broken, I was aware of all my ribs, and would have sworn to a twist in the backbone. The boats, fast astern, lay in a deep shadow, and all around I could see the circle of the sea lighted by the fire. A gigantic flame arose forward straight and clear. It flared fierce, with noises like the whirr of wings, with rumbles as of thunder. There were cracks, detonations, and from the cone of flame the sparks flew upwards, as man is born to trouble, to leaky ships, and to ships that burn.

"What bothered me was that the ship, lying broadside to the swell and to such wind as there was—a mere breath—the boats would not keep astern where they were safe, but persisted, in a pigheaded way boats have, in getting under the counter and then swinging alongside. They were knocking about dangerously and coming near the flame, while the ship rolled on them, and, of course, there was always the danger of the masts going over the side at any moment. I and my two boat keepers kept them off as best we could, with oars and boathooks; but to be constantly at it became exasperating, since there was no reason why we should not leave at once. We could not see those on board, nor could we imagine what caused the delay. The boatkeepers were swearing feebly, and I had not only my share of the work but also had to keep at it two men who showed a constant inclination to lay themselves down and let things slide.

"At last I hailed, 'On deck there,' and someone looked over. 'We're ready here,' I said. The head disappeared, and very soon popped up again. 'The captain says, All right, sir, and to keep the boats well clear of the ship.'

"Half an hour passed. Suddenly there was a frightful racket, rattle, clanking of chain, hiss of water, and millions of sparks flew up into the shivering column of smoke that stood leaning slightly above the ship. The catheads had burned away, and the two red-hot anchors had gone to the bottom, tearing out after them two hundred fathom of red-hot chain. The ship trembled, the mass of flame swayed as if ready to collapse, and the fore topgallant mast fell. It darted down like an arrow of fire, shot under, and instantly leaping up within an oar's length of the boats, floated quietly, very black on the luminous sea. I hailed the deck again. After some time a man in an unexpectedly cheerful but also muffled tone, as though he had been trying to speak with his mouth shut, informed me, 'Coming directly, sir,' and vanished. For a long time I heard nothing but the whirr and roar of the fire. There were also whistling sounds. The boats jumped, tugged at the painters, ran at each other playfully, knocked their sides together, or, do what we would, swung in a bunch against the ship's side. I couldn't stand it any longer, and swarming up a rope, clambered aboard over the stern.

"It was as bright as day. Coming up like this, the sheet of fire facing me was a terrifying sight, and the heat seemed hardly bearable at first. On a settee cushion dragged out of the cabin Captain Beard, his legs drawn up and one arm under his head, slept with the light playing on him. Do you know what the rest were busy about? They were sitting on deck right aft, round an open case, eating bread and cheese and drinking bottled stout.

"On the background of flames twisting in fierce tongues above their heads they seemed at home like salamanders, and looked like a band of desperate pirates. The fire sparkled in the whites of their eyes, gleamed on patches of white skin seen through the torn shirts. Each had the marks as of a battle about him—bandaged heads, tied up arms, a strip of dirty rag round a knee—and each man had a bottle between his legs and a chunk of cheese in his hand. Mahon got up. With his handsome and disreputable head, his hooked profile, his long white beard, and with an uncorked bottle in his hand, he resembled one of those reckless sea robbers of old making merry amidst violence and disaster. 'The last meal on board,' he explained solemnly. 'We had nothing to eat all day, and it was no use leaving all this.' He flourished the bottle and indicated the sleeping skipper. 'He said he couldn't swallow anything, so I got him to lie down,' he went on; and as I stared, 'I don't know whether you are aware, young fellow, the man had no sleep to speak of for days—and there will be dam' little sleep in the boats.' 'There will be no boats by and by if you fool about much longer,' I said, indignantly. I walked up to the skipper and shook him by the shoulder. At last he opened his eyes, but did not move. 'Time to leave her, sir,' I said quietly.

"He got up painfully, looked at the flames, at the sea sparkling round the ship, and black, black as ink farther away; he looked at the stars shining dim through a thin veil of smoke in a sky black, black as Erebus.

" 'Youngest first,' he said.

"And the ordinary seaman, wiping his mouth with the back of his hand, got up, clambered over the taffrail, and vanished. Others followed. One, on the point of going over, stopped short to drain his bottle, and with a great swing of his arm flung it at the fire. 'Take this!' he cried.

"The skipper lingered disconsolately, and we left him to commune alone for a while with his first command. Then I went up again and brought him away at last. It was time. The ironwork on the poop was hot to the touch.

"Then the painter of the longboat was cut, and the three boats, tied together, drifted clear of the ship. It was just sixteen hours after the explosion when we abandoned her. Mahon had charge of the second boat, and I had the smallest —the 14-foot thing. The longboat would have taken the lot of us; but the skipper said we must save as much property as we could—for the underwriters —and so I got my first command. I had two men with me, a bag of biscuits, a few tins of meat, and a beaker of water. I was ordered to keep close to the longboat, that in case of bad weather we might be taken into her.

"And do you know what I thought? I thought I would part company as soon as I could. I wanted to have my first command all to myself. I wasn't going to sail in a squadron if there were a chance for independent cruising. I would make land by myself. I would beat the other boats. Youth! All youth! The silly, charming, beautiful youth.

"But we did not make a start at once. We must see the last of the ship. And so the boats drifted about that night, heaving and setting on the swell. The men dozed, waked, sighed, groaned. I looked at the burning ship.

"Between the darkness of earth and heaven she was burning fiercely upon a disc of purple sea shot by the blood-red play of gleams; upon a disc of water glittering and sinister. A high, clear flame, an immense and lonely flame, ascended from the ocean, and from its summit the black smoke poured continuously at the sky. She burned furiously; mournful and imposing like a funeral pile kindled in the night, surrounded by the sea, watched over by the stars. A magnificent death had come like a grace, like a gift, like a reward to that old ship at the end of her laborious days. The surrender of her weary ghost to the keeping of stars and sea was stirring like the sight of a glorious triumph. The masts fell just before daybreak, and for a moment there was a burst and turmoil of sparks that seemed to fill with flying fire the night patient and watchful, the vast night lying silent upon the sea. At daylight she was only a charred shell, floating still under a cloud of smoke and bearing a glowing mass of coal within.

"Then the oars were got out, and the boats forming in a line moved round her remains as if in procession—the longboat leading. As we pulled across her stern a slim dart of fire shot out viciously at us, and suddenly she went down, head first, in a great hiss of steam. The unconsumed stern was the last to sink; but the paint had gone, had cracked, had peeled off, and there were no letters, there was no word, no stubborn device that was like her soul, to flash at the rising sun her creed and her name.

"We made our way north. A breeze sprang up, and about noon all the boats came together for the last time. I had no mast or sail in mine, but I made a mast out of a spare oar and hoisted a boat awning for a sail, with a boathook for a yard. She was certainly overmasted, but I had the satisfaction of knowing that with the wind aft I could beat the other two. I had to wait for them. Then we all had a look at the captain's chart, and, after a sociable meal of hard bread and water, got our last instructions. These were simple: steer north, and keep together as much as possible. 'Be careful with that jury rig, Marlow,' said the captain; and Mahon, as I sailed proudly past his boat, wrinkled his curved nose and hailed, 'You will sail that ship of yours under water, if you don't look out, young fellow.' He was a malicious old man—and may the deep sea where he sleeps now rock him gently, rock him tenderly to the end of time!

"Before sunset a thick rainsquall passed over the two boats, which were far astern, and that was the last I saw of them for a time. Next day I sat steering my cockleshell—my first command—with nothing but water and sky around me. I did sight in the afternoon the upper sails of a ship far away, but said nothing, and my men did not notice her. You see I was afraid she might be homeward bound, and I had no mind to turn back from the portals of the East. I was steering for Java—another blessed name—like Bankok, you know. I steered many days.

"I need not tell you what it is to be knocking about in an open boat. I remember nights and days of calm, when we pulled, we pulled, and the boat seemed to stand still, as if bewitched within the circle of the sea horizon. I remember the heat, the deluge of rainsqualls that kept us bailing for dear life (but filled our water cask), and I remember sixteen hours on end with a mouth dry as a cinder and a steering oar over the stern to keep my first command head on to a breaking sea. I did not know how good a man I was till then. I remember the drawn faces, the dejected figures of my two men, and I remember my youth and the feeling that will never come back any more—the feeling that I could last forever, outlast the sea, the earth, and all men; the deceitful feeling that lures us on to joys, to perils, to love, to vain effort—to death; the triumphant conviction of strength, the heat of life in the handful of dust, the glow in the heart that with every year grows dim, grows cold, grows small, and expires—and expires, too soon, too soon—before life itself.

"And this is how I see the East. I have seen its secret places and have looked into its very soul; but now I see it always from a small boat, a high outline of mountains, blue and afar in the morning; like faint mist at noon; a jagged wall of purple at sunset. I have the feel of the oar in my hand, the vision of a scorching blue sea in my eyes. And I see a bay, a wide bay, smooth as glass and polished like ice, shimmering in the dark. A red light burns far off upon the gloom of the land, and the night is soft and warm. We drag at the oars with aching arms, and suddenly a puff of wind, a puff faint and tepid and laden with strange odours of blossoms, of aromatic wood, comes out of the still night —the first sigh of the East on my face. That I can never forget. It was impalpable and enslaving, like a charm, like a whispered promise of mysterious delight.

"We had been pulling this finishing spell for eleven hours. Two pulled, and he whose turn it was to rest sat at the tiller. We had made out the red light in that bay and steered for it, guessing it must mark some small coasting port. We passed two vessels, outlandish and high sterned, sleeping at anchor, and, approaching the light, now very dim, ran the boat's nose against the end of a jutting wharf. We were blind with fatigue. My men dropped the oars and fell off the thwarts as if dead. I made fast to a pile. A current rippled softly. The scented obscurity of the shore was grouped into vast masses, a density of colossal clumps of vegetation, probably—mute and fantastic shapes. And at their foot the semicircle of a beach gleamed faintly, like an illusion. There was not a light, not a stir, not a sound. The mysterious East faced me, perfumed like a flower, silent like death, dark like a grave.

"And I sat weary beyond expression, exulting like a conqueror, sleepless and entranced as if before a profound, a fateful enigma.

"A splashing of oars, a measured dip reverberating on the level of water, intensified by the silence of the shore into loud claps, made me jump up. A boat, a European boat, was coming in. I invoked the name of the dead: I hailed: *Judea* ahoy! A thin shout answered.

"It was the captain. I had beaten the flagship by three hours, and I was glad to hear the old man's voice again, tremulous and tired. 'Is it you, Marlow?' 'Mind the end of that jetty, sir,' I cried.

"He approached cautiously, and brought up with the deep sea lead line which we had saved—for the underwriters. I eased my painter and fell along-side. He sat, a broken figure at the stern, wet with dew, his hands clasped in his lap. His men were asleep already. 'I had a terrible time of it,' he murmured. 'Mahon is behind—not very far.' We conversed in whispers, in low whispers, as if afraid to wake up the land. Guns, thunder, earthquakes would not have awakened the men just then.

"Looking round as we talked, I saw away at sea a bright light travelling in the night. 'There's a steamer passing the bay,' I said. She was not passing, she was entering, and she even came close and anchored. 'I wish,' said the old man, 'you would find out whether she is English. Perhaps they could give us passage somewhere.' He seemed nervously anxious. So by dint of punching and kicking I started one of my men into a state of somnambulism, and giving him an oar, took another and pulled towards the lights of the steamer.

"There was a murmur of voices in her, metallic hollow clangs of the engine room, footsteps on the deck. Her ports shone, round like dilated eyes. Shapes moved about, and there was a shadowy man high up on the bridge. He heard my oars.

"And then, before I could open my lips, the East spoke to me, but it was in a Western voice. A torrent of words was poured into the enigmatical, the fateful silence; outlandish, angry words, mixed with words and even whole sentences of good English, less strange but even more surprising. The voice swore and cursed violently; it riddled the solemn peace of the bay by a volley of abuse. It began by calling me Pig, and from that went crescendo into unmentionable adjectives—in English. The man up there raged aloud in two languages, and with a sincerity in his fury that almost convinced me I had, in some way, sinned against the harmony of the universe. I could hardly see him, but began to think he would work himself into a fit.

"Suddenly he ceased, and I could hear him snorting and blowing like a porpoise. I said:

" 'What steamer is this, pray?'

" 'Eh? What's this? And who are you?'

" 'Castaway crew of an English barque burnt at sea. We came here tonight. I am the second mate. The captain is in the longboat, and wishes to know if you would give us a passage somewhere.'

" 'Oh, my goodness! I say. . . . This is the *Celestial* from Singapore on her return trip. I'll arrange with your captain in the morning, . . . and . . . I say . . . did you hear me just now?

" 'I should think the whole bay heard you.'

" 'I thought you were a shoreboat. Now, look here—this infernal lazy scoundrel of a caretaker has gone to sleep again—curse him. The light is out, and I nearly ran foul of the end of this damned jetty. This is the third time he plays me this trick. Now, I ask you, can anybody stand this kind of thing? It's enough to drive a.man out of his mind. I'll report him. . . I'll get the Assistant Resident to give him the sack, by . . . ! See—there's no light. It's out, isn't it? I take you to witness the light's out. There should be a light, you know. A red light on the—'

" 'There was a light,' I said, mildly.

" 'But it's out, man! What's the use of talking like this? You can see for yourself it's out—don't you? If you had to take a valuable steamer along this Godforsaken coast you would want a light, too. I'll kick him from end to end of his miserable wharf. You'll see if I don't. I will—'

" 'So I may tell my captain you'll take us?' I broke in.

" 'Yes, I'll take you. Good-night,' he said, brusquely.

"I pulled back, made fast again to the jetty, and then went to sleep at last. I had faced the silence of the East. I had heard some of its language. But when I opened my eyes again the silence was as complete as though it had never been broken. I was lying in a flood of light, and the sky had never looked so far, so high, before. I opened my eyes and lay without moving.

"And then I saw the men of the East—they were looking at me. The whole length of the jetty was full of people. I saw brown, bronze, yellow faces, the black eyes, the glitter, the colour of an Eastern crowd. And all these beings stared without a murmur, without a sigh, without a movement. They stared down at the boats, at the sleeping men who at night had come to them from the sea. Nothing moved. The fronds of palms stood still against the sky. Not a branch stirred along the shore, and the brown roofs of hidden houses peeped through the green foliage, through the big leaves that hung shining and still like leaves forged of heavy metal. This was the East of the ancient navigators, so old, so mysterious, resplendent and sombre, living and unchanged, full of danger and promise. And these were the men. I sat up suddenly. A wave of movement passed through the crowd from end to end, passed along the heads, swayed the bodies, ran along the jetty like a ripple on the water, a breath of wind on a field—and all was still again. I see it now—the wide sweep of the bay, the glittering sands, the wealth of green infinite and varied, the sea blue like the sea of a dream, the crowd of attentive faces, the blaze of vivid colour— the water reflecting it all, the curve of the shore, the jetty, the high-sterned outlandish craft floating still, and the three boats with the tired men from the West sleeping, unconscious of the land and the people and of the violence of sunshine. They slept thrown across the thwarts, curled on bottom boards, in the careless attitudes of death. The head of the old skipper, leaning back in the stern of the longboat, had fallen on his breast, and he looked as though he would never wake. Farther out old Mahon's face was upturned to the sky, with the long white beard spread out on his breast, as though he had been shot where he sat at the tiller; and a man, all in a heap in the bows of the boat, slept with both arms embracing the stemhead and with his cheek laid on the gunwale. The East looked at them without a sound.

"I have known its fascination since; I have seen the mysterious shores, the still water, the lands of brown nations, where a stealthy Nemesis lies in wait, pursues, overtakes so many of the conquering race, who are proud of their wisdom, of their knowledge, of their strength. But for me all the East is contained in that vision of my youth. It is all in that moment when I opened my young eyes on it. I came upon it from a tussle with the sea—and I was young— and I saw it looking at me. And this is all that is left of it! Only a moment; a moment of strength, of romance, of glamour—of youth! . . . A flick of sunshine upon a strange shore, the time to remember, the time for a sigh, and—good-bye!—Night—Good-bye . . . !"

He drank.

"Ah! The good old time—the good old time. Youth and the sea. Glamour and the sea! The good, strong sea, the salt, bitter sea, that could whisper to you and roar at you and knock your breath out of you."

He drank again.

"By all that's wonderful it is the sea, I believe, the sea itself—or is it youth alone? Who can tell? But you here—you all had something out of life: money, love—whatever one gets on shore—and, tell me, wasn't that the best time, that time when we were young at sea; young and had nothing, on the sea that gives nothing, except hard knocks—and sometimes a chance to feel your strength— that only—what you all regret?"

And we all nodded at him: the man of finance, the man of accounts, the man of law, we all nodded at him over the polished table that like a still sheet of brown water reflected our faces, lined, wrinkled; our faces marked by toil, by deceptions, by success, by love; our weary eyes looking still, looking always, looking anxiously for something out of life, that while it is expected is already gone—has passed unseen, in a sigh, in a flash—together with the youth, with the strength, with the romance of illusions.

William Faulkner

OLD MAN

Preface

Reading Faulkner's *Old Man* and Conrad's *Youth*, though their titles suggest otherwise, puts both short novels literally in the same boat. Our equation of the Old Man, the Mississippi River, with Conrad's sea, of each young protagonist's struggle with nature revealed in its fundamental reality, identifies the passage to adulthood as the central issue of both fictions—and growing up is the central issue in all of Faulkner's major works. But there resemblance ends: reading also reveals a fundamental difference in each author's vision of the way to maturity. In Faulkner youth comes of age by its rediscovery of the old man within itself, rather than by the recognition of external fate and its codetermined hope. The difference between *Old Man* and *Youth* is not simply owing to the forty years and First World War that come between the two short novels, nor to the passage from European to American authors, nor to the change in the techniques of these writers—Faulkner achieving significance with the dense symbolism of myth, Conrad with the open symbolism of everyday. It is not simply that Faulkner's world is more modern, more complex and complicated, with its women and politicians: in fact, quite the reverse is true. The old man within each of us is very old indeed, being primitive or natural man, who struggles with ancient snakes on an Indian mound and with prehistoric alligators in a primeval swamp. *Old Man* disagrees with *Youth* because so many old men are embodied in its title: the hillman convict who is prehistoric but young, the Governor's young man, who is modern old man trying to be young forever, and the oldest man of all—the Father of the Waters, who floods Mother Earth to bring all men into being. Faulkner's final question is not who is older than whom, but who is man?

The question of manhood is central and trifold: how does an individual grow up?; for all individuals collectively, what is Man?; finally, can modern man become an old—that is natural or real—man? William Faulkner (1897–1962) labored with these questions in his masterpieces: *The Sound and the Fury* (1929), *As I Lay Dying* (1930), *Light in August* (1932), and *Absalom, Absalom!* (1936). For his answers, Faulkner received the Nobel Prize for Literature in 1950. Because nothing in Faulkner's fiction can be considered in isolation, looking back to the novel that brought him his first fame, *Sanctuary* (1931), and ahead to his last, *The Reivers* (1962), reveals the trends that help to locate the success of *Old Man*. Most important among these are its place in the evolution of Faulkner's narrative art, its contribution to the root issues of his mythic landscape, and lastly its fulfillment of the positive dreams of his earlier, despairing masterpieces. Primarily a local tale teller, Faulkner wove his stories into the history of an imaginary Mississippi land, Yoknapatawpha County, in which the present-day action of his narratives is short—but significant because so much past goes into its making. His montage structure brings the cubism of modern art to literature. Faulkner started writing with the encouragement of Sherwood Anderson, whom he met in New Orleans in the twenties, went on with his own work after a period in Paris, and achieved greatness with his creation of mythic Yoknapatawpha. Fifteen novels and many stories deal with life in that small region of northern Mississippi, Faulkner over the years recording imaginary history, filling in missing details, and always seeking greater unity and continuity in his history of white and black, of rural and town, of Southern aristocrat and sharecropper. Because history is convoluted, Faulkner's fiction is convoluted. Its essential narratives are short: his masterpieces are short novels. These fictions expand because they fuse several short stories into one, or because the same theme is repeated in them, repeated with variation in a cycle of chronology or family history. *Old Man* is part of a double novel entitled *The Wild Palms* (1939) that begins with the first chapter of *Wild Palms*, followed in turn by the first chapter of *Old Man*, alternating chapter by chapter until we read the convict's last words—words which apply to both stories. One tale counterpoints the other, in particular because *Wild Palms*, unlike almost all of Faulkner's fiction, is set beyond the American South to which *Old Man*, like the Mississippi, belongs; so that mythic Yoknapatawpha rebukes modern America, but shows us hope as well. In *Wild Palms* a young intern falls in love with a married woman, and together they escape to different parts of the country, running from the civilization that they fear will kill their love. The woman finally dies as the result of an abortion performed on her by her lover, who is imprisoned for life. The convict of *Old Man* makes a similar journey with a woman—one he doesn't want—is carried as far as New Orleans by natural flood, not unnatural passion, because all he wants to do is to return to Mississippi, and successfully helps to deliver the woman's child without doctor and with bailing can, to end up with ten extra years in jail. But unlike his intern counterpart, in jail again, the convict is paradoxically free.

The freedom of Faulkner's convict is as central to the Yoknapatawpha myth as Old Man River is to the real world counterpart of the myth's geography. As primitive man, the young convict opposes anxious, consciousness-ridden, and divided modern man; he is the heir of Dilsey in *The Sound and the Fury*, of Lena Grove in *Light in August*, and of Sam Fathers in *Go Down, Moses*. The achievement of *Old Man* is to make natural man the protagonist, to move him to the center of Faulkner's stage then and thereafter. He says very little there, but we can believe him precisely because there is so much empty rhetoric in the narcissistic self-lovers of *Wild Palms*. Nor does his taciturn talk mean that he is new to Yoknapatawpha, for he has been there from the start. Faulkner's myth begins about 1800 with the Chickasaw Indians, and Faulkner was never one to underestimate Indian cultural contributions and the loss that followed White destruction of Indian values, as his brilliant short story, *Red Leaves*, demonstrates. The Chickasaw Ikkemotubbe travels to New Orleans where he is introduced to rivermen and gamblers by a Frenchman, who calls him Du Homme, the Man. Ikkemotubbe likes the title, that Faulkner has him corrupt to "Doom," and this doom, in the form of a potent white powder provided by the White man, falls on the current Chickasaw chief and his heir, leaving the tribe in the hands of Ikkemotubbe and poisoned with exploitation. The primitive convict of *Old Man* travels back to a time before the Indians, by flood into the time of the Flood, and the connection of Du Homme, the Man, Doom, and Old Man tells us that man's doom does not extend that far: Natural Man has neither a French nor an existential name. Older in Faulkner's work, he comes later, but older than Faulkner he comes earlier, to reveal a way back that is a way ahead—not circular and self-centered, but naturally cyclic.

The message of going forward backward is the message of the first flooded stream encountered by the evacuated convicts: "Here they both saw and heard movement—the slow profound eastward and upsteam ('It's running backward,' one convict said quietly) set of the still rigid surface, from beneath which came a deep faint subaquean rumble which . . . sounded like a subway train passing far beneath the street. . . . It was as if the water itself were in three strata, separate and distinct, the bland and unhurried surface bearing a frothy scum and a miniature flotsam of twigs and screening as though by vicious calculation the rush and fury of the flood itself, and beneath this in turn the original stream, trickle, murmuring along in the opposite direction, following undisturbed and unaware its appointed course and serving its Lilliputian end, like a tread of ants between the rails on which an express train passes, they (the ants) as unaware of the power and the fury as if it were a cyclone crossing Saturn." The three strata correspond to the convict's three capitulations to and regurgitations by Old Man, that hurl him from present to past, from past to Eden, and from there on his terms back to the present, and that form the body of Faulkner's narrative. He takes so long to understand Old Man River, though he soon hears his sound, because of the novel's initial setting. Seeing the flood for the first time, the prisoners "both saw and heard movement," for on the prison farm men are divided—from society, from meaning (true work versus toil) and within themselves perceptually: they live "beneath the shadow of the levee itself, knowing only that there was water beyond it from hearsay." And hearsay in the form of dime crime novels has first put the convict in jail, wrongly convincing him that he might thwart the river's express power and make a mark in the "fluid world of our time" by a *train holdup.* His failure is complete when he is hauled to the Old Man by another train "with that same quality of unreality with which it had appeared, running backward now though with the engine in front where before it had moved forward but with the engine behind." In this way he comes to hear the River's "profound deep whisper" that is one with the "murmuring" of the deepest layer of the stratified stream—and the murmur is first a rebuke: " 'He don't have to brag.' " But as the convict stares across the River for the first time, he sees himself for the first time: "That's what we look like from there. That's what I am standing on looks like from there." The new perspective makes him no less unwilling to get his feet wet, and so "all of a sudden the boat whirled clean around and began to run fast backward like it was hitched to a train and it whirled around again," casting the separated convict into the flood and preparing him to be his Father's true and original son.

To be son the convict must father himself. Regaining his boat, he thus finds a pregnant woman waiting: " 'It's taken you awhile,' " she says. Because she is no moviestar, the convict wants no part of her, wishing "to turn his back . . . on all pregnant and female life forever and return to that monastic existence of shotguns and shackles where he would be secure from it"—and from creation. But Faulkner tells us that the choice is not given to man, only to rivers: "Man always has been drawn to dwell beside water . . . drawn to the living water, the course of his destiny and his actual physical appearance rigidly coerced and postulated by it." Learning this, the convict learns that he cannot surrender the woman, meeting the shanty boat, and that he cannot surrender himself, meeting the machine gun. Surrender is by acceptance, by the deepest strata "following undisturbed and unaware its appointed course." The hillman must learn that the code he calls "the right way" is the law of nature: "That was when it occurred to him that its [the Old Man's] present condition was no phenomenon of a decade, but that the intervening years during which it con- sented to bear upon its placid and sleepy bosom the frail mechanicals of man's clumsy contriving was the phenomenon and this the norm and the river was now doing what it liked to do, had waited patiently ten years in order to do," and this is exactly how we find the convict at the close of *Old Man* waiting out his extra ten years. Then he is the river, now he is shown a deer that leads him to the Indian mound, and on that refuge of the past he helps the nature within us meet the nature without as the woman's child is born: "so that at last he stood above them both, looking down at the tiny terra-cotta colored creature resembling nothing, and thought, *And this is all. This is what severed me*

*violently from all I ever knew and did not wish to leave and cast me upon a
medium I was born to fear, to fetch up at last in a place I never saw before and
where I do not even know where I am.* If this sounds as though our earthborn
time "is a tale told by an idiot, full of sound and fury, signifying nothing," so
it is in *Macbeth,* in *The Sound and the Fury,* and in *Old Man.* But in *Old Man*
the one birth begets another, delivering the convict to the Cajan's swamp, where
all existence is naturally equal: "hill-billy and bayou-rat the two one and identical because of the same grudged dispensation and niggard fate of hard and
unceasing travail not to gain future security . . . but just permission to endure
and endure to buy air to feel and sun to drink for each's little while," and the
woman too "because she too had stemmed at some point from the same dim
hill-bred Abraham." "Circumscribed by this environment, accepted by this
environment and accepting it in turn," the convict ultimately alone in the swamp
gives up the life that "was not his life," winning the privilege of saying "I told
you so" to the world of our time, and Faulkner returns a celebration of Old
Man River's primal fertility—"the Old Man . . . brown and rich as chocolate
between levees . . . beyond them . . . the richened soil which would not need to
be planted, which would need only to be shown a cotton seed to sprout and
make." What follows in *Old Man* is Faulkner's ironic coda that shows both
society outside and inside the prison deaf to his convict's final understanding.
For all of them he would be better off dead. He is given ten years by a society
that thinks he can't do anything, and the ten years mean ten years of doing
without to his fellow prisoners. But the convict knows that the Old Man had
"waited patiently the ten years in order to do." His last words repeat his I told
you so by rejecting the values of prisoners and society alike; the women denied
are their women: natural men and women alike share the burden of creation's
"subterranean outrage." What matters is knowing, knowing that Old Man
River is on the other side of the levee: "And you ain't never close to this river
without knowing it . . . I don't care who you are nor where you have been all
your life." Close to the river without knowing it, the convict wasn't anywhere
—now he knows that much.

Faulkner

OLD MAN

Once (it was in Mississippi, in May, in the flood year 1927) there were two convicts. One of them was about twenty-five, tall, lean, flat-stomached, with a sunburned face and Indian-black hair and pale, china-colored outraged eyes—an outrage directed not at the men who had foiled his crime, not even at the lawyers and judges who had sent him here, but at the writers, the uncorporeal names attached to the stories, the paper novels—the Diamond Dicks and Jesse Jameses and such—whom he believed had led him into his present predicament through their own ignorance and gullibility regarding the medium in which they dealt and took money for, in accepting information on which they placed the stamp of verisimilitude and authenticity (this so much the more criminal since there was no sworn notarised statement attached and hence so much the quicker would the information be accepted by one who expected the same unspoken good faith, demanding, asking, expecting no certification, which he extended along with the dime or fifteen cents to pay for it) and retailed for money and which on actual application proved to be impractical and (to the convict) criminally false; there would be times when he would halt his mule and plow in midfurrow (there is no walled penitentiary in Mississippi; it is a cotton plantation which the convicts work under the rifles and shotguns of guards and trusties) and muse with a kind of enraged impotence, fumbling among the rubbish left him by his one and only experience with courts and law, fumbling until the meaningless and verbose shibboleth took form at last (himself seeking justice at the same blind fount where he had met justice and been hurled back and down): Using the mails to defraud: who felt that he had been defrauded by the third-class mail system not of crass and stupid money which he did not particularly want anyway, but of liberty and honor and pride.

He was in for fifteen years (he had arrived shortly after his nineteenth birthday) for attempted train robbery. He had laid his plans in advance, he had followed his printed (and false) authority to the letter; he had saved the paperbacks for two years, reading and rereading them, memorising them, comparing and weighing story and method against story and method, taking the good from each and discarding the dross as his workable plan emerged, keeping his mind open to make the subtle last-minute changes, without haste and without impatience, as the newer pamphlets appeared on their appointed days as a conscientious dressmaker makes the subtle alterations in a court presentation costume as the newer bulletins appear. And then when the day came, he did not even have a chance to go through the coaches and collect the watches and the rings, the brooches and the hidden money-belts, because he had been captured as soon as he entered the express car where the safe and the gold would be. He had shot no one because the pistol which they took away from him was not that kind of a pistol although it was loaded; later he admitted to the District Attorney that he had got it, as well as the dark lantern in which a candle burned and the black handkerchief to wear over the face, by peddling among his pine-hill neighbors subscriptions to the *Detectives' Gazette*. So now from time to time (he had ample leisure for it) he mused with that raging impotence, because there was something else he could not tell them at the trial, did not know how to tell them. It was not the money he had wanted. It was not riches, not the crass loot; that would have been merely a bangle to wear upon the breast of his pride like the Olympic runner's amateur medal—a symbol, a badge to show that he too was the best at his chosen gambit in the living and fluid world of his time. So that at times as he trod the richly shearing black earth behind his plow or with a hoe thinned the sprouting cotton and corn or lay on his sullen back in his bunk after supper, he cursed in a harsh steady unrepetitive stream, not at the living men who had put him where he was but at what he did not even know were pennames, did not even know were not actual men but merely the designations of shades who had written about shades.

The second convict was short and plump. Almost hairless, he was quite white. He looked like something exposed to light by turning over rotting logs or planks and he too carried (though not in his eyes like the first convict) a sense of burning and impotent outrage. So it did not show on him and hence none knew it was there. But then nobody knew very much about him, including the people who had sent him here. His outrage was directed at no printed word but at the paradoxical fact that he had been forced to come here of his own free choice and will. He had been forced to choose between the Mississippi State penal farm and the Federal Penitentiary at Atlanta, and the fact that he, who resembled a hairless and pallid slug, had chosen the out-of-doors and the sunlight was merely another manifestation of the close-guarded and solitary enigma of his character, as something recognisable roils momentarily into view from beneath stagnant and opaque water, then sinks again. None of his fellow prisoners knew what his crime had been, save that he was in for a hundred and ninety-nine years—this incredible and impossible period of punishment or restraint itself carrying a vicious and fabulous quality which indicated that his reason for being here was such that the very men, the paladins and pillars of justice and equity who had sent him here had during that moment become blind apostles not of mere justice but of all human decency, blind instruments not of equity but of all human outrage and vengeance, acting in a savage personal concert, judge, lawyer and jury, which certainly abrogated justice and possibly even law. Possibly only the Federal and State's Attorneys knew what the crime actually was. There had been a woman in it and a stolen automobile transported across a state line, a filling station robbed and the attendant shot to death. There had been a second man in the car at the time and anyone could have looked once at the convict (as the two attorneys did) and known he would not even have had the synthetic courage of alcohol to pull trigger on anyone. But he and the woman and the stolen car had been captured while the second man, doubtless the actual murderer, had escaped, so that, brought to bay at last in the State's Attorney's office, harried, dishevelled and snarling, the two grimly implacable and viciously gleeful attorneys in his front and the now raging woman held by two policemen in the anteroom in his rear, he was given his choice. He could be tried in Federal Court under the Mann Act and for the automobile, that is, by electing to pass through the anteroom where the woman raged he could take his chances on the lesser crime in Federal Court, or by accepting a sentence for manslaughter in the State Court he would be permitted to quit the room by a back entrance, without having to pass the woman. He had chosen; he stood at the bar and heard a judge (who looked down at him as if the District Attorney actually had turned over a rotten plank with his toe and exposed him) sentence him to a hundred and ninety-nine years at the State Farm. Thus (he has ample leisure too; they had tried to teach him to plow and had failed, they had put him in the blacksmith shop and the foreman trusty himself had asked to have him removed: so that now, in a long apron like a woman, he cooked and swept and dusted in the deputy wardens' barracks) he too mused at times with the sense of impotence and outrage though it did not show on him as on the first convict since he leaned on no halted broom to do it and so none knew it was there.

It was this second convict who, toward the end of April, began to read aloud to the others from the daily newspapers when, chained ankle to ankle and herded by armed guards, they had come up from the fields and had eaten supper and were gathered in the bunkhouse. It was the Memphis newspaper which the deputy wardens had read at breakfast; the convict read aloud from it to his companions who could have had but little active interest in the outside world, some of whom could not have read it for themselves at all and did not even know where the Ohio and Missouri river basins were, some of whom had never even seen the Mississippi River, although for past periods ranging from a few days to ten and twenty and thirty years (and for future periods ranging from a few months to life) they had plowed and planted and eaten and slept beneath the shadow of the levee itself, knowing only that there was water beyond it from hearsay and because now and then they heard the whistles of steamboats from beyond it and during the last week or so had seen the stacks and pilot houses moving along the sky sixty feet above their heads.

But they listened, and soon even those who like the taller convict had probably never before seen more water than a horse pond would hold knew what thirty feet on a river gauge at Cairo or Memphis meant and could (and did) talk glibly of sandboils. Perhaps what actually moved them was the accounts of the conscripted levee gangs, mixed blacks and whites working in double shifts against the steadily rising water; stories of men, even though they were Negroes, being forced like themselves to do work for which they received no other pay than coarse food and a place in a mudfloored tent to sleep on—stories, pictures, which emerged from the shorter convict's reading voice: the mud-splashed white men with the inevitable shotguns, the antlike lines of Negroes carrying sandbags, slipping and crawling up the steep face of the revetment to hurl their futile ammunition into the face of a flood and return for more. Or perhaps it was more than this. Perhaps they watched the approach of the disaster with that same amazed and incredulous hope of the slaves—the lions and bears and elephants, the grooms and bathmen and pastrycooks—who watched the mounting flames of Rome from Ahenobarbus' gardens. But listen they did and presently it was May and the wardens' newspaper began to talk in headlines two inches tall—those black staccato slashes of ink which, it would almost seem, even the illiterate should be able to read: *Crest Passes Memphis at Midnight 4000 Homeless in White River Basin Governor Calls out National Guard Martial Law Declared in Following Counties Red Cross Train with Secretary Hoover Leaves Washington Tonight*; then, three evenings later (It had been raining all day—not the vivid brief thunderous downpours of April and May, but the slow steady gray rain of November and December before a cold north wind. The men had not gone to the fields at all during the day, and the very secondhand optismism of the almost twenty-four-hour-old news seemed to contain its own refutation.): *Crest Now Below Memphis 22,000 Refugees Safe at Vicksburg Army Engineers Say Levees Will Hold.*

"I reckon that means it will bust tonight," one convict said.

"Well, maybe this rain will hold on until the water gets here," a second said. They all agreed to this because what they meant, the living unspoken thought among them, was that if the weather cleared, even though the levees broke and the flood moved in upon the Farm itself, they would have to return to the fields and work, which they would have had to do. There was nothing paradoxical in this, although they could not have expressed the reason for it which they instinctively perceived: that the land they farmed and the substance they produced from it belonged neither to them who worked it nor to those who forced them at guns' point to do so, that as far as either—convicts or guards—were concerned, it could have been pebbles they put into the ground and papier-mâché cotton- and corn-sprouts which they thinned. So it was that, what between the sudden wild hoping and the idle day and the evening's headlines, they were sleeping restlessly beneath the sound of the rain on the tin roof when at midnight the sudden glare of the electric bulbs and the guards' voices waked them and they heard the throbbing of the waiting trucks.

"Turn out of there!" the deputy shouted. He was fully dressed—rubber boots, slicker and shotgun. "The levee went out at Mound's Landing an hour ago. Get up out of it!"

When the belated and streaming dawn broke, the two convicts, along with twenty others, were in a truck. A trusty drove, two armed guards sat in the cab with him. Inside the high, stall-like topless body the convicts stood, packed like matches in an upright box or like the pencil-shaped ranks of cordite in a shell, shackled by the ankles to a single chain which wove among the motionless feet and swaying legs and a clutter of picks and shovels among which they stood, and was riveted by both ends to the steel body of the truck.

Then and without warning they saw the flood about which the plump convict had been reading and they listening for two weeks or more. The road ran south. It was built on a raised levee, known locally as a dump, about eight feet above the flat surrounding land, bordered on both sides by the barrow pits from which the earth of the levee had been excavated. These barrow pits had held water all winter from the fall rains, not to speak of the rain of yesterday, but now they saw that the pit on either side of the road had vanished and instead there lay a flat still sheet of brown water which extended into the fields beyond the pits, ravelled out into long motionless shreds in the bottom of the plow furrows and gleaming faintly in the gray light like the bars of a prone and enormous grating. And then (the truck was moving at good speed) as they watched quietly (they had not been talking much anyway but now they were all silent and quite grave, shifting and craning as one to look soberly off to the west side of the road) the crests of the furrows vanished too and they now looked at a single perfectly flat and motionless steel-colored sheet in which the telephone poles and the straight hedgerows which marked section lines seemed to be fixed and rigid as though set in concrete.

It was perfectly motionless, perfectly flat. It looked, not innocent, but bland. It looked almost demure. It looked as if you could walk on it. It looked so still that they did not realise it possessed motion until they came to the first bridge. There was a ditch under the bridge, a small stream, but ditch and stream were both invisible now, indicated only by the rows of cypress and bramble which marked its course. Here they both saw and heard movement—the slow profound eastward and upstream ("It's running backward," one convict said quietly.) set of the still rigid surface, from beneath which came a deep faint subaquean rumble which (though none in the truck could have made the comparison) sounded like a subway train passing far beneath the street and which implied a terrific and secret speed. It was as if the water itself were in three strata, separate and distinct, the bland and unhurried surface bearing a frothy scum and a miniature flotsam of twigs and screening as though by vicious calculation the rush and fury of the flood itself, and beneath this in turn the original stream, trickle, murmuring along in the opposite direction, following undisturbed and unaware its appointed course and serving its Lilliputian end, like a thread of ants between the rails on which an express train passes, they (the ants) as unaware of the power and fury as if it were a cyclone crossing Saturn.

Now there was water on both sides of the road and now, as if once they had become aware of movement in the water the water seemed to have given over deception and concealment, they seemed to be able to watch it rising up the flanks of the dump; trees which a few miles back had stood on tall trunks above the water now seemed to burst from the surface at the level of the lower branches like decorative shrubs on barbered lawns. The truck passed a Negro cabin. The water was up to the window ledges. A woman clutching two children squatted on the ridgepole, a man and a half-grown youth, standing waist-deep, were hoisting a squealing pig onto the slanting roof of a barn, on the ridgepole of which sat a row of chickens and a turkey. Near the barn was a haystack on which a cow stood tied by a rope to the center pole and bawling steadily; a yelling Negro boy on a saddleless mule which he flogged steadily, his legs clutching the mule's barrel and his body leaned to the drag of a rope attached to a second mule, approached the haystack, splashing and floundering. The woman on the housetop began to shriek at the passing truck, her voice carrying faint and melodious across the brown water, becoming fainter and fainter as the truck passed and went on, ceasing at last, whether because of distance or because she had stopped screaming those in the truck did not know.

Then the road vanished. There was no perceptible slant to it yet it had slipped abruptly beneath the brown surface with no ripple, no ridgy demarcation, like a flat thin blade slipped obliquely into flesh by a delicate hand, annealed into the water without disturbance, as if it had existed so for years, had been built that way. The truck stopped. The trusty descended from the cab and came back and dragged two shovels from among their feet, the blades clashing against the serpentining of the chain about their ankles. "What is it?" one said. "What are you fixing to do?" The trusty didn't answer. He returned to the cab, from which one of the guards had descended, without his shotgun. He and the trusty, both in hip boots and each carrying a shovel, advanced into the water, gingerly, probing and feeling ahead with the shovel handles. The same convict spoke again. He was a middle-aged man with a wild thatch of iron-gray hair and a slightly mad face. "What the hell are they doing?" he said. Again nobody answered him. The truck moved, on into the water, behind the guard and the trusty, beginning to push ahead of itself a thick slow viscid ridge of chocolate water. Then the gray-haired convict began to scream. "God damn it, unlock the chain!" He began to struggle, thrashing violently about him, striking at the men nearest him until he reached the cab, the roof of which he now hammered on with his fists, screaming. "God damn it, unlock us! Unlock us! Son of a bitch!" he screamed, addressing no one. "They're going to drown us! Unlock the chain!" But for all the answer he got the men within radius of his voice might have been dead. The truck crawled on, the guard and the trusty feeling out the road ahead with the reversed shovels, the second guard at the wheel, the twenty-two convicts packed like sardines into the truck bed and padlocked by the ankles to the body of the truck itself. They crossed another bridge—two delicate and paradoxical iron railings slanting out of the water, travelling parallel to it for a distance, then slanting down into it again with an outrageous quality almost significant yet apparently meaningless like something in a dream not quite nightmare. The truck crawled on.

Along toward noon they came to a town, their destination. The streets were paved; now the wheels of the truck made a sound like tearing silk. Moving faster now, the guard and the trusty in the cab again, the truck even had a slight bone in its teeth, its bow-wave spreading beyond the submerged sidewalks and across the adjacent lawns, lapping against the stoops and porches of houses where people stood among piles of furniture. They passed through the business district; a man in hip boots emerged knee-deep in water from a store, dragging a flat-bottomed skiff containing a steel safe.

At last they reached the railroad. It crossed the street at right angles, cutting the town in two. It was on a dump, a levee, also, eight or ten feet above the town itself; the street ran blankly into it and turned at right angles beside a cotton compress and a loading platform on stilts at the level of a freight-car door. On this platform was a khaki army tent and a uniformed National Guard sentry with a rifle and bandolier.

The truck turned and crawled out of the water and up the ramp which cotton wagons used and where trucks and private cars filled with household goods came and unloaded onto the platform. They were unlocked from the chain in the truck and shackled ankle to ankle in pairs they mounted the platform and into an apparently inextricable jumble of beds and trunks, gas and electric stoves, radios and tables and chairs and framed pictures which a chain of Negroes under the eye of an unshaven white man in muddy corduroy and hip boots carried piece by piece into the compress, at the door of which another guardsman stood with his rifle, they (the convicts) not stopping here but herded on by the two guards with their shotguns, into the dim and cavernous building where among the piled heterogeneous furniture the ends of cotton bales and the mirrors on dressers and sideboards gleamed with an identical mute and unreflecting concentration of pallid light.

They passed on through, onto the loading platform where the army tent and the first sentry were. They waited here. Nobody told them for what nor why. While the two guards talked with the sentry before the tent the convicts sat in a line along the edge of the platform like buzzards on a fence, their shackled feet dangling above the brown motionless flood out of which the railroad embankment rose, pristine and intact, in a kind of paradoxical denial and repudiation of change and portent, not talking, just looking quietly across the track to where the other half of the amputated town seemed to float, house shrub and tree, ordered and pageant-like and without motion, upon the limitless liquid plain beneath the thick gray sky.

After a while the other four trucks from the Farm arrived. They came up, bunched closely, radiator to tail light, with their four separate sounds of tearing silk and vanished beyond the compress. Presently the ones on the platform heard the feet, the mute clashing of the shackles, the first truckload emerged from the compress, the second, the third; there were more than a hundred of them now in their bed-ticking overalls and jumpers and fifteen or twenty guards with rifles and shotguns. The first lot rose and they mingled, paired, twinned by their clanking and clashing umbilicals; then it began to rain, a slow steady gray drizzle like November instead of May. Yet not one of them made any move toward the open door of the compress. They did not even look toward it, with longing or hope or without it. If they thought at all, they doubtless knew that the available space in it would be needed for furniture, even if it were not already filled. Or perhaps they knew that, even if there were room in it, it would not be for them, not that the guards would wish them to get wet but that the guards would not think about getting them out of the rain. So they just stopped talking and with their jumper collars turned up and shackled in braces like dogs at a field trial they stood, immobile, patient, almost ruminant, their backs turned to the rain as sheep and cattle do.

After another while they became aware that the number of soldiers had increased to a dozen or more, warm and dry beneath rubberised ponchos, there was an officer with a pistol at his belt, then and without making any move toward it, they began to smell food and, turning to look, saw an army field kitchen set up just inside the compress door. But they made no move, they waited until they were herded into line, they inched forward, their heads lowered and patient in the rain, and received each a bowl of stew, a mug of coffee, two slices of bread. They ate this in the rain. They did not sit down because the platform was wet, they squatted on their heels as country men do, hunching forward, trying to shield the bowls and mugs into which nevertheless the rain splashed steadily as into miniature ponds and soaked, invisible and soundless, into the bread.

After they had stood on the platform for three hours, a train came for them. Those nearest the edge saw it, watched it—a passenger coach apparently running under its own power and trailing a cloud of smoke from no visible stack, a cloud which did not rise but instead shifted slowly and heavily aside and lay upon the surface of the aqueous earth with a quality at once weightless and completely spent. It came up and stopped, a single old-fashioned open-ended wooden car coupled to the nose of a pushing switch engine considerably smaller. They were herded into it, crowding forward to the other end where there was a small cast-iron stove. There was no fire in it, nevertheless they crowded about it—the cold and voiceless lump of iron stained with fading tobacco and hovered about by the ghosts of a thousand Sunday excursions to Memphis or Moorhead and return—the peanuts, the bananas, the soiled garments of infants—huddling, shoving for places near it. "Come on, come on," one of the guards shouted. "Sit down now." At last three of the guards, laying aside their guns, came among them and broke up the huddle, driving them back and into seats.

There were not enough seats for all. The others stood in the aisle, they stood braced, they heard the air hiss out of the released brakes, the engine whistled four blasts, the car came into motion with a snapping jerk; the platform, the compress fled violently as the train seemed to transpose from immobility to full speed with that same quality of unreality with which it had appeared, running backward now though with the engine in front where before it had moved forward but with the engine behind.

When the railroad in its turn ran beneath the surface of the water, the convicts did not even know it. They felt the train stop, they heard the engine blow a long blast which wailed away unechoed across the waste, wild and forlorn, and they were not even curious; they sat or stood behind the rain-streaming windows as the train crawled on again, feeling its way as the truck had while the brown water swirled between the trucks and among the spokes of the driving wheels and lapped in cloudy steam against the dragging fire-filled belly of the engine; again it blew four short harsh blasts filled with the wild triumph and defiance yet also with repudiation and even farewell, as if the articulated steel itself knew it did not dare stop and would not be able to return. Two hours later in the twilight they saw through the streaming windows a burning plantation house. Juxtaposed to nowhere and neighbored by nothing it stood, a clear steady pyre-like flame rigidly fleeing its own reflection, burning in the dusk above the watery desolation with a quality paradoxical, outrageous and bizarre.

Some time after dark the train stopped. The convicts did not know where they were. They did not ask. They would no more have thought of asking where they were than they would have asked why and what for. They couldn't even see, since the car was unlighted and the windows fogged on the outside by rain and on the inside by the engendered heat of the packed bodies. All they could see was a milky and sourceless flick and glare of flashlights. They could hear shouts and commands, then the guards inside the car began to shout; they were herded to their feet and toward the exit, the ankle chains clashing and clanking. They descended into a fierce hissing of steam, through ragged wisps of it blowing past the car. Laid-to alongside the train and resembling a train itself was a thick blunt motor launch to which was attached a string of skiffs and flat boats. There were more soldiers; the flashlights played on the rifle barrels and bandolier buckles and flicked and glinted on the ankle chains of the convicts as they stepped gingerly down into knee-deep water and entered the boats; now car and engine both vanished completely in steam as the crew began dumping the fire from the firebox.

After another hour they began to see lights ahead—a faint wavering row of red pin-pricks extending along the horizon and apparently hanging low in the sky. But it took almost another hour to reach them while the convicts squatted in the skiffs, huddled into the soaked garments (they no longer felt the rain any more at all as separate drops) and watched the lights draw nearer and nearer until at last the crest of the levee defined itself; now they could discern a row of army tents stretching along it and people squatting about the fires, the wavering reflections from which, stretching across the water, revealed an involved mass of other skiffs tied against the flank of the levee which now stood high and dark overhead. Flashlights glared and winked along the base, among the tethered skiffs; the launch, silent now, drifted in.

When they reached the top of the levee they could see the long line of khaki tents, interspersed with fires about which people—men, women and children, Negro and white—crouched or stood among shapeless bales of clothing, their heads turning, their eyeballs glinting in the firelight as they looked quietly at the striped garments and the chains; further down the levee, huddled together too though untethered, was a drove of mules and two or three cows. Then the taller convict became conscious of another sound. He did not begin to hear it all at once, he suddenly became aware that he had been hearing it all the time, a sound so much beyond all his experience and his powers of assimilation that up to this point he had been as oblivious of it as an ant or a flea might be of the sound of the avalanche on which it rides; he had been travelling upon water since early afternoon and for seven years now he had run his plow and harrow and planter within the very shadow of the levee on which he now stood, but this profound deep whisper which came from the further side of it he did not at once recognise. He stopped. The line of convicts behind jolted into him like a line of freight cars stopping, with an iron clashing like cars. "Get on!" a guard shouted.

"What's that?" the convict said. A Negro man squatting before the nearest fire answered him:

"Dat's him. Dat's de Ole Man."

"The old man?" the convict said.

"Get on! Get on up there!" the guard shouted. They went on; they passed another huddle of mules, the eyeballs rolling too, the long morose faces turning into and out of the firelight; they passed them and reached a section of empty tents, the light pup tents of a military campaign, made to hold two men. The guards herded the convicts into them, three brace of shackled men to each tent.

They crawled in on all fours, like dogs into cramped kennels, and settled down. Presently the tent became warm from their bodies. Then they became quiet and then all of them could hear it, they lay listening to the bass whisper deep, strong and powerful. "The old man?" the train-robber convict said.

"Yah," another said. "He dont have to brag."

At dawn the guards waked them by kicking the soles of the projecting feet. Opposite the muddy landing and the huddle of skiffs an army field kitchen was set up, already they could smell the coffee. But the taller convict at least, even though he had had but one meal yesterday and that at noon in the rain, did not move at once toward the food. Instead and for the first time he looked at the River within whose shadow he had spent the last seven years of his life but had never seen before; he stood in quiet and amazed surmise and looked at the rigid steel-colored surface not broken into waves but merely slightly undulant. It stretched from the levee on which he stood, further than he could see—a slowly and heavily roiling chocolate-frothy expanse broken only by a thin line a mile away as fragile in appearance as a single hair, which after a moment he recognised. *It's another levee,* he thought quietly. *That's what we look like from there. That's what I am standing on looks like from there.* He was prodded from the rear; a guard's voice carried forward: "Go on! Go on! You'll have plenty of time to look at that!"

They received the same stew and coffee and bread as the day before; they squatted again with their bowls and mugs as yesterday, though it was not raining yet. During the night an intact wooden barn had floated up. It now lay jammed by the current against the levee while a crowd of Negroes swarmed over it, ripping off the shingles and planks and carrying them up the bank; eating steadily and without haste, the taller convict watched the barn dissolve rapidly down to the very water-line exactly as a dead fly vanished beneath the moiling industry of a swarm of ants.

They finished eating. Then it began to rain again, as upon a signal, while they stood or squatted in their harsh garments which had not dried out during the night but had merely become slightly warmer than the air. Presently they were haled to their feet and told off into two groups, one of which was armed from a stack of mud-clogged picks and shovels nearby, and marched away up the levee. A little later the motor launch with its train of skiffs came up across what was, fifteen feet beneath its keel, probably a cotton field, the skiffs loaded to the gunwales with Negroes and a scattering of white people nursing bundles on their laps. When the engine shut off the faint plinking of a guitar came across the water. The skiffs warped in and unloaded; the convicts watched the men and women and children struggle up the muddy slope, carrying heavy tow-sacks and bundles wrapped in quilts. The sound of the guitar had not ceased and now the convicts saw him—a young, black, lean-hipped man, the guitar slung by a piece of cotton plowline about his neck. He mounted the levee, still picking it. He carried nothing else, no food, no change of clothes, not even a coat.

The taller convict was so busy watching this that he did not hear the guard until the guard stood directly beside him shouting his name. "Wake up!" the guard shouted. "Can you fellows paddle a boat?"

"Paddle a boat where?" the taller convict said.

"In the water," the guard said. "Where in hell do you think?"

"I aint going to paddle no boat nowhere out yonder," the tall convict said, jerking his head toward the invisible river beyond the levee behind him.

"No, it's on this side," the guard said. He stooped swiftly and unlocked the chain which joined the tall convict and the plump hairless one. "It's just down the road a piece." He rose. The two convicts followed him down to the boats. "Follow them telephone poles until you come to a filling station. You can tell it, the roof is still above water. It's on a bayou and you can tell the bayou because the tops of the trees are sticking up. Follow the bayou until you come to a cypress snag with a woman in it. Pick her up and then cut straight back west until you come to a cotton house with a fellow sitting on the ridge-pole—" He turned, looking at the two convicts, who stood perfectly still, looking first at the skiff and then at the water with intense sobriety. "Well? What are you waiting for?"

"I cant row a boat," the plump convict said.

"Then it's high time you learned," the guard said. "Get in."

The tall convict shoved the other forward. "Get in," he said. "That water aint going to hurt you. Aint nobody going to make you take a bath."

As, the plump one in the bow and the other in the stern, they shoved away from the levee, they saw other pairs being unshackled and manning the other skiffs. "I wonder how many more of them fellows are seeing this much water for the first time in their lives too," the tall convict said. The other did not answer. He knelt in the bottom of the skiff, pecking gingerly at the water now and then with his paddle. The very shape of his thick soft back seemed to wear that expression of wary and tense concern.

Some time after midnight a rescue boat filled to the guard rail with homeless men and women and children docked at Vicksburg. It was a steamer, shallow of draft; all day long it had poked up and down cypress- and gum-choked bayous and across cotton fields (where at times instead of swimming it waded) gathering its sorry cargo from the tops of houses and barns and even out of trees, and now it warped into that mushroom city of the forlorn and despairing where kerosene flares smoked in the drizzle and hurriedly strung electrics glared upon the bayonets of martial policemen and the Red Cross brassards of doctors and nurses and canteen-workers. The bluff overhead was almost solid with tents, yet still there were more people than shelter for them; they sat or lay, single and by whole families, under what shelter they could find or sometimes under the rain itself, in the little death of profound exhaustion while the doctors and nurses and the soldiers stepped over and around and among them.

Among the first to disembark was one of the penitentiary deputy wardens, followed closely by the plump convict and another white man—a small man with a gaunt unshaven wan face still wearing an expression of incredulous outrage. The deputy warden seemed to know exactly where he wished to go. Followed closely by his two companions he threaded his way swiftly among the piled furniture and the sleeping bodies and stood presently in a fiercely lighted and hastily established temporary office, almost a military post of command in fact, where the Warden of the Penitentiary sat with two army officers wearing majors' leaves. The deputy warden spoke without preamble. "We lost a man," he said. He called the tall convict's name.

"Lost him?" the Warden said.

"Yah. Drowned." Without turning his head he spoke to the plump convict. "Tell him," he said.

"He was the one that said he could row a boat," the plump convict said. "I never. I told him myself—" he indicated the deputy warden with a jerk of his head "—I couldn't. So when we got to the bayou—"

"What's this?" the Warden said.

"The launch brought word in," the deputy warden said. "Woman in a cypress snag on the bayou, then this fellow—" he indicated the third man; the Warden and the two officers looked at the third man "—on a cotton house. Never had room in the launch to pick them up. Go on."

"So we come to where the bayou was," the plump convict continued in a voice perfectly flat, without any inflection whatever. "Then the boat got away from him. I dont know what happened. I was just sitting there because he was so positive he could row a boat. I never saw any current. Just all of a sudden the boat whirled clean around and begun to run fast backward like it was hitched to a train and it whirled around again and I happened to look up and there was a limb right over my head and I grabbed it just in time and that boat was snatched out from under me like you'd snatch off a sock and I saw it one time more upside down and that fellow that said he knew all about rowing holding to it with one hand and still holding the paddle in the other—" He ceased. There was no dying fall to his voice, it just ceased and the convict stood looking quietly at a half-full quart of whiskey sitting on the table.

"How do you know he's drowned?" the Warden said to the deputy. "How do you know he didn't just see his chance to escape, and took it?"

"Escape where?" the other said. "The whole Delta's flooded. There's fifteen foot of water for fifty miles, clean back to the hills. And that boat was upside down."

"That fellow's drowned," the plump convict said. "You dont need to worry about him. He's got his pardon; it wont cramp nobody's hand signing it, neither."

"And nobody else saw him?" the Warden said. "What about the woman in the tree?"

"I dont know," the deputy said. "I aint found her yet. I reckon some other boat picked her up. But this is the fellow on the cotton house."

Again the Warden and the two officers looked at the third man, at the gaunt, unshaven wild face in which an old terror, an old blending of fear and impotence and rage still lingered. "He never came for you?" the Warden said. "You never saw him?"

"Never nobody came for me," the refugee said. He began to tremble though at first he spoke quietly enough. "I set there on that sonabitching cotton house, expecting hit to go any minute. I saw that launch and them boats come up and they never had no room for me. Full of bastard niggers and one of them setting there playing a guitar but there wasn't no room for me. A guitar!" he cried; now he began to scream, trembling, slavering, his face twitching and jerking. "Room for a bastard nigger guitar but not for me—"

"Steady now," the Warden said. "Steady now."

"Give him a drink," one of the officers said. The Warden poured the drink. The deputy handed it to the refugee, who took the glass in both jerking hands and tried to raise it to his mouth. They watched him for perhaps twenty seconds, then the deputy took the glass from him and held it to his lips while he gulped, though even then a thin trickle ran from each corner of his mouth, into the stubble on his chin.

"So we picked him and—" the deputy called the plump convict's name now "—both up just before dark and come on in. But that other fellow is gone."

"Yes," the Warden said. "Well. Here I haven't lost a prisoner in ten years, and now, like this—I'm sending you back to the Farm tomorrow. Have his family notified, and his discharge papers filled out at once."

"All right," the deputy said. "And listen, chief. He wasn't a bad fellow and maybe he never had no business in that boat. Only he did say he could paddle one. Listen. Suppose I write on his discharge, Drowned while trying to save lives in the great flood of nineteen twenty-seven, and send it down for the Governor to sign it. It will be something nice for his folks to have, to hang on the wall when neighbors come in or something. Maybe they will even give his folks a cash bonus because after all they sent him to the Farm to raise cotton, not to fool around in a boat in a flood."

"All right," the Warden said. "I'll see about it. The main thing is to get his name off the books as dead before some politician tries to collect his food allowance."

"All right," the deputy said. He turned and herded his companions out. In the drizzling darkness again he said to the plump convict: "Well, your partner beat you. He's free. He's done served his time out but you've got a right far piece to go yet."

"Yah," the plump convict said. "Free. He can have it."

As the short convict had testified, the tall one, when he returned to the surface, still retained what the short one called the paddle. He clung to it, not instinctively against the time when he would be back inside the boat and would need it, because for a time he did not believe he would ever regain the skiff or anything else that would support him, but because he did not have time to think about turning it loose. Things had moved too fast for him. He had not been warned, he had felt the first snatching tug of the current, he had seen the skiff begin to spin and his companion vanish violently upward like in a translation out of Isaiah, then he himself was in the water, struggling against the drag of the paddle which he did not know he still held each time he fought back to the surface and grasped at the spinning skiff which at one instant was ten feet away and the next poised above his head as though about to brain him, until at last he grasped the stern, the drag of his body becoming a rudder to the skiff, the two of them, man and boat and with the paddle perpendicular above them like a jackstaff, vanishing from the view of the short convict (who had vanished from that of the tall one with the same celerity though in a vertical direction) like a tableau snatched offstage intact with violent and incredible speed.

He was now in the channel of a slough, a bayou, in which until today no current had run probably since the old subterranean outrage which had created the country. There was plenty of current in it now though; from his trough behind the stern he seemed to see the trees and sky rushing past with vertiginous speed, looking down at him between the gouts of cold yellow in lugubrious and mournful amazement. But they were fixed and secure in something; he thought of that, he remembered in an instant of despairing rage the firm earth fixed and founded strong and cemented fast and stable forever by the generations of laborious sweat, somewhere beneath him, beyond the reach of his feet, when, and again without warning, the stern of the skiff struck him a stunning blow across the bridge of his nose. The instinct which had caused him to cling to it now caused him to fling the paddle into the boat in order to grasp the gunwale with both hands just as the skiff pivoted and spun away again. With both hands free he now dragged himself over the stern and lay prone on his face, streaming with blood and water and panting, not with exhaustion but with that furious rage which is terror's aftermath.

But he had to get up at once because he believed he had come much faster (and so farther) than he had. So he rose, out of the watery scarlet puddle in which he had lain, streaming, the soaked denim heavy as iron on his limbs, the black hair plastered to his skull, the blood-infused water streaking his jumper, and dragged his forearm gingerly and hurriedly across his lower face and glanced at it then grasped the paddle and began to try to swing the skiff back upstream. It did not even occur to him that he did not know where his companion was, in which tree among all which he had passed or might pass. He did not even speculate on that for the reason that he knew so incontestably that the other was upstream from him, and after his recent experience the mere connotation of the term upstream carried a sense of such violence and force and speed that the conception of it as other than a straight line was something which the intelligence, reason, simply refused to harbor, like the notion of a rifle bullet the width of a cotton field.

The bow began to swing back upstream. It turned readily, it outpaced the aghast and outraged instant in which he realised it was swinging far too easily, it had swung on over the arc and lay broadside to the current and began again that vicious spinning while he sat, his teeth bared in his bloody streaming face while his spent arms flailed the impotent paddle at the water, that innocent-appearing medium which at one time had held him in iron-like and shifting convolutions like an anaconda yet which now seemed to offer no more resistance to the thrust of his urge and need than so much air, like air; the boat which had threatened him and at last actually struck him in the face with the shocking violence of a mule's hoof now seemed to poise weightless upon it like a thistle bloom, spinning like a wind vane while he flailed at the water and thought of, envisioned, his companion safe, inactive and at ease in the tree with nothing to do but wait, musing with impotent and terrified fury upon that arbitrariness of human affairs which had abrogated to the one the secure tree and to the other the hysterical and unmanageable boat for the very reason that it knew that he alone of the two of them would make any attempt to return and rescue his companion.

The skiff had paid off and now ran with the current again. It seemed again to spring from immobility into incredible speed, and he thought he must already be miles away from where his companion had quitted him, though actually he had merely described a big circle since getting back into the skiff, and the object (a clump of cypress trees choked by floating logs and debris) which the skiff was now about to strike was the same one it had careened into before when the stern had struck him. He didn't know this because he had not yet ever looked higher than the bow of the boat. He didn't look higher now, he just saw that he was going to strike; he seemed to feel run through the very insentient fabric of the skiff a current of eager gleeful vicious incorrigible wilfulness; and he who had never ceased to flail at the bland treacherous water with what he had believed to be the limit of his strength now from somewhere, some ultimate absolute reserve, produced a final measure of endurance, will to endure which adumbrated mere muscle and nerves, continuing to flail the paddle right up to the instant of striking, completing one last reach thrust and recover out of pure desperate reflex, as a man slipping on ice reaches for his hat and money-pocket, as the skiff struck him and hurled him once more flat on his face in the bottom of it.

This time he did not get up at once. He lay flat on his face, slightly spread-eagled and in an attitude almost peaceful, a kind of abject meditation. He would have to get up sometime, he knew that, just as all life consists of having to get up sooner or later and then having to lie down again sooner or later after a while. And he was not exactly exhausted and he was not particularly without hope and he did not especially dread getting up. It merely seemed to him that he had accidentally been caught in a situation in which time and environment, not himself, was mesmerised; he was being toyed with by a current of water going nowhere, beneath a day which would wane toward no evening; when it was done with him it would spew him back into the comparatively safe world he had been snatched violently out of and in the meantime it did not much matter just what he did or did not do. So he lay on his face, now not only feeling but hearing the strong quiet rustling of the current on the underside of the planks, for a while longer. Then he raised his head and this time touched his palm gingerly to his face and looked at the blood again, then he sat up onto his heels and leaning over the gunwale he pinched his nostrils between thumb and finger and expelled a gout of blood and was in the act of wiping his fingers on his thigh when a voice slightly above his line of sight said quietly, "It's taken you a while," and he who up to this moment had had neither reason nor time to raise his eyes higher than the bows looked up and saw, sitting in a tree and looking at him, a woman. She was not ten feet away. She sat on the lowest limb of one of the trees holding the jam he had grounded on, in a calico wrapper and an army private's tunic and a sunbonnet, a woman whom he did not even bother to examine since that first startled glance had been ample to reveal to him all the generations of her life and background, who could have been his sister if he had a sister, his wife if he had not entered the penitentiary at an age scarcely out of adolescence and some years younger than that at which even his prolific and monogamous kind married—a woman who sat clutching the trunk of the tree, her stockingless feet in a pair of man's unlaced brogans less than a yard from the water, who was very probably somebody's sister and quite certainly (or certainly should have been) somebody's wife, though this too he had entered the penitentiary too young to have had more than mere theoretical female experience to discover yet. "I thought for a minute you wasn't aiming to come back."

"Come back?"

"After the first time. After you run into this brush pile the first time and got into the boat and went on." He looked about, touching his face tenderly again; it could very well be the same place where the boat had hit him in the face.

"Yah," he said. "I'm here now though."

"Could you maybe get the boat a little closer? I taken a right sharp strain getting up here; maybe I better . . ." He was not listening; he had just discovered that the paddle was gone; this time when the skiff hurled him forward he had flung the paddle not into it but beyond it. "It's right there in them brush tops," the woman said. "You can get it. Here. Catch a holt of this." It was a grapevine. It had grown up into the tree and the flood had torn the roots loose. She had taken a turn with it about her upper body; she now loosed it and swung it out until he could grasp it. Holding to the end of the vine he warped the skiff around the end of the jam, picking up the paddle, and warped the skiff on beneath the limb and held it and now he watched her move, gather herself heavily and carefully to descend—that heaviness which was not painful but just excruciatingly careful, that profound and almost lethargic awkwardness which added nothing to the sum of that first aghast amazement which had served already for the catafalque of invincible dream since even in durance he had continued (and even with the old avidity, even though they had caused his downfall) to consume the impossible pulp-printed fables carefully censored and as carefully smuggled into the penitentiary; and who to say what Helen, what living Garbo, he had not dreamed of rescuing from what craggy pinnacle or dragoned keep when he and his companion embarked in the skiff. He watched her, he made no further effort to help her beyond holding the skiff savagely steady while she lowered herself from the limb—the entire body, the deformed swell of belly bulging the calico, suspended by its arms, thinking, *And this is what I get. This, out of all the female meat that walks, is what I have to be caught in a runaway boat with.*

"Where's that cottonhouse?" he said.

"Cottonhouse?"

"With that fellow on it. The other one."

"I don't know. It's a right smart of cottonhouses around here. With folks on them too, I reckon." She was examining him. "You're bloody as a hog," she said. "You look like a convict."

"Yah," he said, snarled. "I feel like I done already been hung. Well, I got to pick up my pardner and then find that cottonhouse." He cast off. That is, he released his hold on the vine. That was all he had to do, for even while the bow of the skiff hung high on the log jam and even while he held it by the vine in the comparatively dead water behind the jam, he felt steadily and constantly the whisper, the strong purring power of the water just one inch beyond the frail planks on which he squatted and which, as soon as he released the vine, took charge of the skiff not with one powerful clutch but in a series of touches light, tentative, and catlike; he realised now that he had entertained a sort of foundationless hope that the added weight might make the skiff more controllable. During the first moment or two he had a wild (and still foundationless) belief that it had; he had got the head upstream and managed to hold it so by terrific exertion continued even after he discovered that they were travelling straight enough now stern-first and continued somehow even after the bow began to wear away and swing: the old irresistible movement which he knew well by now, too well to fight against it, so that he let the bow swing on downstream with the hope of utilising the skiff's own momentum to bring it through the full circle and so upstream again, the skiff travelling broadside then bow-first then broadside again, diagonally across the channel, toward the other wall of submerged trees; it began to flee beneath him with terrific speed, they were in an eddy but did not know it; he had no time to draw conclusions or even wonder; he crouched, his teeth bared in his blood-caked and swollen face, his lungs bursting, flailing at the water while the trees stooped hugely down at him. The skiff struck, spun, struck again; the woman half lay in the bow, clutching the gunwales, as if she were trying to crouch behind her own pregnancy; he banged now not at the water but at the living sap-blooded wood with the paddle, his desire now not to go anywhere, reach any destination, but just to keep the skiff from beating itself to fragments against the tree trunks. Then something exploded, this time against the back of his head, and stooping trees and dizzy water, the woman's face and all, fled together and vanished in bright soundless flash and glare.

An hour later the skiff came slowly up an old logging road and so out of the bottom, the forest, and into (or onto) a cottonfield—a gray and limitless desolation now free of turmoil, broken only by a thin line of telephone poles like a wading millipede. The woman was now paddling, steadily and deliberately, with that curious lethargic care, while the convict squatted, his head between his knees, trying to stanch the fresh and apparently inexhaustible flow of blood from his nose with handfuls of water. The woman ceased paddling, the skiff drifted on, slowing, while she looked about. "We're done out," she said.

The convict raised his head and also looked about. "Out where?"

"I thought maybe you might know."

"I dont even know where I used to be. Even if I knowed which way was north, I wouldn't know if that was where I wanted to go." He cupped another handful of water to his face and lowered his hand and regarded the resulting crimson marbling on his palm, not with dejection, not with concern, but with a kind of sardonic and vicious bemusement. The woman watched the back of his head.

"We got to get somewhere."

"Dont I know it? A fellow on a cottonhouse. Another in a tree. And now that thing in your lap."

"It wasn't due yet. Maybe it was having to climb that tree quick yesterday, and having to set in it all night. I'm doing the best I can. But we better get somewhere soon."

"Yah," the convict said. "I thought I wanted to get somewhere too and I aint had no luck at it. You pick out a place to get to now and we'll try yours. Gimme that oar." The woman passed him the paddle. The boat was a double-ender; he had only to turn around.

"Which way you fixing to go?" the woman said.

"Never you mind that. You just keep on holding on." He began to paddle, on across the cottonfield. It began to rain again, though not hard at first. "Yah," he said. "Ask the boat. I been in it since breakfast and I aint never knowed, where I aimed to go or where I was going either."

That was about one o'clock. Toward the end of the afternoon the skiff (they were in a channel of some sort again, they had been in it for some time; they had got into it before they knew it and too late to get out again, granted there had been any reason to get out, as, to the convict anyway, there was certainly none and the fact that their speed had increased again was reason enough to stay in it) shot out upon a broad expanse of debris-filled water which the convict recognised as a river and, from its size, the Yazoo River though it was little enough he had seen of this country which he had not quitted for so much as one single day in the last seven years of his life. What he did not know was that it was now running backward. So as soon as the drift of the skiff indicated the set of the current, he began to paddle in that direction which he believed to be downstream, where he knew there were towns—Yazoo City, and as a last resort, Vicksburg, if his luck was that bad, if not, smaller towns whose names he did not know but where there would be people, houses, something, anything he might reach and surrender his charge to and turn his back on her forever, on all pregnant and female life forever and return to that monastic existence of shotguns and shackles where he would be secure from it. Now, with the imminence of habitations, release from her, he did not even hate her. When he looked upon the swelling and unmanageable body before him it seemed to him that it was not the woman at all but rather a separate demanding threatening inert yet living mass of which both he and she were equally victims; thinking, as he had been for the last three or four hours, of that minute's —nay, second's—aberration of eye or hand which would suffice to precipitate her into the water to be dragged down to death by that senseless millstone which in its turn would not even have to feel agony, he no longer felt any glow of revenge toward her as its custodian, he felt sorry for her as he would for the living timber in a barn which had to be burned to rid itself of vermin.

He paddled on, helping the current, steadily and strongly, with a calculated husbandry of effort, toward what he believed was downstream, towns, people, something to stand upon, while from time to time the woman raised herself to bail the accumulated rain from the skiff. It was raining steadily now though still not hard, still without passion, the sky, the day itself dissolving without grief: the skiff moved in a nimbus, an aura of gray gauze which merged almost without demarcation with the roiling spittle-frothed debris-choked water. Now the day, the light, definitely began to end and the convict permitted himself an extra notch or two of effort because it suddenly seemed to him that the speed of the skiff had lessened. This was actually the case though the convict did not know it. He merely took it as a phenomenon of the increasing obfuscation, or at most as a result of the long day's continuous effort with no food, complicated by the ebbing and fluxing phases of anxiety and impotent rage at his absolutely gratuitous predicament. So he stepped up his stroke a beat or so, not from alarm but on the contrary, since he too had received that lift from the mere presence of a known stream, a river known by its ineradicable name to generations of men who had been drawn to live beside it as man always has been drawn to dwell beside water, even before he had a name for water and fire, drawn to the living water, the course of his destiny and his actual physical appearance rigidly coerced and postulated by it. So he was not alarmed. He paddled on, upstream without knowing it, unaware that all the water which for forty hours now had been pouring through the levee break to the north was somewhere ahead of him, on its way back to the River.

It was full dark now. That is, night had completely come, the gray dissolving sky had vanished, yet as though in perverse ratio surface visibility had sharpened, as though the light which the rain of the afternoon had washed out of the air had gathered upon the water as the rain itself had done, so that the yellow flood spread on before him now with a quality almost phosphorescent, right up to the instant where vision ceased. The darkness in fact had its advantages; he could now stop seeing the rain. He and his garments had been wet for more than twenty-four hours now so he had long since stopped feeling it, and now that he could no longer see it either it had in a certain sense ceased for him. Also, he now had to make no effort even not to see the swell of his passenger's belly. So he was paddling on, strongly and steadily, not alarmed and not concerned but just exasperated because he had not yet begun to see any reflection on the clouds which would indicate the city or cities which he believed he was approaching but which were actually now miles behind him, when he heard a sound. He did not know what it was because he had never heard it before and he would never be expected to hear such again since it is not given to every man to hear such at all and to none to hear it more than once in his life. And he was not alarmed now either because there was not time, for although the visibility ahead, for all its clarity, did not extend very far, yet in the next instant to the hearing he was also seeing something such as he had never seen before. This was that the sharp line where the phosphorescent water met the darkness was now about ten feet higher than it had been an instant before and that it was curled forward upon itself like a sheet of dough being rolled out for a pudding. It reared, stooping; the crest of it swirled like the mane of a galloping horse and, phosphorescent too, fretted and flickered like fire. And while the woman huddled in the bows, aware or not aware the convict did not know which, he (the convict), his swollen and blood-streaked face gaped in an expression of aghast and incredulous amazement, continued to paddle directly into it. Again he simply had not had time to order his rhythm-hypnotised muscles to cease. He continued to paddle though the skiff had ceased to move forward at all but seemed to be hanging in space while the paddle still reached thrust recovered and reached again; now instead of space the skiff became abruptly surrounded by a welter of fleeing debris—planks, small buildings, the bodies of drowned yet antic animals, entire trees leaping and diving like porpoises above which the skiff seemed to hover in weightless and airy indecision like a bird above a fleeing countryside, undecided where to light or whether to light at all, while the convict squatted in it still going through the motions of paddling, waiting for an opportunity to scream. He never found it. For an instant the skiff seemed to stand erect on its stern and then shoot scrabbling and scrambling up the curling wall of water like a cat, and soared on above the licking crest itself and hung cradled into the high actual air in the limbs of a tree, from which bower of new-leafed boughs and branches the convict, like a bird in its nest and still waiting his chance to scream and still going through the motions of paddling though he no longer even had the paddle now, looked down upon a world turned to furious motion and in incredible retrograde.

Some time about midnight, accompanied by a rolling cannonade of thunder and lightning like a battery going into action, as though some forty hours' constipation of the elements, the firmament itself, were discharging in clapping and glaring salute to the ultimate acquiescence to desperate and furious motion, and still leading its charging welter of dead cows and mules and outhouses and cabins and hen-coops, the skiff passed Vicksburg. The convict didn't know it. He wasn't looking high enough above the water; he still squatted, clutching the gunwales and glaring at the yellow turmoil about him out of which entire trees, the sharp gables of houses, the long mornful heads of mules which he fended off with a splintered length of plank snatched from he knew not where in passing (and which seemed to glare reproachfully back at him with sightless eyes, in limber-lipped and incredulous amazement) rolled up and then down again, the skiff now travelling forward now sideways now sternward, sometimes in the water, sometimes riding for yards upon the roofs of houses and trees and even upon the backs of the mules as though even in death they were not to escape that burden-bearing doom with which their eunuch race was cursed. But he didn't see Vicksburg; the skiff, travelling at express speed, was in a seething gut between soaring and dizzy banks with a glare of light above them but he did not see it; he saw the flotsam ahead of him divide violently and begin to climb upon itself, mounting, and he was sucked through the resulting gap too fast to recognize it as the trestling of a railroad bridge; for a horrible moment the skiff seemed to hang in static indecision before the looming flank of a steamboat as though undecided whether to climb over it or dive under it, then a hard icy wind filled with the smell and taste and sense of wet and boundless desolation blew upon him; the skiff made one long bounding lunge as the convict's native state, in a final paroxysm, regurgitated him onto the wild bosom of the Father of Waters.

This is how he told about it seven weeks later, sitting in new bed-ticking garments, shaved and with his hair cut again, on his bunk in the barracks:

During the next three or four hours after the thunder and lightning had spent itself the skiff ran in pitch streaming darkness upon a roiling expanse which, even if he could have seen, apparently had no boundaries. Wild and invisible, it tossed and heaved about and beneath the boat, ridged with dirty phosphorescent foam and filled with a debris of destruction—objects nameless and enormous and invisible which struck and slashed at the skiff and whirled on. He did not know he was now upon the River. At that time he would have refused to believe it, even if he had known. Yesterday he had known he was in a channel by the regularity of the spacing between the bordering trees. Now, since even by daylight he could have seen no boundaries, the last place under the sun (or the streaming sky rather) he would have suspected himself to be would have been a river; if he had pondered at all about his present whereabouts, about the geography beneath him, he would merely have taken himself to be travelling at dizzy and inexplicable speed above the largest cottonfield in the world; if he who yesterday had known he was in a river, had accepted that fact in good faith and earnest, then had seen that river turn without warning and rush back upon him with furious and deadly intent like a frenzied stallion in a lane—if he had suspected for one second that the wild and limitless expanse on which he now found himself was a river, consciousness would simply have refused; he would have fainted.

When daylight—a gray and ragged dawn filled with driving scud between icy rain-squalls—came and he could see again, he knew he was in no cottonfield. He knew that the wild water on which the skiff tossed and fled flowed above no soil tamely trod by man, behind the straining and surging buttocks of a mule. That was when it occurred to him that its present condition was no phenomenon of a decade, but that the intervening years during which it consented to bear upon its placid and sleepy bosom the frail mechanicals of man's clumsy contriving was the phenomenon and this the norm and the river was now doing what it liked to do, had waited patiently the ten years in order to do, as a mule will work for you ten years for the privilege of kicking you once. And he also learned something else about fear too, something he had even failed to discover on that other occasion when he was really afraid—that three or four seconds of that night in his youth while he looked down the twice-flashing pistol barrel of the terrified mail clerk before the clerk could be persuaded that his (the convict's) pistol would not shoot: that if you just held on long enough a time would come in fear after which it would no longer be agony at all but merely a kind of horrible outrageous itching, as after you have been burned bad.

He did not have to paddle now, he just steered (who had been without food for twenty-four hours now and without any sleep to speak of for fifty) while the skiff sped on across that boiling desolation where he had long since begun to not dare believe he could possibly be where he could not doubt he was, trying with his fragment of splintered plank merely to keep the skiff intact and afloat among the houses and trees and dead animals (the entire towns, stores, residences, parks and farmyards, which leaped and played about him like fish), not trying to reach any destination, just trying to keep the skiff afloat until he did. He wanted so little. He wanted nothing for himself. He just wanted to get rid of the woman, the belly, and he was trying to do that in the right way, not for himself, but for her. He could have put her back into another tree at any time—

"Or you could have jumped out of the boat and let her and it drown," the plump convict said. "Then they could have given you the ten years for escaping and then hung you for the murder and charged the boat to your folks."

"Yah," the tall convict said.—but he had not done that. He wanted to do it the right way, find somebody, anybody he could surrender her to, something solid he could set her down on and then jump back into the river, if that would please anyone. That was all he wanted—just to come to something, anything. That didn't seem like a great deal to ask. And he couldn't do it. He told how the skiff fled on—

"Didn't you pass nobody?" the plump convict said. "No steamboat, nothing?"

"I don't know," the tall one said.—while he tried merely to keep it afloat, until the darkness thinned and lifted and revealed—

"Darkness?" the plump convict said. "I thought you said it was already daylight?"

"Yah," the tall one said. He was rolling a cigarette, pouring the tobacco carefully from a new sack, into the creased paper. "This was another one. They had several while I was gone."—the skiff to be moving still rapidly up a winding corridor bordered by drowned trees which the convict recognised again to be a river running again in the direction that, until two days ago, had been upstream. He was not exactly warned through instinct that this one, like that of two days ago, was in reverse. He would not say that he now believed himself to be in the same river, though he would not have been surprised to find that he did believe this, existing now, as he did and had and apparently was to continue for an unnamed period, in a state in which he was toy and pawn on a vicious and inflammable geography. He merely realised that he was in a river again, with all the subsequent inferences of a comprehensible, even if not familiar, portion of the earth's surface. Now he believed that all he had to do would be to paddle far enough and he would come to something horizontal and above water even if not dry and perhaps even populated; and, if fast enough, in time, and that his only other crying urgency was to refrain from looking at the woman who, as vision, the incontrovertible and apparently inescapable presence of his passenger, returned with dawn, had ceased to be a human being and (you could add twenty-four more hours to the first twenty-four and the first fifty now, even counting the hen. It was dead, drowned, caught by one wing under a shingle on a roof which had rolled momentarily up beside the skiff yesterday and he had eaten some of it raw though the woman would not) had become instead one single inert monstrous sentient womb which, he now believed, if he could only turn his gaze away and keep it away, would disappear, and if he could only keep his gaze from pausing again at the spot it had occupied, would not return. That's what he was doing this time when he discovered the wave was coming.

He didn't know how he discovered it was coming back. He heard no sound, it was nothing felt nor seen. He did not even believe that finding the skiff to be now in slack water—that is, that the motion of the current which, whether right or wrong, had at least been horizontal, had now stopped that and assumed a vertical direction—was sufficient to warn him. Perhaps it was just an invincible and almost fanatic faith in the inventiveness and innate vicious- ness of that medium on which his destiny was now cast, apparently forever; a sudden conviction far beyond either horror or surprise that now was none too soon for it to prepare to do whatever it was it intended doing. So he whirled the skiff, spun it on its heel like a running horse, whereupon, reversed, he could not even distinguish the very channel he had come up. He did not know whether he simply could not see it or if it had vanished some time ago and he was not aware at the time; whether the river had become lost in a drowned world or if the world had become drowned in one limitless river. So now he could not tell if he were running directly before the wave or quartering across its line of charge; all he could do was keep that sense of swiftly accumulating ferocity behind him and paddle as fast as his spent and now numb muscles could be driven, and try not to look at the woman, to wrench his gaze from her and keep it away until he reached something flat and above water. So, gaunt, hollow-eyed, striving and wrenching almost physically at his eyes as if they were two of those suction-tipped rubber arrows shot from the toy gun of a child, his spent muscles obeying not will now but that attenuation beyond mere exhaustion which, mesmeric, can continue easier than cease, he once more drove the skiff full tilt into something it could not pass and, once more hurled violently forward onto his hands and knees, crouching, he glared with his wild swollen face up at the man with the shotgun and said in a harsh, croaking voice: "Vicksburg? Where's Vicksburg?"

Even when he tried to tell it, even after the seven weeks and he safe, secure, riveted warranted and doubly guaranteed by the ten years they had added to his sentence for attempted escape, something of the old hysteric incredulous outrage came back into his face, his voice, his speech. He never did even get on the other boat. He told how he clung to a strake (it was a dirty unpainted shanty boat with a drunken rake of tin stove pipe, it had been moving when he struck it and apparently it had not even changed course even though the three people on it must have been watching him all the while—a second man, bare- foot and with matted hair and beard also at the steering sweep, and then—he did not know how long—a woman leaning in the door, in a filthy assortment of men's garments, watching him too with the same cold speculation) being dragged violently along, trying to state and explain his simple (and to him at least) reasonable desire and need; telling it, trying to tell it, he could feel again the old unforgettable affronting like an ague fit as he watched the abortive tobacco rain steadily and faintly from between his shaking hands and then the paper itself part with a thin dry snapping report:

"Burn my clothes?" the convict cried. "Burn them?"

"How in hell do you expect to escape in them billboards?" the man with the shotgun said. He (the convict) tried to tell it, tried to explain as he had tried to explain not to the three people on the boat alone but to the entire circumambi- ence—desolate water and forlorn trees and sky—not for justification because he needed none and knew that his hearers, the other convicts, required none from him, but rather as, on the point of exhaustion, he might have picked dreamily and incredulously at a suffocation. He told the man with the gun how he and his partner had been given the boat and told to pick up a man and a woman, how he had lost his partner and failed to find the man, and now all in the world he wanted was something flat to leave the woman on until he could find an officer, a sheriff. He thought of home, the place where he had lived almost since childhood, his friends of years whose ways he knew and who knew his ways, the familiar fields where he did work he had learned to do well and to like, the mules with characters he knew and respected as he knew and respected the characters of certain men; he thought of the barracks at night, with screens against bugs in summer and good stoves in winter and someone to supply the fuel and the food too; the Sunday ball games and the picture shows—things which, with the exception of the ball games, he had never known before. But most of all, his own character (Two years ago they had offered to make a trusty of him. He would no longer need to plow or feed stock, he would only follow those who did with a loaded gun, but he declined. "I reckon I'll stick to plowing," he said, absolutely without humor. "I done already tried to use a gun one time too many."), his good name, his responsibility not only toward those who were responsible toward him but to himself, his own honor in the doing of what was asked of him, his pride in being able to do it, no matter what it was. He thought of this and listened to the man with the gun talking about escape and it seemed to him that, hanging there, being dragged violently along (It was here he said that he first noticed the goats' beards of moss in the trees, though it could have been there for several days so far as he knew. It just happened that he first noticed it here.), he would simply burst.

"Cant you get it into your head that the last thing I want to do is run away?" he cried. "You can set there with that gun and watch me; I give you fair lief. All I want is to put this woman—"

"And I told you she could come aboard," the man with the gun said in his level voice. "But there aint no room on no boat of mine for nobody hunting a sheriff in no kind of clothes, let alone a penitentiary suit."

"When he steps aboard, knock him in the head with the gun barrel," the man at the sweep said. "He's drunk."

"He aint coming aboard," the man with the gun said. "He's crazy."

Then the woman spoke. She didn't move, leaning in the door, in a pair of faded and patched and filthy overalls like the two men: "Give them some grub and tell them to get out of here." She moved, she crossed the deck and looked down at the convict's companion with her cold sullen face. "How much more time have you got?"

"It wasn't due till next month," the woman in the boat said. "But I—" The woman in overalls turned to the man with the gun.

"Give them some grub," she said. But the man with the gun was still looking down at the woman in the boat.

"Come on," he said to the convict. "Put her aboard, and beat it."

"And what'll happen to you," the woman in overalls said, "when you try to turn her over to an officer? When you lay alongside a sheriff and the sheriff asks you who you are?" Still the man with the gun didn't even look at her. He hardly even shifted the gun across his arm as he struck the woman across the face with the back of his other hand, hard. "You son of a bitch," she said. Still the man with the gun did not even look at her.

"Well?" he said to the convict.

"Don't you see I cant?" the convict cried. "Cant you see that?"

Now, he said, he gave up. He was doomed. That is, he knew now that he had been doomed from the very start never to get rid of her, just as the ones who sent him out with the skiff knew that he never would actually give up; when he recognised one of the objects which the woman in overalls was hurling into the skiff to be a can of condensed milk, he believed it to be a presage, gratuitous and irrevocable as a death-notice over the telegraph, that he was not even to find a flat stationary surface in time for the child to be born on it. So he told how he held the skiff alongside the shanty boat while the first tentative toying of the second wave made up beneath him, while the woman in overalls passed back and forth between house and rail, flinging the food—the hunk of salt meat, the ragged and filthy quilt, the scorched lumps of cold bread which she poured into the skiff from a heaped dishpan like so much garbage—while he clung to the strake against the mounting pull of the current, the new wave which for the moment he had forgotten because he was still trying to state the incredible simplicity of his desire and need until the man with the gun (the only one of the three who wore shoes) began to stamp at his hands, he snatching his hands away one at a time to avoid the heavy shoes, then grasping the rail again until the man with the gun kicked at his face, he flinging himself sideways to avoid the shoe and so breaking his hold on the rail, his weight canting the skiff off at a tangent on the increasing current so that it began to leave the shanty boat behind and he paddling again now, violently, as a man hurries toward the precipice for which he knows at last he is doomed, looking back at the other boat, the three faces sullen derisive and grim and rapidly diminishing across the widening water and at last, apoplectic, suffocating with the intolerable fact not that he had been refused but that he had been refused so little, had wanted so little, asked for so little, yet there had been demanded of him in return the one price out of all breath which (they must have known) if he could have paid it, he would not have been where he was, asking what he asked, raising the paddle and shaking it and screaming curses back at them even after the shotgun flashed and the charge went scuttering past along the water to one side.

So he hung there, he said, shaking the paddle and howling, when suddenly he remembered that other wave, the second wall of water full of houses and dead mules building up behind him back in the swamp. So he quit yelling then and went back to paddling. He was not trying to outrun it. He just knew from experience that when it overtook him, he would have to travel in the same direction it was moving in anyway, whether he wanted to or not, and when it did overtake him, he would begin to move too fast to stop, no matter what places he might come to where he could leave the woman, land her in time. Time: that was his itch now, so his only chance was to stay ahead of it as long as he could and hope to reach something before it struck. So he went on, driving the skiff with muscles which had been too tired so long they had quit feeling it, as when a man has had bad luck for so long that he ceases to believe it is even bad, let alone luck. Even when he ate—the scorched lumps the size of baseballs and the weight and durability of cannel coal even after having lain in the skiff's bilge where the shanty boat woman had thrown them—the iron-like lead-heavy objects which no man would have called bread outside of the crusted and scorched pan in which they had cooked—it was with one hand, begrudging even that from the paddle.

He tried to tell that too—that day while the skiff fled on among the bearded trees while every now and then small quiet tentative exploratory feelers would come up from the wave behind and toy for a moment at the skiff, light and curious, then go on with a faint hissing sighing, almost a chuckling, sound, the skiff going on, driving on with nothing to see but trees and water and solitude: until after a while it no longer seemed to him that he was trying to put space and distance behind him or shorten space and distance ahead but that both he and the wave were now hanging suspended simultaneous and unprogressing in pure time, upon a dreamy desolation in which he paddled on not from any hope even to reach anything at all but merely to keep intact what little of distance the length of the skiff provided between himself and the inert and inescapable mass of female meat before him; then night and the skiff rushing on, fast since any speed over anything unknown and invisible is too fast, with nothing before him and behind him the outrageous idea of a volume of moving water toppling forward, its crest frothed and shredded like fangs, and then dawn again (another of those dreamlike alterations day to dark then back to day again with that quality truncated, anachronic and unreal as the waxing and waning of lights in a theatre scene) and the skiff emerging now with the woman no longer supine beneath the shrunken soaked private's coat but sitting bolt upright, gripping the gunwales with both hands, her eyes closed and her lower lip caught between her teeth and he driving the splintered board furiously now, glaring at her out of his wild swollen sleepless face and crying, croaking, "Hold on! For God's sake hold on!"

"I'm trying to," she said. "But hurry! Hurry!" He told it, the unbelievable: hurry, hasten: the man falling from a cliff being told to catch onto something and save himself; the very telling of it emerging shadowy and burlesque, ludicrous, comic and mad, from the ague of unbearable forgetting with a quality more dreamily furious than any fable behind proscenium lights:

He was in a basin now—"A basin?" the plump convict said. "That's what you wash in."

"All right," the tall one said, harshly, above his hands. "I did." With a supreme effort he stilled them long enough to release the two bits of cigarette paper and watched them waft in light fluttering indecision to the floor between his feet, holding his hands motionless even for a moment longer—a basin, a broad peaceful yellow sea which had an abruptly and curiously ordered air, giving him, even at the moment, the impression that it was accustomed to water even if not total submersion; he even remembered the name of it, told to him two or three weeks later by someone: Atchafalaya—

"Louisiana?" the plump convict said. "You mean you were clean out of Mississippi? Hell fire." He stared at the tall one. "Shucks," he said. "That aint but just across from Vicksburg."

"They never named any Vicksburg across from where I was," the tall one said. "It was Baton Rouge they named." And now he began to talk about a town, a little neat white portrait town nestling among enormous very green trees, appearing suddenly in the telling as it probably appeared in actuality, abrupt and airy and miragelike and incredibly serene before him behind a scattering of boats moored to a line of freight cars standing flush to the doors in water. And now he tried to tell that too: how he stood waist-deep in water for a moment looking back and down at the skiff in which the woman half lay, her eyes still closed, her knuckles white on the gunwales and a tiny thread of blood creeping down her chin from her chewed lip, and he looking down at her in a kind of furious desperation.

"How far will I have to walk?" she said.

"I dont know, I tell you!" he cried. "But it's land somewhere yonder! It's land, houses."

"If I try to move, it wont even be born inside a boat," she said. "You'll have to get closer."

"Yes," he cried, wild, desperate, incredulous. "Wait. I'll go and surrender, then they will have—" He didn't finish, wait to finish; he told that too: himself splashing, stumbling, trying to run, sobbing and gasping; now he saw it— another loading platform standing above the yellow flood, the khaki figures on it as before, identical, the same; he said how the intervening days since that first innocent morning telescoped, vanished as if they had never been, the two contiguous succeeding instants (succeeding? simultaneous) and he transported across no intervening space but merely turned in his own footsteps, plunging, splashing, his arms raised, croaking harshly. He heard the startled shout, "There's one of them!", the command, the clash of equipment, the alarmed cry: "There he goes! There he goes!"

"Yes!" he cried, running, plunging. "Here I am! Here! Here!" running on, into the first scattered volley, stopping among the bullets, waving his arms, shrieking, "I want to surrender! I want to surrender!" watching not in terror but in amazed and absolutely unbearable outrage as a squatting clump of the khaki figures parted and he saw the machine gun, the blunt thick muzzle slant and drop and probe toward him and he still screaming in his hoarse crow's voice, "I want to surrender! Cant you hear me?" continuing to scream even as he whirled and plunged splashing, ducking, went completely under and heard the bullets going thuck-thuck-thuck on the water above him and he scrabbling still on the bottom, still trying to scream even before he regained his feet and still all submerged save his plunging unmistakable buttocks, the outraged screaming bubbling from his mouth and about his face since he merely wanted to surrender. Then he was comparatively screened, out of range, though not for long.

That is (he didn't tell how nor where) there was a moment in which he paused, breathed for a second before running again, the course back to the skiff open for the time being though he could still hear the shouts behind him and now and then a shot, and he panting, sobbing, a long savage tear in the flesh of one hand, got when and how he did not know, and he wasting precious breath, speaking to no one now any more than the scream of the dying rabbit is addressed to any mortal ear but rather an indictment of all breath and its folly and suffering, its infinite capacity for folly and pain, which seems to be its only immortality: "All in the world I want is just to surrender."

He returned to the skiff and got in and took up his splintered plank. And now when he told this, despite the fury of element which climaxed it, it (the telling) became quite simple; he now even creased another cigarette paper between fingers which did not tremble at all and filled the paper from the tobacco sack without spilling a flake, as though he had passed from the machine-gun's barrage into a bourne beyond any more amazement: so that the subsequent part of his narrative seemed to reach his listeners as though from beyond a sheet of slightly milky though still transparent glass, as something not heard but seen—a series of shadows, edgeless yet distinct, and smoothly flowing, logical and unfrantic and making no sound: They were in the skiff, in the center of the broad placid trough which had no boundaries and down which the tiny forlorn skiff flew to the irresistible coercion of a current going once more he knew not where, the neat small liveoak-bowered towns unattainable and miragelike and apparently attached to nothing upon the airy and unchanging horizon. He did not believe them, they did not matter, he was doomed; they were less than the figments of smoke or of delirium, and he driving his unceasing paddle without destination or even hope now, looking now and then at the woman sitting with her knees drawn up and locked and her entire body one terrific clench while the threads of bloody saliva crept from her teeth-clenched lower lip. He was going nowhere and fleeing from nothing, he merely continued to paddle because he had paddled so long now that he believed if he stopped his muscles would scream in agony. So when it happened he was not surprised. He heard the sound which he knew well (he had heard it but once before, true enough, but no man needed hear it but once) and he had been expecting it; he looked back, still driving the paddle, and saw it, curled, crested with its straw-like flotsam of trees and debris and dead beasts, and he glared over his shoulder at it for a full minute out of that attenuation far beyond the point of outragement where even suffering, the capability of being further affronted, had ceased, from which he now contemplated with savage and invulnerable curiosity the further extent to which his now anesthetised nerves could bear, what next could be invented for them to bear, until the wave actually began to rear above his head into its thunderous climax. Then only did he turn his head. His stroke did not falter, it neither slowed nor increased; still paddling with that spent hypnotic steadiness, he saw the swimming deer. He did not know what it was nor that he had altered the skiff's course to follow it, he just watched the swimming head before him as the wave boiled down and the skiff rose bodily in the old familiar fashion on a welter of tossing trees and houses and bridges and fences, he still paddling even while the paddle found no purchase save air and still paddled even as he and the deer shot forward side by side at arm's length, he watching the deer now, watching the deer begin to rise out of the water bodily until it was actually running along upon the surface, rising still, soaring clear of the water altogether, vanishing upward in a dying crescendo of splashings and snapping branches, its damp scut flashing upward, the entire animal vanishing upward as smoke vanishes. And now the skiff struck and canted and he was out of it too, standing knee-deep, springing out and falling to his knees, scrambling up, glaring after the vanished deer. "Land!" he croaked. "Land! Hold on! Just hold on!" He caught the woman beneath the arms, dragging her out of the boat, plunging and panting after the vanished deer. Now earth actually appeared—an acclivity smooth and swift and steep, bizarre, solid and unbelievable; an Indian mound, and he plunging at the muddy slope, slipping back, the woman struggling in his muddy hands.

"Let me down!" she cried. "Let me down!" But he held her, panting, sobbing, and rushed again at the muddy slope; he had almost reached the flat crest with his now violently unmanageable burden when a stick under his foot gathered itself with thick convulsive speed. *It was a snake*, he thought as his feet fled beneath him and with the indubitable last of his strength he half pushed and half flung the woman up the bank as he shot feet first and face down back into that medium upon which he had lived for more days and nights than he could remember and from which he himself had never completely emerged, as if his own failed and spent flesh were attempting to carry out his furious unflagging will for severance at any price, even that of drowning, from the burden with which, unwitting and without choice, he had been doomed. Later it seemed to him that he had carried back beneath the surface with him the sound of the infant's first mewling cry.

When the woman asked him if he had a knife, standing there in the streaming bed-ticking garments which had got him shot at, the second time by a machine gun, on the two occasions when he had seen any human life after leaving the levee four days ago, the convict felt exactly as he had in the fleeing skiff when the woman suggested that they had better hurry. He felt the same outrageous affronting of a condition purely moral, the same raging impotence to find any answer to it; so that, standing above her, spent suffocating and inarticulate, it was a full minute before he comprehended that she was now crying, "The can! The can in the boat!" He did not anticipate what she could want with it; he did not even wonder nor stop to ask. He turned running; this time he thought, *It's another moccasin* as the thick body truncated in that awkward reflex which had nothing of alarm in it but only alertness, he not even shifting his stride though he knew his running foot would fall within a yard of the flat head. The bow of the skiff was well up the slope now where the wave had set it and there was another snake just crawling over the stern into it and as he stooped for the bailing can he saw something else swimming toward the mound, he didn't know what—a head, a face at the apex of a vee of ripples. He snatched up the can; by pure juxtaposition of it and water he scooped it full, already turning. He saw the deer again, or another one. That is, he saw a deer—a side glance, the light smoke-colored phantom in a cypress vista then gone, vanished, he not pausing to look after it, galloping back to the woman and kneeling with the can to her lips until she told him better.

It had contained a pint of beans or tomatoes, something, hermetically sealed and opened by four blows of an axe heel, the metal flap turned back, the jagged edges razor-sharp. She told him how, and he used this in lieu of a knife, he removed one of his shoelaces and cut it in two with the sharp tin. Then she wanted warm water—"If I just had a little hot water," she said in a weak serene voice without particular hope; only when he thought of matches it was again a good deal like when she had asked him if he had a knife, until she fumbled in the pocket of the shrunken tunic (it had a darker double vee on one cuff and a darker blotch on the shoulder where service stripes and a divisional emblem had been ripped off but this meant nothing to him) and produced a match-box contrived by telescoping two shotgun shells. So he drew her back a little from the water and went to hunt wood dry enough to burn, thinking this time, *It's just another snake*, only, he said, he should have thought *ten thousand other snakes*: and now he knew it was not the same deer because he saw three at one time, does or bucks he did not know which since they were all antlerless in May and besides he had never seen one of any kind anywhere before except on a Christmas card; and then the rabbit, drowned, dead anyway, already torn open, the bird, the hawk, standing upon it—the erected crest, the hard vicious patrician nose, the intolerant omnivorous yellow eye—and he kicking at it, kicking it lurching and broadwinging into the actual air.

When he returned with the wood and the dead rabbit, the baby, wrapped in the tunic, lay wedged between two cypress-knees and the woman was not in sight, though while the convict knelt in the mud, blowing and nursing his meagre flame, she came slowly and weakly from the direction of the water. Then, the water heated at last and there produced from some where he was never to know, she herself perhaps never to know until the need comes, no woman perhaps ever to know, only no woman will even wonder, that square of something somewhere between sackcloth and silk—squatting, his own wet garments steaming in the fire's heat, he watched her bathe the child with a savage curiosity and interest that became amazed unbelief, so that at last he stood above them both, looking down at the tiny terra-cotta-colored creature resembling nothing, and thought, *And this is all. This is what severed me violently from all I ever knew and did not wish to leave and cast me upon a medium I was born to fear, to fetch up at last in a place I never saw before and where I do not even know where I am.*

Then he returned to the water and refilled the bailing can. It was drawing toward sunset now (or what would have been sunset save for the high prevailing overcast) of this day whose beginning he could not even remember; when he returned to where the fire burned in the interlaced gloom of the cypresses, even after this short absence, evening had definitely come, as though darkness too had taken refuge upon that quarter-acre mound, that earthen Ark out of Genesis, that dim wet cypress-choked life-teeming constricted desolation in what direction and how far from what and where he had no more idea than of the day of the month, and had now with the setting of the sun crept forth again to spread upon the waters. He stewed the rabbit in sections while the fire burned redder and redder in the darkness where the shy wild eyes of small animals—once the tall mild almost plate-sized stare of one of the deer—glowed and vanished and glowed again, the broth hot and rank after the four days; he seemed to hear the roar of his own saliva as he watched the woman sip the first canful. Then he drank too; they ate the other fragments which had been charring and scorching on willow twigs; it was full night now. "You and him better sleep in the boat," the convict said. "We want to get an early start to-morrow." He shoved the bow of the skiff off the land so it would lie level, he lengthened the painter with a piece of grapevine and returned to the fire and tied the grapevine about his wrist and lay down. It was mud he lay upon, but it was solid underneath, it was earth, it did not move; if you fell upon it you broke your bones against its incontrovertible passivity sometimes but it did not accept you substanceless and enveloping and suffocating, down and down and down; it was hard at times to drive a plow through, it sent you spent, weary, and cursing its light-long insatiable demands back to your bunk at sunset at times but it did not snatch you violently out of all familiar knowing and sweep you thrall and impotent for days against any returning. *I dont know where I am and I dont reckon I know the way back to where I want to go,* he thought. *But at least the boat has stopped long enough to give me a chance to turn it around.*

He waked at dawn, the light faint, the sky jonquil-colored; the day would be fine. The fire had burned out; on the opposite side of the cold ashes lay three snakes motionless and parallel as underscoring, and in the swiftly making light others seemed to materialise: earth which an instant before had been mere earth broke up into motionless coils and loops, branches which a moment before had been mere branches now become immobile ophidian festoons even as the convict stood thinking about food, about something hot before they started. But he decided against this, against wasting this much time, since there still remained in the skiff quite a few of the rocklike objects which the shanty woman had flung into it; besides (thinking this), no matter how fast nor successfully he hunted, he would never be able to lay up enough food to get them back to where they wanted to go. So he returned to the skiff, paying himself back to it by his vine-spliced painter, back to the water on which a low mist thick as cotton batting (though apparently not very tall, deep) lay, into which the stern of the skiff was already beginning to disappear although it lay with its prow almost touching the mound. The woman waked, stirred. "We fixing to start now?" she said.

"Yah," the convict said. "You aint aiming to have another one this morning, are you?" He got in and shoved the skiff clear of the land, which immediately began to dissolve into the mist. "Hand me the oar," he said over his shoulder, not turning yet.

"The oar?"

He turned his head. "The oar. You're laying on it." But she was not, and for an instant during which the mound, the island continued to fade slowly into the mist which seemed to enclose the skiff in weightless and impalpable wool like a precious or fragile bauble or jewel, the convict squatted not in dismay but in that frantic and astonished outrage of a man who, having just escaped a falling safe, is struck by the following two-ounce paper weight which was sitting on it: this the more unbearable because he knew that never in his life had he less time to give way to it. He did not hesitate. Grasping the grapevine end he sprang into the water, vanishing in the violent action of climbing, and reappeared still climbing and (who had never learned to swim) plunged and threshed on toward the almost-vanished mound, moving through the water then upon it as the deer had done yesterday and scrabbled up the muddy slope and lay gasping and panting, still clutching the grapevine end.

Now the first thing he did was to choose what he believed to be the most suitable tree (for an instant in which he knew he was insane he thought of trying to saw it down with the flange of the bailing can) and build a fire against the butt of it. Then he went to seek food. He spent the next six days seeking it while the tree burned through and fell and burned through again at the proper length and he nursing little constant cunning flames along the flanks of the log to make it paddle-shaped, nursing them at night too while the woman and baby (it was eating, nursing now, he turning his back or even returning into the woods each time she prepared to open the faded tunic) slept in the skiff. He learned to watch for stooping hawks and so found more rabbits and twice possums; they ate some drowned fish which gave them both a rash and then a violent flux and one snake which the woman thought was turtle and which did them no harm, and one night it rained and he got up and dragged brush, shaking the snakes (he no longer thought, *It aint nothing but another moccasin*, he just stepped aside for them as they, when there was time, telescoped sullenly aside for him) out of it with the old former feeling of personal invulnerability and built a shelter and the rain stopped at once and did not recommence and the woman went back to the skiff.

Then one night—the slow tedious charring log was almost a paddle now—one night and he was in bed, in his bed in the bunkhouse and it was cold, he was trying to pull the covers up only his mule wouldn't let him, prodding and bumping heavily at him, trying to get into the narrow bed with him and now the bed was cold too and wet and he was trying to get out of it only the mule would not let him, holding him by his belt in its teeth, jerking and bumping him back into the cold wet bed and, leaning, gave him a long swipe across the face with its cold limber musculated tongue and he waked to no fire, no coal even beneath where the almost-finished paddle had been charring and something else prolonged and coldly limber passed swiftly across his body where he lay in four inches of water while the nose of the skiff alternately tugged at the grapevine tied about his waist and bumped and shoved him back into the water again. Then something else came up and began to nudge at his ankle (the log, the oar, it was) even as he groped frantically for the skiff, hearing the swift rustling going to and fro inside the hull as the woman began to thrash about and scream. "Rats!" she cried. "It's full of rats!"

"Lay still!" he cried. "It's just snakes. Cant you hold still long enough for me to find the boat?" Then he found it, he got into it with the unfinished paddle; again the thick muscular body convulsed under his foot; it did not strike; he would not have cared, glaring astern where he could see a little— the faint outer luminosity of the open water. He poled toward it, thrusting aside the snake-looped branches, the bottom of the skiff resounding faintly to thick solid plops, the woman shrieking steadily. Then the skiff was clear of the trees, the mound, and now he could feel the bodies whipping about his ankles and hear the rasp of them as they went over the gunwale. He drew the log in and scooped it forward along the bottom of the boat and up and out; against the pallid water he could see three more of them in lashing convolutions before they vanished. "Shut up!" he cried. "Hush! I wish I was a snake so I could get out too!"

When once more the pale and heatless wafer disc of the early sun stared down at the skiff (whether they were moving or not the convict did not know) in its nimbus of fine cotton batting, the convict was hearing again that sound which he had heard twice before and would never forget—that sound of deliberate and irresistible and monstrously disturbed water. But this time he could not tell from what direction it came. It seemed to be everywhere, waxing and fading; it was like a phantom behind the mist, at one instant miles away, the next on the point of overwhelming the skiff within the next second; suddenly, in the instant he would believe (his whole weary body would spring and scream) that he was about to drive the skiff point-blank into it and with the unfinished paddle of the color and texture of sooty bricks, like something gnawed out of an old chimney by beavers and weighing twenty-five pounds, he would whirl the skiff frantically and find the sound dead ahead of him again. Then something bellowed tremendously above his head, he heard human voices, a bell jangled and the sound ceased and the mist vanished as when you draw your hand across a frosted pane, and the skiff now lay upon a sunny glitter of brown water flank to flank with, and about thirty yards away from, a steamboat. The decks were crowded and packed with men women and children sitting or standing beside and among a homely conglomeration of hurried furniture, who looked mournfully and silently down into the skiff while the convict and the man with a megaphone in the pilot house talked to each other in alternate puny shouts and roars above the chuffing of the reversed engines:

"What in hell are you trying to do? Commit suicide?"

"Which is the way to Vicksburg?"

"Vicksburg? Vicksburg? Lay alongside and come aboard."

"Will you take the boat too?"

"Boat? Boat?" Now the megaphone cursed, the roaring waves of blasphemy and biological supposition empty cavernous and bodiless in turn, as if the water, the air, the mist had spoken it, roaring the words then taking them back to itself and no harm done, no scar, no insult left anywhere. "If I took aboard every floating sardine can you sonabitchin mushrats want me to I wouldn't even have room forrard for a leadsman. Come aboard! Do you expect me to hang here on stern engines till hell freezes?"

"I aint coming without the boat," the convict said. Now another voice spoke, so calm and mild and sensible that for a moment it sounded more foreign and out of place than even the megaphone's bellowing and bodiless profanity:

"Where is it you are trying to go?"

"I aint trying," the convict said. "I'm going. Parchman." The man who had spoken last turned and appeared to converse with a third man in the pilot house. Then he looked down at the skiff again.

"Carnarvon?"

"What?" the convict said. "Parchman?"

"All right. We're going that way. We'll put you off where you can get home. Come aboard."

"The boat too?"

"Yes, yes. Come along. We're burning coal just to talk to you." So the convict came alongside then and watched them help the woman and baby over the rail and he came aboard himself, though he still held to the end of the vine-spliced painter until the skiff was hoisted onto the boiler deck. "My God," the man, the gentle one, said, "is that what you have been using for a paddle?"

"Yah," the convict said. "I lost the plank."

"The plank," the mild man (the convict told how he seemed to whisper it), "the plank. Well. Come along and get something to eat. Your boat is all right now."

"I reckon I'll wait here," the convict said. Because now, he told them, he began to notice for the first time that the other people, the other refugees who crowded the deck, who had gathered in a quiet circle about the upturned skiff on which he and the woman sat, the grapevine painter wrapped several times about his wrist and clutched in his hand, staring at him and the woman with queer hot mournful intensity, were not white people—

"You mean niggers?" the plump convict said.

"No. Not Americans."

"Not Americans? You was clean out of *America* even?"

"I don't know," the tall one said. "They called it Atchafalaya."—Because after a while he said, "What?" to the man and the man did it again, gobble-gobble—

"Gobble-gobble?" the plump convict said.

"That's the way they talked," the tall one said. "Gobble-gobble, whang, caw-caw-to-to."—And he sat there and watched them gobbling at one another and then looking at him again, then they fell back and the mild man (he wore a Red Cross brassard) entered, followed by a waiter with a tray of food. The mild man carried two glasses of whiskey.

"Dring this," the mild man said. "This will warm you." The woman took hers and drank it but the convict told how he looked at his and thought, *I aint tasted whiskey in seven years.* He had not tasted it but once before that; it was at the still itself back in a pine hollow; he was seventeen, he had gone there with four companions, two of whom were grown men, one of twenty-two or -three, the other about forty; he remembered it. That is, he remembered perhaps a third of that evening—a fierce turmoil in the hell-colored firelight, the shock and shock of blows about his head (and likewise of his own fists on other hard bone), then the waking to a splitting and blinding sun in a place, a cowshed, he had never seen before and which later turned out to be twenty miles from his home. He said he thought of this and he looked about at the faces watching him and he said,

"I reckon not."

"Come, come," the mild man said. "Drink it."

"I dont want it."

"Nonsense," the mild man said. "I'm a doctor. Here. Then you can eat." So he took the glass and even then he hesitated but again the mild man said, "Come along, down with it; you're still holding us up," in that voice still calm and sensible but a little sharp too—the voice of a man who could keep calm and affable because he wasn't used to being crossed—and he drank the whiskey and even in the second between the sweet full fire in his belly and when it began to happen he was trying to say, "I tried to tell you! I tried to!" But it was too late now in the pallid sun-glare of the tenth day of terror and hopelessness and despair and impotence and rage and outrage and it was himself and the mule, his mule (they had let him name it—John Henry) which no man save he had plowed for five years now and whose ways and habits he knew and respected and who knew his ways and habits so well that each of them could anticipate the other's very movements and intentions; it was himself and the mule, the little gobbling faces flying before him, the familiar hard skull-bones shocking against his fists, his voice shouting, "Come on, John Henry! Plow them down! Gobble them down, boy!" even as the bright hot red wave turned back, meeting it joyously, happily, lifted, poised, then hurling through space, triumphant and yelling, then again the old shocking blow at the back of his head: he lay on the deck, flat on his back and pinned arm and leg and cold sober again, his nostrils gushing again, the mild man stooping over him with behind the thin rimless glasses the coldest eyes the convict had ever seen—eyes which the convict said were not looking at him but at the gushing blood with nothing in the world in them but complete impersonal interest.

"Good man," the mild man said. "Plenty of life in the old carcass yet, eh? Plenty of good red blood too. Anyone ever suggest to you that you were hemophilic?" ("What?" the plump convict said. "Hemophilic? You know what that means?" The tall convict had his cigarette going now, his body jackknifed backward into the coffinlike space between the upper and lower bunks, lean, clean, motionless, the blue smoke wreathing across his lean dark aquiline shaven face. "That's a calf that's a bull and a cow at the same time."

"No, it aint," a third convict said. "It's a calf or a colt that aint neither one."

"Hell fire," the plump one said. "He's got to be one or the other to keep from drounding." He had never ceased to look at the tall one in the bunk; now he spoke to him again: "You let him call you that?") The tall one had done so. He did not answer the doctor (this was where he stopped thinking of him as the mild man) at all. He could not move either, though he felt fine, he felt better than he had in ten days. So they helped him to his feet and steadied him over and lowered him onto the upturned skiff beside the woman, where he sat bent forward, elbows on knees in the immemorial attitude, watching his own bright crimson staining the mud-trodden deck, until the doctor's clean clipped hand appeared under his nose with a phial.

"Smell," the doctor said. "Deep." The convict inhaled, the sharp ammoniac sensation burned up his nostrils and into his throat. "Again," the doctor said. The convict inhaled obediently. This time he choked and spat a gout of blood, his nose now had no more feeling than a toenail, other than it felt about the size of a ten-inch shovel, and as cold.

"I ask you to excuse me," he said. "I never meant—"

"Why?" the doctor said. "You put up as pretty a scrap against forty or fifty men as I ever saw. You lasted a good two seconds. Now you can eat something. Or do you think that will send you haywire again?"

They both ate, sitting on the skiff, the gobbling faces no longer watching them now, the convict gnawing slowly and painfully at the thick sandwich, hunched, his face laid sideways to the food and parallel to the earth as a dog chews; the steamboat went on. At noon there were bowls of hot soup and bread and more coffee; they ate this too, sitting side by side on the skiff, the grapevine still wrapped about the convict's wrist. The baby waked and nursed and slept again and they talked quietly:

"Was it Parchman he said he was going to take us?"

"That's where I told him I wanted to go."

"It never sounded exactly like Parchman to me. It sounded like he said something else." The convict had thought that too. He had been thinking about that fairly soberly ever since they boarded the steamboat and soberly indeed ever since he had remarked the nature of the other passengers, those men and women definitely a little shorter than he and with skin a little different in pigmentation from any sunburn, even though the eyes were sometimes blue or gray, who talked to one another in a tongue he had never heard before and who apparently did not understand his own, people the like of whom he had never seen about Parchman nor anywhere else and who he did not believe were going there or beyond there either. But after his hillbilly country fashion and kind he would not ask, because to his raising asking information was asking a favor and you did not ask favors of strangers; if they offered them perhaps you accepted and you expressed gratitude almost tediously recapitulant, but you did not ask. So he would watch and wait, as he had done before, and do or try to do to the best of his ability what the best of his judgment dictated.

So he waited, and in midafternoon the steamboat chuffed and thrust through a willow-choked gorge and emerged from it, and now the convict knew it was the River. He could believe it now—the tremendous reach, yellow and sleepy in the afternoon—("Because it's too big," he told them soberly. "Aint no flood in the world big enough to make it do more than stand a little higher so it can look back and see just where the flea is, just exactly where to scratch. It's the little ones, the little piddling creeks that run backward one day and forward the next and come busting down on a man full of dead mules and hen houses.") —and the steamboat moving up this now (*like a ant crossing a plate*, the convict thought, sitting beside the woman on the upturned skiff, the baby nursing again, apparently looking too out across the water where, a mile away on either hand, the twin lines of levee resembled parallel unbroken floating thread) and then it was nearing sunset and he began to hear, to notice, the voices of the doctor and of the man who had first bawled at him through the megaphone now bawling again from the pilot house overhead:

"Stop? Stop? Am I running a street car?"

"Stop for the novelty then," the doctor's pleasant voice said. "I dont know how many trips back and forth you have made in yonder nor how many of what you call mushrats you have fetched out. But this is the first time you ever had two people—no, three—who not only knew the name of some place they wished to go to but were actually trying to go there." So the convict waited while the sun slanted more and more and the steamboat-ant crawled steadily on across its vacant and gigantic plate turning more and more to copper. But he did not ask, he just waited. *Maybe it was Carrollton he said*, he thought. *It begun with a C*. But he did not believe that either. He did not know where he was, but he did know that this was not anywhere near the Carrollton he remembered from that day seven years ago when, shackled wrist to wrist with the deputy sheriff, he had passed through it on the train—the slow spaced repeated shattering banging of trucks where two railroads crossed, a random scattering of white houses tranquil among trees on green hills lush with summer, a pointing spire, the finger of the hand of God. But there was no river there. *And you aint never close to this river without knowing it*, he thought. *I dont care who you are nor where you have been all your life*. Then the head of the steamboat began to swing across the stream, its shadow swinging too, travelling long before it across the water, toward the vacant ridge of willow-massed earth empty of all life. There was nothing there at all, the convict could not even see either earth or water beyond it; it was as though the steamboat were about to crash slowly through the thin low frail willow barrier and embark into space, or lacking this, slow and back and fill and disembark him into space, granted it was about to disembark him, granted this was that place which was not near Parchman and was not Carrollton either, even though it did begin with C. Then he turned his head and saw the doctor stooping over the woman, pushing the baby's eyelid up with his forefinger, peering at it.

"Who else was there when he came?" the doctor said.

"Nobody," the convict said.

"Did it all yourselves, eh?"

"Yes," the convict said. Now the doctor stood up and looked at the convict.

"This is Carnarvon," he said.

"Carnarvon?" the convict said. "That aint—" Then he stopped, ceased. And now he told about that—the intent eyes as dispassionate as ice behind the rimless glasses, the clipped quick-tempered face that was not accustomed to being crossed or lied to either. ("Yes," the plump convict said. "That's what I was aiming to ask. Them clothes. Anybody would know them. How if this doctor was as smart as you claim he was—"

"I had slept in them for ten nights, mostly in the mud," the tall one said. "I had been rowing since midnight with that sapling oar I had tried to burn out that I never had time to scrape the soot off. But it's being scared and worried and then scared and then worried again in clothes for days and days and days that changes the way they look. I dont mean just your pants." He did not laugh. "Your face too. That doctor knowed."

"All right," the plump one said. "Go on.")

"I know it," the doctor said. "I discovered that while you were lying on the deck yonder sobering up again. Now dont lie to me. I dont like lying. This boat is going to New Orleans."

"No," the convict said immediately, quietly, with absolute finality. He could hear them again—the thuck-thuck-thuck on the water where an instant before he had been. But he was not thinking of the bullets. He had forgotten them, forgiven them. He was thinking of himself crouching, sobbing, panting before running again—the voice, the indictment, the cry of final and irrevocable repudiation of the old primal faithless Manipulator of all the lust and folly and injustice: *All in the world I wanted was just to surrender;* thinking of it, remembering it but without heat now, without passion now and briefer than an epitaph: *No. I tried that once. They shot at me.*

"So you dont want to go to New Orleans. And you didn't exactly plan to go to Carnarvon. But you will take Carnarvon in preference to New Orleans." The convict said nothing. The doctor looked at him, the magnified pupils like the heads of two bridge nails. "What were you in for? Hit him harder than you thought, eh?"

"No. I tried to rob a train."

"Say that again." The convict said it again. "Well? Go on. You dont say that in the year 1927 and just stop, man." So the convict told it, dispassionately too—about the magazines, the pistol which would not shoot, the mask and the dark lantern in which no draft had been arranged to keep the candle burning so that it died almost with the match but even then left the metal too hot to carry, won with subscriptions. *Only it aint my eyes or my mouth either he's watching,* he thought. *It's like he is watching the way my hair grows on my head.* "I see," the doctor said. "But something went wrong. But you've had plenty of time to think about it since. To decide what was wrong, what you failed to do."

"Yes," the convict said. "I've thought about it a right smart since."

"So next time you are not going to make that mistake."

"I dont know," the convict said. "There aint going to be a next time."

"Why? If you know what you did wrong, they wont catch you next time."
The convict looked at the doctor steadily. They looked at each other steadily;
the two sets of eyes were not so different after all. "I reckon I see what you
mean," the convict said presently. "I was eighteen then. I'm twenty-five now."

"Oh," the doctor said. Now (the convict tried to tell it) the doctor did not
move, he just simply quit looking at the convict. He produced a pack of cheap
cigarettes from his coat. "Smoke?" he said.

"I wouldn't care for none," the convict said.

"Quite," the doctor said in that affable clipped voice. He put the cigarettes
away. "There has been conferred upon my race (the Medical race) also the
power to bind and to loose, if not by Jehovah perhaps, certainly by the American Medical Association—on which incidentally, in this day of Our Lord, I
would put my money, at any odds, at any amount, at any time. I dont know
just how far out of bounds I am on this specific occasion but I think we'll put it
to the touch." He cupped his hands to his mouth, toward the pilot house overhead. "Captain!" he shouted. "We'll put these three passengers ashore here."
He turned to the convict again. "Yes," he said, "I think I shall let your native
state lick its own vomit. Here." Again his hand emerged from his pocket, this
time with a bill in it.

"No," the convict said.

"Come, come; I dont like to be disputed either."

"No," the convict said. "I aint got any way to pay it back."

"Did I ask you to pay it back?"

"No," the convict said. "I never asked to borrow it either."

So once more he stood on dry land, who had already been toyed with twice
by that risible and concentrated power of water, once more than should have
fallen to the lot of any one man, any one lifetime, yet for whom there was
reserved still another unbelievable recapitulation, he and the woman standing
on the empty levee, the sleeping child wrapped in the faded tunic and the
grapevine painter still wrapped about the convict's wrist, watching the steamboat back away and turn and once more crawl onward up the platter-like reach
of vacant water burnished more and more to copper, its trailing smoke roiling
in slow copper-edged gouts, thinning out along the water, fading, stinking
away across the vast serene desolation, the boat growing smaller and smaller
until it did not seem to crawl at all but to hang stationary in the airy substanceless sunset, dissolving into nothing like a pellet of floating mud.

Then he turned and for the first time looked about him, behind him, recoiling,
not through fear but through pure reflex and not physically but the soul, the
spirit, that profound sober alert attentiveness of the hillman who will not ask
anything of strangers, not even information, thinking quietly, *No. This aint
Carrollton neither.* Because he now looked down the almost perpendicular landward slope of the levee through sixty feet of absolute space, upon a surface,
a terrain flat as a waffle and of the color of a waffle or perhaps of the summer
coat of a claybank horse and possessing that same piled density of a rug or
peltry, spreading away without undulation yet with that curious appearance

of imponderable solidity like fluid, broken here and there by thick humps of arsenical green which nevertheless still seemed to possess no height and by writhen veins of the color of ink which he began to suspect to be actual water but with judgment reserved, with judgment still reserved even when presently he was walking in it. That's what he said, told: So they went on. He didn't tell how he got the skiff singlehanded up the revetment and across the crown and down the opposite sixty-foot drop, he just said he went on, in a swirling cloud of mosquitoes like hot cinders, thrusting and plunging through the saw-edged grass which grew taller than his head and which whipped back at his arms and face like limber knives, dragging by the vine-spliced painter the skiff in which the woman sat, slogging and stumbling knee-deep in something less of earth than water, along one of those black winding channels less of water than earth: and then (he was in the skiff too now, paddling with the charred log, what footing there had been having given away beneath him without warning thirty minutes ago, leaving only the air-filled bubble of his jumperback ballooning lightly on the twilit water until he rose to the surface and scrambled into the skiff) the house, the cabin a little larger than a horse-box, of cypress boards and an iron roof, rising on ten-foot stilts slender as spiders' legs, like a shabby and death-stricken (and probably poisonous) wading creature which had got that far into that flat waste and died with nothing nowhere in reach or sight to lie down upon, a pirogue tied to the foot of a crude ladder, a man standing in the open door holding a lantern (it was that dark now) above his head, gobbling down at them.

He told it—of the next eight or nine or ten days, he did not remember which, while the four of them—himself and the woman and baby and the little wiry man with rotting teeth and soft wild bright eyes like a rat or a chipmunk, whose language neither of them could understand—lived in the room and a half. He did not tell it that way, just as he apparently did not consider it worth the breath to tell how he had got the hundred-and-sixty-pound skiff single-handed up and across and down the sixty-foot levee. He just said, "After a while we come to a house and we stayed there eight or nine days then they blew up the levee with dynamite so we had to leave." That was all. But he remembered it, but quietly now, with the cigar now, the good one the Warden had given him (though not lighted yet) in his peaceful and steadfast hand, remembering that first morning when he waked on the thin pallet beside his host (the woman and baby had the one bed) with the fierce sun already latticed through the warped rough planking of the wall, and stood on the rickety porch looking out upon that flat fecund waste neither earth nor water, where even the senses doubted which was which, which rich and massy air and which mazy and impalpable vegetation, and thought quietly, *He must do something here to eat and live. But I dont know what. And until I can go on again, until I can find where I am and how to pass that town without them seeing me I will have to help him do it so we can eat and live too, and I dont know what.* And he had a change of clothing too, almost at once on that first morning, not telling any more than he had about the skiff and the levee how he had begged borrowed or bought from the man whom he had not laid eyes on twelve hours ago and with whom on the day he saw him for the last time he still could exchange no word, the pair of dungaree pants which even the Cajan had discarded as no longer wearable, filthy, buttonless, the legs slashed and frayed into fringe like that on an 1890 hammock, in which he stood naked from the waist up and holding out to her the mud-caked and soot-stained jumper and overall when the woman waked on that first morning in the crude bunk nailed into one corner and filled with dried grass, saying, "Wash them. Good. I want all them stains out. All of them."

"But the jumper," she said. "Ain't he got ere old shirt too? That sun and them mosquitoes—" But he did not even answer, and she said no more either, though when he and the Cajan returned at dark the garments were clean, stained a little still with the old mud and soot, but clean, resembling again what they were supposed to resemble as (his arms and back already a fiery red which would be blisters by tomorrow) he spread the garments out and examined them and then rolled them up carefully in a six-months-old New Orleans paper and thrust the bundle behind a rafter, where it remained while day followed day and the blisters on his back broke and suppurated and he would sit with his face expressionless as a wooden mask beneath the sweat while the Cajan doped his back with something on a filthy rag from a filthy saucer, she still saying nothing since she too doubtless knew what his reason was, not from that rapport of the wedded conferred upon her by the two weeks during which they had jointly suffered all the crises emotional social economic and even moral which do not always occur even in the ordinary fifty married years (the old married: you have seen them, the electroplate reproductions, the thousand identical coupled faces with only a collarless stud or a fichu out of Louisa Alcott to denote the sex, looking in pairs like the winning braces of dogs after a field trial, out from among the packed columns of disaster and alarm and baseless assurance and hope and incredible insensitivity and insulation from tomorrow propped by a thousand morning sugar bowls or coffee urns; or singly, rocking on porches or sitting in the sun beneath the tobacco-stained porticoes of a thousand county courthouses, as though with the death of the other having inherited a sort of rejuvenescence, immortality; relict, they take a new lease on breath and seem to live forever, as though that flesh which the old ceremony or ritual had morally purified and made legally one had actually become so with long tedious habit and he or she who entered the ground first took all of it with him or her, leaving only the old permanent enduring bone, free and tramelless)—not because of this but because she too had stemmed at some point from the same dim hill-bred Abraham.

So the bundle remained behind the rafter and day followed day while he and his partner (he was in partnership now with his host, hunting alligators on shares, on the halvers he called it—"Halvers?" the plump convict said. "How could you make a business agreement with a man you claim you couldn't even talk to?"

"I never had to talk to him," the tall one said. "Money aint got but one language.") departed at dawn each day, at first together in the pirogue but later singly, the one in the pirogue and the other in the skiff, the one with the battered and pitted rifle, the other with the knife and a piece of knotted rope and a lightwood club the size and weight and shape of a Thuringian mace, stalking their pleistocene nightmares up and down the secret inky channels which writhed the flat brass-colored land. He remembered that too: that first morning when turning in the sunrise from the rickety platform he saw the hide nailed drying to the wall and stopped dead, looking at it quietly, thinking quietly and soberly, *So that's it. That's what he does in order to eat and live,* knowing it was a hide, a skin, but from what animal, by association, ratiocination or even memory of any picture out of his dead youth, he did not know but knowing that it was the reason, the explanation, for the little lost spider-legged house (which had already begun to die, to rot from the legs upward almost before the roof was nailed on) set in that teeming and myriad desolation, enclosed and lost within the furious embrace of flowing mare earth and stallion sun, divining through pure rapport of kind for kind, hillbilly and bayou rat, the two one and identical because of the same grudged dispensation and niggard fate of hard and unceasing travail not to gain future security, a balance in the bank or even in a buried soda can for slothful and easy old age, but just permission to endure and endure to buy air to feel and sun to drink for each's little while, thinking (the convict), *Well, anyway I am going to find out what it is sooner than I expected to,* and did so, re-entered the house where the woman was just waking in the one sorry built-in straw-filled bunk which the Cajan had surrendered to her, and ate the breakfast (the rice, a semi-liquid mess violent with pepper and mostly fish considerably high, the chicory-thickened coffee) and, shirtless, followed the little scuttling bobbing bright-eyed rotten-toothed man down the crude ladder and into the pirogue. He had never seen a pirogue either and he believed that it would not remain upright—not that it was light and precariously balanced with its open side upward but that there was inherent in the wood, the very log, some dynamic and unsleeping natural law, almost will, which its present position outraged and violated—yet accepting this too as he had the fact that that hide had belonged to something larger than any calf or hog and that anything which looked like that on the outside would be more than likely to have teeth and claws too, accepting this, squatting in the pirogue, clutching both gunwales, rigidly immobile as though he had an egg filled with nitroglycerin in his mouth and scarcely breathing, thinking, *If that's it, then I can do it too and even if he cant tell me how I reckon I can watch him and find out.* And he did this too, he remembered it, quietly even yet, thinking, *I thought that was how to do it and I reckon I would still think that even if I had it to do again now for the first time*—the brazen day already fierce upon his naked back, the crooked channel like a voluted thread of ink, the pirogue moving steadily to the paddle which both entered and left the water without a sound; then the sudden cessation of the paddle behind him and the fierce hissing gobble of the Cajan at his back and he squatting bate-breathed and with that intense immobility of complete sobriety of a blind man listening while the frail wooden shell stole on at the dying apex of its own parted water. Afterward he remembered the rifle too—the rust-pitted single-shot weapon with a clumsily wired stock and a muzzle you could have driven a whiskey cork into, which the Cajan had brought into the boat—but not now; now he just squatted, crouched, immobile, breathing with infinitesimal care, his sober unceasing gaze going here and there constantly as he thought, *What? What? I not only dont know what I am looking for, I dont even know where to look for it.* Then he felt the motion of the pirogue as the Cajan moved and then the tense gobbling hissing actually, hot rapid and repressed, against his neck and ear, and glancing downward saw projecting between his own arm and body from behind, the Cajan's hand holding the knife, and glaring up again saw the flat thick spit of mud which as he looked at it divided and became a thick mud-colored log which in turn seemed, still immobile, to leap suddenly against his retinae in three—no, four—dimensions: volume, solidity, shape, and another: not fear but pure and intense speculation and he looking at the scaled motionless shape, thinking not, *It looks dangerous* but *It looks big*, thinking, *Well, maybe a mule standing in a lot looks big to a man that never walked up to one with a halter before*, thinking, *Only if he could just tell me what to do it would save time*, the pirogue drawing nearer now, creeping now, with no ripple now even and it seemed to him that he could even hear his companion's held breath and he taking the knife from the other's hand now and not even thinking this since it was too fast, a flash; it was not a surrender, not a resignation, it was too calm, it was a part of him, he had drunk it with his mother's milk and lived with it all his life: *After all a man cant only do what he has to do, with what he has to do it with, with what he has learned, to the best of his judgment. And I reckon a hog is still a hog, no matter what it looks like. So here goes*, sitting still for an instant longer until the bow of the pirogue grounded lighter than the falling of a leaf and stepped out of it and paused just for one instant while the words *It does look big* stood for just a second, unemphatic and trivial, somewhere where some fragment of his attention could see them and vanished, and stooped straddling, the knife driving even as he grasped the near foreleg, this all in the same instant when the lashing tail struck him a terrific blow upon the back. But the knife was home, he knew that even on his back in the mud, the weight of the thrashing beast longwise upon him, its ridged back clutched to his stomach, his arm about its throat, the hissing head clamped against his jaw, the furious tail lashing and flailing, the knife in his other hand probing for the life and finding it, the hot fierce gush: and now sitting beside the profound up-bellied carcass, his head again between his knees in the old attitude while his own blood freshened the other which drenched him, thinking, *It's my durn nose again.*

So he sat there, his head, his streaming face, bowed between his knees in an attitude not of dejection but profoundly bemused, contemplative, while the shrill voice of the Cajan seemed to buzz at him from an enormous distance; after a time he even looked up at the antic wiry figure bouncing hysterically about him, the face wild and grimacing, the voice gobbling and high; while the convict, holding his face carefully slanted so the blood would run free, looked at him with the cold intentness of a curator or custodian paused before one of his own glass cases, the Cajan threw up the rifle, cried "Boom-boom-boom!" flung it down and in pantomime re-enacted the recent scene then whirled his hands again, crying "Magnifique! Magnifique, Cent d'argent! Mille d'argent! Tout l'argent sous le ciel de Dieu!" But the convict was already looking down again, cupping the coffee-colored water to his face, watching the constant bright carmine marble it, thinking, *It's a little late to be telling me that now,* and not even thinking this long because presently they were in the pirogue again, the convict squatting again with that unbreathing rigidity as though he were trying by holding his breath to decrease his very weight, the bloody skin in the bows before him and he looking at it, thinking, *And I cant even ask him how much my half will be.*

But this not for long either, because as he was to tell the plump convict later, money has but one language. He remembered that too (they were at home now, the skin spread on the platform, where for the woman's benefit now the Cajan once more went through the pantomime—the gun which was not used, the hand-to-hand battle; for the second time the invisible alligator was slain amid cries, the victor rose and found this time that not even the woman was watching him. She was looking at the once more swollen and inflamed face of the convict. "You mean it kicked you right in the face?" she said.

"Nah," the convict said harshly, savagely. "It never had to. I done seem to got to where if that boy was to shoot me in the tail with a bean blower my nose would bleed.")—remembered that too but he did not try to tell it. Perhaps he could not have—how two people who could not even talk to one another made an agreement which both not only understood but which each knew the other would hold true and protect (perhaps for this reason) better than any written and witnessed contract. They even discussed and agreed somehow that they should hunt separately, each in his own vessel, to double the chances of finding prey. But this was easy: the convict could almost understand the words in which the Cajan said, "You do not need me and the rifle; we will only hinder you, be in your way." And more than this, they even agreed about the second rifle: that there was someone, it did not matter who—friend, neighbor, perhaps one in business in that line—from whom they could rent a second rifle; in their two patois, the one bastard English, the other bastard French—the one volatile, with his wild bright eyes and his voluble mouth full of stumps of teeth, the other sober, almost grim, swollen-faced and with his naked back blistered and scoriated like so much beef—they discussed this, squatting on either side of the pegged-out hide like two members of a corporation facing each other across a mahogany board table, and decided against it, the convict deciding: "I reckon not," he said. "I reckon if I had knowed enough to wait to start out with a gun, I still would. But since I done already started out without one, I dont reckon I'll change." Because it was a question of the money in terms of time, days. (Strange to say, that was the one thing which the Cajan could not tell him:

how much the half would be. But the convict knew it was half.) He had so little of them. He would have to move on soon, thinking (the convict), *All this durn foolishness will stop soon and I can get on back,* and then suddenly he found that he was thinking, *Will have to get on back,* and he became quite still and looked about at the rich strange desert which surrounded him, in which he was temporarily lost in peace and hope and into which the last seven years had sunk like so many trivial pebbles into a pool, leaving no ripple, and he thought quietly, with a kind of bemused amazement, *Yes. I reckon I had done forgot how good making money was. Being let to make it.*

So he used no gun, his the knotted rope and the Thuringian mace, and each morning he and the Cajan took their separate ways in the two boats to comb and creep the secret channels about the lost land from (or out of) which now and then still other pint-sized dark men appeared gobbling, abruptly and as though by magic from nowhere, in other hollowed logs, to follow quietly and watch him at his single combats—men named Tine and Toto and Theule, who were not much larger than and looked a good deal like the muskrats which the Cajan (the host did this too, supplied the kitchen too, he expressed this too like the rifle business, in his own tongue, the convict comprehending this too as though it had been English: "Do not concern yourself about food, O Hercules. Catch alligators; I will supply the pot.") took now and then from traps as you take a shoat pig at need from a pen, and varied the eternal rice and fish (the convict did tell this: how at night, in the cabin, the door and one sashless window battened against mosquitoes—a form, a ritual, as empty as crossing the fingers or knocking on wood—sitting beside the bug-swirled lantern on the plank table in a temperature close to blood heat he would look down at the swimming segment of meat on his sweating plate and think, *It must be Theule. He was the fat one.*)—day following day, unemphatic and identical, each like the one before and the one which would follow while his theoretical half of a sum to be reckoned in pennies, dollars, or tens of dollars he did not know, mounted—the mornings when he set forth to find waiting for him like the *matador* his *aficionados* the small clump of constant and deferential pirogues, the hard noons when ringed half about by little motionless shells he fought his solitary combats, the evenings, the return, the pirogues departing one by one into inlets and passages which during the first few days he could not even distinguish, then the platform in the twilight where before the static woman and the usually nursing infant and the one or two bloody hides of the day's take the Cajan would perform his ritualistic victorious pantomime before the two growing rows of knife-marks in one of the boards of the wall; then the nights when, the woman and child in the single bunk and the Cajan already snoring on the pallet and the reeking lantern set close, he (the convict) would sit on his naked heels, sweating steadily, his face worn and calm, immersed and indomitable, his bowed back raw and savage as beef beneath the suppurant old blisters and the fierce welts of tails, and scrape and chip at the charred sapling which was almost a paddle now, pausing now and then to raise his head while the cloud of mosquitoes about it whined and whirled, to stare at the wall before him until after a while the crude boards themselves must have dissolved away and let his blank unseeing gaze go on and on unhampered, through the rich oblivious darkness, beyond it even perhaps, even perhaps beyond the seven wasted years during which, so he had just realised, he had been permitted to toil but not to work. Then he would retire himself, he would take a last look at the rolled bundle behind the rafter and blow out the lantern and lie down as he was beside his snoring partner, to lie sweating (on his stomach, he could not bear the touch of anything to his back) in the whining ovenlike darkness filled with the forlorn bellowing of alligators, thinking not, *They never gave me time to learn* but *I had forgot how good it is to work.*

Then on the tenth day it happened. It happened for the third time. At first he refused to believe it, not that he felt that now he had served out and discharged his apprenticeship to mischance, had with the birth of the child reached and crossed the crest of his Golgotha and would now be, possibly not permitted so much as ignored, to descend the opposite slope free-wheeling. That was not his feeling at all. What he declined to accept was the fact that a power, a force such as that which had been consistent enough to concentrate upon him with deadly undeviation for weeks, should with all the wealth of cosmic violence and disaster to draw from, have been so barren of invention and imagination, so lacking in pride of artistry and craftsmanship, as to repeat itself twice. Once he had accepted, twice he even forgave, but three times he simply declined to believe, particularly when he was at last persuaded to realise that this third time was to be instigated not by the blind potency of volume and motion but by human direction and hands: that now the cosmic joker, foiled twice, had stooped in its vindictive concentration to the employing of dynamite.

He did not tell that. Doubtless he did not know himself how it happened, what was happening. But he doubtless remembered it (but quietly above the thick rich-colored pristine cigar in his clean steady hand), what he knew, divined of it. It would be evening, the ninth evening, he and the woman on either side of their host's empty place at the evening meal, he hearing the voices from without but not ceasing to eat, still chewing steadily, because it would be the same as though he were seeing them anyway—the two or three or four pirogues floating on the dark water beneath the platform on which the host stood, the voices gobbling and jabbering, incomprehensible and filled not with alarm and not exactly with rage or even perhaps absolute surprise but rather just cacophony like those of disturbed marsh fowl, he (the convict) not ceasing to chew but just looking up quietly and maybe without a great deal of interrogation or surprise too as the Cajan burst in and stood before them, wild-faced, glaring, his blackened teeth gaped against the inky orifice of his distended mouth, watching (the convict) while the Cajan went through his violent pantomime of violent evacuation, ejection, scooping something invisible into his arms and hurling it out and downward and in the instant of completing the gesture changing from instigator to victim of that which he had set into pantomimic motion, clasping his head and, bowed over and not otherwise moving, seeming to be swept on and away before it, crying "Boom! Boom! Boom!", the convict watching him, his jaw not chewing now, though for just that moment, thinking, *What? What is it he is trying to tell me?* thinking (this a flash too, since he could not have expressed this, and hence did not even know that he had ever thought it) that though his life had been cast here, circumscribed by this environment, accepted by this environment and accepting it in turn (and he had done well here—this quietly, soberly indeed, if he had been able to phrase it, think it instead of merely knowing it—better than he had ever done, who had not even known until now how good work, making money, could be), yet it was not his life, he still and would ever be no more than the water bug upon the surface of the pond, the plumbless and lurking depths of which he would never know, his only actual contact with it being the instants when on lonely and glaring mud-spits under the pitiless sun and amphitheatred by his motionless and riveted semicircle of watching pirogues, he accepted the gambit which he had not elected, entered the lashing radius of the armed tail and beat at the thrashing and hissing head with his lightwood club, or this failing, embraced without hesitation the armored body itself with the frail web of flesh and bone in which he walked and lived and sought the raging life with an eight-inch knife-blade.

So he and the woman merely watched the Cajan as he acted out the whole charade of eviction—the little wiry man gesticulant and wild, his hysterical shadow leaping and falling upon the rough wall as he went through the pantomime of abandoning the cabin, gathering in pantomime his meagre belongings from the walls and corners—objects which no other man would want and only some power or force like blind water or earthquake or fire would ever dispossess him of, the woman watching too, her mouth slightly open upon a mass of chewed food, on her face an expression of placid astonishment, saying, "What? What's he saying?"

"I don't know," the convict said. "But I reckon if it's something we ought to know we will find it out when it's ready for us to." Because he was not alarmed, though by now he had read the other's meaning plainly enough. *He's fixing to leave,* he thought. *He's telling me to leave too*—this later, after they had quitted the table and the Cajan and the woman had gone to bed and the Cajan had risen from the pallet and approached the convict and once more went through the pantomime of abandoning the cabin, this time as one repeats a speech which may have been misunderstood, tediously, carefully repetitional as to a child, seeming to hold the convict with one hand while he gestured, talked, with the other, gesturing as though in single syllables, the convict (squatting, the knife open and the almost-finished paddle across his lap) watching, nodding his head, even speaking in English: "Yah; sure. You bet. I got you."—trimming again at the paddle but no faster, with no more haste than on any other night, serene in his belief that when the time came for him to know whatever it was, that would take care of itself, having already and without even knowing it, even before the possibility, the question, ever arose, declined, refused to accept even the thought of moving also, thinking about the hides, thinking, *If there was just some way he could tell me where to carry my share to get the money* but thinking this only for an instant between two delicate strokes of the blade because almost at once he thought, *I reckon as long as I can catch them I wont have no big trouble finding whoever it is that will buy them.*

So the next morning he helped the Cajan load his few belongings—the pitted rifle, a small bundle of clothing (again they traded, who could not even converse with one another, this time the few cooking vessels, a few rusty traps by definite allocation, and something embracing and abstractional which included the stove, the crude bunk, the house or its occupancy—something—in exchange for one alligator hide)—into the pirogue, then, squatting and as two children divide sticks they divided the hides, separating them into two piles, one-for-me-and-one-for-you, two-for-me-and-two-for-you, and the Cajan loaded his share and shoved away from the platform and paused again, though this time he only put the paddle down, gathered something invisibly into his two hands and flung it violently upward, crying "Boom? Boom?" on a rising inflection, nodding violently to the half-naked and savagely scoriated man on the platform who stared with a sort of grim equability back at him and said, "Sure. Boom. Boom." Then the Cajan went on. He did not look back. They watched him, already paddling rapidly, or the woman did; the convict had already turned.

"Maybe he was trying to tell us to leave too," she said.

"Yah," the convict said. "I thought of that last night. Hand me the paddle." She fetched it to him—the sapling, the one he had been trimming at nightly, not quite finished yet though one more evening would do it (he had been using a spare one of the Cajan's. The other had offered to let him keep it, to include it perhaps with the stove and the bunk and the cabin's freehold, but the convict had declined. Perhaps he had computed it by volume against so much alligator hide, this weighed against one more evening with the tedious and careful blade.) —and he departed too with his knotted rope and mace, in the opposite direction, as though not only not content with refusing to quit the place he had been warned against, he must establish and affirm the irrevocable finality of his refusal by penetrating even further and deeper into it. And then and without warning the high fierce drowsing of his solitude gathered itself and struck at him.

He could not have told this if he had tried—this not yet midmorning and he going on, alone for the first time, no pirogue emerging anywhere to fall in behind him, but he had not expected this anyway, he knew that the others would have departed too; it was not this, it was his very solitude, his desolation which was now his alone and in full since he had elected to remain; the sudden cessation of the paddle, the skiff shooting on for a moment yet while he thought, *What? What?* Then, *No. No. No,* as the silence and solitude and emptiness roared down upon him in a jeering bellow: and now reversed, the skiff spun violently on its heel, he the betrayed driving furiously back toward the platform where he knew it was already too late, that citadel where the very crux and dear breath of his life—the being allowed to work and earn money, that right and privilege which he believed he had earned to himself unaided, asking no favor of anyone or anything save the right to be let alone to pit his will and strength against the sauric protagonist of a land, a region, which he had not asked to be projected into—was being threatened, driving the homemade paddle in grim fury, coming in sight of the platform at last and seeing the motor launch lying alongside it with no surprise at all but actually with a kind of pleasure as though at a visible justification of his outrage and fear, the privilege of saying *I told you so* to his own affronting, driving on toward it in a dreamlike state in which there seemed to be no progress at all, in which, unimpeded and suffocating, he strove dreamily with a weightless oar, with muscles without strength or resiliency, at a medium without resistance, seeming to watch the skiff creep infinitesimally across the sunny water and up to the platform while a man in the launch (there were five of them in all) gobbled at him in that same tongue he had been hearing constantly now for ten days and still knew no word of, just as a second man, followed by the woman carrying the baby and dressed again for departure in the faded tunic and the sunbonnet, emerged from the house, carrying (the man carried several other things but the convict saw nothing else) the paper-wrapped bundle which the convict had put behind the rafter ten days ago and no other hand had touched since, he (the convict) on the platform too now, holding the skiff's painter in one hand and the bludgeon-like paddle in the other, contriving to speak to the woman at last in a voice dreamy and suffocating and incredibly calm: "Take it away from him and carry it back into the house."

"So you can talk English, can you?" the man in the launch said. "Why didn't you come out like they told you to last night?"

"Out?" the convict said. Again he even looked, glared, at the man in the launch, contriving even again to control his voice: "I aint got time to take trips. I'm busy," already turning to the woman again, his mouth already open to repeat as the dreamy buzzing voice of the man came to him and he turning once more, in a terrific and absolutely unbearable exasperation, crying, "Flood? What flood? Hell a mile, it's done passed me twice months ago! It's gone! What flood?" and then (he did not think this in actual words either but he knew it, suffered that flashing insight into his own character or destiny: how there was a peculiar quality of repetitiveness about his present fate, how not only the almost seminal crises recurred with a certain monotony, but the very physical circumstances followed a stupidly unimaginative pattern) the man in the launch said, "Take him" and he was on his feet for a few minutes yet, lashing and striking in panting fury, then once more on his back on hard unyielding planks while the four men swarmed over him in a fierce wave of hard bones and panting curses and at last the thin dry vicious snapping of handcuffs.

"Damn it, are you mad?" the man in the launch said. "Can't you understand they are going to dynamite that levee at noon today?—Come on," he said to the others. "Get him aboard. Let's get out of here."

"I want my hides and boat," the convict said.

"Damn your hides and boat," the man in the launch said. "If they dont get that levee blowed pretty soon you can hunt plenty more of them on the capitol steps at Baton Rouge. And this is all the boat you will need and you can say your prayers about it."

"I aint going without my boat," the convict said. He said it calmly and with complete finality, so calm, so final that for almost a minute nobody answered him, they just stood looking quietly down at him as he lay, half-naked, blistered and scarred, helpless and manacled hand and foot, on his back, delivering his ultimatum in a voice peaceful and quiet as that in which you talk to your bed-fellow before going to sleep. Then the man in the launch moved; he spat quietly over the side and said in a voice as calm and quiet as the convict's:

"All right. Bring his boat." They helped the woman, carrying the baby and the paper-wrapped parcel, into the launch. Then they helped the convict to his feet and into the launch too, the shackles on his wrists and ankles clashing. "I'd unlock you if you'd promise to behave yourself," the man said. The convict did not answer this at all.

"I want to hold the rope," he said.

"The rope?"

"Yes," the convict said. "The rope." So they lowered him into the stern and gave him the end of the painter after it had passed the towing cleat, and they went on. The convict did not look back. But then, he did not look forward either, he lay half sprawled, his shackled legs before him, the end of the skiff's painter in one shackled hand. The launch made two other stops; when the hazy wafer of the intolerable sun began to stand once more directly overhead there were fifteen people in the launch; and then the convict, sprawled and motionless, saw the flat brazen land begin to rise and become a greenish-black mass of swamp, bearded and convoluted, this in turn stopping short off and there spread before him an expanse of water embraced by a blue dissolution of shoreline and glittering thinly under the noon, larger than he had ever seen before, the sound of the launch's engine ceasing, the hull sliding on behind its fading bow-wave. "What are you doing?" the leader said.

"It's noon," the helmsman said. "I thought we might hear the dynamite." So they all listened, the launch lost of all forward motion, rocking slightly, the glitter-broken small waves slapping and whispering at the hull, but no sound, no tremble even, came anywhere under the fierce hazy sky; the long moment gathered itself and turned on and noon was past. "All right," the leader said. "Let's go." The engine started again, the hull began to gather speed. The leader came aft and stooped over the convict, key in hand. "I guess you'll have to behave now, whether you want to or not," he said, unlocking the manacles. "Wont you?"

"Yes," the convict said. They went on; after a time the shore vanished completely and a little sea got up. The convict was free now but he lay as before, the end of the skiff's painter in his hand, bent now with three or four turns about his wrist; he turned his head now and then to look back at the towing skiff as it slewed and bounced in the launch's wake; now and then he even looked out over the lake, the eyes alone moving, the face grave and expression-less, thinking, *This is a greater immensity of water, of waste and desolation, than I have ever seen before;* perhaps not; thinking three or four hours later, the shoreline raised again and broken into a clutter of sailing sloops and power cruisers, *These are more boats than I believed existed, a maritime race of which I also had no cognizance* or perhaps not thinking it but just watching as the launch opened the shored gut of the ship canal, the low smoke of the city beyond it, then a wharf, the launch slowing in; a quiet crowd of people watching with that same forlorn passivity he had seen before and whose race he did recognise even though he had not seen Vicksburg when he passed it—the brand, the unmistakable hallmark of the violently homeless, he more so than any, who would have permitted no man to call him one of them.

"All right," the leader said to him. "Here you are."

"The boat," the convict said.

"You've got it. What do you want me to do—give you a receipt for it?"

"No," the convict said. "I just want the boat."

"Take it. Only you ought to have a bookstrap or something to carry it in." ("Carry it in?" the plump convict said. "Carry it where? Where would you have to carry it?")

He (the tall one) told that: how he and the woman disembarked and how one of the men helped him haul the skiff up out of the water and how he stood there with the end of the painter wrapped around his wrist and the man bustled up, saying, "All right. Next load! Next load!" and how he told this man too about the boat and the man cried, "Boat? Boat?" and how he (the convict) went with them when they carried the skiff over and racked, berthed, it with the others and how he lined himself up by a Coca-Cola sign and the arch of a draw bridge so he could find the skiff again quick when he returned, and how he and the woman (he carrying the paper-wrapped parcel) were herded into a truck and after a while the truck began to run in traffic, between close houses, then there was a big building, an armory—

"Armory?" the plump one said. "You mean a jail."

"No. It was a kind of warehouse, with people with bundles laying on the floor." And how he thought maybe his partner might be there and how he even looked about for the Cajan while waiting for a chance to get back to the door again, where the soldier was and how he got back to the door at last, the woman behind him and his chest actually against the dropped rifle.

"Gwan, gwan," the soldier said. "Get back. They'll give you some clothes in a minute. You cant walk around the streets that way. And something to eat too. Maybe your kinfolks will come for you by that time." And he told that too: how the woman said,

"Maybe if you told him you had some kinfolks here he would let us out." And how he did not; he could not have expressed this either, it was too deep, too ingrained; he had never yet had to think into words through all the long generations of himself—his hill-man's sober and jealous respect not for truth but for the power, the strength, of lying—not to be niggard with lying but rather to use it with respect and even care, delicate quick and strong, like a fine and fatal blade. And how they fetched him clothes—a blue jumper and overalls, and then food too (a brisk starched young woman saying, "But the baby must be bathed, cleaned. It will die if you dont," and the woman saying, "Yessum.

He might holler some, he aint never been bathed before. But he's a good baby.")
and now it was night, the unshaded bulbs harsh and savage and forlorn above
the snorers and he rising, gripping the woman awake, and then the window.
He told that: how there were doors in plenty, leading he did not know where,
but he had a hard time finding a window they could use but he found one at
last, he carrying the parcel and the baby too while he climbed through first—
"You ought to tore up a sheet and slid down it," the plump convict said. But
he needed no sheet, there were cobbles under his feet now, in the rich darkness.
The city was there too but he had not seen it yet and would not—the low constant glare; Bienville had stood there too, it had been the figment of an emas-
culate also calling himself Napoleon but no more, Andrew Jackson had found it
one step from Pennsylvania Avenue. But the convict found it considerably
further than one step back to the ship canal and the skiff, the Coca-Cola sign
dim now, the draw bridge arching spidery against the jonquil sky at dawn: nor
did he tell, any more than about the sixty-foot levee, how he got the skiff back
into the water. The lake was behind him now; there was but one direction he
could go. When he saw the River again he knew it at once. He should have; it
was now ineradicably a part of his past, his life; it would be a part of what he
would bequeath, if that were in store for him. But four weeks later it would
look different from what it did now, and did: he (the Old Man) had recovered
from his debauch, back in banks again, the Old Man, rippling placidly toward
the sea, brown and rich as chocolate between levees whose inner faces were
wrinkled as though in a frozen and aghast amazement, crowned with the rich
green of summer in the willows; beyond them, sixty feet below, slick mules
squatted against the broad pull of middle-busters in the richened soil which
would not need to be planted, which would need only to be shown a cotton seed
to sprout and make; there would be the symmetric miles of strong stalks by
July, purple bloom in August, in September the black fields snowed over, spilled,
the middles dragged smooth by the long sacks, the long black limber hands
plucking, the hot air filled with the whine of gins, the September air then but
now June air heavy with locust and (the towns) the smell of new paint and the
sour smell of the paste which holds wall paper—the towns, the villages, the
little lost wood landings on stilts on the inner face of the levee, the lower storeys
bright and rank under the new paint and paper and even the marks on spile
and post and tree of May's raging water-height fading beneath each bright
silver gust of summer's loud and inconstant rain; there was a store at the levee's
lip, a few saddled and rope-bridled mules in the sleepy dust, a few dogs, a
handful of Negroes sitting on the steps beneath the chewing tobacco and malaria medicine signs, and three white men, one of them a deputy sheriff can-
vassing for votes to beat his superior (who had given him his job) in the August
primary, all pausing to watch the skiff emerge from the glitter-glare of the afternoon water and approach and land, a woman carrying a child stepping out, then
a man, a tall man who, approaching, proved to be dressed in a faded but recently
washed and quite clean suit of penitentiary clothing, stopping in the dust where
the mules dozed and watching with pale cold humorless eyes while the

deputy sheriff was still making toward his armpit that gesture which everyone present realised was to have produced a pistol in one flashing motion for a considerable time while still nothing came of it. It was apparently enough for the newcomer, however.

"You a officer?" he said.

"You damn right I am," the deputy said. "Just let me get this damn gun—"

"All right," the other said. "Yonder's your boat, and here's the woman. But I never did find that bastard on the cottonhouse."

One of the Governor's young men arrived at the Penitentiary the next morning. That is, he was fairly young (he would not see thirty again though without doubt he did not want to, there being that about him which indicated a character which never had and never would want anything it did not, or was not about to, possess), a Phi Beta Kappa out of an Eastern university, a colonel on the Governor's staff who did not buy it with a campaign contribution, who had stood in his negligent Eastern-cut clothes and his arched nose and lazy contemptuous eyes on the galleries of any number of little lost backwoods stores and told his stories and received the guffaws of his overalled and spitting hearers and with the same look in his eyes fondled infants named in memory of the last administration and in honor (or hope) of the next, and (it was said of him and doubtless not true) by lazy accident the behinds of some who were not infants any longer though still not old enough to vote. He was in the Warden's office with a briefcase, and presently the deputy warden of the levee was there too. He would have been sent for presently though not yet, but he came anyhow, without knocking, with his hat on, calling the Governor's young man loudly by a nickname and striking him with a flat hand on the back and lifted one thigh to the Warden's desk, almost between the Warden and the caller, the emissary. Or the vizier with the command, the knotted cord, as began to appear immediately.

"Well," the Governor's young man said, "you've played the devil, haven't you?" The Warden had a cigar. He had offered the caller one. It had been refused, though presently, while the Warden looked at the back of his neck with hard immobility even a little grim, the deputy leaned and reached back and opened the desk drawer and took one.

"Seems straight enough to me," the Warden said. "He got swept away against his will. He came back as soon as he could and surrendered."

"He even brought that damn boat back," the deputy said. "If he'd a throwed the boat away he could a walked back in three days. But no sir. He's got to bring the boat back. 'Here's your boat and here's the woman but I never found no bastard on no cottonhouse.'" He slapped his knee, guffawing. "Them convicts. A mule's got twice as much sense."

"A mule's got twice as much sense as anything except a rat," the emissary said in his pleasant voice. "But that's not the trouble."

"What is the trouble?" the Warden said.

"This man is dead."

"Hell fire, he aint dead," the deputy said. "He's up yonder in that bunkhouse right now, lying his head off probly. I'll take you up there and you can see him." The Warden was looking at the deputy.

"Look," he said. "Bledsoe was trying to tell me something about that Kate mule's leg. You better go up to the stable and—"

"I done tended to it," the deputy said. He didn't even look at the Warden. He was watching, talking to, the emissary. "No sir. He aint—"

"But he has received an official discharge as being dead. Not a pardon nor a parole either: a discharge. He's either dead, or free. In either case he doesn't belong here." Now both the Warden and the deputy looked at the emissary, the deputy's mouth open a little, the cigar poised in his hand to have its tip bitten off. The emissary spoke pleasantly, extremely distinctly: "On a report of death forwarded to the Governor by the Warden of the Penitentiary." The deputy closed his mouth, though otherwise he didn't move. "On the official evidence of the officer delegated at the time to the charge and returning of the body of the prisoner to the Penitentiary." Now the deputy put the cigar into his mouth and got slowly off the desk, the cigar rolling across his lip as he spoke:

"So that's it. I'm to be it, am I?" He laughed shortly, a stage laugh, two notes. "When I done been right three times running through three separate administrations? That's on a book somewhere too. Somebody in Jackson can find that too. And if they cant, I can show—"

"Three administrations?" the emissary said. "Well, well. That's pretty good."

"You damn right it's good," the deputy said. "The woods are full of folks that didn't." The Warden was again watching the back of the deputy's neck.

"Look," he said. "Why dont you step up to my house and get that bottle of whiskey out of the sideboard and bring it down here?"

"All right," the deputy said. "But I think we better settle this first. I'll tell you what we'll do—"

"We can settle it quicker with a drink or two," the Warden said. "You better step on up to your place and get a coat so the bottle—"

"That'll take too long," the deputy said. "I wont need no coat." He moved to the door, where he stopped and turned. "I'll tell you what to do. Just call twelve men in here and tell him it's a jury—he never seen but one before and he wont know no better—and try him over for robbing that train. Hamp can be the judge."

"You cant try a man twice for the same crime," the emissary said. "He might know that even if he doesn't know a jury when he sees one."

"Look," the Warden said.

"All right. Just call it a new train robbery. Tell him it happened yesterday, tell him he robbed another train while he was gone and just forgot it. He couldn't help himself. Besides, he wont care. He'd just as lief be here as out. He wouldn't have nowhere to go if he was out. None of them do. Turn one loose and be damned if he aint right back here by Christmas like it was a reunion or something, for doing the very same thing they caught him at before." He guffawed again. "Them convicts."

"Look," the Warden said. "While you're there, why dont you open the bottle and see if the liquor's any good. Take a drink or two. Give yourself time to feel it. If it's not good, no use in bringing it."

"O.K.," the deputy said. He went out this time.

"Couldn't you lock the door?" the emissary said. The Warden squirmed faintly. That is, he shifted his position in his chair.

"After all, he's right," he said. "He's guessed right three times now. And he's kin to all the folks in Pittman County except the niggers."

"Maybe we can work fast then." The emissary opened the briefcase and took out a sheaf of papers. "So there you are," he said.

"There what are?"

"He escaped."

"But he came back voluntarily and surrendered."

"But he escaped."

"All right," the Warden said. "He escaped. Then what?" Now the emissary said look. That is, he said,

"Listen. I'm on per diem. That's taxpayers, votes. And if there's any possible chance for it to occur to anyone to hold an investigation about this, there'll be ten senators and twenty-five representatives here on a special train maybe. On per diem. And it will be mighty hard to keep some of them from going back to Jackson by way of Memphis or New Orleans—on per diem."

"All right," the Warden said. "What does he say to do?"

"This. The man left here in charge of one specific officer. But he was delivered back here by a different one."

"But he surren—" This time the Warden stopped of his own accord. He looked, stared almost, at the emissary. "All right. Go on."

"In specific charge of an appointed and delegated officer, who returned here and reported that the body of the prisoner was no longer in his possession; that, in fact, he did not know where the prisoner was. That's correct, isn't it?" The Warden said nothing. "Isn't that correct?" the emissary said, pleasantly, insistently.

"But you cant do that to him. I tell you he's kin to half the—"

"That's taken care of. The Chief has made a place for him on the highway patrol."

"Hell," the Warden said. "He cant ride a motorcycle. I dont even let him try to drive a truck."

"He wont have to. Surely an amazed and grateful state can supply the man who guessed right three times in succession in Mississippi general elections with a car to ride in and somebody to run it if necessary. He wont even have to stay in it all the time. Just so he's near enough so when an inspector sees the car and stops and blows the horn of it he can hear it and come out."

"I still dont like it," the Warden said.

"Neither do I. Your man could have saved all of this if he had just gone on and drowned himself, as he seems to have led everybody to believe he had. But he didn't. And the Chief says do. Can you think of anything better?" The Warden sighed.

"No," he said.

"All right." The emissary opened the papers and uncapped a pen and began to write. "Attempted escape from the Penitentiary, ten years' additional sentence," he said. "Deputy Warden Buckworth transferred to highway patrol. Call it for meritorious service even if you want to. It wont matter now. Done?"

"Done," the Warden said.

"Then suppose you send for him. Get it over with." So the Warden sent for the tall convict and he arrived presently, saturnine and grave, in his new bed-ticking, his jowls blue and close under the sunburn, his hair recently cut and neatly parted and smelling faintly of the prison barber's (the barber was in for life, for murdering his wife, still a barber) pomade. The Warden called him by name.

"You had bad luck, didn't you?" The convict said nothing. "They are going to have to add ten years to your time."

"All right," the convict said.

"It's hard luck. I'm sorry."

"All right," the convict said. "If that's the rule." So they gave him the ten years more and the Warden gave him the cigar and now he sat, jackknifed backward into the space between the upper and lower bunks, the unlighted cigar in his hand while the plump convict and four others listened to him. Or questioned him, that is, since it was all done, finished, now and he was safe again, so maybe it wasn't even worth talking about any more.

"All right," the plump one said. "So you come back into the River. Then what?"

"Nothing. I rowed."

"Wasn't it pretty hard rowing coming back?"

"The water was still high. It was running pretty hard still. I never made much speed for the first week or two. After that it got better." Then, suddenly and quietly, something—the inarticulateness, the innate and inherited reluctance for speech, dissolved and he found himself, listened to himself, telling it quietly, the words coming not fast but easily to the tongue as he required them: how he paddled on (he found out by trying it that he could make better speed, if you could call it speed, next the bank—this after he had been carried suddenly and violently out to midstream before he could prevent it and found himself, the skiff, travelling back toward the region from which he had just escaped and he spent the better part of the morning getting back inshore and up to the canal again from which he had emerged at dawn) until night came and they tied up to the bank and ate some of the food he had secreted in his jumper before leaving the armory in New Orleans and the woman and the infant slept in the boat as usual and when daylight came they went on and tied up again that night too and the next day the food gave out and he came to a landing, a town, he didn't notice the name of it, and he got a job. It was a cane farm—

"Cane?" one of the other convicts said. "What does anybody want to raise cane for? You cut cane. You have to fight it where I come from. You burn it just to get shut of it."

"It was sorghum," the tall convict said.

"Sorghum?" another said. "A whole farm just raising sorghum? *Sorghum?* What did they do with it?" The tall one didn't know. He didn't ask, he just came up the levee and there was a truck waiting full of niggers and a white man said, "You there. Can you run a shovel plow?" and the convict said, "Yes," and the man said, "Jump in then," and the convict said, "Only I've got a—"

"Yes," the plump one said. "That's what I been aiming to ask. What did—" The tall convict's face was grave, his voice was calm, just a little short:

"They had tents for the folks to live in. They were behind." The plump one blinked at him.

"Did they think she was your wife?"

"I don't know. I reckon so." The plump one blinked at him.

"Wasn't she your wife? Just from time to time kind of, you might say?" The tall one didn't answer this at all. After a moment he raised the cigar and appeared to examine a loosening of the wrapper because after another moment he licked the cigar carefully near the end. "All right," the plump one said. "Then what?" So he worked there four days. He didn't like it. Maybe that was why: that he too could not quite put credence in that much of what he believed to be sorghum. So when they told him it was Saturday and paid him and the white man told him about somebody who was going to Baton Rouge the next day in a motor boat, he went to see the man and took the six dollars he had earned and bought food with it and tied the skiff behind the motor boat and went to Baton Rouge. It didn't take long and even after they left the motor boat at Baton Rouge and he was paddling again it seemed to the convict that the River was lower and the current not so fast, so hard, so they made fair speed, tying up to the bank at night among the willows, the woman and baby sleeping in the skiff as of old. Then the food gave out again. This time it was a wood landing, the wood stacked and waiting, a wagon and team being unladen of another load. The men with the wagon told him about the sawmill and helped him drag the skiff up the levee; they wanted to leave it there but he would not so they loaded it onto the wagon too and he and the woman got on the wagon too and they went to the sawmill. They gave them one room in a house to live in here. They paid two dollars a day and furnish. The work was hard. He liked it. He stayed there eight days.

"If you liked it so well, why did you quit?" the plump one said. The tall convict examined the cigar again, holding it up where the light fell upon the rich chocolate-colored flank.

"I got in trouble," he said.

"What trouble?"

"Woman. It was a fellow's wife."

"You mean you had been toting one piece up and down the country day and night for over a month, and now the first time you have a chance to stop and catch your breath almost you got to get in trouble over another one?" The tall convict had thought of that. He remembered it: how there were times, seconds, at first when if it had not been for the baby he might have, might have tried. But they were just seconds because in the next instant his whole

being would seem to flee the very idea in a kind of savage and horrified revulsion; he would find himself looking from a distance at this millstone which
the force and power of blind and risible Motion had fastened upon him, thinking, saying aloud actually, with harsh and savage outrage even though it had
been two years since he had had a woman and that a nameless and not young
Negress, a casual, a straggler whom he had caught more or less by chance on
one of the fifth-Sunday visiting days, the man—husband or sweetheart—whom
she had come to see having been shot by a trusty a week or so previous and
she had not heard about it: "She aint even no good to me for that."

"But you got this one, didn't you?" the plump convict said.

"Yah," the tall one said. The plump one blinked at him.

"Was it good?"

"It's all good," one of the others said. "Well? Go on. How many more did
you have on the way back? Sometimes when a fellow starts getting it it looks
like he just cant miss even if—" That was all, the convict told them. They left
the sawmill fast, he had no time to buy food until they reached the next landing. There he spent the whole sixteen dollars he had earned and they went on.
The River was lower now, there was no doubt of it, and sixteen dollars' worth
looked like a lot of food and he thought maybe it would do, would be enough.
But maybe there was more current in the River still than it looked like. But
this time it was Mississippi, it was cotton; the plow handles felt right to his
palms again, the strain and squat of the slick buttocks against the middle-
buster's blade was what he knew, even though they paid but a dollar a day
here. But that did it. He told it: they told him it was Saturday again and paid
him and he told about it—night, a smoked lantern in a disc of worn and barren
earth as smooth as silver, a circle of crouching figures, the importunate mur-
murs and ejaculations, the meagre piles of worn bills beneath the crouching
knees, the dotted cubes clicking and scuttering in the dust; that did it. "How
much did you win?" the second convict said.

"Enough," the tall one said.

"But how much?"

"Enough," the tall one said. It was enough exactly; he gave it all to the man
who owned the second motor boat (he would not need food now), he and the
woman in the launch now and the skiff towing behind, the woman with the
baby and the paper-wrapped parcel beneath his peaceful hand, on his lap;
almost at once he recognised, not Vicksburg because he had never seen Vicksburg, but the trestle beneath which on his roaring wave of trees and houses
and dead animals he had shot, accompanied by thunder and lightning, a month
and three weeks ago; he looked at it once without heat, even without interest
as the launch went on. But now he began to watch the bank, the levee. He
didn't know how he would but he knew he would, and then it was early afternoon and sure enough the moment came and he said to the launch owner: "I
reckon this will do."

"Here?" the launch owner said. "This dont look like anywhere to me."

"I reckon this is it," the convict said. So the launch put inshore, the engine ceased, it drifted up and lay against the levee and the owner cast the skiff loose.

"You better let me take you on until we come to something," he said. "That was what I promised."

"I reckon this will do," the convict said. So they got out and he stood with the grapevine painter in his hand while the launch purred again and drew away, already curving; he did not watch it. He laid the bundle down and made the painter fast to a willow root and picked up the bundle and turned. He said no word, he mounted the levee, passing the mark, the tide-line of the old raging, dry now and lined, traversed by shallow and empty cracks like foolish and deprecatory senile grins, and entered a willow clump and removed the overalls and shirt they had given him in New Orleans and dropped them without even looking to see where they fell and opened the parcel and took out the other, the known, the desired, faded a little, stained and worn, but clean, recognisable, and put them on and returned to the skiff and took up the paddle. The woman was already in it.

The plump convict stood blinking at him. "So you come back," he said. "Well well." Now they all watched the tall convict as he bit the end from the cigar neatly and with complete deliberation and spat it out and licked the bite smooth and damp and took a match from his pocket and examined the match for a moment as though to be sure it was a good one, worthy of the cigar perhaps, and raked it up his thigh with the same deliberation—a motion almost too slow to set fire to it, it would seem—and held it until the flame burned clear and free of sulphur, then put it to the cigar. The plump one watched him, blinking rapidly and steadily. "And they give you ten years more for running. That's bad. A fellow can get used to what they give him at first, to start off with, I dont care how much it is, even a hundred and ninety-nine years. But ten more years. Ten years more, on top of that. When you never expected it. Ten more years to have to do without no society, no female companionship—" He blinked steadily at the tall convict. But he (the tall convict) had thought of that too. He had had a sweetheart. That is, he had gone to church singings and picnics with her—a girl a year or so younger than he, short-legged, with ripe breasts and a heavy mouth and dull eyes like ripe muscadines, who owned a baking-powder can almost full of earrings and brooches and rings bought (or presented at suggestion) from ten-cent stores. Presently he had divulged his plan to her, and there were times later when, musing, the thought occurred to him that possibly if it had not been for her he would not actually have attempted it—this a mere feeling, unworded, since he could not have phrased this either: that who to know what Capone's uncandled bridehood she might not have dreamed to be her destiny and fate, what fast car filled with authentic colored glass and machine guns, running traffic lights. But that was all past and done when the notion first occurred to him, and in the third month of his incarceration she came to see him. She wore earrings and a bracelet or so which he had never seen before and it never became quite clear how she had got that far from home, and she cried violently for the first three minutes though presently (and without his ever knowing either exactly how they had got separated or how she had made the acquaintance) he saw her in animated conversation with one of the guards. But she kissed him before she left that evening and said she would return the first chance she got, clinging to him, sweating a little, smelling of scent and soft young female flesh, slightly pneumatic. But she didn't come back though he continued to write to her, and seven months later he got an answer. It was a postcard, a colored lithograph of a Birmingham hotel, a childish X inked heavily across one window, the heavy writing on the reverse slanted and primer-like too: *This is where were honnymonning at. Your friend (Mrs) Vernon Waldrip*

The plump convict stood blinking at the tall one, rapidly and steadily. "Yes, sir," he said. "It's them ten more years that hurt. Ten more years to do without a woman, no woman a tall a fellow wants—" He blinked steadily and rapidly, watching the tall one. The other did not move, jackknifed backward between the two bunks, grave and clean, the cigar burning smoothly and richly in his clean steady hand, the smoke wreathing upward across his face saturnine, humorless, and calm. "Ten more years—"

"Women,—!" the tall convict said.

Richard Wright

DOWN BY THE RIVERSIDE

Preface

Richard Wright's *Down by the Riverside* provides a unique opportunity for the study of black and white perspectives, by virtue of its singular parallels with William Faulkner's *Old Man*. To "a Negro man squatting before the nearest fire" Faulkner gives the original identification of "de Ole Man." But it is Wright, not Faulkner, who asks how much suffering has been the source of the black man's wisdom. In *Old Man*, the prison truck drives right past the initial setting of Wright's short novel: "a Negro cabin. The water was up to the window ledges. A woman clutching two children squatted on the ridgepole, a man and a halfgrown youth, standing waist-deep, were hoisting a squealing pig onto the slanting roof . . . the woman on the housetop began to shriek at the passing truck, her voice . . . becoming fainter and fainter as the truck passed and went on, ceasing at last, whether because of distance or because she had stopped screaming those in the truck did not know." The implication is that the white men don't know because they don't want to know. Wright knew that the most vicious form of oppression is the refusal to recognize the fundamental humanity of the oppressed. The flood that ought to expose common humanity reveals, in *Down by the Riverside*, the violence that wants to totally destroy the last tragic vestiges of the black man's humanity. Time and again Mann, Wright's protagonist, is warned by a racist world: "Shucks, nigger! You ought to be glad youre not dead in a flood like this." And Mann himself asks: "What would they do to a black man who had killed a white

101

man in a flood? He did not know. But whatever it was must be something far more terrible than at other times." Wright's *Down by the Riverside* tells us just how terrible.

Richard Wright (1908–1960), the son of an illiterate Mississippi sharecropper, became the most significant black writer of the twentieth century. He knew firsthand the terror of uncertainty. He had learned "that perhaps even a kick was better than uncertainty"; refusing to submit, Wright "embraced the daily horror of anxiety, of tension, of eternal disquiet. I could now sympathize with—though I could never bring myself to approve—those tortured blacks who had given up and had gone to their white tormentors and had said: 'Kick me, if that's all there is for me; kick me and let me feel at home, let me have peace!' " Part of the message of *Down by the Riverside*, and of the collection to which it belongs, *Uncle Tom's Children* (1938), is the horrible truth that there is no difference between enough kicks and the violent burning and dismemberment suffered in *Big Boy Leaves Home*, the collection's first short novel. With concentrated intensity Wright exposes the hideous terror of white oppression in the rural South, but that is not the only purpose of *Uncle Tom's Children*, as its epigraph indicates: "Uncle Tom! . . . has been supplanted by a new word from another generation which says—Uncle Tom is dead!" Because Wright sympathized without approving, because he thought of himself as one of his collection's children with the purpose of leading his oppressed elders out of downtrodden paths, his new word is more than the revelation that Uncle Tomism is living death. The four short novels of *Uncle Tom's Children* add up to a single conclusion, progressing from Big Boy's individual initiation into the reality of violence, to Mann's flood-shaped confrontation and his lone failure, to the chosen confrontation of Silas in *Long Black Song*, to the victorious solidarity of *Fire and Cloud*, where the new word is given: "Freedom belongs to the strong!" Strength comes from union: " 'Its the *people*, son! Wes too much erlone this way! Wes los when wes erlone! Wes gotta be wid our folks.' " *Bright and Morning Star*, a fifth tale added to the original collection, portrays both generations taking united action against oppression. Wright's literary realism is realism with a purpose, and in *Uncle Tom's Children* his genius makes that purpose one with his art.

Wright's greatness, as in his masterpiece *Native Son* (1940), was his knowledge of the essential tragedy of oppression and his decision to make American literature reflect that tragedy: "We do have in the Negro the embodiment of a past tragic enough to appease the spiritual hunger of even a [Henry] James; and we have in the oppression of the Negro a shadow athwart our national life dense and heavy enough to satisfy even the gloomy broodings of a Hawthorne. And if Poe were alive, he would not have to invent horror; horror would invent him." Here Wright tells us that horror is the American tragedy, and that tragedy is particularly evident in *Down by the Riverside*, a study of the psychology of fear, which points directly to Wright's existential novel, *The Outsider* (1953). Wright's flood intensifies inevitable black-white persecution to make plain Mann's alienation from both whites and blacks alike.

His crippling alienation, generated by the interaction of fear and anxiety, makes it impossible for him either to escape *or* destroy what he fears. Wright knew this to be the deepest destructive power of the oppressive flood, from his Mississippi youth, and from his observation of the great flood of 1927 from the vantage point of Memphis. But that particular flood was to help Wright embody his private experience in literature. *Black Boy* (1945), the autobiography of his youth, tells us that in 1927 Wright read a Southern attack on columnist H. L. Mencken, who had written that Northern sympathy for Southern flood victims had been less than generous because of Southern racial oppression. Wright was deeply interested—"Had not the South, which had assigned me the role of a non-man, cast at him its hardest words?"—and his interest led him to struggle his way into the public library, from which he was barred by race, to read Mencken's social criticism. That reading renewed Wright's desire to write and his hunger for literature, for Sinclair Lewis, and for Sherwood Anderson, Joseph Conrad, and Theodore Dreiser. "All my life," Wright explains, "had shaped me for the realism, the naturalism of the modern novel, and I could not read enough of them." Thus from the flood of 1927 come both the experience and the reading that combine in *Down by the Riverside*, but the unique power of Wright's realism comes from Wright himself. When *Down by the Riverside* analyzes the crippling alienation of terror from a combined perspective, the key to that united perspective is Wright's own fear. "The Ethics of Living Jim Crow," the powerful essay that serves as the introduction to *Uncle Tom's Children*, explains: "Even today when I think of white folks, the hard, sharp outlines of white houses surrounded by trees, lawns, hedges are present somewhere in the background of my mind. Through the years they grew into an overreaching symbol of fear." In *Down by the Riverside* the combined power of the flood makes Wright's short novel an epic by allowing the same white houses to come alive and violently turn upon black men.

Mann's story begins with his house creaking "as though the earth beneath the foundation were soggy. He wondered how long the logs which supported the house could stand against the water. But what really worried him were the steps; they might wash away at any moment, and then they would be trapped." Mann's fear is that the flood will leave him with no exit, but Wright wants us to see that this immediate fear is being used to obscure a more fundamental source of terror: the flood collects violence to warn that oppression will wash away all blacks unless they stand together. That all black life is threatened is clear from Wright's complication of Mann's problem. His wife, Lulu, is unable to deliver; man-child is trapped in her womb. "It just did not seem fair that one man should be hit so hard and on so many sides at once," thinks Mann, but this is necessary for Wright if Mann is to understand that the house of the oppressed is never home. Mann knows that the flood means violence: "Shucks, in times like these they'll shoota nigger down jus lika dog n think nothin of it." But his fear of violence keeps him from its meaning. Only "for a moment he had the illusion that that water had always been there, and would always be there . . . and this was just the first time he had noticed it. . . . a nervous shudder went through him." Oppressed religion adds to this passive resignation by separating black men and teaching them to evade confrontation. Mann might switch his stolen white boat with Elder Murray's but for the prayer—"Lawd, only clean hearts kin come t Yuh fer Mercy." The Uncle Tomism of this faith is revealed by Wright's choice of the hymn that follows for his title. Its message—"Ahm gonna lay down mah sword n shiel . . . Ah ain gonna study war no more"—is not Wright's new word. Flood means that the war is real, and must be studied by all blacks together, and that those who hope to go it alone and be left alone will end up as Mann does sprawled dead exactly by the riverside. His tragedy is the tragedy of fear that wishes to ignore the white current and the need for an opposing black one: "I always heard that a niggerd do anything, but I never thought anybody was fool enough to row against that current"—so the white world denigrates black achievement, calling it stupid and futile, blinding black men with a crippling image. Against this image, Mann yearns "for something to come out of the darkness to match an inner vision," but what comes out time and again is the image of his fear in the form of a cyclopean shooting white light. Mann can defeat one, but they are everywhere leagued against him. He escapes Heartfield, but pays a price—Lulu dead on arrival at the hospital. Wright suggests that Lulu dies at the same time as the white man, and then suggests that "Lulu lying stretched out on the marble table with her arm hanging limp" becomes Mann, "one black palm sprawled limply outward and upward, trailing in the brown current." The point is that Mann's confrontation is ultimately with himself, and his tragedy, the tragedy of self-division. Mann can't act because he is afraid and he is afraid because he can't act. When he does act he destroys himself, but why can't he act with others? Wright makes us ask this question to demonstrate the need for a collective response to oppression. He answers with a story that finds alienation in individualism, fear in alienation, and in fear a nihilism that is a living death. The black men conscripted to work on the levee are shown to be digging their own grave, and Mann is "encased . . . in a narrow black coffin that moved with him as he moved." Mann cannot cut his way out of this coffin with an axe, as he does at the hospital to speed the evacuation. Alone and impotent, the symbol of Wright's "overreaching fear" soon catches up with him to announce his crucifixion: "The house was floating down the middle of the street. . . . it seemed like a living thing, spinning slowly with a long, indrawn, sucking noise . . . turning to the light and then going into the darkness." Mann will drown because his foundation has been undermined all along. He can lift his axe, but "then he felt himself being lifted violently up and swung around as though by the gravity of the earth itself and flung face downward into black space. A loud commotion filled his ears: his body rolled over and over and he saw the flashlight . . . its one eye whirling: then he lay flat. . . . the house had tilted, had tilted in the rushing black water." Knocked flat here, Mann enacts exactly what will happen to him when the soldiers jerk him violently from behind and he is swung up in the commotion of a lynch mob to end up rolling and then flat, dead down by the riverside. But his final thoughts demonstrate last-gasp consciousness: "For a split second he was there among those blunt and hazy black faces looking silently and fearfully at the white folks take some poor black man away. Why don they hep me? Yet he knew that they would not and could not help him, even as he in times past had not helped other black men being taken by the white folks to their death." Mann has known all along: that, says Wright, is the tragedy of fear.

DOWN BY THE RIVERSIDE

I

Each step he took made the old house creak as though the earth beneath the foundations were soggy. He wondered how long the logs which supported the house could stand against the water. But what really worried him were the steps; they might wash away at any moment, and then they would be trapped. He had spent all that morning trying to make them secure with frayed rope, but he did not have much faith. He walked to the window and the half-rotten planks sagged under his feet. He had never realized they were that shaky. He pulled back a tattered curtain, wishing the dull ache would leave his head. Ah been feverish all day. Feels like Ah got the flu. Through a dingy pane he saw yellow water swirling around a corner of the barn. A steady drone filled his ears. In the morning the water was a deep brown. In the afternoon it was a clayey yellow. And at night it was black, like a restless tide of liquid tar. It was about six feet deep and still rising; it had risen two feet that day. He squinted at a tiny ridge of white foam where the yellow current struck a side of the barn and veered sharply. For three days he had been watching that tiny ridge of white foam. When it shortened he had hopes of seeing the ground soon; but when it lengthened he knew that the current was flowing strong again. All the seeds for spring planting were wet now. They gonna rot, he thought with despair. The morning before he had seen his only cow, Sally, lowing, wagging her head, rolling her eyes, and pushing through three feet of water for the hills. It was then that Sister Jeff had said that a man who would not follow a cow was a fool. Well, he had not figured it that way. This was his home. But now he would have to leave, for the water was rising and there was no telling when or where it would stop.

Two days ago he had told Bob to take the old mule to Bowman's plantation and sell it, or swap it for a boat, any kind of a boat. N Bob ain back here yit. Ef it ain one thing its ernother. When it rains it pos. But, Lawd, ef only tha ol levee don break. Ef only tha ol levee don break . . .

He turned away from the window, rubbing his forehead. A good dose of quinine would kill that fever. But he had no quinine. Lawd, have mercy!

And worst of all there was Lulu flat on her back these four days, sick with a child she could not deliver. His lips parted in silent agony. It just did not seem fair that one man should be hit so hard and on so many sides at once. He shifted the weight of his body from his right foot to his left, listening for sounds from the front room, wondering how Lulu was. Ef she don have the baby soon Ahma have t git her outta here, some way . . .

He leaned against a damp wall. Whut in the worls keepin Bob so long? Well, in a way all of this was his own fault. He had had a chance to get away and he had acted like a fool and had not taken it. He had figured that the water would soon go down. He had thought if he stayed he would be the first to get back to the fields and start spring plowing. But now even the mule was gone. Yes, he should have cleared-out when the Government offered him the boat. Now he had no money for a boat, and Bob had said that he could not even get near that Red Cross.

He took a gourd from the wall and dipped some muddy water out of a bucket. It tasted thick and bitter and he could not swallow it. He hung the gourd back and spat the water into a corner. He cocked his head, listening. It seemed he had heard the sound of a shot. There it was again. Something happenin in town, he thought. Over the yellow water he heard another shot, thin, dry, far away. Mus be trouble, mus be trouble somewhere. He had heard that the white folks were threatening to conscript all Negroes they could lay their hands on to pile sand- and cement-bags on the levee. And they were talking about bringing in soldiers, too. They were afraid of stores and homes being looted. Yes, it was hard to tell just what was happening in town. Shucks, in times like these they'll shoota nigger down jus lika dog n think nothin of it. Tha shootin might mean anything. But likely as not its jus some po black man gone . . .

He faced the window again, thinking, Ahma git mah pistol outta the dresser drawer when Ah go inter Lulus room. He rolled the tattered curtain up as far as it would go; a brackish light seeped into the kitchen. He looked out; his house was about twelve feet above the water. And water was everywhere. Yellow water. Swirling water. Droning water. For four long days and nights it had been there, flowing past. For a moment he had the illusion that that water had always been there, and would always be there. Yes, it seemed that the water had always been there and this was just the first time he had noticed it.

Mabbe somebody jus *dropped* them houses n tree down inter tha watah . . . He felt giddy and a nervous shudder went through him. He rubbed his eyes. Lawd, Ah got fever. His head ached and felt heavy; he wanted sleep and rest.

The view opposite his window was clear for half a mile. Most of the houses had already washed away. Nearby a few trees stood, casting black shadows into the yellow water. The sky was gray with the threat of rain. Suddenly every muscle in his body stretched taut as a low rumble of thunder rose and died away. He shook his head. Nothin could be worsen rain right now. A heavy rainll carry tha old levee erway sho as hell . . .

"Brother Mann!"

He turned and saw Sister Jeff standing in the hall door.

"How Lulu?" he asked.

The old woman shook her head.

"She poly."

"Yuh reckon she'll have it soon?"

"Cant say, Brother Mann. Mabbe she will n mabbe she wont. She havin the time of her life."

"Cant we do nothin fer her?"

"Naw. We jus have t wait, thas all. Lawd, Ahm scared she'll never have tha baby widout a doctah. Her hips is jus too little."

"There ain no way t git a doctah now."

"But yuh gotta do something, Brother Mann."

"Ah don know whut t do," he sighed. "Where Peewee?"

"He sleep, in Lulus room."

She came close to him and looked hard into his face.

"Brother Mann, there ain nothin t eat in the house. Yuh gotta do something."

He turned from her, back to the window.

"Ah sent Bob wid the mule t try t git a boat," he said.

She sighed. He swallowed with effort, hearing the whisper of her soft shoes die away down the hall. No boat. No money. No doctah. Nothin t eat. N Bob ain back here yit. Lulu could not last much longer this way. If Bob came with a boat he would pile Lulu in and row her over to that Red Cross Hospital, no matter *what*. The white folks would take her in. They would *have* to take her in. They would not let a woman die just because she was black; they would not let a baby kill a woman. They would *not*. He grew rigid, looking out of the window, straining to listen. He thought he had heard another shot. But the only sound was the drone of swirling water. The water was darkening. In the open stretches it was a muddy yellow; but near the houses and trees it was growing black. Its gittin night, he thought. Then came the sound of shots, thin, dry, distant. Wun . . . Tuh . . . Three . . .

"Brother Mann! Its Bob!"

He hurried to the front door, walking heavily on the heels of his big shoes. He saw Bob standing far down on the long steps near the water, bending over and fumbling with a coil of rope. Behind him a white rowboat trembled in the current.

"How yuh come out, Bob?"

Bob looked up and flashed a white grin.

"See?" he said, pointing to the white boat.

Mann's whole body glowed. Thank Gawd, we gotta boat! Now we kin git erway . . .

"Who yuh git from?"

Bob did not answer. He drew the rope tight and came up the steps.

"Ahm one tired soul," Bob said.

They went into the hall. Mann watched Bob pull out a pocket handkerchief and mop his black face. Peewee came in, rubbing his eyes and looking at Bob.

"Yuh git a boat, Uncle Bob?"

"Keep quiet, Peewee," said Mann.

Sister Jeff and Grannie came and stood behind Peewee. They looked from Bob to Mann. Bob tucked his handkerchief away, taking his time to do it, laughing a little.

"Lawd, Ahm one tired soul," he said again.

"Who bought the mule?" asked Mann.

"Ol man Bowman bought the mule, but he didnt wanna pay me much." Bob paused and pulled out a crumpled wad of one-dollar bills. "He gimme fifteen dollars . . ."

"Is that *all* he give yuh?"

"Every penny, so hep me Gawd! N tha ol stingy white ape didnt wanna gimme tha, neither. Lawd, ol man Bowman hada pila dough on im big ernuff t choka cow! Ah swear t Gawd Ah never wanted t rob a man so much in all mah life . . ."

"Don yuh go thinkin sin, Bob!" said Grannie. "Wes got ernuff trouble here now widout yuh thinkin sin!"

Bob looked at her.

"Its a boat!" cried Peewee, running from the front door.

Mann stood fingering the bills.

"But how yuh git tha boat, Bob?" he asked.

"Is it our boat?" Peewee asked.

"Hush, Peewee!" Grannie said.

"Don worry! Yuhll git a chance t ride in tha boat, Peewee," said Bob. He laughed and caught Peewee in his arms. He looked around, then dropped into a chair. "When Ah lef Bowmans place Ah caughta ride downtown in a motorboat wid Brother Hall. Ah went everwheres, lookin high n low fer a boat. Some wanted forty dollahs. Some fifty. Ah met one man whut wanted a hundred. Ah couldn't buy a boat nowheres, so Ah ups n steals a boat when nobody wuz lookin . . ."

"Yuh *stole* the boat? asked Mann.

"There wouldnt be no boat out there now ef Ah hadnt."

"Son, yuh a fool t go stealin them white folks boats in times like these," said Grannie.

Bob slapped his thigh and laughed.

"Awright, Ma, Ahll take the boat back. Hows tha? Wan me t take it back?"
Grannie turned away.

"Ah ain gonna ride in it," she said.

"Awright. Stay here n drown in the watah," said Bob.

Mann sighed.

"Bob, Ah sho wished yuh hadnt stole it."

"Aw," said Bob with an impatient wave of his hand. "Whut yuh so scared fer? Ain nobody gonna see yuh wid it. All yuh gotta do is git in n make fer the hills n make fer em quick. Ef Ah hadnt stole tha boat yuh all woulda had t stay here till the watah washed yuh erway . . ." He pushed Peewee off his knee and looked up seriously. "How Lulu?"

"She poly," said Sister Jeff.

Grannie came forward.

"Whutcha gonna do, Mann? Yuh gonna take Lulu in the boat Bob done stole? Yuh know them white folks is gonna be lookin fer tha boat. Sistah James boy got killed in a flood jus like this . . ."

"She cant stay here in the fix she in," said Mann.

"Is Ah goin, Pa?" asked Peewee.

"Shut up fo Ah slaps yuh!" said Grannie.

"Whutcha gonna do, Brother Mann?" asked Sister Jeff.

Mann hesitated.

"Wrap her up," he said. "Ahma row her over t the Red Cross Hospital . . ."

Bob stood up.

"Red Cross Hospital? Ah thought yuh said yuh wuz gonna make fer the hills?"

"We gotta git Lulu t a doctah," said Mann.

"Yuh mean t take her in the boat Ah *stole*?"

"There ain nothin else t do."

Bob scratched his head.

"Mann, Ahm mighty scared yuhll git in trouble takin tha boat thu town. Ah stole tha boat from the Pos Office. Its old man Heartfields, n yuh know how he hates niggers. Everybody knows his boat when they see it; its white n yuh couldn't git erway wid it. N lissen, theres trouble a-startin in town, too. The levees still over-flowin in the Noth, n theys spectin the one by the cement plant t go any minute. They done put ever nigger they could fin on the levee by the railroad, pilin san n cement bags. They drivin em like slaves. Ah heard they done killed two-three awready whut tried t run erway. N ef anything happened t yuh, yuh just couldn't git erway, cause two mo bridges done washed erway this mawnin n ain no trains runnin. Things awful bad there in town. A lotta them white folks done took down wid typhoid, n tha Red Cross is vaxinatin everybody, black n white. Everywhere Ah looked wuznt nothin but white men wid guns. They wuz a-waiting fer the soljers when Ah lef, n yuh know whut tha means . . ."

Bob's voice died away and they could hear Lulu groaning in the front room.

"Is yuh gonna take her, Brother Mann?" asked Sister Jeff.

"There ain nothin else t do," said Mann. "Ahll try t take tha boat back t the white folks aftah Ah git Lulu t the hospital. But Ah sho wish yuh hadnt stole tha boat, Bob. But we gotta use it now. Ah don like t rile them white folks . . ."

"Ah ain goin in tha boat!" said Grannie. "Ah ain goin outta here t meet mah death today!"

"Stay here n drown, then!" said Mann. "Ahm takin Lulu t the hospital!"

Grannie cried and went into the front room. Sister Jeff followed.

"Pa, is Ah goin?" asked Peewee.

"Yeah. Git yo cloes. N tell Grannie t git hers if she don wanna stay here, cause Ahm gittin ready t leave!"

Bob was restless. He pursed his lips and looked at the floor.

"Yuh gotta hard job, rowin tha boat from here t the hospital. Yuhll be rowin ergin the current ever inch, n wid a boat full itll be the Devil t pay. The watahs twelve foot deep n flowing strong n tricky."

"There ain nothin else t do," sighed Mann.

"Yuh bettah take something wid yuh. Tha ain nobodys plaything there in town."

"Ahma take mah gun," said Mann. "But Ahm sho sorry yuh had t steal them white folks boat . . ."

Like a far away echo a voice floated over the water.

"Brother Mann! Yuh there, Brother Mann!"

"Thas Elder Murray," said Bob.

Mann opened the door. It was pitch black outside. A tall man was standing in a rowboat, his hand holding onto a rope by the steps.

"Tha yuh, Brother Mann?"

"How yuh, Elder?"

"Yuh all ain gone yit?"

"We jus fixin t go. Won't yuh come up?"

"Jes fer a minute."

Murray came up the steps and stood in the doorway, rubbing his hands.

"How Sistah Lulu?"

"We aimin t take her t the Red Cross . . ."

"Yuh mean t say she ain had tha baby *yit*?"

"She too little t have it widout a doctah, Elder."

"Lawd, have mercy! Kin Ah see her?"

Mann led the way into Lulu's room where a smoking pine-knot made shadows blink on the walls. Bob, Peewee, Sister Jeff, Grannie, Murray and Mann stood about the bed. Lulu lay on top of the bed-covers, wrapped in a heavy quilt. Her hair was disordered and her face wet. Her breath came fast.

"How yuh feelin, Sistah Lulu?" asked Murray.

Lulu looked at him weakly. She was a small woman with large shining eyes. Her arms were stretched out at her sides and her hands clutched the quilt.

"How yuh feelin?" asked Murray again.

"She awful weak," said Grannie.

Murray turned to Mann.

"Lissen, yuh bettah be mighty careful takin that boat thu town. Them white folks is makin trouble n that currents strong."

Mann turned from the bed to the dresser, eased his pistol out of the top drawer and slipped it into his pocket.

"Pa, whuts that?" asked Peewee.

"Hush!" said Mann.

"Brothers n Sistahs, les all kneel n pray," said Murray.

They all got to their knees. Lulu groaned. For a split second a blue sheet of lightning lit up the room, then a hard clap of thunder seemed to rock the earth. No one spoke until the last rumble had rolled away.

"Lawd Gawd Awmighty in Heaven, wes a-bowin befo Yuh once ergin, humble in Yo sight, a-pleadin fer fergiveness n mercy! Hear us today, Lawd! Hear us today ef Yuh ain never heard us befo! We needs Yuh now t hep us n guide us! N hep these po folks, Lawd! Deys Yo Chillun! Yuh made em n Yuh made em in Yo own image! Open up their hearts n hep em t have faith in Yo word! N hep this po woman, Lawd! Ease her labor, fer Yuh said, Lawd, she has t bring foth her chillun in pain . . ."

Mann closed his eyes and rested his hands on his hips. That slow dull ache had come back to his head. He wished with all his heart that Elder Murray would hurry up and get through with the prayer, for he wanted to be in that boat. He would not feel safe until he was in that boat. It was too bad Bob had to steal it. But there was no help for that now. The quicker wes in tha boat the bettah, he thought. Ef them white folks come by here n take it back well all be jus where we wuz befo. Yeah, Ahma take tha boat back to the white folks aftah Ah git Lulu t the hospital. Oh, yeah! Mabbe the Elderll take *mah* boat n lemme have *his* since hes on his way t the hills? Lawd, yeah! Thall be a good way to dodge them white folks! Ahma ast im . . .

". . . Lawd, Yuh said call on Yo name n Yuhd answer! Yuh said seek n fin! Today wes callin on Yuh n wes seekin Yuh, Lawd! Yuh said believe in the blooda Yo son Jesus, n today wes believin n waitin fer Yuh t hep us! N soften the hard hearts of them white folks there in town, Lawd! Purify their hearts! Fer Yuh said, Lawd, only clean hearts kin come t Yuh fer mercy . . ."

Mann rubbed his eyes and cleared his throat. Naw, he thought, ain no use astin the Elder t take mah boat. Hell wanna know why n then Ahll have t tell im Bob stole it. N the Elder ain gonna hep noboby he thinks ain doin right. Mabbe ef Ah tol ol man Heartfiel just why Bob stole his boat mabbe he wont hol it ergin me? Yeah, he oughta be glad ef Ah brings im his boat back. N yeah, mabbe the Elder kin take Sistah Jeff n Bob t the hills in his boat? Thad hep a lots . . .

". . . n save our souls for Jesus sake! Ahmen!"

Murray stood up and began to sing. The others chimed in softly.

Ahm gonna lay down mah sword n shiel
Down by the riverside
Down by the riverside

Down by the riverside
Ahm gonna lay down mah sword n shiel
Down by the riverside
Ah ain gonna study war no mo . . .

Ah ain gonna study war no mo
Ah ain gonna study war no mo
Ah ain gonna study war no mo
Ah ain gonna study war no mo
Ah ain gonna study war no mo
Ah ain gonna study war no mo . . .

Murray wiped his mouth with the back of his hand and fumbled with his hat.

"Waal, Brothers n Sistahs. Ahm gittin on t the hills. Mah folks is there awreaady. Ah gotta boatloada stuff outside, but theres room fer two-three mo ef anybody wanna go."

"Kin yuh take Sistah Jeff n Bob erlong?" asked Mann.

"Sho!"

Grannie was crying; she pulled on her coat and went into the hall. Bob came from the kitchen with a bundle. Mann lifted Lulu in his arms. Murray held the door for him. Peewee followed, holding a ragged teddy bear. Sister Jeff put out the pine-knot. They all paused in the front doorway.

"Bob, yuh bettah go down n steady tha boat," said Mann.

"Lemme go wid yuh!" said Peewee.

"Yuh c mere!" said Grannie, grabbing his arm.

Bob pulled the boat close to the steps. Mann went down sideways, slowly.

"Take it easy, Brother Mann!" called Murray.

Mann stepped into the boat and rested Lulu in the back seat. Bob held her by the shoulders.

"C mon, yuh all!" Mann called to Grannie and Peewee.

They came, stepping gingerly. Murray helped them down.

"Ahll see yuh all at the hills!" he said.

Bob and Sister Jeff got into Murray's boat. Murray was first to shove off.

"Ahm gone, folks! Good-bye n Gawd bless yuh!"

"Good-bye!"

Mann grasped the oars, wet the handles to prevent creaking, dipped, pulled, and the boat glided outward, over the darkening flood.

II

To all sides of Mann the flood rustled, gurgled, droned, glistening blackly like an ocean of bubbling oil. Above his head the sky was streaked with faint grey light. The air was warm, humid, blowing in fitful gusts. All around he was ringed in by walls of solid darkness. He knew that houses and trees were hidden by those walls and he knew he had to be careful. As he rowed he could feel the force of the current tugging at his left. With each sweep of the oars he weighed the bulk of the boat in his back, his neck, his shoulders. And fear flowed under everything. Lawd, ef only tha ol levee don break! An oak tree loomed ghostily, its leaves whispering. He remembered it had stood at the fork of a road. His mind weaved about the clue of the tree a quick image of cornfield in sunshine. He would have to turn here at a sharp angle and make for the railroad. With one oar resting, he turned by paddling with the other. The boat struck the current full, and spun. He bent to with the oars, straining, sweeping hard, feeling that now he must fight. He would have to keep the boat moving at a steady pace if he wanted to row in a straight line. And the strokes of the oars would have to be timed, not a second apart. He bent to, lifting the oars; he leaned back, dipping them; then he pulled with tight fingers, feeling the glide of the boat over the water in darkness. Lawd, ef only tha old levee don break!

He began to look for the cotton-seed mill that stood to the left of the railroad. He peered, longing to see black stack-pipes. They were along here somewhere. Mabbe Ah done passed it? He turned to the right, bending low, looking. Then he twisted about and squinted his eyes. He stopped the boat; the oars dangled. He felt a sudden swerve that tilted him.

"Peewee, keep still!" Grannie whispered.

Lulu groaned. Mann felt wild panic. Quickly he retraced in his mind the route over which he thought he had come, and wondered what could be on the ground, what landmarks the water hid. He looked again, to the right, to the left, and over his shoulder. Then he looked straight upward. Two tall, black stack-pipes loomed seemingly a foot from his eyes. Ah wuznt lookin high ernuff, he thought. Westward would be houses. And straight down would be Pikes' Road. That would be the shortest way.

"Pa, is we there?" asked Peewee.

"Hush!"

He rowed from the stack-pipes, rowed with the houses in his mind, yearning for something to come out of the darkness to match an inner vision. Every six or seven strokes he twisted around to look. The current became stiff and the darkness thickened. For awhile he had the feeling that the boat was not moving. He set his heels, bent to as far as he could go, and made his sweeps with the oars as long as his arms could reach. His back was getting tired. His fingers burned; he paused a second and dipped them into the cold black water. That helped some. But there was only darkness ahead of him each time he turned to look for the houses on Pikes' Road. He wondered if he were on the *wrong* side of the mill! Mabbe Ahm headin the wrong way? He could not tell. And with each yard forward the current grew stiffer. He thought of the levee. Suddenly the boat swerved and spun. He caught his breath and plied the oars, losing all sense of direction. Is tha ol levee lunc broke? He heard Grannie cry: "Mann!" The boat leaped: his head hit something: stars danced in the darkness: the boat crashed with a bang: he clung to the oars, one was loose: but the other was jammed and would not move. The boat was still save for a hollow banging against a wall he could not see. He dropped the oars and groped his hands ahead in the darkness. Wood. Ridged wood. Is these them houses? He sensed that he was drifting backwards and clutched with his fingers, wincing from the sharp entry of splinters. Then he grabbed something round, cold, smooth, wet . . . It was wood. He clung tightly and stopped the boat. He could feel the tugging and trembling of the current vibrating through his body as his heart gave soft, steady throbs. He breathed hard, trying to build in his mind something familiar around the cold, wet, smooth pieces of wood. A series of pictures flashed through his mind, but none fitted. He groped higher, thinking with his fingers. Then suddenly he saw the whole street: sunshine, wagons and buggies tied to a water trough. This is old man Toms sto. And these were the railings that went around the front porch he was holding in his hands. Pikes' Road was around the house, in front of him. He thought a moment before picking up the oars, wondering if he could make it in that wild current.

"Whuts the mattah, Mann?" Grannie asked.

"Its awright," he said.

He wanted to reassure them, but he did not know what to say. Instead he grabbed the oars and placed one of them against an invisible wall. He set himself, flexed his body, and gave a shove that sent the boat spinning into the middle of the current. He righted it, striving to keep away from the houses, seeking for the street. He strained his eyes till they ached; but all he could see were dark bulks threatening on either side. Yet, that was enough to steer him clear of them. And he rowed, giving his strength to the right oar and then to the left, trying to keep in the middle.

"Look, Pa!"

"Whut?"

"Hush, Peewee!" said Grannie.

"There's lights, see?"

"Where?"

"See? Right there, over yonder!"

Mann looked, his chin over his shoulder. There were two squares of dim, yellow light. For a moment Mann was puzzled. He plied the oars and steadied the boat. Those lights seemed *too* high up. He could not associate them. But they were on Pikes' Road and they seemed about a hundred yards away. Wondah whut kin tha be? Maybe he could get some help there. He rowed again, his back to the lights; but their soft, yellow glow was in his mind. They helped him, those lights. For awhile he rowed without effort. Where there were lights there were people, and where there were people there was help. Wondah whose house is tha? Is they white folks? Fear dimmed the lights for a moment; but he rowed on and they glowed again, their soft sheen helping him to sweep the oars.

"Pa, cant we go there?"

"Hush, Peewee!"

The closer the lights came the lower they were. His mind groped frantically in the past, sought for other times on Pikes' Road and for other nights to tell him who lived where those yellow lights gleamed. But the lights remained alone, and the past would tell him nothing. Mabbe they kin phone t town n git a boat t come n git Lulu? Mabbe she kin res some there. The lights were close now.

Square yellow lights framed in darkness. They were windows. He steered for the lights, feeling hunger, fatigue, thirst. The dull ache came back to his head: the oars were heavy, almost too heavy to hold: the boat glided beneath the windows: he looked, sighing.

"Is this the hospital, Pa?" asked Peewee.

"We goin in there, Mann?" asked Grannie.

"Ahma call," said Mann.

He cupped his hands to his mouth.

"Hello!"

He waited and looked at the windows; he heard the droning water swallow his voice.

"Hello!" he hollered again.

A window went up with a rasping noise. A white face came into the light. Lawd! Its a white man . . .

"Whos there?"

"Mann!"

"Who?"

"Mann! Mah wifes sick! Shes in birth! Ahm takin her t the hospital! Yuh gotta phone in there?"

"Wait a minute!"

The window was empty. There was silence; he waited, his face turned upward. He plied the oars and steadied the boat in the swift current. Again a white face came through. A pencil of light shot out into the darkness; a spot of yellow caught the boat. He blinked, blinded.

"Yuh gotta phone there, Mistah?" he called again, dodging the glare of the flash-light.

Silence.

"Mah wifes sick! Yuh gotta phone!"

A voice came, cold, angry.

"Nigger, where you steal that boat?"

The window became filled with white faces. Mann saw a white woman with red hair. He fumbled for the oars in fear. He blinked his eyes as the light jumped to and fro over his face.

"Where you steal that boat, nigger! Thats *my* boat!"

Then Mann heard softer voices.

"Thats our boat, Father! Its *white!*"

"Thats our boat, Henry! Thats *our* boat . . ."

"Don't you hear me, nigger! Bring that boat back here!"

There were two pistol shots. Grannie screamed. Mann swept the oars blindly; the boat spun. Lawd, thas Heartfiel! N hes gotta gun! Mann felt the water rocking him away.

"Nigger, dont you take that boat! Ill kill you!"

He heard two more shots: loudly the boat banged against wood: he was thrown flat on his back. He jerked up and tried to keep the yellow windows in sight. For a moment he thought the windows were dark, but only the flash-light had gone out. He held his breath and felt the boat skidding along a wall, shaking with the current. Then it was still: it seemed it had become wedged between two walls: he touched a solid bulk and tried to shove away: the boat lurched: a shower of cold water sprayed him: the boat became wedged again: he looked for the windows: a third square of light burst out: he watched a white man with a hard, red face come out onto a narrow second-story porch and stand framed in a light-flooded doorway. The man was wearing a white shirt and was playing the yellow flare over the black water. In his right hand a gun gleamed. The man walked slowly down an outside stairway and stopped, crouching, at the water's edge. A throaty voice bawled:

"Nigger, bring that boat here! You *nigger!*"

Mann held still, frozen. He stared at the gun in the white man's hand. A cold lump forced its way up out of his stomach into his throat. He saw the disc of yellow sweep over the side of a house. The white man stooped, aimed and shot. He thinks Ahm over there! Lawd! Mann's mouth hung open and his lips dried as he breathed.

"You sonofabitch! Bring my boat here!"

"Mann!" Grannie whispered.

Mann fumbled in his pocket for his gun and held it ready. His hand trembled. He watched the yellow disc jump fitfully over the black water some fifty feet from him. It zigzagged, pausing for instants only, searching every inch of the water. As it crept closer Mann raised his gun. The flare flickered to and fro. His throat tightened and he aimed. Then the flare hovered some five feet from him. He fired, twice. The white man fell backwards on the steps and slipped with an abrupt splash into the water. The flashlight went with him, its one eye swooping downward, leaving a sudden darkness. There was a scream. Mann dropped the gun into the bottom of the boat, grabbed the oars, threw his weight desperately, shoved out from the wall and paddled against the current.

"Henry! Henry!"

Mann rowed: he heard Grannie crying: he felt weak from fear: he had a choking impulse to stop: he felt he was lost because he had shot a white man: he felt there was no use in his rowing any longer: but the current fought the boat and he fought back with the oars.

"Henry! Henry!"

It was a woman's voice, pleading; then a younger voice, shrill, adolescent, insistent.

"The nigger killed him! The nigger killed father!"

Mann rowed on into the darkness, over the black water. He could not see the lights now; he was on the other side of the building. But the screams came clearly.

"Stop, nigger! *Stop!* You killed my father! You bastard! You nigger!"

"Henry! Henry!"

Mann heard Grannie and Peewee crying. But their weeping came to him from a long way off, as though it were as far away as the voices that were screaming. It was difficult for him to get his breath as he bent on the left oar, then the right, keeping the boat in the middle of the bulks of darkness. Then all at once he was limp, nerveless; he felt that getting the boat to the hospital now meant nothing. Two voices twined themselves in his ears: Stop, nigger! Stop, nigger! Henry! Henry! They echoed and re-echoed even after he was long out of earshot.

Then suddenly the rowing became a little easier. He was in the clear again, away from the houses. He did not worry about directions now, for he knew exactly where he was. Only one-half mile across Barrett's Pasture, and he would strike streets and maybe lights. He rowed on, hearing Grannie's crying and seeing Heartfield coming down the narrow steps with the flash-light and the gun. But he shot at me fo Ah shot im . . . Another thought made him drop the oars. Spose Heartfields folks phone to town n tell em Ah shot im? He looked around hopelessly in the darkness. Lawd, Ah don wanna ride mah folks right inter death! The boat drifted sideways, shaking with the tug of the current.

"Lulu," Grannie was whispering.

"How Lulu?" Mann asked.

"She sleep, Ah reckon," sighed Grannie.

Naw, Ahm goin on, no mattah *whut!* He could not turn back now for the hills, not with Lulu in this boat. Not with Lulu in the fix she was in. He gritted his teeth, caught the oars, and rowed. High over his head a plane zoomed; he looked up and saw a triangle of red and green lights winging through the darkness. His fingers were hot and loose, as though all the feeling in his hands had turned into fire. But his body was cool; a listless wind was drying the sweat on him.

"There the lights o town, Mann!" Grannie spoke.

He twisted about. Sure enough, there they were. Shining, barely shining. Dim specks of yellow buried in a mass of blackness. Lawd only knows whut wes ridin inter . . . If he could only get Lulu to the hospital, if he could only get Grannie and Peewee safely out of this water, then he would take a chance on getting away. He knew that that was what they would want him to do. He swept the oars, remembering hearing tales of whole families being killed because some relative had done something wrong.

A quick, blue fork of lightning lit up the waste of desolate and tumbling waters. Then thunder exploded, loud and long, like the sound of a mountain falling. It began to rain. A sudden, sharp rain. Water trickled down the back of his neck. He felt Grannie moving; she was covering Lulu with her coat. He rowed faster, peering into the rain, wanting to reach safety before the boat caught too much water. Another fifty yards or so and he would be among the houses. Yeah, ef they ast me erbout Heartfiel Ahma tell em the truth . . . But he knew he did not want to do that. He knew that that would not help him. But what else was there for him to do? Yes, he would have to tell the truth and trust God. Nobody but God could see him through this. Bob shouldna stole this boat . . . But here Ah am in it now . . . He sighed, rowing. N this rain! Tha ol levee might go wid this rain . . . Lawd, have mercy! He lowered his chin and determined not to think. He would have to trust God and keep on and go through with it, that was all. His feet and clothes were wet. The current stiffened and brought the boat almost to a standstill. Yeah, he thought, theres Rose Street. He headed the boat between two rows of houses.

"Halt! Who goes there?"

He pulled the oars. A glare of light shot from a second-story porch and made him blink. Two white soldiers in khaki uniforms leaned over the banisters. Their faces were like square blocks of red and he could see the dull glint of steel on the tips of their rifles. Well, he would know now. Mabbe they done foun out erbout Heartfiel?

"Where you going, nigger?"

"Ahm takin mah wife t the hospital, suh. Shes in birth, suh!"

"What?"

"Mah wifes in birth, suh! Ahm takin her t the Red Cross!"

"Pull up to the steps!"

"Yessuh!"

He turned the boat and paddled toward steps that led down to the water. The two soldiers loomed over him.

"Whats your name?"

"Mann, suh."

"You got a pass?"

"Nawsuh."

"Dont you know you're violating curfew?"

"Nawsuh."

"What was all that shooting back there a little while ago?"

"Ah don know, suh."

"Didnt you hear it?"

"Nawsuh."

"Frisk im, Mac," said one of the soldiers.

"O.K. Stand up, nigger!"

One of the soldiers patted Mann's hips. Lawd, Ah hope they don see tha gun in the boat . . .

"Hes awright."

"What you say your name was?"

"Mann, suh."

"Where you from?"

"The South En, suh."

"I mean where you bring that boat from?"

"The South En, suh."

"You *rowed* here?"

"Yessuh."

"In *that* boat?"

"Yessuh."

The soldiers looked at each other.

"You aint lying, are you, nigger?"

"Oh, nawsuh," said Mann.

"What wrong with your woman?"

"Shes in birth, suh."

One of the soldiers laughed.

"Well, Ill be Goddamned! Nigger, you take the prize! I always heard that a niggerd do anything, but I never thought anybody was fool enough to row a boat against that current . . ."

"But Mistah, mah wifes sick! She been sick fo days!"

"O.K. Stay here. Ill phone for a boat to take you in."

"Yessuh."

One of the soldiers ran up the steps and the other hooked Mann's boat to a rope.

"Nigger, you dont know how lucky you are," he said. "Six men were drowned today trying to make it to town in rowboats. And here you come, rowing *three* people . . ."

The soldier who had gone to telephone came back.

"Mistah, please!" said Mann. "Kin Ah take mah wife in there, outta the rain?"

The soldier shook his head.

"Im sorry, boy. Orders is that nobody but soldiers can be in these houses. Youll have to wait for the boat. Its just around the corner; it wont be long. But I dont see how in hell you rowed that boat between those houses without drowning! It mustve been tough, hunh?"

"Yessuh."

Mann saw a motorboat swing around a curve, its headlight sweeping a wide arc, its motor yammering. It glided up swiftly in a churn of foam. It was manned by two soldiers whose slickers gleamed with rain.

"Whats the rush?"

"Boy," said one of the soldiers, "I got a nigger here who beat everybody. He rowed in from the South End, against the current. Can you beat that?"

The soldiers in the boat looked at Mann.

"Says you!" said one, with a scornful wave of his white palm.

"Im telling the truth!" said the soldier. "Didnt you, boy?"

"Yessuh."

"Well, what you want us to do about it? Give im a medal?"

"Naw; his bitch is sick. Having a picaninny. Shoot em over to the Red Cross Hospital."

The soldiers in the boat looked at Mann again.

"They crowded out over there, boy . . ."

"Lawd, have mercy!" Grannie cried, holding Lulu's head on her lap.

"Mistah, please! Mah wife cant las much longer like this," said Mann.

"Awright! Hitch your boat, nigger, and lets ride!"

Mann grabbed the rope that was thrown at him and looped it to a hook on the end of his boat. He was standing when one of the soldiers yelled:

"Watch yourself, nigger!"

The motor roared and the boat shot forward; he fell back against Grannie,

Lulu and Peewee. He straightened just as they made the turn. His boat leaned, scooping water, wetting him; then it righted itself. The rest of the drive was straight ahead, into darkness. He had hardly wiped the water out of his eyes before they slowed to a stop. His fingers groped nervously in the bottom of the boat for the gun; he found it and slipped it into his pocket.

"Awright, nigger, unload!"

He stood up and fronted a row of wide steps.

"Is this the hospital, suh?"

"Yeah; straight up!"

He lifted Lulu and stepped out. Grannie followed, leading Peewee by the hand. When he reached the top of the steps the door was opened by another white soldier.

"Where you going?"

"Ah got mah wife, suh. She sick . . ."

"Straight on to the back, till you see the sign."

"Yessuh."

He walked down a dim-lit hall. Grannie and Peewee shuffled behind. He smelled the warm scent of ether and disinfectant and it made him dizzy. Finally, he saw the sign:

FOR COLORED

He pushed open a door with his shoulder and stood blinking in a blaze of bright lights. A white nurse came.

"What you want?"

"Please, Mam . . . Mah wife . . . She sick!"

The nurse threw back the quilt and felt Lulu's pulse. She looked searchingly at Mann, then turned quickly, calling:

"Doctor Burrows!"

A white doctor came. He looked at Lulu's face. Her eyes were closed and her mouth was open.

"Bring her here, to the table," said the doctor.

Mann stretched Lulu out. Her face, her hair, and her clothes were soaking wet. Her left arm fell from the table and hung limp. The doctor bent over and pushed back the lids of her eyes.

"This your woman?"

"Yessuh."

"How long was she in birth?"

"Bout fo days, suh."

"Why didnt you bring her sooner?"

"Ah didnt hava boat n the watah had me trapped, suh."

The doctor lifted his eyes, rubbed his chin, and looked at Mann quizzically.

"Well, boy, shes dead."

"Suh?"

Grannie screamed and grabbed Peewee. The doctor straightened and laid the stethoscope on a white, marble-topped table. Lightning flicked through the room and thunder rolled rumblingly away, leaving a silence filled with the drone of hard, driving rain.

"*Suh!*" said Mann.

III

"Well, boy, it's all over," said the doctor. "Maybe if you could have gotten her here a little sooner we could have saved her. The baby, anyway. But it's all over now, and the best thing for you to do is get your folks to the hills."

Mann stared at the thin, black face; at the wet clothes; at the arm hanging still and limp. His lips moved, but he could not speak. Two more white nurses and another white doctor came and stood. Grannie ran to the table.

"Lulu!"

"Its awright, Aunty," said the doctor, pulling her away.

Grannie sank to the floor, her head on her knees.

"Lawd . . ."

Mann stood like stone now. Lulu dead? He seemed not to see the white doctors and nurses gathering around, looking at him. He sighed and the lids of his eyes drooped halfway down over the pupils.

"Poor nigger," said a white nurse.

Blankly, Mann stared at her. He wet his lips and swallowed. Something pressed against his knee and he looked down. Peewee was clinging to him, his little black face tense with fear. He caught Peewee by the hand, went over to the wall and stood above Grannie, hesitating. His fingers touched her shoulders.

"Awright," said the doctor. "Roll her out."

Mann turned and saw two white nurses rolling Lulu through a door. His throat tightened. Grannie struggled up and tried to follow the body. Mann pulled her back and she dropped to the floor again, crying.

"It's awright, Grannie," said Mann.

"You got a boat, boy?" asked the doctor.

"Yessuh," said Mann.

"Youre lucky. You ought to start out right now for the hills, before that current gets stronger."

"Yessuh."

Again Mann looked at Grannie and twice his hands moved toward her and stopped. It seemed that he wanted ever so much to say something, to do something, but he did not know what.

"C mon, Grannie," he said.

She did not move. A white nurse giggled, nervously. Mann stood squeezing his blistered palms, taking out of the intense pain a sort of consolation, a sort of forgetfulness. A clock began to tick. He could hear Grannie's breath catching softly in her throat; he could hear the doctors and nurses breathing; and beyond the walls of the room was the beat of sweeping rain. Somewhere a bell tolled, faint and far off.

Crash!

Everybody jumped. One of the nurses gave a short scream.

"What's that?"

"Aw, just a chair fell over. Thats all . . ."

"Oh!"

The doctors looked at the nurses and the nurses looked at the doctors. Then all of them laughed, uneasily. There was another silence. The doctor spoke.

"Is that your mother there, boy?"

"Yessuh. Mah ma-in-law."

"Youll have to get her out of here."

"C mon, Grannie," he said again.

She did not move. He stooped and picked her up.

"C mon, Peewee."

He went through the door and down the hall with Peewee pulling at the tail of his coat.

"Hey, you!"

He stopped. A white soldier came up.

"Where you going?"

"Ahm gittin mah boat t take mah family t the hills . . ."

"Your boat was commandeered. Come over here and wait awhile."

"Comman . . ."

"We were short of boats and the boys had to take yours. But Ill get a motor-boat to take you and your family to the hills. Wait right here a minute . . ."

He waited with Grannie in his arms. Lawd, they got me now! They knowed that was Heartfiel's boat! Mabbe they fixin t take me erway? What would they do to a black man who had killed a white man in a flood? He did not know. But whatever it was must be something far more terrible than at other times. He shifted his weight from foot to foot. He was more tired than he could ever remember having been. Well, boy, shes dead. His eyes burned. Lawd, Ah don care whut they do t me! Ah don care . . .

"Pa, where ma?"

"She gone, Peewee."

"Ain she comin wid us?"

"Naw, Peewee."

"How come, Pa?"

"She gonna stay wid Gawd now, Peewee."

"Awways?"

"Awways, Peewee."

Peewee cried.

"Hush, Peewee! Be a good boy, now! Don cry! Ahm here! N Grannies here . . ."

The white soldier came back with the colonel.

"Is this the nigger?"

"Thats him."

"Was that your rowboat outside?"

Mann hesitated.

"Yessuh, Capm."

"A white boat?"

"Yessuh."

"Are you sure it was yours?"

Mann swallowed and hesitated again.

"Yessuh."

"What was it worth?"

"Ah don know, Capm."

"What did you pay for it?"

"Bout f-fifty dollahs, Ah reckon."

"Here, sign this," said the colonel, extending a piece of paper and a pencil. "We can give you thirty-five dollars as soon as things are straightened out. We had to take your boat. We were short of boats. But I've phoned for a motorboat to take you and your family to the hills. Youll be safer in that anyway."

"Yessuh."

He sat Grannie on the floor and sighed.

"Is that your mother there?"

"Yessuh. Mah ma-in-law."

"What's wrong with her?"

"She jus ol, Capm. Her gal jus died n she takes it hard."

"When did she die?"

"Jus now, suh."

"Oh, I see . . . but whats wrong with you? Are you sick?"

"Nawsuh."

"Well, you dont have to go to the hills. Your folksll go on to the hills and you can stay here and help on the levee . . ."

"Capm, please! Ahm tired!"

"This is martial law," said the colonel, turning to the white soldier. "Put this woman and boy into a boat and ship them to the hills. Give this nigger some boots and a raincoat and ship him to the levee!"

The soldier saluted.

"Yessir, Colonel!"

"CAPM, PLEASE! HAVE MERCY ON ME, CAPM!"

The colonel turned on his heels and walked away.

"AHM TIRED! LEMME GO WID MAH FOLKS, PLEASE!"

The soldier glared at Mann.

"Aw, c mon, nigger! What in hells wrong with you? All the rest of the niggers are out there, how come you dont want to go?"

Mann watched the soldier go to the door, open it and look out into the rain.

"Mann!" Grannie whispered.

He leaned to her, his hands on his knees.

"Yuh go on t the levee! Mabbe them Heartfiel folks is out t the hills by now. Git over t where our folks is n mabbe yuh kin git erway . . ."

"C mon!" called the soldier. "Heres your boat!"

"*Here*, Grannie," whispered Mann. He slipped the fifteen dollars he had gotten from Bob into her hands.

"Naw," she said. "*Yuh* keep it!"

"Naw, *take* it!" said Mann. He pushed the money into the pocket of her coat.

"C MON, NIGGER! THIS BOAT CANT WAIT ALL NIGHT FOR YOU!"

He picked Grannie up again and carried her down the steps. Peewee followed, crying. It was raining hard. After he had helped them into the boat he stood on the steps. Lawd, Ah wished Ah could go!

"All set?"

"All set!"

The motor droned and the boat shot out over the water, its spotlight cutting ahead into the rain.

"Good-bye!" Peewee called.

"Good-bye!" Mann was not sure that Peewee had heard and he called again. "Good-bye!"

"C mon, boy! Lets get your boots and raincoat. Youre going to the levee."

"Yessuh."

He followed the soldier into the office.

"Jack, get some hip-boots and a raincoat for this nigger and call for a boat to take him to the levee," the soldier spoke to another soldier sitting behind a desk.

"O.K. Heres some boots. And heres a raincoat."

The first soldier went out. Mann hoisted the boots high on his legs and put on the raincoat.

"Tired, nigger?" asked the soldier.

"Yessuh."

"Well, youve got a hard night ahead of you, and thats no lie."

"Yessuh."

Mann sat down, rested his head against a wall, and closed his eyes. Lawd . . . He heard the soldier talking over the telephone.

"Yeah. Yeah."

". . ."

"The Red Cross Hospital."

"The niggers here now, waiting."

". . ."

"O.K."

Mann heard the receiver click.

"The boatll be along any minute," said the soldier. "And while youre resting, unpack those boxes and lay the stuff on the floor."

"Yessuh."

Mann stood up and shook his head. A sharp pain stabbed at the front of his eyes and would not leave. He went to the back of the room where a pile of wooden boxes was stacked and got a crowbar. He pried open the top of a box and began to pull out raincoats and rubber boots. He worked mechanically, slowly, leaning against boxes, smelling fresh rubber and stale tobacco smoke. He felt the pistol in his pocket and remembered Heartfield. Ah got t git outta here some way. Go where they cant fin me. Lawd, take care Grannie! Take care Peewee, Lawd! Take care Bob! N hep me, Lawd. He thought of Lulu lying stretched out on the marble table with her arm hanging limp. He dropped the bundle of raincoats he was holding and bent over, sobbing.

"Whats the matter, nigger?"

"Ahm tired, Capm! Gawd knows Ahm tired!"

He slipped to the floor.

"What you crying about?"

"Capm, mah wifes dead; *Dead!*"

"Shucks, nigger! You ought to be glad youre not dead in a flood like this," said the soldier.

Mann stared at the blurred boots and raincoats. Naw, Lawd! Ah cant break down now! They'll know somethings wrong ef Ah keep acting like this . . . Ah cant cry bout Lulu now . . . He wiped tears from his eyes with his fingers.

"Kin Ah have some watah, Capm?"

"Theres no water anywhere. You hungry?"

He was not hungry, but he wanted to reassure the soldier.

"Yessuh."

"Heres a sandwich you can have."

"Thank you, suh."

He took the sandwich and bit it. The dry bread balled in his mouth. He chewed and tried to wet it. Ef only that old soljerd quit lookin at me . . . He swallowed and the hard lump went down slowly, choking him.

"Thatll make you feel better," said the soldier.

"Yessuh."

The door swung in.

"Awright, boy! Here's your boat! Lets go!"

"Yessuh."

He put the sandwich in his pocket and followed the soldier to the steps.

"Is this the nigger?"

"Yeah!"

"O.K. Pile in, boy!"

He got in; the boat turned; rain whipped his face. He bent low, holding onto the sides of the boat as it sped through water. He closed his eyes and again saw Heartfield come out on the narrow porch and down the steps. He heard again the two shots of his gun. But he shot at me fo Ah shot im! Then again he saw Lulu lying on the table with her arm hanging limp. Then he heard Peewee calling. Good-bye! Hate welled up in him; he saw the two soldiers in the front seat. Their heads were bent low. They might fin out any minute now . . . His gun nestled close to his thigh. Spose Ah shot em n took the boat? Naw! Naw! It would be better to wait till he got to the levee. He would know some-body there. And they would help him. He knew they would. N them white folks might be too busy botherin wid tha levee t think erbout jus one po black man . . . Mabbe Ah kin slip thu . . .

The boat slowed. Ahead loomed the dark stackpipe of the cement plant. Above his head a hundred spot-lights etched a wide fan of yellow against the rain. As the boat swerved through a gate entrance and pulled to a platform, he saw lights and soldiers, heard voices calling. Black men stood on the edges of the platforms and loaded bags of sand and cement into boats. Long lines of boats were running to and fro between the levee and the cement plant. He felt giddy; the boat rocked. Soldiers yelled commands. An officer stepped forward and bawled:

"You get im!"

"Yeah!"

"O.K.! We got another one here. C mon, boy, hop in!"

A black boy moved forward.

"Mistah, kin Ah hava drinka watah?" asked the boy.

"Hell, naw! There's no water anywhere! Get in the boat!'

"Yessuh."

Mann moved over to make room. He felt better already. He was with his people now. Maybe he could get away yet. He heard the officer talking to the soldiers.

"Hows things?"

"Pretty bad!"

"Hows it going?"

"Still overflowing from the North!"

"You think itll hold?"

"Im scared it wont!"

"Any cracks yet?"

"Shes cracking in two places!"

One of the soldiers whistled.

"Awright, let her go."

"O.K."

The boat started out, churning water.

"Yuh gotta cigarette, Mistah?"

Mann turned and looked at the boy sitting at his side.

"Naw; Ah don smoke."

"Shucks, Ah sho wish theyd lemme handle one of these boats," said the boy.

As they neared the levee Mann could see long, black lines of men weaving snake-fashion about the levee-top. In front of him he could feel the river as though it were a live, cold hand touching his face. The levee was a ridge of dry land between two stretches of black water. The men on the levee-top moved slowly, like dim shadows. They were carrying heavy bags on their shoulders and when they reached a certain point the bags were dumped down. Then they turned around slowly, with bent backs, going to get more bags. Yellow lanterns swung jerkily, blinking out and then coming back on when someone passed in front of them. At the water's edge men unloaded boats; behind them stood soldiers with rifles. Mann held still, looking; the boat stopped and waited for its turn to dock at the levee.

Suddenly a wild commotion broke out. A siren screamed. On the levee-top the long lines of men merged into one whirling black mass. Shouts rose in a mighty roar. There came a vague, sonorous drone, like the far away buzzing in a sea-shell. Each second it grew louder. Lawd! thought Mann. That levees gone! He saw boats filling with men. There was a thunder-like clatter as their motors started up. The soldiers in the front seat were yelling at each other.

"You better turn around, Jim!"

The boat turned and started back.

"Wait for that boat and see whats happened!"

They slowed and a boat caught up with them.

"What's happened?"

"The levees gone!"

"Step on it, Jim!"

Mann held his breath; behind him were shouts, and over the shouts was the siren's scream, and under the siren's scream was the loud roar of loosened waters.

IV

The boat shot back. The siren shrieked at needle-pitch, high, thin, shrill, quivering in his ears; and yellow flares turned restlessly in the sky. The boat slowed for the platform. There was a loud clamor and men rushed about. An officer bawled:

"Line up the boats for rescue work!"

"Its risin! Cant yuh *see* it risin?" The boy at Mann's side was nudging him. Mann looked at the water; a series of slow, heaving swells was rocking the boat. He remembered that the water had been some inches below the level of the platform when he had first come; now it was rising above it. As the men worked their boats splashed in the water.

"Who can handle a boat?" the officer asked.

"Ah kin, Mistah!" yelled the boy.

"Get a partner and come on!"

The boy turned to Mann.

"Yuh wanna go?"

Mann hesitated.

"Yeah. Ahll go."

"C mon!"

He climbed out and followed the boy to the end of the platform.

"Where are we sending em, General?" the officer asked.

"Shoot the first twenty to the Red Cross Hospital!"

"O.K.!" said the officer. "Whos the driver here?"

"Ahm the driver!" said the boy.

"Can you really handle a boat?"

"Yessuh!"

"Is he all right?" asked the general.

"Ah works fer Mistah Bridges," said the boy.

"We dont want too many niggers handling these boats," said the general.

"We havent enough drivers," said the officer.

"All right; let him go! Whos next?"

"Yours is the Red Cross Hospital, boy! Get there as fast as you can and get as many people out as you can and take em to the hills, see?"

"Yessuh!"

"You know the way?"

"Yessuh!"

"Whats your name?"

"Brinkley, suh!"

"All right! Get going!"

They ran to a boat and scrambled in. Brinkley fussed over the motor a minute, then raced it.

"All set!"

"O.K.!"

The boat swung out of the wide gate entrance; they were the first to go. They went fast, against the current, fronting the rain. They were back among the houses before Mann realized it. As they neared the hospital Mann wondered about the boy at his side. Would he help him to get away? Could he trust him enough to tell? If he could only stay in the boat until they carried the first load to the hills, he could slip off. He tried to see Brinkley's face, but the rain and darkness would not let him. Behind him the siren still screamed and it seemed that a thousand bells were tolling. Then the boat stopped short; Mann looked around, tense, puzzled.

"This ain the hospital," he said.

"Yeah, tis," said Brinkley.

Then he understood. He had been watching for the steps up which he had carried Lulu. But the water had already covered the steps and was making for the first floor. He looked up. The same white soldier who had led him in before was standing guard.

"C mon in!"

They went in. The hospital was in an uproar. Down the hall a line of soldiers pushed the crowds back, using their rifles long-wise. The colonel came running out; he carried an axe in his hand.

"How many boats are coming?"

"Bout twenty, suh," said Brinkley.

"Are they on the way?"

"Yessuh."

"Theyll have to hurry. That water is rising at the rate of five feet an hour!"

The colonel turned to Mann.

"Come here, boy!"

"Yessuh!"

Mann followed the colonel up a flight of stairs. They stopped in a hall.

"Listen," began the colonel. "I want you . . ."

The lights went out, plunging them in darkness.

"Goddamn!"

Mann could hear the colonel breathing in heavy gasps. Then a circle of yellow light played over a wall. The colonel was standing in front of him with a flash-light.

"Get two of those tables from back there and pile one on top of the other, right here," said the colonel, indicating a spot just left of the stairway.

When the tables were up the colonel gave Mann the axe.

"Get up there and knock a hole through that ceiling!"

"Yessuh!"

He scampered up and fumbled for a hold on the rickety tables. When he was on top the colonel set the beam of the flash-light on the ceiling.

"Work fast, boy! You've got to cut a hole through there so we can take people out if that water beats the boats!"

"Yessuh!"

He whacked upward; with each blow the axe stuck in the wood; he set his feet wide apart on the tables and jerked downward to pull it out. He forgot everything but that he must cut a hole through this ceiling to save people. Even the memory of Lulu and Heartfield was gone from him. Then the lights came back just as suddenly as they had gone. He knew that that meant that the electric plant at the South End was threatened by water. As he swung the axe he felt sweat breaking out all over his body. He heard the colonel below him, fidgeting. The lights dimmed and flared again.

"Keep that light on me, Capm!"

"Awright; but hurry!"

He had six planks out of the ceiling now. He used his hands and broke them off; his fingers caught splinters. He heard someone running up the steps. He looked down; a soldier was talking to the colonel.

"Its above the steps, Colonel! Its traveling for the first floor!"

"Any boats here yet?"

"Just three, sir!"

"Order everybody to this floor, and keep them quiet even if you have to shoot!"

"Yessir!"

Mann heard the soldier running down the steps.

"C mon, boy! Get that hole bigger than that! Youve got to cut a hole through that roof yet!"

"Yessuh!"

When the hole was big enough he pushed the axe through and pulled himself into the loft. It was dark and he could hear the rain pounding. Suddenly the siren stopped. He had been hearing it all along and had grown used to it; but now that he could hear it no longer the silence it left in his mind was terrifying.

"Ah need some light up here, Capm!"

"Keep cutting! Ill get somebody to bring the flash-light up!"

The roof was easier to cut than the ceiling. He heard someone climbing up behind him. It was a white soldier with a flash-light.

"Where you want it, boy?"

"Right here, suh!"

Quickly he tore a wide hole: he felt a rush of air: rain came into his face: droning water filled his ears: he climbed onto the roof and looked below. Opposite the hospital a bunch of motorboats danced in the current. He stiffened. There was a loud cracking noise, as of timber breaking. He stretched flat on the roof and clung to the wet shingles. Moving into one of the paths of yellow light was a small house, turning like a spool in the wild waters. Unblinkingly he watched it whirl out of sight. *Mabbe Ahll never git outta here . . .* More boats were roaring up, rocking. Then he stared at the water rising; he could *see* it rising. Across from him the roofs of one-story houses were barely visible.

"Here, give a lift!"

Mann caught hold of a white hand and helped to pull a soldier through. He heard the colonel hollering.

"All set?"

"Yessuh!"

"Send the boats to the side of the hospital! We are taking em from the roof!"

Boats roared and came slowly to the wall of the hospital.

"Awright! Coming through!"

On all fours Mann helped a white woman struggle through. She was wrapped in sheets and blankets. The soldier whipped the rope around the woman's body, high under her arms. She whimpered. *Lawd, Lulu down there somewhere,* Mann thought. *Dead! She gonna be lef here in the flood . . .*

"C mon, nigger, n give me a hand!"

"Yessuh!"

Mann caught hold of the woman and they took her to the edge of the roof. She screamed and pulled back.

"Let her go!"

They shoved her over and eased her down with the rope. She screamed again and hung limp. They took another, tied the rope, and eased her over. One woman's face was bleeding; she had scratched herself climbing through the hole. Mann could hear the soldier's breath coming in short gasps as he worked. When six had been let down a motor roared. A boat, loaded to capacity, crawled slowly away. The water was full of floating things now. Objects swirled past, were sucked out of sight. The second boat was filled. The third. Then the fourth. The fifth. Sixth. When the women and children were gone they began to ease the men over. The work went easier and faster with the men. Mann heard them cursing grimly. Now and then he remembered Lulu and Heartfield and he felt dizzy; but he would urge himself and it would pass.

"How many more, Colonel?" asked a soldier.

"About twelve! You got enough boats?"

"Just enough!"

Mann knew they had gotten them all out safely when he saw the colonel climb through. Brinkley came through last.

"Heres one more boat, without a driver!" a soldier called.

"Thas mah boat!" said Brinkley.

"Then you go next!" said the colonel.

Mann looped one end of the rope around a chimney and tied it. Brinkley caught hold and slid down, monkey-like. The colonel crawled over to Mann and caught his shoulder.

"You did well! I wont forget you! If you get out of this, come and see me, hear?"

"Yessuh!"

"Here, take this!"

Mann felt a piece of wet paper in his fingers. He tried to read it, but it was dark.

"Thats the address of a woman with two children who called in for help," said the colonel. "If you and that boy think you can save 'em, then do what you can. If you cant, then try to make it to the hills . . ."

"Yessuh!"

The colonel went down. Mann was alone. For a moment a sense of what he would have to face if he was saved from the flood came to him. Would it not be better to stay here alone like this and go down into the flood with Lulu? Would not that be better than having to answer for killing a white man?

"Yuh comin?" Brinkley called.

Mann fumbled over the roof for the axe, found it, and stuck it in his belt. He put the piece of paper in his pocket, caught hold of the rope, and crawled to the edge. Rain peppered his face as he braced his feet against the walls of the house. He held still for a second and tried to see the boat.

"C mon!"

He slumped into the seat; the boat lurched. He sighed and shed a tension which had gripped him for hours. The boat was sailing against the current.

"Here's somebody callin fer hep," said Mann, holding the piece of paper in front of Brinkley.

"Take the flash-light! Switch it on n lemme see if Ah kin read it!"

Mann held the flash-light.

"Its Pikes' Road!" said Brinkley. "Its the Pos Office! Its Miz Heartfiel . . ."

Mann stared at Brinkley, open-mouthed; the flash-light dropped into the bottom of the boat. His fingers trembled and the wind blew the piece of paper away.

"Heartfiel?"

"Ahma try to make it!" said Brinkley.

The boat slowed, turned; they shot in the opposite direction, with the current. Mann watched the head-light cut a path through the rain. Heartfiel?

V

"Watch it!"

Mann threw his hands before his eyes as though to ward off a blow. Brinkley jerked the boat to the right and shut off the motor. The current swept them backwards. In front the head-light lit a yellow circle of wet wood, showing the side of a house. The house was floating down the middle of the street. The motor raced, the boat turned and sailed down the street, going back over the route they had come. Behind them the house followed, revolving slowly, looming large. They stopped at a telegraph pole and Mann stood up and held the boat steady by clinging to a strand of cable wire that stretched above his head in the dark. All about him the torrent tumbled, droned, surged. Then the spot of light caught the house full; it seemed like a living thing, spinning slowly with a long, indrawn, sucking noise; its doors, its windows, its porch turning to the light and then going into the darkness. It passed. Brinkley swung the boat around and they went back down the street, cautiously this time, keeping in the middle of the current. Something struck. They looked. A chair veered, spinning, and was sucked away. An uprooted tree loomed. They dodged it. They heard noises, but could not tell the direction from which they came. When they reached Barrett's Pasture they went slower. The rain had slackened and they could see better.

"Reckon we kin make it?" asked Brinkley.

"Ah don know," whispered Mann.

They swung a curve and headed for Pikes' Road. Mann thought of Heartfield. He saw the woman with red hair standing in the lighted window. He heard her scream. Thats our boat, Henry! Thats our boat! The boat slowed, swerving for Pikes' Road. Mann had the feeling that he was in a dream. Spose Ah tol the boy? The boat rushed on into the darkness. Ef we take that woman t the hills Ahm caught! Ahead he saw a box bob up out of water and shoot under again. But mabbe they didnt see me good? He could not be sure of that. The light had been on him a long time while he was under that window. And they knew his name; he had called it out to them, twice. He ought to tell Brinkley. Ahm black like he is. He oughta be willin t hep me fo he would them . . . He tried to look into Brinkley's face; the boy was bent forward, straining his eyes, searching the surface of the black water. Lawd, Ah *got* t tell im! The boat lurched and dodged something. Its mah life ergin theirs! The boat slid on over the water. Mann swallowed; then he felt that there would not be any use in his telling; he had waited too long. Even if he spoke now Brinkley would not turn back; they had come too far. Wild-eyed, he gazed around in the watery darkness, hearing the white boy yell, You nigger! You bastard! Naw. Lawd! *Ah got t tell im!* He leaned forward to speak and touched Brinkley's arm. The boat veered again, dodging an object that spun away. Mann held tense, waiting, looking; the boat slid on over the black water. Then he sighed and wished with all his life that he had thrown that piece of paper away.

"Yuh know the place?" asked Brinkley.

"Ah reckon so," whispered Mann.

Mann looked at the houses, feeling that he did not want to look, but looking anyway. All he could see of the one-story houses were their roofs. There were wide gaps between them; some had washed away. But most of the two-story houses were still standing. Mann craned his neck, looking for Mrs. Heartfield's house, yet dreading to see it.

"Its erlong here somewhere," said Brinkley.

Brinkley turned the boat sideways and let the spot-light play over the fronts of the two-story houses. Mann wanted to tell him to turn around, to go back, to make for the hills. But he looked, his throat tight; he looked, gripping the sides of the boat; he looked for Mrs. Heartfield's house, seeing her hair framed in the lighted window.

"There it is!" yelled Brinkley.

At first Mann did not believe it was Mrs. Heartfield's house. It was dark. And he had been watching for two squares of yellow light, two lighted windows. And now, there it was, all dark. Mabbe they ain there? A hot wish rose in his blood, a wish that they were gone. Just gone anywhere, as long as they were not there to see him. He wished that their white bodies were at the bottom of the black waters. They were now ten feet from the house; the boat slowed.

"Mabbe they ain there," whispered Mann.

"We bettah call," said Brinkley.

Brinkley cupped his hand to his mouth and hollered:

"Miz Heartfiel!"

They waited, listening, looking at the dark, shut windows. Brinkley must have thought that his voice had not carried, for he hollered again:

"Miz Heartfiel!"

"They ain there," whispered Mann.

"Look! Somebody's there! See?" breathed Brinkley. "Look!"

The window was opening; Brinkley centered the spot of light on it; a red head came through. Mann sat with parted lips, looking. He leaned over the side of the boat and waited for Mrs. Heartfield to call, Henry! Henry!

"Miz Heartfiel!" Brinkley called again.

"Can you see us? Can you get us?" she was calling.

"We comin! Wait a . . ."

A deafening noise cut out his voice. It was long, vibrant, like the sound of trees falling in storm. A tide of water swept the boat backwards. Mann heard Mrs. Heartfield scream. He could not see the house now; the spot-light lit a path of swirling black water. Brinkley raced the motor and jerked the boat around, playing the light again on the window. It was empty. There was another scream, but it was muffled.

"The watahs got em!" said Brinkley.

Again the boat headed into the middle of the current. The light was on the empty window. The house was moving down the street. Mann held his breath, feeling himself suspended over a black void. The house reached the center of the street and turned violently. It floated away from them, amid a sucking rush of water and the sound of splitting timber. It floundered; it shook in a trembling grip; then it whirled sharply to the left and crashed, jamming itself between two smaller houses. Mann heard the motor race; he was gliding slowly over the water, going toward the house.

"Yuh reckon yuh kin make it? Reckon we can save em?" asked Brinkley.

Mann did not answer. Again they were ten feet from the house. The current speeding between the cracks emitted a thunderous roar. The outside walls tilted at an angle of thirty degrees. Brinkley carried the boat directly under the window and held it steady by clinging to a piece of jutting timber. Mann sat frozen, staring: in his mind he saw Mrs. Heartfield; something tickled his throat: he saw her red hair: he saw her white face: then he heard Brinkley speaking:

"Ahll hol the boat! Try t git in the windah!"

As though he were outside of himself watching himself, Mann felt himself stand up. He saw his hands reaching for the window ledge.

"Kin yuh make it? Here . . . Take the flash-light!"

Mann put the flash-light in his pocket and reached again. He could not make it. He tip-toed, standing on the top of the boat, hearing the rush of water below. His legs trembled; he stretched his arms higher.

"Kin yuh make it?"

"Naw . . ."

He rested a moment, looking at the window, wondering how he could reach it. Then he took the axe from his belt and thrust it into the window; he twisted the handle sideways and jerked. The blade caught. He leaned his weight against it. It held. He pulled up into the window and sat poised for a moment on his toes. He eased his feet to the floor. He stood a second in the droning darkness and something traveled over the entire surface of his body; it was cold, like the touch of wet feathers. He brought out the flash-light and focused it on the floor. He tried to call out Mrs. Heartfield's name, but could not. He swept the light: he saw a broken chair: a crumpled rug: strewn clothing: a smashed dresser: a tumbled bed: then a circle of red hair and a white face. Mrs. Heartfield sat against a wall, her arms about her two children. Her eyes were closed. Her little girl's head lay on her lap. Her little boy sat at her side on the floor, blinking in the light.

"Take my mother!" he whimpered.

The voice startled Mann; he stiffened. It was the same voice that had yelled, You nigger! You bastard! The same wild fear he had known when he was in the boat rowing against the current caught him. He wanted to run from the room and tell Brinkley that he could find no one; he wanted to leave them here for the black waters to swallow.

"Take my mother! Take my mother!"

Mann saw the boy's fingers fumbling; a match flared. The boy's eyes grew big. His jaw moved up and down. The flame flickered out.

"Its the nigger! Its the nigger!" the boy screamed.

Mann gripped the axe. He crouched, staring at the boy, holding the axe stiffly in his right fist. Something hard began to press against the back of his head and he saw it all in a flash while staring at the white boy and hearing him scream, "Its the nigger!" Yes, now, if he could swing that axe they would never tell on him and the black waters of the flood would cover them forever and he could tell Brinkley he had not been able to find them and the whites would never know he had killed a white man . . . His body grew taut with indecision. Yes now, he would swing that axe and they would never tell and he had his gun and if Brinkley found out he would point the gun at Brinkley's head. He saw himself in the boat with Brinkley; he saw himself pointing the gun at Brinkley's head; he saw himself in the boat going away; he saw himself in the boat, alone, going away . . . His muscles flexed and the axe was over his head and he heard the white boy screaming, "Its the nigger! Its the nigger!" Then he felt himself being lifted violently up and swung around as though by gravity of the earth itself and flung face downward into black space. A loud commotion filled his ears: his body rolled over and over and he saw the flashlight for an instant, its one eye whirling: then he lay flat, stunned; he turned over, pulled to his knees, dazed, surprised, shocked. He crawled to the flashlight and picked it up with numbed fingers. A voice whispered over and over in his ears, Ah gotta git outa here . . . He sensed he was at an incline. He swayed to his feet and held onto a wall. He heard the sound of rushing water. He swept the spot of yellow. Mrs. Heartfield was lying face downward in a V-trough to his right, where the floor joined the wall at a slant. The boy was crawling in the dark, whimpering "Mother! Mother!" Mann saw the axe, but seemed not to realize that he had been about to use it. He knew what had happened now; the house had tilted, had tilted in the rushing black water. He saw himself as he had stood a moment before, saw himself standing with the axe raised high over Mrs. Heartfield and her two children . . .

"Yuh fin em? Say, yuh fin em?"

Mann flinched, jerking his head around, trembling. Brinkley was calling. A chill went over Mann. He turned the spot on the window and saw a black face and beyond the face a path of light shooting out over the water. Naw . . . Naw . . . He could not kill now; he could not kill if someone were looking. He stood as though turned to steel. Then he sighed, heavily, as though giving up his last breath, as though giving up the world.

Brinkley was clinging to the window, still calling:

"C mon! Bring em out! The boats at the windah! C mon, Ah kin hep t take em out!"

Like a sleepwalker, Mann moved over to the white boy and grabbed his arm. The boy shrank and screamed:

"Leave me alone, you nigger!"

Mann stood over him, his shoulders slumped, his lips moving.

"Git in the boat," he mumbled.

The boy stared; then he seemed to understand.

"Get my mother . . ."

Like a child, Mann obeyed and dragged Mrs. Heartfield to the window. He saw white hands helping.

"Get my sister!"

He brought the little girl next. Then the boy went. Mann climbed through last.

He was again in the boat, beside Brinkley. Mrs. Heartfield and her two children were in the back. The little girl was crying, sleepily. The boat rocked.

Mann looked at the house; it was slanting down to the water; the window through which he had just crawled was about a foot from the level of the rushing current. The motor raced, but the roar came to him from a long ways off, from out of a deep silence, from out of a time long gone by. The boat slid over the water and he was in it; but it was a far away boat, and it was someone else sitting in that boat; not he. He saw the light plunging ahead into the darkness and felt the lurch of the boat as it plowed through water. But none of it really touched him; he was beyond it all now; it simply passed in front of his eyes like silent, moving shadows; like dim figures in a sick dream. He felt nothing; he sat, looking and seeing nothing.

"Yuh hardly made it," said Brinkley.

He looked at Brinkley as though surprised to see someone at his side.

"Ah thought yuh wuz gone when tha ol house went over," said Brinkley.

The boat was in the clear now, speeding against the current. It had stopped raining.

"Its gittin daylight," said Brinkley.

The darkness was thinning to a light haze.

"Mother? Mother . . ."

"Hush!" whispered Mrs. Heartfield.

Yes, Mann knew they were behind him. He felt them all over his body, and especially like something hard and cold weighing on top of his head; weighing so heavily that it seemed to blot out everything but one hard, tight thought: They got me now . . .

"Theres the hills!" said Brinkley.

Green slopes lay before him in the blurred dawn. The boat sped on and he saw jagged outlines of tents. Smoke drifted upward. Soldiers moved. Out of the depths of his tired body a prayer rose up in him, a silent prayer. Lawd, save me now! Save me now . . .

VI

It was broad daylight. The boat had stopped. The motor had stopped. And when Mann could no longer feel the lurch or hear the drone he grew hysterically tense.

"Waal, wes here," said Brinkley.

With fear Mann saw the soldiers running down the slopes. He felt the people in the seat behind him, felt their eyes on his back, his head. He knew that the white boy back there was hating him to death for having killed his father. He knew the white boy was waiting to scream, "You nigger! You bastard!" The soldiers closed in. Mann grabbed the side of the boat; Brinkley was climbing out.

"C mon," said Brinkley.

Mann stood up, swaying a little. They got me now, he thought. He stumbled on dry land. He took a step and a twig snapped. He looked around and tried to fight off a feeling of unreality. Mrs. Heartfield was crying.

"Here, take this blanket, Mrs. Heartfield," said one of the soldiers.

Mann walked right past them, waiting as he walked to hear the word that would make him stop. The landscape lay before his eyes with a surprising and fateful solidity. It was like a picture which might break. He walked on in blind faith. He reached level ground and went on past white people who stared sullenly. He wanted to look around, but could not turn his head. His body seemed encased in a tight vise, in a narrow black coffin that moved with him as he moved. He wondered if the white boy was telling the soldiers now. He was glad when he reached the tents. At least the tents would keep them from seeing him.

"Hey, you! Halt, there!"

He caught his breath, turning slowly. A white soldier walked toward him with a rifle. Lawd, this is it . . .

"Awright, you can take off that stuff now!"

"Suh?"

"You can take off that stuff, I say!"

"Suh? Suh?"

"Take off those boots and that raincoat, God-dammit!"

"Yessuh."

He pulled off the raincoat. He was trembling. He pushed the boots as far down his legs as they would go; then he stooped on his right knee while he pulled off the left boot, and on his left knee while he pulled off the right.

"Throw em over there in that tent!"

"Yessuh."

He walked on again, feeling the soldier's eyes on his back. Ahead, across a grassy square, were black people, his people. He quickened his pace. Mabbe Ah kin fin Bob. Er Elder Murray . . . Lawd, Ah wondah whuts become of Pee-wee? N Grannie? He thought of Lulu and his eyes blurred. He elbowed into a crowd of black men gathered around a kitchen tent. He sighed and a weight seemed to go from him. He looked into black faces, looked for hope. He had to get away from here before that white boy had the soldiers running him to the ground. He thought of the white boats he had seen tied down at the water's edge. Lawd, if Ah kin git inter one of them . . .

"Yuh had some cawfee?"

A small black woman stood in front of him holding a tin cup. He smelt steam curling up from it.

"Yuh had yo cawfee yit?" the woman asked again. "There ain nothin here but cawfee."

"Nom."

"Here."

He took the extended cup and stood watching the steam curl. The woman turned to walk away.

"Mam, yuh seen a man by the name of Bob Cobb?"

"Lawd knows, Mistah. We don know whos here n who ain. Why don yuh ast over t the Red Cross Station? Thas where everybody signing in at."

No, he could not go to the Red Cross. They would catch him there surely.

He walked a few steps, sipping the coffee, watching for white faces over the brim of his cup. Then suddenly he felt confused, as though all that had happened a few hours ago was but a dream. He had no need to be afraid now, had he? Just to imagine that it was all a dream made him feel better. Lawd. Ahm sho tired! He finished the cup and looked over to the tent. Heat was expanding in his stomach. He looked around again. There were no white faces. Black men stood, eating, talking, Ahma ast some of em t hep me . . . He went over and extended his cup for another helping. The black woman stared, her eyes looking beyond him, wide with fear. He heard her give a short, stifled scream. Then he was jerked violently from behind; he heard the soft clink of tin as the cup bounded from his fingers. The back of his head hit the mud.

"Is this the nigger?"

"Yeah; thats the one! Thats the nigger!"

He was on his back and he looked up into the faces of four white soldiers. Muzzles of rifles pointed at his chest. The white boy was standing, pointing into his face.

"Thats the nigger that killed father!"

They caught his arms and yanked him to his feet. Hunched, he looked up out of the corners of his eyes, his hands shielding his head.

"Get your hands up, nigger!"

He straightened.

"Move on!"

He walked slowly, vaguely, his hands high in the air. Two of the soldiers were in front of him, leading the way. He felt a hard prod on his backbone.

"Walk up, nigger, and dont turn rabbit!"

They led him among the tents. He marched, staring straight, hearing his shoes and the soldiers' shoes sucking in the mud. And he heard the quick steps of the white boy keeping pace. The black faces he passed were blurred and merged one into the other. And he heard tense talk, whispers. For a split second he was there among those blunt and hazy black faces looking silently and fearfully at the white folks take some poor black man away. Why don they hep me? Yet he knew that they would not and could not help him, even as he in times past had not helped other black men being taken by the white folks to their death . . . Then he was back among the soldiers again, feeling the sharp prod of the muzzle on his backbone. He was led across the grassy square that separated the white tents from the black. There were only white faces now. He could hardly breathe.

"Look! They caughta coon!"

"C mon, they gotta nigger!"

He was between the soldiers, being pushed along, stumbling. Each step he took he felt his pistol jostling gently against his thigh. A thought circled round and round in his mind, circled so tightly he could hardly think it! They goin t kill me . . . They goin t kill me . . .

"This way!"

He turned. Behind him were voices; he knew a crowd was gathering. He saw Mrs. Heartfield looking at him; he saw her red hair. The soldiers stopped him in front of her. He looked at the ground.

"Is this the nigger, Mrs. Heartfield?"

"Yes, hes the one."

More white faces gathered around. The crowd blurred and wavered before his eyes. There was a rising mutter of talk. Then he could not move; they were pressing in.

"What did he do?"

"Did he bother a white woman?"

"She says he did something!"

He heard the soldiers protesting.

"Get back now and behave! Get back!"

The crowd closed in tightly; the soldiers stood next to him, between him and the yelling faces. He grabbed a soldier, clinging, surging with the crowd. They were screaming in his ears.

"Lynch im!"

"Kill the black bastard!"

The soldiers struggled.

"Get back! You cant do that!"

"Let us have im!"

He was lifted off his feet in a tight circle of livid faces. A blow came to his mouth. The crowd loosened a bit and he fell to all fours. He felt a dull pain in his thigh and he knew he had been kicked. Out of the corners of his eyes he saw a moving tangle of feet and legs.

"Kill the sonofabitch!"

"GET BACK! GET BACK OR WE WILL SHOOT!"

They were away from him now. Blood dripped from his mouth.

"The general says bring him in his tent!"

He was snatched up and pushed into a tent. Two soldiers held his arms. A red face behind a table looked at him. He saw Mrs. Heartfield, her boy, her little girl. He heard a clamor of voices.

"Keep those people back from this tent!"

"Yessir!"

It grew quiet. He felt faint and grabbed his knees to keep from falling. The soldiers were shaking him. He felt warm blood splashing on his hands.

"Cant you talk, you black bastard! Cant you talk!"

"Yessuh."

"Whats your name?"

"Mann, suh."

"Whats the charge against this nigger?"

"Looting and murder, General."

"Whom did he kill?"

"Heartfield, the Post Master, sir."

"*Heart*field?"

"Yessir."

"He stole our boat and killed father!" said the boy.

"Do you confess that, nigger?"

"Capm, he shot at me fo Ah shot im! He shot at me . . ."

"He stole our boat!" yelled the boy. "He stole our boat and killed father when he told him to bring it back!"

"Are you sure this is the man?"

"Hes the one, General! His name is Mann and I saw him under our window!"

"When was this?"

"Last night at the Post Office."

"Who saw this?"

"I did," said Mrs. Heartfield.

"I saw im!" said the boy.

"Ah didnt steal that boat, Capm! Ah swear fo Gawd, Ah didnt!"

"You did! You stole our boat and killed father and left us in the flood . . ."

The boy ran at Mann. The soldiers pulled him back.

"Ralph, come here!" called Mrs. Heartfield.

"Keep still, sonny," said a soldier. "We can handle this!"

"Did you have that boat, nigger?" asked the general.

"Yessuh, but . . ."

"Where did you get it?"

He did not answer.

"What did you do with the boat?"

"The man at the hospital took it. But Ah didnt steal it, Capm . . ."

"Get Colonel Davis!" the general ordered.

"Yessir!"

"Nigger, do you know the meaning of this?"

Mann opened his mouth, but no words came.

"Do you know this means your life?"

"Ah didnt mean t kill im! Ah wuz takin mah wife t the hospital . . ."

"What did you do with the gun?"

Again he did not answer. He had a wild impulse to pull it out and shoot, blindly; to shoot and be killed while shooting. But before he could act a voice stopped him.

"Search im!"

They found the gun and laid it on the table. There was an excited buzz of conversation. He saw white hands pick up the gun and break it. Four cartridges spilled out.

"He shot daddy twice! He shot im twice!" said the boy.

"Did he *bother* you, Mrs. Heartfield?"

"No; not *that* way."

"The little girl?"

"No; but he came back to the house and got us out. Ralph says he had an axe . . ."

"When was *this?*"

"Early this morning."

"What did you go back there for, nigger?"

He did not answer.

"Did he *bother* you *then*, Mrs. Heartfield?"

"He was going to kill us!" said the boy. "He was holding the axe over us and then the house went over in the flood . . ."

There was another buzz of conversation.

"Heres Colonel Davis, General!"

"You know this nigger, Colonel?"

Mann looked at the ground. A soldier knocked his head up. .

"He was at the hospital."

"What did he do there?"

"He helped us on the roof."

"Did he have a boat?"

"Yes; but we took it and sent him to the levee. Here, he signed for it . . ."

"What kind of a boat was it?"

"A white rowboat."

"That was *our* boat!" said the boy.

The piece of paper Mann had signed in the hospital was shoved under his eyes.

"Did you sign this, nigger?"

He swallowed and did not answer.

A pen scratched on paper.

"Take im out!"

"White folks, have mercy! Ah didnt mean t kill im! Ah swear fo Awmighty Gawd, Ah didnt . . . He shot at me! Ah wuz takin mah wife t the hospital . . ."

"Take im out!"

He fell to the ground, crying.

"Ah didnt mean t kill im! Ah didnt . . ."

"When shall it be, General?"

"Take im out *now!* Whos next?"

They dragged him from the tent. He rolled in the mud. A soldier kicked him.

"Git up and walk, nigger! You aint dead yet!"

He walked blindly with bent back, his mouth dripping blood, his arms dangling loose. There were four of them and he was walking in between. Tears clogged his eyes. Down the slope to his right was a wobbly sea of brown water stretching away to a trembling sky. And there were boats, white boats, free boats, leaping and jumping like fish. There were boats and they were going to kill him. The sun was shining, pouring showers of yellow into his eyes. Two soldiers floated in front of him, and he heard two walking in back. He was between, walking, and the sun dropped spangles of yellow into his eyes. They goin t kill me! They goin . . . His knees buckled and he went forward on his face. For a moment he seemed not to breathe. Then with each heave of his chest he cried:

"Gawd, don let em kill me! Stop em from killin black folks!"

"Get up and walk, nigger!"

"Ah didnt mean to do it! Ah swear fo Gawd, Ah didnt!"

They jerked him up; he slipped limply to the mud again.

"What we going to do with this black bastard?"

"We will have to carry im."

"Ill be Goddam if *I* carry im."

One of them grabbed Mann's right arm and twisted it up the center of his back.

"Gawd!" he screamed. "Gawd, have mercy!"

"You reckon you can walk now, nigger?"

He pulled up and stumbled off, rigid with pain. They were among trees now, going up a slope. Through tears he saw the hazy tents of the soldiers' camp. Lawd, have mercy! Once there and he would be dead. There and then the end. Gawd Awmighty . . .

"Gotta cigarette, Charley?"

"Yeah."

A tiny flame glowed through spangles of yellow sunshine. A smoking match flicked past his eyes and hit waves of green, wet grass. His fear subsided into a cold numbness. Yes, now! Yes, through the trees? Right thu them trees! Gawd! They were going to kill him. Yes, now, he would die! He would die before he would let them kill him. Ahll die fo they kill me! Ahll *die* . . . He ran straight to the right, through the trees, in the direction of the water. He heard a shot.

"You sonofabitch!"

He ran among the trees, over the wet ground, listening as he ran for the crack of rifles. His shoes slipped over waves of green grass. Then came a shot. He heard it hit somewhere. Another sang by his head. He felt he was not running fast enough; he held his breath and ran, ran. He left the hazy trees and ran in the open over waves of green. He veered, hearing rifles cracking. His right knee folded; he fell, rolling over. He scrambled up, limping. His eyes caught a whirling glimpse of brown water and shouting white boats. Then he was hit again, in the shoulder. He was on all fours, crawling to the edge of the slope. Bullets hit his side, his back, his head. He fell, his face buried in the wet, blurred green. He heard the sound of pounding feet growing fainter and felt something hot bubbling in his throat; he coughed and then suddenly he could feel and hear no more.

The soldiers stood above him.

"You shouldntve run, nigger!" said one of the soldiers. "You shouldntve run, Goddammit! You shouldntve run . . ."

One of the soldiers stooped and pushed the butt of his rifle under the body and lifted it over. It rolled heavily down the wet slope and stopped about a foot from the water's edge; one black palm sprawled limply outward and upward, trailing in the brown current . . . joining the flood

Fyodor Dostoevsky

NOTES FROM
THE UNDERGROUND

Preface

Notes from the Underground (1864) intends to overpower us with questions. Can a work written at the time of the American Civil War, to which it makes a passing reference as a current event, be the first and foremost example of modern literature? Beginning with a confusing intellectual monologue (in the form of imagined dialogue) and ending with a seemingly insignificant selection of random events from one man's life, can it be fiction at all? Finally, if *Notes from the Underground* is fiction, how then do its two parts go together? The many who agree to the preeminence of Dostoevsky's short novel are deliberately forced to ask these questions. For Dostoevsky realized that a truly modern novel does not simply embody a modern perspective in a modern experience; what he sought was a continuous restatement of the questions shaping that perspective. Eternally problematic, Dostoevsky's short novel teaches that modern consciousness is problematic. Arguing again the classic arguments of man, we are made to end without achievement—only with the same problem. Recognizing that problem's eternality, Dostoevsky knew, is precisely what makes us modern. By creating modern consciousness, and by presenting that consciousness in ultimate abstraction, *Notes from the Underground* is at once father and heir to the fiction of Conrad, Faulkner, and Wright. Dostoevsky makes the flesh and blood protagonists of their novels possible at the same time

that he bares the bones of those characters' existence. Conrad gives us innocent man, Faulkner natural man, Wright tragic man, but Dostoevsky shows us
that the essential contour of modern man includes all these men at once, and
others as well. Modern man is endlessly faceted because endlessness is the
goal of modern self-division, and *Notes from the Underground* expresses this
both with perfection and with the irony of its final parenthesis: self-definition
and self-division are incompatible.

Dostoevsky abandoned the nineteenth-century conviction that literature is
the mirror of life. His fiction is about people, who in turn make life in their
perception of it. Their perception is their experience. Life does not make man:
rather man creates life, for it is what he believes it to be. These conclusions
of an earlier Romanticism drove the heads of Victorian novelists into the sand.
Dostoevsky is modern because he understands man's self-created image; he
creates man in the image of his time, by recognizing that man himself has
created that image. Simultaneously he rediscovers and rewrites the Bible of
his day, in which it is written that man is made in God's image, and in which
it is understood by Dostoevsky that God is man's necessary fiction. *Notes from
the Underground* repeats the eternal conflict between fate and the need to
eternalize that fate, and Dostoevsky's union of form and content recognizes
that a debate *on* free will is the debate *of* free will. That debate is an Hegelian
nightmare in which every thesis generates an antithesis, and every synthesis
a new thesis. Hegel contributed the dialectic to Marx's materialism, and it is
Dostoevsky's point that the materialism he thought of as nineteenth-century
utilitarianism should never forget its Hegelian component. The utilitarianism of
Jeremy Bentham and John Stuart Mill in England, the doctrine that actions
are just or good as they are useful to the extension of happiness, the doctrine
of the greatest good for the greatest number, and the oversimplification of
that doctrine were satirized by Charles Dickens in the brilliant short novel
Hard Times (1845). The same doctrine, explosive in the landlocked atmosphere of Czarist Russia attempting and failing to resist Westernization, is put
forth in Nicolai Chernyshevsky's utopian novel *What Is To Be Done?* (1863),
in turn the specific focus of Dostoevsky's critique in *Notes from the Underground*. Dickens's attack on pure reason makes love its antithesis, rationally
irrational as it reflects the complexity of human needs. Dostoevsky went one
better by showing man to be totally irrational in make-up, and by showing
just why he is made that way.

As the conservative analyst of man's irrationality in opposition to schemes
of utopian socialist self-interest, Fyodor Dostoevsky (1821–1881) makes *Notes
from the Underground* the prelude to the major works of his maturity. *Crime
and Punishment* (1866), *The Idiot* (1868), *The Devils* (1871), and *The
Brothers Karamazov* (1880) extend the fundamental dialectic of his short novel
masterpiece with both brilliant realism and acutely modern psychology. Connections between such characters as Lisa of *Notes from the Underground* and
the prostitute Sonya of *Crime and Punishment*, and between Raskolnikov of
the same novel, Ivan Karamazov, and the underground man are readily ob-

served. But the excellence of *Notes from the Underground* that most contributes to the mature novels has its source in Dostoevsky's complete knowledge of revolutionary and conservative. He achieved fame with the publication of his first novel, *Poor Folk* (1846), written shortly after his graduation from Military Engineering School, and signaling the end of the career chosen for him by his father. Recognition involved Dostoevsky with a group of utopian socialist intellectuals known as the Petrashevski circle. In 1849 members of the group, including Dostoevsky, were imprisoned, and suffered a mock execution at which all received last-minute reprieves in the form of labor camp sentences and forced military enlistments. For Dostoevsky these amounted to a ten-year exile from St. Petersburg, ending in 1859. The novel of his prison and camp experience, *The House of the Dead* (1861–62), was published in the journal *Vremya* (*Time*) established by Dostoevsky and his brother Mikhail on his return. *Vremya* was shut down by the government in 1863; in 1864 both Dostoevsky's first wife and his brother died—in the year of *Notes from the Underground*. The temptation is to find in the novel a turning point in Dostoevsky's thought, occasioned by political difficulties and personal tragedy and marked by the recantation of earlier utopian beliefs. Dostoevsky himself did not see it that way. Attacking the creed of rational self-interest and its displacement of religious values, he sought a revolution that would not make the oppressed a new oppressor—such as Foma Fomich Opiskin in his *The Village of Stepanchikovo* (1859). Native Russian feeling and the doctrine of Christ must, Dostoevsky advocated, be used by the free-thinking intellectual to contain the selfish actions that feed his vanity. *Notes from the Underground* sets the stage for revolution that is redemption, and redemption is a function of saintly ridiculousness. "In Christian literature," wrote Dostoevsky, "the most perfect character is Don Quixote, but he is perfect simply because he is at the same time also ridiculous . . . one feels a sense of pity towards a man who is unaware of his own perfection and who is constantly held up to ridicule." Christ is the one positively perfect man, and Prince Myshkin of *The Idiot*, whom Dostoevsky is talking about here, and Alyosha of *The Brothers Karamazov*, must both be understood in the holy light of the ridiculous. Dostoevsky's redemptive revolution was at work particularly in the original version of *Crime and Punishment*, before publisher-dictated cuts erased it. Dostoevsky meant to show an explicit parallel between the raising of Lazarus by Christ and the moral regeneration of Raskolnikov by Sonya. These same two characters are, in abstract, the central figures of *Notes from the Underground*, where, Dostoevsky tells us in a letter, the censor mangled a passage on "the necessity of belief in Christ." In that short novel, both the underground man's obsession with Lisa's envisioned grave and with coffins emerging from dark cellars, and the stronger funereal image of the literally translated title (*Notes from a Dark Cellar*) hint at the association of Lazarus awaiting resurrection and the anti-hero whose very self deprives him of that resurrection, because all his admission of his own ridiculousness is designed to keep him from that saintly state.

Anonymity is both the state and the condition of the voice of *Notes from the Underground*. Dostoevsky's speaker has no name because he has no identity. His self-image is that of a man made of "innumerable elements . . . absolutely contrary," and his virtuoso monologue enlists his endless oscillation in the service of free will against reason. But absolute freedom paralyzes absolutely, because modern "consciousness is a disease" that leads to masochism: "Despair too has its moments of intense pleasure . . . especially if you happen to be acutely conscious of the hopelessness of your position." To avoid the pleasure of pain, Dostoevsky's speaker takes pleasure in talking about himself endlessly; although he is "cleverer than any one else in the world," the world ignores him, refusing to listen at all, and may at any moment destroy him with its masochistic excesses—war—for no other purpose than to make an innocent bystander its victim. The choices appear to be narcissism or alienation: the problem is which comes first. Are we alienated because of our narcissism, or are we driven to narcissism by the cosmic scope of alienation? The labels don't matter: what Dostoevsky's speaker wants is the self-image of a man vacillating for forty years over the question of chicken and egg *"ad infinitum."* The *and so on* is Dostoevsky's theme because irrationality makes man endless. Death is the center of the dialectic, and all responses to it from any extreme are strategies of self-love. The self that loves itself does not want to die, so it embraces endless non-self or non-sense. "Can a man of acute sensibility respect himself at all?" asks underground man and answers simultaneously: "The direct, the inevitable, and the legitimate result of consciousness is to make all action impossible." The actual question is how can I love myself forever, and the answer is talk about yourself endlessly in a dark cellar. Genuine feeling is the way out, not the pure "blind emotion" that opposes an equally pure reason, but genuine feeling verified by relation with another that results in identity: having an officer knock you down only proves that you are still alive. But the ultimate dialectic of self and other entraps the speaker, because the trouble with the other is that it's you too. In Dostoevsky's terms, "Human nature acts as a whole," and so the other implies a law of nature, and that law is death— what comes of genuine feeling for other people. Back to chickens, eggs, and non-self argues the speaker.

Part I of *Notes from the Underground* is a dramatic monologue in which what is said is less important than how it is said, for the point of any such monologue is self-revelation. Dostoevsky's genius is to understand that his speaker wishes to conceal precisely by that revelation. Each layer exposed finds another actor, and the actors do not want to be real at any cost. Their collective uniqueness makes them totally unreal, their facade is desperately desired. Being like other people means being ridiculous. Ridiculousness means humility—the last straw for the conscribed ego. Knowledge of our unimportance, implies Dostoevsky, is just too much to bear or bare. What keeps the underground man from being an individual is his paranoid defense of individualism. Having opted for non-self, he screams time and again: "Twice-two-makes-four is not life . . . it is the beginning of death." The speaker's dramatic monologue is followed by Part II, identified as "confessions." As readers, we take the monologue for the confession because we understand that one confession justifies another. Our collective goal is to escape judgment, penance in the form of humility, and so we typically find that Part I defends inaction, and Part II shows that action when attempted is impossible. What we all don't wish to discover is that the heading "Apropos of the wet snow" means "apropos of nothing and everything"; wet snow is neither rain nor snow and both. The essential point is that the half-dozen characters of the narrative—prostitute, servant, school-fellows, officer, colleague, *et al.*—are all identified as the speaker. The officer is "tied to him by a string"; the servant "formed one chemical substance with me." Most of all he is Lisa—first two detached eyes confronting the speaker in the dark that make him feel like "when you enter a damp and stale cellar," and finally: "Our parts were now completely changed . . . she was the heroine now, while I was exactly the same crushed and humiliated creature as she had appeared to me." Truly the enemy we have met is us. That is the paradox of self-definition through self-division, what comes of the speaker's insistence on "the quite incontestable fact that I was unlike anyone and that there was no one like me." That insistence ultimately boils down to the point of his confession: "What I wanted was that you should all go to hell!" "We have lost touch so much that occasionally we cannot help feeling a sort of disgust with 'real life,' and that is why we are so angry when people remind us of it," explains the speaker, and Dostoevsky explains that the life we are disgusted with is other people. Ultimately we are *stillborn*; cause is always effect and the effect always cause, one side of the coin the other, and the coin spins to a manic-depressive rhapsody on the modern fear to live: "When you are really dying, they'll drag you to the most foul-smelling corner of the cellar, in the damp and darkness, and what will your thoughts be as you are lying by yourself?"—they will be *Notes from the Underground.*

Dostoevsky

NOTES FROM
THE UNDERGROUND

Translated by David Magarshack

Part I Underground*

I

I am a sick man. . . . I am a spiteful man. No, I am not a pleasant man at all. I believe there is something wrong with my liver. However, I don't know a damn thing about my liver; neither do I know whether there is anything really wrong with me. I am not under medical treatment, and never have been, though I do respect medicine and doctors. In addition, I am extremely superstitious, at least sufficiently so to respect medicine. (I am well educated enough not to be superstitious, but I am superstitious for all that.) The truth is, I refuse medical treatment out of spite. I don't suppose you will understand that. Well, I do. I don't expect I shall be able to explain to you who it is I am actually trying to annoy in this case by my spite; I realise full well that I can't "hurt" the doctors by refusing to be treated by them; I realise better than any one that by all this I am only hurting myself and no one else. Still, the fact remains that if I refuse to be medically treated, it is only out of spite. My liver hurts me—well, let it damn well hurt—the more it hurts the better.

Reprinted by permission of the translator.

---

*Both the author of the *Notes* and the *Notes* themselves are, of course, fictitious. Nevertheless, such persons as the author of such memoirs not only may, but must, exist in our

I have been living like this a long time—about twenty years, I should think. I am forty now. I used to be in the Civil Service, but I am no longer there now. I was a spiteful civil servant. I was rude and took pleasure in being rude. Mind you, I never accepted any bribes, so that I had at least to find something to compensate myself for that. (A silly joke, but I shan't cross it out. I wrote it thinking it would sound very witty, but now that I have seen myself that I merely wanted to indulge in a bit of contemptible bragging, I shall let it stand on purpose!)

Whenever people used to come to my office on some business, I snarled at them and felt as pleased as Punch when I succeeded in making one of them really unhappy. I nearly always did succeed. They were mostly a timid lot: what else can you expect people who come to a government office to be? But among the fine gentlemen who used to come to me to make inquiries there was one officer in particular whom I could not bear. He would not submit with a good grace and he had a disgusting habit of rattling his sword. For sixteen months I waged a regular war with him over that sword. In the end, I got the better of him. He stopped rattling. However, all this happened a long time ago when I was still a young man. And do you know, gentlemen, what was the chief point about my spitefulness? Well, the whole point of it, I mean, the whole nasty, disgusting part of it was that all the time I was shamefully conscious—even at the moments of my greatest exasperation—that I was not at all a spiteful or even an exasperated man, but that I was merely frightening sparrows for no reason in the world, and being hugely amused by this pastime. I might foam at the mouth, but just present me with some little toy, give me a cup of tea with sugar in it, and I shouldn't be at all surprised if I calmed down completely, even be deeply touched, though afterwards I should most certainly snarl at myself and be overcome with shame and suffer from insomnia for months. That's the sort of man I am.

Incidentally, I was rather exaggerating just now when I said that I was a spiteful civil servant. All I did, as a matter of fact, was to indulge in a little innocent fun at the expense of the officer and the people who came to my office on business, for actually I never could become a spiteful man. I was always conscious of innumerable elements in me which were absolutely contrary to that. I felt them simply swarming in me all my life and asking to be allowed to come out, but I wouldn't let them. I would not let them! I would deliberately not let them. They tormented me to the point of making me ashamed of myself; they reduced me to a state of nervous exhaustion and, finally, I got fed

---

society, if we take into consideration the circumstances which led to the formation of our society. It was my intention to bring before our reading public, more conspicuously than is usually done, one of the characters of our recent past. He is one of the representatives of a generation that is still with us. In this extract, entitled *Underground*, this person introduces himself and his views and, as it were, tries to explain those causes which have not only led, but also were bound to lead, to his appearance in our midst. In the subsequent extract (apropos of the Wet Snow) we shall reproduce this person's *Notes* proper, dealing with certain events of his life.   FYODOR DOSTOEVSKY

up with them. Oh, how thoroughly I got fed up with them in the end! But doesn't it seem to you, gentlemen, that I might possibly be apologising to you for something? Asking you to forgive me for something? Yes, I'm sure it does. . . . Well, I assure you I don't care a damn whether it does seem so to you or not. . . .

Not only did I not become spiteful, I did not even know how to become anything, either spiteful or good, either a blackguard or an honest man, either a hero or an insect. And now I've been spending the last four years of my life in my funk-hole, consoling myself with the rather spiteful, though entirely useless, reflection that an intelligent man cannot possibly become anything in particular and that only a fool succeeds in becoming anything. Yes, a man of the nineteenth century must be, and is indeed morally bound to be, above all a characterless person; a man of character, on the other hand, a man of action, is mostly a fellow with a very circumscribed imagination. This is my conviction as a man of forty. I am forty now and, mind you, forty years is a whole lifetime. It is extreme old age. It is positively immoral, indecent, and vulgar to live more than forty years. Who lives longer than forty? Answer me that—sincerely and honestly. I'll tell you who—fools and blackguards—they do! I don't mind telling that to all old men to their face—all those worthy old men, all those silver-haired and ambrosial old men! I'll tell it to the whole world, damned if I won't. I have a right to say so, for I shall live to the age of sixty myself. I'll live to be seventy! I'll live to be eighty! Wait a minute, let me take breath. . . .

I expect you must be thinking, gentlemen, that I want to amuse you. Well, you're mistaken there too. I'm not at all the jolly sort of person you think I am, or may think I am. However, if irritated with all this idle talk (and I feel that you are irritated), you were to ask me who I really am, then I should reply, I'm a retired civil servant of humble rank, a collegiate assessor. I got myself a job in the Civil Service because I had to eat (and only for that reason), and when a distant relative of mine left me six thousand roubles in his will last year, I immediately resigned from the Civil Service and settled in my little corner. I used to live in this corner before, but now I'm settled permanently here. My room is a dreadful, horrible hole, on the very outskirts of the town. My maid-servant is an old country woman, bad-tempered from sheer stupidity, and there is, besides, always a bad smell about her. I'm told the Petersburg climate isn't good for me any more and that with my small means it is very expensive to live in Petersburg. I know that perfectly well, much better than all those experienced and wise mentors and counsellors. But I'm staying in Petersburg. I shall never leave Petersburg! I shan't leave it—oh, but it really makes no damned difference whether I leave it or not.

By the way, what does a decent chap talk about with the greatest possible pleasure?

Answer: about himself.

Very well, so I will talk about myself.

II

I should like to tell you now, gentlemen, whether you want to listen to me or not, why I've never been able to become even an insect. I declare to you solemnly that I've wished to become an insect many times. But even that has not been vouchsafed to me. I assure you, gentlemen, that to be too acutely conscious is a disease, a real, honest-to-goodness disease. It would have been quite sufficient for the business of everyday life to possess the ordinary human consciousness, that is to say, half or even a quarter of the share which falls to the lot of an intelligent man of our unhappy nineteenth century who, besides, has the double misfortune of living in Petersburg, the most abstract and premeditated city in the whole world. (There are premeditated and unpremeditated cities.) It would have been quite sufficient, for instance, to possess the sort of consciousness with which all the so-called plain men and men of action are endowed. I bet you think I'm writing all this just out of a desire to show off or to crack a joke at the expense of our men of action, and that if I'm rattling my sword like my army officer it is merely because I want to show off, and in rather bad taste, too. But, gentlemen, who wants to show off his own infirmities, let alone boast about them?

However, what am I talking about? Everyone does it; everyone does show off his infirmities, and I more than anyone else perhaps. But don't let us quibble about it; the point I raised was absurd. Still, I firmly believe that not only too much consciousness, but any sort of consciousness is a disease. I insist upon that. But let us leave that, too, for a moment. Tell me this: why did it invariably happen that just at those moments—yes, at those very moments—when I was acutely conscious of "the sublime and beautiful," as we used to call it in those days, I was not only conscious but also guilty of the most contemptible actions which—well, which, in fact, everybody is guilty of, but which, as though on purpose, I only happened to commit when I was most conscious that they ought not to be committed? The more conscious I became of goodness and all that was "sublime and beautiful," the more deeply did I sink into the mire and the more ready I was to sink into it altogether. And the trouble was that all this did not seem to happen to me by accident, but as though it couldn't possibly have happened otherwise. As though it were my normal condition, and not in the least a disease or a vice, so that at last I no longer even attempted to fight against this vice. It ended by my almost believing (and perhaps I did actually believe) that this was probably my normal condition. At first, at the very outset, I mean, what horrible agonies I used to suffer in that struggle! I did not think others had the same experience, and afterwards I kept it to myself as though it were a secret. I was ashamed (and quite possibly I still am ashamed); it got so far that I felt a sort of secret, abnormal, contemptible delight when, on coming home on one of the foulest nights in Petersburg, I used to realise intensely that again I had been guilty of some particularly dastardly action that day, and that once more it was no earthly use crying over spilt milk; and inwardly, secretly, I used to go on nagging myself, worrying myself, accusing myself, till at last the bitterness I felt turned into a sort of shameful, damnable sweetness, and finally, into real, positive delight! Yes, into delight. Into delight! I'm certain of it. As a matter of fact, I've mentioned this because I should like to know for certain whether other people feel the same sort of delight. Let me explain it to you. The feeling of delight was there just because I was so intensely aware of my own degradation; because I felt myself that I had come up against a blank wall; that no doubt, it was bad, but that it couldn't be helped; that there was no escape, and that I should never become a different man; that even if there still was any time or faith left to make myself into something different, I should most likely have refused to do so; and even if I wanted to I should still have done nothing, because as a matter of fact there was nothing I could change into. And above all—and this is the final point I want to make—whatever happened, happened in accordance with the normal and fundamental laws of intensified consciousness and by a sort of inertia which is a direct consequence of those laws, and that therefore you not only could not change yourself, but you simply couldn't make any attempt to. Hence it follows that as a result of that intensified consciousness you are quite right in being blackguard, as though it were any consolation to the blackguard that he actually is a blackguard. But enough. . . . Good Lord, I have talked a lot, haven't I? But have I explained anything? How is one to explain this feeling of delight? But I shall explain myself. I shall pursue the matter to the bitter end! That is why I've taken up my pen. . . .

Now, for instance, I'm very vain. I'm as suspicious and as quick to take offence as a hunchback or a dwarf, but as a matter of fact there were moments in my life when, if someone had slapped my face, I should perhaps have been glad even of that. I'm saying this seriously: I should quite certainly have found even there a sort of pleasure, the pleasure of despair, no doubt, but despair too has its moments of intense pleasure, intense delight, especially if you happen to be acutely conscious of the hopelessness of your position. And there, too, I mean, after you'd had your face slapped, you'd be overwhelmed by the consciousness of having been utterly humiliated and snubbed. The trouble is, of course, that however much I tried to find some excuse for what had happened, the conclusion I'd come to would always be that it was my own fault to begin with, and what hurt most of all was that though innocent I was guilty and, as it were, guilty according to the laws of nature. I was guilty, first of all, because I was cleverer than all the people round me. (I have always considered myself cleverer than any one else in the world, and sometimes, I assure you, I've been even ashamed of it. At least, all my life I looked away and I could never look people straight in the face.) I was, finally, guilty because even if I had had a grain of magnanimity in me, I should have suffered a thousand times more from the consciousness of its uselessness. For I should most certainly not have known what to do with my magnanimity—neither to forgive, since the man who would have slapped my face, would most probably have done it in obedience to the laws of nature; nor to forget, since though even if it is the law of nature, it hurts all the same. Finally, even if I had wanted to be utterly ungenerous and, on the contrary, had desired to avenge myself on the man who had offended me, I couldn't have avenged myself on anyone for anything because I should never have had the courage to do anything even if I could. Why shouldn't I have had the courage? Well, I'd like to say a few words about that by itself.

III

You see, people who know how to avenge themselves and, generally, how to stand up for themselves—how do they, do you think, do it? They are, let us assume, so seized by the feeling of revenge that while that feeling lasts there is nothing but that feeling left in them. Such a man goes straight to his goal, like a mad bull, with lowered horns, and only a stone wall perhaps will stop him. (Incidentally, before such a stone wall such people, that is to say, plain men and men of action, as a rule capitulate at once. To them a stone wall is not a challenge as it is, for instance, to us thinking men who, because we are thinking men, do nothing; it is not an excuse for turning aside, an excuse in which one of our sort does not believe himself, but of which he is always very glad. No, they capitulate in all sincerity. A stone wall exerts a sort of calming influence upon them, a sort of final and morally decisive influence, and perhaps even a mystic one. . . . But of the stone wall later.) Well, that sort of plain man I consider to be the real, normal man, such as his tender mother nature herself wanted to see him when she so lovingly brought him forth upon the earth. I envy such a man with all the forces of my embittered heart. He is stupid— I am not disputing that. But perhaps the normal man should be stupid. How are you to know? Why, perhaps this is even beautiful. And I'm all the more convinced of that—shall we say?—suspicion, since if we take, for instance, the antithesis of the normal man, that is to say, the man of great sensibility, who of course has sprung not out of the lap of nature, but out of a test tube (this is almost mysticism, gentlemen, but I, too, suspect it), then this test-tube-begotten man sometimes capitulates to his antithesis to such an extent that for all his intense sensibility he frankly considers himself a mouse and not a man. I grant you it is an intensely conscious mouse, but it's a mouse all the same, whereas the other is a man, and consequently . . . etc. And, above all, he himself—oh, yes, he in his own person—considers himself a mouse; no one asks him to do so; and this is an important point.

Well, let us now have a look at this mouse in action. Let us suppose, for instance, that its feelings are hurt (and its feelings are almost always hurt), and that it also wants to avenge itself. There will perhaps be a greater accumulation of spite in it than in *l'homme de la nature et de la vérité*. A nasty, mean little desire to repay whoever has offended it in his own coin stirs within it more nastily perhaps than in *l'homme de la nature et de la vérité*; for because of his inborn stupidity *l'homme de la nature et de la vérité* looks upon his revenge merely as a matter of justice whereas because of its intense sensibility the mouse denies that there is any question of justice here. At last we come to the business itself, to the act of revenge. The unhappy mouse has already succeeded in piling up—in the form of questions and doubts—a large number of dirty tricks in addition to its original dirty trick; it has accumulated such a large number of insoluble questions round every one question that it is drowned in a sort of deadly brew, a stinking puddle made up of its doubts, its flurries of emotion, and lastly, the contempt with which the plain men of action cover it from head to foot while they stand solemnly round as judges and dictators and split their sides with laughter at it. Well, of course, all that is left for it to do is to dismiss it with a disdainful wave of its little paw and with a smile of simulated contempt, in which it does not believe itself, and to scurry back ingloriously into its hole. There, in its stinking, disgusting, subterranean hole, our hurt, ridiculed, and beaten mouse plunges into cold, venomous, and, above all, unremitting spite. For forty years it will continuously remember its injury to the last and most shameful detail, and will, besides, add to it still more shameful details, worrying and exciting itself spitefully with the aid of its own imagination. It will be ashamed of its own fancies, but it will nevertheless remember everything, go over everything with the utmost care, think up all sorts of imaginary wrongs on the pretext that they, too, might have happened, and will forgive nothing. Quite likely it will start avenging itself, but, as it were, by fits and starts, in all sorts of trivial ways, from behind the stove, incognito, without believing in its right to avenge itself, nor in the success of its vengeance, and knowing beforehand that it will suffer a hundred times more itself from all its attempts at revenge than the person on whom it is revenging itself, who will most probably not care a hang about it. Even on its deathbed it will remember everything with the interest accumulated during all that time, and.... And it is just in that cold and loathsome half-despair and half-belief—in that conscious burying oneself alive for grief for forty years—in that intensely perceived, but to some extent uncertain, helplessness of one's position—in all that poison of unsatisfied desires that have turned inwards—in that fever of hesitations, firmly taken decisions, and regrets that follow almost instantaneously upon them—that the essence of that delight I have spoken of lies. It is so subtle and sometimes so difficult to grasp by one's conscious mind that people whose mental horizon is even a little bit circumscribed, or simply people with strong nerves will not understand anything of it. "Perhaps," you will add with a grin, "those who have never had their faces slapped will not understand it, either," and in that polite way give me a hint that I too have perhaps had my face slapped in my life and that for that reason I'm speaking about it with authority. I bet that's what you are thinking. But don't worry, gentlemen, I've never had my face slapped, and I don't care a damn what you may think about it. Very likely I am sorry not to have boxed the ears of a sufficient number of people in my lifetime. But enough! Not another word about this subject which seems to interest you so much.

Let me continue calmly about the people with strong nerves who do not understand the subtleties of the pleasure I have been speaking of. Though on some occasions these gentlemen may roar at the top of their voices like bulls, and though this, let us assume, does them the greatest credit, yet as I've already said, they at once capitulate in face of the impossible. The impossible is to them equivalent to a stone wall. What stone wall? Why, the laws of nature, of course, the conclusions of natural science, mathematics. When, for instance, it is proved to you that you are descended from a monkey, then it's no use pulling a long face about it: you just have to accept it. When they prove to you that one drop of your own fat must, as a matter of course, be dearer to you than a hundred thousand of your fellow-men and that all the so-called virtues and duties and other vain fancies and prejudices are, as a result of that consideration, of no importance whatever, then you have to accept it whether you like it or not, because twice-two—mathematics. Just try to refute that.

"Good Lord," they'll scream at you, "you can't possibly deny that: twice two *is* four! Never does nature ask you for your opinion; she does not care a damn for your wishes, or whether you like her laws or not. You are obliged to accept her as she is and, consequently, all her results. A stone wall, that is, is a stone wall . . . etc., etc." But, goodness gracious me, what do I care for the laws of nature and arithmetic if for some reason or other I don't like those laws of twice-two? No doubt I shall never be able to break through such a stone wall with my forehead, if I really do not possess the strength to do it, but I shall not reconcile myself to it just because I have to deal with a stone wall and haven't the strength to knock it down.

As though such a stone wall were really the same thing as peace of mind, and as though it really contained some word of comfort simply because a stone wall is merely the equivalent of twice-two-makes-four. Oh, what stuff and nonsense this is! Is it not much better to understand everything, to be aware of everything, to be conscious of all the impossibilities and stone walls? Not to be reconciled to any of those impossibilities or stone walls if you hate being reconciled to them? To reach by way of the most irrefutable logical combinations the most hideous conclusions on the eternal theme that it is somehow your own fault if there is a stone wall, though again it is abundantly clear that it is not your fault at all, and therefore to abandon yourself sensuously to doing nothing, silently and gnashing your teeth impotently, hugging the illusion that there isn't really anyone you can be angry with; that there is really no object for your anger and that perhaps there never will be an object for it; that the whole thing is nothing but some imposition, some hocus-pocus, some card-sharping trick, or simply some frightful mess—no one knows what and no one knows who. But in spite of these uncertainties and this hocus-pocus, you have still got a headache, and the less you know the more splitting the headache!

IV

"Ha-ha-ha! After this you'll no doubt be finding some pleasure in toothache too!" you cry with a laugh.

"Well, why not? There's pleasure even in toothache," I reply.

I had toothache for a whole month, and I know there is pleasure in it. For, you see, if you have toothache, you don't lose your temper in silence. You groan. But these groans of yours are not sincere groans. They are groans mixed with malice. And it is the malice here that matters. By these groans the sufferer expresses his pleasure. If he did not feel any pleasure, he would not groan. That is an excellent example, gentlemen, and I'm going to develop it.

In these groans there is expressed, in the first place, the whole purposelessness of your pain which is so humiliating to your consciousness; the crowning stroke of nature, for which you, of course, don't care, but from which you suffer all the same, while she goes scot free. They express the consciousness of the fact that even though you had no enemies, you do have pain; the consciousness that for all the dentists in the world you are entirely at the mercy of your teeth; that if someone should desire it, your teeth would stop aching, and if he does not, they will go on aching another three months; and that, finally, if you are still unconvinced and still keep on protesting, all that is left for your own gratification is to give yourself a thrashing or hit the wall with your fist as hard as you can, and absolutely nothing more.

Well, it is from these mortal injuries, from those gibes that come from goodness knows whom, that pleasure at last arises, pleasure that sometimes reaches the highest degree of voluptuousness. I beg of you, gentlemen, listen sometimes to the groans of an educated man of the nineteenth century who is suffering from toothache on—shall we say?—the second or third day of his indisposition, when he is beginning to groan in quite a different way from the way he groaned on the first day, that is, not simply because he has toothache, not like some coarse peasant, but like a man of culture and European civilisation, like a man "who has divorced himself from the soil and uprooted himself from his people," to use a phrase which is at present in vogue. His groans become nasty and offensively ill-tempered groans, and go on for days and nights. And yet he knows perfectly well that he is doing no good with his groaning; he knows better than anyone that he is merely irritating and worrying himself and others for nothing; he knows that the audience before whom he is performing with such zeal and all his family are listening to him with disgust, that they don't believe him in the least, and that in their hearts they know that, if he wished, he could have groaned differently and more naturally, without such trills and flourishes, and that he is only amusing himself out of spite and malice. Well, all those apprehensions and infamies are merely the expression of sensual pleasure. "I'm worrying you, am I?" he seems to say. "I'm breaking your hearts, I'm not letting anyone in the house sleep, am I? All right, don't sleep. I want you, too, to feel every minute that I have toothache. I'm no longer the same hero to you now as I tried to appear before, but just a loathsome little fellow, a nuisance? Very well then. So be it. I'm very glad you've found me out at last. You hate to listen to my mean little groans, do you? Well, all right. Hate it if you like. Just you listen to my next flourish. It'll be much worse than the one before, I promise you. . . ." You still don't understand, gentlemen? Well, it seems we have to develop still further and more thoroughly, we have to sharpen our consciousness still more, before we can fully appreciate all the twists and turns of this sort of voluptuous pleasure.

You are laughing? I'm very glad, I'm sure. I'm afraid, gentlemen, my jokes are in very bad taste, they are lame and a bit confused, and show a lack of self-confidence, too. That is because I have no self-respect. But can a man of acute sensibility respect himself at all?

V

Well, can you expect a man who tries to find pleasure even in the feeling of his own humiliation to have an atom of respect for himself? I'm not saying this now from any hypersensitive feeling of remorse. And, anyway, I never could stand saying, "Sorry, father, I won't do it again,"—not because I'm not capable of saying it; on the contrary, because I'm too capable of saying it. Yes, indeed! I used to get into awful trouble on such occasions though I was not even remotely to be blamed for anything. That was the most horrible part of it. But every time that happened, I used to be touched to the very depth of my soul, I kept on repeating how sorry I was, shedding rivers of tears, and of course deceiving myself, though I was not pretending at all. It was my heart that somehow was responsible for all that nastiness. . . . Here one could not blame even the laws of nature, though the laws of nature have, in fact, always and more than anything else caused me infinite worry and trouble all through my life. It is disgusting to call to mind all this, and as a matter of fact it was a disgusting business even then. For after a minute or so I used to realise bitterly that it was all a lie, a horrible lie, a hypocritical lie, I mean, all those repentances, all those emotional outbursts, all those promises to turn over a new leaf. And if you ask why I tormented myself like that, the answer is because I was awfully bored sitting about and doing nothing, and that is why I started on that sort of song and dance. I assure you it is true. You'd better start watching yourselves more closely, gentlemen, and you will understand that it is so. I used to invent my own adventures, I used to devise my own life for myself, so as to be able to carry on somehow. How many times, for instance, used I to take offence without rhyme or reason, deliberately; and of course I realised very well that I had taken offence at nothing, that the whole thing was just a piece of play-acting, but in the end I would work myself up into such a state that I would be offended in good earnest. All my life I felt drawn to play such tricks, so that in the end I simply lost control of myself. Another time I tried hard to fall in love. This happened to me twice, as a matter of fact. And I can assure you, gentlemen, I suffered terribly. In my heart of hearts, of course, I did not believe that I was suffering, I'd even sneer at myself in a vague sort of way, but I suffered agonies none the less, suffered in the most genuine manner imaginable, as though I were really in love. I was jealous. I made scenes. And all because I was so confoundedly bored, gentlemen, all because I was so horribly bored. Crushed by doing nothing. For the direct, the inevitable, and the legitimate result of consciousness is to make all actions impossible, or—to put it differently—consciousness leads to thumb-twiddling. I've already said so before, but let me repeat, and repeat most earnestly: all plain men and men of action are active only because they are dull-witted and mentally undeveloped. How is that to be explained? Why, like this: owing to their arrested mental development they mistake the nearest and secondary causes for primary causes and in this way persuade themselves much more easily and quickly than other people that they have found a firm basis for whatever business they have in hand and, as a result, they are no longer worried, and that is really the main thing. For to start being active you must first of all be completely composed in mind and never be in doubt. But how can I, for instance, compose myself? Where am I to find the primary cause to lean against? Where am I to get the basis from? I am constantly exercising my powers of thought and, consequently, every primary cause with me at once draws another one after itself, one still more primary, and so *ad infinitum*. That, in fact, is the basis of every sort of consciousness and analysis. That, too, therefore is a law of nature. What is the result of it then? Why, the same. Remember I was speaking of revenge just now. (I don't suppose you grasped that.) I argued that a man revenges himself because he finds justice in it. This of course means that he has found a primary cause, a basis, namely justice. It follows therefore that now he is absolutely calm and, consequently, he revenges himself calmly and successfully, being convinced that what he does is both right and just. But I can't for the life of me see any justice here, and therefore if I should start revenging myself, it would be merely out of spite. Now spite, of course, could get the better of anything, of all my doubts, and so could very well take the place of any primary cause just because it is not a cause. But what can I do if I have not even spite (I began with that just now). Besides, my feeling of bitterness, too, is subject to the process of disintegration as a result of those damned laws of consciousness. One look and the object disappears into thin air, your reasons evaporate, there is no guilty man, the injury is no longer an injury but just fate, something in the nature of toothache for which no one can be blamed, and consequently there is only one solution left, namely, knocking your head against the wall as hard as you can. Well, so you just give it up because you've failed to find the primary cause. But try letting yourself be carried away by your emotions blindly, without reasoning, without any primary cause, letting your consciousness go hang at least for a time; hate or love just for the sake of not having to twiddle your thumbs. What will happen, of course, is that the day after tomorrow (and that at the latest) you will begin despising yourself for having knowingly duped yourself. As a result—a soap bubble and doing nothing again. As a matter of fact, gentlemen, the reason why I consider myself a clever man is simply because I could never in my life finish anything I'd started. All right, I am a talker, a harmless, boring talker as we all are. But what can I do if the direct and sole purpose of every intelligent man is to talk, that is to say, to waste his time deliberately?

VI

Oh, if only I had done nothing merely out of laziness! Lord, how I should have respected myself then. I should have respected myself just because I should at least have been able to be lazy; I should at least have possessed one quality which might be mistaken for a positive one and in which I could have believed myself. Question—who is he? Answer—a loafer. I must say it would have been a real pleasure to have heard that said about myself, for it would have meant that a positive definition had been found for me and that there was something one could say about me. "A loafer!"—why, it's a title, a purpose in life. It's a career, gentlemen, a career! Don't joke about it. It is so. I should then be a member of the most exclusive club by right and should have done nothing but gone on respecting myself continually. I knew a gentleman who all through his life was proud of the fact that he was a great connoisseur of Château Lafitte. He considered it a positive virtue and never had any misgivings. He died not only with a clear, but positively with a triumphant conscience, and he was absolutely right. So I, too, should have chosen a career for myself: I should have been a loafer and a glutton, but would, for instance, admire the sublime and beautiful in everything. How do you like that? I've been dreaming about it a long time. The "sublime and beautiful" has been a great worry to me during my forty years, but that was only *during* my forty years, at one time—oh, at one time it would have been different! I should at once have found an appropriate occupation for myself, namely, to drink to the health of the sublime and the beautiful. I should have made use of every opportunity to drop a tear into my glass and then drain it to all that was sublime and beautiful. I should then have turned everything in the world into something sublime and beautiful; I should have found the sublime and beautiful in the foulest and most unmistakable rubbish. I should have oozed tears like a sponge. The artist G., for instance, paints a picture. At once I drink to the health of the artist G. who has painted a picture because I love all that is sublime and beautiful. An author writes something to please "everybody"; at once I drink to the health of "everybody" because I love all that is sublime and beautiful.

I should demand respect for myself for acting like that, and I should persecute anyone who would not show me respect. I should be at peace with the world and die in the odour of sanctity—why, it's delightful, it's simply delightful! And I should have grown such a monumental belly, I should have propagated such a double chin, I should have acquired such a fiery nose that every man in the street would have said as he looked at me, "Now that's a fine chap! Here's something real, something positive!"

And say what you like, gentlemen, it is very pleasant to hear such tributes in this negative age.

VII

But these are just golden dreams. Oh, tell me who was it first said, who was it first proclaimed that the only reason man behaves dishonourably is because he does not know his own interests, and that if he were enlightened, if his eyes were opened to his real normal interests, he would at once cease behaving dishonourably and would at once become good and honourable because, being

enlightened and knowing what is good for him, he would see that his advantage
lay in doing good, and of course it is well known that no man ever knowingly
acts against his own interests and therefore he would, as it were, willy-nilly
start doing good. Oh, the babe! Oh, the pure innocent child! When, to begin
with, in the course of all these thousands of years has man ever acted in accordance with his own interests? What is one to do with the millions of facts
that bear witness that man *knowingly*, that is, fully understanding his own
interests, has left them in the background and rushed along a different path
to take a risk, to try his luck, without being in any way compelled to do it by
anyone or anything, but just as though he deliberately refused to follow the
appointed path, and obstinately, wilfully, opened up a new, a difficult, and
an utterly preposterous path, groping for it almost in the dark. Well, what
does it mean but that to man this obstinacy and wilfulness is pleasanter than
any advantage. . . . Advantage! What is advantage? Can you possibly give an
exact definition of the nature of human advantage? And what if *sometimes* a
man's ultimate advantage not only may, but even must, in certain cases consist
in his desiring something that is immediately harmful and not advantageous
to himself? If that is so, if such a case can arise, then the whole rule becomes
utterly worthless. What do you think? Are there cases where it is so? You
are laughing? Well, laugh away, gentlemen, only tell me this: have men's advantages ever been calculated with absolute precision? Are there not some
which have not only not fitted in, but cannot possibly be fitted in any classification? You, gentlemen, have, so far as I know, drawn up your entire list of
positive human values by taking the averages of statistical figures and relying
on scientific and economic formulae. What are your values? They are peace,
freedom, prosperity, wealth and so on and so forth. So that any man who
should, for instance, openly and knowingly act contrary to the whole of that
list would, in your opinion, and in mine, too, for that matter, be an obscurantist
or a plain madman, wouldn't he? But the remarkable thing surely is this: why
does it always happen that when all these statisticians, sages, and lovers of
the human race reckon up human values they always overlook one value?
They don't even take it into account in the form in which it should be taken
into account, and the whole calculation depends on that. What harm would
there be if they did take it, that value, I mean, and add it to their list? But the
trouble, you see, is that this particular good does not fall under any classification
and cannot be included in any list. Now, I have a friend, for instance—why,
good gracious, gentlemen, he is also a friend of yours, and indeed whose friend
is he not? In undertaking any business, this gentleman at once explains to
you in high-sounding and clear language how he intends to act in accordance
with the laws of truth and reason. And not only that. He will talk to you, passionately and vehemently, all about real and normal human interests; he will
scornfully reproach the shortsighted fools for not understanding their own advantages, nor the real meaning of virtue, and—exactly a quarter of an hour
later, without any sudden or external cause but just because of some inner impulse which is stronger than any of his interests, he will do something quite
different, that is to say, he will do something that is exactly contrary to what

he has been saying himself: against the laws of reason and against his own interests, in short, against everything. . . . I'd better warn you, though, that my friend is a collective entity and that for that reason it is a little difficult to blame him alone. That's the trouble, gentlemen, that there exists something which is dearer to almost every man than his greatest good, or (not to upset the logic of my argument) that there exists one most valuable good (and one, too, that is being constantly overlooked, namely, the one we are talking about) which is greater and more desirable than all other goods, and for the sake of which a man, if need be, is ready to challenge all laws, that is to say, reason, honour, peace, prosperity—in short, all those excellent and useful things, provided he can obtain that primary and most desirable good which is dearer to him than anything in the world.

"Well," you say, "but they are values all the same, aren't they?"

Very well, I believe we shall soon understand each other, and, besides, this isn't a matter for quibbling. What is important is that this good is so remark- able just because it sets at naught all our classifications and shatters all the systems set up by the lovers of the human race for the happiness of the human race. In fact, it plays havoc with everything. But before I tell you what this good is, I should like to compromise myself personally and I therefore bluntly declare that all these fine systems, all these theories which try to explain to man all his normal interests so that, in attempting to obtain them by every possible means, he should at once become good and honourable, are in my opinion nothing but mere exercises in logic. Yes, exercises in logic. For to assert that you believed this theory of the regeneration of the whole human race by means of the system of its own advantages is, in my opinion, almost the same as—well, asserting, for instance, with Buckle, that civilisation softens man, who con- sequently becomes less bloodthirsty and less liable to engage in wars. I believe he argues it very logically indeed. But man is so obsessed by systems and abstract deductions that he is ready to distort the truth deliberately, he is ready to deny the evidence of his senses, so long as he justifies his logic. That is why I take this example, for it is a most striking example. Well, just take a good look round you: rivers of blood are being spilt, and in the jolliest imag- inable way, like champagne. Take all our nineteenth century in which Buckle lived. Look at Napoleon, the Great and the present one. Look at North America —the everlasting union. Look, finally, at Schleswig-Holstein. . . . And what, pray, does civilisation soften in us? All civilisation does is to develop in man the many-sidedness of his sensations, and nothing, absolutely nothing more. And through the development of his many-sidedness man, for all we know, may reach the stage when he will find pleasure in bloodshed. This has already hap- pened to him. Have you noticed that the most subtle shedders of blood have almost invariably been most civilised men, compared with whom all the Attilas and Stenka Razins were just innocent babes, and if they are not so outstanding as Attila or Stenka Razin it is because we meet them so often, because they are *too* ordinary, and because we have got used to them. At any rate, civilisation has made man, if not more bloodthirsty, then certainly more hideously and more contemptibly bloodthirsty. In the past he looked on bloodshed as an act of justice and exterminated those he thought necessary to exterminate with a clear conscience; but now we consider bloodshed an abomination and we engage in this abomination more than ever. Which is worse? You'd better decide for yourselves. They say that Cleopatra (if I may take an instance from Roman history) loved to stick golden pins into the breasts of her slave girls and enjoyed their screams and contortions. You will say that this happened in relatively speaking barbarous times; but today, too, we live in barbarous times because (again relatively speaking) today, too, we stick pins into people; today, too, though man has learnt to see things more clearly than in barbarous times, he is still very far from having learnt to act in accordance with the dictates of reason and science. But I daresay you are firmly convinced that he will most certainly learn to do so as soon as his so-called bad old habits completely disappear and as soon as common sense and science have completely re-educated human nature and directed it along the road of normal behaviour. You are convinced that, when this happens, man will stop making *deliberate* mistakes and perforce refuse to allow his will to act contrary to his normal interests. And that is not all. You say that science itself will then teach man (though in my opinion it is an unnecessary luxury) that as a matter of fact he possesses neither will nor uncontrollable desires, and never has done, and that he himself is nothing more than a sort of piano-key or organ-stop, and that, in addition, there are the laws of nature in the world; so that whatever he does is not done of his own will at all, but of itself, according to the laws of nature. Consequently, as soon as these laws of nature are discovered, man will no longer have to answer for his actions and will find life exceedingly easy. All human actions will then, no doubt, be computed according to these laws, mathematically, something like the tables of logarithms, up to 108,000, and indexed accordingly. Or, better still, certain well-intentioned works will be published, something like our present encyclopaedic dictionaries, in which everything will be calculated and specified with such an exactness that there will be no more independent actions or adventures in the world.

Then—it is still you who are saying this—new economic relations will be established, relations all ready for use and calculated with mathematical exactitude, so that all sorts of problems will vanish in a twinkling simply because ready-made solutions will be provided for all of them. It is then that the Crystal Palace will be built. Then—why, in fact, the Golden Age will have dawned again. Of course, it is quite impossible to guarantee (it is I who am speaking now) that even then people will not be bored to tears (for what will they have to do when everything is calculated and tabulated), though, on the other hand, everything will be so splendidly rational. Of course, when you are bored, you are liable to get all sort of ideas into your head. Golden pins, too, are after all stuck into people out of boredom. But all that would not matter. What is bad (and it is again I who am saying this) is that I'm afraid they will be glad even of golden pins then. For man is stupid, phenomenally stupid; I mean, he may not be really stupid, but on the other hand he is so ungrateful that you won't find anything like him in the whole wide world. I would not be at all surprised, for instance, if suddenly and without the slightest possible reason a gentleman of an ignoble or rather a reactionary and sardonic countenance were to arise amid all that future reign of universal common sense and, gripping his sides firmly with his hands, were to say to us all, "Well, gentlemen, what about giving all this common sense a mightly kick and letting it scatter in the dust before our feet simply to send all these logarithms to the devil so that we can again live according to our foolish will?" That wouldn't matter, either, but for the regrettable fact that he would certainly find followers: for man is made like that. And all, mind you, for the most stupid of reasons which seems hardly worth mentioning, namely, because man has always and everywhere—whoever he may be—preferred to do as he chose, and not in the least as his reason or advantage dictated; and one may choose to do something even if it is against one's own advantage, and sometimes one *positively should* (that is my idea). One's own free and unfettered choice, one's own whims, however wild, one's own fancy, overwrought though it sometimes may be to the point of madness— that is that same most desirable good which we overlooked and which does not fit into any classification, and against which all theories and systems are continually wrecked. And why on earth do all those sages assume that man must needs strive after some normal, after some rationally desirable good? All man wants is an absolutely *free* choice, however dear that freedom may cost him and wherever it may lead him to. Well, of course, if it is a matter of choice, then the devil only knows . . .

VIII

"Ha-ha-ha! But there's really no such thing as choice, as a matter of fact, whatever you may say," you interrupt me with a laugh. "Today science has succeeded in so far dissecting man that at least we now know that desire and the so-called free will are nothing but——"

One moment, gentlemen. I am coming to that myself, and I don't mind telling you that I was even feeling a little nervous. I was just about to say that choice depended on the devil only knows what and that that was all to the good, but I suddenly remembered science and—the words died on my lips. And you took advantage of it and began to speak. It is, of course, quite true that if one day they really discover some formula of all our desires and whims, that is to say, if they discover what they all depend on, by what laws they are governed, how they are disseminated, what they are aiming at in one case and another, and so on, that is, a real mathematical formula, man may perhaps at once stop feeling any desire and, I suppose, most certainly will. For who would want to desire according to a mathematical formula? And that is not all. He will at once be transformed from a man into an organ-stop, or something of the sort. For what is man without desires, without free will, and without the power of choice but a stop in an organ pipe? What do you think? Let us calculate the probabilities: is it or is it not likely to happen?

"Well," you decide, "in the majority of cases our desires are mistaken from a mistaken idea of what is to our advantage. Sometimes we desire absolute nonsense because in our stupidity we see in this nonsense the easiest way of attaining some conjectural good."

Very well, and when all that is explained and worked out on paper (which is quite possible, for it would be absurd and unreasonable to assume that man will never discover other laws of nature), the so-called desires will of course no longer exist. For when one day desire comes completely to terms with reason we shall of course reason and not desire, for it is obviously quite impossible to *desire* nonsense while retaining our reason and in that way knowingly go against our reason and wish to harm ourselves. And when all desires and reasons can be actually calculated (for one day the laws of our so-called free will are bound to be discovered) something in the nature of a mathematical table may in good earnest be compiled so that all our desires will in effect arise in accordance with this table. For if it is one day calculated and proved to me, for instance, that if I thumb my nose at a certain person it is because I cannot help thumbing my nose at him, and that I have to thumb my nose at him with that particular thumb, what *freedom* will there be left to me, especially if I happen to be a scholar and have taken my degree at a university? In that case, of course, I should be able to calculate my life for thirty years ahead. In short, if this were really to take place, there would be nothing left for us to do: we should have to understand everything whether we wanted to or not. And, generally speaking, we must go on repeating to ourselves incessantly that at a certain moment and in certain circumstances nature on no account asks us for our permission to do anything; that we have got to take her as she is, and not as we imagine her to be; and that if we are really tending towards mathematical tables and rules of thumb and—well—even towards test tubes, then what else is there left for us to do but to accept everything, test tube and all. Or else the test tube will come by itself and will be accepted whether you like it or not. . . .

Quite right, but there's the rub! I'm sorry, gentlemen, to have gone on philosophising like this: remember my forty years in the dark cellar! Do let me indulge my fancy for a moment. You see, gentlemen, reason is an excellent thing. There is no doubt about it. But reason is only reason, and it can only satisfy the reasoning ability of man, whereas volition is a manifestation of the whole of life, I mean, of the whole of human life, including reason with all its concomitant head-scratchings. And although our life, thus manifested, very often turns out to be a sorry business, it is life none the less and not merely extractions of square roots. For my part, I quite naturally want to live in order to satisfy all my faculties and not my reasoning faculty alone, that is to say, only some twentieth part of my capacity for living. What does reason know? Reason only knows what it has succeeded in getting to know (certain things, I suppose, it will never know; this may be poor comfort, but why not admit it frankly?), whereas human nature acts as a whole, with everything that is in it, consciously, and unconsciously, and though it may commit all sorts of absurdities, it persists. I cannot help thinking, gentlemen, that you look upon me with pity; you go on telling me over and over again that an enlightened and mentally developed man, such a man, in short, as the future man can be expected to be, cannot possibly desire deliberately something which is not a real "good," and that, you say, is mathematics. I quite agree. It is mathematics. But I repeat for the hundredth time that here is one case, one case only, when man can deliberately and consciously desire something that is injurious, stupid, even outrageously stupid, just because he wants *to have the right* to desire for himself even what is very stupid and not to be bound by an obligation to desire only what is sensible. For this outrageously stupid thing, gentlemen, this whim of ours, may really be more accounted by us than anything else on earth, especially in certain cases. And in particular it may be more valuable than any good even when it is quite obviously bad for us and contradicts the soundest conclusions of our reason about what is to our advantage, for at all events it preserves what is most precious and most important to us, namely, our personality and our individuality. Indeed some people maintain that this is more precious than anything else to man. Desire, of course, can, if it chooses, come to terms with reason, especially if people do not abuse it and make use of it in moderation; this is useful and sometimes even praiseworthy. But very often and indeed mostly desire is utterly and obstinately at loggerheads with reason and—and, do you know, that, too, is useful and occasionally even praiseworthy. Let us suppose, gentlemen, that man is not stupid. (As a matter of fact, it cannot possibly be said that man is stupid, if only from the one consideration that if he is, then who is wise?) But if he is not stupid, he is monstrously ungrateful. Phenomenally ungrateful. I'm even inclined to believe that the best definition of man is— a creature who walks on two legs and is ungrateful. But that is not all, that is not his principal failing; his greatest failing is his constant lack of moral sense, constant from the days of the Flood to the Schleswig-Holstein period of human history. Lack of moral sense and, consequently, lack of good sense; for it has long been known that lack of good sense is really the result of lack of moral sense. Well, try and cast your eye upon the history of mankind and what will you see? Grandeur? Yes, perhaps even grandeur. The Colossus of Rhodes, for instance, is worth something, isn't it? Well may Mr. Anayevsky bear witness to the fact that some people maintain that it is the work of human hands, while others assert that it was wrought by nature herself. Gaiety? Well, yes. Perhaps gaiety, too. One has only to think of the dress uniforms, military and civilian, of all peoples in all ages—that alone is worth something, and if we throw in the undress uniforms as well, we can only gasp in astonishment at the gaiety of it all; no historian, I am sure, will be able to resist it. Monotonous? Well, I suppose it is monotonous: they fight and fight, they are fighting now, they fought before, and they will fight again—you must admit this is rather monotonous. In short, you can say anything you like about world history, anything that might enter the head of a man with the most disordered imagination. One thing, though, you cannot possibly say about it: you cannot say that it is sensible. If you did, you would choke at the first word. And, moreover, this is the sort of curious thing you come across almost every minute: continually there crop up in life such sensible and moral people, such sages and lovers of humanity whose only object seems to be to live all their lives as sensibly and morally as possible, to be, as it were, a shining light to their neighbours for the sole purpose of proving to them that it is really possible to live morally and sensibly in the world. And what happens? We know that many of these altruists, sooner or later, towards the end of their lives, were untrue to themselves, committing some folly, sometimes indeed of a most indecent nature. Now let me ask you this question: what can you expect of man seeing that he is a being endowed with such strange qualities? Why, shower all the earthly blessings upon him, drown him in happiness, head over ears, so that only bubbles should be visible on its surface, as on the surface of water; bestow such economic prosperity upon him as would leave him with nothing else to do but sleep, eat cakes, and only worry about keeping world history going—and even then he will, man will, out of sheer ingratitude, out of sheer desire to injure you personally, play a dirty trick on you. He would even risk his cakes and ale and deliberately set his heart on the most deadly trash, the most uneconomic absurdity, and do it, if you please, for the sole purpose of infusing into this positive good sense his deadly fantastic element. It is just his fantastic dreams, his most patent absurdities, that he will desire above all else for the sole purpose of proving to himself (as though that were so necessary) that men are still men and not keys of a piano on which the laws of nature are indeed playing any tune they like, but are in danger of going on playing until no one is able to desire anything except a mathematical table. And that is not all: even if he really were nothing but a piano-key, even if this were proved to him by natural science and mathematically, even then he would refuse to come to his senses, but would on purpose, just in spite of everything, do something out of sheer ingratitude; actually, to carry his point. And if he has no other remedy, he will plan destruction and chaos, he will devise all sorts of sufferings, and in the end he will carry his point! He will send a curse over the world, and as only man can curse (this is his privilege which distinguishes him from other animals) he may by his curse alone attain his object, that is, really convince himself that he is a man and not a piano-key! If you say that this, too, can be calculated by the mathematical table—chaos, and darkness, and curses—so that the mere possibility of calculating it all beforehand would stop it all and reason would triumph in the end—well, if that were to happen man would go purposely mad in order to rid himself of reason and carry his point! I believe this is so, I give you my word for it; for it seems to me that the whole meaning of human life can be summed up in the one statement that man only exists for the purpose of proving to himself every minute that he is a man and not an organ-stop! Even if it means physical suffering, even if it means turning his back on civilisation, he will prove it. And how is one after that to resist the temptation to rejoice that all this has not happened yet and that so far desire depends on the devil alone knows what.

You shout at me (if, that is, you will deign to favour me with raising voices) that no one wants to deprive me of my free will, that all they are concerned with is to arrange things in such a way that my will should of itself, of its own will, coincide with my normal interests, with the laws of nature and arithmetic.

But, good Lord, gentlemen, what sort of a free will can it be once it is all a matter of mathematical tables and arithmetic, when the only thing to be taken into account will be that twice-two-makes-four? Twice-two will make four even without my will. Surely, free will does not mean that!

IX

Gentlemen, I am joking of course, and I'm afraid my jokes are rather poor, but you can't after all take everything as a joke. How do you know I'm not joking with a heavy heart? Gentlemen, I'm worried by all sorts of questions; please, answer them for me. For instance, you want to cure man of his old habits and reform his will in accordance with the demands of science and commonsense. But how do you know that man not only could but *should* be remade like that? And what leads you to conclude that human desires must *necessarily* be reformed? In short, how do you know that such a reformation will be a gain to man? And, if one is to put all one's cards on the table, why are you so *utterly* convinced that not to go counter to the real normal gains guaranteed by the conclusions of reason and arithmetic is always so certainly right for man and is a universal law so far as mankind is concerned? For at present it is only a supposition on your part. Let us assume it is a law of logic, but how do you know that it is also a human law? You don't by any chance think I'm mad, do you? Let me explain myself. I agree that man is above all a creative animal, condemned consciously to strive towards a goal and to occupy himself with the art of engineering, that is, always and incessantly clear with a path for himself *wherever it may lead.* And I should not be at all surprised if that were not the reason why he sometimes cannot help wishing to turn aside from the path just because he is condemned to clear it, and perhaps, too, because, however stupid the plain man of action may be as a rule, the thought will sometimes occur to him that the path almost always seems to lead *nowhere in particular*, and that the important point is not where it leads but that it should lead somewhere, and that a well-behaved child, disdaining the art of engineering, should not indulge in the fatal idleness which, as we all know, is the mother of all vices. Man likes to create and to clear paths—that is undeniable. But why is he also so passionately fond of destruction and chaos? Tell me that. But, if you don't mind, I'd like to say a few words about that myself. Is he not perhaps so fond of destruction and chaos (and it cannot be denied that he is sometimes very fond of it—that is a fact) because he is instinctively afraid of reaching the goal and completing the building he is erecting? How do you know, perhaps he only loves the building from a distance and not by any means at close quarters; perhaps he only loves building it and not living in it, preferring to leave it later *aux animaux domestiques*, such as ants, sheep, etc., etc. Now, ants are quite a different matter. They have one marvelous building of this kind, a building that is for ever indestructible—the ant-hill.

The excellent ants began with the ant-hill and with the ant-hill they will most certainly end, which does great credit to their steadfastness and perseverance. But man is a frivolous and unaccountable creature, and perhaps, like a chess-player, he is only fond of the process of achieving his aim, but not of the aim itself. And who knows (it is impossible to be absolutely sure about it), perhaps the whole aim mankind is striving to achieve on earth merely lies in this incessant process of achievement, or (to put it differently) in life itself, and not really in the attainment of any goal, which, needless to say, can be nothing else but twice-two-makes-four, that is to say, a formula; but twice-two-makes-four is not life, gentlemen. It is the beginning of death. At least, man seems always to have been afraid of this twice-two-makes-four, and I am afraid of it now. Let us assume that man does nothing but search for this twice-two-makes-four, sails across oceans and sacrifices his life in this search; but to succeed in his quest, really to find what he is looking for, he is afraid—yes, he really seems to be afraid of it. For he feels that when he has found it there will be nothing more for him to look for. When workmen have finished their work they at least receive their wages, and they go to a pub and later find themselves in a police cell—well, there's an occupation for a week. But where can man go? At all events, one observes a certain awkwardness about him every time he achieves one of these aims. He loves the process of achievement but not achievement itself, which, I'm sure you will agree, is very absurd. In a word, man is a comical creature; I expect there must be some sort of jest hidden in it all. But twice-two-makes-four is for all that a most insupportable thing. Twice-two-makes-four is, in my humble opinion, nothing but a piece of impudence. Twice-two-makes-four is a farcical, dressed-up fellow who stands across your path with arms akimbo and spits at you. Mind you, I quite agree that twice-two-makes-four is a most excellent thing; but if we are to give everything its due, then twice-two-makes-five is sometimes a most charming little thing, too.

And why are you so firmly, so solemnly, convinced that only the normal and positive, in short, only prosperity, is of benefit to man? Does not reason make mistakes about benefits? It is not possible that man loves something besides prosperity? Perhaps he is just as fond of suffering? Perhaps suffering is just as good for him as prosperity? And man does love suffering very much sometimes. He loves it passionately. That is an undeniable fact. You need not even look up world history to prove that; ask yourself, if you are a man and have lived at all. As for my own personal opinion, I believe that to be fond of prosperity is, somehow, indecent even. Whether it is good or bad, it is sometimes very pleasant to smash things, too. Not that I'm particularly anxious to plead the cause of suffering, or of happiness, for that matter. All I plead for is that I should be allowed my whims, and that they should be guaranteed to me whenever I want them. In light comedies, for instance, suffering is not permitted, and I accept that. In the Crystal Palace it is unthinkable: suffering is doubt, it is negation, and what sort of Crystal Palace would it be if one were to have any doubts about it? And yet I am convinced that man will never renounce real suffering, that is to say, destruction and chaos. Suffering! Why, it's the sole cause of consciousness! And though at the beginning I did argue that consciousness was the greatest misfortune to man, yet I know that man loves it and will not exchange it for any satisfaction. Consciousness, for instance, is infinitely superior to twice-two. After twice-two there is nothing left for you to do, or even to learn. All you could do then would be to stop up your five senses and sink into contemplation. While if you hang on to your consciousness you may achieve the same result, that is to say, there will be nothing for you to do, either, you could at least administer a good thrashing to yourself from time to time, and that at any rate livens you up a bit. It may be a reactionary step, but it is better than nothing, isn't it?

X[1]

You believe in the Crystal Palace, forever indestructible, that is to say, in one at which you won't be able to stick out your tongue even by stealth or cock a snook even in your pocket. Well, perhaps I am afraid of this palace just because it is made of crystal and is forever indestructible, and just because I shan't be able to poke my tongue out at it even by stealth.

You see, if it were not a palace but a hencoop, and if it should rain, I might crawl into it to avoid getting wet, but I would never pretend that the hencoop was a palace out of gratitude to it for sheltering me from the rain. You laugh and you tell me that in such circumstances even a hencoop is as good as a palace. Yes, I reply, it certainly is if the only purpose in life is not to get wet.

But what is to be done if I've got it into my head that that is not the only purpose in life, and that if one has to live, one had better live in a palace? That is my choice; that is my desire. You can only force me to give it up when you change my desire. All right, do it. Show me something more attractive. Give me another ideal. For the time being, however, I refuse to accept a hencoop for a palace. The Crystal Palace may be just an idle dream, it may be against all laws of nature, I may have invented it because of my own stupidity, because of certain old and irrational habits of my generation. But what do I care whether it is against the laws of nature? What does it matter so long as it exists in my desires, or rather exists while my desires exist? You are not laughing again, are you? Laugh by all means; I am quite ready to put up with any jeers, but I will still refuse to say that I'm satisfied when I'm hungry. At all events I know that I shall never be content with a compromise, with an everlasting and recurring zero because it exists according to the laws of nature and *actually* exists. I will not accept as the crown of all my desires a big house with model flats for the poor on a lease of ninety-nine hundred and ninety-nine years, and, in case of emergency, with the dental surgeon Wagenheim on a signboard. Destroy my desires, eradicate my ideals, show me something better, and I will follow you. I daresay you will probably declare that it isn't worth your while having anything to do with me; but in that case I, too, can say the same to you. We are discussing this seriously; and if you are too proud to give me your attention, I shall have to do without it.

But while I'm still alive and have desires, I'd rather my right hand withered than let it bring even one small brick to such a house of model flats! I know that

---

[1] The censor so mangled this chapter that Dostoevsky later complained that he was made to contradict himself several times. *Translator.*

a short time ago I rejected the Crystal Palace myself for the sole reason that one would not be allowed to stick one's tongue out at it. But I did not say that because I am so fond of sticking out my tongue. Perhaps what I resented was that among all our buildings there has never been one at which one could not stick out one's tongue. On the contrary, I'd gladly have let my tongue be cut off out of gratitude if things could be so arranged that I should have no wish to stick it out at all. It is not my business if things cannot be arranged like that and if one has to be satisfied with model flats. Why then am I made with such desires? Surely, I have not been made for the sole purpose of drawing the conclusion that the way I am made is a piece of rank deceit? Can this be the sole purpose? I don't believe it.

However, do you know what? I am convinced that fellows like me who live in dark cellars must be kept under restraint. They may be able to live in their dark cellars for forty years and never open their mouths, but the moment they get into the light of day and break out they talk and talk and talk. . . .

XI

And, finally, gentlemen, it is much better to do nothing at all! Better passive awareness! And so three cheers for the dark cellar! Though I have said that I envy the normal man to the point of exasperation, I wouldn't care to be in his place in the circumstances in which I find him (though I shall never cease envying him. No, no, the dark cellar is, at any rate, of much greater advantage to me!). In the dark cellar one can at least. . . . Sorry, I'm afraid I am exaggerating. I am exaggerating because I know, as well as twice-two, that it is not the dark cellar that is better, but something else, something else altogether, something I long for but cannot find. To hell with the dark cellar!

Do you know what would be better? It would be better if I myself believed in anything I had just written. I assure you most solemnly, gentlemen, that there is not a word I've just writen I believe in! What I mean is that perhaps I do believe, but at the same time I cannot help feeling and suspecting for some unknown reason that I'm lying like a cobbler.

"Then why have you written all this?" you ask me.

"Well, suppose I put you in a dark cellar for forty years without anything to do and then came to see you in your dark cellar after the forty years to find out what had become of you. Can a man be left for forty years with nothing to do?"

"But aren't you ashamed? Don't you feel humiliated?" you will perhaps say, shaking your head contemptuously. "You long for life, yet you try to solve the problems of life by a logical tangle! And how tiresome, how insolent your tricks are, and, at the same time, how awfully frightened you are! You talk a lot of nonsense and you seem to be very pleased with it; you say a lot of impudent things, and you are yourself always afraid and apologising for them. You assure us that you are afraid of nothing, and at the same time you try to earn our good opinion. You assure us that you are gnashing your teeth, but at the same time you crack jokes to make us laugh. You know your jokes are not amusing, but you seem to be highly pleased with their literary merit. You may perhaps have really suffered, but you don't seem to have the slightest respect for your suffering. There may be some truth in you, but there is no humility. You carry your truth to the market place out of the pettiest vanity to make a public show of it and to discredit it. No doubt you mean to say something, but you conceal your last word out of fear, because you haven't the courage to say it, but only craven insolence. You boast about your sensibility, but you merely don't know your own mind. For though your mind is active enough, your heart is darkened with corruption, and without a pure heart there can be no full or genuine sensibility. And how tiresome you are! How you impose yourself on people! The airs you give yourself! Lies, lies, lies!"

Now, of course, I've made up all this speech of yours myself. It, too, comes from the dark cellar. I've been listening to your words for forty years through a crack in the ceiling. I have invented them myself. It is the only thing I did invent. No wonder I got it pat and dressed it up in a literary form.

But are you really so credulous as to imagine that I would print all of this, and let you read it into the bargain? And there is another puzzle I'd like to solve: why on earth do I address you as "gentlemen," as though you really were my readers? Such confessions which I am now about to make are not printed, nor given to other people to read. At least I have not enough pluck for that, nor do I consider it necessary to have it. But, you see, a strange fancy has come into my head and I want to realise it, cost what may. It's like this:—

There are certain things in a man's past which he does not divulge to everybody but, perhaps, only to his friends. Again there are certain things he will not divulge even to his friends; he will divulge them perhaps only to himself, and that, too, as a secret. But, finally, there are things which he is afraid to divulge even to himself, and every decent man has quite an accumulation of such things in his mind. I can put it even this way: the more decent a man is, the larger will the number of such things be. At least I have allowed myself only recently to remember some of my early adventures, having till now avoided them rather uneasily. I'm afraid. Now, however, when I have not only remembered them, but have also made up my mind to write them down, I particularly want to put the whole thing to the test to see whether I can be absolutely frank with myself and not be afraid of the whole truth. Let me add, by the way: Heine says that true biographies are almost impossible, and that a man will most certainly tell a lot of lies about himself. In his view, Rousseau told a lot of lies about himself in his Confessions, and told them deliberately, out of vanity. I am sure Heine is right; I can understand perfectly how sometimes one tells all sorts of lies about oneself out of sheer vanity, even going so far as to confess to all sorts of crimes, and I can perfectly understand that sort of vanity. But Heine had in mind a man who made his confessions to the public. I, however, am writing for myself, and I should like to make it clear once and for all that if I address myself in my writings to a reader, I'm doing it simply as a matter of form, because I find it much easier to write like that.

It is only a form, an empty show, for I know that I shall never have any readers. I have already intimated as much. . . .

I don't want to be hampered by any considerations in the editing of my Memoirs. I shan't bother about order or system. I shall put down whatever I remember.

Now, of course, I might, for instance, be taken at my word and asked if I really do not count on any readers, why do I now put down all sorts of conditions, and on paper, too, such as not to pay any attention to order or system, to write down what I remember, etc., etc. Why all these explanations? Why all these apologies?

"Ah," I reply, "now you're asking!"

There is, incidentally, a whole psychology in all this. Perhaps it's simply that I am a coward. Again, perhaps it is simply that I'm imagining an audience on purpose so as to observe the proprieties while I write. There are thousands of reasons, no doubt.

Then again there is this further puzzle: what do I want to write it down for? What is the object of it all? If I'm not writing for the reading public, why not simply recall these things in my mind without putting them down on paper?

Well, I suppose I could do that, but it will look more dignified on paper. There is something imposing about that. There will be a greater sense of passing judgment on myself. The whole style, I'm sure, will be better. Moreover, I really may feel easier in my mind if I write it down. I have, for instance, been latterly greatly oppressed by the memory of some incident that happened to me a long time ago. I remembered it very vividly the other day, as a matter of fact, and it has since been haunting me like some annoying tune you can't get out of your head. And yet I simply must get rid of it. I have hundreds of such memories, but at times one of them stands out from the rest and oppresses me. So why shouldn't I try?

And, lastly, I'm awfully bored, and I have nothing to do. Writing down things is, in fact, a sort of work. People say work makes man better and more honest. Well, here's a chance for me at any rate.

Snow is falling today, almost wet snow, yellow, dirty. It was snowing yesterday, too, and the other day. I think it is because of the wet snow that I remembered the incident which gives me no rest now. So let it be a story apropos of the wet snow.

Part II   Apropos of the Wet Snow

> When with a word of fervent conviction,
> From the lowest dregs of dark affliction,
> A soul from eternal doom I saved;
> And in horror and in torments steeped,
> Wringing your hands, you curses heaped

Upon the life that once you craved;
When your unheeding conscience at last
With your guilty memories flaying,
The dreadful story of your sin-stained past
To me you narrated, pardon praying;
And full of horror, full of shame,
Quickly in your hands you hid your face,
Unconscious of the flood of tears that came,
Shaken and indignant at your own disgrace. . . . etc., etc.
FROM THE POETRY OF N. A. NEKRASSOV.

I

I was only twenty-four at the time. My life even then was gloomy, disorderly, and solitary to the point of savagery. I had no friends or acquaintances, avoided talking to people, and buried myself more and more in my hole. When at work in the office I tried not to look at anyone and I knew perfectly well that my colleagues not only regarded me as a queer fellow, but also—I couldn't help feeling that, too—looked upon me with a sort of loathing. I wondered why no one except me had ever had this feeling that people looked upon him with loathing. One of the clerks at the office had a repulsive, pock-marked face, the face, I should say, of a real villain. I should not have dared to look at anyone with such an indecent face. Another had such a filthy old uniform that one could not go near him without becoming aware of a bad smell. And yet these gentlemen did not seem to be in the least upset either about their clothes, or their faces, or the impression they created. Neither of them ever imagined that people looked at him with loathing; and I daresay it would not have made any difference to them if they had imagined it, so long as their superiors deigned to look at them. It is of course clear that, owing to my unbounded vanity and hence also to my over-sensitiveness where my own person was concerned, I often looked at myself with a sort of furious dissatisfaction which verged on loathing, and for that reason I could not help attributing my own views to other people. I hated my own face, for instance, finding it odious to a degree and even suspecting that it had rather a mean expression, and so every time I arrived at the office I went through agonies in my efforts to assume as independent an air as possible so as to make sure that my colleagues did not suspect me of meanness and so as to give my face as noble an expression as possible. "What do I care," I thought to myself, "whether my face is ugly or not, so long as it is also noble, expressive, and, above all, *extremely* intelligent." But I knew very well, I knew it agonisingly well, that it was quite impossible for my face to express such high qualities. But the really dreadful part of it was that I thought my face looked absolutely stupid. I would have been completely satisfied if it looked intelligent. Indeed, I'd have reconciled myself even to a mean expression so long as my face was at the same time generally admitted to be awfully intelligent.

I need hardly say that I hated all my colleagues at the office, one and all, and that I despised them all, and yet at the same time I was also in a way afraid of them. It sometimes happened that I thought of them more highly than of myself. It was a feeling that somehow came upon me suddenly: one moment I despised them and the next moment I thought of them as above me. A decent, educated man cannot afford the luxury of vanity without being exceedingly exacting with himself and without occasionally despising himself to the point of hatred. But whether I despised them or thought them superior to me, I used to drop my eyes almost every time I met any one of them. I even used to make experiments to see whether I would be able to meet without flinching the look of one or another of my colleagues, and it was always I who dropped my eyes first. That irritated me to the point of madness. I was also morbidly afraid of appearing ridiculous and for that reason I slavishly observed all the social conventions; I enthusiastically followed in the beaten track and was mortally afraid of any eccentricity. But how could I hope to keep it up? I was so highly developed mentally, as indeed a man of our age should be. They, on the other hand, were all so stupidly dull and as like one another as so many sheep. Perhaps I was the only one in our office who constantly thought that he was a coward and a slave, and I thought that just because I was so highly developed mentally. But the truth is that it was not only a matter of my imagining it, but that it actually was so: I was a coward and a slave. I say this without the slighest embarrassment. Every decent man of our age is, and indeed has to be, a coward and a slave. That is his normal condition. I am absolutely convinced of that. He is made like that, and he has been created for that very purpose. And not only at the present time or as a result of some fortuitous circumstances, but at all times and in general a decent man has to be a coward and a slave. This is the law of nature for all decent men on earth. If one of them does sometimes happen to pluck up courage about something or other, he need not derive any comfort from it or be pleased about it: he is quite sure to make a fool of himself over something else. Such is the inevitable and eternal result of his being what he is. Only donkeys and mules pretend not to be afraid, and even they do it only up to a point. It is hardly worth while taking any notice of them, however, since they do not amount to anything, anyway.

Another thing that used to worry me very much at that time was the quite incontestable fact that I was unlike anyone and that there was no one like me. "I am one, and they are *all*," I thought and—fell into a melancholy muse.

From all that it can be seen that I was still a very young man.

Sometimes, though, quite the reverse used to happen. I would loathe the thought of going to the office, and things went so far that many times I used to come home ill. But suddenly and for no reason at all a mood of scepticism would come upon me (everything was a matter of moods with me), and I would myself laugh at my intolerance and sensitiveness and reproach myself with being a *romantic*. Sometimes I'd hate to talk to anyone, and at other times I'd not only talk to people, but would even take it into my head to be friends with them. All my fastidiousness would suddenly and for no reason in the world disappear. Who knows, maybe I really had never been fastidious, but just acquired a taste for appearing fastidious out of books. I haven't thought of an answer to this question to this day. Once I got very friendly with them, began visiting their homes, playing preference, drinking vodka, talking of promotions. . . . But here you must let me make a digression.

We Russians, generally speaking, have never had those stupid starry-eyed German and, still more, French romantics on whom nothing produces any effect; though the very ground cracked beneath their feet, though the whole of France perished at the barricades, they would still be the same and would not change even for the sake of appearances, and they would go on singing their highly romantic songs to their last breath, as it were, because they were fools. In Russia, however, there are no fools; that is a well known fact and that is what makes us so different from other countries. Therefore no starry-eyed natures, pure and simple, can be found among us. All that has been invented by our "positive" publicists and critics who at the time were chasing after Gogol's and Goncharov's idealised landowners and, in their folly, mistook them for our ideal; they have traduced our romantics, thinking them the same starry-eyed sort as in Germany or France. On the contrary, the characteristics of our romantics are the exact and direct opposite of the starry-eyed European variety, and not a single European standard applies here. (I hope you don't mind my using the word "romantic"—it is an old, honourable, and highly estimable word and is familiar to all.) The characteristics of our romantic are to understand everything, *to see everything and to see it incomparably more clearly than the most positive of our thinkers*; to refuse to take anyone or anything for granted, but at the same time not to despise anything; to go round and round everything and to yield to everything out of policy; never to lose sight of the useful and the practical (rent-free quarters for civil servants, pensions of a sort, decorations)—and to discern this aim through all the enthusiasms and volumes of lyrical verses, and at the same time to preserve to his dying day a profound and indestructible respect for "the sublime and the beautiful," and, incidentally, also to preserve himself like some precious jewel wrapt in cotton-wool for the benefit, for instance, of the same "sublime and beautiful." Our romantic is a man of great breadth of vision and the most consummate rascal of all our rascals, I assure you—from experience. That, of course, is all true if our romantic is intelligent. Good Lord, what am I saying? The romantic is always intelligent. I only meant to observe that even if there were fools among our romantics, they need not be taken into account for the simple reason that they had transformed themselves into Germans when still in their prime and, to preserve that pristine jewel-like purity of theirs, gone and settled somewhere abroad, preferably in Weimar or the Black Forest.

Now, for instance, I had a sincere contempt for the Civil Service and if I did not show it, it was only out of sheer necessity, for I was myself sitting at a desk in a Government office and getting paid for it. As a result—note that, please!—I refrained from showing my contempt in any circumstances. Our romantic would sooner go off his head (which does not happen often, though) than show his contempt for his job if he has no other job in prospect, and he is never kicked out of a job, either, unless indeed he is carried off to a lunatic asylum as "the King of Spain," but even then only if he should go stark raving mad. However, only the very thin and fair people go off their heads in Russia. An innumerable host of romantics, on the other hand, usually end up by becoming civil servants of the highest grade. Quite a remarkable versatility! And what an ability they possess for the most contradictory sensations! Even in those days this thought used to console me mightily, and I am still of the same opinion. That is why we have such a great number of "expansive" natures who do not lose sight of their ideal even when faced with the most catastrophic disaster; and though they never lift a finger for their ideal, though they are the most thorough-paced villains and thieves, they respect their original ideal, are ready to shed bitter tears for it and are, besides, quite remarkably honest at heart. Yes, gentlemen, it is only among us that the most arrant knave can be perfectly and even sublimely honest at heart without at the same time ceasing to be a knave. I repeat, I have seen our romantics over and over again grown into the most businesslike rascals (I use the word "rascals" affectionately); they suddenly acquire such a wonderful grasp of reality and such a thorough knowledge of the practical world that their astonished superiors in the Civil Service and the public at large can only click their tongues in utter stupefaction.

Their many-sidedness is truly amazing, and goodness only knows into what it may be transformed and developed later on and what, as a result of it, the future may hold in store for us. And the material is far from unpromising! I do not say this out of some ridiculous or blustering patriotism. However, I'm sure you must be thinking again that I am pulling your legs. Well, I don't know. Perhaps I am wrong. I mean, perhaps you are convinced that this really is my opinion. In either case, gentlemen, I shall consider both these views as a singular honour and a matter of special gratification to me. And you will forgive me for my digression, won't you?

My friendship with my colleagues did not of course last. Within a very short time I was at loggerheads with them again and, owing to my youthful inexperience at the time, I even stopped exchanging greetings with them and, so to speak, cut them. That, however, only happened to me once. Generally speaking, I was always alone.

At home I mostly spent my time reading. I tried to stifle all that was seething within me by all sorts of outside distractions, and of all outside distractions reading was the most easily available to me. My reading of course helped a lot: it excited, delighted, and tormented me. But at times it also bored me terribly. I got heartily sick of sitting in my room; I wanted to go somewhere, to move about; and so I plunged into a sort of sombre, secret, disgusting—no, not dissipation, but vile, petty vice. My mean lusts were always acute and burning as a result of my continual morbid irritability. My outbursts of passion were hysterical, and always accompanied by tears and convulsions. Apart from my reading, I had nothing to occupy me. I mean, there was nothing in my surroundings which I could respect or to which I could feel attracted. In addition, I was terribly sick at heart; I felt a terrible craving for conflicts and contrasts, and so I plunged into a life of mean debauchery. Mind you, I have spoken at such great length now not at all because of any desire to justify myself. And yet—no! It's a lie! Of course I wanted to justify myself. I'm speaking this little note for my own use, gentlemen. I don't want to lie. I promised not to.

I pursued my vile amusements in solitude, at night, in secret, fearfully, filthily, with a feeling of shame that did not desert me in the most sickening moments and that brought me in such moments to the point of calling down curses on my own head. Even in these days I carried the dark cellar about with me in my soul. I was terribly afraid of being seen, of meeting someone I knew, of being recognised. I frequented all sorts of rather obscure dens of vice.

One night as I was passing a small pub, I saw through a lighted window some men having a fight with billiard cues and one of them being thrown out of the window. At any other time I should have felt very much disgusted; but at the time I could not help feeling envious of the fellow who had been thrown out of the window. Indeed, so envious did I feel that I even went into the pub, walked straight into the billiard room, thinking that perhaps I too could pick a quarrel with the men there and be thrown out of the window.

I was not drunk, but what was I to do? To such a state of hysteria had my depression brought me! But nothing happened. It seemed that I was not even capable of jumping out of the window, and I went away without having a fight.

An army officer in the pub put me in my place from the very first.

I was standing beside the billiard table and, in my ignorance, was blocking the way. As he had to pass me, he took me by the shoulders and, without a word of warning or explanation, silently carried me bodily from where I was standing to another place and passed by as though he had not even noticed me. I could have forgiven him if he had given me a beating, but I could not forgive him for having moved me from one place to another as if I were a piece of furniture. I would have given anything at that moment for a real, a more regular, a more decent, and a more, so to speak, *literary* quarrel! But I had been treated like a fly. The army officer was over six foot, and I am a short, thin little fellow. The quarrel, however, was in my hands: if I had uttered one word of protest, I should most certainly have been thrown out of the window. But I changed my mind and preferred—to efface myself angrily.

I left the pub feeling wild and embarrassed and went straight home. On the following day I carried on with my mean dissipation even more timidly, more abjectly and miserably than before, as though with tears in my eyes, but I did carry on with it. Do not imagine, however, that I was afraid of the army officer because I am a coward; I never was a coward at heart, although I have in-variably been a coward in action, but—don't be in such a hurry to laugh; I have an explanation for everything, don't you worry.

Oh, if that army officer had only been one of those who would accept a challenge to a duel! But no. He was most decidedly one of those gentlemen (alas, long extinct!) who preferred action with billiard cues or, like Gogol's lieutenant Pirogov, by lodging a complaint with the authorities. They never accepted a challenge, and in any case would have considered a duel with me, a low grade civil servant, as quite improper; as for duelling in general, they regarded it as something unthinkable, something that only a freethinker or a Frenchman would indulge in. But that did not prevent them from treading on any man's corns, and painfully, too, particularly as they were over six foot.

No, I was not afraid because I was a coward, but because of my unbounded vanity. I was not afraid of his six foot, nor of getting soundly thrashed and being thrown out of the window; I should have had sufficient physical courage for that, what I lacked was moral courage. What I was afraid of was that every one in the billiard room from the cheeky marker to the last rotten, pimply little government clerk in a greasy collar who was fawning upon everybody in the room, would misunderstand me and jeer at me when I protested and began addressing them in literary language. For even today we cannot speak of a point of honour—not of honour, mind you, but of a point of honour (*point d'honneur*) except in literary language. You cannot even mention a "point of honour" in ordinary language. I was absolutely convinced (the sense of reality in spite of all romanticism!) that they would all simply split their sides with laughter and that the officer would not just simply, that is to say, not inoffensively, thrash me, but would certainly push me round the billiard table with his knee and perhaps only then would he have taken pity on me and thrown me out of the window. With me a wretched incident like this would never, of course, end there. I often met that army officer in the street afterwards and made a careful note of him. What I am not quite sure about is whether he recognised me. I don't think he did, and I have come to this conclusion by certain signs. But I—I stared at him with hatred and malice, and that went on— oh, for several years. At first I began finding out quietly all I could about this officer. It was a difficult job, for I did not know anyone. But one day someone called him by his surname in the street just as I was trailing after him at a distance, as though I were tied to him by a string, and so I learnt his name. Another day I followed him to his home and for ten copecks I found out from the caretaker where he lived, on which floor, whether alone or with somebody, etc., in fact, everything one could learn from a caretaker. One morning, though I had never indulged in literary work, it suddenly occurred to me to write a story round this officer, a story in a satiric vein, in order to show him up for what he was. I wrote this story with real pleasure. I exposed, I did not hesitate even to libel him; at first I gave him a name which could be immediately recognised as his, but later, on second thoughts, I changed it, and sent the story to "Homeland Notes." But at that time exposures were not in fashion yet, and my story was not published. I felt very sore about it.

Sometimes my resentment became quite unbearable. At last I made up my mind to challenge my enemy to a duel. I wrote him a most beautiful, most charming letter, demanding an apology from him and, if he refused to apologise, hinting rather plainly at a duel. The letter was written in such a way that if the officer had had the least notion of "the sublime and the beautiful," he would certainly have come running to me, fallen on my neck, and offered me his friendship. And how wonderful that would have been! Oh, how wonderfully we should have got on together! He would have protected me by his rank of an army officer, and I would have enlarged his mind by my superior education and—well—by my ideas, and lots of things could have happened! Just consider, this was two years after he had insulted me, and my challenge was absurdly out of date, a pure anachronism, in fact, in spite of the cleverness of my letter explaining away and concealing the lapse of time. But, thank God (to this day I thank the Almighty with tears in my eyes!), I did not send my letter. A shiver runs down my spine when I think of what might have happened if I had sent it. And suddenly—suddenly I revenged myself in the simplest and most extraordinarily clever way! A most brilliant idea suddenly occurred to me.

Sometimes on a holiday I used to take a walk on Nevsky Avenue, on the sunny side of it, and about four o'clock in the afternoon. As a matter of fact, I did not really take a walk there, but went through a series of torments, humiliations, and bilious attacks; but I suppose that was really what I wanted. I darted along like a groundling in the most unbecoming manner imaginable among the people on the pavement, continuously making way for generals, officers of the guards and hussars, and ladies. At those moments I used to have sharp shooting pains in my heart and I used to feel all hot down the back at the mere thought of the miserable appearance of my clothes and the wretchedness of my darting little figure. It was a most dreadful torture, an incessant, unbearable humiliation at the thought, which grew into an uninterrupted and most palpable sensation, that in the eyes of all those high society people I was just a fly, an odious, obscene fly, more intelligent, more highly developed, more noble than anyone else (I had no doubts about that), but a fly that was always making way for everyone, a fly insulted and humiliated by every one. Why I suffered this torment, why I went for my walks on Nevsky Avenue, I do not know. But I was simply *drawn* there at every possible opportunity.

Already at that time I began experiencing the sudden onrush of those keen delights of which I spoke in the first part. But after the incident with the army officer, I felt drawn there more than ever: it was on Nevsky Avenue that I met him most frequently, and it was there that I took such delight in looking at him. He, too, used to take a walk there mostly on holidays. And though he, too, made way for generals and other persons of high rank, though he, too, darted like a groundling among them, he simply bore down on people like me, or even those who were a cut above me; he walked straight at them as though there were just an empty space in front of him, and never in any circumstances did he make way for them. I gloated spitefully as I looked at him and—made way for him resentfully every time he happened to bear down on me. I was tortured by the thought that even in the street I could not be on the same footing as he. "Why do you always have to step aside first?" I asked myself over and over again in a sort of hysterical rage, sometimes waking up at three o'clock in the morning. "Why always you and not he? There is no law about it, is there? There's nothing written down about it, is there? Why can't you arrange it so that each of you should make way for the other, as usually happens when two well-bred men meet in the street? He yields you half of his pavement and you half of yours, and you pass one another with mutual respect." But it never happened like that. It was always I who stepped aside, while he did not even notice that I made way for him.

And it was then the brilliant idea occurred to me. "And what," thought I, "what if I should meet him and—and not move aside? Just not do it on purpose, even if I have to give him a push. Well, what would happen then?" This brazen thought took such a hold of me that it gave me no rest. I thought of it continually and went for a walk on Nevsky Avenue more frequently so as to make quite sure of the way in which I was going to do it when I did do it. I felt transported. This plan seemed to me more and more feasible and promising. "Of course I'm not going to give him a real push," I thought, feeling much kindlier disposed towards him in my joy. "I'll simply not make way for him. Knock against him, taking good care not to hurt him very much, just shoulder against shoulder, just as much as the laws of propriety allow. I shall only knock against him as much as he knocks against me."

At last my mind was firmly made up. But my preparations took a long time. The first thing I had to take into account was that when I carried out my plan I had to take good care to be as well dressed as possible. I had therefore to see about my clothes. "Just in case, for instance, there should be a public scandal (and there was sure to be quite an audience there: a countess taking a walk, Prince D. taking a walk, the whole literary world taking a walk), one had to be decently dressed. Good clothes impress people and will immediately put us on an equal footing in the eyes of society." Accordingly, I obtained an advance of salary and bought myself a pair of black gloves and a smart hat at Churkin's. Black gloves seemed to me more impressive and more elegant than canary-coloured ones which I had thought of buying first. "Too bright a colour. Looks as though a man wants to show off too much!" So I did not take the canary-coloured ones. I had long ago got ready an excellent shirt with white bone studs; but my overcoat delayed the carrying out of my plan for a long time. My overcoat was not at all bad. It kept me warm. But it was wadded and had a raccoon collar, which made one look altogether too much a flunkey. The collar had to be changed at all costs for a beaver one, like one of those army officers wore. To acquire such a collar, I began visiting the Arcade, and after a few attempts decided to buy a cheap German beaver. These German beavers may soon look shabby and worn, but at first, when new, they look very decent indeed. And I wanted it for one occasion only. I asked the price: it was much too expensive. On thinking it over, I decided to sell my raccoon collar and to borrow the rest of the money (and a considerable sum it was, too) from the head of my department, Anton Antonovich Setochkin, a quiet man, but serious and dependable, who never lent any money to any one, but to whom I had been particularly recommended years ago on entering the service by an important personage who got me the job. I went through hell before taking this step. To ask Anton Antonovich for a loan seemed to me a monstrous and shameful thing. I did not sleep for two or three nights and, as a matter of fact, I did not sleep well at the time generally, feeling very feverish. My heart seemed to be either beating very faintly or suddenly began thumping, thumping, thump-ing! . . . Anton Antonovich looked rather surprised at first, then he frowned, then he pondered, and in the end he did lend me the money, having made me sign a promissory note authorising him to deduct the money from my salary in a fortnight. In this way everything was settled at last; the beautiful beaver reigned in the place of the odious raccoon, and gradually I set about making the final arrangements. This sort of thing could not be done without careful preparation, without thought. It had to be done skilfully and without hurry. But I must admit that after many attempts to carry my plan into execution, I began to give way to despair: however much I tried, we just did not knock against each other, and there seemed to be nothing I could do about it! Hadn't I got everything ready? Hadn't I made up my mind to go through with it? And did it not now seem that we ought to knock against each other any minute? And yet, when the moment came I made way for him again and he passed without taking any notice of me. I even offered up a prayer when I approached him, beseeching God to fill me with the necessary determination to see the business through. Once I had quite made up my mind, but it all ended by my tripping up and falling down in front of him, for at the last moment, at a dis-tance of only a few feet, my courage failed me. He calmly strode over me, and I was hurled to one side like a ball. That night I was again in a fever and de-lirious. And suddenly everything came to a most satisfactory conclusion. The night before I had made up my mind most definitely not to go through with my luckless enterprise and to forget all about it, and with that intention I went for a walk on Nevsky Avenue for the last time, just to see how I would forget all about it. Suddenly, only three paces from my enemy, I quite unexpectedly made up my mind, shut my eyes, and—we knocked violently against each other, shoulder to shoulder. I did not budge an inch and passed him absolutely on an equal footing! He did not even look round and pretended not to have noticed anything. But he was only pretending: I am quite sure of that. Yes, to this day I am quite sure of that! Of course I got the worst of it, for he was stronger. But that was not the point. The point was that I had done what I had set out to do, that I had kept up my dignity, that I had not yielded an inch, and that I had put myself publicly on the same social footing as he. I came back home feeling that I had completely revenged myself for everything. I was beside myself with delight. I was in the seventh heaven and sang Italian arias. I shall not, of course, describe to you what happened to me three days later. If you have read my first chapter, you will be able to guess for your-selves. The officer was afterwards transferred somewhere. I have not seen him for fourteen years now. I wonder how the dear fellow is getting on now. Who is he bullying now?

II

But when my mood for odious little dissipations came to an end I used to feel dreadfully flat and miserable. I had an awful conscience about it, but I did my best not to think of it: I felt too miserable for that. Little by little, however, I got used to that, too. I got used to everything, or rather I did not really get used to it, but just made up my mind to grin and bear it. But I had a solution which made up for everything, and that was to seek salvation in all that was "sublime and beautiful," in my dreams, of course. I would give myself up entirely to dreaming. I would dream for three months on end, skulking in my corner. And, believe me, at those moments I bore no resemblance to the gentleman who in his pigeon-livered confusion had sewed a piece of German beaver to the collar of his overcoat. I suddenly became a hero. I shouldn't have admitted my six-foot lieutenant to my rooms even if he had come to pay a call on me. I could not even picture him before me at the time. What exactly my dreams were about, or how I could be content with them, it is difficult to say now, but I was content with them at the time. As a matter of fact, I feel even now a certain glow of satisfaction at the memory of it. It was after my phase of dissipation had passed that I took special pleasure in my dreams which seemed sweeter and more vivid then. They came to me with repentance and tears, with curses and transports of delight. I had moments of such positive intoxication, of such intense happiness, that, I assure you, I did not feel even the faintest stir of derision within me. What I had was faith, hope, and love. The trouble was that in those days I believed blindly that by some miracle, by some outside event, all this would suddenly draw apart and expand, that I would suddenly catch a glimpse of a vista of some suitable activity, beneficent and beautiful, and, above all, an activity that was absolutely ready-made (what sort of activity I never knew, but the great thing was that it was to be all ready-made), and then I would suddenly emerge into the light of day, almost mounted on a white horse and with a laurel wreath on my head. I could not even imagine any place of secondary importance for myself, and for that very reason I quite contentedly occupied the most insignificant one in real life. Either a hero or dirt —there was no middle way. That turned out to be my undoing, for while wallowing in dirt I consoled myself with the thought that at other times I was a hero, and the hero overlaid the dirt: an ordinary mortal, as it were, was ashamed to wallow in dirt, but a hero was too exalted a person to be entirely covered in dirt, and hence I could wallow in dirt with an easy conscience. It is a remarkable fact that these attacks of the "sublime and beautiful" came to me even during my spells of odious dissipation, and more particularly at the time when I was touching bottom. They came quite unexpectedly, in separate outbursts, as though reminding me of themselves, but their appearance never brought my debauch to an end; on the contrary, they seemed to stimulate it by contrast, and they only lasted for as long as it was necessary for them to carry out the function of a good sauce. In this case the sauce consisted of contradictions and suffering, of torturing inner analysis, and all these pangs and torments added piquancy and even meaning to my odious little dissipation— in short, fully carried out the function of a good sauce. All this had a certain profundity, too. For I could never have been content to indulge in the simple, vulgar, direct, sordid debauchery of some office clerk and reconcile myself to all that filth! What else could I have found so attractive in it to draw me into the street at night? No, gentlemen, I had a noble loophole for every thing. . . .

But how much love, good Lord, how much love I used to experience in those dreams of mine, during those hours of "salvation through the sublime and the beautiful"; fantastic though that sort of love was and though in reality it had no relation whatever to anything human, there was so much of it, so much of this love, that one did not feel the need of applying it in practice afterwards; that would indeed have been a superfluous luxury. Everything, however, always ended most satisfactorily in an indolent and rapturous transition to art, that is, to the beautiful forms of existence, all ready-made, snatched forcibly from the poets and novelists and adapted to every possible need and requirement. For instance, I triumphed over everything; all of course lay in the dust at my feet, compelled of their own free will to acknowledge all my perfections, and I forgave them all. I was a famous poet and court chamberlain, and I fell in love; I became a multi-millionaire and at once devoted all my wealth to the improvement of the human race, and there and then confessed all my hideous and shameful crimes before all the people; needless to say, my crimes were, of course, not really hideous or shameful, but had much in them that was "sublime and beautiful," something in the style of Manfred. All would weep and kiss me (what damned fools they'd have been otherwise!), and I'd go off, barefoot and hungry, to preach new ideas and inflict another Waterloo on the reactionaries. Then the band would be brought out and strike up a march, a general amnesty would be granted, and the Pope would agree to leave Rome for Brazil; then there would be a ball for the whole of Italy at the Villa Borghese on the banks of Lake Como, Lake Como being specially transferred for that occasion to the neighborhood of Rome; this would be followed by the scene in the bushes, and so on and so forth—don't tell me you don't know it! You will say it is mean and contemptible now to shout it all from the housetops after all the raptures and tears which I have myself confessed to. But why, pray, is it mean? Surely, you don't think I'm ashamed of it, do you? You don't imagine by any chance that all this was much sillier than what ever happened in your life, gentlemen? And let me assure you that certain things were not so badly worked out by me, either. . . . It did not all take place on the banks of Lake Como. Of course, on the other hand, you are quite right. As a matter of fact, it is mean and contemptible. And what is even meaner is that now I should be trying to justify myself to you. Enough of this, though, or I should never finish: things are quite sure to get meaner and meaner anyway.

I was never able to spend more than three months of dreaming at a time without feeling an irresistible urge to plunge into social life. To me plunging into social life meant paying a call on the head of my department, Anton Antonovich Setochkin. He was the only permanent acquaintance I have had in my life, and I can't help being surprised at it myself now. But I used to call on him only when I was in the right mood for such a visit, when, that is, my dreams had reached such a pinnacle of bliss that I felt an instant and irresistible urge to embrace all my fellow-men and all humanity. But to do that one had at least to have one man who actually existed. However, it was only on Tuesdays that one could call on Anton Antonovich (Tuesday was his at home day), and therefore it was necessary to work myself up into the right mood for embracing all mankind on that day. This Anton Antonovich Setochkin lived at Five Corners, on the fourth floor, in four little rooms with low ceilings, one smaller than the other, and all of a most frugal and jaundiced appearance. He had two daughters and their aunt who used to pour out the tea. One of the daughters was thirteen and the other fourteen; both had snub noses and both used to embarrass me terribly because they kept whispering to each other and giggling. The master of the house was usually in his study. He sat on a leather sofa in front of his desk, with some grey-haired visitor, a civil servant from our department or, occasionally, from some other department. I never saw more than two or three visitors there, and always the same. The usual topic of conversation was excise duties, the hard bargaining in the Senate, salaries, promotions, His Excellency, the best way to please him, etc., etc. I had the patience to sit like a damn fool beside these people for hours, listening to them, neither daring to speak to them, nor knowing what to say. I got more and more bored, broke out into a sweat, and was in danger of getting an apoplectic stroke. But all this was good and useful to me. When I came home, I would put off for a time my desire to embrace all mankind.

I had, by the way, another acquaintance of a sort, a fellow by the name of Simonov, an old schoolfellow of mine. I suppose I must have had quite a lot of schoolfellows in Petersburg, but I had nothing to do with them and even stopped exchanging greetings with them in the street. I expect the real reason why I had got myself transferred to another department in the Civil Service was that I did not want to have anything to do with them any more. I wanted to cut myself off completely from the hateful years of my childhood. To hell with that school and those terrible years of slavery! In short, I broke with my schoolfellows as soon as I began to shift for myself. There were only two or three of them left with whom I still exchanged greetings in the street. One of them was Simonov, who was a very quiet boy at school, of an equable nature and not particularly brilliant, but I discerned in him a certain independence of character and even honesty. I don't think he was a dull fellow at all. Not very dull, anyway. We had had some bright times together, but I'm afraid they did not last long and somehow or other got lost in a mist rather suddenly. I had a feeling that he did not exactly relish being reminded of those times and that he seemed to be always afraid that I might adopt the same tone with him again. I suspected that he really loathed the sight of me, but as I was never quite sure about it, I went on visiting him.

So that one Thursday afternoon, unable to bear my solitude any longer and knowing that on Thursdays Anton Antonovich's door would be closed, I thought of Simonov. As I was climbing up to his rooms on the fourth floor, I could not help thinking that this particular gentleman must be sick and tired of me and that I was wasting my time going to see him. But as it invariably happened that such reflections merely spurred me on to put myself into an equivocal position, I went in. It was almost a year since I had last seen Simonov.

III

I found two more of my former schoolfellows with him. They seemed to be discussing some highly important matter. None of them took any particular notice of my arrival, which struck me as rather odd considering that I had not seen them for years. No doubt they regarded me as some sort of common fly. I had never been treated like that even at school, though they all hated me there. I realised, of course, that they could not help despising me now for my failure to get on in the Civil Service, for my having sunk so low, going about shabbily dressed, etc., which in their eyes was, as it were, an advertisement of my own incompetence and insignificance. But all the same I had never expected so great a contempt for me. Simonov could not even disguise his surprise at my visit. He always used to be surprised at my visits, at least that was the impression I got. All this rather upset me. I sat down, feeling somewhat put out, and began listening to their conversation.

They were discussing very earnestly, and even with some warmth, the question of a farewell dinner which they wanted to give next day to a friend of theirs, an army officer by the name of Zverkov, who was due to leave for some remote place in the provinces. Zverkov too had been at school with me all the time, but I grew to hate him particularly in the upper forms. In the lower forms he had been just a good-looking, high-spirited boy, who was a favourite with everybody. I had hated him, however, even in the lower forms just because he was so good-looking and high-spirited a boy. He was never good at lessons, and as time went on he got worse and worse. But he got his school certificate all right because he had powerful connections. During his last year at school he came into an inheritance, an estate with two hundred peasants, and as almost all of us were poor, he even began showing off to us. He was superlatively vulgar, but a good fellow in spite of it, even when he gave himself airs. And in spite of the superficial, fantastic, and rather silly ideas of honour and fair play we had at school, all but a few of us grovelled before Zverkov, and the more he showed off, the more anxious were they to get into his good books. And they did it not because of any selfish motives, but simply because he had been favoured with certain gifts by nature. Besides, Zverkov was for some reason looked upon by us as an authority on smartness and good manners. The last point in particular used to infuriate me. I hated the brusque, self-assured tone of his voice, the way he enjoyed his own jokes, which, as a matter of fact, were awfully silly, though he always was rather daring in his expressions; I hated his handsome but rather vapid face (for which, by the way, I would have gladly exchanged my *clever one*) and his free and easy military manners which were in vogue in the forties. I hated the way in which he used to talk of his future conquests (he did not have the courage to start an affair with a woman before getting his officer's epaulettes, and was looking forward to them with impatience), and of the duels he would be fighting almost every minute. I remember how I, who had always been so reserved and taciturn, had a furious argument with Zverkov when he was discussing his future love affairs with his cronies during playtime and, becoming as playful as a puppy in the sun, suddenly declared that on his estate he would not leave a single peasant girl who was a virgin without his attentions, that that was his *droit de seigneur*, and that if any of his peasants dared to protest he would have them flogged and double the tax on them, too, the bearded rascals. Our oafs applauded him, but I got my teeth into him not because I was sorry for the virgins or their fathers, but just because they were applauding such an insect. I got the better of him then, but though a great fool, Zverkov was an impudent and jolly fellow, so he laughed the whole affair off, and did it so well that I didn't really get the better of him in the end: the laugh was against me. He got the better of me several times afterwards, but without malice and as though it were all a great lark, with a casual sort of laugh. I would not reply to him, keeping resentfully and contemptuously silent. When we left school, Zverkov seemed anxious to be friends with me, and feeling flattered, I did not object; but we soon, and quite naturally, drifted apart. Afterward I heard of his barrackroom successes as a lieutenant and of the *gay* life he was leading. Then other rumours reached me of his *progress* in the army. Already he began cutting me dead in the street, and I suspected he was afraid of compromising himself by greeting so insignificant a person as me. I also saw him at the theatre once, in the circle, already wearing shoulder-straps. He was bowing and scraping to the daughters of some ancient general. In three years he had lost his youthful looks, though he still was quite handsome and smart. He was beginning to put on weight and looked somewhat bloated. It was pretty clear that by the time he was thirty he would go completely fat and flabby. It was to this Zverkov, who was now leaving the capital, that our friends were going to give a dinner. They had been his boon companions, though I felt sure that in their hearts they never thought themselves his equal.

Of Simonov's two friends one was Ferfichkin, a Russian of German origin, a little fellow with the face of a monkey and one of my worst enemies from our earliest days at school. He was an utterly contemptible, impudent, conceited fellow who liked to parade his claims to a most meticulous sense of honour, but who really was a rotten little coward at heart. He belonged to those of Zverkov's admirers who fawned on him for selfish reasons and who, in fact, often borrowed money from him. Simonov's other visitor, Trudolyubov, was not in any way remarkable. He was an army officer, tall, with rather a cold countenance, fairly honest, but a great admirer of every kind of success and only capable of discussing promotions. He seemed to be a distant relative of Zverkov's, and that, foolish as it may sound, invested him with a certain prestige among us. He always regarded me as a man of no importance, but if not polite, his treatment of me was tolerant.

"Well," said Trudolyubov, "I suppose if we contribute seven roubles each we'll have twenty-one roubles, and for that we ought to be able to get a damn good dinner. Zverkov, of course, won't pay."

"Naturally," Simonov agreed, "if we're inviting him."

"Surely you don't suppose," Ferfichkin interjected superciliously and with some warmth, like an impudent footman who was boasting about the decorations of his master the general, "surely you don't suppose Zverkov will let us pay for him, do you? He might let us pay for the dinner out of a feeling of delicacy, but I bet you anything he'll contribute half a dozen bottles of champagne."

"Half a dozen for the four of us is a bit too much, isn't it?" remarked Trudolyubov, paying attention only to the half-dozen.

"So the three of us then, with Zverkov making four, twenty-one roubles, at the Hôtel de Paris at five o'clock tomorrow," Simonov, who had been chosen as the organiser of the dinner, concluded finally.

"How do you mean twenty-one?" I said in some agitation, pretending to be rather offended. "If you count me, you'll have twenty-eight roubles, and not twenty-one."

I felt that to offer myself suddenly and so unexpectedly as one of the contributors to the dinner was rather a handsome gesture on my part and that they would immediately accept my offer with enthusiasm and look at me with respect.

"You don't want to contribute, too, do you?" Simonov observed without concealing his displeasure and trying not to look at me.

He could read me like a book.

I felt furious that he should be able to read me like a book.

"But why shouldn't I? I'm an old school friend of his, am I not? I must say I can't help resenting being passed over like that!" I spluttered again.

"And where do you suppose were we to find you?" Ferfichkin broke in, rudely.

"You were never on good terms with Zverkov, you know," Trudolyubov added, frowning.

But I had got hold of the idea and I was not to give it up so easily.

"I don't think anyone has a right to express an opinion about that," I replied with a tremor in my voice, as though goodness knows what had happened. "It is just because I was not on very good terms with him before that I might like to meet him now."

"Well," Trudolyubov grinned, "who can make you out—all those fine ideals——"

"Very well," Simonov made up his mind, "we'll put your name down. Tomorrow at five o'clock at the Hôtel de Paris. Don't forget."

"But the money!" Ferfichkin began in an undertone, addressing Simonov and nodding in my direction, but he stopped short, for even Simonov felt embarrassed.

"All right," Trudolyubov said, getting up, "let him come, if he really wants to so much."

"But, damn it all, it's only a dinner for a few intimate friends," Ferfichkin remarked crossly as he, too, picked up his hat. "It's not an official gathering. How do you know we want you at all?"

They went away. As he went out, Ferfichkin did not even think it necessary to say goodbye to me. Trudolyubov just nodded, without looking at me. Simonov, with whom I now remained alone, seemed perplexed and puzzled, and he gave me a strange look. He did not sit down, nor did he ask me to take a seat.

"Mmmm—yes—tomorrow then. Will you let me have the money now? I mean, I'd like to know—" he murmured, looking embarrassed.

I flushed and, as I did so, I remembered that I had owed Simonov fifteen roubles for years, which, incidentally I never forgot, though I never returned the money.

"But look here, Simonov, you must admit that I couldn't possibly have known when I came here that—I mean, I am of course very sorry I forgot——"

"All right, all right! It makes no difference. You can pay me tomorrow at the dinner. I just want to know, that's all. Please, don't——"

He stopped short and began pacing the room noisily, looking more vexed than ever. As he paced the room, he raised himself on his heels and stamped even more noisily.

"I'm not keeping you, am I?" I asked after a silence of two minutes.

"Oh, no, not at all!" He gave a sudden start. "I mean, as a matter of fact, you are. You see I have an appointment with someone,—er—not far from here," he added in an apologetic sort of voice, a little ashamed.

"Good Lord, why didn't you tell me?" I cried, seizing my cap with rather a nonchalant air, though goodness only knows where I got it from.

"Oh, it's not far really—only a few steps from here," Simonov repeated, seeing me off to the front door with a bustling air, which did not become him at all. "So tomorrow at five o'clock sharp!" he shouted after me as I was going down the stairs.

He seemed very glad indeed to see me go, but I was mad with rage.

"What possessed me to do it?" I muttered, grinding my teeth, as I walked along the street. "And for such a rotter, such a swine as Zverkov. Of course I mustn't go. Of course to hell with the lot of them. Why should I? I'm not obliged to, am I? I'll let Simonov know tomorrow. Drop him a line by post."

But the reason why I was so furious was because I knew perfectly well that I should go, that I should go deliberately; and that the more tactless, the more indecent my going was, the more certainly would I go.

And there was a good reason why I should not go: I had not got the money. All in all, I had nine roubles, but of that I had to give seven to my servant Apollon tomorrow for his monthly wages, out of which he paid for his board. Not to pay him was quite out of the question, knowing as I did the sort of man Apollon was. But of that fiend, of that scourge of mine, I shall speak another time.

Anyway, I knew very well that I wouldn't pay him, but would quite certainly go to the dinner.

That night I had the most hideous dreams. And no wonder. The whole evening I was haunted by memories of my hateful days at school, and I could not get rid of them. I was sent to the school by some distant relations of mine, on whom I was dependent and of whom I have not heard anything since. They dumped me there, an orphan already crushed by their reproaches, already accustomed to brood for hours on end, always silent, one who looked sullenly on everything around him. My schoolmates overwhelmed me with spiteful and pitiless derision because I was not like any of them. And derision was the only thing I could not stand. I did not find it at all as easy to make friends with people as they did to make friends among themselves. I at once conceived a bitter hatred for them and withdrew from them all into my own shell of wounded, timid, and excessive pride. Their coarseness appalled me. They laughed cynically at my face, at my ungainly figure. And yet how stupid their own faces were! At our school the faces of the boys seemed to undergo an extraordinary change and grow particularly stupid. Lots of nice looking children entered our school, but after a few years one could not look at them without a feeling of revulsion. Even at the age of sixteen I wondered morosely at them. Even at that time I was amazed at the pettiness of their thoughts, the silliness of their occupations, their games, their conversations. They did not understand even the most necessary things; they were not interested in anything that was out of the ordinary, in anything that was conducive to thought, so that I could not help looking on them as my inferiors. It was not injured vanity that drove me to it, and don't for goodness' sake come to me with your hackneyed and nauseating objections, such as, for instance, that I was only dreaming, while they understood the real meaning of life even then. They understood nothing. They had not the faintest idea of real life. Indeed, it was just that I could not stand most of all about them. On the contrary, they had a most fantastic and absurd notion of the most simple, most ordinary facts, and already at that early age they got into the habit of admiring success alone. Everything that was just but looked down upon and oppressed, they laughed at shamelessly and heartlessly. Rank they mistook for brains. Even at sixteen all they were discussing was cushy jobs. A great deal of it, no doubt, was due to their stupidity, to the bad examples with which they had been surrounded in their childhood and adolescence. And they were abominably vicious. I suppose much of that, too, was only on the surface, much of their depravity was just affected cynicism, and even in their vices one could catch a glimpse of youth and a certain freshness. But that freshness had nothing attractive about it, and it took the form of a kind of rakishness. I hated them terribly, though I suppose I was really much worse than they. They repaid me in the same coin and did not conceal their loathing of me. But I was no longer anxious for them to like me; on the contrary, I longed continually to humiliate them. To escape their ridicule, I purposely began to apply myself more diligently to my studies and was soon among the top boys in my form. This did make an impression on them. Moreover, they all began gradually to realise that I was already reading books they could not read, and that I understood things (not included in our school curriculum) of which they had not even heard. They looked sullenly and sardonically on all this, but they had to acknowledge my moral superiority, particularly as even the teachers took notice of me on account of it. Their jeering stopped, but their hostility remained, and henceforth our relations became strained and frigid. In the end I could no longer stand it myself: the older I became, the more I longed for the society of men and the more I was in need of friends. I tried to become friends with some of them, but my friendship with them always somehow appeared unnatural and came to an end of itself. I did have a sort of a friend once, but by that time I was already a tyrant at heart: I wanted to exercise complete authority over him, I wanted to implant a contempt for his surroundings in his heart, I demanded that he should break away from these surroundings, scornfully and finally. I frightened him with my passionate friendship. I reduced him to tears, to hysterics. He was a simple and devoted soul, but the moment I felt that he was completely in my power I grew to hate him and drove him from me, as though I only wanted him for the sake of gaining a victory over him, for the sake of exacting his complete submission to me. But I could not get the better of them all. My friend, too, was unlike any of the others; he was, in fact, a rare exception. The first thing I did on leaving school was to give up the career for which I had been trained so as to break all the ties that bound me to my past, which I loathed and abominated. . . . And I'm damned if I know why after all that I should go trotting off to see that Simonov! . . .

Early next morning I jumped out of bed in a state of tremendous excitement, as though everything were about to happen there and then. But I really did believe that there was going to be some radical break in my life and that it would most certainly come that day. Whether it was because I was not used to change or for some other reason, but all through my life I could not help feeling that any extraneous event, however trivial, would immediately bring about some radical alteration in my life. However, I went to the office as usual, but slipped away home two hours early to get ready. The important thing, I thought, was not to arrive there first, or they might think that I was really glad to be in their company. But there were thousands of such important things to think of, and they excited me so much that in the end I felt a physical wreck. I gave my boots another polish with my own hands; Apollon would not have cleaned them twice a day for anything in the world, for he considered that a most irregular procedure. I polished them with the brushes I had sneaked from the passage to make sure he did not know anything about it, for I did not want him to despise me for it afterwards. Then I submitted my clothes to a most meticulous inspection and found that everything was old, worn, and covered with stains. I had certainly grown much too careless of my appearance. My Civil Service uniform was not so bad, but I could not go out to dinner in my uniform, could I? The worst of it was that there was a huge yellow stain on the knee of my trousers. I had a presentiment that the stain alone would rob me of nine-tenths of my self-respect. I knew, too, that it was a thought unworthy of me. "But this is no time for thinking: now I have to face reality," I thought with a sinking heart. I knew, of course, perfectly well at the time that I was monstrously exaggerating all these facts. But what could I do? It was too late for me to control my feelings, and I was shaking with fever. I imagined with despair how patronisingly and how frigidly that "rotter" Zverkov would meet me; with what dull and irresistible contempt that blockhead Trudolyubov would look at me; with what unbearable insolence that insect Ferfichkin would titter at me in order to curry favour with Zverkov; how perfectly Simonov would understand it all and how he would despise me for the baseness of my vanity and want of spirit, and, above all, how paltry, *unliterary*, and commonplace the whole affair would be. Of course, the best thing would be not to go at all. But that was most of all out of the question: once I felt drawn into something, I was drawn into it head foremost. All my life I should have jeered at myself afterwards: "So you were afraid, were you? Afraid of *life!* Afraid!" On the contrary, I longed passionately to show all that "rabble" that I was not such a coward as even I imagined myself to be. And that was not all by any means: in the most powerful paroxysms of my cowardly fever I dreamed of getting the upper hand, of sweeping the floor with them, of forcing them to admire and like me—if only for my "lofty thoughts and indisputable wit." They would turn their backs on Zverkov, he would be left sitting by himself in some corner, silent and ashamed, utterly crushed by me. Afterwards, no doubt, I would make it up with him and we would drink to our everlasting friendship. But what was most galling and infuriating to me was that even then I knew without a shadow of doubt that, as a matter of fact, I did not want any of this at all, that, as a matter of fact, I had not the least desire to get the better of them, to crush them, to make them like me, and that if I ever were to do so, I should not give a rap for it. Oh, how I prayed for the day to pass quickly! Feeling utterly miserable I walked up again and again to the window, opened the small ventilating pane, and peered out into the murky haze of the thickly falling wet snow. . . .

At last my cheap clock wheezed out five. I seized my hat and, trying not to look at Apollon, who had been waiting for his wages ever since the morning but was too big a fool to speak to me about it first, slipped past him through the door, and in a smart sledge, which cost me my last fifty copecks, drove up in great style to the Hôtel de Paris.

IV

I had had a feeling the day before that I'd be the first to arrive. But it was no longer a question of arriving first. For not only were they not there, but I could hardly find the room. Nor was the table laid. What did it mean? After many inquiries I found out at last from the waiters that the dinner had been ordered for six and not for five o'clock. I had that confirmed at the bar, too. I even began feeling ashamed to go on making those inquiries. It was only twenty-five minutes past five. If they had changed the dinner hour, they should at least have let me know—what was the post for?—and not have exposed me to such "humiliation" in my own eyes and—and certainly not in the eyes of the waiters. I sat down. A waiter began laying the table. I felt even more humiliated in his presence. Towards six o'clock they brought in candles in addition to the burning lamps. The waiter, however, had never thought of bringing them in as soon as I arrived. In the next room two gloomy gentlemen were having dinner at separate tables; they looked angry and were silent. People in one of the other rooms were kicking up a terrible shindy, shouting at the top of their voices; I could hear the loud laughter of a whole crowd of people, interspersed with some disgustingly shrill shrieks in French: there were ladies at the dinner. The whole thing, in short, could not have been more nauseating. I don't remember ever having had such a bad time, so that when, punctually at six, they arrived all together, I was at first very glad to see them, as though they were my deliverers, and I almost forgot that I ought to be looking offended.

Zverkov entered the room ahead of everybody, quite obviously the leading spirit of the whole company. He and his companions were laughing. But as soon as he caught sight of me, he pulled himself up and, walking up to me unhurriedly, bent his body slightly from the waist, as though showing off what a fine gentleman he was. He shook hands with me affably, though not too affably, with a sort of watchful politeness, almost as though he were already a general, and as though in giving me his hand he was protecting himself against something. I had imagined that as soon as he came in he would, on the contrary, break into his customary high-pitched laugh, intermingled with shrill shrieks, and at once start making his insipid jokes and witticisms. It was to deal with this that I had been preparing myself since last evening, but I had never expected such condescending affability, such grand manners of a person of the highest rank. So he already considered himself infinitely superior to me in every respect, did he? If he only meant to insult me with the superior airs of a general, it would not matter, I thought to myself; but what if, without the least desire to offend me, the fool had really got the preposterous idea into his head that he was immeasurably superior to me and could not look at me but with a patronising air? The very thought of it made me choke with resentment.

"I was surprised to hear of your desire to join us," he began, mouthing and lisping, which he never used to do before. "I'm afraid we haven't seen much of each other recently. You seem to avoid us. A pity. We're not so terrible as you think. Anyway, I'm glad to—er—re-e-sume—er——" and he turned away casually to put down his hat on the windowsill.

"Been waiting long?" asked Trudolyubov.

"I arrived at precisely five o'clock as I was told to yesterday," I replied in a loud voice and with an irritation that threatened an early explosion.

"Didn't you let him know that we had changed the hour?" Trudolyubov asked, turning to Simonov.

"I'm afraid I didn't—forgot all about it," Simonov replied unrepentantly and, without a word of apology to me, went off to order the *hors d'œuvres*.

"You poor fellow, so you've been waiting here for a whole hour, have you?" Zverkov exclaimed sarcastically, for, according to his notions, this was really very funny.

That awful cad Ferfichkin broke into a nasty, shrill chuckle, like the yapping of a little dog. My position seemed to him too ludicrous and too embarrassing for words.

"It isn't funny at all!" I cried to Ferfichkin, getting more and more irritated. "It was somebody else's fault, not mine. I expect I wasn't considered important enough to be told. This—this—this is simply idiotic!"

"Not only idiotic, but something else as well," Trudolyubov muttered, naïvely taking my part. "You're much too nice about it. It's simply insulting. Unintentional, no doubt. And how could Simonov—well!"

"If anyone had played that kind of joke on me," observed Ferfichkin, "I'd——"

"You'd have ordered something for yourself," Zverkov interrupted him, "or simply asked for dinner without waiting for us."

"But you must admit I could have done as much without your permission," I rapped out. "If I waited, I——"

"Let's take our seats, gentlemen," Simonov cried, coming in. "Everything's ready. I can answer for the champagne—it's been excellently iced. . . . I'm sorry," he suddenly turned to me, but again somehow avoiding looking at me, "but I didn't know your address, and so I couldn't possibly have got hold of you, could I?"

He must have had something against me. Must have changed his mind after my visit last night.

All sat down; so did I. The table was a round one. Trudolyubov was on my left and Simonov on my right. Zverkov was sitting opposite with Ferfichkin next to him, between him and Trudolyubov.

"Tell me plea-ea-se are you—er—in a Government department?" Zverkov continued to be very attentive to me.

He saw how embarrassed I was and he seriously imagined that it was his duty to be nice to me and, as it were, cheer me up.

"Does he want me to throw a bottle at his head?" I thought furiously. As I was unaccustomed to these surroundings, I was getting irritated somehow unnaturally quickly.

"In the . . . office," I replied abruptly, my eyes fixed on my plate.

"Good Lord, and do-o-o you find it re-mu-nerative? Tell me, plea-ea-se, what indu-u-uced you to give up your old job?"

"What indu-u-uced me was simply that I got fed up with my old job," I answered, drawing out the words three times as much as he and scarcely able to control myself.

Ferfichkin snorted. Simonov glanced ironically at me. Trudolyubov stopped eating and began observing me curiously.

Zverkov winced, but pretended not to have noticed anything.

"We-e-e-ell, and what's your screw?"

"Which screw?"

"I mean, what's your sa-a-alary?"

"You're not by any chance cross-examining me, are you?"

However, I told him at once what my salary was. I was blushing terribly.

"Not much," Zverkov observed importantly.

"No," Ferfichkin added insolently, "hardly enough to pay for your dinners at a restaurant."

"I think it's simply beggarly," Trudolyubov said, seriously.

"And how thin you've grown, how you've changed since—er—those days," added Zverkov, no longer without venom, examining my clothes with a sort of impudent compassion.

"Stop embarrassing the poor fellow," Ferfichkin exclaimed, giggling.

"You're quite mistaken, sir," I burst out at last, "I'm not at all embarrassed. Do you hear? I'm dining here at this restaurant, sir, at my own expense, and not at other people's. Make a note of that, Mr. Ferfichkin."

"What do you mean?" Ferfichkin flew at me, turning red as a lobster and glaring furiously at me. "And who, sir, isn't dining at his own expense here? You seem to——"

"I mean what I said," I replied, feeling that I had gone too far, "and I think we'd better talk of something more intelligent."

"You're not by any chance anxious to show off your intelligence, are you?"

"I shouldn't worry about that, if I were you. It would be entirely out of place here."

"What are you talking about, my dear sir? You haven't gone out of your mind at that *le*partment of yours, have you?"

"Enough, enough, gentlemen!" Zverkov cried in a commanding voice.

"How damn silly!" Simonov muttered.

"It is damn silly," Trudolyubov said, addressing himself rudely to me alone. "Here we are, a few good friends, met to wish godspeed to a comrade, and you're trying to settle old scores! It was you who invited yourself to join us yesterday, so why are you now upsetting the friendly atmosphere of this dinner?"

"Enough, enough!" Zverkov cried again. "Drop it, gentlemen. This is hardly the time or place for a brawl. Let me rather tell you how I nearly got married the other day!"

And off he went to tell some scandalous story of how he had nearly got married a few days before. There was, by the way, not a word about the marriage. The story was all about generals, colonels, and even court chamberlains, and Zverkov, of course, played the most important part among them. It was followed by a burst of appreciative laughter, Ferfichkin's high-pitched laugh breaking into loud shrieks.

None of them paid any attention to me, and I sat there feeling crushed and humiliated.

"Good heavens, is this the sort of company for me?" I thought. "And what an ass I've made of myself in front of them! I let Ferfichkin go too far, though. The idiots think they do me an honour by letting me sit down at the same table with them. They don't seem to realize that it is I who am doing them an honour, and not they me. 'You look so thin! Your clothes!' Damn my trousers! I'm sure Zverkov noticed the stain on the knee the moment he came in. . . . But what the hell am I doing here? I'd better get up at once, this minute, take my hat, and simply go without a word. . . . Show them how much I despise them! Don't care a damn if I have to fight a duel tomorrow. The dirty rotters! Do they really think I care about the seven roubles? They might, though. . . . To hell with it! I don't care a damn about the seven roubles! I'll go this minute!"

But, of course, I stayed.

In my despair I drank glass after glass of sherry and Château Lafitte. As I was unused to drink, I got drunk very quickly, and the more drunk I got the hotter did my resentment grow. I suddenly felt like insulting them in the most insolent way and then going. Waiting for the right moment, then showing them the kind of man I was, and in that way forcing them to admit that, though I might be absurd, I was clever and—and—oh, to hell with them!

I looked impudently at them with leaden eyes. But they seemed to have entirely forgotten me. *They* were noisy, clamorous, happy. Zverkov was talking all the time. I started listening. He was talking about some ravishingly beautiful woman whom he had brought to the point of declaring her love to him at last (he was of course lying like a trooper), and how an intimate friend of his, a prince of sorts, a hussar by the name of Kolya, who owned three thousand peasants, was particularly helpful to him in this affair.

"And yet this friend of yours, the chap with the three thousand peasants, isn't here, is he? To see you off, I mean," I broke into the conversation.

For a minute there was dead silence.

"I believe you're quite tight now." Trudolyubov at last condescended to notice me, throwing a disdainful glance in my direction.

Zverkov stared at me in silence, examining me as though I were an insect. Simonov quickly began pouring out the champagne.

Trudolyubov raised his glass, all the others except myself following his example.

"To your health and a pleasant journey!" he cried to Zverkov. "To our past, gentlemen, and to our future! Hurrah!"

They drained their glasses and rushed to embrace Zverkov. I did not stir; my full glass stood untouched before me.

"Aren't you going to drink?" roared Trudolyubov, losing patience and addressing me menacingly.

"I want to make a speech too—er—a special speech and—and then I'll drink, Mr. Trudolyubov."

"Unmannerly brute!" muttered Simonov.

I drew myself up in my chair and took up my glass feverishly, preparing myself for something extraordinary, though I hardly knew myself what I was going to say.

"Silence!" cried Ferfichkin. "Now we're going to hear something really clever!"

Zverkov waited gravely, realising what was in the wind.

"Lieutenant Zverkov," I began, "I'd like you to know that I hate empty phrases, phrasemongers, and tight waists. . . . That is the first point I should like to make. The second will follow presently."

They all stirred uneasily.

"My second point: I hate smutty stories and the fellows who tell them. Especially the fellows who tell them. My third point: I love truth, frankness, and honesty," I went on almost mechanically, for I was beginning to freeze with terror myself, quite at a loss how I came to talk like this. "I love thought, Mr. Zverkov. I love true comradeship where all are equal, and not—er—yes. I love—but what the hell! Why not? I'll drink to your health too, Mr. Zverkov. Seduce the Caucasian maidens, shoot the enemies of our country and—and—to your health, Mr. Zverkov!"

Zverkov got up from his seat, bowed, and said, "Very much obliged to you, I'm sure."

He was terribly offended and even turned pale.

"Damn it all!" Trudolyubov roared, striking the table with his fist.

"Why, sir," Ferfichkin squealed, "people get a punch on the nose for that!"

"Let's kick him out!" muttered Simonov.

"Not another word, gentlemen, please!" Zverkov cried solemnly, putting a stop to the general indignation. "I thank you all, but leave it to me to show him how much value I attach to his words."

"Mr. Ferfichkin," I said in a loud voice, addressing myself importantly to Ferfichkin, "I expect you to give me full satisfaction tomorrow for your words just now!"

"You mean a duel, do you? With pleasure, sir!" Ferfichkin replied, but I must have looked so ridiculous as I challenged him, and the whole thing, in fact, must have looked so incongruous in view of my small stature, that everyone, including Ferfichkin, roared with laughter.

"Oh, leave him alone for goodness' sake," Trudolyubov said with disgust. "The fellow's tight!"

"I shall never forgive myself for having put his name down," Simonov muttered again.

"Now is the time to throw a bottle at them," I thought, picked up the bottle and—poured myself out another glass.

"... No, I'd better see it through to the end!" I went on thinking to myself. "You'd be pleased if I went away, gentlemen, wouldn't you? But I shan't go. Oh, no. Not for anything in the world. I'll go on sitting here on purpose—and drinking—to the end just to show you that I don't care a damn for you. I'll go on sitting and drinking because this is nothing but a low-class pub and, besides, I paid for everything. I'll sit and drink because I think you're a lot of nobodies, a lot of miserable, paltry nobodies. I'll sit and drink and—and sing, if I like. Yes, sing! For, damn it, I've a right to sing—er—yes."

But I did not sing. I just did my best not to look at them, assumed most independent attitudes, and waited patiently for them to speak to me *first*. But, alas, they did not speak to me. And how I longed—oh, how I longed at that moment to be reconciled to them! It struck eight, then at last nine. They moved from the table to the sofa. Zverkov made himself comfortable on the sofa, placing one foot on a little round table. They took the wine with them. Zverkov did actually stand them three bottles of champagne. He did not of course invite me to join them. They all sat round him on the sofa, listening to him almost with reverence. It was clear that they were fond of him. "But why? Why?" I asked myself. From time to time they were overcome with drunken enthusiasm and kissed each other. They talked about the Caucasus, about the nature of real passion, about cards, about cushy jobs in the service; about the income of the hussar Podkharzhevsky, whom none of them knew personally, and they were glad he had such a large income; about the marvellous grace and beauty of princess D., whom none of them had ever seen, either; and at last they finished up with the statement that Shakespeare was immortal.

I was smiling contemptuously, walking up and down at the other end of the room, directly opposite the sofa, along the wall, from the table to the stove, and back again. I did my best to show them that I could do without them, at the same time deliberately stamping on the floor, raising myself up and down on my heels. But it was all in vain. *They* paid no attention to me. I had the patience to pace the room like that right in front of them from eight till eleven o'clock, always in the same place, from the table to the stove, and back again. "Here I am, walking up and down, just as I please, and no one can stop me!" The waiter, who kept coming into the room, stopped and looked at me a few times. I was beginning to feel giddy from turning round so frequently, and there were moments when I thought I was delirious. Three times during those three hours I got wet through with perspiration and three times I got dry again. At times the thought would flash through my mind and stab my heart with fierce, intense pain that ten, twenty, forty years would pass and I would still remember after forty years with humiliation and disgust those beastly, ridiculous and horrible moments of my life. It was quite impossible for anyone to abase himself more disgracefully and do it more willingly, and I realised it fully —fully—and yet I went on pacing the room from the table to the stove, and from the stove to the table. "Oh, if only you knew the thoughts and feelings I'm capable of and how intelligent I am!" I thought again and again, addressing myself mentally to the sofa on which my enemies were sitting. But my enemies behaved as though I were not in the room at all. Once, only once, they turned to me, just when Zverkov began talking about Shakespeare and I burst out laughing contemptuously. I guffawed in so affected and disgusting a manner that they at once interrupted their conversation and watched me silently for a couple of minutes, with a grave air and without laughing, walking up and down along the wall from the table to the stove, *taking no notice of them.* But nothing came of it: they said nothing to me, and two minutes later stopped taking any notice of me again. It struck eleven.

"Gentlemen," Zverkov cried, getting up from the sofa, "now let's all go *there!*"

"Of course, of course," the others said.

I turned abruptly to Zverkov. I was so exhausted, so dead beat, that I would have gladly cut my own throat to put an end to my misery. I was feverish. My hair, wet with perspiration, stuck to my forehead and temples.

"Zverkov," I said sharply and determinedly, "I'm sorry. Ferfichkin and all of you, all of you, I hope you'll forgive me—I've offended you all!"

"Aha! Got frightened of the duel, have you?" Ferfichkin hissed venomously. I felt as though he had stabbed me to the heart.

"No, Ferfichkin, I'm not afraid of the duel. I'm ready to fight you tomorrow, if you like, but only after we've made it up. Yes, I even insist on it, and you can't possibly refuse me. I want to show you that I'm not afraid of a duel. You can fire first, and I'll fire in the air!"

"Pleased with himself, isn't he?" Simonov remarked.

"Talking through his hat, if you ask me," Trudolyubov declared.

"Get out of my way, will you?" Zverkov said contemptuously. "What are you standing in my way for? What do you want?"

They were all red in the face; their eyes were shining; they had been drinking heavily.

"I ask you for your friendship, Zverkov. I offended you, but——"

"Offended me? *You* offended *me*? Don't you realise, sir, that you couldn't possibly offend me under any circumstances?"

"We've had enough of you," Trudolyubov summed up the position. "Get out! Come on, let's go!"

"Olympia's mine, gentlemen! Agreed?" Zverkov exclaimed.

"Agreed! Agreed!" they answered him, laughing.

I stood there utterly humiliated. The whole party left the room noisily. Trudolyubov began singing some stupid song. Simonov stayed behind for a second to tip the waiters. I suddenly went up to him.

"Simonov," I said firmly and desperately, "let me have six roubles!"

He gazed at me in utter amazement, with a sort of stupefied look in his eyes. He, too, was drunk.

"But you're not coming *there* with us, are you?"

"Yes, I am!"

"I haven't any money!" he snapped out with a contemptuous grin, and left the room.

I caught him by the overcoat. It was a nightmare.

"Simonov, I saw you had money. Why do you refuse me? Am I a scoundrel? Be careful how you refuse me: if you knew, if you knew why I'm asking! Everything depends on it, my whole future, all my plans! . . ."

Simonov took out the money and almost flung it at me.

"Take it if you're so utterly without shame!" he said, pitilessly, and rushed away to overtake them.

For a moment I remained alone. The general disorder in the room, the remains of the dinner, the broken wineglass on the floor, the cigarette-stubs, the fumes of wine and the delirium in my head, the piercing anguish in my heart, and, finally, the waiter who had seen and heard everything and was now peering curiously into my eyes.

"*There!*" I cried. "Either they'll implore me for my friendship on their knees or—or I'll slap Zverkov's face!"

V

"So this is it—this is it at last—a head-on clash with real life!" I murmured, racing down the stairs. "This is quite a different proposition from your Pope leaving Rome for Brazil! This isn't your ball on Lake Como!"

"You're a swine," the thought flashed through my mind, "if you laugh at this now!"

"I don't care," I cried in answer to myself. "Now everything is lost anyway!"

There was not a trace of them to be seen in the street, but that did not worry me: I knew where they had gone.

At the front steps of the hotel stood a solitary nightsledge with its driver in a rough, peasant coat, thickly covered with wet and, as it were, warm snow which was still falling. It was steamy and close. His little shaggy, piebald horse was also covered thickly with snow and was coughing—I remember it all very well. I rushed to the wooden sledge, raised a leg to get into it, and was suddenly so stunned by the memory of how Simonov had just given me the six roubles that I fell into the sledge like a sack.

"Oh, I shall have to do a lot to get my own back," I cried. "But I shall do it or perish on the spot tonight. Come on, driver, start!"

We started. My thoughts were in a whirl.

"They won't go down on their knees to ask me to be their friend. That's an illusion, a cheap, romantic, fantastic, horrible illusion—just another ball on Lake Como. And that's why I *must* slap Zverkov's face! I simply must do it. Well, that's settled then. I'm flying now to slap his face! Hurry up, driver!"

The driver tugged at the reins.

"As soon as I go in I'll slap his face. Ought I perhaps to say a few words before slapping his face by way of introduction? No. I'll just go in and slap his face. They'll be all sitting in the large room, and he'll be on the sofa with Olympia. That blasted Olympia! She made fun of my face once and refused me. I shall drag Olympia by the hair and then drag Zverkov by the ears. No. Better by one ear. I shall take him all round the room by the ear. Quite likely they'll all start beating me and will kick me out. That's almost certain. But never mind. I'd have slapped his face first all the same. My initiative. And by the rules of honour that's everything. He would be branded for life and he couldn't wipe off the slap by any blows—no, by nothing but a duel. We will have to fight. Yes, let them beat me now. Let them, the ungrateful swine! I expect Trudolyubov will do most of the beating: he's so strong. Ferfichkin will hang on to me from the side and quite certainly by the hair—yes, quite certainly by the hair. Well, let him. Let him. That's the whole idea of my going there. The silly fools will be forced to realize at last that there's something tragic here! When they're dragging me to the door, I'll shout to them that as a matter of fact they're not worth my little finger. Come on, driver, hurry up!" I cried to the sledge-driver.

He gave a start and whipped up his horse—I shouted so fiercely.

"We shall fight at dawn, that's settled. It's all over with the department. Ferfichkin had said *le*partment instead of *de*partment at dinner. But where am I to get the pistols? Nonsense! I'll ask for an advance of salary and buy them. But the powder, the bullets? That's not my business. Let the second worry about that. But how can I get it all done by daybreak? And where am I to get a second? I have no friends. . . . Nonsense!" I cried, getting more and more carried away. "Nonsense! The first man I meet in the street is bound to be my second, as he would be bound to drag a drowning man out of the water. I must make allowances for the most improbable incidents. Why, even if I were to ask the head of my department himself tomorrow morning to be my second, he too would have to agree, if only from a feeling of chivalry, and keep the secret into the bargain! Anton Antonovich——"

The truth is that at that very moment the whole hideous absurdity of my plans became clearer and more obvious to me than to anyone else in the world. I saw clearly the other side of the medal, and yet——

"Faster, driver! Faster, you rascal! Faster!"

"Lord, sir," said the son of the soil.

A cold shiver ran suddenly down my spine.

"But wouldn't it be better—wouldn't it be a hundred times better to—to go straight home? Oh, dear God, why did I have to invite myself to this dinner yesterday? But no—that's impossible! And what about my walking up and down the room from the table to the stove for three hours? No, they—they alone will have to make amends to me for that walk! They must wipe out that dishonour! Drive on!

". . . And what if they should hand me over to the police? They won't dare! They'll be afraid of a scandal! And what if Zverkov contemptuously refused to fight a duel? That's most likely, but if that happens I'll show them—I'll go to the posting station when he is leaving tomorrow, seize him by the leg, drag his overcoat off him when he gets into the carriage. I'll hang on to his arm with my teeth. I'll bite him. 'See to what lengths a desperate man can be driven?' Let him punch me on the head and the others on the back. I'll shout to all the people around, 'Look, here's a young puppy who's going off to the Caucasus to captivate the girls there with my spit on his face!'

"Of course, after that everything will be over. The department will have vanished off the face of the earth. I shall be arrested. I shall be tried. I shall be dismissed from the Civil Service, thrown into prison, sent to Siberia, to one of the convict settlements there. Never mind. Fifteen years later, after they let me out of jail, I shall set out in search of him, in rags, a beggar, and at last I shall find him in some provincial city. He will be married and happy. He will have a grown-up daughter. I shall say, 'Look, monster, look at my hollow cheeks and my rags! I've lost everything—my career, my happiness, art, science, *the woman I loved*, and all through you. Here are the pistols. I've come to discharge my pistol and—and I forgive you!' And then I shall fire into the air, and he won't hear of me again. . . ."

I almost broke into tears, though I knew very well at that moment that the whole thing was from *Silvio* and from Lermontov's *Masquerade*. And all of a sudden I felt terribly ashamed, so ashamed that I stopped the sledge, got out of it, and stood in the snow in the middle of the road. The driver sighed and looked at me in astonishment.

"What am I to do? I can't go there, for the whole thing is absurd. But I couldn't leave things like that, either, because if I did, it would——Good Lord, how could I possibly leave it like that? And after such insults, too! No!" I cried, rushing back to the sledge. "It's ordained! It's fate! Drive on! Drive on, there!"

And in my impatience I hit the driver in the back with my fist.

"What's the matter with you? What are you hitting me for?" the poor man shouted, but he whipped up the horse so that it began kicking.

The wet snow was falling in large flakes. I unbuttoned my overcoat—I didn't mind the snow. I forgot everything, for I had finally made up my mind to slap Zverkov in the face, and I couldn't help feeling with horror that now it was going to happen *for certain* and that *nothing in the world could stop it*. Solitary street-lamps flickered gloomily in the snowy haze like torches at a funeral. The snow was drifting under my overcoat, under my coat, and under my collar where it melted. I did not button myself up: all was lost, anyway!

At last we arrived. I jumped out and, hardly knowing what I was doing, rushed up the steps and began banging at the door with my fists and feet. My legs, especially at the knees, felt terribly weak. The door was opened more quickly than I expected, as though they knew about my arrival. (Simonov, as a matter of fact, had warned them that someone else might arrive, and in this place it was necessary to give notice beforehand and, generally, to take precautions. It was one of those "fashion shops" which were long ago closed by the police. In the daytime it really was a shop, but at night those who had an introduction could go there to be entertained.) I walked rapidly through the dark shop into the familiar large room where there was only one candle burning and stopped dead, looking utterly bewildered: there was no one there.

"But where are they?" I asked someone.

But, of course, they had already gone their separate ways.

Before me was standing a person who looked at me with a stupid smirk on her face. It was the proprietress herself who knew me slightly. A moment later a door opened and another person came in.

I walked up and down the room without paying any attention to them and, I believe, I was talking to myself. It was as though I had been saved from death, and I felt it joyfully with every fibre of my being. For I should most certainly have slapped his face—oh, most certainly! But they were not there and everything—everything had vanished, everything had changed! I looked round. I was still unable to think clearly. I looked up mechanically at the girl who had just entered: I caught sight of a fresh, young, somewhat pale face, with straight dark eyebrows, and with a serious, as it were, surprised look in her eyes. I liked that at once. I should have hated her if she had been smiling. I began looking at her more intently and with a certain effort: I could not collect my thoughts even yet. There was something kind and good-humoured about her face, but also something strangely serious. I was sure that was to her disadvantage here, and that not one of those fools had noticed her. However, you could hardly have called her a beauty, although she was tall, strong, and well-built. She was dressed very simply. Something vile came over me: I went straight up to her.

I caught sight of myself accidentally in a mirror. My flustered face looked utterly revolting to me: pale, evil, mean, with dishevelled hair. "It's all right, I'm glad of it," I thought. "I'm glad that I'll seem repulsive to her. I like that. . . ."

wakes up almost reborn

VI

Somewhere behind the partition, as though under some great pressure, as though someone were strangling it, the clock began wheezing. After the unnaturally protracted wheezing there came a thinnish, disagreeable, and, somehow, unexpectedly rapid chime, as though it had suddenly taken a leap forward. It struck two. I woke up, though I hadn't been really asleep and had only lain in a state of semi-consciousness.

The small, narrow, low-ceilinged room, filled with a huge wardrobe and cluttered up with cardboard boxes, clothes, and all sorts of rags, was almost completely dark. The guttered end of a candle which was burning on the table at the other end of the room was on the point of going out, and only from time to time did it flicker faintly. In a few moments the room would be plunged in darkness.

It did not take me long to recover: everything came back to me in a flash, without the slightest effort, as though it had only been waiting for an opportunity to pounce upon me again. And even while I was fast asleep there always remained some sort of a point in my memory which I never forgot and round which my drowsy dreams revolved wearily. But the strange thing was that everything that had happened to me during the previous day seemed to me now, on awakening, to have occurred a long, long time ago, as though I had long ago shaken it all off.

My head was heavy. Something seemed to be hovering over me, provoking me, exciting and worrying me. Resentment and black despair were again surging up in me and seeking an outlet. Suddenly, close beside me, I saw two wide-open eyes observing me intently and curiously. The look in those eyes was coldly indifferent and sullen, as though it were utterly detached, and it made me feel terribly depressed.

A peevish thought stirred in my mind and seemed to pass all over my body like some vile sensation, resembling the sensation you experience when you enter a damp and stale cellar. It seemed somehow unnatural that those two eyes should have been scrutinising me only now. I remembered, too, that for two whole hours I had never said a word to this creature, and had not even thought it necessary to do so; that, too, for some reason appealed to me. Now, however, I suddenly saw clearly how absurd and hideous like a spider was the idea of vice which, without love, grossly and shamelessly begins where true love finds its consummation. We went on looking at each other like that for a long time, but she did not drop her eyes before mine, nor did she change her expression, so that in the end it made me for some reason feel creepy.

"What's your name?" I asked abruptly, to put an end to this unbearable situation.

"Lisa," she replied, almost in a whisper, but somehow without attempting to be agreeable, and turned her eyes away.

I said nothing for the next few moments.

"The weather was beastly yesterday—snow—horrible!" I said, almost as though I were speaking to myself, putting my arm disconsolately under my head and staring at the ceiling.

She made no answer. The whole thing was hideous.

"Were you born here?" I asked after a minute's silence, almost angry with her, and turning my head slightly towards her.

"No."

"Where do you come from?"

"Riga," she replied reluctantly.

"German?"

"No, I'm a Russian."

"Have you been here long?"

"Where?"

"In this house."

"A fortnight."

She spoke more and more abruptly. The candle went out. I could no longer make out her face.

"Have you any parents?"

"No—yes—I have."

"Where are they?"

"They are there—in Riga."

"Who are they?"

"Oh——"

"Oh? How do you mean? Who are they? What are they?"

"Tradespeople."

"Did you live with them all the time?"

"Yes."

"How old are you?"

"Twenty."

"Why did you leave them?"

"Oh——"

This "oh" meant leave me alone, I'm fed up. We were silent.

Goodness only knows why I did not go away. I felt more and more cheerless and disconsolate myself. The events of the previous day passed disjointedly through my mind, as though of themselves and without any effort on my part. I suddenly remembered something I had seen in the street that morning when, worried and apprehensive, I was hurrying to the office.

"I saw them carrying out a coffin yesterday and they nearly dropped it," I suddenly said aloud, without wishing to start a conversation and almost, as it were, by accident.

"A coffin?"

"Yes, in the Hay Market. They were carrying it out of a cellar."

"A cellar?"

"Well, not exactly a cellar. A basement—you know—down there, below—from a disorderly house. There was such filth everywhere—litter, bits of shell—an evil smell—oh, it was horrible."

Silence.

"It was a rotten day for a funeral," I began again, simply because I did not want to be silent.

"Why rotten?"

"Snow—slush——" I yawned.

"What difference does it make?" she said suddenly after a moment's silence.

"No, it was horrible—(I yawned again)—I expect the grave-diggers must have been swearing at getting wet by the snow. And there must have been water in the grave."

"Why should there be water in the grave?" she asked with a strange sort of curiosity, but speaking even more abruptly and harshly than before.

Something inside me suddenly began egging me on to carry on with the conversation.

"Of course there's water there. About a foot of water at the bottom. You can't dig a dry grave in Volkovo cemetery."

"Oh? Why not?"

"How do you mean? The whole place is a swamp. Marshy ground everywhere. Saw it for myself—many a time."

(I had never seen it, nor have I ever been in Volkovo cemetery. All I knew about it was from what I had heard people say.)

"Don't you mind it at all—dying, I mean?"

"But why should I die?" she replied, as though defending herself.

"You will die one day, you know, and I expect you'll die the same way as that girl whose coffin I saw yesterday morning. She too was a—a girl like you. Died of consumption."

"The slut would have died in the hospital too," she said.

("She knows all about it," I thought to myself, "and she said 'slut' and not girl.")

"She owed money to the woman who employed her," I replied, feeling more and more excited by the discussion. "She worked for her to the very end, though she was in a consumption. The cabmen were talking about it with some soldiers in the street, and they told them that. They were laughing. Promised to have a few drinks to her memory at the pub."

(Much of that was pure invention on my part.)

Silence. Profound silence. She did not even stir.

"You don't suppose it's better to die in a hospital, do you?" she asked, adding a little later, irritably, "What difference does it make? And why on earth should I die?"

"If not now, then later——"

"Later? Oh, well——"

"Don't be so sure of yourself! Now you're young, good-looking, fresh, and that's why they put such a high value on you. But after a year of this sort of life you'll be different. You'll lose your looks."

"After one year?"

"Well, after one year your price will have dropped, anyway," I went on maliciously. "You'll find yourself in some lower establishment then. In another house. In another year—in a third house, lower and lower. And in about seven years you'll get to the cellar in the Hay Market. That wouldn't be so terrible, but, you see, the trouble is that you may fall ill—a weakness in the chest—or catch a cold, or something. In this sort of life it's not so easy to shake off an illness. Once you fall ill you'll find it jolly difficult to get well again. And so you will die."

"All right, so I'll die," she replied, very spitefully, and made a quick movement.

"But aren't you sorry?"

"Sorry? For what?"

"For your life."

Silence.

"You've been engaged to be married, haven't you?"

"Why don't you mind your own business?"

"I'm sorry. I'm not trying to cross-examine you. What the hell do I care? Why are you so angry? I expect you must have all sorts of trouble. It's not my business, of course. But I can't help feeling sorry. That's all."

"Sorry for whom?"

"Sorry for you."

"Not worth it," she whispered in a hardly audible voice and stirred again.

That incensed me. Good Lord, I had been so gentle with her, and she. . . .

"Well, what do you think about it? You think you're on the right path, do you?"

"I don't think anything."

"That's what's wrong with you—you don't think. Come, get back your senses while there's still time. You're still young, you're good-looking, you might fall in love, be married, be happy——"

"Not all married women are happy, are they?" she snapped out, in her former harsh, quick, and abrupt manner.

"Why, no. Not all, of course. But it's much better than here, anyway. A hundred times better. For if you love, you can live even without happiness. Life is sweet even in sorrow. It's good to be alive, however hard life is. But what have you got here? Nothing but foulness. Phew!"

I turned away in disgust. I was no longer reasoning coldly. I was myself beginning to react emotionally to my words and getting worked up. I was already longing to expound my own favourite *little* notions which I had nursed so lovingly in my funk-hole. Suddenly something flared up in me, a sort of aim had *appeared*.

"Don't pay any attention to me," I said. "I mean, that I am here. I'm not an example for you. I'm probably much worse than you. Anyway, I was drunk when I came here," I hastened, however, to justify myself. "Besides, a man is no example for a woman. It's different. Though I may be defiling and degrading myself, I'm not anyone's slave: now I'm here, but I shall be gone soon and you won't see me again. I can shake it all off and be a different man. But you—why, you're a slave from the very start. Yes, a slave! You give away everything. All your freedom. And even if one day you should want to break your chains, you won't be able to: you'll only get yourself more and more entangled in them. That's the kind of damnable chain it is! I know it. And I'm not mentioning anything else, for I don't suppose you'll understand it. Tell me one thing, though. Do you owe money to the woman who employs you? You do, don't you? Ah, there you are!" I added, though she did not reply, but merely listened in silence, with all her being. "So that's your chain. You'll never be able to pay off your debt. They'll see to that. Why, it's the same as selling your soul to the devil! And, besides, perhaps for all you know I'm every bit as wretched as you are and wallow in filth on purpose—because I, too, am sick at heart. People take to drink because they are unhappy, don't they? Well, I, too, am here because I am unhappy. Now, tell me what is there so good about all this? Here you and I were making love to one another—a few hours ago—and we never said a word to each other all the time, and it was only afterwards that you began staring at me like a wild thing. And I at you. Is that how people love one another? Is that how one human being should make love to another? It's disgusting, that's what it is!"

"Yes!" she agreed with me, sharply and promptly.

The promptness with which she had uttered that "yes" even surprised me. So the same thought must have occurred to her too when she was looking so intently at me. So she, too, was capable of the same thoughts. "Damn it, this is interesting—this means that we are *akin* to one another," I thought, almost rubbing my hands with glee. And how indeed should I not be able to cope with a young creature like that?

What appealed to me most was the sporting side of it.

She turned her head closer to me—so it seemed to me in the dark—propping herself up on her arm. Perhaps she was examining me. I was so sorry I could not see her eyes. I heard her deep breathing.

"Why did you come here?" I began, already with a certain note of authority in my voice.

"Oh——"

"But it's nice to be living in your father's house, isn't it? Warm, free—your own home."

"But what if it's much worse than it is here?"

"I must find the right tone," the thought flashed through my mind. "I shan't get far by being sentimental with her, I'm afraid."

However, it was only a momentary thought. She most certainly did interest me. Besides, I was feeling rather exhausted and irritable, and guile accommodates itself so easily to true feeling.

"I don't doubt it for a moment," I hastened to reply. "Everything's possible. You see, I'm sure someone must have wronged you and it's *their* fault rather than yours. Mind, I don't know anythink of your story, but it's quite clear to me that a girl like you wouldn't have come here of her own inclination, would she?"

"What kind of girl am I?" she murmured in a hardly audible whisper, but I heard it.

Damn it all, I was flattering her! That was horrible. But perhaps it was not. Perhaps it was all right. . . . She was silent.

"Look here, Lisa, I'll tell you about myself. If I had had a home when I was a child, I should not be what I am now. I often think of it. For however bad life in a family can be your father and your mother are not your enemies, are they? They are not strangers, are they? Though perhaps only once a year, they will still show their love for you. And however bad it may be, you know you are at home. But I grew up without a home. That's why I suppose I am what I am— a man without feeling. . . ."

Again I waited for some response.

"I don't suppose she understands what I am talking about, after all," I thought. "Besides, it's ridiculous—all this moralising!"

"If I were a father and had a daughter of my own, I think I'd love my daughter more than my sons—I would indeed!" I began indirectly as though I never intended to draw her out at all. I must confess, I blushed.

"But why's that?" she asked.

Oh, so she was listening!

"Just—well, I don't really know, Lisa. You see, I once knew a father who was very strict, a very stern man he was, but he used to go down on his knees to his daughter, kiss her hands and feet, never grew tired of looking at her. Yes, indeed. She would spend the evening dancing at some party, and he'd stand for five hours in the same place without taking his eyes off her. He was quite mad about her. I can understand that. At night she'd get tired and fall asleep, and he's go and kiss her in her sleep and make the sign of the cross over her. He would go about in a dirty old coat, he was a miser to everyone else, but on her he'd lavish everything he had. He'd buy her expensive presents and be overjoyed if she were pleased with them. Fathers always love their daughters more than mothers do. Many a girl finds life at home very pleasant indeed. I don't think I'd ever let my daughter marry!"

"But why ever not?" she asked with a faint smile.

"I'd be jealous. Indeed I would. I mean I'd hate the thought of her kissing someone else. Loving a stranger more than her father. Even the thought of it is painful to me. Of course, it's all nonsense. Of course, every father would come to his senses in the end. But I'm afraid I'd worry myself to death before I'd let her marry. I'd certainly find fault with all the men who proposed to her. But in the end I daresay I should let her marry the man she herself loved. For the man whom his daughter loves always seems to be the worst to the father. That's how it is. There's a lot of trouble in families because of that."

"Some parents are glad to sell their daughters, let alone marry them honourably," she said suddenly.

Oh, so that's what it was!

"That, Lisa, only happens in those infamous families where there is neither God nor love," I interjected warmly. "For where there's no love, there's no decency, either. It's true there are such families, but I'm not speaking of them. You can't have known any kindness in your family, if you talk like that. Indeed, you must be very unlucky. Yes, I expect this sort of thing mostly happens because of poverty."

"But is it any better in rich families? Honest people live happily even if they are poor."

"Well, yes, I suppose so. And come to think of it, Lisa, a man only remembers his misfortunes. He never remembers his good fortune. If he took account of his good fortune as well, he'd have realised that there's a lot of that too for his share. But what if all goes well with the family? If with the blessing of God your husband is a good man, loves you, cherishes you, never leaves you for a moment? Oh, such a family is happy, indeed! Even if things don't turn out so well sometimes, it is still all right. For where is there no sorrow? If you ever get married, *you'll find it out for yourself.* Then again if you take the first years of your marriage to a man you love—oh, what happiness, what happiness there is in it sometimes! Why, it's a common enough experience. At first even your quarrels with your husband end happily. There are many women who the more they love their husbands, the more ready they are to quarrel with them. I tell you I knew such a woman myself. 'You see,' she used to say, 'I love you very much, and it's just because I love you so much that I'm tormenting you, and you ought to realise that!' Do you know that one can torment a person just because one loves him? Women do it mostly. They say to themselves, 'But I shall love him so dearly, I shall cherish him so much afterwards that it doesn't matter if I torment him a little now.' And everyone in the house is happy looking at you, everything's so nice, so jolly, so peaceful, and so honest. . . . Other women, of course, are jealous. If her husband happens to go off somewhere (I knew a woman who was like that), she won't be happy till she runs out of the house at night and finds out on the quiet where he is, whether he is in that house or with that woman. That's bad. That's very bad. And she knows herself it is wrong. Her heart fails her and she suffers agonies, but, you see, she loves him: it's all through love. And how nice it is to make it up after a quarrel, to admit that she was wrong, or to forgive him! And how happy they are suddenly. So happy that it seems as though they had met for the first time, as though they had only just got married, as though they had fallen in love for the first time. And no one, no one ought to know what passes between man and wife, if they love one another. And however much they quarrel, they ought not to call in their own mother to adjudicate between them, and to tell tales of one another. They are their own judges. Love is a mystery that God alone only comprehends and should be hidden from all eyes whatever happens. If that is done, it is more holy, and better. They are more likely to respect one another, and a lot depends on their respect for one another. And if once there has been love, if at first they married for love, there is no reason why their love should pass away. Surely, they can keep it! It hardly ever happens that it cannot be kept. Well, and if the husband is a good and honest man, why should love pass away? It is true they will not love one another as they did when they were married, but afterwards their love will be better still, for then they will be united in soul as well as in body, they will manage their affairs in common, there will be no secrets between them—the important thing is to love and have courage. In such circumstances even hard work is a joy; even if you have to go hungry sometimes for the sake of your children, it is a joy. For they will love you for it afterwards; for you are merely laying up treasures for yourself: as the children grow up, you feel that you are an example for them, that you are their support, that even when you die your thoughts and feelings will live with them, for they have received them from you, for they are like you in everything. It is therefore a duty, a great duty. Indeed, the father and the mother cannot help drawing closer together. People say children are a great trouble. But who says it? It is the greatest happiness people can have on earth! Are you fond of little children, Lisa? I am very fond of them. Just imagine a rosy little baby boy sucking at your breast—what husband's heart is not touched at the sight of his wife nursing his child? Oh, such a plump and rosy baby! He sprawls, he snuggles up to you, his little hands are so pink and chubby, his nails are so clean and tiny—so tiny that it makes you laugh to look at them, and his eyes gaze at you as if he understands everything. And while he sucks he pulls at your breast with his sweet little hand—plays. If his father comes near, he tears himself away from the breast, flings himself back, looks at his father and laughs as if goodness only knows how funny it is—and then he begins sucking greedily again. Or again, when his teeth are beginning to come through he will just bite his mother's breast, looking slyly at her with his eyes—'See? I'm biting you!' Isn't everything here happiness when the three of them—husband, wife, and child—are together? One can forgive a great deal for the sake of these moments. Yes, Lisa, one has to learn to live first before blaming others."

"It is with pictures, with pictures like these, that you will beguile her," I thought to myself, though, goodness knows, I spoke with real feeling, and suddenly blushed. "And what if she should suddenly burst out laughing? What a priceless ass I'd look then!" This thought made me furious. Towards the end of my speech I really grew excited, and now my vanity was somewhat hurt. I almost felt like nudging her.

"What are you——" she began suddenly and stopped.

But I understood everything: there was quite a different note in her trembling voice, something that was no longer harsh and crude and unyielding as a short while ago, but something soft and shy, so that I suddenly felt somehow ashamed of her myself. I felt guilty.

"What?" I asked with curiosity.

"Why, you——"

"What?"

"Why, you—you're speaking as though you were reading from a book," she said, and something that sounded like irony could suddenly be heard in her voice.

I resented that remark very deeply. It was not what I was expecting.

I did not realise that by her irony she was deliberately concealing her own feelings, that this was the usual last stratagem of people with pure and chaste hearts against those who impudently and unceremoniously attempt to pry into the inmost recesses of their minds, and that, out of pride, such people do not give in till the very last moment, that they are afraid to show their feelings before you. I should have guessed that from the timidity with which after several tries she approached her ironic remark, and from the shy way in which she made it at last. But I did not guess, and a feeling of vicious spite took possession of me.

"You wait!" I thought.

VII

"Good Lord, Lisa, what sort of a book am I supposed to be reading from when I, who cannot possibly have any interest in what happens to you, feel so sick myself. But as a matter of fact I'm not indifferent, either. All that has now awakened in my heart——Surely, surely, you yourself must be sick to death of being here. Or does habit really mean so much? Hang it all, habit can apparently make anything of a man! Do you really seriously believe that you will never grow old, that you will always be good-looking, and that they will keep you here for ever and ever? To say nothing of the vileness of your present way of life. However, let me tell you this about this business here, about your present way of life. Though you are now young, attractive, pretty, sensitive, warm-hearted, I—well, you know, the moment I woke up a few minutes ago, I couldn't help feeling disgusted at being with you here! It is only when you're drunk that you come to a place like this. But if you were anywhere else, if you lived as all good, decent people live, I should not only have taken a fancy to you, but fallen head over ears in love with you. I'd have been glad if you'd only looked at me, let alone spoken to me. I'd have hung round your door. I'd have gone down on my knees before you. I'd have been happy if you'd have consented to marry me, and deemed it an honour, too. I shouldn't have dared to harbour a single indecent thought about you. But here I know that I have only to whistle and, whether you like it or not, you'll have to come with me, and that it is not I who have to consult your wishes, but you mine. Even if the meanest peasant hires himself out as a labourer, he does not make a slave of himself entirely, and, besides, he knows that after a certain time he will be his own master again. But when can you say as much for yourself? Just think what you are giving up here. What is it you're enslaving? Why, it is your soul, your soul over which you have no power, together with your body! You're giving your love to every drunkard to mock at! Love? Why, that's everything, that's a precious jewel, a girl's dearest treasure—that's what love is! To win this love, a man would be ready to give his soul, to face death itself! And how much is your love worth now? You can be all bought, all of you! And why should anyone try to win your love when he can get everything without love? Why, there is no greater insult for a girl than that. Don't you see it? I am told that to please you, poor fools, they let you have lovers here. But good Lord, what is it but just insulting you? What is it but sheer deceit? Why, they are just laughing at you, and you believe them! Or do you really believe that lover of yours loves you? I don't believe it. How can he love you when he knows that you can be called away from him any moment? He'd be nothing but a pimp after that! And could such a man have an atom of respect for you? What have you in common with him? He's just laughing at you, and robbing you into the bargain—that's what his love amounts to. You're lucky if he doesn't beat you. Perhaps he does, too. Ask him, if you have such a lover, whether he will marry you. Why, he'll laugh in your face, if, that is, he doesn't spit in it or give you a beating, and he himself is probably not worth twopence. And why have you ruined your life here? For what? For the coffee they give you to drink? For the good meals? Have you ever thought why they feed you so well here? Another woman, an honest woman, could not swallow such food, for she would know why she was being fed so well. You are in debt here—well, take my word for it, you'll never be able to repay your debt, you'll remain 'n debt to the very end, till the visitors here begin to scorn you. And all that wi'l be much sooner than you think. You need not count on your good looks. They don't last very long here, you know. And then you'll be kicked out. And that's not all by any means: long before you're kicked out they'll start finding fault with you, reproaching you, reviling you, as though you had not sacrificed your health for them, ruined your youth and your soul for them, without getting anything in return, but as though you had ruined them, robbed them, beggared them. And don't expect any of the other girls to take your part: they, those friends of yours, will turn against you, too, for the sake of currying favour with your employer, for you are all slaves here, you've all lost all conscience and pity long ago. They have sunk too low, and there's nothing in the world filthier, more odious, and more insulting than their abuse. And you'll leave everything here, everything you possess, without any hope of ever getting it back—your health, your beauty, and your hopes, and at twenty-two you'll look like a woman of thirty-five, and you'll be lucky if you're not ill—pray God for that. I shouldn't be at all surprised if you were not thinking now that you're having a lovely time—no work, just a life of pleasure! But let me tell you that there is no work in the world harder or more oppressive—and there never has been. It is a wonder you haven't long ago cried your heart out. And when they turn you out you won't dare to say a word, not even as much as a syllable, and you'll go away as though it is you who were to blame. You'll pass on to another place, then to a third, then again to some other place, till at last you'll find yourself in the Hay Market. And there they'll start beating you as a matter of course. It's a lovely custom they have there. A visitor there does not know how to be kind without first giving you a good thrashing. You don't believe it's so horrible there? Well, go and have a look for yourself some time and you'll perhaps see with your own eyes. Once, on New Year's Eve, I saw a girl there. She had been turned out by her friends as a joke, to cool off a little in the frost, because she had been howling too much, and they locked the door behind her. At nine o'clock in the morning she was already dead drunk, dishevelled, half naked, beaten black and blue. Her face was made up, but she had two black eyes; she was bleeding from the nose and mouth; she sat down on the stone steps, holding some salt fish in her hands; she was shrieking at the top of her voice bewailing her 'bad luck,' and striking the salt fish against the steps, while a crowd of cabmen and drunken soldiers were standing round and making fun of her. You don't believe that you, too, will be like her one day? Well, I shouldn't like to believe it, either, but how do you know? Perhaps ten or eight years ago the same girl, the girl with the salt fish, arrived here as fresh as a child, innocent and pure, knowing no evil and blushing at every word. Perhaps she was like you, proud, quick to take offence, quite unlike the others, looking like a queen, and quite certain that she would make the man who fell in love with her and whom she loved the happiest man in the world. But you see how it all ended, don't you? And what if at the very moment when she was striking the grimy steps with that fish, dirty and dishevelled, what if at that moment she recalled all the innocent years she had once spent at her father's house, when she used to go to school and the son of their neighbours waited for her on the way and assured her that he would love her as long as he lived, that he would devote his whole future to her, and when they vowed to love one another for ever and be married as soon as they grew up? No, Lisa, you'd be lucky, you'd be very lucky, if you were to die soon, very soon, of consumption, in some corner, in some cellar like that woman I told you of. In a hospital, you say? You'll be fortunate if they take you to a hospital, for, you see, you may still be wanted by your employer. Consumption is a queer sort of illness. It is not like a fever. A consumptive goes on hoping to the last minute. To the very last he goes on saying that there is nothing the matter with him, that he is not ill—deceiving himself. And your employers are only too pleased. Don't worry, it is so. I assure you. You've sold your soul and you owe money into the bargain, so you daren't say a word. But when you are dying, all will abandon you, all will turn away from you, for what more can they get out of you? If anything, they'll reproach you for taking up room without paying for it, for not dying quickly enough. You beg and beg for a drink of water, and when at last they bring it to you they'll abuse you at the same time. 'When are you going to die, you dirty baggage, you? You don't let us sleep, moaning all the time, and the visitors don't like it.' That's true. I've heard such things said myself. And when you are really dying, they'll drag you to the most foul-smelling corner of the cellar, in the damp and the darkness, and what will your thoughts be as you are lying by yourself? When you die, strangers will lay you out, hurriedly, impatiently, grumbling. No one will bless you. No one will sigh for you. Get you quickly out of the way—that's all they'll be concerned about. They'll buy a cheap coffin, take you to the cemetery as they took that poor girl yesterday, and then go to a pub to talk about you. Your grave will be full of slush and dirt and wet snow—they won't put themselves out for you—not they! 'Let her down, boy! Lord, just her "bad luck," I suppose. Gone with her legs up here too, the slut! Shorten the ropes, you young rascal!' 'It's all right!' 'All right, is it? Can't you see she's lying on her side? She's been a human being herself once, ain't she? Oh, all right, fill it up!' And they won't be wasting much time in abusing each other over you, either. They will fill in your grave with wet blue clay and go off to a pub. . . . That will be the end of your memory on earth. Other women have children to visit their graves, fathers, husbands, but there will be neither tears, nor sighs, nor any remembrance for you. No one, no one in the world will ever come to you. Your name will vanish from the face of the earth as though you had never been born! Dirt and mud, dirt and mud, though you knock at your coffin lid at night when the dead arise as hard as you please, crying, 'Let me live in the world, good people! I lived, but I knew no real life. I spent my life as a doormat for people to wipe their dirty boots on. My life has been drunk away at a pub in the Hay Market. Let me live in the world again, good people!' "

I worked myself up into so pathetic a state that I felt a lump rising to my throat and—all of a sudden I stopped, raised myself in dismay, and, bending over apprehensively, began to listen with a violently beating heart. I had good reason to feel embarrassed.

I had felt for a long while that I had cut her to the quick and wrung her heart, and the more I became convinced of it, the more eager I was to finish what I had set out to do as expeditiously and as thoroughly as possible. It was the sport of it, the sport of it, that carried me away. However, it was not only the sport of it.

I knew I was speaking in a stiff, affected, even bookish manner, but as a matter of fact I could not speak except "as though I was reading from a book." But that did not worry me, for I knew, I had a feeling that I would be understood, that this very bookishness would assist rather than hinder matters. But now that I had succeeded in making an impression, I got frightened. No, never, never had I witnessed such despair! She lay prone on the bed, with her face buried in the pillow, which she clasped tightly with both her hands. Her bosom was heaving spasmodically. Her young body was writhing as though in convulsions. The sobs which she tried to suppress seemed to deprive her of breath and rend her bosom, and suddenly they broke out into loud moans and cries. It was then that she clung more tightly to the pillow. She did not want anyone here, not a soul, to know of her agonies and tears. She bit the pillow, she bit her arm till it bled (I saw it afterwards), or clutching at her dishevelled hair with her fingers, went rigid with that superhuman effort, holding her breath and clenching her teeth. I began saying something to her, asking her to calm herself, but I felt that I dared not go on, and all at once, shivering as though in a fever and almost in terror, I began groping for my clothes, intending to dress myself quickly and go. It was dark. However much I tried, I could not finish dressing quickly. Suddenly my hand touched a box of matches and a candle-stick with a new unused candle. The moment the candle lit up the room, Lisa jumped up, sat up on the bed, and with a strangely contorted face and a half-crazy smile looked at me with an almost vacant expression. I sat down beside her and took her hands. She recollected herself, flung herself at me as though wishing to embrace me, but did not dare and slowly bowed her head before me.

"Lisa, my dear, I'm sorry, I—I shouldn't have——" I began, but she squeezed my hands in her fingers with such force that I realised that I was saying the wrong thing and stopped.

"Here's my address, Lisa. Come and see me."

"I will," she whispered firmly, but still not daring to raise her head.

"I'm going now. Goodbye. You will come, won't you?"

I got up. She too got up, and suddenly blushed crimson, gave a shudder, seized a shawl from a chair, threw it over her shoulders and muffled herself up to the chin. Having done that, she again smiled a rather sickly smile, blushed and looked at me strangely. I was deeply sorry for her. I was longing to go, to sink through the floor.

"Wait a minute," she said suddenly in the entrance hall, at the very door, and stopped me by catching hold of my overcoat.

She quickly put down the candle and ran off. She must have remembered something or wanted to show me something. As she was running away, she again blushed all over, her eyes were shining, a smile flitted over her lips—what could it mean? I waited against my will. She came back in a minute and looked at me as though asking forgiveness for something. It was altogether a different face, altogether a different look from a few hours ago—sullen, mistrustful, and obstinate. Now her eyes were soft and beseeching, and at the same time trustful, tender, and shy. So do children look at people they are very fond of and from whom they expect some favour. She had light-brown eyes, beautiful and full of life, eyes which could express love as well as sullen hatred.

Without a word of explanation, as though I, like a sort of higher being, ought to know everything without explanations, she held out a piece of paper to me. At that moment her whole face was radiant with the most naïve, most childlike, triumph. I unfolded it. It was a letter to her from some medical student or someone of the sort—a highly flamboyant and flowery, but also extremely respectful declaration of love. I cannot recall its exact words now, but I remember very well that through that grandiloquent style there peered a genuine feeling which cannot be faked. When I had finished reading the letter, I met her fervent, curious, and childishly impatient gaze fixed on me. Her eyes were glued to my face, and she was waiting with impatience to hear what I had to say. In a few words, hurriedly, but, somehow, joyfully and as though proudly, she explained to me that she had been to a dance in a private house, a family of "very, very nice people, who *knew nothing*, nothing at all," for she had only been here a short time and she did not really intend to stay— no, she had made up her mind not to stay, and she was indeed quite certainly going to leave as soon as she paid her debt. . . . Well, anyway, at that party she had met a student who had danced the whole evening with her. He had talked to her, and it appeared that he had known her as a child in Riga when they used to play together, but that was a long time ago. And he knew her parents too, but he knew nothing, nothing whatever about *this*, and he had not the slightest suspicion even! And the day after the dance (three days ago) he had sent her that letter through a girl friend of hers with whom she had gone to the dance and—and—"well, that is all."

She lowered her shining eyes somewhat shyly as she finished telling me her story.

Poor child, she was keeping the letter of that student as a treasure and ran to fetch that one treasure of hers not wishing that I should go away without knowing that she, too, was loved sincerely and honestly, that people addressed her, too, with respect. That letter, I knew, would most certainly remain in her box without leading to anything. But that did not matter. I was sure she would keep it all her life, guarding it as a priceless treasure, as her pride and justification, and now at such a moment she had remembered it and brought it to boast about naïvely to me, to vindicate herself in my eyes, so that I should see it and commend her for it. I said nothing, pressed her hand, and went out. I longed to get away. . . .

I walked home all the way, though the wet snow kept falling all the time in large flakes. I felt dead tired, depressed, bewildered. But the truth was already blazing through my bewilderment. The disgusting truth!

VIII

However, it took me some time before I acknowledged that truth to myself. Waking up next morning after a few hours of heavy, leaden sleep and immediately remembering all that had occurred the previous day, I was utterly amazed at my *sentimentality* with Lisa the night before, and all "those horrors and commiserations of last night."

"I must have been suffering from an attack of nerves just like a silly old woman," I decided. "Lord, what a fool I was! And why did I give her my address? What if she should come? However, what does it matter if she does come? Let her come, I don't mind. . . ."

But *obviously* that was not the chief and most important thing. What I had to do now, and that quickly, too, was to save my reputation in the eyes of Zverkov and Simonov. That was the chief thing. And so preoccupied was I with the other affair that I forgot all about Lisa that morning.

First of all I had immediately to return the money I had borrowed from Simonov the day before. I decided on a desperate step: to borrow fifteen roubles from Anton Antonovich. As it happened, he was in an excellent mood that morning and lent me the money as soon as I asked him for it. That made me feel so happy that, as I signed the promissory note, I told him *casually* with a sort of devil-may-care air that "we had a very gay party last night at the Hôtel de Paris; seeing off a friend, I suppose I might almost say a friend of my childhood. An awful rake, you know, terribly spoilt and, well, of course, of a good family, a man of considerable means, a brilliant career, witty, charming, has affairs with society women, you understand. Drank an additional 'half-dozen' and——And it went off all right," I said it all very glibly, confidently, and complacently.

As soon as I got home I wrote to Simonov.

To this day, as I recall that letter of mine to Simonov, I am lost in admiration at the gentlemanly, good-humoured, frank tone of it. Very dexterously, with perfect grace, and, above all, without any superfluous words, I candidly acknowledged myself to have been completely in the wrong. My only excuse, "if there can possibly be an excuse for the way I behaved," was that, being utterly unaccustomed to drink, I got drunk after the first glass which (I lied) I had drunk before they arrived, while I was waiting for them at the Hôtel de Paris between five and six o'clock. I apologised principally to Simonov, and I asked him to convey my explanations to all the others, especially to Zverkov, whom "I remember as though in a dream" I seem to have insulted. I added that I would have apologised personally to every one of them myself, but I had a terrible headache and—to be quite frank—was too ashamed to face them. I was particularly pleased with the "certain lightness," almost off-handedness (by no means discourteous, by the way) which was so unexpectedly reflected in my style and gave them to understand at once better than any arguments that I took a very detached view of "all that ghastly business of last night"; that I was not at all so crushed as you, gentlemen, probably imagine, but on the contrary look upon it just as any self-respecting gentleman ought to look on it. "A young man," as it were, "can hardly be blamed for every indiscretion he commits."

"Damned if there isn't a certain marquis-like playfulness about it!" I thought admiringly as I read over my letter. "And it's all because I'm such a well-educated person! Others in my place wouldn't have known how to extricate themselves, but I've wriggled out of it and I'm as bright and merry as ever, and all because I am 'an educated man, a modern intellectual.' "

And really the whole ghastly business had most probably been due to the wine. Well, perhaps not to the wine. As a matter of fact, I didn't have any drinks between five and six when I was waiting for them. I had lied to Simonov. I had told him the most shameless lie, but I'm not in the least sorry for it even now. . . .

Anyway, to hell with it! The main thing is that I've got out of it.

I put six roubles in the letter, sealed it, and asked Apollon to take it to Simonov. When he learnt that there was money in the letter, Apollon became more respectful and agreed to take it to Simonov. Towards evening I went out for a walk. My head was still aching from the night before and I was feeling sick. But the further the evening wore on and the darker it grew, the more my impressions and—after them—my thoughts changed and grew confused. Inside me, deep down in my heart and conscience, something kept stirring, would not die, and manifested itself in a feeling of poignant anguish. Mostly I walked aimlessly along the most crowded business streets, along Meshchanskaya, Sadovaya, and Yussupov Park. I always particularly liked taking a stroll along these streets at dusk just when crowds of workers and tradespeople with cross and worried faces were going home from their daily work. What I liked about it was just that common bustle, the every-day, prosaic nature of it all. That evening all that rush and bustle in the streets irritated me more than ever. I could not cope with my own feelings. I could not find an explanation for them. Something was rising up, rising up incessantly in my soul, painfully, something that wouldn't quieten down. I returned home feeling greatly upset. It was as though I had a crime on my conscience.

The thought that Lisa might come worried me constantly. I found it very strange that of all the memories of the day before, the memory of her seemed to torment me in particular, and, as it were, apart from the rest. Everything else I had been successful in dismissing from my mind completely by the evening; I just dismissed it all and was still perfectly satisfied with my letter to Simonov. But so far as Lisa was concerned, I somehow did not feel satisfied. As if it were the thought of Lisa alone that made me so unhappy. "What if she comes?" I kept thinking all the time. "Well, what if she does? Let her. H'm ... For one thing, I don't want her to see how I live. Last night I seemed—er— a hero to her and—er—now—h'm! It is certainly a nuisance that I let myself go to pieces like that. Everything in my room is so poor and shabby. And how could I have gone out to dinner in such clothes last night! And that American cloth sofa of mine with the stuffing sticking out of it! And my dressing gown in which I can't even wrap myself decently! Rags and tatters. . . . And she will see it all, and she will see Apollon, too. The swine will probably insult her. He'll be rude to her just to be rude to me. And I, of course, will get into a funk as usual, start striking attitudes before her, drape myself in the skirts of my dressing gown, start smiling, start telling lies. Ugh! Sickening! And it isn't this that's really so sickening. There's something more important, more horrible, more contemptible! Yes, more contemptible! And again to assume that dishonest, lying mask—again, again!"

Having come thus far in my thoughts, I couldn't help flaring up.

"Why dishonest? In what way is it dishonest? I was speaking sincerely last night. I remember there was some genuine feeling in me, too. I wanted to awaken honourable feelings in her. . . . If she cried a little, it was all to the good. It's sure to have a highly beneficent effect on her. . . ."

All that evening, even when I had returned home, even after nine o'clock when I knew that Lisa could not possibly come, I still could not get her out of my mind, and, above all, I remembered her in one and the same position. Yes, one moment of that night's incident seemed to stand out in my memory with particular clarity, namely, when I struck a match and saw her pale, contorted face and that tortured look in her eyes. What a pitiful, what an unnatural, what a twisted smile she had at that moment! But I did not know then that fifteen years later I should still see Lisa in my mind's eye with the same pitiful, inappropriate smile which was on her face at that moment.

Next day I was once more quite ready to dismiss it all as nonsense, as a result of overstrained nerves, and, above all, as—an *exaggeration*. I was always aware of that weakness of mine, and sometimes I was very much afraid of it. "I always exaggerate—that's my trouble," I used to remind myself almost every hour. But still—"still, Lisa will probably show up all the same," that was the constant refrain of my thoughts at the time. I was so worried about it that I sometimes flew into a blind rage: "She'll come! She's quite certain to come!" I stormed, pacing my room. "If not today, then tomorrow, but come she will! She'll seek me out! For such is the damned romanticism of all those *pure hearts!* Oh, the loathsomeness, oh, the stupidity, oh, the insensibility of these blasted 'sentimental souls!' How could she fail to understand? Why, anyone would have seen through it!"

But here I would stop, overcome with embarrassment.

And how few, how few words were necessary, I thought in passing, how few idyllic descriptions were necessary (and those, too, affected, bookish, insincere) to shape a whole human life at once according to my will! There's innocence for you! Virgin soil!

Sometimes I wondered whether I ought not to go and see her, "tell her everything," and ask her not to come to me. But there, at that thought, I'd fly into such a rage that it seemed to me that I should have crushed that "damned" Lisa if she had happened to be near me at the time. I should have humiliated her. I should have heaped mortal insults upon her, driven her out, beaten her!

However, one day passed, and another, and a third, and she did not come, and I was beginning to feel easier in my mind. I felt particularly cheerful and let my fancy run riot after nine o'clock, and at times I even began indulging in rather sweet daydreams. For instance, "I'm saving Lisa just because she's coming regularly to see me and I'm talking to her. . . . I'm educating her, enlarging her mind. At last I notice that she is in love with me. I pretend not to understand (I don't know why I am pretending, though, just for the sheer beauty of it, I suppose). In the end, all embarrassed, beautiful, trembling and sobbing, she flings herself at my feet and says that I have saved her and that she loves me more than anything in the world. I look surprised, but—'Lisa,' I say, 'surely you don't imagine I haven't noticed that you love me, do you? I saw everything, I guessed everything, but I did not dare lay claim to your heart first because I knew you were under my influence and was afraid that, out of gratitude, you would deliberately force yourself to respond to my love, that you would rouse a feeling in your heart which perhaps did not really exist, and I did not want this because it—it would be sheer despotism on my part—it would have been indelicate. . . . (Well, in short, here I got myself entangled in a sort of European, George-Sandian, inexpressibly noble subtleties.) But now, now you're mine, you are my creation, you are pure and beautiful, you are—my beautiful wife!"

> And my house, fearlessly and freely,
> As mistress you can enter now!

And then we live happily ever after, go abroad, etc., etc. In short, I got so thoroughly fed up with myself in the end that I finished up by sticking out my tongue at myself.

"Besides, they won't let her go, the 'tart!'" I thought to myself. "I don't think they are allowed to go out very much and certainly not in the evening (for some reason I took it into my head that she would come in the evening and exactly at seven o'clock). However, she told me herself that she was not entirely at their beck and call and that she was given special privileges, and that means—h'm! Damn it, she will come! She will most certainly turn up!"

Fortunately, Apollon took my mind off Lisa by his churlish behaviour. I lost my patience with him completely! He was the bane of my life, the punishment Providence had imposed upon me. For years on end we had been continually squabbling, and I hated him. Lord, how I hated him! I don't think I ever hated anyone as much as him, particularly at certain times. He was an elderly, pompous man, who did some tailoring in his spare time. For some unknown reason he despised me beyond measure, and looked down upon me in a way that was simply maddening. He looked down upon everyone, as a matter of fact. Take one look at that fair, smoothly brushed head, at the tuft of hair which he fluffed out over his forehead and smeared with lenten oil, at that gravely pursed mouth, always compressed into the shape of the letter V—and you felt that you were in the presence of a creature who was never in doubt. He was pedantic to a degree, the greatest pedant, in fact, I ever met in my life, and, in addition, possessed of a vanity that was worthy only of Alexander the Great. He was in love with every button on his coat, with every hair on his head. Yes, in love, most decidedly in love with them! And he looked it. His attitude towards me was utterly despotic. He hardly ever spoke to me, and if occasionally he did deign to look at me, his look was so hard, so majestically self-confident, and invariably so contemptuous, that it alone was sometimes sufficient to drive me into a fury. He carried out his duties with an air of conferring the greatest favour upon me. As a matter of fact, he hardly ever did anything for me, and he did not even consider himself bound to do anything for me. There could be no doubt whatever that he looked upon me as the greatest fool on earth, and if he graciously permitted me to "live with him," it was only because he could get his wages from me every month. He did not mind "doing nothing" for me for seven roubles a month. I'm certain many of my sins will be forgiven me for what I suffered from him. At times I hated him so bitterly that I was almost thrown into a fit when I heard him walking about. But what I loathed most of all was his lisp. His tongue must have been a little too long, or something of the sort, and because of that he always lisped and minced his words, and, I believe, he was terribly proud of it, imagining that it added to his dignity. He spoke in a slow, measured voice, with his hands behind his back and his eyes fixed on the ground. He infuriated me particularly when he began reading the psalter in his room behind the partition. I have fought many battles over that reading. But he was terribly fond of reading aloud of an evening, in a slow, even, sing-song voice, as though he were chanting psalms for the dead. It is interesting that he is doing just that at present: he hires himself out to read psalms over the dead and exterminates rats and manufactures a boot polish as well. But at that time I could not get rid of him, as though he formed one chemical substance with me. Besides, he would never have consented to leave me for anything in the world. I could not afford to live in furnished rooms. I lived in an unfurnished self-contained flat—it was my shell, the case into which I hid from humanity, and for some confounded reason Apollon seemed to be an integral part of my flat, and for seven years I could not get rid of him.

To be behind with his wages even for two or three days, for instance, was quite out of the question. He'd have made such a fuss that I shouldn't have known how to keep out of his way. But at that time I was feeling so exasperated with everyone that for a reason I did not myself clearly understand I made up my mind to *punish* Apollon by withholding his wages for a whole fortnight. I had been intending to do it for a long time, for the last two years, just to show him that he had no business to treat me with such insolence and that if I liked I could always refuse to pay him his wages. I decided to say nothing to him about it and to ignore the whole thing deliberately so as to crush his pride and force him to speak about his wages first. Then I would take the seven roubles out of the drawer, show him that I had the money, that I had purposely put it aside, and say that "I won't, I won't, I simply won't give you your wages! I won't just because *I don't want to,*" because I was the master in this house, because he had been disrespectful, because he had been rude; but if he were to ask me nicely, I might relent and give it to him; otherwise he would have to wait a fortnight, or three weeks, or maybe a month even. . . .

But furious though I was with him, he got the better of me in the end. I could not hold out for four days even. He started, as he always did start in such circumstances, for they had already happened before, I had already tried it on before (and, let me add, I knew all this beforehand, I knew all his contemptible tactics by heart)—he started by fixing me with a stern glare which he kept up for several minutes at a time, particularly when he used to meet me or when I went out of the house. If I did not shrink back and pretended not to notice his glances, he would set about—still in silence—to inflict more tortures upon me. He would suddenly and without any excuse whatever enter my room quietly and smoothly when I was either reading or pacing my room, and remain standing at the door, with one hand behind his back and one foot thrust forward, and stare fixedly at me. This time his stare was not only stern, but witheringly contemptuous. If I suddenly asked him what he wanted, he would not reply, but continue to stare straight at me for a few more seconds, then he would purse his lips with a specially significant expression, turn round slowly, and slowly go back to his room. About two hours later he would leave his room again, and again appear before me in the same manner. Sometimes, beside myself with rage, I did not even ask him what he wanted, but just raised my head sharply and imperiously and began staring back at him. We would thus stare at each other for about two minutes till at last he would turn round, slowly and pompously, and again go back for two hours.

If that did not make me come to my senses and I continued to be rebellious, he would suddenly break into sighs as he stared at me, as though measuring with each sigh the whole depth of my moral turpitude and, of course, it all ended in his complete victory over me: I raved, I shouted, but I still had to do what was expected of me.

No sooner did this manœuvre of stern looks begin this time than I lost my temper at once and flew at him in a blind rage.

"Stop!" I shouted, beside myself, as he was turning round slowly and silently, with one hand behind his back, to go back to his room. "Stop! Come back, I tell you! Come back!"

I must have roared at him in so unnatural a voice that he turned round again and began looking at me with surprise. He still said nothing, and that maddened me.

"How dare you come into my room without knocking and stare at me like that? Come on, answer me!"

But after looking calmly at me for half a minute, he started turning round again.

"Stop!" I roared, rushing up to him. "Don't you dare to move! Ah, that's better! Now answer me: what did you come in to look at me for?"

"If there is anything, sir, you want me to do for you now, it is my duty to carry it out," he replied, once more pausing a little before speaking, with his slow and measured lisp, raising his eyebrows and calmly inclining his head first to one side and then to another, and all this with the most exasperating self-composure.

"That's not what I asked you about, you tormentor!" I screamed, trembling with rage. "I'll tell you myself, you tormentor, why you come here. You see I'm not giving you your wages, and being too proud to come and ask for them yourself, you come here to stare at me stupidly in order to punish me, in order to torment me, without suspecting, tormentor that you are, how damned silly, silly, silly, silly it all is!"

He was about to turn round again silently, but I caught hold of him.

"Look," I shouted to him, "here's the money! Do you see? Here it is! (I took it out of the table drawer.) All the seven roubles. But you won't get them, you—will—not—get—them, until you come to me respectfully, acknowledge your fault, and say you are sorry! Do you hear?"

"That will never be!" he answered with a sort of unnatural self-confidence.

"It shall be!" I screamed. "I give you my word of honour—it shall be!"

"There's nothing I have to apologise for," he went on, as though not noticing my screams, "because you, sir, called me 'tormentor,' for which I can lodge a complaint against you at the police station."

"Go and lodge your complaint!" I roared. "Go at once, this very minute, this very second! You are a tormentor! A tormentor! A tormentor!"

But he only gave me a look, then turned round and, without paying any attention to my screams to stop, went out to his room with a measured step and without turning round.

"But for Lisa this would never have happened!" I said to myself. Then, after standing still for a minute, I went myself to his room behind the partition, gravely and solemnly, and without hurrying, though my heart was thumping slowly and violently. "Apollon," I said quietly and with great emphasis, though rather breathlessly, "go at once and fetch the police inspector. At once!"

He had in the meantime seated himself at his table, put on his spectacles, and settled down to his sewing. But, hearing my order, he burst into a loud guffaw.

"Go at once! This minute! Go, I say, or I shan't be responsible for what happens!"

"You must be off your head, sir," he remarked, without even raising his head, with his usual, slow lisp, calmly threading the needle. "Whoever heard of a man going to report to the police against himself! But, of course, sir, if you want to frighten me, then you might as well save yourself the trouble, for nothing will come of it."

"Go!" I screamed, grasping him by the shoulder. I felt that I was going to strike him any minute.

But I did not hear the door from the passage open quietly and slowly at that instant and someone come in, stand still, and start gazing at us in bewilderment. I looked up, nearly fainted with shame, and rushed back to my room. There, clutching at my hair with both hands and leaning my head against the wall, I remained motionless in that position.

About two minutes later I heard Apollon's slow footsteps.

"There's a certain young lady to see you, sir," he said, looking rather severely at me.

He then stood aside to let Lisa in. He did not seem to want to go, and stood staring at us sarcastically.

"Go! Go!" I ordered him, completely thrown off my balance.

At that moment my clock made a tremendous effort, and, wheezing, struck seven.

IX

And my house, fearlessly and freely,
As mistress you can enter now!
                    BY THE SAME POET.

I stood before her, feeling utterly crushed, disgraced, and shockingly embarrassed, and, I think, I smiled, trying desperately to wrap myself in the skirts of my tattered, wadded old dressing gown, exactly as a short while ago in one of the moments of complete depression I had imagined I would do. After watching us for a few minutes, Apollon went away, but that did not make me feel any better. Worst of all, she too was suddenly overcome with confusion, which I had hardly expected.

"Sit down," I said mechanically, placing a chair for her near the table.

I myself sat down on the sofa. She sat down at once, obediently, looking at me with wide-open eyes and evidently expecting something from me at any moment. It was this naïve expectancy of hers that incensed me, but I controlled myself.

If she had had any sense, she would have pretended not to have noticed anything, as though everything had been as usual, but instead she . . .

And I felt vaguely that I would make her pay dearly for *all this.*

"I'm afraid you've found me in a rather strange situation, Lisa," I began, stammering, and realising perfectly well that I shouldn't have opened the conversation like that. "No, no, don't think there's anything wrong," I exclaimed, seeing that she had suddenly blushed. "I'm not ashamed of my poverty. On the contrary, I look on it with pride. I'm a poor but honourable man. One can be poor and honourable, you know," I stammered. "However, will you have some tea?"

"No, thank you," she began.

"Wait a minute!"

I jumped up and ran out to Apollon. I had to get out of her sight somehow.

"Apollon," I whispered feverishly, talking very fast and flinging down on the table before him the seven roubles I had been keeping in my clenched hand all the time, "here are your wages. You see, I give them to you. But for that you must save me: go at once and fetch a pot of tea and a dozen rusks from the tea-shop. If you won't go, you'll make me the unhappiest man in the world! You don't know what a fine woman she is! She's wonderful! You may be thinking there's something—er—but you don't know what a fine woman she is!"

Apollon, who had sat down to his work and put on his spectacles again, at first looked silently at the money without putting down the needle; then, without paying any attention to me or replying to me, he went on busying himself with the needle, which he was still threading. I waited for three minutes, standing in front of him with my hands crossed *à la Napoléon.* My temples were wet with perspiration; I was very pale—I could feel it. But, thank God, he must have felt sorry as he looked at me, for having finished threading his needle, he slowly rose from his place, slowly pushed back his chair, slowly took off his glasses, slowly counted the money, and at last, asking me over his shoulder whether he should get a pot of tea for two, slowly left the room. As I was going back to Lisa, the thought occurred to me whether it would not be a good idea to run away just as I was in my dressing gown, run away no matter where, and let things take their course.

I sat down again. She regarded me uneasily. For a few minutes neither of us spoke.

"I'll murder him!" I suddenly screamed, banging my fist on the table with such violence that the ink spurted out of the ink-well.

"Good heavens, what are you saying?" she cried, startled.

"I'll murder him! I'll murder him!" I screamed, banging the table, beside myself with rage, but realising very well at the same time how stupid it was to be in such a rage.

"You can't imagine, Lisa, what a tormentor he is to me. He's my tormentor. He's gone out for some rusks now—he——"

And suddenly I burst into tears. It was a nervous attack. In between my sobs I felt awfully ashamed, but I could do nothing to stop them.

She was frightened. "What's the matter? What's the matter?" she kept asking, standing helplessly over me.

"Water . . . Give me some water, please. It's over there!" I murmured in a weak voice, realising very well at the same time that I could have managed without a drink of water and without murmuring in a weak voice. But I was, what is called, *play-acting* to save appearances, though my fit was real enough.

She gave me water, looking at me in utter confusion. At that moment Apollon brought in the tea. I felt that this ordinary, prosaic tea was very inappropriate and paltry after all that had happened, and I blushed. Lisa looked at Apollon almost in terror. He went out without a glance at us.

"Do you despise me, Lisa?" I said, looking straight at her and trembling with impatience to know what she was thinking of.

She was overcome with confusion and did not know what to say.

"Drink your tea," I said, angrily.

I was angry with myself, but of course it was she who would suffer for it. A terrible resentment against her suddenly blazed up in my heart. I believe I could have killed her. To revenge myself on her, I took a silent vow not to say a single word to her while she was in my room. "She's to blame for everything," I thought.

Our silence went on for almost five minutes. The tea stood on the table, but she did not touch it. I had got so far that I deliberately did not want to start drinking it in order to make her feel even more embarrassed. And she could not very well start drinking it alone. She glanced at me a few times in mournful perplexity. I kept obstinately silent. I was, of course, the chief sufferer, for I fully realised the whole despicable meanness of my spiteful stupidity, and yet I could do nothing to restrain myself.

"I—I want to get away from that—place for good," she began in an effort to do something to break the silence, but, poor thing, that was just what she should not have spoken about at the moment, for it was a stupid thing to say and especially to a man who was as stupid as I. Even I felt a pang of pity in my heart for her clumsiness and unnecessary frankness. But something hideous inside me at once stifled my feeling of pity. It provoked me even more—to hell with it all! Another five minutes passed.

"I haven't come at the wrong time, have I?" she began shyly in a hardly audible whisper, and made to get up.

But the moment I saw the first signs of injured dignity, I shook with spite and burst out at once.

"What have you come here for? Answer me! Answer!" I began, gasping for breath and paying no attention to the logical order of my words. I wanted to blurt it all out at once, and I didn't care a damn what I started with, "I'll tell you, my dear girl, what you have come for. You've come because I made *pathetic speeches* to you the other night. So you were softened and now you want more of these pathetic speeches. Well, I may as well tell you at once that I was laughing at you then. And I'm laughing at you now. What are you shuddering for? Yes, I was laughing at you! I had been insulted before, at dinner, by the fellows who came before me that night. I came to your place intending to thrash one of them, an army officer, but I was too late. He had already gone. So to avenge my wounded pride on someone, to get my own back, I vented my spite on you and I laughed at you. I had been humiliated, so I too wanted to humiliate someone; they wiped the floor with me, so I too wanted to show my power. That's what happened, and you thought I'd come there specially to save you, did you? You thought so, didn't you? You did, didn't you?"

I knew that she would probably be confused and unable to make head or tail of it, but I knew, too, that she would grasp the gist of it perfectly. And so it was. She turned white as a sheet, tried to say something, her lips painfully twisted. But before she could say anything, she collapsed in a chair as though she had been felled by an axe. And afterwards she listened to me all the time with parted lips and wide-open eyes, trembling with terror. The cynicism, the cynicism of my words crushed her. . . .

"To save you!" I went on, jumping up from my chair and running up and down the room in front of her. "Save you from what? Why, I'm probably much worse than you. Why didn't you throw it in my teeth when I was reading that lecture to you? 'But why did you come to us yourself? To read me a lecture on morality?' I wanted power. Power was what I wanted then. I wanted sport. I wanted to see you cry. I wanted to humiliate you. To make you hysterical. That's what I wanted. I couldn't keep it up because I'm nothing but a rag myself. I got frightened, and I'm damned if I know why I told you where I lived. I was a bloody fool. That's why, I suppose. So even before I got home that night I was cursing and swearing at you for having given you my address. I hated you already because of the lies I had been telling you. For all I wanted was to make a few fine speeches, to have something to dream about. And do you know what I really wanted? What I wanted was that you should all go to hell! That's what I wanted. The thing I must have at any cost is peace of mind. To get that peace of mind, to make sure that no one worried me, I'd sell the whole world for a farthing. Is the world to go to rack and ruin or am I to have my cup of tea? Well, so far as I'm concerned, blow the world so long as I can have my cup of tea. Did you know that, or didn't you? Well, anyway, I know I'm a blackguard, a cad, an egoist, a loafer. Here I've been shivering in a fever for the last three days for fear that you might come. And do you know what I was so worried about in particular during those three days? I'll tell you. What I was so worried about was that I was making myself out to be such a hero before you and that you'd find me here in this torn old dressing gown of mine, poor and loathsome. Only a few minutes ago I told you that I was not ashamed of my poverty. Well, it's not true. I am ashamed of my poverty. I'm ashamed of it more than of anything. I'm afraid of it more than of anything, more than of being a thief, because I'm so confoundedly vain that at times I feel as though I had been skinned and every puff of air hurt me. Don't you realise now that I shall never forgive you for having found me in this tattered old dressing gown and just when, like a spiteful cur, I flew at Apollon's throat? Your saviour, your former hero, flings himself like some mangy, shaggy mongrel on his valet, and his valet is laughing at him! And I shall never forgive you for the tears which I was shedding before you a minute ago, like some silly old woman who had been put to shame. Nor shall I ever forgive *you* for what I'm now confessing to you! Yes, you alone must answer for it all because you just happened to come at that moment, because I'm a rotter, because I'm the most horrible, the most ridiculous, the most petty, the most stupid, the most envious of all the worms on earth who are not a bit better than me, but who—I'm damned if I know why—are never ashamed or embarrassed, while I shall be insulted all my life by every louse because that's the sort of fellow I am! And what the hell do I care if you don't understand what I'm talking about? And what the hell do I care what happens to you? Whether you're going to rack and ruin there or not? And do you realise that now that I've told you all this I shall hate you for having been here and listened to me? Why, it's only once in a lifetime that a man speaks his mind like this, and that, too, when he is in hysterics. What more do you want? Why after all this do you still stand here before me torturing me? Why don't you get out of here?"

But here a very odd thing happened.

I was so used to imagining everything and to thinking of everything as it happened in books, and to picturing to myself everything in the world as I had previously made it up in my dreams, that at first I could not all at once grasp the meaning of this occurrence. What occurred was this: Lisa, humiliated and crushed by me, understood much more than I imagined. She understood from all this what a woman who loves sincerely always understands first of all, namely, that I was unhappy.

The frightened and resentful look on her face first gave place to one of sorrowful astonishment. But when I began to call myself a cad and a black-guard and my tears began to flow (I had spoken the whole of that tirade with tears), her whole face began to work convulsively. She was about to get up and stop me, and when I finished, it was not my cries of why she was here and why she did not go away to which she paid attention; what she felt was that I must have found it very hard indeed to say all this. And besides, she was so crushed, poor girl. She considered herself so inferior to me. Why should she feel angry or offended? She suddenly jumped up from her chair with a kind of irresistible impulse and, all drawn towards me but still feeling very shy and not daring to move from her place, held out her hands to me. . . . It was here that my heart failed me. Then she rushed to me, flung her arms round my neck, and burst into tears. I could not restrain myself, either, and burst out sobbing as I had never in my life sobbed before. . . .

"They—they won't let me—I—I can't be good!" I could hardly bring myself to say, then I stumbled to the sofa, fell on it face downwards, and for a quarter of an hour sobbed hysterically. She clung to me, put her arms round me, and seemed to remain frozen in that embrace.

But the trouble was that my hysterical fit could not go on for ever. And so (it is the loathsome truth I am writing), lying prone on the sofa, clinging tightly to it, and my face buried in my cheap leather cushion, I began gradually, remotely, involuntarily but irresistibly to feel that I should look an awful ass if I raised my head now and looked Lisa straight in the face. What was I ashamed of? I don't know. All I know is that I was ashamed. It also occurred to me just then, overwrought as I was, that our parts were now completely changed, that she was the heroine now, while I was exactly the same crushed and humiliated creature as she had appeared to me that night—four days before. . . . And all this flashed through my mind while I was still lying prone on the sofa!

Good God, was I really envious of her then?

I don't know. To this day I cannot possibly say whether I was envious of her or not, and at the time of course I was less able to understand it than now. I cannot live without feeling that I have someone completely in my power, that I am free to tyrannise over some human being. But—you can't explain anything by reasoning and consequently it is useless to reason.

I soon pulled myself together, however, and raised my head; I had to do it sooner or later. . . . And, well, to this day I can't help thinking that it was because I was ashamed to look at her that another feeling was suddenly kindled and blazed up in my heart—a feeling of domination and possession! My eyes flashed with passion and I clasped her hands violently. How I hated her and how I was drawn to her at that moment! One feeling intensified the other. This was almost like vengeance! . . . At first she looked bewildered and even frightened, but only for one moment. She embraced me warmly and rapturously.

X

A quarter of an hour later I was rushing up and down the room in furious impatience. Every minute I walked up to the screen and looked through the narrow slit at Lisa. She was sitting on the floor, her head leaning against the edge of the bed, and, I suppose, was crying. But she did not go away, and that irritated me. This time she knew everything. I had insulted her finally, but— there is no need to speak about it. She guessed that my outburst of passion was nothing but revenge, a fresh insult for her, and that to my earlier, almost aimless, hatred, there was now added a *personal, jealous* hatred of her. . . . However, I can't be certain that she did understand it all so clearly; what she certainly did understand was that I was a loathsome man and that, above all, I was incapable of loving her.

I know I shall be told that it is incredible—that it is incredible that anyone could be as spiteful and as stupid as I was; and I daresay it will be added that it was improbable that I should not love her or, at any rate, appreciate her love. But why is it improbable? First of all, I could not possibly have loved anyone because, I repeat, to me love meant to tyrannise and to be morally superior. I have never in my life been able to imagine any other sort of love, and I have reached the point that sometimes I cannot help thinking even now that love only consists in the right to tyrannise over the woman you love, who grants you this right of her own free will. Even in my most secret dreams I could not imagine love except as a struggle, and always embarked on it with hatred and ended it with moral subjugation, and afterwards I did not have the faintest idea what to do with the woman I had subjugated. And indeed what is there improbable about it when I had at last reached such a state of moral depravity, when I had lost touch so much with "real life," that only a few hours before I had thought of reproaching her for having come to me to listen to "pathetic speeches," and did not even guess that she had not come to listen to my pathetic speeches at all, but to love me, for it is only in love that a woman can find her true resurrection, her true salvation from any sort of calamity, and her moral regeneration, and she cannot possibly find it in anything else. Still, I did not hate her so much after all when I was pacing the room and looked at her through the chink in the screen. I merely felt unbearably distressed at her being there. I wanted her to disappear. I longed for "peace." I wanted to be left alone in my funk-hole. "Real life"—so unaccustomed was I to it—had crushed me so much that I found it difficult to breathe.

But a few minutes passed and still she did not get up, as though she were unconscious. I had the meanness to knock quietly at the screen to remind her. . . . She gave a start, got up quickly, and began looking for her kerchief, her hat, her fur coat, as though her only thought were how to run away from me as quickly as possible. . . .

Two minutes later she came out slowly from behind the screen and looked hard at me. I grinned maliciously, though I must confess I had to force myself to do it, *for the sake of appearances*, and turned away from her gaze.

"Goodbye," she said, going to the door.

I ran up to her suddenly, seized her hand, opened it, put something in it and —closed it again. Then I turned at once and rushed away quickly to the other corner of the room so as not to see her at least.

I almost told a lie this very minute. I was about to write that I did not do it deliberately, that I did it because I did not realise what I was doing, having in my folly completely lost my head. But I don't want to lie, and therefore I say frankly that I opened her hand and put something in it—out of spite. The thought came into my head when I was running up and down the room and she was sitting behind the screen. But this I can say in all truth: I did that cruel thing deliberately, I did it not because my heart, but because my wicked brain prompted me to do it. This cruelty was so insincere, so much thought out, so deliberately invented, so *bookish*, that I couldn't stand it myself even for a minute, but first rushed away to a corner so as not to see anything, and then, overwhelmed with shame and despair, rushed after Lisa. I opened the front door and began listening.

"Lisa! Lisa!" I cried down the stairs, but in a halting voice, in an undertone.

There was no answer, but I thought I heard her footsteps, lower down on the stairs.

"Lisa!" I called in a louder voice.

No answer. But at that moment I heard the heavy glass street-door open with a creak and with difficulty and slam heavily. The noise reverberated on the stairs.

She was gone. I returned musing to my room, feeling terribly ill at ease.

I stopped at the table beside the chair on which she had sat and looked disconsolately before me. A minute passed. Suddenly I gave a start: straight before me on the table I saw a crumpled blue five-rouble note, the same which a minute before I had pressed into her hand. It *was* the same note. It could be no other, for there was no other in the house. She therefore had just enough time to fling it on the table at the moment when I rushed to the other end of the room.

Well, of course, I might have expected it of her. Might have expected it? No, I was too great an egoist, I had too little respect for people to have been able even to imagine that she would do it. That was too much. That I could not bear. A moment later I began to dress madly, putting on hurriedly whatever clothes I could lay my hands on, and rushed headlong after her. She had hardly had time to walk more than a hundred yards when I ran out into the street.

The street was quiet and deserted. It was snowing heavily, the snowflakes falling almost perpendicularly and piling up in deep drifts on the pavement and on the empty road. There was not a soul to be seen, not a sound to be heard. The street-lamps twinkled desolately and uselessly. I ran about a hundred yards to the cross-roads and stopped.

Where had she gone? And why was I running after her?

Why? To fall on my knees before her, to sob with remorse, to kiss her feet, to beseech her to forgive me! I wanted to do so, my breast was being torn to pieces, and never, never shall I be able to recall that moment with indifference. But—why? I could not help thinking. Would I not hate her fiercely tomorrow perhaps just because I had been kissing her feet today? Could I make her happy? Had I not learnt today for the hundredth time what I was really worth? Should I not torture her to death?

I stood in the snow, peering into the dim haze, and thought of that.

"And will it not be better, will it not be much better," I thought afterwards at home, giving full rein to my imagination and suppressing the living pain in my heart, "will it not be much better that she should now carry that insult away with her for ever? What is an insult but a sort of purification? It is the most corrosive and painful form of consciousness! Tomorrow I should have bespattered her soul with mud, I should have wearied her heart by thrusting myself upon her, while now the memory of the insult will never die in her, and

however horrible the filth that lies in store for her, the memory of that humiliation will raise her and purify her—by hatred, and, well, perhaps also by forgiveness. Still, will that make things easier for her?"

And, really, here am I already putting the idle question to myself—which is
better: cheap happiness or exalted suffering? Well, which is better?

So I went on dreaming as I sat at home that evening, almost dead with the
pain in my heart. Never before had I endured such suffering and remorse. But
didn't I know perfectly well when I ran out of my flat that I should turn back
half-way? I never met Lisa again, and have heard nothing of her. I may as well
add that I remained for a long time pleased with the *phrase* about the useful-
ness of insults and hatred in spite of the fact that I almost fell ill at the time
from blank despair.

Even now, after all these years, I somehow feel *unhappy* to recall all this.
Lots of things make me unhappy now when I recall them, but—why not finish
my "memoirs" at this point? I can't help thinking that I made a mistake in
starting to write them. At any rate, I have felt ashamed all the time I have been
writing this *story:* so it seems this is no longer literature, but a corrective punishment. For to tell long stories and how I have, for instance, spoilt my life by a
moral disintegration in my funk-hole, by my unsociable habits, by losing touch
with life, and by nursing my spite in my dark cellar—all this, I'm afraid, is not
interesting. A novel must have a hero, and here I seemed to have *deliberately*
gathered together all the characteristics of an anti-hero, and, above all, all this
is certain to produce a most unpleasant impression because we have all lost
touch with life, we are all cripples, every one of us—more or less. We have lost
touch so much that occasionally we cannot help feeling a sort of disgust with
"real life," and that is why we are so angry when people remind us of it. Why,
we have gone so far that we look upon "real life" almost as a sort of burden,
and we are all agreed that "life" as we find it in books is much better. And why
do we make such a fuss sometimes? Why do we make fools of ourselves? What
do we want? We don't know ourselves. For as a matter of fact we should fare
much worse if our nonsensical prayers were granted. Why, just try, just give
us, for instance, more independence, untie the hands of any one of us, widen
the sphere of our activities, relax discipline, and we—yes, I assure you—we
should immediately be begging for the discipline to be reimposed upon us.
I know that very likely you will be angry with me for saying this, that you will
start shouting and stamping, "Speak for yourself and for your miserable life
in that dark cellar of yours and don't you dare to say 'all of us.' " But, good
Lord, gentlemen, I'm not trying to justify myself by this *all-of-usness.* For my
part, I have merely carried to extremes in my life what you have not dared to
carry even halfway, and, in addition, you have mistaken your cowardice for
common sense and have found comfort in that, deceiving yourselves. So that,
as a matter of fact, I seem to be much more alive than you. Come, look into it
more closely! Why, we do not even know where we are to find real life, or
what it is, or what it is called. Leave us alone without any books, and we shall
at once get confused, lose ourselves in a maze, we shall not know what to cling

to, what to hold on to, what to love and what to hate, what to respect and what to despise. We even find it hard to be men, men of *real* flesh and blood, *our own* flesh and blood. We are ashamed of it. We think it a disgrace. And we do our best to be some theoretical "average" men. We are stillborn, and for a long time we have been begotten not by living fathers, and that's just what we seem to like more and more. We are getting a taste for it. Soon we shall invent some way of being somehow or other begotten by an idea. But enough—I don't want to write any more "from a Dark Cellar. . . ."

(This is not, by the way, the end of the "Memoirs" of this paradoxical fellow. He could not resist and went on and on. But it seems to us, too, that we may stop here.)

Thomas Mann

TONIO KRÖGER

Preface

The division of modern consciousness, that which separates man within himself and without from other people, continues to plague us whatever it is called —dialectical necessity, relativity, contingency, schizophrenia, or existentialism. Dostoevsky's subject in *Notes from the Underground* is again Thomas Mann's in his distinguished short novel *Tonio Kröger* (1903). Mann's protagonist "bore within himself the possibility of a thousand ways of life, together with the private conviction that they were all sheer impossibilities." Tonio is "eaten up with intellect and introspection, ravaged and paralysed by insight . . . helpless and in anguish of conscience between two extremes." Dostoevsky's underground man used an identical mirror to draw his own portrait, and we can suspect that Thomas Mann took a look into it too—considering his praise of Russian literature in *Tonio Kröger*. From Mann's own notebooks, we know that he himself planned to write the work he assigns to his character Gustav Aschenbach in the great short novel *Death in Venice* (1912)—a "stark tale which is called *The Wretch*," which overcame consciousness and "pointed out . . . the possibility of some moral certainty beyond pure knowledge." The title's satiric reference to Dostoevsky, keeping in mind that Mann's first writing job (1898– 1899) was on the staff of the Munich satirical magazine *Simplicissimus*, should not prevent us from believing in Mann's quest for certainty. Mann's version of *Notes from the Underground* would be a novel by an artist and about himself, very much the shape of *Tonio Kröger*, and the difference would be the conversion of talking about yourself into writing about yourself. For Mann that difference is art, and art and the artist are the continual subject of his work.

To reduce the moral implications of Mann's aestheticism to a preference for art over life is as unfair as asking how does it work. Mann is not called the ironic German for nothing, nor can he spell out the meaning of aesthetic faith in life. But the intricately woven satiric, ironic, and magical maze of his fiction never ceases to amaze us with life. Mann knew that magic requires that the magician never show his hand as much as it requires its audience to look the other way. Irony keeps Mann's hand steady, and pseudo-autobiography distracts us, and so the trick of his fiction is played on us just as it is played by life on his artist characters. These artists are variously called magicians, swindlers, jugglers, and confidence men, and we can find them in such short novels as *Tristan* (1903)—the origin of Mann's masterpiece, *The Magic Mountain* (1924)—*Mario and the Magician* (1929), *Death in Venice*, and *Tonio Kröger*. The *Confessions of Felix Krull, Confidence Man*, started in 1909, was first published as a fragment in 1922, and the novel's first and only volume was completed in 1954; its history alone suggests the continuity of Mann's analysis of the meaning of the artist. The depth of that same analysis is fully revealed in Mann's most powerful novel, *Doctor Faustus* (1947), subtitled the "Life of the Composer Adrian Leverkun, as Told by a Friend." But it is Tonio Kröger, speaking of himself, who most defines the collective artist of all Mann's fictional biographies as "this vain and frigid charlatan."

Mann's charlatan artists' lives have one trick to pull on us, and that is to convince that all are the life of one writer—Thomas Mann (1875–1955). It is a hard trick not to succumb to, considering the blatant autobiography of *Tonio Kröger*, that makes Mann's native Lübeck Tonio's as well (in *Death in Venice* it is called simply L - - - -), and Tonio's parents into Mann's, whose father, a Senator and merchant, was of typical German stock, while his mother was born in Brazil of a part-German, part-Creole family. Tonio thus finds a north-south dialectic in his blood and name from the start of his story, which is often called Mann's "Portrait of the Artist as a Young Man." Similarly, the old official artist is Aschenbach, whose achievements prefigure Mann's Nobel Prize, awarded in 1929. Again, the trick makes Hans Castorp's conversion in *The Magic Mountain* equivalent to Mann's shift from apolitical writer to critic of rising Nazism in the twenties and thirties, and *Mario and the Magician* becomes one of his anti-Hitler radio broadcasts on the subject of the artist as tool of a fascist dictator. The flight from Egypt of the *Joseph Tetralogy* (1933–1943), Mann's scholarly reenactment of Biblical myth, is in turn seen as his journey from Nazi Germany to Czech, then American, and ultimately to Swiss citizenship. Finally, *Doctor Faustus*, with its theme of the solitary, is then made to anticipate Mann's last years, following the deaths of his son, the writer Klaus Mann, by suicide, and of his brother, political novelist Heinrich Mann. Mann's biography is real, not fictitious. His fiction seduces us by seeming to put us in the know—so that if we know a little about his life we think that we know a lot about his work. "It is a kind of mimicry that I love and spontaneously practise,"

Mann wrote, but he never fell for his own trick. Always "Art is a heightened mode of existence": The life of art is not the life of man or Mann, only the life of his fictions. But by seeming to confuse the two, Mann achieved his purpose. Tricked into thinking that art is life, that fictional self is self, we can be shocked by the discovery that truth *is* stranger than fiction.

All Mann's artists are driven to and away from the humiliating discovery that wonder is what makes all men artists, and it is Life's wonder that enables man to live in the shadow of eternal doubt. In the many novels, many different artists develop individual responses to this truth of *Tonio Kröger*. To simply call that novel a "Portrait of the Artist as a Young Man" is to ignore that in two of its three parts Tonio is over thirty. Similarly, to find Adrian Leverkun's solitude a consequence of age is to ignore his decision to pursue the lonely reaches of pure form and random abstraction in his art. Counterpoint we will miss as well, and nowhere is that counterpoint more brilliantly manifest than in the interplay of Mann's two greatest short novels, *Death in Venice* and *Tonio Kröger*. In both, Mann's old and young hometown artists find themselves ultimately in two seaside "bath-hotels," one north in Hamlet country, the other south in Venice, city of art, and for Mann the city of composer Richard Wagner's death—Wagner is also in both stories. Each artist must confront his obsession with an identical fourteen-year-old blonde boy in a sailor suit. Face to face with Mann's blue boy, each finds the doctrine of the artist as a man of frozen feeling insufficient. Tonio's mythic biography is exploded by real life, and Aschenbach's real-life biography is exploded by mythmaking. Each learns that love is a humiliating and thus thoroughly human experience—most of all for those who have renounced it precisely in order to obtain it. Frustrated by rejection, Tonio meditates: "For happiness, he told himself, is not in being loved—which is a satisfaction of the vanity and mingled with disgust. Happiness is in loving, and perhaps in snatching fugitive little approaches to the beloved object." If we think this mere adolescent rationalizing, we have only to remember Aschenbach's memory of Plato's dialogue of Socrates and young Phaedrus on love: "And then this crafty suitor made the neatest remark of all; it was this, that the lover is more divine than the beloved, since the god is in the one, but not in the other—perhaps the most delicate, the most derisive thought which has ever been framed, and the one from which spring all the cunning and the profoundest pleasures of desire." In both Tonio and Aschenbach, the suitor's irony turns back upon itself as each is given a classic lesson on the meaning of his own classicism. The price of Life is the flawed beauty that is human.

Plato's *Phaedrus* is more than one dialogue on love. Rhetoric, not love, is its actual subject, and so it discusses love twice to distinguish conventional rhetoric, that attempts to persuade regardless of truth, and true rhetoric based on dialectic. Mann's dialogue on the problem "of the artist and his human aspect," *Tonio Kröger*, makes the same distinction with two similar dialogues formed from the novel's three parts: Tonio's adolescence, his discussion with the painter Lisabeta Ivanova, and his trip back home and to the Danish seaside town of his adolescent summer vacations. Mann's false dialogue is the actual talk with Lisabeta, in which Tonio's rhetoric is mainly to persuade himself; the true dialogue is in the interplay of the novel's first and last sections, where past and past-in-present debate to expose the novel's false center. Talking with Lisabeta in Munich, Tonio is talking to himself: "She was about the same age as himself . . . her brown hair . . . framing a sensitive, sympathetic, dark-skinned face . . . and little bright black eyes." This is an exact portrait of the *bellezza* side of Tonio, the side of himself he attacks with a blonde portrait of the artist: "feeling, warm, heartfelt feeling, is always banal and futile; only the irritations and icy ecstasies of the artist's corrupted nervous system are artistic. The artist must be unhuman, extra-human"—anything but sensitive and sympathetic. As Tonio sees it, the audience pays for a trick that excuses its feelings by rendering them up to the frozen charlatan: "Honestly, don't you think there's a good deal of cool cheek in the prompt and superficial way a writer can get rid of his feelings by turning them into literature? . . . He will analyze and formulate your affair, label it and express it . . . and make you indifferent to it. . . . If the whole world could be expressed, it would be saved, finished, and done." But Tonio's dark side, in the guise of Lisabeta, turns his desires back upon themselves by expressing him! For Lisabeta is metaphorically painting Tonio while he speaks, as he remarks: "Inside my head it looks just the way it does on this canvas." If Lisabeta does not finish the actual painting, she finishes Tonio with brilliant irony: "The solution of the problem that has been upsetting you . . . is that you, as you sit there, are, quite simply, a bourgeois. . . . a bourgeois *manqué.*" The portrait is a ludicrous one, but Tonio knows its truth. His earlier words turn even his hurt parting irony back upon him: "Now I can go home in peace. I am expressed." He has wanted the canvas to represent "Hamlet the Dane, that typical literary man," who must know more than he wants to, and write it down while the blondes are kissing. And irrespective of Lisabeta's expression, Tonio will still go to Denmark, "to stand on the terrace at Kronberg, where the ghost appeared to Hamlet, bringing despair and death to that poor, noble-souled youth." But, as Lisabeta has shown, the ghost of Tonio's desires is very middle-class, and it cannot be laid to rest in the world of art—there it is lost, until Tonio finds it.

The opening line of *Tonio Kröger* tells us: "The winter sun, poor ghost of itself, hung milky and wan . . . above the . . . roofs of the town," and it is seeking his own ghost that brings Tonio back home. There at fourteen he loved Hans Hansen, who loved horses more than Tonio, and books of "instantaneous photography" more than Schiller's *Don Carlos*—so Tonio learns that love means painful betrayal. By sixteen he loves Ingeborg Holm, who loves Knaak the Dancing Master, while Magdalena, who loves Tonio, doesn't get the affection that Hans Hansen gave to a horse. So Tonio formulates Aschenbach's ultimate *Phaedrus:* stupid is lovable, smart unlovable except by what it finds stupid, and to try to make the stupid smart is as impossible as loving yourself—what is most desired and most inadmissible. Wishing that Ingeborg would "come back," Tonio leaves for the life of art. But stop-motion photography is all that he can get there; even Hans Hansen knew that it shows only what "you never can get to see in life." On the return journey from art to life Tonio, however, gets exactly the opposite of what he expects: "And now the present refused to distinguish itself in any way from one of those tantalizing dream fabrications." In the dream that is life, Tonio returns home to find that his home has been turned into a public library, and in his own room in that library he takes down and reads a copy of a novel that he has written himself. He is subsequently detained by a policeman, who accuses him of being a gypsy charlatan on the run from Munich, and the only way in which Tonio can prove his identity—actual identity—is with a *proof*-sheet giving his literary identity. This is as ironic as Mann can be, and as solipsistic as Tonio can become in seeking a way back to life that is not ridiculously human. The denouement following Mann's ironic climax comes finally with Tonio near Helsingör, modern Elsinore. In the paralysis that his art has become, Tonio there "hovered disembodied above space and time," until life reproduces Hans Hansen and Ingeborg Holm for him, to teach who is the supreme artist. We find them among a group of tourists who have stopped at Tonio's bath-hotel for lunch. "So they are coming back?" asks Tonio, again missing Mann's irony, and discovers that the tourists will return for an evening festival. Guess who hides behind a curtained glass door, observing the dance—the very dance of his adolescence, the quadrille, with its *moulinet*—life's inescapable windmill? Hamlet Kröger in a dream within a dream is watching a play within a play—and so Mann's theme is realized *in him:* "Did you laugh, Ingeborg the blonde . . . even if I in my own person had written the nine symphonies . . . and painted the Last Judgment, you would still be eternally right to laugh." Tonio's obsession laughs in his own face to teach him to laugh at himself. He is finally ridiculous in his own eyes, and "without being allowed to forget the melancholy conflict within oneself," he can live in the world of doubt, knowing that "if anything is capable of making a poet of a literary man," that is, a Shakespeare out of a Hamlet, "it is my *bourgeois* love of the human, the living, the usual."

TONIO KRÖGER

Translated by H. T. Lowe-Porter

The winter sun, poor ghost of itself, hung milky and wan behind layers of cloud above the huddled roofs of the town. In the gabled streets it was wet and windy and there came in gusts a sort of soft hail, not ice, not snow.

School was out. The hosts of the released streamed over the paved court and out at the wrought-iron gate, where they broke up and hastened off right and left. Elder pupils held their books in a strap high on the left shoulder and rowed, right arm against the wind, towards dinner. Small people trotted gaily off, splashing the slush with their feet, the tools of learning rattling amain in their walrus-skin satchels. But one and all pulled off their caps and cast down their eyes in awe before the Olympian hat and ambrosial beard of a master moving homewards with measured stride. . . .

"Ah, there you are at last, Hans," said Tonio Kröger. He had been waiting a long time in the street and went up with a smile to the friend he saw coming out of the gate in talk with other boys and about to go off with them. . . . "What?" said Hans, and looked at Tonio. "Right-oh! We'll take a little walk, then."

Tonio said nothing and his eyes were clouded. Did Hans forget, had he only just remembered that they were to take a walk together today? And he himself had looked forward to it with almost incessant joy.

"Well, good-bye, fellows," said Hans Hansen to his comrades. "I'm taking a walk with Kröger." And the two turned to their left, while the others sauntered off in the opposite direction.

Hans and Tonio had time to take a walk after school because in neither of their families was dinner served before four o'clock. Their fathers were prominent business men, who held public office and were of consequence in the town. Hans's people had owned for some generations the big wood-yards down by the river, where powerful machine-saws hissed and spat and cut up timber; while Tonio was the son of Consul Kröger, whose grain-sacks with the firm name in great black letters you might see any day driven through the streets; his large, old ancestral home was the finest house in all the town. The two friends had to keep taking off their hats to their many acquaintances; some folk did not even wait for the fourteen-year-old lads to speak first, as by rights they should.

Both of them carried their satchels across their shoulders and both were well and warmly dressed: Hans in a short sailor jacket, with the wide blue collar of his sailor suit turned out over shoulders and back, and Tonio in a belted grey overcoat. Hans wore a Danish sailor cap with black ribbons, beneath which streamed a shock of straw-coloured hair. He was uncommonly handsome and well built, broad in the shoulders and narrow in the hips, with keen, far-apart, steel-blue eyes; while beneath Tonio's round fur cap was a brunette face with the finely chiselled features of the south; the dark eyes, with delicate shadows and too heavy lids, looked dreamily and a little timorously on the world. Tonio's walk was idle and uneven, whereas the other's slim legs in their black stockings moved with an elastic, rhythmic tread.

Tonio did not speak. He suffered. His rather oblique brows were drawn together in a frown, his lips were rounded to whistle, he gazed into space with his head on one side. Posture and manner were habitual.

Suddenly Hans shoved his arm into Tonio's, with a sideways look—he knew very well what the trouble was. And Tonio, though he was silent for the next few steps, felt his heart soften.

"I hadn't forgotten, you see, Tonio," Hans said, gazing at the pavement, "I only thought it wouldn't come off today because it was so wet and windy. But I don't mind that at all, and it's jolly of you to have waited. I thought you had gone home, and I was cross. . . ."

Everything in Tonio leaped and jumped for joy at the words.

"All right; let's go over the wall," he said with a quaver in his voice. "Over the Millwall and the Holstenwall, and I'll go as far as your house with you, Hans. Then I'll have to walk back alone, but that doesn't matter; next time you can go round my way."

At bottom he was not really convinced by what Hans said; he quite knew the other attached less importance to this walk than he did himself. Yet he saw Hans was sorry for his remissness and willing to be put in a position to ask pardon, a pardon that Tonio was far indeed from withholding.

The truth was, Tonio loved Hans Hansen, and had already suffered much on his account. He who loves the more is the inferior and must suffer; in this hard and simple fact his fourteen-year-old soul had already been instructed by life; and he was so organized that he received such experiences consciously, wrote them down as it were inwardly, and even, in a certain way, took pleasure in them, though without ever letting them mould his conduct, indeed, or drawing any practical advantage from them. Being what he was, he found this knowledge far more important and far more interesting than the sort they made him learn in school; yes, during his lesson hours in the vaulted Gothic classrooms he was mainly occupied in feeling his way about among these intuitions of his and penetrating them. The process gave him the same kind of satisfaction as that he felt when he moved about in his room with his violin—for he played the violin —and made the tones, brought out as softly as ever he knew how, mingle with the plashing of the fountain that leaped and danced down there in the garden beneath the branches of the old walnut tree.

The fountain, the old walnut tree, his fiddle, and away in the distance the North Sea, within sound of whose summer murmurings he spent his holidays— these were the things he loved, within these he enfolded his spirit, among these things his inner life took its course. And they were all things whose names were effective in verse and occurred pretty frequently in the lines Tonio Kröger sometimes wrote.

The fact that he had a note-book full of such things, written by himself, leaked out through his own carelessness and injured him no little with the masters as well as among his fellows. On the one hand, Consul Kröger's son found their attitude both cheap and silly, and despised his schoolmates and his masters as well, and in his turn (with extraordinary penetration) saw through and disliked their personal weaknesses and bad breeding. But then, on the other hand, he himself felt his verse-making extravagant and out of place and to a certain extent agreed with those who considered it an unpleasing occupation. But that did not enable him to leave off.

As he wasted his time at home, was slow and absent-minded at school, and always had bad marks from the masters, he was in the habit of bringing home pitifully poor reports, which troubled and angered his father, a tall, fastidiously dressed man, with thoughtful blue eyes, and always a wild flower in his button-hole. But for his mother, she cared nothing about the reports—Tonio's beautiful black-haired mother, whose name was Consuelo, and who was so absolutely different from the other ladies in the town, because father had brought her long ago from some place far down on the map.

Tonio loved his dark, fiery mother, who played the piano and mandolin so wonderfully, and he was glad his doubtful standing among men did not distress her. Though at the same time he found his father's annoyance a more dignified and respectable attitude and despite his scoldings understood him very well, whereas his mother's blithe indifference always seemed just a little wanton. His thoughts at times would run something like this: "It is true enough that I am what I am and will not and cannot alter: heedless, self-willed, with my mind on things nobody else thinks of. And so it is right they should scold and punish me and not smother things all up with kisses and music. After all, we are not gypsies living in a green wagon; we're respectable people, the family of Consul Kröger." And not seldom he would think: "Why is it I am different, why do I fight everything, why am I at odds with the masters and like a stranger among the other boys? The good scholars, and the solid majority—they don't find the masters funny, they don't write verses, their thoughts are all about things that people do think about and can talk about out loud. How regular and comfortable they must feel, knowing that everybody knows just where they stand! It must be nice! But what is the matter with me, and what will be the end of it all?"

These thoughts about himself and his relation to life played an important part in Tonio's love for Hans Hansen. He loved him in the first place because he was handsome; but in the next because he was in every respect his own opposite and foil. Hans Hansen was a capital scholar, and a jolly chap to boot, who was head at drill, rode and swam to perfection, and lived in the sunshine of popularity. The masters were almost tender with him, they called him Hans and were partial to him in every way; the other pupils curried favour with him; even grown people stopped him on the street, twitched the shock of hair beneath his Danish sailor cap, and said: "Ah, here you are, Hans Hansen, with your pretty blond hair! Still head of the school? Remember me to your father and mother, that's a fine lad!"

Such was Hans Hansen; and ever since Tonio Kröger had known him, from the very minute he set eyes on him, he had burned inwardly with a heavy, envious longing. "Who else has blue eyes like yours, or lives in such friendliness and harmony with all the world? You are always spending your time with some right and proper occupation. When you have done your prep you take your riding lesson, or make things with a fret-saw; even in the holidays, at the seashore, you row and sail and swim all the time, while I wander off somewhere and lie down in the sand and stare at the strange and mysterious changes that whisk over the face of the sea. And all that is why your eyes are so clear. To be like you . . ."

He made no attempt to be like Hans Hansen, and perhaps hardly even seriously wanted to. What he did ardently, painfully want was that just as he was, Hans Hansen should love him; and he wooed Hans Hansen in his own way, deeply, lingeringly, devotedly, with a melancholy that gnawed and burned more terribly than all the sudden passion one might have expected from his exotic looks.

And he wooed not in vain. Hans respected Tonio's superior power of putting certain difficult matters into words; moreover, he felt the lively presence of an uncommonly strong and tender feeling for himself; he was grateful for it, and his response gave Tonio much happiness—though also many pangs of jealousy and disillusion over his futile efforts to establish a communion of spirit between them. For the queer thing was that Tonio, who after all envied Hans Hansen for being what he was, still kept on trying to draw him over to his own side; though of course he could succeed in this at most only at moments and superficially. . . .

"I have just been reading something so wonderful and splendid . . ." he said. They were walking and eating together out of a bag of fruit toffees they had bought at Iverson's sweet-shop in Mill Street for ten pfennigs. "You must read it, Hans, it is Schiller's *Don Carlos* . . . I'll lend it you if you like. . . ."

"Oh, no," said Hans Hansen, "you needn't, Tonio, that's not anything for me. I'll stick to my horse books. There are wonderful cuts in them, let me tell you. I'll show them to you when you come to see me. They are instantaneous photography—the horse in motion; you can see him trot and canter and jump, in all positions, that you never can get to see in life, because they happen so fast. . . ."

"In all positions?" asked Tonio politely. "Yes, that must be great. But about *Don Carlos*—it is beyond anything you could possibly dream of. There are places in it that are so lovely they make you jump . . . as though it were an explosion—"

"An explosion?" asked Hans Hansen. "What sort of an explosion?"

"For instance, the place where the king has been crying because the marquis betrayed him . . . but the marquis did it only out of love for the prince, you see, he sacrifices himself for his sake. And the word comes out of the cabinet into the antechamber that the king has been weeping. 'Weeping? The king been weeping?' All the courtiers are fearfully upset, it goes through and through you, for the king has always been so frightfully stiff and stern. But it is so easy to understand why he cried, and I feel sorrier for him than for the prince and the marquis put together. He is always so alone, nobody loves him, and then he thinks he has found one man, and then *he* betrays him. . . ."

Hans Hansen looked sideways into Tonio's face, and something in it must have won him to the subject, for suddenly he shoved his arm once more into Tonio's and said:

"How had he betrayed him, Tonio?"

Tonio went on.

"Well," he said, "you see all the letters for Brabant and Flanders—"

"There comes Irwin Immerthal," said Hans.

Tonio stopped talking. If only the earth would open and swallow Immerthal up! "Why does he have to come disturbing us? If he only doesn't go with us all the way and talk about the riding-lessons!" For Irwin Immerthal had riding-lessons too. He was the son of the bank president and lived close by, outside the city wall. He had already been home and left his bag, and now he walked towards them through the avenue. His legs were crooked and his eyes like slits.

" 'lo, Immerthal," said Hans. "I'm taking a little walk with Kröger. . . ."

"I have to go into town on an errand," said Immerthal. "But I'll walk a little way with you. Are those fruit toffees you've got? Thanks, I'll have a couple. Tomorrow we have our next lesson, Hans." He meant the riding-lesson.

"What larks!" said Hans. "I'm going to get the leather gaiters for a present, because I was top lately in our papers."

"You don't take riding-lessons, I suppose, Kröger?" asked Immerthal, and his eyes were only two gleaming cracks.

"No . . ." answered Tonio, uncertainly.

"You ought to ask your father," Hans Hansen remarked, "so you could have lessons too, Kröger."

"Yes . . ." said Tonio. He spoke hastily and without interest; his throat had suddenly contracted, because Hans had called him by his last name. Hans seemed conscious of it too, for he said by way of explanation: "I call you Kröger because your first name is so crazy. Don't mind my saying so, I can't do with it all. Tonio—why, what sort of name is that? Though of course I know it's not your fault in the least."

"No, they probably called you that because it sounds so foreign and sort of something special," said Immerthal, obviously with intent to say just the right thing.

Tonio's mouth twitched. He pulled himself together and said:

"Yes, it's a silly name—Lord knows I'd rather be called Heinrich or Wilhelm. It's all because I'm named after my mother's brother Antonio. She comes from down there, you know. . . ."

There he stopped and let the others have their say about horses and saddles. Hans had taken Immerthal's arm; he talked with a fluency that *Don Carlos* could never have roused in him. . . . Tonio felt a mounting desire to weep pricking his nose from time to time; he had hard work to control the trembling of his lips.

Hans could not stand his name—what was to be done? He himself was called Hans, and Immerthal was called Irwin; two good, sound, familiar names, offensive to nobody. And Tonio was foreign and queer. Yes, there was always something queer about him, whether he would or no, and he was alone, the regular and usual would none of him; although after all he was no gypsy in a green wagon, but the son of Consul Kröger, a member of the Kröger family. But why did Hans call him Tonio as long as they were alone and then feel ashamed as soon as anybody else was by? Just now he had won him over, they had been close together, he was sure. "How had he betrayed him, Tonio?" Hans asked, and took his arm. But he had breathed easier directly Immerthal came up, he had dropped him like a shot, even gratuitously taunted him with his outlandish name. How it hurt to have to see through all this! . . . Hans Hansen did like him a little, when they were alone, that he knew. But let a third person come, he was ashamed, and offered up his friend. And again he was alone. He thought of King Philip. The king had wept. . . .

"Goodness, I have to go," said Irwin Immerthal. "Good-bye, and thanks for the toffee." He jumped upon a bench that stood by the way, ran along it with his crooked legs, jumped down, and trotted off.

"I like Immerthal," said Hans, with emphasis. He had a spoilt and arbitrary way of announcing his likes and dislikes, as though graciously pleased to confer them like an order on this person and that. . . . He went on talking about the riding-lessons where he had left off. Anyhow, it was not very much farther to his house; the walk over the walls was not a long one. They held their caps and bent their heads before the strong, damp wind that rattled and groaned in the leafless trees. And Hans Hansen went on talking, Tonio throwing in a forced yes or no from time to time. Hans talked eagerly, had taken his arm again; but the contact gave Tonio no pleasure. The nearness was only apparent, not real; it meant nothing. . . .

They struck away from the walls close to the station, where they saw a train puff busily past, idly counted the coaches, and waved to the man who was perched on top of the last one bundled in a leather coat. They stopped in front of the Hansen villa on the Lindenplatz, and Hans went into detail about what fun it was to stand on the bottom rail of the garden gate and let it swing on its creaking hinges. After that they said good-bye.

"I must go in now," said Hans. "Good-bye, Tonio. Next time I'll take you home, see if I don't."

"Good-bye, Hans," said Tonio. "It was a nice walk."

They put out their hands, all wet and rusty from the garden gate. But as Hans looked into Tonio's eyes, he bethought himself, a look of remorse came over his charming face.

"And I'll read *Don Carlos* pretty soon, too," he said quickly. "That bit about the king in his cabinet must be nuts." Then he took his bag under his arm and ran off through the front garden. Before he disappeared he turned and nodded once more.

And Tonio went off as though on wings. The wind was at his back; but it was not the wind alone that bore him along so lightly.

Hans would read *Don Carlos*, and then they would have something to talk about, and neither Irwin Immerthal nor another could join in. How well they understood each other! Perhaps—who knew?—some day he might even get Hans to write poetry!... No, no, that he did not ask. Hans must not become like Tonio, he must stop just as he was, so strong and bright, everybody loved him as he was, and Tonio most of all. But it would do him no harm to read *Don Carlos*. . . . Tonio passed under the squat old city gate, along by the harbour, and up the steep, wet, windy, gabled street to his parents' house. His heart beat richly: longing was awake in it, and a gentle envy; a faint contempt, and no little innocent bliss.

Ingeborg Holm, blonde little Inge, the daughter of Dr. Holm, who lived on Market Square opposite the tall old Gothic fountain with its manifold spires— she it was Tonio Kröger loved when he was sixteen years old.

Strange how things come about! He had seen her a thousand times; then one evening he saw her again; saw her in a certain light, talking with a friend in a certain saucy way, laughing and tossing her head; saw her lift her arm and smooth her back hair with her schoolgirl hand, that was by no means particularly fine or slender, in such a way that the thin white sleeve slipped down from her elbow; heard her speak a word or two, a quite indifferent phrase, but with a certain intonation, with a warm ring in her voice; and his heart throbbed with ecstasy, far stronger than that he had once felt when he looked at Hans Hansen long ago, when he was still a little, stupid boy.

That evening he carried away her picture in his eye: the thick blonde plait, the longish, laughing blue eyes, the saddle of pale freckles across the nose. He could not go to sleep for hearing that ring in her voice; he tried in a whisper to imitate the tone in which she had uttered the commonplace phrase, and felt a shiver run through and through him. He knew by experience that this was love. And he was accurately aware that love would surely bring him much pain, affliction, and sadness, that it would certainly destroy his peace, filling his heart to overflowing with melodies which would be no good to him because he would never have the time or tranquillity to give them permanent form. Yet he received this love with joy, surrendered himself to it, and cherished it with all the strength of his being; for he knew that love made one vital and rich, and he longed to be vital and rich, far more than he did to work tranquilly on anything to give it permanent form.

Tonio Kröger fell in love with merry Ingeborg Holm in Frau Consul Hustede's drawing-room on the evening when it was emptied of furniture for the weekly dancing-class. It was a private class, attended only by members of the first families; it met by turns in the various parental houses to receive instruction from Knaak, the dancing-master, who came from Hamburg expressly for the purpose.

François Knaak was his name, and what a man he was! *"J'ai l'honneur de me vous représenter,"* he would say, *"mon nom est Knaak. . . .* This is not said during the bowing, but after you have finished and are standing up straight again. In a low voice, but distinctly. Of course one does not need to introduce oneself in French every day in the week, but if you can do it correctly and faultlessly in French you are not likely to make a mistake when you do it in German." How marvellously the silky black frock-coat fitted his chubby hips! His trouser-legs fell down in soft folds upon his patent-leather pumps with their wide satin bows, and his brown eyes glanced about him with languid pleasure in their own beauty.

All this excess of self-confidence and good form was positively overpowering. He went trippingly—and nobody tripped like him, so elastically, so weavingly, rockingly, royally—up to the mistress of the house, made a bow, waited for a hand to be put forth. This vouchsafed, he gave murmurous voice to his gratitude, stepped buoyantly back, turned on his left foot, swiftly drawing the right one backwards on its toe-tip, and moved away, with his hips shaking.

When you took leave of a company you must go backwards out at the door; when you fetched a chair, you were not to shove it along the floor or clutch it by one leg; but gently, by the back, and set it down without a sound. When you stood, you were not to fold your hands on your tummy or seek with your tongue the corners of your mouth. If you did, Herr Knaak had a way of showing you how it looked that filled you with disgust for that particular gesture all the rest of your life.

This was deportment. As for dancing, Herr Knaak was, if possible, even more of a master at that. The salon was emptied of furniture and lighted by a gas-chandelier in the middle of the ceiling and candles on the mantel-shelf. The floor was strewn with talc, and the pupils stood about in a dumb semicircle. But in the next room, behind the portières, mothers and aunts sat on plush-upholstered chairs and watched Herr Knaak through their lorgnettes, as in little springs and hops, curtsying slightly, the hem of his frock-coat held up on each side by two fingers, he demonstrated the single steps of the mazurka. When he wanted to dazzle his audience completely he would suddenly and unexpectedly spring from the ground, whirling his two legs about each other with bewildering swiftness in the air, as it were trilling with them, and then, with a subdued bump, which nevertheless shook everything within him to its depths, return to earth.

"What an unmentionable monkey!" thought Tonio Kröger to himself. But he saw the absorbed smile on jolly little Inge's face as she followed Herr Knaak's movements; and that, though not that alone, roused in him something like admiration of all this wonderfully controlled corporeality. How tranquil, how imperturbable was Herr Knaak's gaze! His eyes did not plumb the depth of things to the place where life becomes complex and melancholy; they knew nothing save that they were beautiful brown eyes. But that was just why his bearing was so proud. To be able to walk like that, one must be stupid; then one was loved, then one was lovable. He could so well understand how it was that Inge, blonde, sweet little Inge, looked at Herr Knaak as she did. But would never a girl look at him like that?

Oh, yes, there would, and did. For instance, Magdalena Vermehren, Attorney Vermehren's daughter, with the gentle mouth and the great, dark, brilliant eyes, so serious and adoring. She often fell down in the dance; but when it was "ladies' choice" she came up to him; she knew he wrote verses and twice she had asked him to show them to her. She often sat at a distance, with drooping head, and gazed at him. He did not care. It was Inge he loved, blonde, jolly Inge, who most assuredly despised him for his poetic effusions . . . he looked at her, looked at her narrow blue eyes full of fun and mockery, and felt an envious longing; to be shut away from her like this, to be forever strange—he felt it in his breast, like a heavy, burning weight.

"First couple *en avant*," said Herr Knaak; and no words can tell how marvellously he pronounced the nasal. They were to practise the quadrille, and to Tonio Kröger's profound alarm he found himself in the same set with Inge Holm. He avoided her where he could, yet somehow was forever near her; kept his eyes away from her person and yet found his gaze ever on her. There she came, tripping up hand-in-hand with red-headed Ferdinand Matthiessen; she flung back her braid, drew a deep breath, and took her place opposite Tonio. Herr Heinzelmann, at the piano, laid bony hands upon the keys, Herr Knaak waved his arm, the quadrille began.

She moved to and fro before his eyes, forwards and back, pacing and swinging; he seemed to catch a fragrance from her hair or the folds of her thin white frock, and his eyes grew sadder and sadder. "I love you, dear, sweet Inge," he said to himself, and put into his words all the pain he felt to see her so intent upon the dance with not a thought of him. Some lines of an exquisite poem by Storm came into his mind: "I would sleep, but thou must dance." It seemed against all sense, and most depressing, that he must be dancing when he was in love. . . .

"First couple *en avant*," said Herr Knaak; it was the next figure. "*Compli-*

ment! Moulinet des dames! Tour de main!" and he swallowed the silent *e* in the *"de,"* with quite indescribable ease and grace.

"Second couple *en avant!"* This was Tonio Kröger and his partner. *"Compliment!"* And Tonio Kröger bowed. *"Moulinet des dames!"* And Tonio Kröger, with bent head and gloomy brows, laid his hand on those of the four ladies, on Ingeborg Holm's hand, and danced the *moulinet.*

Roundabout rose a tittering and laughing. Herr Knaak took a ballet pose conventionally expressive of horror. "Oh, dear! Oh, dear!" he cried. "Stop! Stop! Kröger among the ladies! *En arrière,* Fräulein Kröger, step back, *fi donc!* Everybody else understood it but you. Shoo! Get out! Get away!" He drew out his yellow silk handkerchief and flapped Tonio Kröger back to his place.

Everyone laughed, the girls and the boys and the ladies beyond the portières; Herr Knaak had made something too utterly funny out of the little episode, it was as amusing as a play. But Herr Heinzelmann at the piano sat and waited, with a dry, business-like air, for a sign to go on; he was hardened against Herr Knaak's effects.

Then the quadrille went on. And the intermission followed. The parlourmaid came clinking in with a tray of wine-jelly glasses, the cook followed in her wake with a load of plum-cake. But Tonio Kröger stole away. He stole out into the corridor and stood there, his hands behind his back, in front of a window with the blind down. He never thought that one could not see through the blind and that it was absurd to stand there as though one were looking out.

For he was looking within, into himself, the theatre of so much pain and longing. Why, why was he here? Why was he not sitting by the window in his own room, reading Storm's *Immensee* and lifting his eyes to the twilight garden outside, where the old walnut tree moaned? That was the place for him! Others might dance, others bend their fresh and lively minds upon the pleasure in hand! . . . But no, no, after all, his place was here, where he could feel near Inge even although he stood lonely and aloof, seeking to distinguish the warm notes of her voice amid the buzzing, clattering, and laughter within. Oh, lovely Inge, blonde Inge of the narrow, laughing blue eyes! So lovely and laughing as you are one can only be if one does not read *Immensee* and never tries to write things like it. And that was just the tragedy!

Ah, she *must* come! She *must* notice where he had gone, must feel how he suffered! She must slip out to him, even pity must bring her, to lay her hand on his shoulder and say: "Do come back to us, ah, don't be sad—I love you, Tonio." He listened behind him and waited in frantic suspense. But not in the least. Such things did not happen on this earth.

Had she laughed at him too like all the others? Yes, she had, however gladly he would have denied it for both their sakes. And yet it was only because he had been so taken up with her that he had danced the *moulinet des dames.* Suppose he had—what did that matter? Had not a magazine accepted a poem of his a little while ago—even though the magazine had failed before his poem could be printed? The day was coming when he would be famous, when they would print everything he wrote; and *then* he would see if that made any im-

pression on Inge Holm! No, it would make no impression at all; that was just
it. Magdalena Vermehren, who was always falling down in the dances, yes,
she would be impressed. But never Ingeborg Holm, never blue-eyed, laughing
Inge. So what was the good of it?

Tonio Kröger's heart contracted painfully at the thought. To feel stirring
within you the wonderful and melancholy play of strange forces and to be
aware that those others you yearn for are blithely inaccessible to all that moves
you—what a pain is this! And yet! He stood there aloof and alone, staring hopelessly at a drawn blind and making, in his distraction, as though he could look
out. But yet he was happy. For he lived. His heart was full; hotly and sadly
it beat for thee, Ingeborg Holm, and his soul embraced thy blonde, simple, pert,
commonplace little personality in blissful self-abnegation.

Often after that he stood thus, with burning cheeks, in lonely corners,
whither the sound of music, the tinkling of glasses and fragrance of flowers
came but faintly, and tried to distinguish the ringing tones of thy voice amid
the distant happy din; stood suffering for thee—and still was happy! Often
it angered him to think that he might talk with Magdalena Vermehren, who
always fell down in the dance. She understood him, she laughed or was serious
in the right places; while Inge the fair, let him sit never so near her, seemed
remote and estranged, his speech not being her speech. And still—he was
happy. For happiness, he told himself, is not in being loved—which is a satisfaction of the vanity and mingled with disgust. Happiness is in loving, and
perhaps in snatching fugitive little approaches to the beloved object. And he
took inward note of this thought, wrote it down in his mind; followed out all
its implications and felt it to the depths of his soul.

"Faithfulness," thought Tonio Kröger. "Yes, I will be faithful, I will love
thee, Ingeborg, as long as I live!" He said this in the honesty of his intentions.
And yet a still small voice whispered misgivings in his ear: after all, he had
forgotten Hans Hansen utterly, even though he saw him every day! And the
hateful, the pitiable fact was that this still, small, rather spiteful voice was right:
time passed and the day came when Tonio Kröger was no longer so uncondi-
tionally ready as once he had been to die for the lively Inge, because he felt in
himself desires and powers to accomplish in his own way a host of wonderful
things in this world.

And he circled with watchful eye the sacrificial altar, where flickered the
pure, chaste flame of his love; knelt before it and tended and cherished it in
every way, because he so wanted to be faithful. And in a little while, unob-
servably, without sensation or stir, it went out after all.

But Tonio Kröger still stood before the cold altar, full of regret and dismay
at the fact that faithfulness was impossible upon this earth. Then he shrugged
his shoulders and went his way.

He went the way that go he must, a little idly, a little irregularly, whistling
to himself, gazing into space with his head on one side; and if he went wrong
it was because for some people there is no such thing as a right way. Asked

what in the world he meant to become, he gave various answers, for he was used to say (and had even already written it) that he bore within himself the possibility of a thousand ways of life, together with the private conviction that they were all sheer impossibilities.

Even before he left the narrow streets of his native city, the threads that bound him to it had gently loosened. The old Kröger family gradually declined, and some people quite rightly considered Tonio Kröger's own existence and way of life as one of the signs of decay. His father's mother, the head of the family, had died, and not long after his own father followed, the tall, thoughtful, carefully dressed gentleman with the field-flower in his buttonhole. The great Kröger house, with all its stately tradition, came up for sale, and the firm was dissolved. Tonio's mother, his beautiful, fiery mother, who played the piano and mandolin so wonderfully and to whom nothing mattered at all, she married again after a year's time; married a musician, moreover, a virtuoso with an Italian name, and went away with him into remote blue distances. Tonio Kröger found this a little irregular, but who was he to call her to order, who wrote poetry himself and could not even give an answer when asked what he meant to do in life?

And so he left his native town and its tortuous, gabled streets with the damp wind whistling through them; left the fountain in the garden and the ancient walnut tree, familiar friends of his youth; left the sea too, that he loved so much, and felt no pain to go. For he was grown up and sensible and had come to realize how things stood with him; he looked down on the lowly and vulgar life he had led so long in these surroundings.

He surrendered utterly to the power that to him seemed the highest on earth, to whose service he felt called, which promised him elevation and honours: the power of intellect, the power of the Word, that lords it with a smile over the unconscious and inarticulate. To this power he surrendered with all the passion of youth, and it rewarded him with all it had to give, taking from him inexorably, in return, all that it is wont to take.

It sharpened his eyes and made him see through the large words which puff out the bosoms of mankind; it opened for him men's souls and his own, made him clairvoyant, showed him the inwardness of the world and the ultimate behind men's words and deeds. And all that he saw could be put in two words: the comedy and the tragedy of life.

And then, with knowledge, its torment and its arrogance, came solitude; because he could not endure the blithe and innocent with their darkened understanding, while they in turn were troubled by the sign on his brow. But his love of the Word kept growing sweeter and sweeter, and his love of form; for he used to say (and had already said it in writing) that knowledge of the soul would unfailingly make us melancholy if the pleasures of expression did not keep us alert and of good cheer.

He lived in large cities and in the south, promising himself a luxuriant ripening of his art by southern suns; perhaps it was the blood of his mother's race that drew him thither. But his heart being dead and loveless, he fell into adventures of the flesh, descended into the depths of lust and searing sin, and suffering unspeakably thereby. It might have been his father in him, that tall, thoughtful, fastidiously dressed man with the wild flower in his buttonhole, that made him suffer so down there in the south; now and again he would feel a faint, yearning memory of a certain joy that was of the soul; once it had been his own, but now, in all his joys, he could not find it again.

Then he would be seized with disgust and hatred of the senses; pant after purity and seemly peace, while still he breathed the air of art, the tepid, sweet air of permanent spring, heavy with fragrance where it breeds and brews and burgeons in the mysterious bliss of creation. So for all results he was flung to and fro forever between two crass extremes: between icy intellect and scorching sense, and what with his pangs of conscience led an exhausting life, rare, extraordinary, excessive, which at bottom he, Tonio Kröger, despised. "What a labyrinth!" he sometimes thought. "How could I possibly have got into all these fantastic adventures? As though I had a wagonful of travelling gypsies for my ancestors!"

But as his health suffered from these excesses, so his artistry was sharpened; it grew fastidious, precious, *raffiné*, morbidly sensitive in questions of tact and taste, rasped by the banal. His first appearance in print elicited much applause; there was joy among the elect, for it was a good and workmanlike performance, full of humour and acquaintance with pain. In no long time his name—the same by which his masters had reproached him, the same he had signed to his earliest verses on the walnut tree and the fountain and the sea, those syllables compact of the north and the south, that good middle-class name with the exotic twist to it—became a synonym for excellence; for the painful thoroughness of the experiences he had gone through, combined with a tenacious ambition and a persistent industry, joined battle with the irritable fastidiousness of his taste and under grinding torments issued in work of a quality quite uncommon.

He worked, not like a man who works that he may live; but as one who is bent on doing nothing but work; having no regard for himself as a human being but only as a creator; moving about grey and unobtrusive among his fellows like an actor without his make-up, who counts for nothing as soon as he stops representing something else. He worked withdrawn out of sight and sound of the small fry, for whom he felt nothing but contempt, because to them a talent was a social asset like another; who, whether they were poor or not, went about ostentatiously shabby or else flaunted startling cravats, all the time taking jolly good care to amuse themselves, to be artistic and charming without the smallest notion of the fact that good work only comes out under pressure of a bad life; that he who lives does not work; that one must die to life in order to be utterly a creator.

"Shall I disturb you?" asked Tonio Kröger on the threshold of the atelier. He held his hat in his hand and bowed with some ceremony, although Lisabeta Ivanovna was a good friend of his, to whom he told all his troubles.

"Mercy on you, Tonio Kröger! Don't be so formal," answered she, with her lilting intonation. "Everybody knows you were taught good manners in your nursery." She transferred her brush to her left hand, that held the palette, reached him her right, and looked him in the face, smiling and shaking her head.

"Yes, but you are working," he said. "Let's see. Oh, you've been getting on," and he looked at the colour-sketches leaning against chairs at both sides of the easel and from them to the large canvas covered with a square linen mesh, where the first patches of colour were beginning to appear among the confused and schematic lines of the charcoal sketch.

This was in Munich, in a back building in Schellingstrasse, several storeys up. Beyond the wide window facing the north were blue sky, sunshine, birds twittering; the young sweet breath of spring streaming through an open pane mingled with the smells of paint and fixative. The afternoon light, bright golden, flooded the spacious emptiness of the atelier; it made no secret of the bad flooring or the rough table under the window, covered with little bottles, tubes, and brushes; it illumined the unframed studies on the unpapered walls, the torn silk screen that shut off a charmingly furnished little living-corner near the door; it shone upon the inchoate work on the easel, upon the artist and the poet there before it.

She was about the same age as himself—slightly past thirty. She sat there on a low stool, in her dark-blue apron, and leant her chin in her hand. Her brown hair, compactly dressed, already a little grey at the sides, was parted in the middle and waved over the temples, framing a sensitive, sympathetic, dark-skinned face, which was Slavic in its facial structure, with flat nose, strongly accentuated cheek-bones, and little bright black eyes. She sat there measuring her work with her head on one side and her eyes screwed up; her features were drawn with a look of misgiving, almost of vexation.

He stood beside her, his right hand on his hip, with the other furiously twirling his brown moustache. His dress, reserved in cut and a soothing shade of grey, was punctilious and dignified to the last degree. He was whistling softly to himself, in the way he had, and his slanting brows were gathered in a frown. The dark-brown hair was parted with severe correctness, but the laboured forehead beneath showed a nervous twitching, and the chiselled southern features were sharpened as though they had been gone over again with a graver's tool. And yet the mouth—how gently curved it was, the chin how softly formed! . . . After a little he drew his hand across his brow and eyes and turned away.

"I ought not to have come," he said.

"And why not, Tonio Kröger?"

"I've just got up from my desk, Lisabeta, and inside my head it looks just the way it does on this canvas. A scaffolding, a faint first draft smeared with corrections and a few splotches of colour; yes, and I come up here and see the same thing. And the same conflict and contradiction in the air," he went on, sniffing, "that has been torturing me at home. It's extraordinary. If you are possessed by an idea, you find it expressed everywhere, you even *smell* it. Fixative and the breath of spring; art and—what? Don't say nature, Lisabeta, 'nature' isn't exhausting. Ah, no, I ought to have gone for a walk, though it's doubtful if it would have made me feel better. Five minutes ago, not far from here, I met a man I know, Adalbert, the novelist. 'God damn the spring!' says he in the aggressive way he has. 'It is and always has been the most ghastly time of the year. Can you get hold of a single sensible idea, Kröger? Can you sit still and work out even the smallest effect, when your blood tickles till it's positively indecent and you are teased by a whole host of irrelevant sensations that when you look at them turn out to be unworkable trash? For my part, I am going to a café. A café is neutral territory, the change of the seasons doesn't affect it; it represents, so to speak, the detached and elevated sphere of the literary man, in which one is only capable of refined ideas.' And he went into the café . . . and perhaps I ought to have gone with him."

Lisabeta was highly entertained.

"I like that, Tonio Kröger. That part about the indecent tickling is good. And he is right, too, in a way, for spring is really not very conducive to work. But now listen. Spring or no spring, I will just finish this little place—work out this little effect, as your friend Adalbert would say. Then we'll go into the 'salon' and have tea, and you can talk yourself out, for I can perfectly well see you are too full for utterance. Will you just compose yourself somewhere—on that chest, for instance, if you are not afraid for your aristocratic garments—"

"Oh, leave my clothes alone, Lisabeta Ivanovna! Do you want me to go about in a ragged velveteen jacket or a red waistcoat? Every artist is as bohemian as the deuce, inside! Let him at least wear proper clothes and behave outwardly like a respectable being. No, I am not too full for utterance," he said as he watched her mixing her paints. "I've told you, it is only that I have a problem and a conflict, that sticks in my mind and disturbs me at any work. . . . Yes, what was it we were just saying? We were talking about Adalbert, the novelist, that stout and forthright man. 'Spring is the most ghastly time of the year,' says he, and goes into a café. A man has to know what he needs, eh? Well, you see he's not the only one; the spring makes me nervous, too; I get dazed with the triflingness and sacredness of the memories and feelings it evokes; only that I don't succeed in looking down on it; for the truth is it makes me ashamed; I quail before its sheer naturalness and triumphant youth. And I don't know whether I should envy Adalbert or despise him for his ignorance. . . .

"Yes, it is true; spring is a bad time for work; and why? Because we are feeling too much. Nobody but a beginner imagines that he who creates must feel. Every real and genuine artist smiles at such naïve blunders as that. A melancholy enough smile, perhaps, but still a smile. For what an artist talks about is never the main point; it is the raw material, in and for itself indifferent, out of which, with bland and serene mastery, he creates the work of art. If you care too much about what you have to say, if your heart is too much in it, you can be pretty sure of making a mess. You get pathetic, you wax sentimental;

something dull and doddering, without roots or outlines, with no sense of humour—something tiresome and banal grows under your hand, and you get nothing out of it but apathy in your audience and disappointment and misery in yourself. For so it is, Lisabeta; feeling, warm, heartfelt feeling, is always banal and futile; only the irritations and icy ecstasies of the artist's corrupted nervous system are artistic. The artist must be unhuman, extra-human; he must stand in a queer aloof relationship to our humanity; only so is he in a position, I ought to say only so would he be tempted, to represent it, to present it, to portray it to good effect. The very gift of style, of form and expression, is nothing else than this cool and fastidious attitude towards humanity; you might say there has to be this impoverishment and devastation as a preliminary condition. For sound natural feeling, say what you like, has no taste. It is all up with the artist as soon as he becomes a man and begins to feel. Adalbert knows that; that's why he betook himself to the café, the neutral territory—God help him!"

"Yes, God help him, Batuschka," said Lisabeta, as she washed her hands in a tin basin. "You don't need to follow his example."

"No, Lisabeta, I am not going to; and the only reason is that I am now and again in a position to feel a little ashamed of the springtime of my art. You see sometimes I get letters from strangers, full of praise and thanks and admiration from people whose feelings I have touched. I read them and feel touched myself at these warm if ungainly emotions I have called up; a sort of pity steals over me at this naïve enthusiasm; and I positively blush at the thought of how these good people would freeze up if they were to get a look behind the scenes. What they, in their innocence, cannot comprehend is that a properly constituted, healthy, decent man never writes, acts, or composes— all of which does not hinder me from using his admiration for my genius to goad myself on; nor from taking it in deadly earnest and aping the airs of a great man. Oh, don't talk to me, Lisabeta. I tell you I am sick to death of depicting humanity without having any part or lot in it. . . . Is an artist a male, anyhow? Ask the females! It seems to me we artists are all of us something like those unsexed papal singers . . . we sing like angels; but—"

"Shame on you, Tonio Kröger. But come to tea. The water is just on the boil, and here are some *papyros*. You were talking about singing soprano, do go on. But really you ought to be ashamed of yourself. If I did not know your passionate devotion to your calling and how proud you are of it—"

"Don't talk about 'calling,' Lisabeta Ivanovna. Literature is not a calling, it is a curse, believe me! When does one begin to feel the curse? Early, horribly early. At a time when one ought by rights still to be living in peace and harmony with God and the world. It begins by your feeling yourself set apart, in a curious sort of opposition to the nice, regular people; there is a gulf of ironic sensibility, of knowledge, scepticism, disagreement between you and the others; it grows deeper and deeper, you realize that you are alone; and from then on any *rapprochement* is simply hopeless! What a fate! That is, if you still have enough heart, enough warmth of affections, to feel how frightful it is!

... Your self-consciousness is kindled, because you among thousands feel the sign on your brow and know that everyone else sees it. I once knew an actor, a man of genius, who had to struggle with a morbid self-consciousness and instability. When he had no rôle to play, nothing to represent, this man, consummate artist but impoverished human being, was overcome by an exaggerated consciousness of his ego. A genuine artist—not one who has taken up art as a profession like another, but artist foreordained and damned—you can pick out, without boasting very sharp perceptions, out of a group of men. The sense of being set apart and not belonging, of being known and observed, something both regal and incongruous shows in his face. You might see something of the same sort on the features of a prince walking through a crowd in ordinary clothes. But no civilian clothes are any good here, Lisabeta. You can disguise yourself, you can dress up like an attaché or a lieutenant of the guard on leave; you hardly need to give a glance or speak a word before everyone knows you are not a human being, but something else: something queer, different, inimical.

"But what is it, to be an artist? Nothing shows up the general human dislike of thinking, and man's innate craving to be comfortable, better than his attitude to this question. When these worthy people are affected by a work of art, they say humbly that that sort of thing is a 'gift.' And because in their innocence they assume that beautiful and uplifting results must have beautiful and uplifting causes, they never dream that the 'gift' in question is a very dubious affair and rests upon extremely sinister foundations. Everybody knows that artists are 'sensitive' and easily wounded; just as everybody knows that ordinary people, with a normal bump of self-confidence, are not. Now you see, Lisabeta, I cherish at the bottom of my soul all the scorn and suspicion of the artist gentry—translated into terms of the intellectual—that my upright old forbears there on the Baltic would have felt for any juggler or mountebank that entered their houses. Listen to this. I know a banker, grey-haired business man, who has a gift for writing stories. He employs this gift in his idle hours, and some of his stories are of the first rank. But despite—I say despite—this excellent gift his withers are by no means unwrung: on the contrary, he has had to serve a prison sentence, on anything but trifling grounds. Yes, it was actually first *in prison* that he became conscious of his gift, and his experiences as a convict are the main theme in all his works. One might be rash enough to conclude that a man has to be at home in some kind of jail in order to become a poet. But can you escape the suspicion that the source and essence of his being an artist had less to do with his life in prison than they had with the reasons that *brought him there?* A banker who writes—that is a rarity, isn't it? But a banker who isn't a criminal, who is irreproachably respectable, and yet writes —he doesn't exist. Yes, you are laughing, and yet I am more than half serious. No problem, none in the world, is more tormenting than this of the artist and his human aspect. Take the most miraculous case of all, take the most typical and therefore the most powerful of artists, take such a morbid and profoundly equivocal work as *Tristan and Isolde,* and look at the effect it has on a healthy young man of thoroughly normal feelings. Exaltation, encouragement, warm, downright enthusiasm, perhaps incitement to 'artistic' creation of his own. Poor young dilettante! In us artists it looks fundamentally different from what he wots of, with his 'warm heart' and 'honest enthusiasm.' I've seen women and youths go mad over artists ... and I *knew* about them ... ! The origin, the accompanying phenomena, and the conditions of the artist life—good Lord, what I haven't observed about them, over and over!"

"Observed, Tonio Kröger? If I may ask, only 'observed'?"

He was silent, knitting his oblique brown brows and whistling softly to himself.

"Let me have your cup, Tonio. The tea is weak. And take another cigarette. Now, you perfectly know that you are looking at things as they do not necessarily have to be looked at. ..."

"That is Horatio's answer, dear Lisabeta. ' 'Twere to consider too curiously, to consider so.' "

"I mean, Tonio Kröger, that one can consider them just exactly as well from another side. I am only a silly painting female, and if I can contradict you at all, if I can defend your own profession a little against you, it is not by saying anything new, but simply by reminding you of some things you very well know yourself: of the purifying and healing influence of letters, the subduing of the passions by knowledge and eloquence; literature as the guide to understanding, forgiveness, and love, the redeeming power of the word, literary art as the noblest manifestation of the human mind, the poet as the most highly developed of human beings, the poet as saint. Is it to consider things not curiously enough, to consider them so?"

"You may talk like that, Lisabeta Ivanovna, you have a perfect right. And with reference to Russian literature, and the words of your poets, one can really worship them; they really come close to being that elevated literature you are talking about. But I am not ignoring your objections, they are part of the things I have in my mind today. ... Look at me, Lisabeta. I don't look any too cheerful, do I? A little old and tired and pinched, eh? Well, now to come back to the 'knowledge.' Can't you imagine a man, born orthodox, mild-mannered, well-meaning, a bit sentimental, just simply over-stimulated by his psychological clairvoyance, and going to the dogs? Not to let the sadness of the world unman you; to read, mark, learn, and put to account even the most torturing things and to be of perpetual good cheer, in the sublime consciousness of moral superiority over the horrible invention of existence—yes, thank you! But despite all the joys of expression once in a while the thing gets on your nerves. '*Tout comprendre c'est tout pardonner.*' I don't know about that. There is something I call being sick of knowledge, Lisabeta; when it is enough for you to see through a thing in order to be sick to death of it, and not in the least in a forgiving mood. Such was the case of Hamlet the Dane, that typical literary man. He knew what it meant to be called to knowledge without being born to it. To see things clear, if even through your tears, to recognize, notice, observe— and have to put it all down with a smile, at the very moment when hands are clinging, and lips meeting, and the human gaze is blinded with feeling—it is infamous, Lisabeta, it is indecent, outrageous—but what good does it do to be outraged?

"Then another and no less charming side of the thing, of course, is your ennui, your indifferent and ironic attitude towards truth. It is a fact that there is no society in the world so dumb and hopeless as a circle of literary people who are hounded to death as it is. All knowledge is old and tedious to them. Utter some truth that it gave you considerable youthful joy to conquer and possess—and they will all chortle at you for your naïveté. Oh, yes, Lisabeta, literature is a wearing job. In human society, I do assure you, a reserved and sceptical man can be taken for stupid, whereas he is really only arrogant and perhaps lacks courage. So much for 'knowledge.' Now for the 'Word.' It isn't so much a matter of the 'redeeming power' as it is of putting your emotions on ice and serving them up chilled! Honestly, don't you think there's a good deal of cool cheek in the prompt and superficial way a writer can get rid of his feelings by turning them into literature? If your heart is too full, if you are overpowered with the emotions of some sweet or exalted moment—nothing simpler! Go to the literary man, he will put it all straight for you instanter. He will analyse and formulate your affair, label it and express it and discuss it and polish it off and make you indifferent to it for time and eternity—and not charge you a farthing. You will go home quite relieved, cooled off, enlightened; and wonder what it was all about and why you were so mightily moved. And will you seriously enter the lists in behalf of this vain and frigid charlatan? What is uttered, so runs this *credo*, is finished and done with. If the whole world could be expressed, it would be saved, finished and done. . . . Well and good. But I am not a nihilist—"

"You are not a—" said Lisabeta. . . . She was lifting a teaspoonful of tea to her mouth and paused in the act to stare at him.

"Come, come, Lisabeta, what's the matter? I say I am not a nihilist, with respect, that is, to lively feeling. You see, the literary man does not understand that life may go on living, unashamed, even after it has been expressed and therewith finished. No matter how much it has been redeemed by becoming literature, it keeps right on sinning—for all action is sin in the mind's eye—

"I'm nearly done, Lisabeta. Please listen. I love life—this is an admission. I present it to you, you may have it. I have never made it to anyone else. People say—people have even written and printed—that I hate life, or fear or despise or abominate it. I liked to hear this, it has always flattered me; but that does not make it true. I love life. You smile; and I know why, Lisabeta. But I implore you not to take what I am saying for literature. Don't think of Cæsar Borgia or any drunken philosophy that has him for a standard-bearer. He is nothing to me, your Cæsar Borgia. I have no opinion of him, and I shall never comprehend how one can honour the extraordinary and dæmonic as an ideal. No, life as the eternal antinomy of mind and art does not represent itself to us as a vision of savage greatness and ruthless beauty; we who are set apart and different do not conceive it as, like us, unusual; it is the normal, respectable, and admirable that is the kingdom of our longing: life, in all its seductive banality! That man is very far from being an artist, my dear, whose last and deepest enthusiasm is the *raffiné*, the eccentric and satanic; who does not know a longing for the innocent, the simple, and the living, for a little friendship, devotion, familiar human happiness—the gnawing, surreptitious hankering, Lisabeta, for the bliss of the commonplace. . . .

"A genuine human friend. Believe me, I should be proud and happy to possess a friend among men. But up to now all the friends I have had have been dæmons, kobolds, impious monsters, and spectres dumb with excess of knowledge—that is to say, literary men.

"I may be standing upon some platform, in some hall in front of people who have come to listen to me. And I find myself looking round among my hearers, I catch myself secretly peering about the auditorium, and all the while I am thinking who it is that has come here to listen to me, whose grateful applause is in my ears, with whom my art is making me one. . . . I do not find what I seek, Lisabeta, I find the herd. The same old community, the same old gathering of early Christians, so to speak: people with fine souls in uncouth bodies, people who are always falling down in the dance, if you know what I mean; the kind to whom poetry serves as a sort of mild revenge on life. Always and only the poor and suffering, never any of the others, the blue-eyed ones, Lisabeta—they do not need mind. . . .

"And, after all, would it not be a lamentable lack of logic to want it otherwise? It is against all sense to love life and yet bend all the powers you have to draw it over to your own side, to the side of finesse and melancholy and the whole sickly aristocracy of letters. The kingdom of art increases and that of health and innocence declines on this earth. What there is left of it ought to be carefully preserved; one ought not to tempt people to read poetry who would much rather read books about the instantaneous photography of horses.

"For, after all, what more pitiable sight is there than life led astray by art? We artists have a consummate contempt for the dilettante, the man who is leading a living life and yet thinks he can be an artist too if he gets the chance. I am speaking from personal experience, I do assure you. Suppose I am in a company in a good house, with eating and drinking going on, and plenty of conversation and good feeling: I am glad and grateful to be able to lose myself among good regular people for a while. Then all of a sudden—I am thinking of something that actually happened—an officer gets up, a lieutenant, a stout, good-looking chap, whom I could never have believed guilty of any conduct unbecoming his uniform, and actually in good set terms asks the company's permission to read some verses of his own composition. Everybody looks disconcerted, they laugh and tell him to go on, and he takes them at their word and reads from a sheet of paper he has up to now been hiding in his coat-tail pocket—something about love and music, as deeply felt as it is inept. But I ask you: a lieutenant! A man of the world! He surely did not need to. . . . Well, the inevitable result is long faces, silence, a little artificial applause, everybody thoroughly uncomfortable. The first sensation I am conscious of is guilt—I feel partly responsible for the disturbance this rash youth has brought upon the company; and no wonder, for I, as a member of the same guild, am a target for some of the unfriendly glances. But next minute I realize something else: this man for whom just now I felt the greatest respect has suddenly sunk in my eyes. I feel a benevolent pity. Along with some other brave and good-natured gentlemen I go up and speak to him. 'Congratulations, Herr Lieutenant,' I say, 'that is a very pretty talent you have. It was charming.' And I am within an ace of clapping him on the shoulder. But is that the way one is supposed to feel towards a lieutenant—benevolent? . . . It was his own fault. There he stood, suffering embarrassment for the mistake of thinking that one may pluck a single leaf from the laurel tree of art without paying for it with his life. No, there I go with my colleague, the convict banker—but don't you find, Lisabeta, that I have quite a Hamlet-like flow of oratory today?"

"Are you done, Tonio Kröger?"

"No. But there won't be any more."

"And quite enough too. Are you expecting a reply?"

"Have you one ready?"

"I should say. I have listened to you faithfully, Tonio, from beginning to end, and I will give you the answer to everything you have said this afternoon and the solution of the problem that has been upsetting you. Now: the solution is that you, as you sit there, are, quite simply, a bourgeois."

"Am I?" he asked a little crestfallen.

"Yes, that hits you hard, it must. So I will soften the judgment just a little. You are a bourgeois on the wrong path, a bourgeois *manqué.*"

Silence. Then he got up resolutely and took his hat and stick.

"Thank you, Lisabeta Ivanovna; now I can go home in peace. I am expressed."

Towards autumn Tonio Kröger said to Lisabeta Ivanovna:

"Well, Lisabeta, I think I'll be off. I need a change of air. I must get away, out into the open."

"Well, well, well, little Father! Does it please your Highness to go down to Italy again?"

"Oh, get along with your Italy, Lisabeta. I'm fed up with Italy, I spew it out of my mouth. It's a long time since I imagined I could belong down there. Art, eh? Blue-velvet sky, ardent wine, the sweets of sensuality. In short, I don't want it—I decline with thanks. The whole *bellezza* business makes me nervous. All those frightfully animated people down there with their black animal-like eyes; I don't like them either. These Romance peoples have no soul in their eyes. No, I'm going to take a trip to Denmark."

"To Denmark?"

"Yes. I'm quite sanguine of the results. I happen never to have been there, though I lived all my youth so close to it. Still I have always known and loved the country. I suppose I must have this northern tendency from my father, for my mother was really more for the *bellezza,* in so far, that is, as she cared very much one way or the other. But just take the books that are written up there, that clean, meaty, whimsical Scandinavian literature, Lisabeta, there's nothing like it, I love it. Or take the Scandinavian meals, those incomparable meals, which can only be digested in strong sea air (I don't know whether I can digest them in any sort of air); I know them from my home too, because we ate that way up there. Take even the names, the given names that people rejoice in up north; we have a good many of them in my part of the country too: Ingeborg, for instance, isn't it the purest poetry—like a harp-tone? And then the sea— up there it's the Baltic! . . . In a word, I am going, Lisabeta, I want to see the Baltic again and read the books and hear the names on their native heath; I want to stand on the terrace at Kronberg, where the ghost appeared to Hamlet, bringing despair and death to that poor, noble-souled youth. . . ."

"How are you going, Tonio, if I may ask? What route are you taking?"

"The usual one," he said, shrugging his shoulders, and blushed perceptibly. "Yes, I shall touch my—my point of departure, Lisabeta, after thirteen years, and that may turn out rather funny."

She smiled.

"That is what I wanted to hear, Tonio Kröger. Well be off, then, in God's name. Be sure to write to me, do you hear? I shall expect a letter full of your experiences in—Denmark."

And Tonio Kröger travelled north. He travelled in comfort (for he was wont to say that anyone who suffered inwardly more than other people had a right to a little outward ease); and he did not stay until the towers of the little town he had left rose up in the grey air. Among them he made a short and singular stay.

The dreary afternoon was merging into evening when the train pulled into the narrow, reeking shed, so marvellously familiar. The volumes of thick smoke rolled up to the dirty glass roof and wreathed to and fro there in long tatters, just as they had, long ago, on the day when Tonio Kröger, with nothing but derision in his heart, had left his native town.— He arranged to have his luggage sent to his hotel and walked out of the station.

There were the cabs, those enormously high, enormously wide black cabs drawn by two horses, standing in a rank. He did not take one, he only looked at them, as he looked at everything: the narrow gables, and the pointed towers peering above the roofs close at hand; the plump, fair, easy-going populace, with their broad yet rapid speech. And a nervous laugh mounted in him, mysteriously akin to a sob.— He walked on, slowly, with the damp wind constantly in his face, across the bridge, with the mythological statues on the railings, and some distance along the harbour.

Good Lord, how tiny and close it all seemed! The comical little gabled streets were climbing up just as of yore from the port to the town! And on the ruffled waters the smoke-stacks and masts of the ships dipped gently in the wind and twilight. Should he go up the next street, leading, he knew, to a certain house? No, tomorrow. He was too sleepy. His head was heavy from the journey, and slow, vague trains of thought passed through his mind.

Sometimes in the past thirteen years, when he was suffering from indigestion, he had dreamed of being back home in the echoing old house in the steep, narrow street. His father had been there too, and reproached him bitterly for his dissolute manner of life, and this, each time, he had found quite as it should be. And now the present refused to distinguish itself in any way from one of those tantalizing dream-fabrications in which the dreamer asks himself if this be delusion or reality and is driven to decide for the latter, only to wake up after all in the end. . . . He paced through the half-empty streets with his head inclined against the wind, moving as though in his sleep in the direction of the hotel, the first hotel in the town, where he meant to sleep. A bow-legged man, with a pole at the end of which burned a tiny fire, walked before him with a rolling, seafaring gait and lighted the gas-lamps.

What was at the bottom of this? What was it burning darkly beneath the ashes of his fatigue, refusing to burst out into a clear blaze? Hush, hush, only no talk. Only don't make words! He would have liked to go on so, for a long time, in the wind, through the dusky, dreamily familiar streets—but everything was so little and close together here. You reached your goal at once.

In the upper town there were arc-lamps, just lighted. There was the hotel with the two black lions in front of it; he had been afraid of them as a child. And there they were, still looking at each other as though they were about to sneeze; only they seemed to have grown much smaller. Tonio Kröger passed between them into the hotel.

As he came on foot, he was received with no great ceremony. There was a porter, and a lordly gentleman dressed in black, to do the honours; the latter, shoving back his cuffs with his little fingers, measured him from the crown of his head to the soles of his boots, obviously with intent to place him, to assign him to his proper category socially and hierarchically speaking and then mete out the suitable degree of courtesy. He seemed not to come to any clear decision and compromised on a moderate display of politeness. A mild-mannered waiter with yellow-white sidewhiskers, in a dress suit shiny with age, and rosettes on his soundless shoes, led him up two flights into a clean old room furnished in patriarchal style. Its windows gave on a twilit view of courts and gables, very mediæval and picturesque, with the fantastic bulk of the old church close by. Tonio Kröger stood awhile before this window; then he sat down on the wide sofa, crossed his arms, drew down his brows, and whistled to himself.

Lights were brought and his luggage came up. The mild-mannered waiter laid the hotel register on the table, and Tonio Kröger, his head on one side, scrawled something on it that might be taken for a name, a station, and a place of origin. Then he ordered supper and went on gazing into space from his sofa-corner. When it stood before him he let it wait long untouched, then took a few bites and walked up and down an hour in his room, stopping from time to time and closing his eyes. Then he very slowly undressed and went to bed. He slept long and had curiously confused and ardent dreams.

It was broad day when he woke. Hastily he recalled where he was and got up to draw the curtains; the pale-blue sky, already with a hint of autumn, was streaked with frayed and tattered cloud; still, above his native city the sun was shining.

He spent more care than usual upon his toilette, washed and shaved and made himself fresh and immaculate as though about to call upon some smart family where a well-dressed and flawless appearance was *de rigueur;* and while occupied in this wise he listened to the anxious beating of his heart.

How bright it was outside! He would have liked better a twilight air like yesterday's, instead of passing through the streets in the broad sunlight, under everybody's eye. Would he meet people he knew, be stopped and questioned and have to submit to be asked how he had spent the last thirteen years? No, thank goodness, he was known to nobody here; even if anybody remembered him, it was unlikely he would be recognized—for certainly he had changed in the meantime! He surveyed himself in the glass and felt a sudden sense of security behind his mask, behind his work-worn face, that was older than his years. . . . He sent for breakfast, and after that he went out; he passed under the disdainful eye of the porter and the gentleman in black, through the vestibule and between the two lions, and so into the street.

Where was he going? He scarcely knew. It was the same as yesterday. Hardly was he in the midst of this long-familiar scene, this stately conglomeration of gables, turrets, arcades, and fountains, hardly did he feel once more the wind in his face, that strong current wafting a faint and pungent aroma from far-off dreams, when the same mistiness laid itself like a veil about his senses. . . . The muscles of his face relaxed, and he looked at men and things with a look grown suddenly calm. Perhaps right there, on that street corner, he might wake up after all. . . .

Where was he going? It seemed to him the direction he took had a connection with his sad and strangely rueful dreams of the night. . . . He went to Market Square, under the vaulted arches of the Rathaus, where the butchers were weighing out their wares red-handed, where the tall old Gothic fountain stood with its manifold spires. He paused in front of a house, a plain narrow building, like many another, with a fretted baroque gable; stood there lost in contemplation. He read the plate on the door, his eyes rested a little while on each of the windows. Then slowly he turned away.

Where did he go? Towards home. But he took a roundabout way outside the walls—for he had plenty of time. He went over the Millwall and over the Holstenwall, clutching his hat, for the wind was rushing and moaning through the trees. He left the wall near the station, where he saw a train puffing busily past, idly counted the coaches, and looked after the man who sat perched upon the last. In the Lindenplatz he stopped at one of the pretty villas, peered long into the garden and up at the windows, lastly conceived the idea of swinging the gate to and fro upon its hinges till it creaked. Then he looked awhile at his moist, rust-stained hand and went on, went through the squat old gate, along the harbour, and up the steep, windy street to his parents' house.

It stood aloof from its neighbors, its gable towering above them; grey and sombre, as it had stood these three hundred years; and Tonio Kröger read the pious, half-illegible motto above the entrance. Then he drew a long breath and went in.

His heart gave a throb of fear, lest his father might come out of one of the doors on the ground floor, in his office coat, with the pen behind his ear, and take him to task for his excesses. He would have found the reproach quite in order; but he got past unchidden. The inner door was ajar, which appeared to him reprehensible though at the same time he felt as one does in certain broken dreams, where obstacles melt away of themselves, and one presses onward in marvellous favour with fortune. The wide entry, paved with great square flags, echoed to his tread. Opposite the silent kitchen was the curious projecting structure, of rough boards, but cleanly varnished, that had been the servants' quarters. It was quite high up and could only be reached by a sort of ladder from the entry. But the great cupboards and carven presses were gone. The son of the house climbed the majestic staircase, with his hand on the white-enamelled, fret-work balustrade. At each step he lifted his hand, and put it down again with the next as though testing whether he could call back his ancient familiarity with the stout old railing. . . . But at the landing of the entresol he stopped. For on the entrance door was a white plate; and on it in black letters he read: "Public Library."

"Public Library?" thought Tonio Kröger. What were either literature or the public doing here? He looked . . . heard a "come in," and obeying it with gloomy suspense gazed upon a scene of most unhappy alteration.

The storey was three rooms deep, and all the doors stood open. The walls were covered nearly all the way up with long rows of books in uniform bindings, standing in dark-coloured bookcases. In each room a poor creature of a man sat writing behind a sort of counter. The farthest two just turned their heads, but the nearest got up in haste and, leaning with both hands on the table, stuck out his hand, pursed his lips, lifted his brows, and looked at the visitor with eagerly blinking eyes.

"I beg pardon," said Tonio Kröger without turning his eyes from the bookshelves. "I am a stranger here, seeing the sights. So this is your Public Library? May I examine your collection a little?"

"Certainly, with pleasure," said the official, blinking still more violently. "It is open to everybody. . . . Pray look about you. Should you care for a catalogue?"

"No, thanks," answered Tonio Kröger, "I shall soon find my way about." And he began to move slowly along the walls, with the appearance of studying the rows of books. After a while he took down a volume, opened it, and posted himself at the window.

This was the breakfast-room. They had eaten here in the morning instead of in the big dining-room upstairs, with its white statues of gods and goddesses standing out against the blue walls. . . . Beyond there had been a bedroom, where his father's mother had died—only after a long struggle, old as she was, for she had been of a pleasure-loving nature and clung to life. And his father too had drawn his last breath in the same room: that tall, correct, slightly melancholy and pensive gentleman with the wild flower in his buttonhole. ... Tonio had sat at the foot of his death-bed, quite given over to unutterable feelings of love and grief. His mother had knelt at the bedside, his lovely, fiery mother, dissolved in hot tears, and after that she had withdrawn with her artist into the far blue south. ... And beyond still, the small third room, likewise full of books and presided over by a shabby man—that had been for years on end his own. Thither he had come after school and a walk—like today's; against that wall his table had stood with the drawer where he had kept his first clumsy, heartfelt attempts at verse. ... The walnut tree ... a pang went through him. He gave a sidewise glance out at the window. The garden lay desolate, but there stood the old walnut tree where it used to stand, groaning and creaking heavily in the wind. And Tonio Kröger let his gaze fall upon the book he had in his hands, an excellent piece of work, and very familiar. He followed the black lines of print, the paragraphs, the flow of words that flowed with so much art, mounting in the ardour of creation to a certain climax and effect and then as artfully breaking off.

"Yes, that was well done," he said; put back the book and turned away. Then he saw that the functionary still stood bolt-upright, blinking with a mingled expression of zeal and misgiving. "A capital collection, I see," said Tonio Kröger. "I have already quite a good idea of it. Much obliged to you. Good-bye." He went out; but it was a poor exit, and he felt sure the official would stand there perturbed and blinking for several minutes.

He felt no desire for further researches. He had been home. Strangers were living upstairs in the large rooms behind the pillared hall; the top of the stairs was shut off by a glass door which used not to be there, and on the door was a plate. He went away, down the steps, across the echoing corridor, and left his parental home. He sought a restaurant, sat down in a corner, and brooded over a heavy, greasy meal. Then he returned to his hotel.

"I am leaving," he said to the fine gentleman in black. "This afternoon." And he asked for his bill, and for a carriage to take him down to the harbour where he should take the boat for Copenhagen. Then he went up to his room and sat there stiff and still, with his cheek on his hand, looking down on the table before him with absent eyes. Later he paid his bill and packed his things. At the appointed hour the carriage was announced and Tonio Kröger went down in travel array.

At the foot of the stairs the gentleman in black was waiting.

"Beg pardon," he said, shoving back his cuffs with his little fingers. ... "Beg pardon, but we must detain you just a moment. Herr Seehaase, the proprietor, would like to exchange two words with you. A matter of form. ... He is back there. ... If you will have the goodness to step this way. ... It is *only* Herr Seehaase, the proprietor."

And he ushered Tonio Kröger into the background of the vestibule. ... There, in fact, stood Herr Seehaase. Tonio Kröger recognized him from old time. He was small, fat, and bow-legged. His shaven side-whisker was white, but he wore the same old low-cut dress coat and little velvet cap embroidered in green. He was not alone. Beside him, at a little high desk fastened into the wall, stood a policeman in a helmet, his gloved right hand resting on a document in coloured inks; he turned towards Tonio Kröger with his honest, soldierly face as though he expected Tonio to sink into the earth at his glance.

Tonio Kröger looked at the two and confined himself to waiting.

"You came from Munich?" the policeman asked at length in a heavy, good-natured voice.

Tonio Kröger said he had.

"You are going to Copenhagen?"

"Yes, I am on the way to a Danish seashore resort."

"Seashore resort? Well, you must produce your papers," said the policeman. He uttered the last word with great satisfaction.

"Papers . . . ?" He had no papers. He drew out his pocketbook and looked into it; but aside from notes there was nothing there but some proof-sheets of a story which he had taken along to finish reading. He hated relations with officials and had never got himself a passport. . . .

"I am sorry," he said, "but I don't travel with papers."

"Ah!" said the policeman. "And what might be your name?"

Tonio replied.

"Is that a fact?" asked the policeman, suddenly erect, and expanding his nostrils as wide as he could. . . .

"Yes, that is a fact," answered Tonio Kröger.

"And what are you, anyhow?"

Tonio Kröger gulped and gave the name of his trade in a firm voice. Herr Seehaase lifted his head and looked him curiously in the face.

"H'm," said the policeman. "And you give out that you are not identical with an individdle named"—he said "individdle" and then, referring to his document in coloured inks, spelled out an involved, fantastic name which mingled all the sounds of all the races—Tonio Kröger forgot it next minute—"of unknown parentage and unspecified means," he went on, "wanted by the Munich police for various shady transactions, and probably in flight towards Denmark?"

"Yes, I give out all that, and more," said Tonio Kröger, wriggling his shoulders. The gesture made a certain impression.

"What? Oh, yes, of course," said the policeman. "You say you can't show any papers—"

Herr Seehaase threw himself into the breach.

"It is only a formality," he said pacifically, "nothing else. You must bear in mind the official is only doing his duty. If you could only identify yourself somehow—some document . . ."

They were all silent. Should he make an end of the business, by revealing to Herr Seehaase that he was no swindler without specified means, no gypsy in a green wagon, but the son of the late Consul Kröger, a member of the Kröger family? No, he felt no desire to do that. After all, were not these guardians of civic order within their right? He even agreed with them—up to a point. He shrugged his shoulders and kept quiet.

"What have you got, then?" asked the policeman. "In your portfoly, I mean?"

"Here? Nothing. Just a proof-sheet," answered Tonio Kröger.

"Proof-sheet? What's that? Let's see it."

And Tonio Kröger handed over his work. The policeman spread it out on the shelf and began reading. Herr Seehaase drew up and shared it with him. Tonio Kröger looked over their shoulders to see what they read. It was a good moment, a little effect he had worked out to a perfection. He had a sense of self-satisfaction.

"You see," he said, "there is my name. I wrote it, and it is going to be published, you understand."

"All right, that will answer," said Herr Seehaase with decision, gathered up the sheets and gave them back. "That will have to answer, Petersen," he repeated crisply, shutting his eyes and shaking his head as though to see and hear no more. "We must not keep the gentleman any longer. The carriage is waiting. I implore you to pardon the little inconvenience, sir. The officer has only done his duty, but I told him at once he was on the wrong track. . . ."

"Indeed!" thought Tonio Kröger.

The officer seemed still to have his doubts; he muttered something else about individdle and document. But Herr Seehaase, overflowing with regrets, led his guest through the vestibule, accompanied him past the two lions to the carriage, and himself, with many respectful bows, closed the door upon him. And then the funny, high, wide old cab rolled and rattled and bumped down the steep, narrow street to the quay.

And such was the manner of Tonio Kröger's visit to his ancestral home.

Night fell and the moon swam up with silver gleam as Tonio Kröger's boat reached the open sea. He stood at the prow wrapped in his cloak against a mounting wind, and looked beneath into the dark going and coming of the waves as they hovered and swayed and came on, to meet with a clap and shoot erratically away in a bright gush of foam.

He was lulled in a mood of still enchantment. The episode at the hotel, their wanting to arrest him for a swindler in his own home, had cast him down a little, even although he found it quite in order—in a certain way. But after he came on board he had watched, as he used to do as a boy with his father, the lading of goods into the deep bowels of the boat, amid shouts of mingled Danish and Plattdeutsch; not only boxes and bales, but also a Bengal tiger and a polar bear were lowered in cages with stout iron bars. They had probably come from Hamburg and were destined for a Danish menagerie. He had enjoyed these distractions. And as the boat glided along between flat river-banks he quite forgot Officer Petersen's inquisition; while all the rest—his sweet, sad, rueful dreams of the night before, the walk he had taken, the walnut tree—had welled up again in his soul. The sea opened out and he saw in the distance the beach where he as a lad had been let to listen to the ocean's summer dreams; saw the flashing of the lighthouse tower and the lights of the Kurhaus where he and his parents had lived. . . . The Baltic! He bent his head to the strong salt wind; it came sweeping on, it enfolded him, made him faintly giddy and a little deaf; and in that mild confusion of the senses all memory of evil, of anguish and error, effort and exertion of the will, sank away into joyous oblivion and were gone. The roaring, foaming, flapping, and slapping all about him came to his ears like the groan and rustle of an old walnut tree, the creaking of a garden gate. . . . More and more the darkness came on.

"The stars! Oh, by Lord, look at the stars!" a voice suddenly said, with a heavy singsong accent that seemed to come out of the inside of a tun. He recognized it. It belonged to a young man with red-blond hair who had been Tonio Kröger's neighbour at dinner in the salon. His dress was very simple, his eyes were red, and he had the moist and chilly look of a person who had just bathed. With nervous and self-conscious movements he had taken unto himself an astonishing quantity of lobster omelet. Now he leaned on the rail beside Tonio Kröger and looked up at the skies, holding his chin between thumb and forefinger. Beyond a doubt he was in one of those rare and festal and edifying moods that cause the barriers between man and man to fall; when the heart opens even to the stranger, and the mouth utters that which otherwise it would blush to speak. . . .

"Look, by dear sir, just look at the stars. There they stahd and glitter; by goodness, the whole sky is full of theb! And I ask you, when you stahd ahd look up at theb, ahd realize that bany of theb are a huddred tibes larger thad the earth, how does it bake you feel? Yes, we have idvehted the telegraph and the telephode and all the triuphs of our bodern tibes. But whed we look up there, after all we have to recogdize and uhderstad that we are worbs, biserable worbs, ahd dothing else. Ab I right, sir, or ab I wrog? Yes, we are worbs," he answered himself, and nodded meekly and abjectly in the direction of the firmament.

"Ah, no, he has no literature in his belly," thought Tonio Kröger. And he recalled something he had lately read, an essay by a famous French writer on cosmological and psychological philosophies, a very delightful *causerie*.

He made some sort of reply to the young man's feeling remarks, and they went on talking, leaning over the rail, and looking into the night with its movement and fitful lights. The young man, it seemed, was a Hamburg merchant on his holiday.

"Y'ought to travel to Copedhagen on the boat, thigks I, and so here I ab, and so far it's been fide. But they shouldn't have given us the lobster obelet, sir, for it's going to be storby—the captain said so hibself—and that's do joke with indigestible food like that in your stobach. . . ."

Tonio Kröger listened to all this engaging artlessness and was privately drawn to it.

"Yes," he said, "all the food up here is too heavy. It makes one lazy and melancholy."

"Belancholy?" repeated the young man, and looked at him, taken aback. Then he asked, suddenly: "You are a stradger up here, sir?"

"Yes, I come from a long way off," answered Tonio Kröger vaguely, waving his arm.

"But you're right," said the youth; "Lord kdows you are right about the belancholy. I am dearly always belancholy, but specially on evedings like this when there are stars in the sky." And he supported his chin again with thumb and forefinger.

"Surely this man writes verses," thought Tonio Kröger; "business man's verses, full of deep feeling and singlemindedness."

Evening drew on. The wind had grown so violent as to prevent them from talking. So they thought they would sleep a bit, and wished each other goodnight.

Tonio Kröger stretched himself out on the narrow cabin bed, but he found no repose. The strong wind with its sharp tang had power to rouse him; he was strangely restless with sweet anticipations. Also he was violently sick with the motion of the ship as she glided down a steep mountain of wave and her screw vibrated as in agony, free of the water. He put on all his clothes again and went up to the deck.

Clouds raced across the moon. The sea danced. It did not come on in fullbodied, regular waves; but far out in the pale and flickering light the water was lashed, torn, and tumbled; leaped upward like great licking flames; hung in jagged and fantastic shapes above dizzy abysses, where the foam seemed to be tossed by the playful strength of colossal arms and flung upward in all directions. The ship had a heavy passage; she lurched and stamped and groaned through the welter; and far down in her bowels the tiger and the polar bear voiced their acute discomfort. A man in an oilskin, with the hood drawn over his head and a lantern strapped to his chest, went straddling painfully up and down the deck. And at the stern, leaning far out, stood the young man from Hamburg suffering the worst. "Lord!" he said, in a hollow, quavering voice, when he saw Tonio Kröger. "Look at the uproar of the elebents, sir!" But he could say no more—he was obliged to turn hastily away.

Tonio Kröger clutched at a taut rope and looked abroad into the arrogance of the elements. His exultation outvied storm and wave; within himself he chanted a song to the sea, instinct with love of her: "O thou wild friend of my youth, Once more I behold thee—" But it got no further, he did not finish it. It was not fated to receive a final form nor in tranquillity to be welded to a perfect whole. For his heart was too full. . . .

Long he stood; then stretched himself out on a bench by the pilot-house and looked up at the sky, where stars were flickering. He even slept a little. And when the cold foam splashed his face it seemed in his half-dreams like a caress.

Perpendicular chalk-cliffs, ghostly in the moonlight, came in sight. They were nearing the island of Möen. Then sleep came again, broken by salty showers of spray that bit into his face and made it stiff. . . . When he really roused, it was broad day, fresh and palest grey, and the sea had gone down. At breakfast he saw the young man from Hamburg again, who blushed rosy-red for shame of the poetic indiscretions he had been betrayed into by the dark, ruffled up his little red-blond moustache with all five fingers, and called out a brisk and soldierly good-morning—after that he studiously avoided him.

And Tonio Kröger landed in Denmark. He arrived in Copenhagen, gave tips to everybody who laid claim to them, took a room at a hotel, and roamed the city for three days with an open guide-book and the air of an intelligent foreigner bent on improving his mind. He looked at the king's New Market and the "Horse" in the middle of it, gazed respectfully up the columns of the Frauenkirch, stood long before Thorwaldsen's noble and beautiful statuary, climbed the round tower, visited castles, and spent two lively evenings in the Tivoli. But all this was not exactly what he saw.

The doors of the houses—so like those in his native town, with open-work gables of baroque shape—bore names known to him of old; names that had a tender and precious quality, and withal in their syllables an accent of plaintive reproach, of repining after the lost and gone. He walked, he gazed, drawing deep, lingering draughts of moist sea air; and everywhere he saw eyes as blue, hair as blond, faces as familiar, as those that had visited his rueful dreams the night he had spent in his native town. There in the open street it befell him that a glance, a ringing word, a sudden laugh would pierce him to his marrow.

He could not stand the bustling city for long. A restlessness, half memory and half hope, half foolish and half sweet, possessed him; he was moved to drop this rôle of ardently inquiring tourist and lie somewhere, quite quietly, on a beach. So he took ship once more and travelled under a cloudy sky, over a black water, northwards along the coast of Seeland towards Helsingör. Thence he drove, at once, by carriage, for three-quarters of an hour, along and above the sea, reaching at length his ultimate goal, the little white "bath-hotel" with green blinds. It stood surrounded by a settlement of cottages, and its shingled turret tower looked out on the beach and the Swedish coast. Here he left the carriage, took possession of the light room they had ready for him, filled shelves and presses with his kit, and prepared to stop awhile.

It was well on in September; not many guests were left in Aalsgaard. Meals were served on the ground floor, in the great beamed dining-room, whose lofty windows led out upon the veranda and the sea. The landlady presided, an elderly spinster with white hair and faded eyes, a faint colour in her cheek and a feeble twittering voice. She was forever arranging her red hands to look well upon the table-cloth. There was a short-necked old gentleman, quite blue in the face, with a grey sailor beard; a fish-dealer he was, from the capital, and strong at the German. He seemed entirely congested and inclined to apoplexy; breathed in short gasps, kept putting his beringed first finger to one nostril, and snorting violently to get a passage of air through the other. Notwithstanding, he addressed himself constantly to the whisky-bottle, which stood at his place at luncheon and dinner, and breakfast as well. Besides him the company consisted only of three tall American youths with their governor or tutor, who kept adjusting his glasses in unbroken silence. All day long he played football with his charges, who had narrow, taciturn faces and reddish-yellow hair parted in the middle. "Please pass the *wurst*," said one. "That's not *wurst*, it's *schinken*," said the other, and this was the extent of their conversation, as the rest of the time they sat there dumb, drinking hot water.

Tonio Kröger could have wished himself no better table-companions. He revelled in the peace and quiet, listened to the Danish palatals, the clear and the clouded vowels in which the fish-dealer and the landlady desultorily conversed; modestly exchanged views with the fish-dealer on the state of the barometer, and then left the table to go through the veranda and onto the beach once more, where he had already spent long, long morning hours.

Sometimes it was still and summery there. The sea lay idle and smooth, in stripes and blue and russet and bottle-green, played all across with glittering silvery lights. The seaweed shrivelled in the sun and the jelly-fish lay steaming. There was a faintly stagnant smell and a whiff of tar from the fishing-boat against which Tonio Kröger leaned, so standing that he had before his eyes not the Swedish coast but the open horizon, and in his face the pure, fresh breath of the softly breathing sea.

Then grey, stormy days would come. The waves lowered their heads like bulls and charged against the beach; they ran and ramped high up the sands and left them strewn with shining wet sea-grass, driftwood, and mussels. All abroad beneath an overcast sky extended ranges of billows, and between them foaming valleys palely green; but above the spot where the sun hung behind the cloud a patch like white velvet lay on the sea.

Tonio Kröger stood wrapped in wind and tumult, sunk in the continual dull, drowsy uproar that he loved. When he turned away it seemed suddenly warm and silent all about him. But he was never unconscious of the sea at his back; it called, it lured, it beckoned him. And he smiled.

He went landward, by lonely meadow-paths, and was swallowed up in the beech-groves that clothed the rolling landscape near and far. Here he sat down on the moss, against a tree, and gazed at the strip of water he could see between the trunks. Sometimes the sound of surf came on the wind—a noise like boards collapsing at a distance. And from the tree-tops over his head a cawing—hoarse, desolate, forlorn. He held a book on his knee, but did not read a line. He enjoyed profound forgetfulness, hovered disembodied above space and time; only now and again his heart would contract with a fugitive pain, a stab of longing and regret, into whose origin he was too lazy to inquire.

Thus passed some days. He could not have said how many and had no desire to know. But then came one on which something happened; happened while the sun stood in the sky and people were about; and Tonio Kröger, even, felt no vast surprise.

The very opening of the day had been rare and festal. Tonio Kröger woke early and suddenly from his sleep, with a vague and exquisite alarm; he seemed to be looking at a miracle, a magic illumination. His room had a glass door and balcony facing the sound; a thin white gauze curtain divided it into living- and sleeping-quarters, both hung with delicately tinted paper and furnished with an airy good taste that gave them a sunny and friendly look. But now to his sleep-drunken eyes it lay bathed in a serene and roseate light, an unearthly brightness that gilded walls and furniture and turned the gauze curtain to radiant pink cloud. Tonio Kröger did not at once understand. Not until he stood at the glass door and looked out did he realize that this was the sunrise.

For several days there had been clouds and rain; but now the sky was like a piece of pale-blue silk, spanned shimmering above sea and land, and shot with light from red and golden clouds. The sun's disk rose in splendour from a crisply glittering sea that seemed to quiver and burn beneath it. So began the day. In a joyous daze Tonio Kröger flung on his clothes, and breakfasting in the veranda before everybody else, swam from the little wooden bathhouse some distance out into the sound, then walked for an hour along the beach. When he came back, several omnibuses were before the door, and from the dining-room he could see people in the parlour next door where the piano was, in the veranda, and on the terrace in front; quantities of people sitting at little tables enjoying beer and sandwiches amid lively discourse. There were whole families, there were old and young, there were even a few children.

At second breakfast—the table was heavily laden with cold viands, roast, pickled, and smoked—Tonio Kröger inquired what was going on.

"Guests," said the fish-dealer. "Tourists and ball-guests from Helsingör. Lord help us, we shall get no sleep this night! There will be dancing and music, and I fear me it will keep up till late. It is a family reunion, a sort of celebration and excursion combined; they all subscribe to it and take advantage of the good weather. They came by boat and bus and they are having breakfast. After that they go on with their drive, but at night they will all come back for a dance here in the hall. Yes, damn it, you'll see we shan't get a wink of sleep."

"Oh, it will be a pleasant change," said Tonio Kröger.

After that there was nothing more said for some time. The landlady arranged her red fingers on the cloth, the fish-dealer blew through his nostril, the Americans drank hot water and made long faces.

Then all at once a thing came to pass: *Hans Hansen and Ingeborg Holm walked through the room.*

Tonio Kröger, pleasantly fatigued after his swim and rapid walk, was leaning back in his chair and eating smoked salmon on toast; he sat facing the veranda and the ocean. All at once the door opened and the two entered hand-in-hand—calmly and unhurried. Ingeborg, blonde Inge, was dressed just as she used to be at Herr Knaak's dancing-class. The light flowered frock reached down to her ankles and it had a tulle fichu draped with a pointed opening that left her soft throat free. Her hat hung by its ribbons over her arm. She, perhaps, was a little more grown up than she used to be, and her wonderful plait of hair was wound round her head; but Hans Hansen was the same as ever. He wore his sailor overcoat with gilt buttons, and his wide blue sailor collar lay across his shoulders and back; the sailor cap with its short ribbons he was dangling carelessly in his hand. Ingeborg's narrow eyes were turned away; perhaps she felt shy before the company at table. But Hans Hansen turned his head straight towards them, and measured one after another defiantly with his steel-blue eyes; challengingly, with a sort of contempt. He even dropped Ingeborg's hand and swung his cap harder than ever, to show what manner of man he was. Thus the two, against the silent, blue-dyed sea, measured the length of the room and passed through the opposite door into the parlour.

This was at half past eleven in the morning. While the guests of the house were still at table the company in the veranda broke up and went away by the side door. No one else came into the dining-room. The guests could hear them laughing and joking as they got into the omnibuses, which rumbled away one by one. . . ." "So they are coming back?" asked Tonio Kröger.

"That they are," said the fish-dealer. "More's the pity. They have ordered music, let me tell you—and my room is right above the dining-room."

"Oh, well, it's a pleasant change," repeated Tonio Kröger. Then he got up and went away.

That day he spent as he had the others, on the beach and in the wood, holding a book on his knee and blinking in the sun. He had but one thought; they were coming back to have a dance in the hall, the fish-dealer had promised they would; and he did nothing but be glad of this, with a sweet and timorous gladness such as he had not felt through all these long dead years. Once he happened, by some chance association, to think of his friend Adalbert, the novelist, the man who had known what he wanted and betaken himself to the café to get away from the spring. Tonio Kröger shrugged his shoulders at the thought of him.

Luncheon was served earlier than usual, also supper, which they ate in the parlour because the dining-room was being got ready for the ball, and the whole house flung in disorder for the occasion. It grew dark; Tonio Kröger sitting in his room heard on the road and in the house the sounds of approaching festivity. The picnickers were coming back; from Helsingör, by bicycle and carriage, new guests were arriving; a fiddle and a nasal clarinet might be heard practising down in the dining-room. Everything promised a brilliant ball. . . .

Now the little orchestra struck up a march; he could hear the notes, faint but lively. The dancing opened with a polonaise. Tonio Kröger sat for a while and listened. But when he heard the march-time go over into a waltz he got up and slipped noiselessly out of his room.

From his corridor it was possible to go by the side stairs to the side entrance of the hotel and thence to the veranda without passing through a room. He took this route, softly and stealthily as though on forbidden paths, feeling along through the dark, relentlessly drawn by this stupid jigging music, that now came up to him loud and clear.

The veranda was empty and dim, but the glass door stood open into the hall, where shone two large oil lamps, furnished with bright reflectors. Thither he stole on soft feet; and his skin prickled with the thievish pleasure of standing unseen in the dark and spying on the dancers there in the brightly lighted room. Quickly and eagerly he glanced about for the two whom he sought. . . .

Even though the ball was only half an hour old, the merriment seemed in full swing; however, the guests had come hither already warm and merry, after a whole day of carefree, happy companionship. By bending forward a little, Tonio Kröger could see into the parlour from where he was. Several old gentlemen sat there smoking, drinking, and playing cards; others were with their wives on the plush-upholstered chairs in the foreground watching the dance. They sat with their knees apart and their hands resting on them, puffing out their cheeks with a prosperous air; the mothers, with bonnets perched on their parted hair, with their hands folded over their stomachs and their heads on one side, gazed into the whirl of dancers. A platform had been erected on the long side of the hall, and on it the musicians were doing their utmost. There was even a trumpet, that blew with a certain caution, as though afraid of its own voice, and yet after all kept breaking and cracking. Couples were dipping and circling about, others walked arm-in-arm up and down the room. No one wore ballroom clothes; they were dressed as for an outing in the summertime: the men in countrified suits which were obviously their Sunday wear; the girls in light-coloured frocks with bunches of field-flowers in their bodices. Even a few children were there, dancing with each other in their own way, even after the music stopped. There was a long-legged man in a coat with a little swallow-tail, a provincial lion with an eye-glass and frizzed hair, a post-office clerk or some such thing; he was like a comic figure stepped bodily out of a Danish novel; and he seemed to be the leader and manager of the ball. He was everywhere at once, bustling, perspiring, officious, utterly absorbed; setting down his feet, in shiny, pointed, military half-boots, in a very artificial and involved manner, toes first; waving his arms to issue an order, clapping his hands for the music to begin; here, there, and everywhere, and glancing over his shoulder in pride at his great bow of office, the streamers of which fluttered grandly in his rear.

Yes, there they were, those two, who had gone by Tonio Kröger in the broad light of day; he saw them again—with a joyful start he recognized them almost at the same moment. Here was Hans Hansen by the door, quite close; his legs apart, a little bent over, he was eating with circumspection a large piece of sponge-cake, holding his hand cupwise under his chin to catch the crumbs. And there by the wall sat Ingeborg Holm, Inge the fair; the post-office clerk was just mincing up to her with an exaggerated bow and asking her to dance. He laid one hand on his back and gracefully shoved the other into his bosom. But she was shaking her head in token that she was a little out of breath and must rest awhile, whereat the post-office clerk sat down by her side.

Tonio Kröger looked at them both, these two for whom he had in time past suffered love—at Hans and Ingeborg. They were Hans and Ingeborg not so much by virtue of individual traits and similarity of costume as by similarity of race and type. This was the blond, fair-haired breed of the steel-blue eyes, which stood to him for the pure, the blithe, the untroubled in life; for a virginal aloofness that was at once both simple and full of pride. . . . He looked at them. Hans Hansen was standing there in his sailor suit, lively and well built as ever, broad in the shoulders and narrow in the hips; Ingeborg was laughing and tossing her head in a certain high-spirited way she had; she carried her hand, a schoolgirl hand, not at all slender, not at all particularly aristocratic, to the back of her head in a certain manner so that the thin sleeve fell away from her elbow—and suddenly such a pang of home-sickness shook his breast that involuntarily he drew farther back into the darkness lest someone might see his features twitch.

"Had I forgotten you?" he asked. "No, never. Not thee, Hans, not thee, Inge the fair! It was always you I worked for; when I heard applause I always stole a look to see if you were there. . . . Did you read *Don Carlos*, Hans Hansen, as you promised me at the garden gate? No, don't read it! I do not ask it any more. What have you to do with a king who weeps for loneliness? You must not cloud your clear eyes or make them dreamy and dim by peering into melancholy poetry. . . . To be like you! To begin again, to grow up like you, regular like you, simple and normal and cheerful, in conformity and understanding with God and man, beloved of the innocent and happy. To take you, Ingeborg Holm, to wife, and have a son like you, Hans Hansen—to live free from the curse of knowledge and the torment of creation, live and praise God in blessed mediocrity! Begin again? But it would do no good. It would turn out the same— everything would turn out the same as it did before. For some go of necessity astray, because for them there is no such thing as a right path."

The music ceased; there was a pause in which refreshments were handed round. The post-office assistant tripped about in person with a trayful of herring salad and served the ladies; but before Ingeborg Holm he even went down on one knee as he passed her the dish, and she blushed for pleasure.

But now those within began to be aware of a spectator behind the glass door; some of the flushed and pretty faces turned to measure him with hostile glances; but he stood his ground. Ingeborg and Hans looked at him too, at almost the same time, both with that utter indifference in their eyes that looks so like contempt. And he was conscious too of a gaze resting on him from a different quarter; turned his head and met with his own the eyes that had sought him out. A girl stood not far off, with a fine, pale little face—he had already noticed her. She had not danced much, she had few partners, and he had seen her sitting there against the wall, her lips closed in a bitter line. She was standing alone now too; her dress was a thin light stuff, like the others, but beneath the transparent frock her shoulders showed angular and poor, and the thin neck was thrust down so deep between those meagre shoulders that as she stood there motionless she might almost be thought a little deformed. She was holding her hands in their thin mitts across her flat breast, with the finger-tips touching; her head was drooped, yet she was looking up at Tonio Kröger with black swimming eyes. He turned away. . . .

Here, quite close to him, were Ingeborg and Hans. He had sat down beside her—she was perhaps his sister—and they ate and drank together surrounded by other rosy-cheeked folk; they chattered and made merry, called to each other in ringing voices, and laughed aloud. Why could he not go up and speak to them? Make some trivial remark to him or her, to which they might at least answer with a smile? It would make him happy—he longed to do it; he would go back more satisfied to his room if he might feel he had established a little contact with them. He thought out what he might say; but he had not the courage to say it. Yes, this too was just as it had been: they would not understand him, they would listen like strangers to anything he was able to say. For their speech was not his speech.

It seemed the dance was about to begin again. The leader developed a comprehensive activity. He dashed hither and thither, adjuring everybody to get partners; helped the waiters to push chairs and glasses out of the way, gave orders to the musicians, even took some awkward people by the shoulders and shoved them aside.... What was coming? They formed squares of four couples each.... A frightful memory brought the colour to Tonio Kröger's cheeks. They were forming for a quadrille.

The music struck up, the couples bowed and crossed over. The leader called off; he called off—Heaven save us—in French! And pronounced the nasals with great distinction. Ingeborg Holm danced close by, in the set nearest the glass door. She moved to and fro before him, forwards and back, pacing and turning; he caught a waft from her hair or the thin stuff of her frock, and it made him close his eyes with the old, familiar feeling, the fragrance and bitter-sweet enchantment he had faintly felt in all these days, that now filled him utterly with irresistible sweetness. And what was the feeling? Longing, tenderness? Envy? Self-contempt?... *Moulinet des dames!* "Did you laugh, Ingeborg the blonde, did you laugh at me when I disgraced myself by dancing the *moulinet?* And would you still laugh today even after I have become something like a famous man? Yes, that you would, and you would be right to laugh. Even if I in my own person had written the nine symphonies and *The World as Will and Idea* and painted the Last Judgment, you would still be eternally right to laugh...." As he looked at her he thought of a line of verse once so familiar to him, now long forgotten: "I would sleep, but thou must dance." How well he knew it, that melancholy northern mood it evoked—its heavy inarticulateness. To sleep.... To long to be allowed to live the life of simple feeling, to rest sweetly and passively in feeling alone, without compulsion to act and achieve— and yet to be forced to dance, dance the cruel and perilous sword-dance of art; without even being allowed to forget the melancholy conflict within oneself; to be forced to dance, the while one loved....

A sudden wild extravagance had come over the scene. The sets had broken up, the quadrille was being succeeded by a galop, and all the couples were leaping and gliding about. They flew past Tonio Kröger to a maddeningly quick tempo, crossing, advancing, retreating, with quick, breathless laughter. A couple came rushing and circling towards Tonio Kröger; the girl had a pale, refined face and lean, high shoulders. Suddenly, directly in front of him, they tripped and slipped and stumbled.... The pale girl fell, so hard and violently it almost looked dangerous; and her partner with her. He must have hurt himself badly, for he quite forgot her, and, half rising, began to rub his knee and grimace; while she, quite dazed, it seemed, still lay on the floor. Then Tonio Kröger came forward, took her gently by the arms, and lifted her up. She looked dazed, bewildered, wretched; then suddenly her delicate face flushed pink.

"*Tak, O, mange tak!*" she said, and gazed up at him with dark, swimming eyes.

"You should not dance any more, Fräulein," he said gently. Once more he looked round at *them*, at Ingeborg and Hans, and then he went out, left the ball and the veranda and returned to his own room.

He was exhausted with jealousy, worn out with the gaiety in which he had had no part. Just the same, just the same as it had always been. Always with burning cheeks he had stood in his dark corner and suffered for you, you blond, you living, you happy ones! And then quite simply gone away. Somebody *must* come now! Ingeborg *must* notice he had gone, must slip after him, lay a hand on his shoulder and say: "Come back and be happy. I love you!" But she came not at all. No, such things did not happen. Yes, all was as it had been, and he too was happy, just as he had been. For his heart was alive. But between that past and this present what had happened to make him become that which he now was? Icy desolation, solitude: mind, and art, forsooth!

He undressed, lay down, put out the light. Two names he whispered into his pillow, the few chaste northern syllables that meant for him his true and native way of love, of longing and happiness; that meant to him life and home, meant simple and heartfelt feeling. He looked back on the years that had passed. He thought of the dreamy adventures of the senses, nerves, and mind in which he had been involved; saw himself eaten up with intellect and introspection, ravaged and paralysed by insight, half worn out by the fevers and frosts of creation, helpless and in anguish of conscience between two extremes, flung to and fro between austerity and lust; *raffiné*, impoverished, exhausted by frigid and artificially heightened ecstasies; erring, forsaken, martyred, and ill—and sobbed with nostalgia and remorse.

Here in his room it was still and dark. But from below life's lulling, trivial waltz-rhythm came faintly to his ears.

Tonio Kröger sat up in the north, composing his promised letter to his friend Lisabeta Ivanovna.

"Dear Lisabeta down there in Arcady, whither I shall shortly return," he wrote: "Here is something like a letter, but it will probably disappoint you, for I mean to keep it rather general. Not that I have nothing to tell; for indeed, in my way, I have had experiences; for instance, in my native town they were even going to arrest me . . . but of that by word of mouth. Sometimes now I have days when I would rather state things in general terms than go on telling stories.

"You probably still remember, Lisabeta, that you called me a *bourgeois, a bourgeois manqué?* You called me that in an hour when, led on by other confessions I had previously let slip, I confessed to you my love of life, or what I call life. I ask myself if you were aware how very close you came to the truth, how much my love of 'life' is one and the same thing as my being a *bourgeois.* This journey of mine has given me much occasion to ponder the subject.

"My father, you know, had the temperament of the north: solid, reflective, puritanically correct, with a tendency to melancholia. My mother, of indeterminate foreign blood, was beautiful, sensuous, naïve, passionate, and careless at once, and, I think, irregular by instinct. The mixture was no doubt extraordinary and bore with it extraordinary dangers. The issue of it, a *bourgeois* who strayed off into art, a bohemian who feels nostalgic yearnings for respectability, an artist with a bad conscience. For surely it is my *bourgeois* conscience makes me see in the artist life, in all irregularity and all genius, something profoundly suspect, profoundly disreputable; that fills me with this lovelorn *faiblesse* for the simple and good, the comfortably normal, the average unendowed respectable human being.

"I stand between two worlds. I am at home in neither, and I suffer in consequence. You artists call me a *bourgeois*, and the *bourgeois* try to arrest me. . . . I don't know which makes me feel worse. The *bourgeois* are stupid; but you adorers of the beautiful, who call me phlegmatic and without aspirations, you ought to realize that there is a way of being an artist that goes so deep and is so much a matter of origins and destinies that no longing seems to it sweeter and more worth knowing than longing after the bliss of the commonplace.

"I admire those proud, cold beings who adventure upon the paths of great and dæmonic beauty and despise 'mankind'; but I do not envy them. For if anything is capable of making a poet of a literary man, it is my *bourgeois* love of the human, the living and usual. It is the source of all warmth, goodness, and humour; I even almost think it is itself that love of which it stands written that one may speak with the tongues of men and of angels and yet having it not is as sounding brass and tinkling cymbals.

"The work I have so far done is nothing or not much—as good as nothing. I will do better, Lisabeta—this is a promise. As I write, the sea whispers to me and I close my eyes. I am looking into a world unborn and formless, that needs to be ordered and shaped; I see into a whirl of shadows of human figures who beckon to me to weave spells to redeem them: tragic and laughable figures and some that are both together—and to these I am drawn. But my deepest and secretest love belongs to the blond and blue-eyed, the fair and living, the happy, lovely, and commonplace.

"Do not chide this love, Lisabeta; it is good and fruitful. There is longing in it, and a gentle envy; a touch of contempt and no little innocent bliss."

Franz Kafka

THE METAMORPHOSIS

Preface

The Metamorphosis (1915) begins with Gregor Samsa waking up to find "himself transformed in his bed into a gigantic insect." In this way Franz Kafka's classic short novel fulfills the dream of Dostoevsky's underground man, who "wished to become an insect many times." Starting with *Notes from the Underground*, Kafka and Mann lead us in opposite directions: Mann's artist leaves Dostoevsky's cellar because life incorporates the possibility of wonder, and thus wonderfulness; Kafka follows the underground man to his grave, not in wet snow, but in a garbage heap. In *The Metamorphosis* the frog-prince of fairy tale cannot recover his humanity because wonder has been defeated by nightmare—by the conviction that what may be wonderful will always be horrible. There is no reality in Kafka's story; Gregor is caught in a nightmare that can never correspond to reality because it is reality understood as one horrible unreality that must be lived and died to be believed. We do not read *The Metamorphosis* again and again for novelty or for fright, but for the ultimate horror of Kafka's revelation that Gregor's fate is self-made. He doesn't wake up because he wants to acquiesce before holocaust, wants to define all martyrdom as masochism, wants finally to die. The twentieth century having shown us that men can treat other men as nothing—not as though they were nothing, but as nothing—our eternal fascination with Kafka's short novel is our fascination with a man, who, given the choice between nightmare and life, prefers to die in bed from unnatural causes. *The Metamorphosis* shows us two transformations: from man into bug, and from human bug into nothing. Kafka's greatness was to understand that the second of these transformations is always the more horrible—in a century that isn't always sure itself.

The Metamorphosis was first published in the series called *Judgment Day,* where Kafka's first story *The Judgment* (1913) was reprinted, and where *The Stoker,* the first chapter of the posthumously published novel *Amerika,* also appeared. The series thus includes most of the works Kafka published in his lifetime (1883–1924), the remaining pieces being the collection of short fiction, *A Country Doctor* (1919), and the important short novel *In the Penal Colony* (1919); a last collection, *A Hunger Artist* (1924), was read in proof by Kafka on his deathbed, but corrected finally by his friend Max Brod. Kafka told Brod to burn the unpublished manuscripts remaining after his death by tuberculosis, but Brod disregarded the request on the grounds that it was made knowingly to the one man who would never comply with it. So understanding Kafka, Brod edited and released the three great novels: *The Trial* (1925), *The Castle* (1926), and *Amerika* (1927). The history of Kafka's fiction can mislead us if we think that only one-quarter of his work was published before his death and forget that all of it was in fact written in the years from 1913 to 1924. The central experience of his life from age thirty to forty was the nightmare called the First World War, with its destruction of the old order and its introduction of the potential for universal death. In Kafka's work we find the fullest understanding of the last great nineteenth-century novel's bitterest prophecy—the prophecy of *Jude the Obscure* (1895), in which Thomas Hardy tells us that the suicide and murder of his novel's children manifests "the coming universal wish not to live." Kafka, of the generation of Hardy's children, was as much a child of the times as of his own family, with its authoritarian old-world father. Originally he planned to publish the three *Judgment Day* pieces in a single volume to be called *The Sons;* his later plan was to publish *The Judgment, The Metamorphosis,* and *In the Penal Colony* as a book entitled *Punishments.* The wider scope of "Punishments" tells us that Kafka had come to understand family conflict as a political metaphor. Both privately and publicly he was an outsider: undermined by his father, a German in Prague, educated in German not Czech, a Jew among Gentiles, and a writer who understood what the anarchy and insanity that followed World War I meant. Kafka's education earned him a Doctor of Jurisprudence in 1906, and soon after he went to work as an administrator in the equivalent of a modern Workmens Compensation System. There his imagination found the endless empty bureaucracies of his last novels— a further symptom of the sickness of the times. After 1917 his tuberculosis led him to the sanitorium world we know so well from Mann's *The Magic Mountain.* The experience confirmed Kafka as a sick man in a sick world. We can find bits and pieces of his history in *The Metamorphosis*—Gregor's name is as much Czech (*sám*—alone; *jsem*—I am) as Kafka, and Gregor's thoughts on "the sick-insurance doctor" certainly reflect Kafka's experiences. But neither biography nor psychology will completely explain *The Metamorphosis.* In that short novel, Kafka concentrated on the interrelationship of public and private neurosis, explaining how despairing pessimism fueled the madness between the wars. His genius isolated the mechanism of repression and its consequent drift toward death in a single character whose name cries out in alienation as his identity is erased by rising madness—while mad himself he lies down before it. "I have powerfully assumed the negativity of my times," wrote Kafka in his own diary.

The measure of Kafka's power is the absolute fiat with which *The Metamorphosis* begins: Gregor Samsa has turned into a bug and that's that. Kafka's *fait accompli* means to foil three questions: did it happen? how did it happen?, and what exactly happened—what kind of bug did Gregor become? These three questions cannot be answered because the event must be taken for granted —taking it for granted is its cause. To take a human being for granted is to treat him as nothing, and such treatment is the very cause of Gregor's metamorphosis. What happened happened because it happened—and with this logic Kafka forces us to acknowledge the world of nightmare metaphor as the only existing world. Gregor's transformation is from life to a state of death-in-life, and Kafka's point is to show us his inability to imagine himself back to manhood. Living death means the death of the imagination, the secret of Gregor's acquiescence. When we seek to make the insect real by giving it a name—bedbug hence commercial traveler hence Gregor the parasite, or cockroach hence the survivor hero of our time hence Gregor as id against superego, or beetle hence fertility scarab hence Gregor castrated by Kierkegaard—we disregard Kafka's statement that the insect could not be drawn. The bug must be imagined in order that the novel awaken our own imagination.

Gregor's initial reaction is deadpan: "What has happened to me? he thought. It was no dream." We immediately want to read—"What have they done to me this time?"—because Gregor's tone knows that persecution has become predictable, and almost immediately it slides into self-pitying complaint. We sense that Gregor would rather indulge than escape: "What about sleeping a little longer and forgetting all this nonsense, he thought, but . . . he was accustomed to sleep on his right side and in his present condition he could not turn himself over." Here Kafka is brilliantly ironic: Gregor's body has revolted against his mind; he cannot sleep longer because he has slept too long in the bed of repression by getting up too early all along. He can't turn over—change, expose, imagine—because he has postponed action with never-realized plans of future escape. Even the underground man knew that those who work to pay off others' debts only end up more deeply in debt themselves. Gregor is a bug because he has slept through the alarm, not heard it though it "had been properly set." His change is a last warning that time will run out completely, but paradoxically Gregor feels healthier as a bug than as the selfish robot he was. So death seduces him by being more comfortable than life. This for Kafka is the consequence of being taught to accept persecution and to think that humanity may still be preserved. Man cannot live on survival alone is the strong warning. It is underlined by irony that reveals Gregor's struggle as a macabre will not to survive at all. Wanting first to go back to sleep, he then struggles to get up without knocking himself out: "At all costs he must not lose consciousness now, precisely now; he would rather stay in bed." But in bed he can't go back to sleep—knocked out he would clearly be better off. The masochism of all his past martyrdom is thus revealed to us. Gregor comes from a family of martyrs all of whom are having trouble breathing because their collective self-sacrifice has paralysis rather than transcendence as its goal. Gregor has made the family helpless, and they remain helpless, just as he as bug struggling to get up is helpless, because they wish to be so. When we ask finally why Gregor doesn't call for first aid, Kafka gives us this answer: "Ought he really to call for help? In spite of his misery he could not suppress a smile at the very idea of it." The smile tells us that language and locked doors are not real problems. Gregor smiles because ultimately he knows that no one can help him but himself, and he will not help himself because he seeks pity precisely by putting himself above it. Kafka's nightmare shows human emotions so far turned back upon themselves as to pervert life into death, and death into a final complaint against being forced to live in the first place. In the first of the three parental confrontations that mark the end of the novel's three cycles, Gregor's "father gave him a strong push which was literally a deliverance and he flew far into the room, bleeding freely." When deliverance forces us back into a locked room in which we must die, we understand that birth has become death. The logic that exchanges the two is the logic of Gregor's smile, and it is equally at work in his sister, who begins to "exaggerate the horror of her brother's circumstances in order that she might do all the more for him." She has learned this selfish style of martyrdom from Gregor, whose death began long ago when he lost his anger. By contrast his family grows increasingly healthy as it becomes more angry with him, moving toward his original state as he towards theirs. Anger makes the father throw an apple into Gregor's back and so crucify him as much as it makes his sister as beauty take no ultimate pity on Gregor the beast—but it is Gregor who turns religion and fable into nightmare by loving himself to death for their sake. So Kafka's irony makes Gregor's sister kill him with his own philosophy: "You must just try to get rid of the idea that this is Gregor. The fact that we've believed it for so long is the root of all our trouble. But how can it be Gregor? If this were Gregor, he would have realized long ago that human beings can't live with such a creature, and he'd have gone away on his own accord." If the bug is Gregor it would have died for us, and because it didn't die we are justified in killing it for it is not human; thinking this way, Grete kills Gregor by replacing him. By showing how a logic that reverses means and ends evolves, Kafka finds a fascist skeleton in the bourgeois family closet. But his most horrible discovery is the knowledge that Gregor wants to be that skeleton: "He thought of his family with tenderness and love. The decision that he must disappear was one that he held to even more strongly than his sister, if that were possible." Kafka' genius is to insist that it *is* possible, and that is to insist that Gregor's desire is not to have existed.

Gregor fulfills his death wish like a spoiled child, starving himself because that way he might receive the "unknown nourishment" denied him. In this way Kafka's punishment fantasy achieves its goal: revelation by and in negation. The operation of the novel succeeds by killing the patient to answer his question: "But what if all the quiet, the comfort, the contentment were now to end in horror?" The enshrinement of quiet is the worship of death, believed Kafka, just as he knew that silence was the ultimate weapon of the middle-class family. He has the maid leave promising to "never say a single word" about Gregor, who is satisfied that the family somehow got rid of the summoned doctor, keeping its curse to itself. A conspiracy of silence, one to which self-abnegating Gregor agrees, keeps him in the family closet where he dies a skeleton without a key. Self-expression is the key because Gregor, who expected equal help from a doctor and a locksmith jointly, manages to open the door of his ever-locked room with his mouth. But he does so thinking: "If they were horrified then the responsibility was no longer his and he could stay quiet. But if they took it calmly, then he had no reason either to be upset." Quiet either way here means that a world which accepts Gregor's delusions recognizes that he is nothing, and recognizing that, it shows itself as insanely neurotic as he is. Gregor's final solution, his ultimate evasion of human responsibility, is to understand others and refuse to have them understand him: "He heard his own voice . . . unmistakably his own voice, it was true, but with a persistent horrible twittering squeak behind it like an undertone, that left the words in their clear shape only for the first moment and then rose up reverberating round them to destroy their sense, so that one could not be sure one had heard them rightly." Gregor speaks this way, and Kafka speaking for him does so exactly. We read *The Metamorphosis* wondering if we have heard rightly, because it wants to remind us of the undertone that destroys sense. Too much sensory repression will destroy us—as ultimately Gregor's undertone destroys him. Only putting his own undertone into words saved Kafka.

Kafka

THE
METAMORPHOSIS

Translated by Willa and Edwin Muir

I

As Gregor Samsa awoke one morning from uneasy dreams he found himself transformed in his bed into a gigantic insect. He was lying on his hard, as it were armor-plated, back and when he lifted his head a little he could see his dome-like brown belly divided into stiff arched segments on top of which the bed quilt could hardly keep in position and was about to slide off completely. His numerous legs, which were pitifully thin compared to the rest of his bulk, waved helplessly before his eyes.

What has happened to me? he thought. It was no dream. His room, a regular human bedroom, only rather too small, lay quiet between the four familiar walls. Above the table on which a collection of cloth samples was unpacked and spread out—Samsa was a commercial traveler—hung the picture which he had recently cut out of an illustrated magazine and put into a pretty gilt frame. It showed a lady, with a fur cap on and a fur stole, sitting upright and holding out to the spectator a huge fur muff into which the whole of her forearm had vanished!

Gregor's eyes turned next to the window, and the overcast sky—one could hear rain drops beating on the window gutter—made him quite melancholy. What about sleeping a little longer and forgetting all this nonsense, he thought, but it could not be done, for he was accustomed to sleep on his right side and in his present condition he could not turn himself over. However violently he forced himself towards his right side he always rolled on to his back again. He tried it at least a hundred times, shutting his eyes to keep from seeing his struggling legs, and only desisted when he began to feel in his side a faint dull ache he had never experienced before.

Oh God, he thought, what an exhausting job I've picked on! Traveling about day in, day out. It's much more irritating work than doing the actual business in the office, and on top of that there's the trouble of constant traveling, of worrying about train connections, the bed and irregular meals, casual acquaintances that are always new and never become intimate friends. The devil take it all! He felt a slight itching up on his belly; slowly pushed himself on his back nearer to the top of the bed so that he could lift his head more easily; identified the itching place which was surrounded by many small white spots the nature of which he could not understand and made to touch it with a leg, but drew the leg back immediately, for the contact made a cold shiver run through him.

He slid down again into his former position. This getting up early, he thought, makes one quite stupid. A man needs his sleep. Other commercials live like harem women. For instance, when I come back to the hotel of a morning to write up the orders I've got, these others are only sitting down to breakfast. Let me just try that with my chief; I'd be sacked on the spot. Anyhow, that might be quite a good thing for me, who can tell? If I didn't have to hold my hand because of my parents I'd have given notice long ago, I'd have gone to the chief and told him exactly what I think of him. That would knock him endways from his desk! It's a queer way of doing, too, this sitting on high at a desk and talking down to employees, especially when they have to come quite near because the chief is hard of hearing. Well, there's still hope; once I've saved enough money to pay back my parents' debts to him—that should take another five or six years—I'll do it without fail. I'll cut myself completely loose then. For the moment, though, I'd better get up, since my train goes at five.

He looked at the alarm clock ticking on the chest. Heavenly Father! he thought. It was half-past six o'clock and the hands were quietly moving on, it was even past the half-hour, it was getting on toward a quarter to seven. Had the alarm clock not gone off? From the bed one could see that it had been properly set for four o'clock; of course it must have gone off. Yes, but was it possible to sleep quietly through that ear-splitting noise? Well, he had not slept quietly, yet apparently all the more soundly for that. But what was he to do now? The next train went at seven o'clock; to catch that he would need to hurry like mad and his samples weren't even packed up, and he himself wasn't feeling particularly fresh and active. And even if he did catch the train he wouldn't avoid a row with the chief, since the firm's porter would have been waiting for the five o'clock train and would have long since reported his failure to turn up. The porter was a creature of the chief's, spineless and stupid. Well, supposing he were to say he was sick? But that would be most unpleasant and would look suspicious, since during his five years' employment he had not been ill once. The chief himself would be sure to come with the sick-insurance doctor, would reproach his parents with their son's laziness and would cut all excuses short by referring to the insurance doctor, who of course regarded all mankind as perfectly healthy malingerers. And would he be so far wrong on this occasion? Gregor really felt quite well, apart from a drowsiness that was utterly superfluous after such a long sleep, and he was even unusually hungry.

As all this was running through his mind at top speed without his being able to decide to leave his bed—the alarm clock had just struck a quarter to seven—there came a cautious tap at the door behind the head of his bed. "Gregor," said a voice—it was his mother's—"it's a quarter to seven. Hadn't you a train to catch?" That gentle voice! Gregor had a shock as he heard his own voice answering hers, unmistakably his own voice, it was true, but with a persistent horrible twittering squeak behind it like an undertone, that left the words in their clear shape only for the first moment and then rose up reverberating round them to destroy their sense, so that one could not be sure one had heard them rightly. Gregor wanted to answer at length and explain everything, but in the circumstances he confined himself to saying: "Yes, yes, thank you, Mother, I'm getting up now." The wooden door between them must have kept the change in his voice from being noticeable outside, for his mother contented herself with this statement and shuffled away. Yet this brief exchange of words had made the other members of the family aware that Gregor was still in the house, as they had not expected, and at one of the side doors his father was already knocking, gently, yet with his fist. "Gregor, Gregor," he called, "what's the matter with you?" And after a little while he called again in a deeper voice: "Gregor! Gregor!" At the other side door his sister was saying in a low, plaintive tone: "Gregor? Aren't you well? Are you needing anything?" He answered them both at once: "I'm just ready," and did his best to make his voice sound as normal as possible by enunciating the words very clearly and leaving long pauses between them. So his father went back to his breakfast, but his sister whispered: "Gregor, open the door, do." However, he was not thinking of opening the door, and felt thankful for the prudent habit he had acquired in traveling of locking all doors during the night, even at home.

His immediate intention was to get up quietly without being disturbed, to put on his clothes and above all eat his breakfast, and only then to consider what else was to be done, since in bed, he was well aware, his meditations would come to no sensible conclusion. He remembered that often enough in bed he had felt small aches and pains, probably caused by awkward postures, which had proved purely imaginary once he got up, and he looked forward eagerly to seeing this morning's delusions gradually fall away. That the change in his voice was nothing but the precursor of a severe chill, a standing ailment of commercial travelers, he had not the least possible doubt.

To get rid of the quilt was quite easy; he had only to inflate himself a little and it fell off by itself. But the next move was difficult, especially because he was so uncommonly broad. He would have needed arms and hands to hoist himself up; instead he had only the numerous little legs which never stopped waving in all directions and which he could not control in the least. When he tried to bend one of them it was the first to stretch itself straight; and did he succeed at last in making it do what he wanted, all the other legs meanwhile waved the more wildly in a high degree of unpleasant agitation. "But what's the use of lying idle in bed," said Gregor to himself.

He thought that he might get out of bed with the lower part of his body first, but this lower part, which he had not yet seen and of which he could form no clear conception, proved too difficult to move; it shifted so slowly; and when finally, almost wild with annoyance, he gathered his forces together and thrust out recklessly, he had miscalculated the direction and bumped heavily against the lower end of the bed, and the stinging pain he felt informed him that precisely this lower part of his body was at the moment probably the most sensitive.

So he tried to get the top part of himself out first, and cautiously moved his head towards the edge of the bed. That proved easy enough, and despite its breadth and mass the bulk of his body at last slowly followed the movement of his head. Still, when he finally got his head free over the edge of the bed he felt too scared to go on advancing, for after all if he let himself fall in this way it would take a miracle to keep his head from being injured. And at all costs he must not lose consciousness now, precisely now; he would rather stay in bed.

But when after a repetition of the same efforts he lay in his former position again, sighing, and watched his little legs struggling against each other more wildly than ever, if that were possible, and saw no way of bringing any order into this arbitrary confusion, he told himself again that it was impossible to stay in bed and that the most sensible course was to risk everything for the smallest hope of getting away from it. At the same time he did not forget meanwhile to remind himself that cool reflection, the coolest possible, was much better than desperate resolves. In such moments he focused his eyes as sharply as possible on the window, but, unfortunately, the prospect of the morning fog, which muffled even the other side of the narrow street, brought him little encouragement and comfort. "Seven o'clock already," he said to himself when the alarm clock chimed again, "seven o'clock already and still such a thick fog." And for a little while he lay quiet, breathing lightly, as if perhaps expecting such complete repose to restore all things to their real and normal condition.

But then he said to himself: "Before it strikes a quarter past seven I must be quite out of this bed, without fail. Anyhow, by that time someone will have come from the office to ask for me, since it opens before seven." And he set himself to rocking his whole body at once in a regular rhythm, with the idea of swinging it out of the bed. If he tipped himself out in that way he could keep his head from injury by lifting it at an acute angle when he fell. His back seemed to be hard and was not likely to suffer from a fall on the carpet. His biggest worry was the loud crash he would not be able to help making, which would probably cause anxiety, if not terror, behind all the doors. Still, he must take the risk.

When he was already half out of the bed—the new method was more a game than an effort, for he needed only to hitch himself across by rocking to and fro—it struck him how simple it would be if he could get help. Two strong people—he thought of his father and the servant girl—would be amply sufficient; they would only have to thrust their arms under his convex back, lever him out of the bed, bend down with their burden and then be patient enough to let him turn himself right over on to the floor, where it was to be hoped his legs would then find their proper function. Well, ignoring the fact that the doors were all locked, ought he really to call for help? In spite of his misery he could not suppress a smile at the very idea of it.

He had got so far that he could barely keep his equilibrium when he rocked himself strongly, and he would have to nerve himself very soon for the final decision since in five minutes' time it would be a quarter past seven—when the front door bell rang. "That's someone from the office," he said to himself, and grew almost rigid, while his little legs only jigged about all the faster. For a moment everything stayed quiet. "They're not going to open the door," said Gregor to himself, catching at some kind of irrational hope. But then of course the servant girl went as usual to the door with her heavy tread and opened it. Gregor needed only to hear the first good morning of the visitor to know immediately who it was—the chief clerk himself. What a fate, to be condemned to work for a firm where the smallest omission at once gave rise to the gravest suspicion! Were all employees in a body nothing but scoundrels, was there not among them one single loyal devoted man who, had he wasted only an hour or so of the firm's time in a morning, was so tormented by conscience as to be driven out of his mind and actually incapable of leaving his bed? Wouldn't it really have been sufficient to send an apprentice to inquire—if any inquiry were necessary at all—did the chief clerk himself have to come and thus indicate to the entire family, an innocent family, that this suspicious circumstance could be investigated by no one less versed in affairs than himself? And more through the agitation caused by these reflections than through any act of will Gregor swung himself out of bed with all his strength. There was a loud thump, but it was not really a crash. His fall was broken to some extent by the carpet, his back, too, was less stiff than he thought, and so there was merely a dull thud, not so very startling. Only he had not lifted his head carefully enough and had hit it; he turned it and rubbed it on the carpet in pain and irritation.

"That was something falling down in there," said the chief clerk in the next room to the left. Gregor tried to suppose to himself that something like what had happened to him today might some day happen to the chief clerk; one really could not deny that it was possible. But as if in brusque reply to this supposition the chief clerk took a couple of firm steps in the next-door room and his patent leather boots creaked. From the right-hand room his sister was whispering to inform him of the situation: "Gregor, the chief clerk's here." "I know," muttered Gregor to himself; but he didn't dare to make his voice loud enough for his sister to hear it.

"Gregor," said his father now from the left-hand room, "the chief clerk has come and wants to know why you didn't catch the early train. We don't know what to say to him. Besides, he wants to talk to you in person. So open the door, please. He will be good enough to excuse the untidiness of your room." "Good morning, Mr. Samsa," the chief clerk was calling amiably meanwhile. "He's not well," said his mother to the visitor, while his father was still speaking through the door, "he's not well, sir, believe me. What else would make him miss a train! The boy thinks about nothing but his work. It makes me almost cross the way he never goes out in the evenings; he's been here the last eight days and has stayed at home every single evening. He just sits there quietly at the table reading a newspaper or looking through railway timetables. The only amusement he gets is doing fretwork. For instance, he spent two or three evenings cutting out a little picture frame; you would be surprised to see how pretty it is; it's hanging in his room; you'll see it in a minute when Gregor opens the door. I must say I'm glad you've come, sir; we should never have got him to unlock the door by ourselves; he's so obstinate; and I'm sure he's unwell, though he wouldn't have it to be so this morning." "I'm just coming," said Gregor slowly and carefully, not moving an inch for fear of losing one word of the conversation. "I can't think of any other explanation, madam," said the chief clerk, "I hope it's nothing serious. Although on the other hand I must say that we men of business—fortunately or unfortunately—very often simply have to ignore any slight indisposition, since business must be attended to." "Well, can the chief clerk come in now?" asked Gregor's father impatiently, again knocking on the door. "No," said Gregor. In the left-hand room a painful silence followed this refusal, in the right-hand room his sister began to sob.

Why didn't his sister join the others? She was probably newly out of bed and hadn't even begun to put on her clothes yet. Well, why was she crying? Because he wouldn't get up and let the chief clerk in, because he was in danger of losing his job, and because the chief would begin dunning his parents again for the old debts? Surely these were things one didn't need to worry about for the present. Gregor was still at home and not in the least thinking of deserting the family. At the moment, true, he was lying on the carpet and no one who knew the condition he was in could seriously expect him to admit the chief clerk. But for such a small discourtesy, which could plausibly be explained away somehow later on, Gregor could hardly be dismissed on the spot. And it seemed to Gregor that it would be much more sensible to leave him in peace for the present than to trouble him with tears and entreaties. Still, of course, their uncertainty bewildered them all and excused their behavior.

"Mr. Samsa," the chief clerk called now in a louder voice, "what's the matter with you? Here you are, barricading yourself in your room, giving only 'yes' and 'no' for answers, causing your parents a lot of unnecessary trouble and neglecting—I mention this only in passing—neglecting your business duties in an incredible fashion. I am speaking here in the name of your parents and of your chief, and I beg you quite seriously to give me an immediate and precise explanation. You amaze me, you amaze me. I thought you were a quiet, dependable person, and now all at once you seem bent on making a disgraceful exhibition of yourself. The chief did hint to me early this morning a possible explanation for your disappearance—with reference to the cash payments that were entrusted to you recently—but I almost pledged my solemn word of honor that this could not be so. But now that I see how incredibly obstinate you are, I no longer have the slightest desire to take your part at all. And your position in the firm is not so unassailable. I came with the intention of telling you all this in private, but since you are wasting my time so needlessly I don't see why your parents shouldn't hear it too. For some time past your work has been most unsatisfactory; this is not the season of the year for a business boom, of course, we admit that, but a season of the year for doing no business at all, that does not exist, Mr. Samsa, must not exist."

"But, sir," cried Gregor, beside himself and in his agitation forgetting everything else, "I'm just going to open the door this very minute. A slight illness, an attack of giddiness, has kept me from getting up. I'm still lying in bed. But I feel all right again. I'm getting out of bed now. Just give me a moment or two longer! I'm not quite so well as I thought. But I'm all right, really. How a thing like that can suddenly strike one down! Only last night I was quite well, my parents can tell you, or rather I did have a slight presentiment. I must have showed some sign of it. Why didn't I report it at the office! But one always thinks that an indisposition can be got over without staying in the house. Oh sir, do spare my parents! All that you're reproaching me with now has no foundation; no one has ever said a word to me about it. Perhaps you haven't looked at the last orders I sent in. Anyhow, I can still catch the eight o'clock train, I'm much the better for my few hours' rest. Don't let me detain you here, sir; I'll be attending to business very soon, and do be good enough to tell the chief so and to make my excuses to him!"

And while all this was tumbling out pell-mell and Gregor hardly knew what he was saying, he had reached the chest quite easily, perhaps because of the practice he had had in bed, and was now trying to lever himself upright by means of it. He meant actually to open the door, actually to show himself and speak to the chief clerk; he was eager to find out what the others, after all their insistence, would say at the sight of him. If they were horrified then the responsibility was no longer his and he could stay quiet. But if they took it calmly, then he had no reason either to be upset, and could really get to the station for the eight o'clock train if he hurried. At first he slipped down a few times from the polished surface of the chest, but at length with a last heave he stood upright; he paid no more attention to the pains in the lower part of his body, however they smarted. Then he let himself fall against the back of a near-by chair, and clung with his little legs to the edges of it. That brought him into control of himself again and he stopped speaking, for now he could listen to what the chief clerk was saying.

"Did you understand a word of it?" the chief clerk was asking; "surely he can't be trying to make fools of us?" "Oh dear," cried his mother, in tears, "perhaps he's terribly ill and we're tormenting him. Grete! Grete!" she called out then. "Yes Mother?" called his sister from the other side. They were calling to each other across Gregor's room. "You must go this minute for the doctor. Gregor is ill. Go for the doctor, quick. Did you hear how he was speaking?" "That was no human voice," said the chief clerk in a voice noticeably low beside the shrillness of the mother's. "Anna! Anna!" his father was calling through the hall to the kitchen, clapping his hands, "get a locksmith at once!" And the two girls were already running through the hall with a swish of skirts—how could his sister have got dressed so quickly?—and were tearing the front door open. There was no sound of its closing again; they had evidently left it open, as one does in houses where some great misfortune has happened.

But Gregor was now much calmer. The words he uttered were no longer understandable, apparently, although they seemed clear enough to him, even clearer than before, perhaps because his ear had grown accustomed to the sound of them. Yet at any rate people now believed that something was wrong with him, and were ready to help him. The positive certainty with which these first measures had been taken comforted him. He felt himself drawn once more into the human circle and hoped for great and remarkable results from both the doctor and the locksmith, without really distinguishing precisely between them. To make his voice as clear as possible for the decisive conversation that was now imminent he coughed a little, as quietly as he could, of course, since this noise too might not sound like a human cough for all he was able to judge. In the next room meanwhile there was complete silence. Perhaps his parents were sitting at the table with the chief clerk, whispering, perhaps they were all leaning against the door and listening.

Slowly Gregor pushed the chair towards the door, then let go of it, caught hold of the door for support—the soles at the end of his little legs were somewhat sticky—and rested against it for a moment after his efforts. Then he set himself to turning the key in the lock with his mouth. It seemed, unhappily, that he hadn't really any teeth—what could he grip the key with?—but on the other hand his jaws were certainly very strong; with their help he did manage to set the key in motion, heedless of the fact that he was undoubtedly damaging them somewhere, since a brown fluid issued from his mouth, flowed over the key and dripped on the floor. "Just listen to that," said the chief clerk next door; "he's turning the key." That was a great encouragement to Gregor; but they should all have shouted encouragement to him, his father and mother too: "Go on, Gregor," they should have called out, "keep going, hold on to that key!" And in the belief that they were all following his efforts intently, he clenched his jaws recklessly on the key with all the force at his command. As the turning of the key progressed he circled round the lock, holding on now only with his mouth, pushing on the key, as required, or pulling it down again with all the weight of his body. The louder click of the finally yielding lock literally quickened Gregor. With a deep breath of relief he said to himself: "So I didn't need the locksmith," and laid his head on the handle to open the door wide.

Since he had to pull the door towards him, he was still invisible when it was really wide open. He had to edge himself slowly round the near half of the double door, and to do it very carefully if he was not to fall plump upon his back just on the threshold. He was still carrying out this difficult manoeuvre, with no time to observe anything else, when he heard the chief clerk utter a loud "Oh!"—it sounded like a gust of wind—and now he could see the man, standing as he was nearest to the door, clapping one hand before his open mouth and slowly backing away as if driven by some invisible steady pressure. His mother—in spite of the chief clerk's being there her hair was still undone and sticking up in all directions—first clasped her hands and looked at his father, then took two steps towards Gregor and fell on the floor among her outspread skirts, her face quite hidden on her breast. His father knotted his fist with a fierce expression on his face as if he meant to knock Gregor back into his room, then looked uncertainly round the living room, covered his eyes with his hands and wept till his great chest heaved.

Gregor did not go now into the living room, but leaned against the inside of the firmly shut wing of the door, so that only half his body was visible and his head above it bending sideways to look at the others. The light had meanwhile strengthened; on the other side of the street one could see clearly a section of the endlessly long, dark gray building opposite—it was a hospital—abruptly punctuated by its row of regular windows; the rain was still falling, but only in large singly discernible and literally singly splashing drops. The breakfast dishes were set out on the table lavishly, for breakfast was the most important meal of the day to Gregor's father, who lingered it out for hours over various newspapers. Right opposite Gregor on the wall hung a photograph of himself on military service, as a lieutenant, hand on sword, a carefree smile on his face, inviting one to respect his uniform and military bearing. The door leading to the hall was open, and one could see that the front door stood open too, showing the landing beyond and the beginning of the stairs going down.

"Well," said Gregor, knowing perfectly that he was the only one who had retained any composure, "I'll put my clothes on at once, pack up my samples and start off. Will you only let me go? You see, sir, I'm not obstinate, and I'm willing to work; traveling is a hard life, but I couldn't live without it. Where are you going, sir? To the office? Yes? Will you give a true account of all this? One can be temporarily incapacitated, but that's just the moment for remembering former services and bearing in mind that later on, when the incapacity has been got over, one will certainly work with all the more industry and concentration. I'm loyally bound to serve the chief, you know that very well. Besides, I have to provide for my parents and my sister. I'm in great difficulties, but I'll get out of them again. Don't make things any worse for me than they are. Stand up for me in the firm. Travelers are not popular there, I know. People think they earn sacks of money and just have a good time. A prejudice there's no particular reason for revising. But you, sir, have a more comprehensive view of affairs than the rest of the staff, yes, let me tell you in confidence, a more comprehensive view than the chief himself, who, being the owner, lets his judgment easily be swayed against one of his employees. And you know very well that the traveler, who is never seen in the office almost the whole year round, can so easily fall a victim to gossip and ill luck and unfounded complaints, which he mostly knows nothing about, except when he comes back exhausted from his rounds, and only then suffers in person from their evil consequences, which he can no longer trace back to the original causes. Sir, sir, don't go away without a word to me to show that you think me in the right at least to some extent!"

But at Gregor's very first words the chief clerk had already backed away and only stared at him with parted lips over one twitching shoulder. And while Gregor was speaking he did not stand still one moment but stole away towards the door, without taking his eyes off Gregor, yet only an inch at a time, as if obeying some secret injunction to leave the room. He was already at the hall, and the suddenness with which he took his last step out of the living room would have made one believe he had burned the sole of his foot. Once in the hall he stretched his right arm before him towards the staircase, as if some supernatural power were waiting there to deliver him.

Gregor perceived that the chief clerk must on no account be allowed to go away in this frame of mind if his position in the firm were not to be endangered to the utmost. His parents did not understand this so well; they had convinced themselves in the course of years that Gregor was settled for life in this firm, and besides they were so preoccupied with their immediate troubles that all foresight had forsaken them. Yet Gregor had this foresight. The chief clerk must be detained, soothed, persuaded and finally won over; the whole future of Gregor and his family depended on it! If only his sister had been there! She was intelligent; she had begun to cry while Gregor was still lying quietly on his back. And no doubt the chief clerk, so partial to ladies, would have been guided by her; she would have shut the door of the flat and in the hall talked him out of his horror. But she was not there, and Gregor would have to handle the situation himself. And without remembering that he was still unaware what powers of movement he possessed, without even remembering that his words in all possibility, indeed in all likelihood, would again be unintelligible, he let go the wing of the door, pushed himself through the opening, started to walk towards the chief clerk, who was already ridiculously clinging with both hands to the railing on the landing; but immediately, as he was feeling for a support, he fell down with a little cry upon all his numerous legs. Hardly was he down when he experienced for the first time this morning a sense of physical comfort; his legs had firm ground under them; they were completely obedient, as he noted with joy; they even strove to carry him forward in whatever direction he chose; and he was inclined to believe that a final relief from all his sufferings was at hand. But in the same moment as he found himself on the floor, rocking with suppressed eagerness to move, not far from his mother, indeed just in front of her, she, who had seemed so completely crushed, sprang all at once to her feet, her arms and fingers outspread, cried: "Help, for God's sake, help!" bent her head down as if to see Gregor better, yet on the contrary kept backing senselessly away; had quite forgotten that the laden table stood

behind her; sat upon it hastily, as if in absence of mind, when she bumped
into it; and seemed altogether unaware that the big coffee pot beside her was
upset and pouring coffee in a flood over the carpet.

"Mother, Mother," said Gregor in a low voice, and looked up at her. The
chief clerk, for the moment, had quite slipped from his mind; instead, he could
not resist snapping his jaws together at the sight of the streaming coffee. That
made his mother scream again, she fled from the table and fell into the arms
of his father, who hastened to catch her. But Gregor had now no time to spare
for his parents; the chief clerk was already on the stairs; with his chin on the
banisters he was taking one last backward look. Gregor made a spring, to be
as sure as possible of overtaking him; the chief clerk must have divined his
intention, for he leaped down several steps and vanished; he was still yelling
"Ugh!" and it echoed through the whole staircase.

Unfortunately, the flight of the chief clerk seemed completely to upset
Gregor's father, who had remained relatively calm until now, for instead of
running after the man himself, or at least not hindering Gregor in his pursuit,
he seized in his right hand the walking stick which the chief clerk had left behind on a chair, together with a hat and greatcoat, snatched in his left hand
a large newspaper from the table and began stamping his feet and flourishing
the stick and the newspaper to drive Gregor back into his room. No entreaty
of Gregor's availed, indeed no entreaty was even understood, however humbly
he bent his head his father only stamped on the floor the more loudly. Behind
his father his mother had torn open a window, despite the cold weather, and
was leaning far out of it with her face in her hands. A strong draught set in
from the street to the staircase, the window curtains blew in, the newspapers
on the table fluttered, stray pages whisked over the floor. Pitilessly Gregor's
father drove him back, hissing and crying "Shoo!" like a savage. But Gregor
was quite unpracticed in walking backwards, it really was a slow business. If
he only had a chance to turn round he could get back to his room at once, but
he was afraid of exasperating his father by the slowness of such a rotation and
at any moment the stick in his father's hand might hit him a fatal blow on the
back or on the head. In the end, however, nothing else was left for him to do
since to his horror he observed that in moving backwards he could not even
control the direction he took; and so, keeping an anxious eye on his father
all the time over his shoulder, he began to turn round as quickly as he could,
which was in reality very slowly. Perhaps his father noted his good intentions,
for he did not interfere except every now and then to help him in the manoeuvre
from a distance with the point of the stick. If only he would have stopped
making that unbearable hissing noise! It made Gregor quite lose his head.
He had turned almost completely round when the hissing noise so distracted
him that he even turned a little the wrong way again. But when at last his head
was fortunately right in front of the doorway, it appeared that his body was too
broad simply to get through the opening. His father, of course, in his present
mood was far from thinking of such a thing as opening the other half of the
door, to let Gregor have enough space. He had merely the fixed idea of driving

Gregor back into his room as quickly as possible. He would never have suffered Gregor to make the circumstantial preparations for standing up on end and perhaps slipping his way through the door. Maybe he was now making more noise than ever to urge Gregor forward, as if no obstacle impeded him; to Gregor, anyhow, the noise in his rear sounded no longer like the voice of one single father; this was really no joke, and Gregor thrust himself—come what might—into the doorway. One side of his body rose up, he was tilted at an angle in the doorway, his flank was quite bruised, horrid blotches stained the white door, soon he was stuck fast and, left to himself, could not have moved at all, his legs on one side fluttered trembling in the air, those on the other were crushed painfully to the floor—when from behind his father gave him a strong push which was literally a deliverance and he flew far into the room, bleeding freely. The door was slammed behind him with the stick, and then at last there was silence.

II

Not until it was twilight did Gregor awake out of a deep sleep, more like a swoon than a sleep. He would certainly have waked up of his own accord not much later, for he felt himself sufficiently rested and well-slept, but it seemed to him as if a fleeting step and a cautious shutting of the door leading into the hall had aroused him. The electric lights in the street cast a pale sheen here and there on the ceiling and the upper surfaces of the furniture, but down below, where he lay, it was dark. Slowly, awkwardly trying out his feelers, which he now first learned to appreciate, he pushed his way to the door to see what had been happening there. His left side felt like one single long, unpleasantly tense scar, and he had actually to limp on his two rows of legs. One little leg, moreover, had been severely damaged in the course of that morning's events—it was almost a miracle that only one had been damaged—and trailed uselessly behind him.

He had reached the door before he discovered what had really drawn him to it: the smell of food. For there stood a basin filled with fresh milk in which floated little sops of white bread. He could almost have laughed with joy, since he was now still hungrier than in the morning, and he dipped his head almost over the eyes straight into the milk. But soon in disappointment he withdrew it again; not only did he find it difficult to feed because of his tender left side—and he could only feed with the palpitating collaboration of his whole body—he did not like the milk either, although milk had been his favorite drink and that was certainly why his sister had set it there for him, indeed it was almost with repulsion that he turned away from the basin and crawled back to the middle of the room.

He could see through the crack of the door that the gas was turned on in the living room, but while usually at this time his father made a habit of reading the afternoon newspaper in a loud voice to his mother and occasionally to his sister as well, not a sound was now to be heard. Well, perhaps his father had recently given up this habit of reading aloud, which his sister had mentioned so often in conversation and in her letters. But there was the same silence all around, although the flat was certainly not empty of occupants. "What a quiet life our family has been leading," said Gregor to himself, and as he sat there motionless staring into the darkness he felt great pride in the fact that he had been able to provide such a life for his parents and sister in such a fine flat. But what if all the quiet, the comfort, the contentment were now to end in horror? To keep himself from being lost in such thoughts Gregor took refuge in movement and crawled up and down the room.

Once during the long evening one of the side doors was opened a little and quickly shut again, later the other side door too; someone had apparently wanted to come in and then thought better of it. Gregor now stationed himself immediately before the living room door, determined to persuade any hesitating visitor to come in or at least to discover who it might be; but the door was not opened again and he waited in vain. In the early morning, when the doors were locked, they had all wanted to come in, now that he had opened one door and the other had apparently been opened during the day, no one came in and even the keys were on the other side of the doors.

It was late at night before the gas went out in the living room, and Gregor could easily tell that his parents and his sister had all stayed awake until then, for he could clearly hear the three of them stealing away on tiptoe. No one was likely to visit him, not until the morning, that was certain; so he had plenty of time to meditate at his leisure on how he was to arrange his life afresh. But the lofty, empty room in which he had to lie flat on the floor filled him with an apprehension he could not account for, since it had been his very own room for the past five years—and with a half-unconscious action, not without a slight feeling of shame, he scuttled under the sofa, where he felt comfortable at once, although his back was a little cramped and he could not lift his head up, and his only regret was that his body was too broad to get the whole of it under the sofa.

He stayed there all night, spending the time partly in a light slumber, from which his hunger kept waking him up with a start, and partly in worrying and sketching vague hopes, which all led to the same conclusion, that he must lie low for the present and, by exercising patience and the utmost consideration, help the family to bear the inconvenience he was bound to cause them in his present condition.

Very early in the morning, it was still almost night, Gregor had the chance to test the strength of his new resolutions, for his sister, nearly fully dressed, opened the door from the hall and peered in. She did not see him at once, yet when she caught sight of him under the sofa—well, he had to be somewhere, he couldn't have flown away, could he?—she was so startled that without being able to help it she slammed the door shut again. But as if regretting her behavior she opened the door again immediately and came in on tiptoe, as if she were visiting an invalid or even a stranger. Gregor had pushed his head forward to the very edge of the sofa and watched her. Would she notice that he had left the milk standing, and not for lack of hunger, and would she bring in some other kind of food more to his taste? If she did not do it of her own accord, he would rather starve than draw her attention to the fact, although he felt a wild impulse to dart out from under the sofa, throw himself at her feet and beg her for something to eat. But his sister at once noticed, with surprise, that the basin was still full, except for a little milk that had been spilt all around it, she lifted it immediately, not with her bare hands, true, but with a cloth and carried it away. Gregor was wildly curious to know what she would bring instead, and made various speculations about it. Yet what she actually did next, in the goodness of her heart, he could never have guessed at. To find out what he liked she brought him a whole selection of food, all set out on an old newspaper. There were old, half-decayed vegetables, bones from last night's supper covered with a white sauce that had thickened; some raisins and almonds; a piece of cheese that Gregor would have called uneatable two days ago; a dry roll of bread, a buttered roll, and a roll both buttered and salted. Besides all that, she set down again the same basin, into which she had poured some water, and which was apparently to be reserved for his exclusive use. And with fine tact, knowing that Gregor would not eat in her presence, she withdrew quickly and even turned the key, to let him understand that he could take his ease as much as he liked. Gregor's legs all whizzed towards the food. His wounds must have healed completely, moreover, for he felt no disability, which amazed him and made him reflect how more than a month ago he had cut one finger a little with a knife and had still suffered pain from the wound only the day before yesterday. Am I less sensitive now? he thought, and sucked greedily at the cheese, which above all the other edibles attracted him at once and strongly. One after another and with tears of satisfaction in his eyes he quickly devoured the cheese, the vegetables and the sauce; the fresh food, on the other hand, had no charms for him, he could not even stand the smell of it and actually dragged away to some little distance the things he could eat. He had long finished his meal and was only lying lazily on the same spot when his sister turned the key slowly as a sign for him to retreat. That roused him at once, although he was nearly asleep, and he hurried under the sofa again. But it took considerable self-control for him to stay under the sofa, even for the short time his sister was in the room, since the large meal had swollen his body somewhat and he was so cramped he could hardly breathe. Slight attacks of breathlessness afflicted him and his eyes were starting a little out of his head as he watched his unsuspecting sister sweeping together with a broom not only the remains of what he had eaten but even the things he had not touched, as if these were now of no use to anyone, and hastily shoveling it all into a bucket, which she covered with a wooden lid and carried away. Hardly had she turned her back when Gregor came from under the sofa and stretched and puffed himself out.

In this manner Gregor was fed, once in the early morning while his parents and the servant girl were still asleep, and a second time after they had all had their midday dinner, for then his parents took a short nap and the servant girl could be sent out on some errand or other by his sister. Not that they would have wanted him to starve, of course, but perhaps they could not have borne to know more about his feeding than from hearsay, perhaps too his sister wanted to spare them such little anxieties wherever possible, since they had quite enough to bear as it was.

Under what pretext the doctor and the locksmith had been got rid of on that first morning Gregor could not discover, for since what he said was not understood by the others it never struck any of them, not even his sister, that he could understand what they said, and so whenever his sister came into his room he had to content himself with hearing her utter only a sigh now and then and an occasional appeal to the saints. Later on, when she had got a little used to the situation—of course she could never get completely used to it— she sometimes threw out a remark which was kindly meant or could be so interpreted. "Well, he liked his dinner today," she would say when Gregor had made a good clearance of his food; and when he had not eaten, which gradually happened more and more often, she would say almost sadly: "Everything's been left standing again."

But although Gregor could get no news directly, he overheard a lot from the neighboring rooms, and as soon as voices were audible, he would run to the door of the room concerned and press his whole body against it. In the first few days especially there was no conversation that did not refer to him somehow, even if only indirectly. For two whole days there were family consultations at every mealtime about what should be done; but also between meals the same subject was discussed, for there were always at least two members of the family at home, since no one wanted to be alone in the flat and to leave it quite empty was unthinkable. And on the very first of these days the household cook—it was not quite clear what and how much she knew of the situation—went down on her knees to his mother and begged leave to go, and when she departed, a quarter of an hour later, gave thanks for her dismissal with tears in her eyes as if for the greatest benefit that could have been conferred on her, and without any prompting swore a solemn oath that she would never say a single word to anyone about what had happened.

Now Gregor's sister had to cook too, helping her mother; true, the cooking did not amount to much, for they ate scarcely anything. Gregor was always hearing one of the family vainly urging another to eat and getting no answer but: "Thanks, I've had all I want," or something similar. Perhaps they drank nothing either. Time and again his sister kept asking his father if he wouldn't like some beer and offered kindly to go and fetch it herself, and when he made no answer suggested that she could ask the concierge to fetch it, so that he need feel no sense of obligation, but then a round "No" came from his father and no more was said about it.

In the course of that very first day Gregor's father explained the family's financial position and prospects to both his mother and his sister. Now and then he rose from the table to get some voucher or memorandum out of the small safe he had rescued from the collapse of his business five years earlier. One could hear him opening the complicated lock and rustling papers out and shutting it again. This statement made by his father was the first cheerful information Gregor had heard since his imprisonment. He had been of the opinion that nothing at all was left over from his father's business, at least his father had never said anything to the contrary, and of course he had not asked him directly. At that time Gregor's sole desire was to do his utmost to help the family to forget as soon as possible the catastrophe which had overwhelmed the business and thrown them all into a state of complete despair. And so he had set to work with unusual ardor and almost overnight had become a commercial traveler instead of a little clerk, with of course much greater chances of earning money, and his success was immediately translated into good round coin which he could lay on the table for his amazed and happy family. These had been fine times, and they had never recurred, at least not with the same sense of glory, although later on Gregor had earned so much money that he was able to meet the expenses of the whole household and did so. They had simply got used to it, both the family and Gregor; the money was gratefully accepted and gladly given, but there was no special uprush of warm feeling. With his sister alone had he remained intimate, and it was a secret plan of his that she, who loved music, unlike himself, and could play movingly on the violin, should be sent next year to study at the Conservatorium, despite the great expense that would entail, which must be made up in some other way. During his brief visits home the Conservatorium was often mentioned in the talks he had with his sister, but always merely as a beautiful dream which could never come true, and his parents discouraged even these innocent references to it; yet Gregor had made up his mind firmly about it and meant to announce the fact with due solemnity on Christmas Day.

Such were the thoughts, completely futile in his present condition, that went through his head as he stood clinging upright to the door and listening. Sometimes out of sheer weariness he had to give up listening and let his head fall negligently against the door, but he always had to pull himself together again at once, for even the slight sound his head made was audible next door and brought all conversation to a stop. "What can he be doing now?" his father would say after a while, obviously turning towards the door, and only then would the interrupted conversation gradually be set going again.

Gregor was now informed as amply as he could wish—for his father tended to repeat himself in his explanations, partly because it was a long time since he had handled such matters and partly because his mother could not always grasp things at once—that a certain amount of investments, a very small amount it was true, had survived the wreck of their fortunes and had even increased a little because the dividends had not been touched meanwhile. And besides that, the money Gregor brought home every month—he had kept only a few dollars for himself—had never been quite used up and now amounted to a small capital sum. Behind the door Gregor nodded his head eagerly, rejoiced at this evidence of unexpected thrift and foresight. True, he could really have paid off some more of his father's debts to the chief with this extra money,

and so brought much nearer the day on which he could quit his job, but doubtless it was better the way his father had arranged it.

Yet this capital was by no means sufficient to let the family live on the
interest of it; for one year, perhaps, or at the most two, they could live on the
principal, that was all. It was simply a sum that ought not to be touched and
should be kept for a rainy day; money for living expenses would have to be
earned. Now his father was still hale enough but an old man, and he had done
no work for the past five years and could not be expected to do much; during
these five years, the first years of leisure in his laborious though unsuccessful
life, he had grown rather fat and become sluggish. And Gregor's old mother,
how was she to earn a living with her asthma, which troubled her even when
she walked through the flat and kept her lying on a sofa every other day panting for breath beside an open window? And was his sister to earn her bread,
she who was still a child of seventeen and whose life hitherto had been so
pleasant, consisting as it did in dressing herself nicely, sleeping long, helping
in the housekeeping, going out to a few modest entertainments and above all
playing the violin? At first whenever the need for earning money was mentioned Gregor let go his hold on the door and threw himself down on the cool
leather sofa beside it, he felt so hot with shame and grief.

Often he just lay there the long nights through without sleeping at all,
scrabbling for hours on the leather. Or he nerved himself to the great effort of
pushing an armchair to the window, then crawled up over the window sill and,
braced against the chair, leaned against the window panes, obviously in some
recollection of the sense of freedom that looking out of a window always used
to give him. For in reality day by day things that were even a little way off
were growing dimmer to his sight; the hospital across the street, which he
used to execrate for being all too often before his eyes, was now quite beyond
his range of vision, and if he had not known that he lived in Charlotte Street,
a quiet street but still a city street, he might have believed that his window gave
on a desert waste where gray sky and gray land blended indistinguishably
into each other. His quick-witted sister only needed to observe twice that
the armchair stood by the window; after that whenever she had tidied the
room she always pushed the chair back to the same place at the window and
even left the inner casements open.

If he could have spoken to her and thanked her for all she had to do for
him, he could have borne her ministrations better; as it was, they oppressed
him. She certainly tried to make as light as possible of whatever was disagreeable in her task, and as time went on she succeeded, of course, more and more,
but time brought more enlightenment to Gregor too. The very way she came in
distressed him. Hardly was she in the room when she rushed to the window,
without even taking time to shut the door, careful as she was usually to shield
the sight of Gregor's room from the others, and as if she were almost suffocating tore the casements open with hasty fingers, standing then in the open
draught for a while even in the bitterest cold and drawing deep breaths. This
noisy scurry of hers upset Gregor twice a day; he would crouch trembling

under the sofa all the time, knowing quite well that she would certainly have spared him such a disturbance had she found it at all possible to stay in his presence without opening the window.

On one occasion, about a month after Gregor's metamorphosis, when there was surely no reason for her to be still startled at his appearance, she came a little earlier than usual and found him gazing out of the window, quite motionless, and thus well placed to look like a bogey. Gregor would not have been surprised had she not come in at all, for she could not immediately open the window while he was there, but not only did she retreat, she jumped back as if in alarm and banged the door shut; a stranger might well have thought that he had been lying in wait for her there meaning to bite her. Of course he hid himself under the sofa at once, but he had to wait until midday before she came again, and she seemed more ill at ease than usual. This made him realize how repulsive the sight of him still was to her, and that it was bound to go on being repulsive, and what an effort it must cost her not to run away even from the sight of the small portion of his body that stuck out from under the sofa. In order to spare her that, therefore, one day he carried a sheet on his back to the sofa—it cost him four hours' labor—and arranged it there in such a way as to hide him completely, so that even if she were to bend down she could not see him. Had she considered the sheet unnecessary, she would certainly have stripped it off the sofa again, for it was clear enough that this curtaining and confining of himself was not likely to conduce to Gregor's comfort, but she left it where it was, and Gregor even fancied that he caught a thankful glance from her eye when he lifted the sheet carefully a very little with his head to see how she was taking the new arrangement.

For the first fortnight his parents could not bring themselves to the point of entering his room, and he often heard them expressing their appreciation of his sister's activities, whereas formerly they had frequently scolded her for being as they thought a somewhat useless daughter. But now, both of them often waited outside the door, his father and his mother, while his sister tidied his room, and as soon as she came out she had to tell them exactly how things were in the room, what Gregor had eaten, how he had conducted himself this time and whether there was not perhaps some slight improvement in his condition. His mother, moreover, began relatively soon to want to visit him, but his father and sister dissuaded her at first with arguments which Gregor listened to very attentively and altogether approved. Later, however, she had to be held back by main force, and when she cried out: "Do let me in to Gregor, he is my unfortunate son! Can't you understand that I must go to him?" Gregor thought that it might be well to have her come in, not every day, of course, but perhaps once a week; she understood things, after all, much better than his sister, who was only a child despite the efforts she was making and had perhaps taken on so difficult a task merely out of childish thoughtlessness.

Gregor's desire to see his mother was soon fulfilled. During the daytime he did not want to show himself at the window, out of consideration for his parents, but he could not crawl very far around the few square yards of floor space he had, nor could he bear lying quietly at rest all during the night, while he was fast losing any interest he had ever taken in food, so that for mere recreation he had formed the habit of crawling crisscross over the walls and ceiling. He especially enjoyed hanging suspended from the ceiling; it was much better than lying on the floor; one could breathe more freely; one's body swung and rocked lightly; and in the almost blissful absorption induced by this suspension it could happen to his own surprise that he let go and fell plump on the floor. Yet he now had his body much better under control than formerly, and even such a big fall did him no harm. His sister at once remarked the new distraction Gregor had found for himself—he left traces behind him of the sticky stuff on his soles wherever he crawled—and she got the idea in her head of giving him as wide a field as possible to crawl in and of removing the pieces of furniture that hindered him, above all the chest of drawers and the writing desk. But that was more than she could manage all by herself; she did not dare ask her father to help her; and as for the servant girl, a young creature of sixteen who had had the courage to stay on after the cook's departure, she could not be asked to help, for she had begged as an especial favor that she might keep the kitchen door locked and open it only on a definite summons; so there was nothing left but to apply to her mother at an hour when her father was out. And the old lady did come, with exclamations of joyful eagerness, which, however, died away at the door of Gregor's room. Gregor's sister, of course, went in first, to see that everything was in order before letting his mother enter. In great haste Gregor pulled the sheet lower and rucked it more in folds so that it really looked as if it had been thrown accidentally over the sofa. And this time he did not peer out from under it; he renounced the pleasure of seeing his mother on this occasion and was only glad that she had come at all. "Come in, he's out of sight," said his sister, obviously leading her mother in by the hand. Gregor could now hear the two women struggling to shift the heavy old chest from its place, and his sister claiming the greater part of the labor for herself, without listening to the admonitions of her mother who feared she might overstrain herself. It took a long time. After at least a quarter of an hour's tugging his mother objected that the chest had better be left where it was, for in the first place it was too heavy and could never be got out before his father came home, and standing in the middle of the room like that it would only hamper Gregor's movements, while in the second place it was not at all certain that removing the furniture would be doing a service to Gregor. She was inclined to think to the contrary; the sight of the naked walls made her own heart heavy, and why shouldn't Gregor have the same feeling, considering that he had been used to his furniture for so long and might feel forlorn without it. "And doesn't it look," she concluded in a low voice—in fact she had been almost whispering all the time as if to avoid letting Gregor, whose exact whereabouts she did not know, hear even the tones of her voice, for she was convinced that he could not understand her words—"doesn't it look as if we were showing him, by taking away his furniture, that we have given up hope of his ever getting better and are just leaving him coldly to himself? I think it would be best to keep his room exactly as it has always been, so that when he comes back to us he will find everything unchanged and be able all the more easily to forget what has happened in between."

On hearing these words from his mother Gregor realized that the lack of all direct human speech for the past two months together with the monotony of family life must have confused his mind, otherwise he could not account for the fact that he had quite earnestly looked forward to having his room emptied of furnishing. Did he really want his warm room, so comfortably fitted with old family furniture, to be turned into a naked den in which he would certainly be able to crawl unhampered in all directions but at the price of shedding simultaneously all recollection of his human background? He had indeed been so near the brink of forgetfulness that only the voice of his mother, which he had not heard for so long, had drawn him back from it. Nothing should be taken out of his room; everything must stay as it was; he could not dispense with the good influence of the furniture on his state of mind; and even if the furniture did hamper him in his senseless crawling round and round, that was no drawback but a great advantage.

Unfortunately his sister was of the contrary opinion; she had grown accustomed, and not without reason, to consider herself an expert in Gregor's affairs as against her parents, and so her mother's advice was now enough to make her determined on the removal not only of the chest and the writing desk, which had been her first intention, but of all the furniture except the indispensable sofa. This determination was not, of course, merely the outcome of childish recalcitrance and of the self-confidence she had recently developed so unexpectedly and at such cost; she had in fact perceived that Gregor needed a lot of space to crawl about in, while on the other hand he never used the furniture at all, so far as could be seen. Another factor might have been also the enthusiastic temperament of an adolescent girl, which seeks to indulge itself on every opportunity and which now tempted Grete to exaggerate the horror of her brother's circumstances in order that she might do all the more for him. In a room where Gregor lorded it all alone over empty walls no one save herself was likely ever to set foot.

And so she was not to be moved from her resolve by her mother, who seemed moreover to be ill at ease in Gregor's room and therefore unsure of herself, was soon reduced to silence and helped her daughter as best she could to push the chest outside. Now, Gregor could do without the chest, if need be, but the writing desk he must retain. As soon as the two women had got the chest out of his room, groaning as they pushed it, Gregor stuck his head out from under the sofa to see how he might intervene as kindly and cautiously as possible. But as bad luck would have it, his mother was the first to return, leaving Grete clasping the chest in the room next door where she was trying to shift it all by herself, without of course moving it from the spot. His mother however was not accustomed to the sight of him, it might sicken her and so in alarm Gregor backed quickly to the other end of the sofa, yet could not prevent the sheet from swaying a little in front. That was enough to put her on the alert. She paused, stood still for a moment and then went back to Grete.

Although Gregor kept reassuring himself that nothing out of the way was happening, but only a few bits of furniture were being changed round, he soon had to admit that all this trotting to and fro of the two women, their little ejaculations and the scraping of furniture along the floor affected him like a vast disturbance coming from all sides at once, and however much he tucked in his head and legs and cowered to the very floor he was bound to confess that he would not be able to stand it for long. They were clearing his room out; taking away everything he loved; the chest in which he kept his fret saw and other tools was already dragged off; they were now loosening the writing desk which had almost sunk into the floor, the desk at which he had done all his homework when he was at the commercial academy, at the grammar school before that, and, yes, even at the primary school—he had no more time to waste in weighing the good intentions of the two women, whose existence he had by now almost forgotten, for they were so exhausted that they were laboring in silence and nothing could be heard but the heavy scuffling of their feet.

And so he rushed out—the women were just leaning against the writing desk in the next room to give themselves a breather—and four times changed his direction, since he really did not know what to rescue first, then on the wall opposite, which was already otherwise cleared, he was struck by the picture of the lady muffled in so much fur and quickly crawled up to it and pressed himself to the glass, which was a good surface to hold on to and comforted his hot belly. This picture at least, which was entirely hidden beneath him, was going to be removed by nobody. He turned his head towards the door of the living room so as to observe the women when they came back.

They had not allowed themselves much of a rest and were already coming; Grete had twined her arm round her mother and was almost supporting her. "Well, what shall we take now?" said Grete, looking round. Her eyes met Gregor's from the wall. She kept her composure, presumably because of her mother, bent her head down to her mother, to keep her from looking up, and said, although in a fluttering, unpremeditated voice: "Come, hadn't we better go back to the living room for a moment?" Her intentions were clear enough to Gregor, she wanted to bestow her mother in safety and then chase him down from the wall. Well, just let her try it! He clung to his picture and would not give it up. He would rather fly in Grete's face.

But Grete's words had succeeded in disquieting her mother, who took a step to one side, caught sight of the huge brown mass on the flowered wallpaper, and before she was really conscious that what she saw was Gregor screamed in a loud, hoarse voice: "Oh God, oh God!" fell with outspread arms over the sofa as if giving up and did not move. "Gregor!" cried his sister, shaking her fist and glaring at him. This was the first time she had directly addressed him since his metamorphosis. She ran into the next room for some aromatic essence with which to rouse her mother from her fainting fit. Gregor wanted to help too—there was still time to rescue the picture—but he was stuck fast to the glass and had to tear himself loose; he then ran after his sister into the next room as if he could advise her, as he used to do; but then had to stand helplessly behind her; she meanwhile searched among various small bottles and when she turned round started in alarm at the sight of him; one bottle fell on the floor and broke; a splinter of glass cut Gregor's face and some kind of corrosive medicine splashed him; without pausing a moment longer Grete gathered up all the bottles she could carry and ran to her mother with them; she banged the door shut with her foot. Gregor was now cut off from his mother, who was perhaps nearly dying because of him; he dared not open the door for fear of frightening away his sister, who had to stay with her mother; there was nothing he could do but wait; and harassed by self-reproach and worry he began now to crawl to and fro, over everything, walls, furniture and ceiling, and finally in his despair, when the whole room seemed to be reeling round him, fell down on to the middle of the big table.

A little while elapsed, Gregor was still lying there feebly and all around was quiet, perhaps that was a good omen. Then the doorbell rang. The servant girl was of course locked in her kitchen, and Grete would have to open the door. It was his father. "What's been happening?" were his first words; Grete's face must have told him everything. Grete answered in a muffled voice, apparently hiding her head on his breast: "Mother has been fainting, but she's better now. Gregor's broken loose." "Just what I expected," said his father, "just what I've been telling you, but you women would never listen." It was clear to Gregor that his father had taken the worst interpretation of Grete's all too brief statement and was assuming that Gregor had been guilty of some violent act. Therefore Gregor must now try to propitiate his father, since he had neither time nor means for an explanation. And so he fled to the door of his own room and crouched against it, to let his father see as soon as he came in from the hall that his son had the good intention of getting back into his room immediately and that it was not necessary to drive him there, but that if only the door were opened he would disappear at once.

Yet his father was not in the mood to perceive such fine distinctions. "Ah!" he cried as soon as he appeared, in a tone which sounded at once angry and exultant. Gregor drew his head back from the door and lifted it to look at his father. Truly, this was not the father he had imagined to himself; admittedly he had been too absorbed of late in his new recreation of crawling over the ceiling to take the same interest as before in what was happening elsewhere in the flat, and he ought really to be prepared for some changes. And yet, and yet, could that be his father? The man who used to lie wearily sunk in bed whenever Gregor set out on a business journey; who welcomed him back of an evening lying in a long chair in a dressing gown; who could not really rise to his feet but only lifted his arms in greeting, and on the rare occasions when he did go out with his family, on one or two Sundays a year and on high holidays, walked between Gregor and his mother, who were slow walkers anyhow, even more slowly than they did, muffled in his old greatcoat, shuffling laboriously forward with the help of his crook-handled stick which he set down most cautiously at every step and, whenever he wanted to say anything, nearly always came to a full stop and gathered his escort around him? Now he was standing there in fine shape; dressed in a smart blue uniform with gold buttons, such as bank messengers wear; his strong double chin bulged over the stiff high collar of his jacket; from under his bushy eyebrows his black eyes darted fresh and penetrating glances; his onetime tangled white hair had been combed flat on either side of a shining and carefully exact parting. He pitched his cap, which bore a gold monogram, probably the badge of some bank, in a wide sweep across the whole room on to a sofa and with the tail-ends of his jacket thrown back, his hands in his trouser pockets, advanced with a grim visage towards Gregor. Likely enough he did not himself know what he meant to do; at any rate he lifted his feet uncommonly high, and Gregor was dumbfounded at the enormous size of his shoe soles. But Gregor could not risk standing up to him, aware as he had been from the very first day of his new life that his father believed only the severest measures suitable for dealing with him. And so he ran before his father, stopping when he stopped and scuttling forward again when his father made any kind of move. In this way they circled the room several times without anything decisive happening, indeed the whole operation did not even look like a pursuit because it was carried out so slowly. And so Gregor did not leave the floor, for he feared that his father might take as a piece of peculiar wickedness any excursion of his over the walls or the ceiling. All the same, he could not stay this course much longer, for while his father took one step he had to carry out a whole series of movements. He was already beginning to feel breathless, just as in his former life his lungs had not been very dependable. As he was staggering along, trying to concentrate his energy on running, hardly keeping his eyes open; in his dazed state never even thinking of any other escape than simply going forward; and having almost forgotten that the walls were free to him, which in this room were well provided with finely carved pieces of furniture full of knobs and crevices— suddenly something lightly flung landed close behind him and rolled before him. It was an apple; a second apple followed immediately; Gregor came to a stop in alarm; there was no point in running on, for his father was determined to bombard him. He had filled his pockets with fruit from the dish on the sideboard and was now shying apple after apple, without taking particularly good aim for the moment. The small red apples rolled about the floor as if magnetized and cannoned into each other. An apple thrown without much force grazed Gregor's back and glanced off harmlessly. But another following immediately landed right on his back and sank in; Gregor wanted to drag himself forward, as if this startling, incredible pain could be left behind him; but he felt as if nailed to the spot and flattened himself out in a complete derangement of all his senses. With his last conscious look he saw the door of his room being torn open and his mother rushing out ahead of his screaming sister, in her underbodice, for her daughter had loosened her clothing to let her breathe more freely and recover from her swoon, he saw his mother rushing towards his father, leaving one after another behind her on the floor her loosened petticoats, stumbling over her petticoats straight to his father and embracing him, in complete union with him—but here Gregor's sight began to fail—with her hands clasped round his father's neck as she begged for her son's life.

III

The serious injury done to Gregor, which disabled him for more than a month— the apple went on sticking in his body as a visible reminder, since no one ventured to remove it—seemed to have made even his father recollect that Gregor was a member of the family, despite his present unfortunate and repulsive shape, and ought not to be treated as an enemy, that, on the contrary, family duty required the suppression of disgust and the exercise of patience, nothing but patience.

And although his injury had impaired, probably for ever, his powers of movement, and for the time being it took him long, long minutes to creep across his room like an old invalid—there was no question now of crawling up the wall—yet in his own opinion he was sufficiently compensated for this worsening of his condition by the fact that towards evening the living-room door, which he used to watch intently for an hour or two beforehand, was always thrown open, so that lying in the darkness of his room, invisible to the family, he could see them all at the lamp-lit table and listen to their talk, by general consent as it were, very different from his earlier eavesdropping.

True, their intercourse lacked the lively character of former times, which he had always called to mind with a certain wistfulness in the small hotel bedrooms where he had been wont to throw himself down, tired out, on damp bedding. They were now mostly very silent. Soon after supper his father would fall asleep in his armchair; his mother and sister would admonish each other to be silent; his mother, bending low over the lamp, stitched at fine sewing for an underwear firm; his sister, who had taken a job as a salesgirl, was learning shorthand and French in the evenings on the chance of bettering herself. Sometimes his father woke up, and as if quite unaware that he had been sleeping said to his mother: "What a lot of sewing you're doing today!" and at once fell asleep again, while the two women exchanged a tired smile.

With a kind of mulishness his father persisted in keeping his uniform on even in the house; his dressing gown hung uselessly on its peg and he slept fully dressed where he sat, as if he were ready for service at any moment and even here only at the beck and call of his superior. As a result, his uniform, which was not brand-new to start with, began to look dirty, despite all the loving care of the mother and sister to keep it clean, and Gregor often spent whole evenings gazing at the many greasy spots on the garment, gleaming with gold buttons always in a high state of polish, in which the old man sat sleeping in extreme discomfort and yet quite peacefully.

As soon as the clock struck ten his mother tried to rouse his father with gentle words and to persuade him after that to get into bed, for sitting there he could not have a proper sleep and that was what he needed most, since he had to go on duty at six. But with the mulishness that had obsessed him since he became a bank messenger he always insisted on staying longer at the table, although he regularly fell asleep again and in the end only with the greatest trouble could be got out of his armchair and into his bed. However insistently Gregor's mother and sister kept urging him with gentle reminders, he would go on slowly shaking his head for a quarter of an hour, keeping his eyes shut, and refuse to get to his feet. The mother plucked at his sleeve, whispering endearments in his ear, the sister left her lessons to come to her mother's help, but Gregor's father was not to be caught. He would only sink down deeper in his chair. Not until the two women hoisted him up by the armpits did he open his eyes and look at them both, one after the other, usually with the remark: "This is a life. This is the peace and quiet of my old age." And leaning on the two of them he would heave himself up, with difficulty, as if he were a great burden to himself, suffer them to lead him as far as the door and then wave them off and go on alone, while the mother abandoned her needlework and the sister her pen in order to run after him and help him farther.

Who could find time, in this overworked and tired-out family, to bother about Gregor more than was absolutely needful? The household was reduced more and more; the servant girl was turned off; a gigantic bony charwoman with white hair flying round her head came in morning and evening to do the rough work; everything else was done by Gregor's mother, as well as great piles of sewing. Even various family ornaments, which his mother and sister used to wear with pride at parties and celebrations, had to be sold, as Gregor discovered of an evening from hearing them all discuss the prices obtained. But what they lamented most was the fact that they could not leave the flat which was much too big for their present circumstances, because they could not think of any way to shift Gregor. Yet Gregor saw well enough that consideration for him was not the main difficulty preventing the removal, for they could have easily shifted him in some suitable box with a few air holes in it; what really kept them from moving into another flat was rather their own complete hopelessness and the belief that they had been singled out for a misfortune such as had never happened to any of their relations or acquaintances. They fulfilled to the uttermost all that the world demands of poor people, the father fetched breakfast for the small clerks in the bank, the mother devoted her energy to making underwear for strangers, the sister trotted to and fro behind the counter at the behest of customers, but more than this they had not the strength to do. And the wound in Gregor's back began to nag at him afresh when his mother and sister, after getting his father into bed, came back again, left their work lying, drew close to each other and sat cheek by cheek; when his mother, pointing towards his room, said: "Shut that door now, Grete," and he was left again in darkness, while next door the women mingled their tears or perhaps sat dry-eyed staring at the table.

Gregor hardly slept at all by night or by day. He was often haunted by the idea that next time the door opened he would take the family's affairs in hand again just as he used to do; once more, after this long interval, there appeared in his thoughts the figures of the chief and the chief clerk, the commercial travelers and the apprentices, the porter who was so dull-witted, two or three friends in other firms, a chambermaid in one of the rural hotels, a sweet and fleeting memory, a cashier in a milliner's shop, whom he had wooed earnestly but too slowly—they all appeared, together with strangers or people he had quite forgotten, but instead of helping him and his family they were one and all unapproachable and he was glad when they vanished. At other times he would not be in the mood to bother about his family, he was only filled with rage at the way they were neglecting him, and although he had no clear idea of what he might care to eat he would make plans for getting into the larder to take the food that was after all his due, even if he were not hungry. His sister no longer took thought to bring him what might especially please him, but in the morning and at noon before she went to business hurriedly pushed into his room with her foot any food that was available, and in the evening cleared it out again with one sweep of the broom, heedless of whether it had been merely tasted, or—as most frequently happened—left untouched. The cleaning of his room, which she now did always in the evenings, could not have been more hastily done. Streaks of dirt stretched along the walls, here and there lay balls of dust and filth. At first Gregor used to station himself in some particularly filthy corner when his sister arrived, in order to reproach her with it, so to speak. But he could have sat there for weeks without getting her to make any improvement; she could see the dirt as well as he did, but she had simply made up her mind to leave it alone. And yet, with a touchiness that was new to her, which seemed anyhow to have infected the whole family, she jealously guarded her claim to be the sole caretaker of Gregor's room. His mother once subjected his room to a thorough cleaning, which was achieved only by means of several buckets of water—all this dampness of course upset Gregor too and he lay widespread, sulky and motionless on the sofa—but she was well punished for it. Hardly had his sister noticed the changed aspect of his room that evening than she rushed in high dudgeon into the living room and, despite the imploringly raised hands of her mother, burst into a storm of weeping, while her parents—her father had of course been startled out of his chair—looked on at first in helpless amazement; then they too began to go into action; the father reproached the mother on his right for not having left the cleaning of Gregor's room to his sister; shrieked at the sister on his left that never again was she to be allowed to clean Gregor's room; while the mother tried to pull the father into his bedroom, since he was beyond himself with agitation; the sister, shaken with sobs, then beat upon the table with her small fists; and Gregor hissed loudly with rage because not one of them thought of shutting the door to spare him such a spectacle and so much noise.

Still, even if the sister, exhausted by her daily work, had grown tired of looking after Gregor as she did formerly, there was no need for his mother's intervention or for Gregor's being neglected at all. The charwoman was there. This old widow, whose strong bony frame had enabled her to survive the worst a long life could offer, by no means recoiled from Gregor. Without being in the least curious she had once by chance opened the door of his room and at the sight of Gregor, who, taken by surprise, began to rush to and fro although no one was chasing him, merely stood there with her arms folded. From that time she never failed to open his door a little for a moment, morning and evening, to have a look at him. At first she even used to call him to her, with words which apparently she took to be friendly, such as: "Come along, then, you old dung beetle!" or "Look at the old dung beetle, then!" To such allocutions Gregor made no answer, but stayed motionless where he was, as if the door had never been opened. Instead of being allowed to disturb him so senselessly whenever the whim took her, she should rather have been ordered to clean out his room daily, that charwoman! Once, early in the morning—heavy rain was lashing on the windowpanes, perhaps a sign that spring was on the way— Gregor was so exasperated when she began addressing him again that he ran at her, as if to attack her, although slowly and feebly enough. But the charwoman instead of showing fright merely lifted high a chair than happened to be beside the door, and as she stood there with her mouth wide open it was clear that she meant to shut it only when she brought the chair down on Gregor's back. "So you're not coming any nearer?" she asked, as Gregor turned away again, and quietly put the chair back into the corner.

Gregor was now eating hardly anything. Only when he happened to pass the food laid out for him did he take a bit of something in his mouth as a pastime, kept it there for an hour at a time and usually spat it out again. At first he thought it was chagrin over the state of his room that prevented him from eating, yet he soon got used to the various changes in his room. It had become a habit in the family to push into his room things there was no room for elsewhere, and there were plenty of these now, since one of the rooms had been let to three lodgers. These serious gentlemen—all three of them with full beards, as Gregor once observed through a crack in the door—had a passion for order, not only in their own room but, since they were now members of the household, in all its arrangements, especially in the kitchen. Superfluous, not to say dirty, objects they could not bear. Besides, they had brought with them most of the furnishings they needed. For this reason many things could be dispensed with that it was no use trying to sell but that should not be thrown away either. All of them found their way into Gregor's room. The ash can likewise and the kitchen garbage can. Anything that was not needed for the moment was simply flung into Gregor's room by the charwoman, who did everything in a hurry; fortunately Gregor usually saw only the object, whatever it was, and the hand that held it. Perhaps she intended to take the things away again as time and opportunity offered, or to collect them until she could throw them all out in a heap, but in fact they just lay wherever she happened to throw them, except when Gregor pushed his way through the junk heap and shifted it somewhat, at first out of necessity, because he had not room enough to crawl, but later with increasing enjoyment, although after such excursions, being sad and weary to death, he would lie motionless for hours. And since the lodgers often ate their supper at home in the common living room, the living-room door stayed shut many an evening, yet Gregor reconciled himself quite easily to the shutting of the door, for often enough on evenings when it was opened he had disregarded it entirely and lain in the darkest corner of his room, quite unnoticed by the family. But on one occasion the charwoman left the door open a little and it stayed ajar even when the lodgers came in for supper and the lamp was lit. They set themselves at the top end of the table where formerly Gregor and his father and mother had eaten their meals, unfolded their napkins and took knife and fork in hand. At once his mother appeared in the other doorway with a dish of meat and close behind her his sister with a dish of potatoes piled high. The food steamed with a thick vapor. The lodgers bent over the food set before them as if to scrutinize it before eating, in fact the man in the middle, who seemed to pass for an authority with the other two, cut a piece of meat as it lay on the dish, obviously to discover if it were tender or should be sent back to the kitchen. He showed satisfaction, and Gregor's mother and sister, who had been watching anxiously, breathed freely and began to smile.

The family itself took its meals in the kitchen. None the less, Gregor's father came into the living room before going into the kitchen and with one prolonged bow, cap in hand, made a round of the table. The lodgers all stood up and murmured something in their beards. When they were alone again they ate their food in almost complete silence. It seemed remarkable to Gregor that among the various noises coming from the table he could always distinguish the sound of their masticating teeth, as if this were a sign to Gregor that one needed teeth in order to eat, and that with toothless jaws even of the finest make one could do nothing. "I'm hungry enough," said Gregor sadly to himself, "but not for that kind of food. How these lodgers are stuffing themselves, and here am I dying of starvation!"

On that very evening—during the whole of his time there Gregor could not remember ever having heard the violin—the sound of violin-playing came from the kitchen. The lodgers had already finished their supper, the one in the middle had brought out a newspaper and given the other two a page apiece, and now they were leaning back at ease reading and smoking. When the violin began to play they pricked up their ears, got to their feet, and went on tiptoe to the hall door where they stood huddled together. Their movements must have been heard in the kitchen, for Gregor's father called out: "Is the violin-playing disturbing you, gentlemen? It can be stopped at once." "On the contrary," said the middle lodger, "could not Fräulein Samsa come and play in this room, beside us, where it is much more convenient and comfortable?" "Oh certainly," cried Gregor's father, as if he were the violin-player. The lodgers came back into the living room and waited. Presently Gregor's father arrived with the music stand, his mother carrying the music and his sister with the violin. His sister quietly made everything ready to start playing; his parents, who had never let rooms before and so had an exaggerated idea of the courtesy due to lodgers, did not venture to sit down on their own chairs; his father leaned against the door, the right hand thrust between two buttons of his livery coat, which was formally buttoned up; but his mother was offered a chair by one of the lodgers and, since she left the chair just where he had happened to put it, sat down in a corner to one side.

Gregor's sister began to play; the father and mother, from either side, intently watched the movements of her hands. Gregor, attracted by the playing, ventured to move forward a little until his head was actually inside the living room. He felt hardly any surprise at his growing lack of consideration for the others; there had been a time when he prided himself on being considerate. And yet just on this occasion he had more reason than ever to hide himself, since owing to the amount of dust which lay thick in his room and rose into the air at the slightest movement, he too was covered with dust; fluff and hair and remnants of food trailed with him, caught on his back and along his sides; his indifference to everything was much too great for him to turn on his back and scrape himself clean on the carpet, as once he had done several times a day. And in spite of his condition, no shame deterred him from advancing a little over the spotless floor of the living room.

To be sure, no one was aware of him. The family was entirely absorbed in the violin-playing; the lodgers, however, who first of all had stationed themselves, hand in pockets, much too close behind the music stand so that they could all have read the music, which must have bothered his sister, had soon retreated to the window, half-whispering with downbent heads, and stayed there while his father turned an anxious eye on them. Indeed, they were making it more than obvious that they had been disappointed in their expectation of hearing good or enjoyable violin-playing, that they had had more than enough of the performance and only out of courtesy suffered a continued disturbance of their peace. From the way they all kept blowing the smoke of their cigars high in the air through nose and mouth one could divine their irritation. And yet Gregor's sister was playing so beautifully. Her face leaned sideways, intently and sadly her eyes followed the notes of music. Gregor crawled a little farther forward and lowered his head to the ground so that it might be possible for his eyes to meet hers. Was he an animal, that music had such an effect upon him? He felt as if the way were opening before him to the unknown nourishment he craved. He was determined to push forward till he reached his sister, to pull at her skirt and so let her know that she was to come into his room with her violin, for no one here appreciated her playing as he would appreciate it. He would never let her out of his room, at least, not so long as he lived; his frightful appearance would become, for the first time, useful to him; he would watch all the doors of his room at once and spit at intruders; but his sister should need no constraint, she should stay with him of her own free will; she should sit beside him on the sofa, bend down her ear to him and hear him confide that he had had the firm intention of sending her to the Conservatorium, and that, but for his mishap, last Christmas—surely Christmas was long past?—he would have announced it to everybody without allowing a single objection. After this confession his sister would be so touched that she would burst into tears, and Gregor would then raise himself to her shoulder and kiss her on the neck, which, now that she went to business, she kept free of any ribbon or collar.

"Mr. Samsa!" cried the middle lodger, to Gregor's father, and pointed, without wasting any more words, at Gregor, now working himself slowly forwards. The violin fell silent, the middle lodger first smiled to his friends with a shake of the head and then looked at Gregor again. Instead of driving Gregor out, his father seemed to think it more needful to begin by soothing down the lodgers, although they were not at all agitated and apparently found Gregor more entertaining than the violin-playing. He hurried towards them and, spreading out his arms, tried to urge them back into their own room and at the same time to block their view of Gregor. They now began to be really a little angry, one could not tell whether because of the old man's behavior or because it had just dawned on them that all unwittingly they had such a neighbor as Gregor next door. They demanded explanations of his father, they waved their arms like him, tugged uneasily at their beards, and only with reluctance backed towards their room. Meanwhile Gregor's sister, who stood there as if lost when her playing was so abruptly broken off, came to life again, pulled herself together all at once after standing for a while holding violin and bow in nervelessly hanging hands and staring at her music, pushed her violin into the lap of her mother, who was still sitting in her chair fighting asthmatically for breath, and ran into the lodgers' room to which they were now being shepherded by her father rather more quickly than before. One could see the pillows and blankets on the beds flying under her accustomed fingers and being laid in order. Before the lodgers had actually reached their room she had finished making the beds and slipped out.

The old man seemed once more to be so possessed by his mulish self-assertiveness that he was forgetting all the respect he should show to his lodgers. He kept driving them on and driving them on until in the very door of the bedroom the middle lodger stamped his foot loudly on the floor and so brought him to a halt. "I beg to announce," said the lodger, lifting one hand and looking also at Gregor's mother and sister, "that because of the disgusting conditions prevailing in this household and family"—here he spat on the floor with emphatic brevity—"I give you notice on the spot. Naturally I won't pay you a penny for the days I have lived here, on the contrary I shall consider bringing an action for damages against you, based on claims—believe me—that will be easily susceptible of proof." He ceased and stared straight in front of him, as if he expected something. In fact his two friends at once rushed into the breach with these words: "And we too give notice on the spot." On that he seized the door-handle and shut the door with a slam.

Gregor's father, groping with his hands, staggered forward and fell into his chair; it looked as if he were stretching himself there for his ordinary evening nap, but the marked jerkings of his head, which was as if uncontrollable, showed that he was far from asleep. Gregor had simply stayed quietly all the time on the spot where the lodgers had espied him. Disappointment at the failure of his plan, perhaps also the weakness arising from extreme hunger, made it impossible for him to move. He feared, with a fair degree of certainty, that at any moment the general tension would discharge itself in a combined attack upon him, and he lay waiting. He did not react even to the noise made by the violin as it fell off his mother's lap from under her trembling fingers and gave out a resonant note.

"My dear parents," said his sister, slapping her hand on the table by way of introduction, "things can't go on like this. Perhaps you don't realize that, but I do. I won't utter my brother's name in the presence of this creature, and so all I say is: we must try to get rid of it. We've tried to look after it and to put up with it as far as is humanly possible, and I don't think anyone could reproach us in the slightest."

"She is more than right," said Gregor's father to himself. His mother, who was still choking for lack of breath, began to cough hollowly into her hand with a wild look in her eyes.

His sister rushed over to her and held her forehead. His father's thoughts seemed to have lost their vagueness at Grete's words, he sat more upright, fingering his service cap that lay among the plates still lying on the table from the lodgers' supper, and from time to time looked at the still form of Gregor.

"We must try to get rid of it," his sister now said explicitly to her father, since her mother was coughing too much to hear a word, "it will be the death of both of you, I can see that coming. When one has to work as hard as we do, all of us, one can't stand this continual torment at home on top of it. At least I can't stand it any longer." And she burst into such a passion of sobbing that her tears dropped on her mother's face, where she wiped them off mechanically.

"My dear," said the old man sympathetically, and with evident understanding, "but what can we do?"

Gregor's sister merely shrugged her shoulders to indicate the feeling of helplessness that had now overmastered her during her weeping fit, in contrast to her former confidence.

"If he could understand us," said her father, half questioningly; Grete, still sobbing, vehemently waved a hand to show how unthinkable that was.

"If he could understand us," repeated the old man, shutting his eyes to consider his daughter's conviction that understanding was impossible, "then perhaps we might come to some agreement with him. But as it is—"

"He must go," cried Gregor's sister, "that's the only solution, Father. You must just try to get rid of the idea that this is Gregor. The fact that we've believed it for so long is the root of all our trouble. But how can it be Gregor? If this were Gregor, he would have realized long ago that human beings can't live with such a creature, and he'd have gone away on his own accord. Then we wouldn't have any brother, but we'd be able to go on living and keep his memory in honor. As it is, this creature persecutes us, drives away our lodgers, obviously wants the whole apartment to himself and would have us all sleep in the gutter. Just look, Father," she shrieked all at once, "he's at it again!" And in an access of panic that was quite incomprehensible to Gregor she even quitted her mother, literally thrusting the chair from her as if she would rather sacrifice her mother than stay so near to Gregor, and rushed behind her father, who also rose up, being simply upset by her agitation, and half-spread his arms out as if to protect her.

Yet Gregor had not the slightest intention of frightening anyone, far less his sister. He had only begun to turn around in order to crawl back to his room, but it was certainly a startling operation to watch, since because of his disabled condition he could not execute the difficult turning movements except by lifting his head and then bracing it against the floor over and over again. He paused and looked around. His good intentions seemed to have been recognized; the alarm had only been momentary. Now they were all watching him in melancholy silence. His mother lay in her chair, her legs stiffly outstretched and pressed together, her eyes almost closing for sheer weariness; his father and his sister were sitting beside each other, his sister's arm around the old man's neck.

Perhaps I can go on turning round now, thought Gregor, and began his labors again. He could not stop himself from panting with the effort, and had to pause now and then to take breath. Nor did anyone harass him, he was left entirely to himself. When he had completed the turn-round he began at once to crawl straight back. He was amazed at the distance separating him from his room and could not understand how in his weak state he had managed to accomplish the same journey so recently, almost without remarking it. Intent on crawling as fast as possible, he barely noticed that not a single word, not an ejaculation from his family, interfered with his progress. Only when he was already in the doorway did he turn his head round, not completely, for his neck muscles were getting stiff, but enough to see that nothing had changed behind him except that his sister had risen to her feet. His last glance fell on his mother, who was quite overcome by sleep.

Hardly was he well inside his room when the door was hastily pushed shut, bolted and locked. The sudden noise in his rear startled him so much that his little legs gave beneath him. It was his sister who had shown such haste. She had been standing ready waiting and had made a light spring forward, Gregor had not even heard her coming, and she cried, "At last!" to her parents as she turned the key in the lock.

"And what now?" said Gregor to himself, looking round in the darkness. Soon he made the discovery that he was now unable to stir a limb. This did not surprise him, rather it seemed unnatural that he should ever actually have been able to move on these feeble little legs. Otherwise he felt relatively comfortable. True, his whole body was aching, but it seemed that the pain was gradually growing less and would finally pass away. The rotting apple in his back and the inflamed area around it, all covered with soft dust, already hardly troubled him. He thought of his family with tenderness and love. The decision that he must disappear was one that he held to even more strongly than his sister, if that were possible. In this state of vacant and peaceful meditation he remained until the tower clock struck three in the morning. The first broadening of light in the world outside the window entered his consciousness once more. Then his head sank to the floor of its own accord and from the nostrils came the last faint flicker of his breath.

When the charwoman arrived early in the morning—what between her strength and her impatience she slammed all the doors so loudly, never mind how often she had been begged not to do so, that no one in the whole apartment could enjoy any quiet sleep after her arrival—she noticed nothing unusual as she took her customary peep into Gregor's room. She thought he was lying motionless on purpose, pretending to be in the sulks; she credited him with every kind of intelligence. Since she happened to have the long-handled broom in her hand she tried to tickle him up with it from the doorway. When that too produced no reaction she felt provoked and poked at him a little harder, and only when she had pushed him along the floor without meeting any resistance was her attention aroused. It did not take her long to establish the truth of the matter, and her eyes widened, she let out a whistle, yet did not waste much time over it but tore open the door of the Samsas' bedroom and yelled into the darkness at the top of her voice: "Just look at this, it's dead; it's lying here dead and done for!"

Mr. and Mrs. Samsa started up in their double bed and before they realized the nature of the charwoman's announcement had some difficulty in overcoming the shock of it. But then they got out of bed quickly, one on either side, Mr. Samsa throwing a blanket over his shoulders, Mrs. Samsa in nothing but her nightgown; in this array they entered Gregor's room. Meanwhile the door of the living room opened, too, where Grete had been sleeping since the advent of the lodgers; she was completely dressed as if she had not been to bed, which seemed to be confirmed also by the paleness of her face. "Dead?" said Mrs. Samsa, looking questioningly at the charwoman, although she could have investigated for herself, and the fact was obvious enough without investigation. "I should say so," said the charwoman, proving her words by pushing Gregor's corpse a long way to one side with her broomstick. Mrs. Samsa made a movement as if to stop her, but checked it. "Well," said Mr. Samsa, "now thanks be to God." He crossed himself, and the three women followed his example. Grete, whose eyes never left the corpse, said: "Just see how thin he was. It's such a long time since he's eaten anything. The food came out again just as it went in." Indeed, Gregor's body was completely flat and dry, as could only now be seen when it was no longer supported by the legs and nothing prevented one from looking closely at it.

"Come in beside us, Grete, for a little while," said Mrs. Samsa with a tremulous smile, and Grete, not without looking back at the corpse, followed her parents into their bedroom. The charwoman shut the door and opened the window wide. Although it was so early in the morning a certain softness was perceptible in the fresh air. After all, it was already the end of March.

The three lodgers emerged from their room and were surprised to see no breakfast; they had been forgotten. "Where's our breakfast?" said the middle lodger peevishly to the charwoman. But she put her finger to her lips and hastily, without a word, indicated by gestures that they should go into Gregor's room. They did so and stood, their hands in the pockets of their somewhat shabby coats, around Gregor's corpse in the room where it was now fully light.

At that the door of the Samsas' bedroom opened and Mr. Samsa appeared in his uniform, his wife on one arm, his daughter on the other. They all looked a little as if they had been crying; from time to time Grete hid her face on her father's arm.

"Leave my house at once!" said Mr. Samsa, and pointed to the door without disengaging himself from the women. "What do you mean by that?" said the middle lodger, taken somewhat aback, with a feeble smile. The two others put their hands behind them and kept rubbing them together, as if in gleeful expectation of a fine set-to in which they were bound to come off the winners. "I mean just what I say," answered Mr. Samsa, and advanced in a straight line with his two companions towards the lodger. He stood his ground at first quietly, looking at the floor as if his thoughts were taking a new pattern in his head. "Then let us go, by all means," he said, and looked up at Mr. Samsa as if in a sudden access of humility he were expecting some renewed sanction for this decision. Mr. Samsa merely nodded briefly once or twice with meaning eyes. Upon that the lodger really did go with long strides into the hall, his two friends had been listening and had quite stopped rubbing their hands for some moments and now went scuttling after him as if afraid that Mr. Samsa might get into the hall before them and cut them off from their leader. In the hall they all three took their hats from the rack, their sticks from the umbrella stand, bowed in silence and quitted the apartment. With a suspiciousness which proved quite unfounded Mr. Samsa and the two women followed them out to the landing; leaning over the banister they watched the three figures slowly but surely going down the long stairs, vanishing from sight at a certain turn of the staircase on every floor and coming into view again after a moment or so; the more they dwindled, the more the Samsa family's interest in them dwindled, and when a butcher's boy met them and passed them on the stairs coming up proudly with a tray on his head, Mr. Samsa and the two women soon left the landing and as if a burden had been lifted from them went back into their apartment.

They decided to spend this day in resting and going for a stroll; they had not only deserved such a respite from work, but absolutely needed it. And so they sat down at the table and wrote three notes of excuse, Mr. Samsa to his board of management, Mrs. Samsa to her employer and Grete to the head of her firm. While they were writing, the charwoman came in to say that she was going now, since her morning's work was finished. At first they only nodded without looking up, but as she kept hovering there they eyed her irritably. "Well?" said Mr. Samsa. The charwoman stood grinning in the doorway as if she had good news to impart to the family but meant not to say a word unless properly questioned. The small ostrich feather standing upright on her hat, which had annoyed Mr. Samsa ever since she was engaged, was waving gaily in all directions. "Well, what is it then?" asked Mrs. Samsa, who obtained more respect from the charwoman than the others. "Oh," said the charwoman, giggling so amiably that she could not at once continue, "just this, you don't need to bother about how to get rid of the thing next door. It's been seen to already." Mrs. Samsa and Grete bent over their letters again, as if preoccupied; Mr. Samsa, who perceived that she was eager to begin describing it all in detail, stopped her with a decisive hand. But since she was not allowed to tell her story, she remembered the great hurry she was in, being obviously deeply huffed: "Bye, everybody," she said, whirling off violently, and departed with a frightful slamming of doors.

"She'll be given notice tonight," said Mr. Samsa, but neither from his wife nor his daughter did he get any answer, for the charwoman seemed to have shattered again the composure they had barely achieved. They rose, went to the window and stayed there, clasping each other tight. Mr. Samsa turned in his chair to look at them and quietly observed them for a little. Then he called out: "Come along, now, do. Let bygones be bygones. And you might have some consideration for me." The two of them complied at once, hastened to him, caressed him and quickly finished their letters.

Then they all three left the apartment together, which was more than they had done for months, and went by tram into the open country outside the town. The tram, in which they were the only passengers, was filled with warm sunshine. Leaning comfortably back in their seats they canvassed their prospects for the future, and it appeared on closer inspection that these were not at all bad, for the jobs they had got, which so far they had never really discussed with each other, were all three admirable and likely to lead to better things later on. The greatest immediate improvement in their condition would of course arise from moving to another house; they wanted to take a smaller and cheaper but also better situated and more easily run apartment than the one they had, which Gregor had selected. While they were thus conversing, it struck both Mr. and Mrs. Samsa, almost at the same moment, as they became aware of their daughter's increasing vivacity, that in spite of all the sorrow of recent times, which had made her cheeks pale, she had bloomed into a pretty girl with a good figure. They grew quieter and half unconsciously exchanged glances of complete agreement, having come to the conclusion that it would soon be time to find a good husband for her. And it was like a confirmation of their new dreams and excellent intentions that at the end of their journey their daughter sprang to her feet first and stretched her young body.

Saul Bellow

SEIZE THE DAY

Preface 🔲🔲🔲🔲🔲🔲🔲🔲🔲🔲🔲🔲🔲🔲🔲🔲🔲🔲🔲🔲

Reading *Seize the Day* (1956), and learning that Saul Bellow was born in the year *The Metamorphosis* (1915) was published, we may think that Bellow begins where Kafka left off. Both short novels, classic modern and classic contemporary, focus on man's condition, using the lens of father-son conflict to examine the death of a salesman. But Bellow did not win the Nobel Prize for Literature in 1976 by joining together Kafka's theme and Arthur Miller's Pulitzer Prize–winning drama, *Death of a Salesman* (1949). His success in *Seize the Day* is to understand how modern becomes contemporary, how man continues to live with and despite the pessimism isolated by Kafka. Bellow uses his novel to analyze his relationship with Kafka as writer and son both. The tradition of literature is another dimension of parent-child conflict. Conrad, Faulkner, Mann, and Kafka are the fathers of contemporary literature—Dostoevsky grandparent—Bellow, Alexander Solzhenitsyn, Carson McCullers, and Yukio Mishima are their son and daughter writers. Bellow's success as a novelist is to recover his literary father by discovering his father's meaning in himself as son. Between *The Metamorphosis* and *Seize the Day*, literature too often pursued the death wish of pure form, endless experiment, and rabid, boring consciousness upon consciousness too easily given. What could be said after Kafka? was the writer's question, and the wrong answer was to repeat him with hollow variation that assumed he had said it all. Bellow, first of classic

319

contemporaries, does not repeat Kafka—he writes, and in writing he rediscovers Kafka not for, but in, our time.

Because Bellow believes in human experience, he puts realism—symbolic, mythic, or aesthetic (Conrad, Faulkner, Mann)—before literary formalism. His characters grapple with life, seeking truth from the human experience in which Bellow has faith. Life may be chaotic, but the novel's job is not to reproduce chaos; for man lives, chaos or not. Literature must love people more than it loves itself, and the genius of Bellow's fiction is to embrace them: "The great, great crowd, the inexhaustible current of millions of every race and kind pouring out, pressing round, of every age, of every genius, possessors of every human secret, antique and future, in every face the refinement of one particular motive or essence—*I labor, I spend, I strive, I design, I love, I cling, I uphold, I give way, I envy, I long, I scorn, I die, I hide, I want.* Faster, much faster than any man could make the tally." Any one human essence may be ridiculous, but for Bellow that is no reason for a literature of the absurd: that only comes from a writer thinking he is fast enough to make the total human tally. Common humanity and its common experiences are worth writing about because they are common—all men share them. Sharing is the value of human experience, and the writer ought to share it. Nowhere is this more expressly put in Bellow's fiction than in his paramount novel, *Henderson the Rain King* (1959), where Eugene Henderson describes his turnabout: "I had a voice that said, I want! *I* want? I? It should have told me *she* wants, *he* wants, *they* want." People want, all both lack and desire because to lack is to desire and to desire is to lack—wanting is human. Recognizing that, we can define living and wanting as one: we *want* to live in every sense of the word. The weight always pressing on Bellow's heroes—what the poet Wordsworth called "the burthen of the mystery . . . the heavy and the weary weight of all this unintelligible world"—can be shared when fiction renews our collective strength by teaching that mankind imaginatively defined is a shared experience.

The climax of *Seize the Day* finds its hero, Tommy Wilhelm, mourning himself in the image of a dead stranger. His grief is genuine because Tommy has found humanity and thus reality. A bystander asks: "The man's brother, maybe?" Another answers: "Oh, I doubt that very much . . . they're not alike at all. Night and day." But Bellow's *Henderson* proclaims that "the opposite makes the opposite." Tommy and the dead man are brothers just because they are not alike. Because men are not like one another mankind is, and in that understanding lies the reality of Tommy's tears. In his earlier novel, *The Victim* (1947), Bellow gives the judgment of Tommy's performance to his theater critic, Schlossberg: "It's bad to be less than human and it's bad to be more than human. . . . Good acting is what is exactly human. And if you say I am a tough critic, you mean I have a high opinion of what is human. This is my whole idea. More than human, can you have any use for life? Less than human, you don't either." Schlossberg's whole idea is Bellow's because Bellow's highest opinion of mankind defines man in the whole. Individual differences in men— their wants—add up to mankind in *Seize the Day.* All of Bellow's fiction treats the conflict of less than human and more than human; between those opposites man dangles, but in dangling man is defined. Caught between civilian life and the army, Joseph of Bellow's first novel, *Dangling Man* (1944), asks: "Who can be the earnest huntsman of himself when he knows he is in turn a quarry?" To show us that paralysis and its opposite—displacement—are the wrong answers to this question is the goal of Bellow's fiction. Vacillating between pig-man and superman, Henderson reflects: "Nobody truly occupies a station in life any more. There are mostly people who feel that they occupy the place that belongs to another by rights. There are displaced persons everywhere." Understanding that to be human is to act so, we may bring order to a world of mismatched places and people. When we are human all places are ours and our places are everyone's: people make and match all places by being themselves.

The heroes of Bellow's fiction are more acted upon than acting. They understand that the human comedy demands this role. *The Adventures of Augie March* (1953), which brought Bellow national recognition, has almost no adventure in it. Just as Augie is no instigator, neither is the immensely suffering protagonist Moses Herzog of *Herzog* (1964); and the same can be said of the more recent heroes of *Mr. Sammler's Planet* (1971), and *Humboldt's Gift* (1975). Faced with their too open suffering and immobility, we very often do not like Bellow's protagonists, suspecting that their martyrdom is made out of a molehill. Even as clowns they seem to fail at both comedy and tragedy, and so we see them as no more than self-pitying bunglers. But Bellow's bunglers come out of the same tradition as Bellow, the Yiddish tradition of the *shlemiehl*, the poor, warmhearted slob who can never do anything right, and Bellow wants us to see that the *shlemiehl* is as much like us as we don't want him to be. For the bungler has one thing going for him—he's no cynic—and it is cynicism that leads dangling man into paralysis and displacement. The *shlemiehl* can be taught to wonder, to grapple with fatality by recognizing Life's mystery. Those who teach him comprise the second voice of the dialogue of Bellow's fiction, a dialogue whose questions and answers remind us of the tradition of the *Torah*, the ultimate tradition of learning that is Judaism. But in Bellow's fictional world, as in ours, religion and its social counterpart the family are on the way out. No rabbis come to instruct the modern American *shlemiehl*; no fathers free such hindered sons as Henderson. Still, insists Bellow, the schoolmen can be found: Schlossberg in *The Victim*, Himmelstein in *Herzog*, King Dahfu in *Henderson*, and in *Seize the Day*, Dr. Tamkin. These are the men whom Herzog styles "Reality-Instructors," and whom Augie March identifies as "those persons who persistently arise before me with life counsels and illumination throughout my earthly pilgrimage." These fast-talking hucksters mix up Socrates and Christ and always make sure to get paid, because taking the *shlemiehl* and telling him that you're doing it is the important lesson. They seem to know everything, and most of all poetry and medicine, because they are all healers with words aplenty. King Dahfu gives Henderson a treatise on Obersteiner's allochiria for the same reason that Tamkin gives Tommy Wilhelm a poem on "Ism vs Hism." The message is always the same: don't be a superman, don't be a robot, be human, seek balance not extremes. Henderson never finds out that allochiria means the reversal of symmetry: hit the right knee and the left leg jerks. The gag is out of vaudeville, and Bellow's instructors are no more than charlatan artists once again who mix con-man with preacher. "Only vanity, is what is," argues Tamkin to teach Tommy not to seek an economic advantage over nature, as Henderson seeks a mechanical one. Henderson gets his chance to be human when a pulley breaks. He succeeds, and so must pay for his lesson by inheriting King Dahfu's throne: "No child of age, makes the Sungo [Henderson] king," reveals Dahfu as he dies. The charlatan artist is thus surrogate father, and to be healed into humanity is to become a genuine son. But the newly schooled son is unhindered, for what is natural can be neither constrained nor exaggerated out of humanity. A cured Henderson gets to "the heart of the water"—and water imagery is dominant in all Bellow's novels—when he knows it to be "the lead-sealed but expanding water," and the same water in Tommy Wilhelm's tears shows that he has risen naturally to the human level.

Rising and falling are major concerns of *Seize the Day*, for fat Tommy Wilhelm's one day desperately awaits the rising of lard on the commodities exchange. Fakir-guru Tamkin has lured him into the market with the dream of making a killing—at the price of a less than half share for an equal partnership—and of course it is Wilhelm who is murdered when lard falls about as far down as the swimming pool in the basement of the Hotel Gloriana, in which Tamkin, Tommy, and his father, Dr. Adler live. Between the hotel and its pool is a movie theater on the street floor that repeats the theater in the brokerage office where Tommy watches his shares sink. His last mistake has been a seven-hundred-dollar check spent on lard on Tamkin's tip; his first seeking a film career instead of finishing college. Tommy's screen test is a flop because he leaks emotion despite his good looks. Instead of a star, he turns into an extra—in a single film. In *Annie Laurie* he played a bagpiper ordered to *drown out* a message of warning. Feeling and falling deeper into guilty brooding, Tommy ends up where Bellow's novel starts: out of job, marriage, love affair, and money—and "Money is"! He wants his father to pay his hotel bill, to love him, and to carry him, but Doctor Adler refuses to take up Tommy as his cross. Tamkin then seems to pick it up, but for the purpose of having Tommy carry him. When Tommy learns the truth, lard falls; but Bellow's point is made. If Tommy can carry Tamkin he ought to be able to carry himself. Old Doctor Adler was famous for internal diagnosis, and Tamkin is no different; when he warns Tommy not to "marry suffering" he repeats Adler's advice to "concentrate on real troubles." Father and surrogate both stand against suffering self-pity, but only Tamkin insists that what is wrong can be made right. Adler is only an advanced case of Tommy's disease: to help Tommy out means admitting his own mistakes, and his silence is the legacy in Tommy that won't deal with his problems precisely by over-admitting them. Tamkin's here-and-now philosophy, and Bellow's title, *Seize the Day*, come from the Latin *carpe diem*—meaning that nothing should be put off until tomorrow. But, as speculators, both Tamkin and Tommy make the mistake of selling out today for tomorrow. Tommy's one day thus turns into a day of reckoning, and in that summing of accounts his money margin is wiped out. But living on margin was what made him less than human, trying to be more than human with typically modern self-destructiveness. The real point of Tamkin's false preaching is its vitality: "Then there's a small percentage of those who want to live. That's the only significant thing in the whole world of today. Those are the only two classes of people there are. Some want to live, but the great majority don't." And, ironically, it is by giving up a margin that seeks tomorrow, by giving up a small percentage paid down, that one joins the small percentage who live. Tommy goes out of business and into life because he was in the wrong business from the start, believing that "to carry his peculiar burden, to feel shame and impotence, to taste . . . quelled tears" was "the only important business." But Tamkin guides Tommy, as Virgil guided Dante for a price, and in the insane hell that is New York City Tommy finds "the right clue . . . something very big. Truth, like."

Neither Tamkin nor Tommy talks to each other; they talk to themselves and hurl their monologues at each other. But the environment of New York City— Bellow's fictional place—turns monologue into true dialogue. Bellow's chalk-on-sidewalk picture of the city is brilliant because it lives, and living it is real. The city's reality powers Bellow's realism, and in turn that realism empowers his characters. Nowhere is Bellow speaking more closely for himself than in Tamkin's exclamation: "Facts always are sensational. I'll say that a second time. Facts *always!* are sensational." This makes the "human tragedy comedy" of New York City as divine as Dante's *Divine Comedy*, as Tommy realizes: "When you are . . . dreaming that everybody is outcast, you realize that this must be one of the small matters. There is a larger body, and from this you cannot be separated. . . . The sons and fathers are themselves. . . . The idea of this larger body had been planted in him a few days ago beneath Times Square. . . . He was going through an underground corridor. . . . And in the dark tunnel, in the haste, heat, and darkness which disfigure . . . all of a sudden, unsought, a general love for all these imperfect and lurid-looking people burst out in Wilhelm's breast. . . . He was imperfect and disfigured himself, but what difference did that make if he was united with them by this blaze of love?" Beneath the sidewalks of New York, Tommy is baptised by Bellow in the deepest current of humanity. The environment communicates the sensational fact of common humanity's most human nature—its dynamic onward streaming. Nature is a giant wave; nature "rolls the waters of the earth. Man is the chief of this. All creations are his just inheritance. You don't know what you've got within you"—so Tamkin and Bellow proclaim. And so Tommy cries to get what's inside him out: His tears make him finally a star—the best and therefore the most human actor.

Bellow

SEIZE THE DAY

I

When it came to concealing his troubles, Tommy Wilhelm was not less capable than the next fellow. So at least he thought, and there was a certain amount of evidence to back him up. He had once been an actor—no, not quite, an extra—and he knew what acting should be. Also, he was smoking a cigar, and when a man is smoking a cigar, wearing a hat, he has an advantage; it is harder to find out how he feels. He came from the twenty-third floor down to the lobby on the mezzanine to collect his mail before breakfast, and he believed—he hoped—that he looked passably well: doing all right. It was a matter of sheer hope, because there was not much that he could add to his present effort. On the fourteenth floor he looked for his father to enter the elevator; they often met at this hour, on the way to breakfast. If he worried about his appearance it was mainly for his old father's sake. But there was no stop on the fourteenth, and the elevator sank and sank. Then the smooth door opened and the great dark red uneven carpet that covered the lobby billowed toward Wilhelm's feet. In the foreground the lobby was dark, sleepy. French drapes like sails kept out the sun, but three high, narrow windows were open, and in the blue air Wilhelm saw a pigeon about to light on the great chain that supported the marquee of the movie house directly underneath the lobby. For one moment he heard the wings beating strongly.

Most of the guests at the Hotel Gloriana were past the age of retirement. Along Broadway in the Seventies, Eighties, and Nineties, a great part of New York's vast population of old men and women lives. Unless the weather is too cold or wet they fill the benches about the tiny railed parks and along the subway gratings from Verdi Square to Columbia University, they crowd the shops and cafeterias, the dime stores, the tea-rooms, the bakeries, the beauty parlors, the reading rooms and club rooms. Among these old people at the Gloriana, Wilhelm felt out of place. He was comparatively young, in his middle forties, large and blond, with big shoulders; his back was heavy and strong, if already a little stooped or thickened. After breakfast the old guests sat down on the green leather armchairs and sofas in the lobby and began to gossip and look into the papers; they had nothing to do but wait out the day. But Wilhelm was used to an active life and liked to go out energetically in the morning. And for several months, because he had no position, he had kept up his morale by rising early; he was shaved and in the lobby by eight o'clock. He bought the paper and some cigars and drank a Coca-Cola or two before he went in to breakfast with his father. After breakfast—out, out, out to attend to business. The getting out had in itself become the chief business. But he had realized that he could not keep this up much longer, and today he was afraid. He was aware that his routine was about to break up and he sensed that a huge trouble long presaged but till now formless was due. Before evening, he'd know.

Nevertheless he followed his daily course and crossed the lobby.

Rubin, the man at the newsstand, had poor eyes. They may not have been actually weak but they were poor in expression, with lacy lids that furled down at the corners. He dressed well. It didn't seem necessary—he was behind the counter most of the time—but he dressed very well. He had on a rich brown suit; the cuffs embarrassed the hairs on his small hands. He wore a Countess Mara painted necktie. As Wilhelm approached, Rubin did not see him; he was looking out dreamily at the Hotel Ansonia, which was visible from his corner, several blocks away. The Ansonia, the neighborhood's great landmark, was built by Stanford White. It looks like a baroque palace from Prague or Munich enlarged a hundred times, with towers, domes, huge swells and bubbles of metal gone green from exposure, iron fretwork and festoons. Black television antennae are densely planted on its round summits. Under the changes of weather it may look like marble or like sea water, black as slate in the fog, white as tufa in sunlight. This morning it looked like the image of itself reflected in deep water, white and cumulous above, with cavernous distortions underneath. Together, the two men gazed at it.

Then Rubin said, "Your dad is in to breakfast already, the old gentleman."

"Oh, yes? Ahead of me today?"

"That's a real knocked-out shirt you got on," said Rubin. "Where's it from, Saks?"

"No, it's a Jack Fagman—Chicago."

Even when his spirits were low, Wilhelm could still wrinkle his forehead in a pleasing way. Some of the slow, silent movements of his face were very attractive. He went back a step, as if to stand away from himself and get a better look at his shirt. His glance was comic, a comment upon his untidiness. He liked to wear good clothes, but once he had put it on each article appeared to go its own way. Wilhelm, laughing, panted a little; his teeth were small; his cheeks when he laughed and puffed grew round, and he looked much younger than his years. In the old days when he was a college freshman and wore a raccoon coat and a beanie on his large blond head his father used to say that, big as he was, he could charm a bird out of a tree. Wilhelm had great charm still.

"I like this dove-gray color," he said in his sociable, good-natured way. "It isn't washable. You have to send it to the cleaner. It never smells as good as washed. But it's a nice shirt. It cost sixteen, eighteen bucks."

This shirt had not been bought by Wilhelm; it was a present from his boss—his former boss, with whom he had had a falling out. But there was no reason why he should tell Rubin the history of it. Although perhaps Rubin knew—Rubin was the kind of man who knew, and knew and knew. Wilhelm also knew many things about Rubin, for that matter, about Rubin's wife and Rubin's business, Rubin's health. None of these could be mentioned, and the great weight of the unspoken left them little to talk about.

"Well, y'lookin' pretty sharp today," Rubin said.

And Wilhelm said gladly, "Am I? Do you really think so?" He could not believe it. He saw his reflection in the glass cupboard full of cigar boxes, among the grand seals and paper damask and the gold-embossed portraits of famous men, García, Edward the Seventh, Cyrus the Great. You had to allow for the darkness and deformations of the glass, but he thought he didn't look too good. A wide wrinkle like a comprehensive bracket sign was written upon his forehead, the point between his brows, and there were patches of brown on his dark blond skin. He began to be half amused at the shadow of his own marveling, troubled, desirous eyes, and his nostrils and his lips. Fair-haired hippopotamus!—that was how he looked to himself. He saw a big round face, a wide, flourishing red mouth, stump teeth. And the hat, too; and the cigar, too. I should have done hard labor all my life, he reflected. Hard honest labor that tires you out and makes you sleep. I'd have worked off my energy and felt better. Instead, I had to distinguish myself—yet.

He had put forth plenty of effort, but that was not the same as working hard, was it? And if as a young man he had got off to a bad start it was due to this very same face. Early in the nineteen-thirties, because of his striking looks, he had been very briefly considered star material, and he had gone to Hollywood. There for seven years, stubbornly, he had tried to become a screen artist. Long before that time his ambition or delusion had ended, but through pride and perhaps also through laziness he had remained in California. At last he turned to other things, but those seven years of persistence and defeat had unfitted him somehow for trades and businesses, and then it was too late to go into one of the professions. He had been slow to mature, and he had lost ground, and so he hadn't been able to get rid of his energy and he was convinced that this energy itself had done him the greatest harm.

"I didn't see you at the gin game last night," said Rubin.

"I had to miss it. How did it go?"

For the last few weeks Wilhelm had played gin almost nightly, but yesterday he had felt that he couldn't afford to lose any more. He had never won. Not once. And while the losses were small they weren't gains, were they? They were losses. He was tired of losing, and tired also of the company, and so he had gone by himself to the movies.

"Oh," said Rubin, "it went okay. Carl made a chump of himself yelling at the guys. This time Doctor Tamkin didn't let him get away with it. He told him the psychological reason why."

"What was the reason?"

Rubin said, "I can't quote him. Who could? You know the way Tamkin talks. Don't ask me. Do you want the *Trib?* Aren't you going to look at the closing quotations?"

"It won't help much to look. I know what they were yesterday at three," said Wilhelm. "But I suppose I better had get the paper." It seemed necessary for him to lift one shoulder in order to put his hand into his jacket pocket. There, among little packets of pills and crushed cigarette butts and strings of cellophane, the red tapes of packages which he sometimes used as dental floss, he recalled that he had dropped some pennies.

"That doesn't sound so good," said Rubin. He meant to be conversationally playful, but his voice had no tone and his eyes, slack and lid-blinded, turned elsewhere. He didn't want to hear. It was all the same to him. Maybe he already knew, being the sort of man who knew and knew.

No, it wasn't good. Wilhelm held three orders of lard in the commodities market. He and Dr. Tamkin had bought this lard together four days ago at 12.96, and the price at once began to fall and was still falling. In the mail this morning there was sure to be a call for additional margin payment. One came every day.

The psychologist, Dr. Tamkin, had got him into this. Tamkin lived at the Gloriana and attended the card game. He had explained to Wilhelm that you could speculate in commodities at one of the uptown branches of a good Wall Street house without making the full deposit of margin legally required. It was up to the branch manager. If he knew you—and all the branch managers knew Tamkin—he would allow you to make short-term purchases. You needed only to open a small account.

"The whole secret of this type of speculation," Tamkin had told him, "is in the alertness. You have to act fast—buy it and sell it; sell it and buy in again. But quick! Get to the window and have them wire Chicago at just the right second. Strike and strike again! Then get out the same day. In no time at all you turn over fifteen, twenty thousand dollars' worth of soy beans, coffee, corn, hides, wheat, cotton." Obviously the doctor understood the market well. Otherwise he could not make it sound so simple. "People lose because they are greedy and can't get out when it starts to go up. They gamble, but I do it scientifically. This is not guesswork. You must take a few points and get out. Why, ye gods!" said Dr. Tamkin with his bulging eyes, his bald head, and his drooping lip. "Have you stopped to think how much dough people are making in the market?"

Wilhelm with a quick shift from gloomy attention to the panting laugh which entirely changed his face had said, "Ho, have I ever! What do you think? Who doesn't know it's way beyond nineteen-twenty-eight—twenty-nine and still on the rise? Who hasn't read the Fulbright investigation? There's money everywhere. Everyone is shoveling it in. Money is—is—"

"And can you rest—can you sit still while this is going on?" said Dr. Tamkin. "I confess to you I can't. I think about people, just because they have a few bucks to invest, making fortunes. They have no sense, they have no talent, they just have the extra dough and it makes them more dough. I get so worked up and tormented and restless, so restless! I haven't even been able to practice my profession. With all this money around you don't want to be a fool while everyone else is making. I know guys who make five, ten thousand a week just by fooling around. I know a guy at the Hotel Pierre. There's nothing to him, but he has a whole case of Mumm's champagne at lunch. I know another guy on Central Park South—But what's the use of talking. They make millions. They have smart lawyers who get them out of taxes by a thousand schemes."

"Whereas I got taken," said Wilhelm. "My wife refused to sign a joint return. One fairly good year and I got into the thirty-two-per-cent bracket and was stripped bare. What of all my bad years?"

"It's a businessmen's government," said Dr. Tamkin. "You can be sure that these men making five thousand a week—"

"I don't need that sort of money," Wilhelm had said. "But oh! if I could only work out a little steady income from this. Not much. I don't ask much. But how badly I need—! I'd be so grateful if you'd show me how to work it."

"Sure I will. *I* do it regularly. I'll bring you my receipts if you like. And do you want to know something? I approve of your attitude very much. You want to avoid catching the money fever. This type of activity is filled with hostile feeling and lust. You should see what it does to some of these fellows. They go on the market with murder in their hearts."

"What's that I once heard a guy say?" Wilhelm remarked. "A man is only as good as what he loves."

"That's it—just it," Tamkin said. "You don't have to go about it their way. There's also a calm and rational, a psychological approach."

Wilhelm's father, old Dr. Adler, lived in an entirely different world from his son, but he had warned him once against Dr. Tamkin. Rather casually— he was a very bland old man—he said, "Wilky, perhaps you listen too much to this Tamkin. He's interesting to talk to. I don't doubt it. I think he's pretty common but he's a persuasive man. However, I don't know how reliable he may be."

It made Wilhelm profoundly bitter that his father should speak to him with such detachment about his welfare. Dr. Adler liked to appear affable. Affable! His own son, his one and only son, could not speak his mind or ease his heart to him. I wouldn't turn to Tamkin, he thought, if I could turn to him. At least Tamkin sympathizes with me and tries to give me a hand, whereas Dad doesn't want to be disturbed.

Old Dr. Adler had retired from practice; he had a considerable fortune and could easily have helped his son. Recently Wilhelm had told him, "Father—it so happens that I'm in a bad way now. I hate to have to say it. You realize that I'd rather have good news to bring you. But it's true. And since it's true, Dad— What else am I supposed to say? It's true."

Another father might have appreciated how difficult this confession was—so much bad luck, weariness, weakness, and failure. Wilhelm had tried to copy the old man's tone and made himself sound gentlemanly, low-voiced, tasteful. He didn't allow his voice to tremble; he made no stupid gesture. But the doctor had no answer. He only nodded. You might have told him that Seattle was near Puget Sound, or that the Giants and Dodgers were playing a night game, so little was he moved from his expression of healthy, handsome, good-humored old age. He behaved toward his son as he had formerly done toward his patients, and it was a great grief to Wilhelm; it was almost too much to bear. Couldn't he see—couldn't he feel? Had he lost his family sense?

Greatly hurt, Wilhelm struggled however to be fair. Old people are bound to change, he said. They have hard things to think about. They must prepare for where they are going. They can't live by the old schedule any longer and all their perspectives change, and other people become alike, kin and acquaintances. Dad is no longer the same person, Wilhelm reflected. He was thirty-two when I was born, and now he's going on eighty. Furthermore, it's time I stopped feeling like a kid toward him, a small son.

The handsome old doctor stood well above the other old people in the hotel. He was idolized by everyone. This was what people said: "That's old Professor Adler, who used to teach internal medicine. He was a diagnostician, one of the best in New York, and had a tremendous practice. Isn't he a wonderful-looking old guy? It's a pleasure to see such a fine old scientist, clean and immaculate. He stands straight and understands every single thing you say. He still has all his buttons. You can discuss any subject with him." The clerks, the elevator operators, the telephone girls and waitresses and chambermaids, the management flattered and pampered him. That was what he wanted. He had always been a vain man. To see how his father loved himself sometimes made Wilhelm madly indignant.

He folded over the *Tribune* with its heavy, black, crashing sensational print and read without recognizing any of the words, for his mind was still on his father's vanity. The doctor had created his own praise. People were primed and did not know it. And what did he need praise for? In a hotel where everyone was busy and contacts were so brief and had such small weight, how could it satisfy him? He could be in people's thoughts here and there for a moment; in and then out. He could never matter much to them. Wilhelm let out a strong, hard breath and raised the brows of his round and somewhat circular eyes. He stared beyond the thick borders of the paper.

. . . love that well which thou must leave ere long.

Involuntary memory brought him this line. At first he thought it referred to his father, but then he understood that it was for himself, rather. *He* should

love that well. "This thou perceivest, which makes *thy* love more strong."
Under Dr. Tamkin's influence Wilhelm had recently begun to remember the
poems he used to read. Dr. Tamkin knew, or said he knew, the great English
poets and once in a while he mentioned a poem of his own. It was a long time
since anyone had spoken to Wilhelm about this sort of thing. He didn't like
to think about his college days, but if there was one course that now made
sense it was Literature I. The textbook was Lieder and Lovett's *British Poetry
and Prose*, a black heavy book with thin pages. Did I read that? he asked himself. Yes, he had read it and there was one accomplishment at least he could
recall with pleasure. He had read "Yet once more, O ye laurels." How pure this
was to say! It was beautiful.

Sunk though he be beneath the wat'ry floor . . .

Such things had always swayed him, and now the power of such words was
far, far greater.

Wilhelm respected the truth, but he could lie and one of the things he lied
often about was his education. He said he was an alumnus of Penn State; in
fact he had left school before his sophomore year was finished. His sister
Catherine had a B. S. degree. Wilhelm's late mother was a graduate of Bryn
Mawr. He was the only member of the family who had no education. This was
another sore point. His father was ashamed of him.

But he had heard the old man bragging to another old man, saying, "My son
is a sales executive. He didn't have the patience to finish school. But he does
all right for himself. His income is up in the five figures somewhere."

"What—thirty, forty thousand?" said his stooped old friend.

"Well, he needs at least that much for his style of life. Yes, he needs that."

Despite his troubles, Wilhelm almost laughed. Why, that boasting old hypocrite. He knew the sales executive was no more. For many weeks there had
been no executive, no sales, no income. But how we love looking fine in the
eyes of the world—how beautiful are the old when they are doing a snow
job! It's Dad, thought Wilhelm, who is the salesman. He's selling me. *He*
should have gone on the road.

But what of the truth? Ah, the truth was that there were problems, and of
these problems his father wanted no part. His father was ashamed of him.
The truth, Wilhelm thought, was very awkward. He pressed his lips together,
and his tongue went soft; it pained him far at the back, in the cords and throat,
and a knot of ill formed in his chest. Dad never was a pal to me when I was
young, he reflected. He was at the office or the hospital, or lecturing. He expected me to look out for myself and never gave me much thought. Now he
looks down on me. And maybe in some respects he's right.

No wonder Wilhelm delayed the moment when he would have to go into
the dining room. He had moved to the end of Rubin's counter. He had opened
the *Tribune*; the fresh pages drooped from his hands; the cigar was smoked
out and the hat did not defend him. He was wrong to suppose that he was more

capable than the next fellow when it came to concealing his troubles. They were clearly written out upon his face. He wasn't even aware of it.

There was the matter of the different names, which, in the hotel, came up frequently. "Are you Doctor Adler's son?" "Yes, but my name is Tommy Wilhelm." And the doctor would say, "My son and I use different monickers. I uphold tradition. He's for the new." The Tommy was Wilhelm's own invention. He adopted it when he went to Hollywood, and dropped the Adler. Hollywood was his own idea, too. He used to pretend that it had all been the doing of a certain talent scout named Maurice Venice. But the scout had never made him a definite offer of a studio connection. He had approached him, but the results of the screen test had not been good. After the test Wilhelm took the initiative and pressed Maurice Venice until he got him to say, "Well, I suppose you might make it out there." On the strength of this Wilhelm had left college and had gone to California.

Someone had said, and Wilhelm agreed with the saying, that in Los Angeles all the loose objects in the country were collected, as if America had been tilted and everything that wasn't tightly screwed down had slid into Southern California. He himself had been one of these loose objects. Sometimes he told people, "I was too mature for college. I was a big boy, you see. Well, I thought, when do you start to become a man?" After he had driven a painted flivver and had worn a yellow slicker with slogans on it, and played illegal poker, and gone out on Coke dates, he had *had* college. He wanted to try something new and quarreled with his parents about his career. And then a letter came from Maurice Venice.

The story of the scout was long and intricate and there were several versions of it. The truth about it was never told. Wilhelm had lied first boastfully and then out of charity to himself. But his memory was good, he could still separate what he had invented from the actual happenings, and this morning he found it necessary as he stood by Rubin's showcase with his *Tribune* to recall the crazy course of the true events.

I didn't seem even to realize that there was a depression. How could I have been such a jerk as not to prepare for anything and just go on luck and inspiration? With round gray eyes expanded and his large shapely lips closed in severity toward himself he forced open all that had been hidden. Dad I couldn't affect one way or another. Mama was the one who tried to stop me, and we carried on and yelled and pleaded. The more I lied the louder I raised my voice, and charged—like a hippopotamus. Poor Mother! How I disappointed her. Rubin heard Wilhelm give a broken sigh as he stood with the forgotten *Tribune* crushed under his arm.

When Wilhelm was aware that Rubin watched him, loitering and idle, apparently not knowing what to do with himself this morning, he turned to the Coca-Cola machine. He swallowed hard at the coke bottle and coughed over it, but he ignored his coughing, for he was still thinking, his eyes upcast and his lips closed behind his hand. By a peculiar twist of habit he wore his coat collar turned up always, as though there were a wind. It never lay flat. But on his broad back, stooped with its own weight, its strength warped almost into deformity, the collar of his sports coat appeared anyway to be no wider than a ribbon.

He was listening to the sound of his own voice as he explained, twenty-five years ago in the living room on West End Avenue, "But Mother, if I don't pan out as an actor I can still go back to school."

But she was afraid he was going to destroy himself. She said, "Wilky, Dad could make it easy for you if you wanted to go into medicine." To remember this stifled him.

"I can't bear hospitals. Besides, I might make a mistake and hurt someone or even kill a patient. I couldn't stand that. Besides, I haven't got that sort of brains."

Then his mother had made the mistake of mentioning her nephew Artie, Wilhelm's cousin, who was an honor student at Columbia in math and languages. That dark little gloomy Artie with his disgusting narrow face, and his moles and self-sniffing ways and his unclean table manners, the boring habit he had of conjugating verbs when you went for a walk with him. "Roumanian is an easy language. You just add a *tl* to everything." He was now a professor, this same Artie with whom Wilhelm had played near the Soldiers' and Sailors' Monument on Riverside Drive. Not that to be a professor was in itself so great. How could anyone bear to know so many languages? And Artie also had to remain Artie, which was a bad deal. But perhaps success had changed him. Now that he had a place in the world perhaps he was better. Did Artie love his languages, and live for them, or was he also, in his heart, cynical? So many people nowadays were. No one seemed satisfied, and Wilhelm was especially horrified by the cynicism of successful people. Cynicism was bread and meat to everyone. And irony, too. Maybe it couldn't be helped. It was probably even necessary. Wilhelm, however, feared it intensely. Whenever at the end of the day he was unusually fatigued he attributed it to cynicism. Too much of the world's business done. Too much falsity. He had various words to express the effect this had on him. Chicken! Unclean! Congestion! he exclaimed in his heart. Rat race! Phony! Murder! Play the Game! Buggers!

At first the letter from the talent scout was nothing but a flattering sort of joke. Wilhelm's picture in the college paper when he was running for class treasurer was seen by Maurice Venice, who wrote to him about a screen test. Wilhelm at once took the train to New York. He found the scout to be huge and oxlike, so stout that his arms seemed caught from beneath in a grip of flesh and fat; it looked as though it must be positively painful. He had little hair. Yet he enjoyed a healthy complexion. His breath was noisy and his voice rather difficult and husky because of the fat in his throat. He had on a double-breasted suit of the type then known as the pillbox; it was chalk-striped, pink on blue; the trousers hugged his ankles.

They met and shook hands and sat down. Together these two big men dwarfed the tiny Broadway office and made the furnishings look like toys.

Wilhelm had the color of a Golden Grimes apple when he was well, and then his thick blond hair had been vigorous and his wide shoulders unwarped; he was leaner in the jaws, his eyes fresher and wider; his legs were then still awkward but he was impressively handsome. And he was about to make his first great mistake. Like, he sometimes thought, I was going to pick up a weapon and strike myself a blow with it.

Looming over the desk in the small office darkened by overbuilt midtown—sheer walls, gray spaces, dry lagoons of tar and pebbles—Maurice Venice proceeded to establish his credentials. He said, "My letter was on the regular stationery, but maybe you want to check on me?"

"Who, *me?*" said Wilhelm. "Why?"

"There's guys who think I'm in a racket and make a charge for the test. I don't ask a cent. I'm no agent. There ain't no commission."

"I never even thought of it," said Wilhelm. Was there perhaps something fishy about this Maurice Venice? He protested too much.

In his husky, fat-weakened voice he finally challenged Wilhelm, "If you're not sure, you can call the distributor and find out who I am, Maurice Venice."

Wilhelm wondered at him. "Why shouldn't I be sure? Of course I am."

"Because I can see the way you size me up, and because this is a dinky office. Like you don't believe me. Go ahead. Call. I won't care if you're cautious. I mean it. There's quite a few people who doubt me at first. They can't really believe that fame and fortune are going to hit 'em."

"But I tell you I do believe you," Wilhelm had said, and bent inward to accommodate the pressure of his warm, panting laugh. It was purely nervous. His neck was ruddy and neatly shaved about the ears—he was fresh from the barbershop; his face anxiously glowed with his desire to make a pleasing impression. It was all wasted on Venice, who was just as concerned about the impression *he* was making.

"If you're surprised, I'll just show you what I mean," Venice had said. "It was about fifteen months ago right in this identical same office when I saw a beautiful thing in the paper. It wasn't even a photo but a drawing, a brassière ad, but I knew right away that this was star material. I called up the paper to ask who the girl was, they gave me the name of the advertising agency; I phoned the agency and they gave me the name of the artist; I got hold of the artist and he gave me the number of the model agency. Finally, finally I got her number and phoned her and said, 'This is Maurice Venice, scout for Kaskaskia Films.' So right away she says, 'Yah, so's your old lady.' Well, when I saw I wasn't getting nowhere with her I said to her, 'Well, miss. I don't blame you. You're a very beautiful thing and must have a dozen admirers after you all the time, boy friends who like to call and pull your leg and give a tease. But as I happen to be a very busy fellow and don't have the time to horse around or argue, I tell you what to do. Here's my number, and here's the number of the Kaskaskia Distributors, Inc. Ask them who am I, Maurice Venice. The scout.' She did it. A little while later she phoned me back, all apologies and excuses, but I didn't want to embarrass her and get off on the wrong foot with an artist. I know better than to do that. So I told her it was a natural precaution, never mind. I wanted to run a screen test right away. Because I seldom am wrong about talent. If I see it, it's there. Get that, please. And do you know who that litle girl is today?"

"No," Wilhelm said eagerly. "Who is she?"

Venice said impressively, " 'Nita Christenberry."

Wilhelm sat utterly blank. This was failure. He didn't know the name, and Venice was waiting for his response and would be angry.

And in fact Venice had been offended. He said, "What's the matter with you! Don't you read a magazine? She's a starlet."

"I'm sorry," Wilhelm answered. "I'm at school and don't have time to keep up. If I don't know her, it doesn't mean a thing. She made a big hit, I'll bet."

"You can say that again. Here's a photo of her." He handed Wilhelm some pictures. She was a bathing beauty—short, the usual breasts, hips, and smooth thighs. Yes, quite good, as Wilhelm recalled. She stood on high heels and wore a Spanish comb and mantilla. In her hand was a fan.

He had said, "She looks awfully peppy."

"Isn't she a divine girl? And what personality! Not just another broad in the show business, believe me." He had a surprise for Wilhelm. "I have found happiness with her," he said.

"You have?" said Wilhelm, slow to understand.

"Yes, boy, we're engaged."

Wilhelm saw another photograph, taken on the beach. Venice was dressed in a terry-cloth beach outfit, and he and the girl, cheek to cheek, were looking into the camera. Below, in white ink, was written "Love at Malibu Colony."

"I'm sure you'll be very happy. I wish you—"

"I *know*," said Venice firmly, "I'm going to be happy. When I saw that drawing, the breath of fate breathed on me. I felt it over my entire body."

"Say, it strikes a bell suddenly," Wilhelm had said. "Aren't you related to Martial Venice the producer?"

Venice was either a nephew of the producer or the son of a first cousin. Decidedly he had not made good. It was easy enough for Wilhelm to see this now. The office was so poor, and Venice bragged so nervously and identified himself so scrupulously—the poor guy. He was the obscure failure of an aggressive and powerful clan. As such he had the greatest sympathy from Wilhelm.

Venice had said, "Now I suppose you want to know where you come in. I seen your school paper, by accident. You take quite a remarkable picture."

"It can't be so much," said Wilhelm, more panting than laughing.

"You don't want to tell me my business," Venice said. "Leave it to me. I studied up on this."

"I never imagined—Well, what kind of roles do you think I'd fit?"

"All this time that we've been talking, I've been watching. Don't think I haven't. You remind me of someone. Let's see who it can be—one of the great old-timers. Is it Milton Sills? No, that's not the one. Conway Tearle, Jack Mulhall? George Bancroft? No, his face was ruggeder. One thing I can tell you, though, a George Raft type you're not—those tough, smooth, black little characters."

"No, I wouldn't seem to be."

"No, you're not that flyweight type, with the fists, from a nightclub, and the glamorous sideburns, doing the tango or the bolero. Not Edward G. Robinson, either—I'm thinking aloud. Or the Cagney fly-in-your-face role, a cabbie, with that mouth and those punches."

"I realize that."

"Not suave like William Powell, or a lyric juvenile like Buddy Rogers. I suppose you don't play the sax? No. But—"

"But what?"

"I have you placed as the type that loses the girl to the George Raft type or the William Powell type. You are steady, faithful, you get stood up. The older women would know better. The mothers are on your side. With what they been through, if it was up to them, they'd take you in a minute. You're very sympathetic, even the young girls feel that. You'd make a good provider. But they go more for the other types. It's as clear as anything."

This was not how Wilhelm saw himself. And as he surveyed the old ground he recognized now that he had been not only confused but hurt. Why, he thought, he cast me even then for a loser.

Wilhelm had said, with half a mind to be defiant, "Is that your opinion?"

It never occurred to Venice that a man might object to stardom in such a role. "Here is your chance," he said. "Now you're just in college. What are you studying?" He snapped his fingers. "Stuff." Wilhelm himself felt this way about it. "You may plug along fifty years before you get anywheres. This way, in one jump, the world knows who you are. You become a name like Roosevelt, Swanson. From east to west, out to China, into South America. This is no bunk. You become a lover to the whole world. The world wants it, needs it. One fellow smiles, a billion people also smile. One fellow cries, the other billion sob with him. Listen, bud—" Venice had pulled himself together to make an effort. On his imagination there was some great weight which he could not discharge. He wanted Wilhelm, too, to feel it. He twisted his large, clean, well-meaning, rather foolish features as though he were their unwilling captive, and said in his choked, fat-obstructed voice, "Listen, everywhere there are people trying hard, miserable, in trouble, downcast, tired, trying and trying. They need a break, right? A break through, a help, luck or sympathy."

"That certainly is the truth," said Wilhelm. He had seized the feeling and he waited for Venice to go on. But Venice had no more to say; he had concluded. He gave Wilhelm several pages of blue hectographed script, stapled together, and told him to prepare for the screen test. "Study your lines in front of a mirror," he said. "Let yourself go. The part should take ahold of you. Don't be afraid to make faces and be emotional. Shoot the works. Because when you start to act you're no more an ordinary person, and those things don't apply to you. You don't behave the same way as the average."

And so Wilhelm had never returned to Penn State. His roommate sent his things to New York for him, and the school authorities had to write to Dr. Adler to find out what had happened.

Still, for three months Wilhelm delayed his trip to California. He wanted to start out with the blessings of his family, but they were never given. He quarreled with his parents and his sister. And then, when he was best aware of the risks and knew a hundred reasons against going and had made himself sick with fear, he left home. This was typical of Wilhelm. After much thought and hesitation and debate he invariably took the course he had rejected innumerable times. Ten such decisions made up the history of his life. He had decided that it would be a bad mistake to go to Hollywood, and then he went. He had made up his mind not to marry his wife, but ran off and got married. He had resolved not to invest money with Tamkin, and then had given him a check.

But Wilhelm had been eager for life to start. College was merely another delay. Venice had approached him and said that the world had named Wilhelm to shine before it. He was to be freed from the anxious and narrow life of the average. Moreover, Venice had claimed that he never made a mistake. His instinct for talent was infallible, he said.

But when Venice saw the results of the screen test he did a quick about-face. In those days Wilhelm had had a speech difficulty. It was not a true stammer, it was a thickness of speech which the sound track exaggerated. The film showed that he had many peculiarities, otherwise unnoticeable. When he shrugged, his hands drew up within his sleeves. The vault of his chest was huge, but he really didn't look strong under the lights. Though he called himself a hippopotamus, he more nearly resembled a bear. His walk was bearlike, quick and rather soft, toes turned inward, as though his shoes were an impediment. About one thing Venice had been right. Wilhelm was photogenic, and his wavy blond hair (now graying) came out well, but after the test Venice refused to encourage him. He tried to get rid of him. He couldn't afford to take a chance on him, he had made too many mistakes already and lived in fear of his powerful relatives.

Wilhelm had told his parents, "Venice says I owe it to myself to go." How ashamed he was now of this lie! He had begged Venice not to give him up. He had said, "Can't you help me out? It would kill me to go back to school now."

Then when he reached the Coast he learned that a recommendation from Maurice Venice was the kiss of death. Venice needed help and charity more than he, Wilhelm, ever had. A few years later when Wilhelm was down on his luck and working as an orderly in a Los Angeles hospital, he saw Venice's picture in the papers. He was under indictment for pandering. Closely following the trial, Wilhelm found out that Venice had indeed been employed by Kaskaskia Films but that he had evidently made use of the connection to organize a ring of call girls. Then what did he want with me? Wilhelm had cried to himself. He was unwilling to believe anything very bad about Venice. Perhaps he was foolish and unlucky, a fall guy, a dupe, a sucker. You didn't give a man fifteen years in prison for that. Wilhelm often thought that he might write him a letter to say how sorry he was. He remembered the breath of fate and Venice's certainty that he would be happy. 'Nita Christenberry was sentenced to three years. Wilhelm recognized her although she had changed her name.

By that time Wilhelm too had taken his new name. In California he became Tommy Wilhelm. Dr. Adler would not accept the change. Today he still called his son Wilky, as he had done for more than forty years. Well, now, Wilhelm was thinking, the paper crowded in disarray under his arm, there's really very little that a man can change at will. He can't change his lungs, or nerves, or constitution or temperament. They're not under his control. When he's young and strong and impulsive and dissatisfied with the way things are he wants to rearrange them to assert his freedom. He can't overthrow the government or be differently born; he only has a little scope and maybe a foreboding, too, that essentially you can't change. Nevertheless, he makes a gesture and becomes Tommy Wilhelm. Wilhelm had always had a great longing to be Tommy. He had never, however, succeeded in feeling like Tommy, and in his soul had always remained Wilky. When he was drunk he reproached himself horribly as Wilky. "You fool, you clunk, you Wilky!" he called himself. He thought that it was a good thing perhaps that he had not become a success as Tommy since that would not have been a genuine success. Wilhelm would have feared that not he but Tommy had brought it off, cheating Wilky of his birthright. Yes, it had been a stupid thing to do, but it was his imperfect judgment at the age of twenty which should be blamed. He had cast off his father's name, and with it his father's opinion of him. It was, he knew it was, his bid for liberty. Adler being in his mind the title of the species, Tommy the freedom of the person. But Wilky was his inescapable self.

In middle age you no longer thought of such thoughts about free choice. Then it came over you that from one grandfather you had inherited such and such a head of hair which looked like honey when it whitens or sugars in the jar; from another, broad thick shoulders; an oddity of speech from one uncle, and small teeth from another, and the gray eyes with darkness diffused even into the whites, and a wide-lipped mouth like a statue from Peru. Wandering races have such looks, the bones of one tribe, the skin of another. From his mother he had gotten sensitive feelings, a soft heart, a brooding nature, a tendency to be confused under pressure.

The changed name was a mistake, and he would admit it as freely as you liked. But this mistake couldn't be undone now, so why must his father continually remind him how he had sinned? It was too late. He would have to go back to the pathetic day when the sin was committed. And where was that day? Past and dead. Whose humiliating memories were these? His and not his father's. What had he to think back on that he could call good? Very, very little. You had to forgive. First, to forgive yourself, and then general forgiveness. Didn't he suffer from his mistakes far more than his father could?

"Oh, God," Wilhelm prayed. "Let me out of my trouble. Let me out of my thoughts, and let me do something better with myself. For all the time I have wasted I am very sorry. Let me out of this clutch and into a different life. For I am all balled up. Have mercy."

II

The mail.

The clerk who gave it to him did not care what sort of appearance he made this morning. He only glanced at him from under his brows, upward, as the letters changed hands. Why should the hotel people waste courtesies on him? They had his number. The clerk knew that he was handing him, along with the letters, a bill for his rent. Wilhelm assumed a look that removed him from all such things. But it was bad. To pay the bill he would have to withdraw money from his brokerage account, and the account was being watched because of the drop in lard. According to the *Tribune's* figures lard was still twenty points below last year's level. There were government price supports. Wilhelm didn't know how these worked but he understood that the farmer was protected and that the SEC kept an eye on the market and therefore he believed that lard would rise again and he wasn't greatly worried as yet. But in the meantime his father might have offered to pick up his hotel tab. Why didn't he? What a selfish old man he was! He saw his son's hardships; he could so easily help him. How little it would mean to him, and how much to Wilhelm! Where was the old man's heart? Maybe, thought Wilhelm, I was sentimental in the past and exaggerated his kindliness—warm family life. It may never have been there.

Not long ago his father had said to him in his usual affable, pleasant way, "Well, Wilky, here we are under the same roof again, after all these years."

Wilhelm was glad for an instant. At last they would talk over old times. But he was also on guard against insinuations. Wasn't his father saying, "Why are you here in a hotel with me and not at home in Brooklyn with your wife and two boys? You're neither a widower nor a bachelor. You have brought me all your confusions. What do you expect me to do with them?"

So Wilhelm studied the remark for a bit, then said, "The roof is twenty-six stories up. But how many years has it been?"

"That's what I was asking you."

"Gosh, Dad, I'm not sure. Wasn't it the year Mother died? What year was that?"

He asked this question with an innocent frown on his Golden Grimes, dark blond face. *What year was it!* As though he didn't know the year, the month, the day, the very hour of his mother's death.

"Wasn't it nineteen-thirty-one?" said Dr. Adler.

"Oh, was it?" said Wilhelm. And in hiding the sadness and the overwhelming irony of the question he gave a nervous shiver and wagged his head and felt the ends of his collar rapidly.

"Do you know?" his father said. "You must realize, an old fellow's memory becomes unreliable. It was in winter, that I'm sure of. Nineteen-thirty-two?"

Yes, it was age. Don't make an issue of it, Wilhelm advised himself. If you were to ask the old doctor in what year he had interned, he'd tell you correctly. All the same, don't make an issue. Don't quarrel with your own father. Have pity on an old man's failings.

"I believe the year was closer to nineteen-thirty-four, Dad," he said.

But Dr. Adler was thinking, Why the devil can't he stand still when we're talking? He's either hoisting his pants up and down by the pockets or jittering with his feet. A regular mountain of tics, he's getting to be. Wilhelm had a habit of moving his feet back and forth as though, hurrying into a house, he had to clean his shoes first on the doormat.

Then Wilhelm had said, "Yes, that was the beginning of the end, wasn't it, Father?"

Wilhelm often astonished Dr. Adler. Beginning of the end? What could he mean—what was he fishing for? Whose end? The end of family life? The old man was puzzled but he would not give Wilhelm an opening to introduce his complaints. He had learned that it was better not to take up Wilhelm's strange challenges. So he merely agreed pleasantly, for he was a master of social behavior, and said, "It was an awful misfortune for us all."

He thought, What business has he to complain to *me* of his mother's death?

Face to face they had stood, each declaring himself silently after his own way. It was: it was not, the beginning of the end—*some* end.

Unaware of anything odd in his doing it, for he did it all the time, Wilhelm had pinched out the coal of his cigarette and dropped the butt in his pocket, where there were many more. And as he gazed at his father the little finger of his right hand began to twitch and tremble; of that he was unconscious, too.

And yet Wilhelm believed that when he put his mind to it he could have perfect and even distinguished manners, outdoing his father. Despite the slight thickness in his speech—it amounted almost to a stammer when he started the same phrase over several times in his effort to eliminate the thick sound— he could be fluent. Otherwise he would never have made a good salesman. He claimed also that he was a good listener. When he listened he made a tight mouth and rolled his eyes thoughtfully. He would soon tire and begin to utter short, loud, impatient breaths, and he would say, "Oh yes . . . yes . . . yes. I couldn't agree more." When he was forced to differ he would declare, "Well, I'm not sure. I don't really see it that way. I'm of two minds about it." He would never willingly hurt any man's feelings.

But in conversation with his father he was apt to lose control of himself. After any talk with Dr. Adler, Wilhelm generally felt dissatisfied, and his dissatisfaction reached its greatest intensity when they discussed family matters. Ostensibly he had been trying to help the old man to remember a date, but in reality he meant to tell him, "You were set free when Ma died. You wanted to forget her. You'd like to get rid of Catherine, too. Me, too. You're not kidding anyone"—Wilhelm striving to put this across, and the old man not having it. In the end he was left struggling, while his father seemed unmoved.

And then once more Wilhelm had said to himself, "But man! you're not a kid. Even then you weren't a kid!" He looked down over the front of his big, indecently big, spoiled body. He was beginning to lose his shape, his gut was fat, and he looked like a hippopotamus. His younger son called him "a hummuspotamus"; that was little Paul. And here he was still struggling with his old dad, filled with ancient grievances. Instead of saying, "Good-by, youth! Oh, good-by those marvelous, foolish wasted days. What a big clunk I was— I *am*."

Wilhelm was still paying heavily for his mistakes. His wife Margaret would not give him a divorce, and he had to support her and the two children. She would regularly agree to divorce him, and then think things over again and set new and more difficult conditions. No court would have awarded her the amounts he paid. One of today's letters, as he had expected, was from her. For the first time he had sent her a postdated check, and she protested. She also enclosed bills for the boys' educational insurance policies, due next week. Wilhelm's mother-in-law had taken out these policies in Beverly Hills, and since her death two years ago he had to pay the premiums. Why couldn't she have minded her own business? They were his kids, and he took care of them and always would. He had planned to set up a trust fund. But that was on his former expectations. Now he had to rethink the future, because of the money problem. Meanwhile, here were the bills to be paid. When he saw the two sums punched out so neatly on the cards he cursed the company and its IBM equipment. His heart and his head were congested with anger. Everyone was supposed to have money. It was nothing to the company. It published pictures of funerals in the magazines and frightened the suckers, and then punched out little holes, and the customers would lie awake to think out ways to raise the dough. They'd be ashamed not to have it. They couldn't let a great company down, either, and they got the scratch. In the old days a man was put in prison for debt, but there were subtler things now. They made it a shame not to have money and set everybody to work.

Well, and what else had Margaret sent him? He tore the envelope open with his thumb, swearing that he would send any other bills back to her. There was, luckily, nothing more. He put the hole-punched cards in his pocket. Didn't Margaret know that he was nearly at the end of his rope? Of course. Her instinct told her that this was her opportunity, and she was giving him the works.

He went into the dining room, which was under Austro-Hungarian management at the Hotel Gloriana. It was run like a European establishment. The pastries were excellent, especially the strudel. He often had apple strudel and coffee in the afternoon.

As soon as he entered he saw his father's small head in the sunny bay at the farther end, and heard his precise voice. It was with an odd sort of perilous expression that Wilhelm crossed the dining room.

Dr. Adler liked to sit in a corner that looked across Broadway down to the Hudson and New Jersey. On the other side of the street was a supermodern cafeteria with gold and purple mosaic columns. On the second floor a private-eye school, a dental laboratory, a reducing parlor, a veteran's club, and a Hebrew school shared the space. The old man was sprinkling sugar on his strawberries. Small hoops of brilliance were cast by the water glasses on the white tablecloth, despite a faint murkiness in the sunshine. It was early summer, and the long window was turned inward; a moth was on the pane; the putty was broken and the white enamel on the frames was streaming with wrinkles.

"Ha, Wilky," said the old man to his tardy son. "You haven't met our neighbor Mr. Perls, have you? From the fifteenth floor."

"How d'do," Wilhelm said. He did not welcome this stranger; he began at once to find fault with him. Mr. Perls carried a heavy cane with a crutch tip. Dyed hair, a skinny forehead—these were not reasons for bias. Nor was it Mr. Perls's fault that Dr. Adler was using him, not wishing to have breakfast with his son alone. But a gruffer voice within Welhelm spoke, asking, "Who is this damn frazzle-faced herring with his dyed hair and his fish teeth and this drippy mustache? Another one of Dad's German friends. Where does he collect all these guys? What is the stuff on his teeth? I never saw such pointed crowns. Are they stainless steel, or a kind of silver? How can a human face get into this condition. Uch!" Staring with his widely spaced gray eyes, Wilhelm sat, his broad back stooped under the sports jacket. He clasped his hands on the table with an implication of suppliance. Then he began to relent a little toward Mr. Perls, beginning at the teeth. Each of those crowns represented a tooth ground to the quick, and estimating a man's grief with his teeth as two per cent of the total, and adding to that his flight from Germany and the probable origin of his wincing wrinkles, not to be confused with the wrinkles of his smile, it came to a sizable load.

"Mr. Perls was a hosiery wholesaler," said Dr. Adler.

"Is this the son you told me was in the selling line?" said Mr. Perls.

Dr. Adler replied, "I have only this one son. One daughter. She was a medical technician before she got married—anesthetist. At one time she had an important position in Mount Sinai."

He couldn't mention his children without boasting. In Wilhelm's opinion, there was little to boast of. Catherine, like Wilhelm, was big and fair-haired. She had married a court reporter who had a pretty hard time of it. She had taken a professional name, too—Philippa. At forty she was still ambitious to become a painter. Wilhelm didn't venture to criticize her work. It didn't do much to him, he said, but then he was no critic. Anyway, he and his sister were generally on the outs and he didn't often see her paintings. She worked very hard, but there were fifty thousand people in New York with paints and brushes, each practically a law unto himself. It was the Tower of Babel in paint. *He* didn't want to go far into this. Things were chaotic all over.

Dr. Adler thought that Wilhelm looked particularly untidy this morning—unrested, too, his eyes red-rimmed from excessive smoking. He was breathing through his mouth and he was evidently much distracted and rolled his redshot eyes barbarously. As usual, his coat collar was turned up as though he had had to go out in the rain. When he went to business he pulled himself together a little; otherwise he let himself go and looked like hell.

"What's the matter, Wilky, didn't you sleep last night?"

"Not very much."

"You take too many pills of every kind—first stimulants and then depressants, anodynes followed by analeptics, until the poor organism doesn't know what's happened. Then the luminal won't put people to sleep, and the Pervitin or Benzedrine won't wake them. God knows! These things get to be as serious as poisons, and yet everyone puts all their faith in them."

"No, Dad, it's not the pills. It's that I'm not used to New York any more. For a native, that's very peculiar, isn't it? It was never so noisy at night as now, and every little thing is a strain. Like the alternate parking. You have to run out at eight to move your car. And where can you put it? If you forget for a minute they tow you away. Then some fool puts advertising leaflets under your windshield wiper and you have heart failure a block away because you think you've got a ticket. When you do get stung with a ticket, you can't argue. You haven't got a chance in court and the city wants the revenue."

"But in your line you have to have a car, eh?" said Mr. Perls.

"Lord knows why any lunatic would want one in the city who didn't need it for his livelihood."

Wilhelm's old Pontiac was parked in the street. Formerly, when on an expense account he had always put it up in a garage. Now he was afraid to move the car from Riverside Drive lest he lose his space, and he used it only on Saturdays when the Dodgers were playing in Ebbets Field and he took his boys to the game. Last Saturday, when the Dodgers were out of town, he had gone out to visit his mother's grave.

Dr. Adler had refused to go along. He couldn't bear his son's driving. Forgetfully, Wilhelm traveled for miles in second gear; he was seldom in the right lane and he neither gave signals nor watched for lights. The upholstery of his Pontiac was filthy with grease and ashes. One cigarette burned in the ashtray, another in his hand, a third on the floor with maps and other waste paper and Coca-Cola bottles. He dreamed at the wheel or argued and gestured, and therefore the old doctor would not ride with him.

Then Wilhelm had come back from the cemetery angry because the stone bench between his mother's and his grandmother's graves had been overturned and broken by vandals. "Those damn teen-age hoodlums get worse and worse," he said. "Why, they must have used a sledgehammer to break the seat smack in half like that. If I could catch one of them!" He wanted the doctor to pay for a new seat, but his father was cool to the idea. He said he was going to have himself cremated.

Mr. Perls said, "I don't blame you if you get no sleep up where you are." His voice was tuned somewhat sharp, as though he were slightly deaf. "Don't you have Parigi the singing teacher there? God, they have some queer elements in this hotel. On which floor is that Estonian woman with all her cats and dogs? They should have made her leave long ago."

"They've moved her down to twelve," said Dr. Adler.

Wilhelm ordered a large Coca-Cola with his breakfast. Working in secret at the small envelopes in his pocket, he found two pills by touch. Much fingering had worn and weakened the paper. Under cover of a napkin he swallowed a Phenaphen sedative and a Unicap, but the doctor was sharp-eyed and said, "Wilky, what are you taking now?"

"Just my vitamin pills." He put his cigar butt in an ashtray on the table behind him, for his father did not like the odor. Then he drank his Coca-Cola.

"That's what you drink for breakfast, and not orange juice?" said Mr. Perls. He seemed to sense that he would not lose Dr. Adler's favor by taking an ironic tone with his son.

"The caffeine stimulates brain activity," said the old doctor. "It does all kinds of things to the respiratory center."

"It's just a habit of the road, that's all," Wilhelm said. "If you drive around long enough it turns your brains, your stomach, and everything else."

His father explained, "Wilky used to be with the Rojax Corporation. He was their northeastern sales representative for a good many years but recently ended the connection."

"Yes," said Wilhelm, "I was with them from the end of the war." He sipped the Coca-Cola and chewed the ice, glancing at one and the other with his attitude of large, shaky, patient dignity. The waitress set two boiled eggs before him.

"What kind of line does this Rojax company manufacture?" said Mr. Perls.

"Kiddies' furniture. Little chairs, rockers, tables, Jungle-Gyms, slides, swings, seesaws."

Wilhelm let his father do the explaining. Large and stiff-backed, he tried to sit patiently, but his feet were abnormally restless. All right! His father had to impress Mr. Perls? He would go along once more, and play his part. Fine! He would play along and help his father maintain his style. Style was the main consideration. That was just fine!

"I was with the Rojax Corporation for almost ten years," he said. "We parted ways because they wanted me to share my territory. They took a son-in-law into the business—a new fellow. It was his idea."

To himself, Wilhelm said, Now God alone can tell why I have to lay my whole life bare to this blasted herring here. I'm sure nobody else does it. Other people keep their business to themselves. Not me.

He continued, "But the rationalization was that it was too big a territory for one man. I had a monopoly. That wasn't so. The real reason was that they had gotten to the place where they would have to make me an officer of the corporation. Vice presidency. I was in line for it, but instead this son-in-law got in, and—"

Dr. Adler thought Wilhelm was discussing his grievances much too openly and said, "My son's income was up in the five figures."

As soon as money was mentioned, Mr. Perls's voice grew eagerly sharper. "Yes? What, the thirty-two-per-cent bracket? Higher even, I guess?" He asked for a hint, and he named the figures not idly but with a sort of hugging relish. Uch! How they love money, thought Wilhelm. They adore money! Holy money! Beautiful money! It was getting so that people were feeble-minded about everything except money. While if you didn't have it you were a dummy, a dummy! You had to excuse yourself from the face of the earth. Chicken! that's what it was. The world's business. If only he could find a way out of it.

Such thinking brought on the usual congestion. It would grow into a fit of passion if he allowed it to continue. Therefore he stopped talking and began to eat.

Before he struck the egg with his spoon he dried the moisture with his napkin. Then he battered it (in his father's opinion) more than was necessary. A faint grime was left by his fingers on the white of the egg after he had picked away the shell. Dr. Adler saw it with silent repugnance. What a Wilky he had given to the world! Why, he didn't even wash his hands in the morning. He used an electric razor so that he didn't have to touch water. The doctor couldn't bear Wilky's dirty habits. Only once—and never again, he swore—had he visited his room. Wilhelm, in pajamas and stockings had sat on his bed, drinking gin from a coffee mug and rooting for the Dodgers on television. "That's two and two on you, Duke. Come on—hit it, now." He came down on the mattress—bam! The bed looked kicked to pieces. Then he drank the gin as though it were tea, and urged his team on with his fist. The smell of dirty clothes was outrageous. By the bedside lay a quart bottle and foolish magazines and mystery stories for the hours of insomnia. Wilhelm lived in worse filth than a savage. When the doctor spoke to him about this he answered, "Well, I have no wife to look after my things." And who—*who!*—had done the leaving? Not Margaret. The doctor was certain that she wanted him back.

Wilhelm drank his coffee with a trembling hand. In his full face his abused bloodshot gray eyes moved back and forth. Jerkily he set his cup back and put half the length of a cigarette into his mouth; he seemed to hold it with his teeth, as though it were a cigar.

"I can't let them get away with it," he said. "It's also a question of morale."

His father corrected him. "Don't you mean a moral question, Wilky?"

"I mean that, too. I have to do something to protect myself. I was promised executive standing." Correction before a stranger mortified him, and his dark blond face changed color, more pale, and then more dark. He went on talking to Perls but his eyes spied on his father. "I was the one who opened the territory for them. I could go back for one of their competitors and take away their customers. *My* customers. Morale enters into it because they've tried to take away my confidence."

"Would you offer a different line to the same people?" Mr. Perls wondered.

"Why not? I know what's wrong with the Rojax product."

"Nonsense," said his father. "Just nonsense and kid's talk, Wilky. You're only looking for trouble and embarrassment that way. What would you gain by such a silly feud? You have to think about making a living and meeting your obligations."

Hot and bitter, Wilhelm said with pride, while his feet moved angrily under the table, "I don't have to be told about my obligations. I've been meeting them for years. In more than twenty years I've never had a penny of help from anybody. I preferred to dig a ditch on the WPA but never asked anyone to meet my obligations for me."

"Wilky has had all kinds of experiences," said Dr. Adler.

The old doctor's face had a wholesome reddish and almost translucent color, like a ripe apricot. The wrinkles beside his ears were deep because the skin conformed so tightly to his bones. With all his might, he was a healthy and fine small old man. He wore a white vest of a light check pattern. His hearing-aid doodad was in the pocket. An unusual shirt of red and black stripes covered his chest. He bought his clothes in a college shop farther uptown., Wilhelm thought he had no business to get himself up like a jockey, out of respect for his profession.

"Well," said Mr. Perls. "I can understand how you feel. You want to fight it out. By a certain time of life, to have to start all over again can't be a pleasure, though a good man can always do it. But anyway you want to keep on with a business you know already, and not have to meet a whole lot of new contacts."

Wilhelm again thought, Why does it have to be me and my life that's discussed, and not him and his life? He would never allow it. But I am an idiot. I have no reserve. To me it can be done. I talk. I must ask for it. Everybody wants to have intimate conversations, but the smart fellows don't give out, only the fools. The smart fellows talk intimately about the fools, and examine them all over and give them advice. Why do I allow it? The hint about his age had hurt him. No, you can't admit it's as good as ever, he conceded. Things do give out.

"In the meanwhile," Dr. Adler said, "Wilky is taking it easy and considering various propositions. Isn't that so?"

"More or less," said Wilhelm. He suffered his father to increase Mr. Perls's respect for him. The WPA ditch had brought the family into contempt. He was a little tired. The spirit, the peculiar burden of his existence lay upon him like an accretion, a load, a hump. In any moment of quiet, when sheer fatigue prevented him from struggling, he was apt to feel this mysterious weight, this growth or collection of nameless things which it was the business of his life to carry about. That must be what a man was for. This large, odd, excited, fleshy, blond, abrupt personality named Wilhelm, or Tommy, was here, present, in the present—Dr. Tamkin had been putting into his mind many suggestions about the present moment, the here and now—this Wilky, or Tommy Wilhelm, forty-four years old, father of two sons, at present living in the Hotel Gloriana, was assigned to be the carrier of a load which was his own self, his characteristic self. There was no figure or estimate for the value of this load. But it is probably exaggerated by the subject, T. W. Who is a visionary sort of animal. Who has to believe that he can know why he exists. Though he has never seriously tried to find out why.

Mr. Perls said, "If he wants to think things over and have a rest, why doesn't he run down to Florida for a while? Off season it's cheap and quiet.

Fairyland. The mangoes are just coming in. I got two acres down there. You'd think you were in India."

Mr. Perls utterly astonished Wilhelm when he spoke of fairyland with a foreign accent. Mangoes—India? What did he mean, India?

"Once upon a time," said Welhelm, "I did some public-relations work for a big hotel down in Cuba. If I could get them a notice in Leonard Lyons or one of the other columns it might be good for another holiday there, gratis. I haven't had a vacation for a long time, and I could stand a rest after going so hard. You know that's true, Father." He meant that his father knew how deep the crisis was becoming; how badly he was strapped for money; and that he could not rest but would be crushed if he stumbled; and that his obligations would destroy him. He couldn't falter. He thought, The money! When I had it, I flowed money. They bled it away from me. I hemorrhaged money. But now it's almost all gone, and where am I supposed to turn for more?

He said, "As a matter of fact, Father, I am tired as hell."

But Mr. Perls began to smile and said, "I understand from Doctor Tamkin that you're going into some kind of investment with him, partners."

"You know, he's a very ingenious fellow," said Dr. Adler. "I really enjoy hearing him go on. I wonder if he really is a medical doctor."

"Isn't he?" said Perls. "Everybody thinks he is. He talks about his patients. Doesn't he write prescriptions?"

"I don't really know what he does," said Dr. Adler. "He's a cunning man."

"He's a psychologist, I understand," said Wilhelm.

"I don't know what sort of psychologist or psychiatrist he may be," said his father. "He's a little vague. It's growing into a major industry, and a very expensive one. Fellows have to hold down very big jobs in order to pay those fees. Anyway, this Tamkin is clever. He never said he practiced here, but I believe he was a doctor in California. They don't seem to have much legislation out there to cover these things, and I hear a thousand dollars will get you a degree from a Los Angeles correspondence school. He gives the impression of knowing something about chemistry, and things like hypnotism. I wouldn't trust him, though."

"And why wouldn't you?" Wilhelm demanded.

"Because he's probably a liar. Do you believe he invented all the things he claims?"

Mr. Perls was grinning.

"He was written up in *Fortune*," said Wilhelm. "Yes, in *Fortune* magazine. He showed me the article. I've seen his clippings."

"That doesn't make him legitimate," said Dr. Adler. "It might have been another Tamkin. Make no mistake, he's an operator. Perhaps even crazy."

"Crazy, you say?"

Mr. Perls put in, "He could be both sane and crazy. In these days nobody can tell for sure which is which."

"An electrical device for truck drivers to wear in their caps," said Dr. Adler, describing one of Tamkin's proposed inventions. "To wake them with a shock when they begin to be drowsy at the wheel. It's triggered by the change in blood-pressure when they start to doze."

"It doesn't sound like such an impossible thing to me," said Wilhelm.

Mr. Perls said, "To me he described an underwater suit so a man could walk on the bed of the Hudson in case of an atomic attack. He said he could walk to Albany in it."

"Ha, ha, ha, ha, ha!" cried Dr. Adler in his old man's voice. "Tamkin's Folly. You could go on a camping trip under Niagara Falls."

"This is just his kind of fantasy," said Wilhelm. "It doesn't mean a thing. Inventors are supposed to be like that. I get funny ideas myself. Everybody wants to make something. Any American does."

But his father ignored this and said to Perls, "What other inventions did he describe?"

While the frazzle-faced Mr. Perls and his father in the unseemly, monkey-striped shirt were laughing, Wilhelm could not restrain himself and joined in with his own panting laugh. But he was in despair. They were laughing at the man to whom he had given a power of attorney over his last seven hundred dollars to speculate for him in the commodities market. They had bought all that lard. It had to rise today. By ten o'clock, or half-past ten, trading would be active, and he would see.

III

Between white tablecloths and glassware and glancing silverware, through overfull light, the long figure of Mr. Perls went away into the darkness of the lobby. He thrust with his cane, and dragged a large built-up shoe which Wilhelm had not included in his estimate of troubles. Dr. Adler wanted to talk about him. "There's a poor man," he said, "with a bone condition which is gradually breaking him up."

"One of those progressive diseases?" said Wilhelm.

"Very bad. I've learned," the doctor told him, "to keep my sympathy for the real ailments. This Perls is more to be pitied than any man I know."

Wilhelm understood he was being put on notice and did not express his opinion. He ate and ate. He did not hurry but kept putting food on his plate until he had gone through the muffins and his father's strawberries, and then some pieces of bacon that were left; he had several cups of coffee, and when he was finished he sat gigantically in a state of arrest and didn't seem to know what he should do next.

For a while father and son were uncommonly still. Wilhelm's preparations to please Dr. Adler had failed completely, for the old man kept thinking, You'd never guess he had a clean upbringing, and, What a dirty devil this son of mine is. Why can't he try to sweeten his appearance a little? Why does he want to drag himself like this? And he makes himself look so idealistic.

Wilhelm sat, mountainous. He was not really so slovenly as his father found him to be. In some aspects he even had a certain delicacy. His mouth, though broad, had a fine outline, and his brow and his gradually incurved nose, dignity, and in his blond hair there was white but there were also shades of gold and chestnut. When he was with the Rojax Corporation Wilhelm had kept a small apartment in Roxbury, two rooms in a large house with a small porch and garden, and on mornings of leisure, in late spring weather like this, he used to sit expanded in a wicker chair with the sunlight pouring through the weave, and sunlight through the slug-eaten holes of the young hollyhocks and as deeply as the grass allowed into small flowers. This peace (he forgot that that time had had its troubles, too), this peace was gone. It must not have belonged to him, really, for to be here in New York with his old father was more gen-uinely like his life. He was well aware that he didn't stand a chance of getting sympathy from his father, who said he kept his for real ailments. Moreover, he advised himself repeatedly not to discuss his vexatious problems with him, for his father, with some justice, wanted to be left in peace. Wilhelm also knew that when he began to talk about these things he made himself feel worse, he became congested with them and worked himself into a clutch. Therefore he warned himself, Lay off, pal. It'll only be an aggravation. From a deeper source, however, came other promptings. If he didn't keep his troubles before him he risked losing them altogether, and he knew by experience that this was worse. And furthermore, he could not succeed in excusing his father on the ground of old age. No. No, he could not. I am his son, he thought. He is my father. He is as much father as I am son—old or not. Affirming this, though in complete silence, he sat, and, sitting, he kept his father at the table with him.

"Wilky," said the old man, "have you gone down to the baths here yet?"

"No, Dad, not yet."

"Well, you know the Gloriana has one of the finest pools in New York. Eighty feet, blue tile. It's a beauty."

Wilhelm had seen it. On the way to the gin game you passed the stairway to the pool. He did not care for the odor of the wall-locked and chlorinated water.

"You ought to investigate the Russian and Turkish baths, and the sun-lamps and massage. I don't hold with sunlamps. But the massage does a world of good, and there's nothing better than hydrotherapy when you come right down to it. Simple water has a calming effect and would do you more good than all the barbiturates and alcohol in the world."

Wilhelm reflected that this advice was as far as his father's help and sym-pathy would extend.

"I thought," he said, "that the water cure was for lunatics."

The doctor received this as one of his son's jokes and said with a smile, "Well, it won't turn a sane man into a lunatic. It does a great deal for me. I couldn't live without my massages and steam."

"You're probaby right. I ought to try it one of these days. Yesterday, late in the afternoon, my head was about to bust and I just had to have a little air, so

I walked around the reservoir, and I sat down for a while in a playground. It rests me to watch the kids play potsy and skiprope."

The doctor said with approval, "Well, now, that's more like the idea."

"It's the end of the lilacs," said Wilhelm. "When they burn it's the beginning of the summer. At least, in the city. Around the time of year when the candy stores take down the windows and start to sell sodas on the sidewalk. But even though I was raised here, Dad, I can't take city life any more, and I miss the country. There's too much push here for me. It works me up too much. I take things too hard. I wonder why you never retired to a quieter place."

The doctor opened his small hand on the table in a gesture so old and so typical that Wilhelm felt it like an actual touch upon the foundations of his life. "I am a city boy myself, you must remember," Dr. Adler explained. "But if you find the city so hard on you, you ought to get out."

"I'll do that," said Wilhelm, "as soon as I can make the right connection. Meanwhile—"

His father interrupted, "Meanwhile I suggest you cut down on drugs."

"You exaggerate that, Dad. I don't really—I give myself a little boost against—" He almost pronounced the word "misery" but he kept his resolution not to complain.

The doctor, however, fell into the error of pushing his advice too hard. It was all he had to give his son and he gave it once more. "Water and exercise," he said.

He wants a young, smart, successful son, thought Wilhelm, and he said, "Oh, Father, it's nice of you to give me this medical advice, but steam isn't going to cure what ails me."

The doctor measurably drew back, warned by the sudden weak strain of Wilhelm's voice and all that the droop of his face, the swell of his belly against the restraint of his belt intimated.

"Some new business?" he asked unwillingly.

Wilhelm made a great preliminary summary which involved the whole of his body. He drew and held a long breath, and his color changed and his eyes swam. "New?" he said.

"You make too much of your problems," said the doctor. "They ought not to be turned into a career. Concentrate on real troubles—fatal sickness, accidents." The old man's whole manner said, Wilky, don't start this on me. I have a right to be spared.

Wilhelm himself prayed for restraint; he knew this weakness of his and fought it. He knew, also, his father's character. And he began mildly, "As far as the fatal part of it goes, everyone on this side of the grave is the same distance from death. No, I guess my trouble is not exactly new. I've got to pay premiums on two policies for the boys. Margaret sent them to me. She unloads everything on me. Her mother left her an income. She won't even file a joint tax return. I get stuck. Etcetera. But you've heard the whole story before."

"I certainly have," said the old man. "And I've told you to stop giving her so much money."

Wilhelm worked his lips in silence before he could speak. The congestion was growing. "Oh, but my kids, Father. My kids. I love them. I don't want them to lack anything."

The doctor said with a half-deaf benevolence, "Well, naturally. And she, I'll bet, is the beneficiary of that policy."

"Let her be. I'd sooner die myself before I collected a cent of such money."

"Ah yes." The old man sighed. He did not like the mention of death. "Did I tell you that your sister Catherine—Philippa—is after me again."

"What for?"

"She wants to rent a gallery for an exhibition."

Stiffly fair-minded, Wilhelm said, "Well, of course that's up to you, Father."

The round-headed old man with his fine, feather-white, ferny hair said, "No, Wilky. There's not a thing on those canvases. I don't believe it; it's a case of the emperor's clothes. I may be old enough for my second childhood, but at least the first is well behind me. I was glad enough to buy crayons for her when she was four. But now she's a woman of forty and too old to be encouraged in her delusions. She's no painter."

"I wouldn't go so far as to call her a born artist," said Wilhelm, "but you can't blame her for trying something worth while."

"Let her husband pamper her."

Wilhelm had done his best to be just to his sister, and he had sincerely meant to spare his father, but the old man's tight, benevolent deafness had its usual effect on him. He said, "When it comes to women and money, I'm completely in the dark. What makes Margaret act like this?"

"She's showing you that you can't make it without her," said the doctor. "She aims to bring you back by financial force."

"But if she ruins me, Dad, how can she expect me to come back? No, I have a sense of honor. What you don't see is that she's trying to put an end to me."

His father stared. To him this was absurd. And Wilhelm thought, Once a guy starts to slip, he figures he might as well be a clunk. A real big clunk. He even takes pride in it. But there's nothing to be proud of—hey, boy? Nothing. I don't blame Dad for his attitude. And it's no cause for pride.

"I understand that. But if you feel like this why don't you settle with her once and for all?"

"What do you mean, Dad?" said Wilhelm, surprised. "I thought I told you. Do you think I'm not willing to settle? Four years ago when we broke up I gave her everything—goods, furniture, savings. I tried to show good will, but I didn't get anywhere. Why when I wanted Scissors, the dog, because the animal and I were so attached to each other—it was bad enough to leave the kids—she absolutely refused me. Not that she cared a damn about the animal. I don't think you've seen him. He's an Australian sheep dog. They usually have one blank or whitish eye which gives a misleading look, but they're the gentlest dogs and have unusual delicacy about eating or talking. Let me at least have the companionship of this animal. Never." Wilhelm was greatly moved. He wiped his face at all corners with his napkin. Dr. Adler felt that his son was indulging himself too much in his emotions.

"Whenever she can hit me, she hits, and she seems to live for that alone. And she demands more and more, and still more. Two years ago she wanted to go back to college and get another degree. It increased my burden but I thought it would be wiser in the end if she got a better job through it. But still she takes as much from me as before. Next thing she'll want to be a Doctor of Philosophy. She says the women in her family live long, and I'll have to pay and pay for the rest of my life."

The doctor said impatiently, "Well, these are details, not principles. Just details which you can leave out. The dog! You're mixing up all kinds of irrelevant things. Go to a good lawyer." *I don't want to hear anymore.*

"But I've already told you, Dad, I got a lawyer, and she got one, too, and both of them talk and send me bills, and I eat my heart out. Oh, Dad, Dad, what a hole I'm in!" said Wilhelm in utter misery. "The lawyers—see?—draw up an agreement, and she says okay on Monday and wants more money on Tuesday. And it begins again."

"I always thought she was a strange kind of woman," said Dr. Adler. He felt that by disliking Margaret from the first and disapproving of the marriage he had done all that he could be expected to do.

"Strange, Father? I'll show you what she's like." Wilhelm took hold of his broad throat with brown-stained fingers and bitten nails and began to choke himself.

"What are you doing?" cried the old man.

"I'm showing you what she does to me."

"Stop that—stop it!" the old man said and tapped the table commandingly.

"Well, Dad, she hates me. I feel that she's strangling me. I can't catch my breath. She just has fixed herself on me to kill me. She can do it at long distance. One of these days I'll be struck down by suffocation or apoplexy because of her. I just can't catch my breath."

"Take your hands off your throat, you foolish man," said his father. "Stop this bunk. Don't expect me to believe in all kinds of voodoo."

"If that's what you want to call it, all right." His face flamed and paled and swelled and his breath was laborious.

"But I'm telling you that from the time I met her I've been a slave. The Emancipation Proclamation was only for colored people. A husband like me is a slave, with an iron collar. The churches go up to Albany and supervise the law. They won't have divorces. The court says, 'You want to be free. Then you have to work twice as hard—twice, at least! Work! you bum.' So then guys kill each other for the buck, and they may be free of a wife who hates them but they are sold to the company. The company knows a guy has got to have his salary, and takes full advantage of him. Don't talk to me about being free. A rich man may be free on an income of a million net. A poor man may be free because nobody cares what he does. But a fellow in my position has to sweat it out until he drops dead."

His father replied to this, "Wilky, it's entirely your own fault. You don't have to allow it."

Stopped in his eloquence, Wilhelm could not speak for a while. Dumb and incompetent, he struggled for breath and frowned with effort into his father's face.

"I don't understand your problems," said the old man. "I never had any like them."

By now Wilhelm had lost his head and he waved his hands and said over and over, "Oh, Dad, don't give me that stuff, don't give me that. Please don't give me that sort of thing."

"It's true," said his father. "I come from a different world. Your mother and I led an entirely different life."

"Oh, how can you compare Mother," Wilhelm said. "Mother was a help to you. Did she harm you ever?"

"There's no need to carry on like an opera, Wilky," said the doctor. "This is only your side of things."

"What? It's the truth," said Wilhelm.

The old man could not be persuaded and shook his round head and drew his vest down over the gilded shirt, and leaned back with a completeness of style that made this look, to anyone out of hearing, like an ordinary conversation between a middle-aged man and his respected father. Wilhelm towered and swayed, big and sloven, with his gray eyes red-shot and his honey-colored hair twisted in flaming shapes upward. Injustice made him angry, made him beg. But he wanted an understanding with his father, and he tried to capitulate to him. He said, "You can't compare Mother and Margaret, and neither can you and I be compared, because you, Dad, were a success. And a success— is a success. I never made a success."

The doctor's old face lost all of its composure and became hard and angry. His small breast rose sharply under the red and black shirt and he said, "Yes. Because of hard work. I was not self-indulgent, not lazy. My old man sold dry goods in Williamsburg. We were nothing, do you understand? I knew I couldn't afford to waste my chances."

"I wouldn't admit for one minute that I was lazy," said Wilhelm. "If anything, I tried too hard. I admit I made many mistakes. Like I thought I shouldn't do things you had done already. Study chemistry. You had done it already. It was in the family."

His father continued, "I didn't run around with fifty women, either. I was not a Hollywood star. I didn't have time to go to Cuba for a vacation. I stayed at home and took care of my children."

Oh, thought Wilhelm, eyes turning upward. Why did I come here in the first place, to live near him? New York is like a gas. The colors are running. My head feels so tight, I don't know what I'm doing. He thinks I want to take away his money or that I envy him. He doesn't see what I want.

"Dad," Wilhelm said aloud, "you're being very unfair. It's true the movies was a false step. But I love my boys. I didn't abandon them. I left Margaret because I had to."

"Why did you have to?"

"Well—" said Wilhelm, struggling to condense his many reasons into a few plain words. "I had to—I had to."

With sudden and surprising bluntness his father said, "Did you have bed-trouble with her? Then you should have stuck it out. Sooner or later everyone has it. Normal people stay with it. It passes. But you wouldn't, so now you pay for your stupid romantic notions. Have I made my view clear?"

It was very clear. Wilhelm seemed to hear it repeated from various sides and inclined his head different ways, and listened and thought. Finally he said, "I guess that's the medical standpoint. You may be right. I just couldn't live with Margaret. I wanted to stick it out, but I was getting very sick. She was one way and I was another. She wouldn't be like me, so I tried to be like her, and I couldn't do it."

"Are you sure she didn't tell *you* to go?" the doctor said.

"I wish she had. I'd be in a better position now. No, it was me. I didn't want to leave, but I couldn't stay. Somebody had to take the initiative. I did. Now I'm the fall guy too."

Pushing aside in advance all the objections that his son would make, the doctor said, "Why did you lose your job with Rojax?"

"I didn't, I've told you."

"You're lying. You wouldn't have ended the connection. You need the money too badly. But you must have got into trouble." The small old man spoke concisely and with great strength. "Since you have to talk and can't let it alone, tell the truth. Was there a scandal—a woman?"

Wilhelm fiercely defended himself. "No, Dad, there wasn't any woman. I told you how it was."

"Maybe it was a man, then," the old man said wickedly.

Shocked, Wilhelm stared at him with burning pallor and dry lips. His skin looked a little yellow. "I don't think you know what you're talking about," he answered after a moment. "You shouldn't let your imagination run so free. Since you've been living here on Broadway you must think you understand life, up to date. You ought to know your own son a little better. Let's drop that, now."

"All right, Wilky, I'll withdraw it. But something must have happened in Roxbury nevertheless. You'll never go back. You're just talking wildly about representing a rival company. You won't. You've done something to spoil your reputation, I think. But you've got girl friends who are expecting you back, isn't that so?"

"I take a lady out now and then while on the road," said Wilhelm. "I'm not a monk."

"No one special? Are you sure you haven't gotten into complications?"

He had tried to unburden himself and instead, Wilhelm thought, he had to undergo an inquisition to prove himself worthy of a sympathetic word. Because his father believed that he did all kinds of gross things.

"There is a woman in Roxbury that I went with. We fell in love and wanted to marry, but she got tired of waiting for my divorce. Margaret figured that. On top of which the girl was a Catholic and I had to go with her to the priest and make an explanation."

Neither did this last confession touch Dr. Alder's sympathies or sway his calm old head or affect the color of his complexion.

"No, no, no, no; all wrong," he said.

Again Wilhelm cautioned himself. Remember his age. He is no longer the same person. He can't bear trouble. I'm so choked up and congested anyway I can't see straight. Will I ever get out of the woods, and recover my balance? You're never the same afterward. Trouble rusts out the system.

"You really *want* a divorce?" said the old man.

"For the price I pay I should be getting something."

"In that case," Dr. Adler said, "it seems to me no normal person would stand for such treatment from a woman."

"Ah, Father, Father!" said Wilhelm. "It's always the same thing with you. Look how you lead me on. You always start out to help me with my problems, and be sympathetic and so forth. It gets my hopes up and I begin to be grateful. But before we're through I'm a hundred times more depressed than before. Why is that? You have no sympathy. You want to shift all the blame on to me. Maybe you're wise to do it." Wilhelm was beginning to lose himself. "All you seem to think about is your death. Well, I'm sorry. But I'm going to die too. And I'm your son. It isn't my fault in the first place. There ought to be a right way to do this, and be fair to each other. But what I want to know is, why do you start up with me if you're not going to help me? What do you want to know about my problems for, Father? So you can lay the whole responsibility on me—so that you won't have to help me? D'you want me to comfort you for having such a son?" Wilhelm had a great knot of wrong tied tight within his chest, and tears approached his eyes but he didn't let them out. He looked shabby enough as it was. His voice was thick and hazy, and he was stammering and could not bring his awful feelings forth.

"You have some purpose of your own," said the doctor, "in acting so unreasonable. What do you want from me? What do you expect?"

"What do I expect?" said Wilhelm. He felt as though he were unable to recover something. Like a ball in the surf, washed beyond reach, his self-control was going out. "I expect *help!*" The words escaped him in a loud, wild, frantic cry and startled the old man, and two or three breakfasters within hearing glanced their way. Wilhelm's hair, the color of whitened honey, rose dense and tall with the expansion of his face, and he said. "When I suffer—you aren't even sorry. That's because you have no affection for me, and you don't want any part of me."

"Why must I like the way you behave? No, I don't like it," said Dr. Adler.

"All right. You want me to change myself. But suppose I could do it—what would I become? What could I? Let's suppose that all my life I have had the wrong ideas about myself and wasn't what I thought I was. And wasn't even careful to take a few precautions, as most people do—like a woodchuck has a few exits to his tunnel. But what shall I do now? More than half my life is over. More than half. And now you tell me I'm not even normal."

The old man too had lost his calm. "You cry about being helped," he said. "When you thought you had to go into the service I sent a check to Margaret every month. As a family man you could have had an exemption. But no! The war couldn't be fought without you and you had to get yourself drafted and be an office-boy in the Pacific theater. Any clerk could have done what you did. You could find nothing better to become than a GI."

Wilhelm was going to reply, and half raised his bearish figure from the chair, his fingers spread and whitened by their grip on the table, but the old man would not let him begin. He said, "I see other elderly people here with children who aren't much good, and they keep backing them and holding them up at a great sacrifice. But I'm not going to make that mistake. It doesn't enter your mind that when I die—a year, two years from now—you'll still be here. I do think of it."

He had intended to say that he had a right to be left in peace. Instead he gave Wilhelm the impression that he meant it was not fair for the better man of the two, and the more useful, the more admired, to leave the world first. Perhaps he meant that, too—a little; but he would not under other circumstances have come out with it so flatly.

"Father," said Wilhelm with an unusual openness of appeal. "Don't you think I know how you feel? I have pity. I want you to live on and on. If you outlive me, that's perfectly okay by me." As his father did not answer this avowal and turned away his glance, Wilhelm suddenly burst out, "No, but you hate me. And if I had money you wouldn't. By God, you have to admit it. The money makes the difference. Then we would be a fine father and son, if I was a credit to you—so you could boast and brag about me all over the hotel. But I'm not the right type of son. I'm too old, I'm too old and too unlucky."

His father said, "I can't give you any money. There would be no end to it if I started. You and your sister would take every last buck from me. I'm still alive, not dead. I am still here. Life isn't over yet. I am as much alive as you or anyone. And I want nobody on my back. Get off! And I give you the same advice, Wilky. Carry nobody on your back."

"Just keep your money," said Wilhelm miserably. "Keep it and enjoy it yourself. That's the ticket!"

IV

Ass! Idiot! Wild boar! Dumb mule! Slave Lousy, wallowing hippopotamus! Wilhelm called himself as his bending legs carried him from the dining room. His pride! His inflamed feelings! His begging and feebleness! And trading insults with his old father—and spreading confusion over everything. Oh, how poor, contemptible, and ridiculous he was! When he remembered how he had said, with great reproof, "You ought to know your own son"—why, how corny and abominable it was.

He could not get out of the sharply brilliant dining room fast enough. He was horribly worked up; his neck and shoulders, his entire chest ached as though they had been tightly tied with ropes. He smelled the salt odor of tears in his nose.

But at the same time, since there were depths in Wilhelm not unsuspected by himself, he received a suggestion from some remote element in his thoughts that the business of life, the real business—to carry his peculiar burden, to feel shame and impotence, to taste these quelled tears—the only important business, the highest business was being done. Maybe the making of mistakes expressed the very purpose of his life and the essence of his being here. Maybe he was supposed to make them and suffer from them on this earth. And though he had raised himself above Mr. Perls and his father because they adored money, still they were called to act energetically and this was better than to yell and cry, pray and beg, poke and blunder and go by fits and starts and fall upon the thorns of life. And finally sink beneath that watery floor—would that be tough luck, or would it be good riddance?

But he raged once more against his father. Other people with money, while they're still alive, want to see it do some good. Granted, he shouldn't support me. But have I ever asked him to do that? Have I ever asked for dough at all, either for Margaret or for the kids or for myself? It isn't the money, but only the assistance; not even assistance, but just the feeling. But he may be trying to teach me that a grown man should be cured of such feelings. Feeling got me in dutch at Rojax. I had the *feeling* that I belonged to the firm, and my *feelings* were hurt when they put Gerber in over me. Dad thinks I'm too simple. But I'm not so simple as he thinks. What about his feelings? He doesn't forget death for one single second, and that's what makes him like this. And not only is death on his mind but through money he forces me to think about it, too. It gives him power over me. He forces me that way, he himself, and then he's sore. If he was poor, I could care for him and show it. The way I *could* care, too, if I only had a chance. He'd see how much love and respect I had in me. It would make him a different man, too. He'd put his hands on me and give me his blessing.

Someone in a gray straw hat with a wide cocoa-colored band spoke to Wilhem in the lobby. The light was dusky, splotched with red underfoot; green, the leather furniture; yellow, the indirect lighting.

"Hey, Tommy. Say, there."

"Excuse me," said Wilhelm, trying to reach a house phone. But this was Dr. Tamkin, whom he was just about to call.

"You have a very obsessional look on your face," said Dr. Tamkin.

Wilhelm thought, Here he is, Here he is. If I could only figure this guy out.

"Oh," he said to Tamkin. "Have I got such a look? Well, whatever it is, you name it and I'm sure to have it."

The sight of Dr. Tamkin brought his quarrel with his father to a close. He found himself flowing into another channel.

"What are we doing?" he said. "What's going to happen to lard today?"

"Don't worry yourself about that. All we have to do is hold on to it and it's sure to go up. But what's made you so hot under the collar, Wilhelm?"

"Oh, one of those family situations." This was the moment to take a new look at Tamkin, and he viewed him closely but gained nothing by the new effort. It was conceivable that Tamkin was everything that he claimed to be, and all the gossip false. But was he a scientific man, or not? If he was not, this might be a case for the district attorney's office to investigate. Was he a liar? That was a delicate question. Even a liar might be trustworthy in some ways. Could he trust Tamkin—could he? He feverishly, fruitlessly sought an answer.

But the time for this question was past, and he had to trust him now. After a long struggle to come to a decision, he had given him the money. Practical judgment was in abeyance. He had worn himself out, and the decision was no decision. How had this happened? But how had his Hollywood career begun? It was not because of Maurice Venice, who turned out to be a pimp. It was because Wilhelm himself was ripe for the mistake. His marriage, too, had been like that. Through such decisions somehow his life had taken form. And so, from the moment when he tasted the peculiar flavor of fatality in Dr. Tamkin, he could no longer keep back the money.

Five days ago Tamkin had said, "Meet me tomorrow, and we'll go to the market." Wilhelm, therefore, had had to go. At eleven o'clock they had walked to the brokerage office. On the way, Tamkin broke the news to Wilhelm that though this was an equal partnership, he couldn't put up his half of the money just yet; it was tied up for a week or so in one of his patents. Today he would be two hundred dollars short; next week he'd make it up. But neither of them needed an income from the market, of course. This was only a sporting proposition anyhow, Tamkin said. Wilhelm had to answer, "Of course." It was too late to withdraw. What else could he do? Then came the formal part of the transaction, and it was frightening. The very shade of green of Tamkin's check looked wrong; it was a false, disheartening color. His handwriting was peculiar, even monstrous; the e's were like i's, the t's and l's the same, and the h's like wasps' bellies. He wrote like a fourth-grader. Scientists, however, dealt mostly in symbols; they printed. This was Wilhelm's explanation.

Dr. Tamkin had given him his check for three hundred dollars. Wilhelm, in a blinded and convulsed aberration, pressed and pressed to try to kill the trembling of his hand as he wrote out his check for a thousand. He set his lips tight, crouched with his huge back over the table, and wrote with crumbling, terrified fingers, knowing that if Tamkin's check bounced his own would not be honored either. His sole cleverness was to set the date ahead by one day to give the green check time to clear.

Next he had signed a power of attorney, allowing Tamkin to speculate with his money, and this was an even more frightening document. Tamkin had never said a word about it, but here they were and it had to be done.

After delivering his signatures, the only precaution Wilhelm took was to come back to the manager of the brokerage office and ask him privately, "Uh, about Doctor Tamkin. We were in here a few minutes ago, remember?"

That day had been a weeping, smoky one and Wilhelm had gotten away from Tamkin on the pretext of having to run to the post office. Tamkin had gone to lunch alone, and here was Wilhelm, back again, breathless, his hat dripping, needlessly asking the manager if he remembered.

"Yes, sir, I know," the manager had said. He was a cold, mild, lean German who dressed correctly and around his neck wore a pair of opera glasses with which he read the board. He was an extremely correct person except that he never shaved in the morning, not caring, probably, how he looked to the fumblers and the old people and the operators and the gamblers and the idlers of Broadway uptown. The market closed at three. Maybe, Wilhelm guessed, he had a thick beard and took a lady out to dinner later and wanted to look fresh-shaven.

"Just a question," said Wilhelm. "A few minutes ago I signed a power of attorney so Doctor Tamkin could invest for me. You gave me the blanks."

"Yes, sir, I remember."

"Now this is what I want to know," Wilhelm had said. "I'm no lawyer and I only gave the paper a glance. Does this give Doctor Tamkin power of attorney over any other assets of mine—money, or property?"

The rain had dribbled from Wilhelm's deformed, transparent raincoat; the buttons of his shirt, which always seemed tiny, were partly broken, in pearly quarters of the moon, and some of the dark, thick golden hairs that grew on his belly stood out. It was the manager's business to conceal his opinion of him; he was shrewd, gray, correct (although unshaven) and had little to say except on matters that came to his desk. He must have recognized in Wilhelm a man who reflected long and then made the decision he had rejected twenty separate times. Silvery, cool, level, long-profiled, experienced, indifferent, observant, with unshaven refinement, he scarcely looked at Wilhelm, who trembled with fearful awkwardness. The manager's face, low-colored, long-nostriled, acted as a unit of perception; his eyes merely did their reduced share. Here was a man like Rubin, who knew and knew and knew. He, a foreigner, knew; Wilhelm, in the city of his birth, was ignorant.

The manager had said. "No, sir, it does not give him."

"Only over the funds I deposited with you?"

"Yes, that is right, sir."

"Thank you, that's what I wanted to find out," Wilhelm had said, grateful.

The answer comforted him. However, the question had no value. None at all. For Wilhelm had no other assets. He had given Tamkin his last money. There wasn't enough of it to cover his obligations anyway, and Wilhelm had reckoned that he might as well go bankrupt now as next month. "Either broke or rich" was how he had figured, and that formula had encouraged him to make the gamble. Well, not rich; he did not expect that, but perhaps Tamkin might really show him how to earn what he needed in the market. By now, however, he had forgotten his own reckoning and was aware only that he stood to lose his seven hundred dollars to the last cent.

Dr. Tamkin took the attitude that they were a pair of gentlemen experimenting with lard and grain futures. The money, a few hundred dollars, meant nothing much to either of them. He said to Wilhelm, "Watch. You'll get a big kick out of this and wonder why more people don't go into it. You think the Wall Street guys are so smart—geniuses? That's because most of us are psychologically afraid to think about the details. Tell me this. When you're on the road, and you don't understand what goes on under the hood of your car, you'll worry what'll happen if something goes wrong with the engine. Am I wrong?" No, he was right. "Well," said Dr. Tamkin with an expression of quiet triumph about his mouth, almost the suggestion of a jeer. "It's the same psychological principle, Wilhelm. They are rich because you don't understand what goes on. But it's no mystery, and by putting in a little money and applying certain principles of observation, you begin to grasp it. It can't be studied in the abstract. You have to take a specimen risk so that you feel the process, the money-flow, the whole complex. To know how it feels to be a seaweed you have to get in the water. In a very short time we'll take out a hundred-percent profit." Thus Wilhelm had had to pretend at the outset that his interest in the market was theoretical.

"Well," said Tamkin when he met him now in the lobby, "what's the problem, what is this family situation? Tell me." He put himself forward as the keen mental scientist. Whenever this happened Wilhelm didn't know what to reply. No matter what he said or did it seemed that Dr. Tamkin saw through him.

"I had some words with my dad."

Dr. Tamkin found nothing extraordinary in this. "It's the eternal same story," he said. "The elemental conflict of parent and child. It won't end, ever. Even with a fine old gentleman like your dad."

"I don't suppose it will. I've never been able to get anywhere with him. He objects to my feelings. He thinks they're sordid. I upset him and he gets mad at me. But maybe all old men are alike."

"Sons, too. Take it from one of them," said Dr. Tamkin. "All the same, you should be proud of such a fine old patriarch of a father. It should give you hope. The longer he lives, the longer your life-expectancy becomes."

Wilhelm answered, brooding, "I guess so. But I think I inherit more from my mother's side, and she died in her fifties."

"A problem arose between a young fellow I'm treating and his dad—I just had a consultation," said Dr. Tamkin as he removed his dark gray hat.

"So early in the morning?" said Wilhelm with suspicion.

"Over the telephone, of course."

What a creature Tamkin was when he took off his hat! The indirect light showed the many complexities of his bald skull, his gull's nose, his rather handsome eyebrows, his vain mustache, his deceiver's brown eyes. His figure was stocky, rigid, short in the neck, so that the large ball of the occiput touched his collar. His bones were peculiarly formed, as though twisted twice where the ordinary human bone was turned only once, and his shoulders rose in two pagoda-like points. At mid-body he was thick. He stood pigeon-toed, a sign perhaps that he was devious or had much to hide. The skin of his hands was aging, and his nails were moonless, concave, clawlike, and they appeared loose. His eyes were as brown as beaver fur and full of strange lines. The two large brown naked balls looked thoughtful—but were they? And honest—but was Dr. Tamkin honest? There was a hypnotic power in his eyes, but this was not always of the same strength, nor was Wilhelm convinced that it was completely natural. He felt that Tamkin tried to make his eyes deliberately conspicuous, with studied art, and that he brought forth his hypnotic effect by an exertion. Occasionally it failed or drooped, and when this happened the sense of his face passed downward to his heavy (possibly foolish?) red underlip.

Wilhelm wanted to talk about the lard holdings, but Dr. Tamkin said, "This father-and-son case of mine would be instructive to you. It's a different psychological type completely than your dad. This man's father thinks that he isn't his son."

"Why not?"

"Because he has found out something about the mother carrying on with a friend of the family for twenty-five years."

"Well, what do you know!" said Wilhelm. His silent thought was, Pure bull. Nothing but bull!

"You must note how interesting the woman is, too. She has two husbands. Whose are the kids? The fellow detected her and she gave a signed confession that two of the four children were not the father's."

"It's amazing," said Wilhelm, but he said it in a rather distant way. He was always hearing such stories from Dr. Tamkin. If you were to believe Tamkin, most of the world was like this. Everybody in the hotel had a mental disorder, a secret history, a concealed disease. The wife of Rubin at the newsstand was supposed to be kept by Carl, the yelling, loud-mouthed gin-rummy player. The wife of Frank in the barbershop had disappeared with a GI while he was waiting for her to disembark at the French Lines' pier. Everyone was like the faces on a playing card, upside down either way. Every public figure had a character-neurosis. Maddest of all were the businessmen, the heartless, flaunting, boisterous business class who ruled this country with their hard manners and their bold lies and their absurd words that nobody could believe. They were crazier than anyone. They spread the plague. Wilhelm, thinking of the Rojax Corporation, was inclined to agree that many businessmen were insane. And he supposed that Tamkin, for all his peculiarities, spoke a kind of truth and did some people a sort of good. It confirmed Wilhelm's suspicions to hear that there was a plague, and he said, "I couldn't agree with you more. They trade on any thing, they steal everything, they're cynical right to the bones."

"You have to realize," said Tamkin, speaking of his patient, or his client, "that the mother's confession isn't good. It's a confession of duress. I try to tell the young fellow he shouldn't worry about a phony confession. But what does it help him if I am rational with him?"

"No?" said Wilhelm, intensely nervous. "I think we ought to go over to the market. It'll be opening pretty soon."

"Oh, come on," said Tamkin. "It isn't even nine o'clock, and there isn't much trading the first hour anyway. Things don't get hot in Chicago until half-past ten, and they're an hour behind us, don't forget. Anyway, I say lard will go up, and it will. Take my word. I've made a study of the guilt-aggression cycle which is behind it. I ought to know *something* about that. Straighten your collar."

"But meantime," said Wilhelm, "we have taken a licking this week. Are you sure your insight is at its best? Maybe when it isn't we should lay off and wait."

"Don't you realize," Dr. Tamkin told him, "you can't march in a straight line to the victory? You fluctuate toward it. From Euclid to Newton there was straight lines. The modern age analyzes the wavers. On my own accounts, I took a licking in hides and coffee. But I have confidence. I'm sure I'll outguess them." He gave Wilhelm a narrow smile, friendly, calming, shrewd, and wizard-like, patronizing, secret, potent. He saw his fears and smiled at them. "It's something," he remarked, "to see how the competition-factor will manifest itself in different individuals."

"So? Let's go over."

"But I haven't had my breakfast yet."

"I've had mine."

"Come, have a cup of coffee."

"I wouldn't want to meet my dad." Looking through the glass doors, Wilhelm saw that his father had left by the other exit. Wilhelm thought, He didn't want to run into me, either. He said to Dr. Tamkin, "Okay, I'll sit with you, but let's hurry it up because I'd like to get to the market while there's still a place to sit. Everybody and his uncle gets in ahead of you."

"I want to tell you about this boy and his dad. It's highly absorbing. The father was a nudist. Everybody went naked in the house. Maybe the woman found men *with* clothes attractive. Her husband didn't believe in cutting his hair, either. He practiced dentistry. In his office he wore riding pants and a pair of boots, and he wore a green eyeshade."

"Oh, come off it," said Wilhelm.

"This is a true case history."

Without warning, Wilhelm began to laugh. He himself had had no premonition of his change of humor. His face became warm and pleasant, and he forgot his father, his anxieties; he panted bearlike, happily, through his teeth. "This sounds like a horse-dentist. He wouldn't have to put on pants to treat a horse. Now what else are you going to tell me? Did the wife play the mandolin? Does the boy join the cavalry? Oh, Tamkin, you really are a killer-diller."

"Oh, you think I'm trying to amuse you," said Tamkin. "That's because you aren't familiar with my outlook. I deal in facts. Facts always are sensational. I'll say that a second time. Facts *always!* are sensational."

Wilhelm was reluctant to part with his good mood. The doctor had little sense of humor. He was looking at him earnestly.

"I'd bet you any amount of money," said Tamkin, "that the facts about you are sensational."

"Oh—ha, ha! You want them? You can sell them to a true confession magazine."

"People forget how sensational things are that they do. They don't see it on themselves. It blends into the background of their daily life."

Wilhelm smiled. "Are you sure this boy tells you the truth?"

"Yes, because I've known the whole family for years."

"And you do psychological work with your own friends? I didn't know that was allowed."

"Well, I'm a radical in the profession. I have to do good wherever I can."

Wilhelm's face became ponderous again and pale. His whitened gold hair lay heavy on his head, and he clasped uneasy fingers on the table. Sensational, but oddly enough, dull, too. Now how do you figure that out? It blends with the background. Funny but unfunny. True but false. Casual but laborious, Tamkin was. Wilhelm was most suspicious of him when he took his driest tone.

"With me," said Dr. Tamkin, "I am at my most efficient when I don't need the fee. When I only love. Without a financial reward. I remove myself from the social influence. Especially money. The spiritual compensation is what I look for. Bringing people into the here-and-now. The real universe. That's the present moment. The past is no good to us. The future is full of anxiety. Only the present is real—the here-and-now. Seize the day."

"Well," said Wilhelm, his earnestness returning. "I know you are a very unusual man. I like what you say about here-and-now. Are all the people who come to see you personal friends and patients too? Like that tall handsome girl, the one who always wears those beautiful broomstick skirts and belts?"

"She was an epileptic, and a most bad and serious pathology, too. I'm curing her successfully. She hasn't had a seizure in six months, and she used to have one every week."

"And that young cameraman, the one who showed us those movies from the jungles of Brazil, isn't he related to her?"

"Her brother. He's under my care, too. He has some terrible tendencies, which are to be expected when you have an epileptic sibling. I came into their lives when they needed help desperately, and took hold of them. A certain man forty years older than she had her in his control and used to give her fits by suggestion whenever she tried to leave him. If you only knew one per cent of what goes on in the city of New York! You see, I understand what it is when the lonely person begins to feel like an animal. When the night comes and he feels like howling from his window like a wolf. I'm taking complete care of that young fellow and his sister. I have to steady him down or he'll go from Brazil to Australia the next day. The way I keep him in the here-and-now is by teaching him Greek."

This was a complete surprise! "What, do you know Greek?"

"A friend of mine taught me when I was in Cairo. I studied Aristotle with him to keep from being idle."

Wilhelm tried to take in these new claims and examine them. Howling from the window like a wolf when night comes sounded genuine to him. That was something really to think about. But the Greek! He realized that Tamkin was watching to see how he took it. More elements were continually being added. A few days ago Tamkin had hinted that he had once been in the underworld, one of the Detroit Purple Gang. He was once head of a mental clinic in Toledo. He had worked with a Polish inventor on an unsinkable ship. He was a technical consultant in the field of television. In the life of a man of genius, all of these things might happen. But had they happened to Tamkin? Was he a genius? He often said that he had attended some of the Egyptian royal family as a psychiatrist. "But everybody is alike, common or aristocrat," he told Wilhelm. "The aristocrat knows less about life."

An Egyptian princess whom he had treated in California, for horrible disorders he had described to Wilhelm, retained him to come back to the old country with her, and there he had had many of her friends and relatives under his care. They turned over a villa on the Nile to him. "For ethical reasons, I can't tell you many of the details about them," he said—but Wilhelm had already heard all these details, and strange and shocking they were, if true. *If true*—he could not be free from doubt. For instance, the general who had to wear ladies' silk stockings and stand otherwise naked before the mirror—and all the rest. Listening to the doctor when he was so strangely factual, Wilhelm had to translate his words into his own language, and he could not translate fast enough or find terms to fit what he heard.

"Those Egyptian big shots invested in the market, too, for the heck of it. What did they need extra money for? By association, I almost became a millionaire myself, and if I had played it smart there's no telling what might have happened. I could have been the ambassador." The American? The Egyptian ambassador? "A friend of mine tipped me off on the cotton. I made a heavy purchase of it. I didn't have that kind of money, but everybody there knew me. It never entered their minds that a person of their social circle didn't have dough. The sale was made on the phone. Then, while the cotton shipment was at sea, the price tripled. When the stuff suddenly became so valuable all hell broke loose on the world cotton market, they looked to see who was the owner of this big shipment. Me! They investigated my credit and found out I was a mere doctor, and they canceled. This was illegal. I sued them. But as I didn't have the money to fight them I sold the suit to a Wall Street lawyer for twenty thousand dollars. He fought it and was winning. They settled with him out of court for more than a million. But on the way back from Cairo, flying, there was a crash. All on board died. I have this guilt on my conscience, of being the murderer of that lawyer. Although he was a crook."

Wilhelm thought, I must be a real jerk to sit and listen to such impossible stories. I guess I am a sucker for people who talk about the deeper things of life, even the way he does.

"We scientific men speak of irrational guilt, Wilhelm," said Dr. Tamkin, as if Wilhelm were a pupil in his class. "But in such a situation, because of the money, I wished him harm. I realize it. This isn't the time to describe all the details, but the money made me guilty. Money and Murder both begin with M. Machinery. Mischief."

Wilhelm, his mind thinking for him at random, said, "What about Mercy? Milk-of-human-kindness?"

"One fact should be clear to you by now. Money-making is aggression. That's the whole thing. The functionalistic explanation is the only one. People come to the market to kill. They say, 'I'm going to make a killing.' It's not accidental. Only they haven't got the genuine courage to kill, and they erect a symbol of it. The money. They make a killing by a fantasy. Now, counting and numbering is always a sadistic activity. Like hitting. In the Bible, the Jews wouldn't allow you to count them. They knew it was sadistic."

"I don't understand what you mean," said Wilhelm. A strange uneasiness tore at him. The day was growing too warm and his head felt dim. "What makes them want to kill?"

"By and by, you'll get the drift," Dr. Tamkin assured him. His amazing eyes had some of the rich dryness of a brown fur. Innumerable crystalline hairs or spicules of light glittered in their bold surfaces. "You can't understand without first spending years on the study of the ultimates of human and animal behavior, the deep chemical, organismic, and spiritual secrets of life. I am a psychological poet."

"If you're this kind of poet," said Wilhelm, whose fingers in his pocket were feeling the little envelopes for the Phenaphen capsules, "what are you doing on the market?"

"That's a good question. Maybe I am better at speculation, because I don't care. Basically, I don't wish hard enough for money, and therefore I come with a cool head to it."

Wilhelm thought, Oh sure! That's an answer, is it? I bet that if I took a strong attitude he'd back down on everything. He'd grovel in front of me. The way he looks at me on the sly, to see if I'm being taken in! He swallowed his Phenaphen pill with a long gulp of water. The rims of his eyes grew red as it went down. And then he felt calmer.

"Let me see if I can give you an answer that will satisfy you," said Dr. Tamkin. His flapjacks were set before him. He spread the butter on them, poured on brown maple syrup, quartered them, and began to eat with hard, active, muscular jaws which sometimes gave a creak at the hinges. He pressed the handle of his knife against his chest and said, "In here, the human bosom—mine, yours, everybody's—there isn't just one soul. There's a lot of souls. But there are two main ones, the real soul and a pretender soul. Now! Every man realizes that he has to love something or somebody. He feels that he must go outward. 'If thou canst not love, what art thou?' Are you with me?"

"Yes, Doc, I think so," said Wilhelm listening—a little skeptically but nonetheless hard.

"'What art thou?' Nothing. That's the answer. Nothing. In the heart of hearts—Nothing! So of course you can't stand that and want to be Something, and you try. But instead of being Something, the man puts it over on everybody instead. You can't be that strict to yourself. You love a *little*. Like you have a dog" (*Scissors!*) "or give some money to a charity drive. Now that isn't love, is it? What is it? Egotism, pure and simple. It's a way to love the pretender soul. Vanity. Only vanity, is what it is. And social control. The interest of the pretender soul is the same as the interest of the social life, the society mechanism. This is the main tragedy of human life. Oh, it is terrible! Terrible! You are not free. Your own betrayer is inside of you and sells you out. You have to obey him like a slave. He makes you work like a horse. And for what? For who?"

"Yes, for what?" The doctor's words caught Wilhelm's heart. "I couldn't agree more," he said. "When do we get free?"

"The purpose is to keep the whole thing going. The true soul is the one that pays the price. It suffers and gets sick, and it realizes that the pretender can't be loved. Because the pretender is a lie. The true soul loves the truth. And when the true soul feels like this, it wants to kill the pretender. The love has turned into hate. Then you become dangerous. A killer. You have to kill the deceiver."

"Does this happen to everybody?"

The doctor answered simply, "Yes, to everybody. Of course, for simplification purposes, I have spoken of the soul; it isn't a scientific term, but it helps you to understand it. Whenever the slayer slays, he wants to slay the soul in him which has gypped and deceived him. Who is his enemy? Him. And his lover? Also. Therefore, all suicide is murder, and all murder is suicide. It's the one and identical phenomenon. Biologically, the pretender soul takes away the energy of the true soul and makes it feeble, like a parasite. It happens unconsciously, unawaringly, in the depths of the organism. Ever take up parasitology?"

"No, it's my dad who's the doctor."

"You should read a book about it."

Wilhelm said, "But this means that the world is full of murderers. So it's not the world. It's a kind of hell."

"Sure," the doctor said, "At least a kind of purgatory. You walk on the bodies. They are all around. I can hear them cry *de profundis* and wring their hands. I hear them, poor human beasts. I can't help hearing. And my eyes are open to it. I have to cry, too. This is the human tragedy-comedy."

Wilhelm tried to capture his vision. And again the doctor looked untrustworthy to him, and he doubted him. "Well," he said, "there are also kind, ordinary, helpful people. They're—out in the country. All over. What kind of morbid stuff do you read, anyway?" The doctor's room was full of books.

"I read the best of literature, science and philosophy," Dr. Tamkin said. Wilhelm had observed that in his room even the TV aerial was set upon a pile of volumes. "Korzybski, Aristotle, Freud, W. H. Sheldon, and all the great poets. You answer me like a layman. You haven't applied your mind strictly to this."

"Very interesting," said Wilhelm. He was aware that he hadn't applied his mind strictly to anything. "You don't have to think I'm a dummy, though. I have ideas, too." A glance at the clock told him that the market would soon open. They could spare a few minutes yet. There were still more things he wanted to hear from Tamkin. He realized that Tamkin spoke faultily, but then scientific men were not always strictly literate. It was the description of the two souls that had awed him. In Tommy he saw the pretender. And even Wilky might not be himself. Might the name of his true soul be the one by which his old grandfather had called him—Velvel? The name of a soul, however, must be only that—soul. What did it look like? Does my soul look like me? Is there a soul that looks like Dad? Like Tamkin? Where does the true soul gets its strength? Why does it have to love truth? Wilhelm was tormented, but tried to be oblivious to his torment. Secretly, he prayed the doctor would give him some useful advice and transform his life. "Yes, I understand you," he said. "It isn't lost on me."

"I never said you weren't intelligent, but only you just haven't made a study of it all. As a matter of fact you're a profound personality with very profound creative capacities but also disturbances. I've been concerned with you, and for some time I've been treating you."

"Without my knowing it? I haven't felt you doing anything. What do you mean? I don't think I like being treated without my knowledge. I'm of two minds. What's the matter, don't you think I'm normal?" And he really was divided in mind. That the doctor cared about him pleased him. This was what he craved, that someone should care about him, wish him well. Kindness, mercy, he wanted. But—and here he retracted his heavy shoulders in his peculiar way, drawing his hands up into his sleeves; his feet moved uneasily under the table—but he was worried, too, and even somewhat indignant. For what right had Tamkin to meddle without being asked? What kind of privileged life did this man lead? He took other people's money and speculated with it. Everybody came under his care. No one could have secrets from him.

The doctor looked at him with his deadly brown, heavy, impenetrable eyes, his naked shining head, his red hanging underlip, and said, "You have lots of guilt in you."

Wilhelm helplessly admitted, as he felt the heat rise to his wide face, "Yes, I think so too. But personally," he added, "I don't feel like a murderer. I always try to lay off. It's the others who get me. You know—-make me feel oppressed. And if you don't mind, and it's all the same to you, I would rather know it when you start to treat me. And now, Tamkin, for Christ's sake, they're putting out the lunch menus already. Will you sign the check, and let's go!"

Tamkin did as he asked, and they rose. They were passing the bookkeeper's desk when he took out a substantial bundle of onionskin papers and said, "These are receipts of the transactions. Duplicates. You'd better keep them as the account is in your name and you'll need them for income taxes. And here is a copy of a poem I wrote yesterday."

"I have to leave something at the desk for my father," Wilhelm said, and he put his hotel bill in an envelope with a note. *Dear Dad, Please carry me this month, Yours, W.* He watched the clerk with his sullen pug's profile and his stiff-necked look push the envelope into his father's box.

"May I ask you really why you and your dad had words?" said Dr. Tamkin, who had hung back, waiting.

"It was about my future," said Wilhelm. He hurried down the stairs with swift steps, like a tower in motion, his hands in his trousers pockets. He was ashamed to discuss the matter. "He says there's a reason why I can't go back to my old territory, and there is. I told everybody I was going to be an officer of the corporation. And I was supposed to. It was promised. But then they welshed because of the son-in-law. I bragged and made myself look big."

"If you was humble enough, you could go back. But it doesn't make much difference. We'll make you a good living on the market."

They came into the sunshine of upper Broadway, not clear but throbbing through the dust and fumes, a false air of gas visible at eye-level as it spurted from the bursting buses. From old habit, Wilhelm turned up the collar of his jacket.

"Just a technical question," Wilhelm said. "What happens if your losses are bigger than your deposit?"

"Don't worry. They have ultra-modern electronic bookkeeping machinery, and it won't let you get in debt. It puts you out automatically. But I want you to read this poem. You haven't read it yet."

Light as a locust, a helicopter bringing mail from Newark Airport to La Guardia sprang over the city in a long leap.

The paper Wilhelm unfolded had ruled borders in red ink. He read:

Mechanism vs Functionalism
Ism vs Hism

If thee thyself couldst only see
Thy greatness that is and yet to be,
Thou would feel joy-beauty-what ecstasy.
They are at thy feet, earth-moon-sea, the trinity.

Why-forth then dost thou tarry
And partake thee only of the crust
And skim the earth's surface narry
When all creations art thy just?

Seek ye then that which art not there
In thine own glory let thyself rest.
Witness. Thy power is not bare.
Thou art King. Thou art at thy best.

Look then right before thee.
Open thine eyes and see.
At the foot of Mt. Serenity
Is thy cradle to eternity.

Utterly confused, Wilhelm said to himself explosively, What kind of mish-mash, claptrap is this! What does he want from me? Damn him to hell, he might as well hit me on the head, and lay me out, kill me. What does he give me this for? What's the purpose? Is it a deliberate test? Does he want to mix me up? He's already got me mixed up completely. I was never good at riddles. Kiss those seven hundred bucks good-by, and call it one more mistake in a long line of mistakes—Oh, Mama, what a line! He stood near the shining window of a fancy fruit store, holding Tamkin's paper, rather dazed, as though a charge of photographer's flash powder had gone up in his eyes.

But he's waiting for my reaction. I have to say something to him about his poem. It really is no joke. What will I tell him? Who is this King? The poem is written *to* someone. But who? I can't even bring myself to talk. I feel too choked and strangled. With all the books he reads, how come the guy is so illiterate? And why do people just naturally assume that you'll know what they're talking about? No. I don't know, and nobody knows. The planets don't, the stars don't, infinite space doesn't. It doesn't square with Planck's Constant or anything else. So what's the good of it? Where's the need of it? What does he mean here by Mount Serenity? Could it be a figure of speech for Mount Everest? As he says people are all committing suicide, maybe those guys who climbed Everest were only trying to kill themselves, and if we want peace we should stay at the foot of the mountain. In the here-and-now. But it's also here-and-now on the slope, and on the top, where they climbed to seize the day. Surface narry is something he can't mean. I don't believe. I'm about to start foaming at the mouth. "Thy cradle . . ." *Who* is resting in his cradle—in his glory? My thoughts are at an end. I feel the wall. No more. So _____k it all! The money and everything. Take it away! When I have the money they eat me alive, like those piranha fish in the movie about the Brazilian jungle. It was hideous when they ate up that Brahma bull in the river. He turned pale, just like clay, and in five minutes nothing was left except the skeleton still in one piece, floating away. When I haven't got it any more, at least they'll let me alone.

"Well, what do you think of this?" said Dr. Tamkin. He gave a special sort of wise smile, as though Wilhelm must now see what kind of man he was dealing with.

"Nice. Very nice. Have you been writing long?"

"I've been developing this line of thought for years and years. You follow it all the way?"

"I'm trying to figure out who this Thou is."

"Thou? Thou is you."

"Me! Why? This applies to *me*?"

"Why shouldn't it apply to you. You were in my mind when I composed it. Of course, the hero of the poem is sick humanity. If it would open its eyes it would be great."

"Yes, but how do I get into this?"

"The main idea of the poem is *construct* or *destruct*. There is no ground in between. Mechanism is *destruct*. Money of course is *destruct*. When the last grave is dug, the gravedigger will have to be paid. If you could have confidence in nature you would not have to fear. It would keep you up. Creative is nature. Rapid. Lavish. Inspirational. It shapes leaves. It rolls the waters of the earth.

Man is the chief of this. All creations are his just inheritance. You don't know what you've got within you. A person either creates or he destroys. There is no neutrality . . ."

"I realized you were no beginner," said Wilhelm with propriety. "I have only one criticism to make. I think 'why-forth' is wrong. You should write 'Wherefore then dost thou . . .'" And he reflected, So? I took a gamble. It'll have to be a miracle, though, to save me. My money will be gone, then it won't be able to destruct me. He can't just take and lose it, though. He's in it, too. I think he's in a bad way himself. He must be. I'm sure because, come to think of it, he sweated blood when he signed that check. But what have I let myself in for? The waters of the earth are going to roll over me.

V

Patiently, in the window of the fruit store, a man with a scoop spread crushed ice between his rows of vegetables. There were also Persian melons, lilacs, tulips with radiant black at the middle. The many street noises came back after a little while from the caves of the sky. Crossing the tide of Broadway traffic, Wilhelm was saying to himself, The reason Tamkin lectures me is that somebody has lectured him, and the reason for the poem is that he wants to give me good advice. Everybody seems to know something. Even fellows like Tamkin. Many people know what to do, but how many can do it?

He believed that he must, that he could and would recover the good things, the happy things, the easy tranquil things of life. He had made mistakes, but he could overlook these. He had been a fool, but that could be forgiven. The time wasted—must be relinquished. What else could one do about it? Things were too complex, but they might be reduced to simplicity again. Recovery was possible. First he had to get out of the city. No, first he had to pull out his money. . . .

From the carnival of the street—pushcarts, accordion and fiddle, shoeshine, begging, the dust going round like a woman on stilts—they entered the narrow crowded theater of the brokerage office. From front to back it was filled with the Broadway crowd. But how was lard doing this morning? From the rear of the hall Wilhelm tried to read the tiny figures. The German manager was looking through his binoculars. Tamkin placed himself on Wilhelm's left and covered his conspicuous bald head. "The guy'll ask me about the margin," he muttered. They passed, however, unobserved. "Look, the lard has held its place," he said.

Tamkin's eyes must be very sharp to read the figures over so many heads and at this distance—another respect in which he was unusual.

The room was always crowded. Everyone talked. Only at the front could you hear the flutter of the wheels within the board. Teletyped news items crossed the illuminated screen above.

"Lard. Now what about rye?" said Tamkin, rising on his toes. Here he was a different man, active and impatient. He parted people who stood in his way.

His face turned resolute, and on either side of his mouth odd bulges formed under his mustache. Already he was pointing out to Wilhelm the appearance of a new pattern on the board. "There's something up today," he said.

"Then why'd you take so long with breakfast?" said Wilhelm.

There were no reserved seats in the room, only customary ones. Tamkin always sat in the second row, on the commodities side of the aisle. Some of his acquaintances kept their hats on the chairs for him.

"Thanks. Thanks," said Tamkin, and he told Wilhelm, "I fixed it up yesterday."

"That was a smart thought," said Wilhelm. They sat down.

With folded hands, by the wall, sat an old Chinese businessman in a seersucker coat. Smooth and fat, he wore a white Vandyke. One day Wilhelm had seen him on Riverside Drive pushing two little girls along in a baby carriage—his grandchildren. Then there were two women in their fifties, supposed to be sisters, shrewd and able money-makers, according to Tamkin. They had never a word to say to Wilhelm. But they would chat with Tamkin. Tamkin talked to everyone.

Wilhelm sat between Mr. Rowland, who was elderly, and Mr. Rappaport, who was very old. Yesterday Rowland had told him that in the year 1908, when he was a junior at Harvard, his mother had given him twenty shares of steel for his birthday, and then he had started to read the financial news and had never practiced law but instead followed the market for the rest of his life. Now he speculated only in soy beans, of which he had made a specialty. By his conservative method, said Tamkin, he cleared two hundred a week. Small potatoes, but then he was a bachelor, retired, and didn't need money.

"Without dependents," said Tamkin. "He doesn't have the problems that you and I do."

Did Tamkin have dependents? He had everything that it was possible for a man to have—science, Greek, chemistry, poetry, and now dependents too. That beautiful girl with epilepsy, perhaps. He often said that she was a pure, marvelous, spiritual child who had no knowledge of the world. He protected her, and, if he was not lying, adored her. And if you encouraged Tamkin by believing him, or even if you refrained from questioning him, his hints became more daring. Sometimes he said that he paid for her music lessons. Sometimes he seemed to have footed the bill for the brother's camera expedition to Brazil. And he spoke of paying for the support of the orphaned child of a dead sweetheart. These hints, made dully as asides, grew by repetition into sensational claims.

"For myself, I don't need much," said Tamkin. "But a man can't live for himself and I need the money for certain important things. What do you figure you have to have, to get by?"

"Not less than fifteen grand, after taxes. That's for my wife and the two boys."

"Isn't there anybody else?" said Tamkin with a shrewdness almost cruel.

But his look grew more sympathetic as Wilhelm stumbled, not willing to recall another grief.

"Well—there was. But it wasn't a money matter."

"I should hope!" said Tamkin. "If love is love, it's free. Fifteen grand, though, isn't too much for a man of your intelligence to ask out of life. Fools, hard-hearted criminals, and murderers have millions to squander. They burn up the world—oil, coal, wood, metal, and soil, and suck even the air and the sky. They consume, and they give back no benefit. A man like you, humble for life, who wants to feel and live, has trouble—not wanting," said Tamkin in his parenthetical fashion, "to exchange an ounce of soul for a pound of social power—he'll never make it without help in a world like this. But don't you worry." Wilhelm grasped at this assurance. "Just you never mind. We'll go easily beyond your figure."

Dr. Tamkin gave Wilhelm comfort. He often said that he had made as much as a thousand a week in commodities. Wilhelm had examined the receipts, but until this moment it had never occurred to him that there must be debit slips too; he had been shown only the credits.

"But fifteen grand is not an ambitious figure," Tamkin was telling him. "For that you don't have to wear yourself out on the road, dealing with narrow-minded people. A lot of them don't like Jews, either, I suppose?"

"I can't afford to notice. I'm lucky when I have my occupation. Tamkin, do you mean you can save our money?"

"Oh, did I forget to mention what I did before closing yesterday? You see, I closed out one of the lard contracts and bought a hedge of December rye. The rye is up three points already and takes some of the sting out. But lard will go up, too."

"Where? God, yes, you're right," said Wilhelm, eager, and got to his feet to look. New hope freshened his heart. "Why didn't you tell me before?"

And Tamkin, smiling like a benevolent magician, said "You must learn to have trust. The slump in lard can't last. And just take a look at eggs. Didn't I predict they couldn't go any lower? They're rising and rising. If we had taken eggs we'd be far ahead."

"Then why didn't we take them?"

"We were just about to. I had a buying order in at .24, but the tide turned at .26¼ and we barely missed. Neved mind. Lard will go back to last year's levels."

Maybe. But when? Wilhelm could not allow his hopes to grow too strong. However, for a little while he could breathe more easily. Late-morning trading was getting active. The shining numbers whirred on the board, which sounded like a huge cage of artificial birds. Lard fluctuated between two points, but rye slowly climbed.

He closed his strained, greatly earnest eyes briefly and nodded his Buddha's head, too large to suffer such uncertainties. For several moments of peace he was removed to his small yard in Roxbury.

He breathed in the sugar of the pure morning.

He heard the long phrases of the birds.

No enemy wanted his life.

Wilhelm thought, I will get out of here. I don't belong in New York any more. And he sighed like a sleeper.

Tamkin said, "Excuse me," and left his seat. He could not sit still in the room but passed back and forth between the stocks and commodities sections. He knew dozens of people and was continually engaging in discussions. Was he giving advice, gathering information, or giving it, or practicing—whatever mysterious profession he practiced? Hypnotism? Perhaps he could put people in a trance while he talked to them. What a rare, peculiar bird he was, with those pointed shoulders, that bare head, his loose nails, almost claws, and those brown, soft, deadly, heavy eyes.

He spoke of things that mattered, and as very few people did this he could take you by surprise, excite you, move you. Maybe he wished to do good, maybe give himself a lift to a higher level, maybe believe his own prophecies, maybe touch his own heart. Who could tell? He had picked up a lot of strange ideas; Wilhelm could only suspect, he could not say with certainty, that Tamkin hadn't made them his own.

Now Tamkin and he were equal partners, but Tamkin had put up only three hundred dollars. Suppose he did this not only once but five times; then an investment of fifteen hundred dollars gave him five thousand to speculate with. If he had power of attorney in every case, he could shift the money from one account to another. No, the German probably kept an eye on him. Nevertheless it was possible. Calculations like this made Wilhelm feel ill. Obviously Tamkin was a plunger. But how did he get by? He must be in his fifties. How did he support himself? Five years in Egypt; Hollywood before that; Michigan; Ohio; Chicago. A man of fifty has supported himself for at least thirty years. You could be sure that Tamkin had never worked in a factory or in an office. How did he make it? His taste in clothes was horrible, but he didn't buy cheap things. He wore corduroy or velvet shirts from Clyde's, painted neckties, striped socks. There was a slightly acid or pasty smell about his person; for a doctor, he didn't bathe much. Also, Dr. Tamkin had a good room at the Gloriana and had had it for about a year. But so was Wilhelm himself a guest, with an unpaid bill at present in his father's box. Did the beautiful girl with the skirts and belts pay him? Was he defrauding his so-called patients? So many questions impossible to answer could not be asked about an honest man. Nor perhaps about a sane man. Was Tamkin a lunatic, then? That sick Mr. Perls at breakfast had said that there was no easy way to tell the sane from the mad, and he was right about that in any big city and especially in New York— the end of the world, with its complexity and machinery, bricks and tubes, wires and stones, holes and heights. And was everybody crazy here? What sort of people did you see? Every other man spoke a language entirely his own, which he had figured out by private thinking; he had his own ideas and peculiar ways. If you wanted to talk about a glass of water, you had to start back with

God creating the heavens and earth; the apple; Abraham; Moses and Jesus; Rome; the Middle Ages; gunpowder; the Revolution; back to Newton; up to Einstein; then war and Lenin and Hitler. After reviewing this and getting it all straight again you could proceed to talk about a glass of water. "I'm fainting, please get me a little water." You were lucky even then to make yourself understood. And this happened over and over and over with everyone you met. You had to translate and translate, explain and explain, back and forth, and it was the punishment of hell itself not to understand or be understood, not to know the crazy from the sane, the wise from the fools, the young from the old or the sick from the well. The fathers were no fathers and the sons no sons. You had to talk with yourself in the daytime and reason with yourself at night. Who else was there to talk to in a city like New York?

A queer look came over Wilhelm's face with its eyes turned up and his silent mouth with its high upper lip. He went several degrees further—when you are like this, dreaming that everybody is outcast, you realize that this must be one of the small matters. There is a larger body, and from this you cannot be separated. The glass of water fades out. You do not go from simple *a* and simple *b* to the great *x* and *y*, nor does it matter whether you agree about the glass but, far beneath such details, what Tamkin would call the real soul says plain and understandable things to everyone. There sons and fathers are themselves, and a glass of water is only an ornament; it makes a hoop of brightness on the cloth; it is an angel's mouth. There truth for everybody may be found, and confusion is only—only temporary, thought Wilhelm.

The idea of this larger body had been planted in him a few days ago beneath Times Square, when he had gone downtown to pick up tickets for the baseball game on Saturday (a doubleheader at the Polo Grounds). He was going through an underground corridor, a place he had always hated and hated more than ever now. On the walls between the advertisements were words in chalk: "Sin No More," and "Do Not Eat the Pig," he had particularly noticed. And in the dark tunnel, in the haste, heat, and darkness which disfigure and make freaks and fragments of nose and eyes and teeth, all of a sudden, unsought, a general love for all these imperfect and lurid-looking people burst out in Wilhelm's breast. He loved them. One and all, he passionately loved them. They were his brothers and his sisters. He was imperfect and disfigured himself, but what difference did that make if he was united with them by this blaze of love? And as he walked he began to say, "Oh my brothers—my brothers and my sisters," blessing them all as well as himself.

So what did it matter how many languages there were, or how hard it was to describe a glass of water? Or matter that a few minutes later he didn't feel anything like a brother toward the man who sold him the tickets?

On that very same afternoon he didn't hold so high an opinion of this same onrush of loving kindness. What did it come to? As they had the capacity and must use it once in a while, people were bound to have such involuntary feelings. It was only another one of those subway things. Like having a hard-on at random. But today, his day of reckoning, he consulted his memory again and thought, I must go back to that. That's the right clue and may do me the most good. Something very big. Truth, like.

The old fellow on the right, Mr. Rappaport, was nearly blind and kept asking Wilhelm, "What's the new figure on November wheat? Give me July soy beans too." When you told him he didn't say thank you. He said, "Okay," instead, or, "Check," and turned away until he needed you again. He was very old, older even than Dr. Adler, and if you believed Tamkin he had once been the Rockefeller of the chicken business and had retired with a large fortune.

Wilhelm had a queer feeling about the chicken industry, that it was sinister. On the road, he frequently passed chicken farms. Those big, rambling, wooden buildings out in the neglected fields; they were like prisons. The lights burned all night in them to cheat the poor hens into laying. Then the slaughter. Pile all the coops of the slaughtered on end, and in one week they'd go higher than Mount Everest or Mount Serenity. The blood filling the Gulf of Mexico. The chicken shit, acid, burning the earth.

How old—old this Mr. Rappaport was! Purple stains were buried in the flesh of his nose, and the cartilage of his ear was twisted like a cabbage heart. Beyond remedy by glasses, his eyes were smoky and faded.

"Read me that soy-bean figure now, boy," he said, and Wilhelm did. He thought perhaps the old man might give him a tip, or some useful advice or information about Tamkin. But no. He only wrote memoranda on a pad, and put the pad in his pocket. He let no one see what he had written. And Wilhelm thought this was the way a man who had grown rich by the murder of millions of animals, little chickens, would act. If there was a life to come he might have to answer for the killing of all those chickens. What if they all were waiting? But if there was a life to come, everybody would have to answer. But if there was a life to come, the chickens themselves would be all right.

Well! What stupid ideas he was having this morning. Phooey!

Finally old Rappaport did address a few remarks to Wilhelm. He asked him whether he had reserved his seat in the synagogue for Yom Kippur.

"No," said Wilhelm.

"Well, you better hurry up if you expect to say *Yiskor* for your parents. I never miss."

And Wilhelm thought, Yes, I suppose I should say a prayer for Mother once in a while. His mother had belonged to the Reform congregation. His father had no religion. At the cemetery Wilhelm had paid a man to say a prayer for her. He was among the tombs and he wanted to be tipped for the *El molai rachamin.* "Thou God of Mercy," Wilhelm thought that meant. *B'gan Aden*— "in Paradise." Singing, they drew it out. *B'gan Ayden.* The broken bench beside the grave made him wish to do something. Wilhelm often prayed in his own manner. He did not go to the synagogue but he would occasionally perform certain devotions, according to his feelings. Now he reflected, In Dad's eyes I am the wrong kind of Jew. He doesn't like the way I act. Only he is the right kind of Jew. Whatever you are, it always turns out to be the wrong kind.

Mr. Rappaport grumbled and whiffed at his long cigar. And the board, like a swarm of electrical bees, whirred.

"Since you were in the chicken business, I thought you'd speculate in eggs, Mr. Rappaport." Wilhelm, with his warm, panting laugh, sought to charm the old man.

"Oh. Yeah. Loyalty, hey?" said old Rappaport. "I should stick to them. I spent a lot of time amongst chickens. I got to be an expert chicken-sexer. When the chick hatches you have to tell the boys from the girls. It's not easy. You need long, long experience. What do you think, it's a joke? A whole industry depends on it. Yes, now and then I buy contract eggs. What have you got today?"

Wilhelm said anxiously, "Lard. Rye."

"Buy? Sell?"

"Bought."

"Uh," said the old man. Wilhelm could not determine what he meant by this. But of course you couldn't expect him to make himself any clearer. It was not in the code to give information to anyone. Sick with desire, Wilhem waited for Mr. Rappaport to make an exception in his case. Just this once! Because it was critical! Silently, by a sort of telepathic concentration, he begged the old man to speak the single word that would save him, give him the merest sign. "Oh, please—please help," he nearly said. If Rappaport would close one eye, or lay his head to one side, or raise his finger and point to a column in the paper or to a figure on his pad. A hint! A hint!

A long perfect ash formed on the end of the cigar, the white ghost of the leaf with all its veins and its fainter pungency. It was ignored, in its beauty, by the old man. For it was beautiful. Wilhelm he ignored as well.

Then Tamkin said to him, "Wilhelm, look at the jump our rye stock just took."

December rye climbed three points as they tensely watched; the tumblers raced and the machine's lights buzzed.

"A point and a half more, and we can cover the lard losses," said Tamkin. He showed him his calculations on the margin of the *Times*.

"I think you should put in the selling order now. Let's get out with a small loss."

"Get out now? Nothing doing."

"Why not? Why should we wait?"

"Because," said Tamkin with a smiling, almost openly scoffing look, "you've got to keep your nerve when the market starts to go places. Now's when you can make something."

"I'd get out while the getting's good."

"No, you shouldn't lose your head like this. It's obvious to me what the mechanism is, back in the Chicago market. There's a short supply of December rye. Look, it's just gone up another quarter. We should ride it."

"I'm losing my taste for the gamble," said Wilhelm. "You can't feel safe when it goes up so fast. It's liable to come down just as quick."

Dryly, as though he were dealing with a child, Tamkin told him in a tone of tiring patience, "Now listen, Tommy. I have it diagnosed right. If you wish I should sell I can give the sell order. But this is the difference between healthiness and pathology. One is objective, doesn't change his mind every minute, enjoys the risk element. But that's not the neurotic character. The neurotic character—"

"Damn it, Tamkin!" said Wilhelm roughly. "Cut that out. I don't like it. Leave my character out of consideration. Don't pull any more of that stuff on me. I tell you I don't like it."

Tamkin therefore went no further; he backed down. "I meant," he said, softer, "that as a salesman you are basically an artist type. The seller is in the visionary sphere of the business function. And then you're an actor, too."

"No matter what type I am—"An angry and yet weak sweetness rose into Wilhelm's throat. He coughed as though he had the flu. It was twenty years since he had appeared on the screen as an extra. He blew the bagpipes in a film called *Annie Laurie*. Annie had come to warn the young Laird; he would not believe her and called the bagpipers to drown her out. He made fun of her while she wrung her hands. Wilhelm, in a kilt, barelegged, blew and blew and blew and not a sound came out. Of course all the music was recorded. He fell sick with the flu after that and still suffered sometimes from chest weakness.

"Something stuck in your throat?" said Tamkin. "I think maybe you are too disturbed to think clearly. You should try some of my 'here-and-now' mental exercises. It stops you from thinking so much about the future and the past and cuts down confusion."

"Yes, yes, yes, yes," said Wilhelm, his eyes fixed on December rye.

"Nature only knows one thing, and that's the present. Present, present, eternal present, like a big, huge, giant wave—colossal, bright and beautiful, full of life and death, climbing into the sky, standing in the seas. You must go along with the actual, the Here-and-Now, the glory—"

. . . chest weakness, Wilhelm's recollection went on. Margaret nursed him. They had had two rooms of furniture, which was later seized. She sat on the bed and read to him. He made her read for days, and she read stories, poetry, everything in the house. He felt dizzy, stifled when he tried to smoke. They had him wear a flannel vest.

> Come then, Sorrow!
> Sweetest Sorrow!
> Like an own babe I nurse thee on my breast!

Why did he remember that? Why?

"You have to pick out something that's in the actual, immediate present moment," said Tamkin. "And say to yourself here-and-now, here-and-now, here-and-now. 'Where am I?' 'Here.' 'When is it?' 'Now.' Take an object or a person. Anybody. 'Here and now I see a person.' 'Here and now I see a man.'

'Here and now I see a man sitting on a chair.' Take me, for instance. Don't let your mind wander. 'Here and now I see a man in a brown suit. Here and now I see a corduroy shirt.' You have to narrow it down, one item at a time, and not let your imagination shoot ahead. Be in the present. Grasp the hour, the moment, the instant."

Is he trying to hypotize or con me? Wilhelm wondered. To take my mind off selling? But even if I'm back at seven hundred bucks, then where am I?

As if in prayer, his lids coming down with raised veins, frayed out, on his significant eyes, Tamkin said, " 'Here and now I see a button. Here and now I see the thread that sews the button. Here and now I see the green thread.' " Inch by inch he contemplated himself in order to show Wilhelm how calm it would make him. But Wilhelm was hearing Margaret's voice as she read, somewhat unwillingly,

Come then, Sorrow!

.   .   .

I thought to leave thee,
And deceive thee,
But now of all the world I love thee best.

Then Mr. Rappaport's old hand pressed his thigh, and he said, "What's my wheat? Those damn guys are blocking the way. I can't see."

VI

Rye was still ahead when they went out to lunch, and lard was holding its own.

They ate in the cafeteria with the gilded front. There was the same art inside as outside. The food looked sumptuous. Whole fishes were framed like pictures with carrots, and the salads were like terraced landscapes or like Mexican pyramids; slices of lemon and onion and radishes were like sun and moon and stars; the cream pies were about a foot thick and the cakes swollen as if sleepers had baked them in their dreams.

"What'll you have?" said Tamkin.

"Not much. I ate a big breakfast. I'll find a table. Bring me some yogurt and crackers and a cup of tea. I don't want to spend much time over lunch."

Tamkin said, "You've got to eat."

Finding an empty place at this hour was not easy. The old people idled and gossiped over their coffee. The elderly ladies were rouged and mascaraed and hennaed and used blue hair rinse and eye shadow and wore costume jewelry, and many of them were proud and stared at you with expressions that did not belong to their age. Were there no longer any respectable old ladies who knitted and cooked and looked after their grandchildren? Wilhelm's grandmother had dressed him in a sailor suit and danced him on her knee, blew on the porridge for him and said, "Admiral, you must eat." But what was the use of remembering this so late in the day? He managed to find a table, and Dr. Tamkin came along with a tray piled with plates and cups. He had Yankee pot roast, purple cabbage, potatoes, a big slice of watermelon, and two cups of coffee. Wilhelm could not even swallow his yogurt. His chest pained him still.

At once Tamkin involved him in a lengthy discussion. Did he do it to stall Wilhelm and prevent him from selling out the rye—or to recover the ground lost when he had made Wilhelm angry by hints about the neurotic character? Or did he have no purpose except to talk?

"I think you worry a lot too much about what your wife and your father will say. Do they matter so much?"

Wilhelm replied, "A person can become tired of looking himself over and trying to fix himself up. You can spend the entire second half of your life recovering from the mistakes of the first half."

"I believe your dad told me he had some money to leave you."

"He probably does have something."

"A lot?"

"Who can tell," said Wilhelm guardedly.

"You ought to think over what you'll do with it."

"I may be too feeble to do anything by the time I get it. If I get anything."

"A thing like this you ought to plan out carefully. Invest it properly." He began to unfold schemes whereby you bought bonds, and used the bonds as security to buy something else and thereby earned twelve per cent safely on your money. Wilhelm failed to follow the details. Tamkin said, "If he made you a gift now, you wouldn't have to pay the inheritance taxes."

Bitterly, Wilhelm told him, "My father's death blots out all other considerations from his mind. He forces me to think about it, too. Then he hates me because he succeeds. When I get desperate—of course I think about money. But I don't want anything to happen to him. I certainly don't want him to die." Tamkin's brown eyes glittered shrewdly at him. "You don't believe it. Maybe it's not psychological. But on my word of honor. A joke is a joke, but I don't want to joke about stuff like this. When he dies, I'll be robbed, like. I'll have no more father."

"You love your old man?"

Wilhelm grasped at this. "Of course, of course I love him. My father. My mother—" As he said this there was a great pull at the very center of his soul. When a fish strikes the line you feel the live force in your hand. A mysterious being beneath the water, driven by hunger, has taken the hook and rushes away and fights, writhing. Wilhelm never identified what struck within him. It did not reveal itself. It got away.

And Tamkin, the confuser of the imagination, began to tell, or to fabricate, the strange history of *his* father. "He was a great singer," he said. "He left us five kids because he fell in love with an opera soprano. I never held it against him, but admired the way he followed the life-principle. I wanted to do the same. Because of unhappiness, at a certain age, the brain starts to die back." (True, true! thought Wilhelm.) "Twenty years later I was doing experiments in Eastman Kodak, Rochester, and I found the old fellow. He had five more children." (False, false!) "He wept; he was ashamed. I had nothing against him. I naturally felt strange."

"My dad is something of a stranger to me, too," said Wilhelm, and he began to muse. Where is the familiar person he used to be? Or I used to be? Catherine —she won't even talk to me any more, my own sister. It may not be so much my trouble that Papa turns his back on as my confusion. It's too much. The ruins of life, and on top of that confusion—chaos and old night. Is it an easier farewell for Dad if we don't part friends? He should maybe do it angrily— "Blast you with my curse!" And why, Wilhelm further asked, should he or anybody else pity me; or why should I be pitied sooner than another fellow? It is my childish mind that thinks people are ready to give it just because you need it.

Then Wilhelm began to think about his own two sons and to wonder how he appeared to them, and what they would think of him. Right now he had an advantage through baseball. When he went to fetch them, to go to Ebbets Field, though, he was not himself. He put on a front but he felt as if he had swallowed a fistful of sand. The strange, familiar house, horribly awkward; the dog, Scissors, rolled over on his back and barked and whined. Wilhelm acted as if there were nothing irregular, but a weary heaviness came over him. On the way to Flatbush he would think up anecdotes about old Pigtown and Charlie Ebbets for the boys and reminiscences of the old stars, but it was very heavy going. They did not know how much he cared for them. No. It hurt him greatly and he blamed Margaret for turning them against him. She wanted to ruin him, while she wore the mask of kindness. Up in Roxbury he had to go and explain to the priest, who was not sympathetic. They don't care about individuals, their rules come first. Olive said she would marry him outside the Church when he was divorced. But Margaret would not let go. Olive's father was a pretty decent old guy, an osteopath, and he understood what it was all about. Finally he said, "See here, I have to advise Olive. She is asking me. I am mostly a free-thinker myself, but the girl has to live in this town." And by now Wilhelm and Olive had had a great many troubles and she was beginning to dread his days in Roxbury, she said. He trembled at offending this small, pretty, dark girl whom he adored. When she would get up late on Sunday morning she would wake him almost in tears at being late for Mass. He would try to help her hitch her garters and smooth out her slip and dress and even put on her hat with shaky hands; then he would rush her to church and drive in second gear in his forgetful way, trying to apologize and to calm her. She got out a block from church to avoid gossip. Even so she loved him, and she would have married him if he had obtained the divorce. But Margaret must have sensed this. Margaret would tell him he did not really want a divorce; he was afraid of it. He cried, "Take everything I've got, Margaret. Let me go to Reno. Don't you want to marry again?" No. She went out with other men, but took his money. She lived in order to punish him.

Dr. Tamkin told Wilhelm, "Your dad is jealous of you."

Wilhelm smiled. "Of *me*? That's rich."

"Sure. People are always jealous of a man who leaves his wife."

"Oh," said Wilhelm scornfully. "When it comes to wives he wouldn't have to envy me."

"Yes, and your wife envies you, too. She thinks, He's free and goes with young women. Is she getting old?"

"Not exactly old," said Wilhelm, whom the mention of his wife made sad. Twenty years ago, in a neat blue wool suit, in a soft hat made of the same cloth—he could plainly see her. He stooped his yellow head and looked under the hat at her clear, simple face, her living eyes moving, her straight small nose, her jaw beautifully, painfully clear in its form. It was a cool day, but he smelled the odor of pines in the sun, in the granite canyon. Just south of Santa Barbara, this was.

"She's forty-some years old," he said.

"I was married to a lush," said Tamkin. "A painful alcoholic. I couldn't take her out to dinner because she'd say she was going to the ladies' toilet and disappear into the bar. I'd ask the bartenders they shouldn't serve her. But I loved her deeply. She was the most spiritual woman of my entire experience."

"Where is she now?"

"Drowned," said Tamkin. "At Provincetown, Cape Cod. It must have been a suicide. She was that way—suicidal. I tried everything in my power to cure her. Because," said Tamkin, "my real calling is to be a healer. I get wounded. I suffer from it. I would like to escape from the sicknesses of others, but I can't. I am only on loan to myself, so to speak. I belong to humanity."

Liar! Wilhelm inwardly called him. Nasty lies. He invented a woman and killed her off and then called himself a healer, and made himself so earnest he looked like a bad-natured sheep. He's a puffed-up little bogus and humbug with smelly feet. A doctor! A doctor would wash himself. He believes he's making a terrific impression, and he practically invites you to take off your hat when he talks about himself; and he thinks he has an imagination, but he hasn't; neither is he smart.

Then what am I doing with him here, and why did I give him the seven hundred dollars? thought Wilhelm.

Oh, this was a day of reckoning. It was a day, he thought, on which, willing or not, he would take a good close look at the truth. He breathed hard and his misshapen hat came low upon his congested dark blond face. A rude look. Tamkin was a charlatan, and furthermore he was desperate. And furthermore, Wilhelm had always known this about him. But he appeared to have worked it out at the back of his mind that Tamkin for thirty or forty years had gotten through many a tight place, that he would get through this crisis too and bring him, Wilhelm, to safety also. And Wilhelm realized that he was on Tamkin's back. It made him feel that he had virtually left the ground and was riding upon the other man. He was in the air. It was for Tamkin to take the steps.

The doctor, if he was a doctor, did not look anxious. But then his face did not have much variety. Talking always about spontaneous emotion and open receptors and free impulses, he was about as expressive as a pincushion. When his hypnotic spell failed, his big underlip made him look weak-minded. Fear stared from his eyes, sometimes, so humble as to make you sorry for him. Once or twice Wilhelm had seen that look. Like a dog, he thought. Perhaps he didn't look it now, but he was very nervous. Wilhelm knew, but he could not afford to recognize this too openly. The doctor needed a little room, a little time. He should not be pressed now. So Tamkin went on, telling his tales.

Wilhelm said to himself, I am on his back—his back. I gambled seven hundred bucks, so I must take this ride. I have to go along with him. It's too late. I can't get off.

"You know," Tamkin said, "that blind old man Rappaport—he's pretty close to totally blind—is one of the most interesting personalities around here. If you could only get him to tell his true story. It's fascinating. This is what he told me. You often hear about bigamists with a secret life. But this old man never hid anything from anybody. He's a regular patriarch. Now, I'll tell you what he did. He had two whole families, separate and apart, one in Williamsburg and the other in The Bronx. The two wives knew about each other. The wife in The Bronx was younger; she's close to seventy now. When he got sore at one wife he went to live with the other one. Meanwhile he ran his chicken business in New Jersey. By one wife he had four kids, and by the other six. They're all grown, but they never have met their half-brothers and sisters and don't want to. The whole bunch of them are listed in the telephone book."

"I can't believe it," said Wilhelm.

"He told me this himself. And do you know what else? While he had his eyesight he used to read a lot, but the only books he would read were by Theodore Roosevelt. He had a set in each of the places where he lived, and he brought his kids up on those books."

"Please," said Wilhelm, "don't feed me any more of this stuff, will you? Kindly do not—"

"In telling you this," said Tamkin with one of his hypnotic subtleties, "I do have a motive. I want you to see how some people free themselves from morbid guilt feelings and follow their instincts. Innately, the female knows how to cripple by sickening a man with guilt. It is a very special *destruct*, and she sends her curse to make a fellow impotent. As if she says, 'Unless I allow it, you will never more be a man.' But men like my old dad or Mr. Rappaport answer, 'Woman, what art thou to me?' You can't do that yet. You're a halfway case. You want to follow your instinct, but you're too worried still. For instance, about your kids—"

"Now look here," said Wilhelm, stamping his feet. "One thing! Don't bring up my boys. Just lay off."

"I was only going to say that they are better off than with conflicts in the home."

"I'm deprived of my children." Wilhelm bit his lip. It was too late to turn away. The anguish struck him. "I pay and pay. I never see them. They grow up without me. She makes them like herself. She'll bring them up to be my enemies. Please let's not talk about this."

But Tamkin said, "Why do you let her make you suffer so? It defeats the original object in leaving her. Don't play her game. Now, Wilhelm, I'm trying to do you some good. I want to tell you, don't marry suffering. Some people do. They get married to it, and sleep and eat together, just as husband and wife. If they go with joy they think it's adultery."

When Wilhelm heard this he had, in spite of himself, to admit that there was a great deal in Tamkin's words. Yes, thought Wilhelm, suffering is the only kind of life they are sure they can have, and if they quit suffering they're afraid they'll have nothing. He knows it. This time the faker knows what he's talking about.

Looking at Tamkin he believed he saw all this confessed from his usually barren face. Yes, yes, he too. One hundred falsehoods, but at last one truth. Howling like a wolf from the city window. No one can bear it any more. Everyone is so full of it that at last everybody must proclaim it. It! It!

Then suddenly Wilhelm rose and said, "That's enough of this. Tamkin, let's go back to the market."

"I haven't finished my melon."

"Never mind that. You've had enough to eat. I want to go back."

Dr. Tamkin slid the two checks across the table. "Who paid yesterday? It's your turn, I think."

It was not until they were leaving the cafeteria that Wilhelm remembered definitely that he had paid yesterday too. But it wasn't worth arguing about.

Tamkin kept repeating as they walked down the street that there were many who were dedicated to suffering. But he told Wilhelm, "I'm optimistic in your case, and I have seen a world of maladjustment. There's hope for you. You don't really want to destroy yourself. You're trying hard to keep your feelings open, Wilhelm. I can see it. Seven per cent of this country is committing suicide by alcohol. Another three, maybe, narcotics. Another sixty just fading away into dust by boredom. Twenty more who have sold their souls to the Devil. Then there's a small percentage of those who want to live. That's the only significant thing in the whole world of today. Those are the only two classes of people there are. Some want to live, but the great majority don't." This fantastic Tamkin began to surpass himself. "They don't. Or else, why these wars? I'll tell you more," he said. "The love of the dying amounts to one thing; they want you to die with them. It's because they love you. Make no mistake."

True, true! thought Wilhelm, profoundly moved by these revelations. How does he know these things? How can he be such a jerk, and even perhaps an operator, a swindler, and understand so well what gives? I believe what he says. It simplifies much—everything. People are dropping like flies. I am trying to stay alive and work too hard at it. That's what's turning my brains. This working hard defeats its own end. At what point should I start over? Let me go back a ways and try once more.

Only a few hundred yards separated the cafeteria from the broker's, and within that short space Wilhelm turned again, in measurable degrees, from these wide considerations to the problems of the moment. The closer he approached to the market, the more Wilhelm had to think about money.

They passed the newsreel theater where the ragged shoeshine kids called after them. The same old bearded man with his bandaged beggar face and his tiny ragged feet and the old press clipping on his fiddle case to prove he had once been a concert violinist, pointed his bow at Wilhelm, saying, "You!" Wilhelm went by with worried eyes, bent on crossing Seventy-second Street. In full tumult the great afternoon current raced for Columbus Circle, where the mouth of midtown stood open and the skyscrapers gave back the yellow fire of the sun.

As they approached the polished stone front of the new office building, Dr. Tamkin said, "Well, isn't that old Rappaport by the door? I think he should carry a white cane, but he will never admit there's a single thing the matter with his eyes."

Mr. Rappaport did not stand well; his knees were sunk, while his pelvis only half filled his trousers. His suspenders held them, gaping.

He stopped Wilhelm with an extended hand, having somehow recognized him. In his deep voice he commanded him, "Take me to the cigar store."

"You want me—? Tamkin!" Wilhelm whispered, "You take him."

Tamkin shook his head. "He wants you. Don't refuse the old gentleman." Significantly he said in a lower voice, "This minute is another instance of the 'here-and-now.' You have to live in this very minute, and you don't want to. A man asks you for help. Don't think of the market. It won't run away. Show your respect to the old boy. Go ahead. That may be more valuable."

"Take me," said the old chicken merchant again.

Greatly annoyed, Wilhelm wrinkled his face at Tamkin. He took the old man's big but light elbow at the bone. "Well, let's step on it," he said. "Or wait—I want to have a look at the board first to see how we're doing."

But Tamkin had already started Mr. Rappaport forward. He was walking, and he scolded Wilhelm, saying, "Don't leave me standing in the middle of the sidewalk. I'm afraid to get knocked over."

"Let's get a move on. Come." Wilhelm urged him as Tamkin went into the broker's.

The traffic seemed to come down Broadway out of the sky, where the hot spokes of the sun rolled from the south. Hot, stony odors rose from the subway grating in the street.

"These teen-age hoodlums worry me. I'm ascared of these Puerto Rican kids, and these young characters who take dope," said Mr. Rappaport. "They go around all hopped up."

"Hoodlums?" said Wilhelm. "I went to the cemetery and my mother's stone bench was split. I could have broken somebody's neck for that. Which store do you go to?"

"Across Broadway. That La Magnita sign next door to the Automat."

"What's the matter with this store here on this side?"

"They don't carry my brand, that's what's the matter."

Wilhelm cursed, but checked the words.

"What are you talking?"

"Those damn taxis," said Wilhelm. "They want to run everybody down."

They entered the cool, odorous shop. Mr. Rappaport put away his large cigars with great care in various pockets while Wilhelm muttered, "Come on, you old creeper. What a poky old character! The whole world waits on him." Rappaport did not offer Wilhelm a cigar, but, holding one up, he asked, "What do you say at the size of these, huh? They're Churchill-type cigars."

He barely crawls along, thought Wilhelm. His pants are dropping off because he hasn't got enough flesh for them to stick to. He's almost blind, and covered with spots, but this old man still makes money in the market. Is loaded with dough, probably. And I bet he doesn't give his children any. Some of them must be in their fifties. This is what keeps middle-aged men as children. He's master over the dough. Think—just think! Who controls everything? Old men of this type. Without needs. They don't need therefore they have. I need, therefore I don't have. That would be too easy.

"I'm older even than Churchill," said Rappaport.

Now he wanted to talk! But if you asked him a question in the market, he couldn't be bothered to answer.

"I bet you are," said Wilhelm. "Come, let's get going."

"I was a fighter, too, like Churchill," said the old man. "When we licked Spain I went into the Navy. Yes, I was a gob that time. What did I have to lose? Nothing. After the battle of San Juan Hill, Teddy Roosevelt kicked me off the beach."

"Come, watch the curb," said Wilhelm.

"I was curious and wanted to see what went on. I didn't have no business there, but I took a boat and rowed myself to the beach. Two of our guys were dead, layin' under the American flag to keep the flies off. So I says to the guy on duty, there, who was the sentry, 'Let's have a look at these guys. I want to see what went on here,' and he says, 'Naw,' but I talked him into it. So he took off the flag and there were these two tall guys, both gentlemen, lying in their boots. They was very tall. The two of them had long mustaches. They were high-society boys. I think one of them was called Fish, from up the Hudson, a big-shot family. When I looked up, there was Teddy Roosevelt, with his hat off, and he was looking at these fellows, the only ones who got killed there. Then he says to me. 'What's the Navy want here? Have you got orders?' 'No, sir,' I says to him. 'Well, get the hell off the beach, then.' "

Old Rappaport was very proud of this memory. "Everything he said had such snap, such class. Man! I love that Teddy Roosevelt," he said, "I love him!"

Ah, what people are! He is almost not with us, and his life is nearly gone, but T. R. once yelled at him, so he loves him. I guess it is love, too. Wilhelm smiled. So maybe the rest of Tamkin's story was true, about the ten children and the wives and the telephone directory.

He said, "Come on, come on, Mr. Rappaport," and hurried the old man back by the large hollow elbow; he gripped it through the thin cotton cloth. Re-entering the brokerage office where under the lights the tumblers were speeding with the clack of drumsticks upon wooden blocks, more than ever resembling a Chinese theater, Wilhelm strained his eyes to see the board.

The lard figures were unfamiliar. That amount couldn't be lard! They must have put the figures in the wrong slot. He traced the line back to the margin. It was down to .19, and had dropped twenty points since noon. And what about the contract of rye? It had sunk back to its earlier position, and they had lost their chance to sell.

Old Mr. Rappaport said to Wilhelm, "Read me my wheat figure."

"Oh, leave me alone for a minute," he said, and positively hid his face from the old man behind one hand. He looked for Tamkin, Tamkin's bald head, or Tamkin with his gray straw and the cocoa-colored band. He couldn't see him. Where was he? The seats next to Rowland were taken by strangers. He thrust himself over the one on the aisle, Mr. Rappaport's former place, and pushed at the back of the chair until the new occupant, a red-headed man with a thin, determined face, leaned forward to get out of his way but would not surrender the seat. "Where's Tamkin?" Wilhelm asked Rowland.

"Gee, I don't know. Is anything wrong?"

"You must have seen him. He came in a while back."

"No, but I didn't."

Wilhelm fumbled out a pencil from the top pocket of his coat and began to make calculations. His very fingers were numb, and in his agitation he was afraid he made mistakes with the decimal points and went over the subtraction and multiplication like a schoolboy at an exam. His heart, accustomed to many sorts of crisis, was now in a new panic. And, as he had dreaded, he was wiped out. It was unnecessary to ask the German manager. He could see for himself that the electronic bookkeeping device must have closed him out. The manager probably had known that Tamkin wasn't to be trusted, and on that first day he might have warned him. But you couldn't expect him to interfere.

"You get hit?" said Mr. Rowland.

And Wilhelm, quite coolly, said, "Oh, it could have been worse, I guess." He put the piece of paper into his pocket with its cigarette butts and packets of pills. The lie helped him out—although, for a moment, he was afraid he would cry. But he hardened himself. The hardening effort made a violent, vertical pain go through his chest, like that caused by a pocket of air under the collar bones. To the old chicken millionaire, who by this time had become acquainted with the drop in rye and lard, he also denied that anything serious had happened. "It's just one of those temporary slumps. Nothing to be scared about," he said, and remained in possession of himself. His need to cry, like someone in a crowd, pushed and jostled and abused him from behind, and Wilhelm did not dare turn. He said to himself, I will not cry in front of these people. I'll be damned if I'll break down in front of them like a kid, even though I never expect to see them again. No! No! And yet his unshed tears rose and rose and he looked like a man about to drown. But when they talked to him, he answered very distinctly. He tried to speak proudly.

". . . going away?" he heard Rowland ask.

"Why?"

"I thought you might be going away too. Tamkin said he was going to Maine this summer for his vacation."

"Oh, going away?"

Wilhelm broke off and went to look for Tamkin in the men's toilet. Across the corridor was the room where the machinery of the board was housed. It hummed and whirred like mechanical birds, and the tubes glittered in the dark. A couple of businessmen with cigarettes in their fingers were having a conversation in the lavatory. At the top of the closet door sat a gray straw hat with a cocoa-colored band. "Tamkin," said Wilhelm. He tried to identify the feet below the door. "Are you in there, Doctor Tamkin?" he said with stifled anger. "Answer me. It's Wilhelm."

The hat was taken down, the latch lifted, and a stranger came out who looked at him with annoyance.

"You waiting?" said one of the businessmen. He was warning Wilhelm that he was out of turn.

"Me? Not me," said Wilhelm. "I'm looking for a fellow."

Bitterly angry, he said to himself that Tamkin would pay him the two hundred dollars at least, his share of the original deposit. "And before he takes the train to Maine, too. Before he spends a penny on vacation—that liar! We went into this as equal partners."

VII

I was the man beneath; Tamkin was on my back, and I thought I was on his. He made me carry him, too, besides Margaret. Like this they ride on me with hoofs and claws. Tear me to pieces, stamp on me and break my bones.

Once more the hoary old fiddler pointed his bow at Wilhelm as he hurried by. Wilhelm rejected his begging and denied the omen. He dodged heavily through traffic and with his quick, small steps ran up the lower stairway of the Gloriana Hotel with its dark-tinted mirrors, kind to people's defects. From the lobby he phoned Tamkin's room, and when no one answered he took the elevator up. A rouged woman in her fifties with a mink stole led three tiny dogs on a leash, high-strung creatures with prominent black eyes, like dwarf deer, and legs like twigs. This was the eccentric Estonian lady who had been moved with her pets to the twelfth floor.

She identified Wilhelm. "You are Doctor Adler's son," she said.

Formally, he nodded.

"I am a dear friend of your father."

He stood in the corner and would not meet her glance, and she thought he was snubbing her and made a mental note to speak of it to the doctor.

The linen-wagon stood at Tamkin's door, and the chambermaid's key with its big brass tongue was in the lock.

"Has Doctor Tamkin been here?" he asked her.

"No, I haven't seen him."

Wilhelm came in, however, to look around. He examined the photos on the desk, trying to connect the faces with the strange people in Tamkin's stories. Big, heavy volumes were stacked under the double-pronged TV aerial. *Science and Sanity*, he read, and there were several books of poetry. The *Wall Street*

Journal hung in separate sheets from the bed-table under the weight of the silver water jug. A bathrobe with lightening streaks of red and white was laid across the foot of the bed with a pair of expensive batik pajamas. It was a box of a room, but from the windows you saw the river as far uptown as the bridge, as far downtown at Hoboken. What lay between was deep, azure, dirty, complex, crystal, rusty, with the red bones of new apartments rising on the bluffs of New Jersey, and huge liners in their berths, the tugs with matted beards of cordage. Even the brackish tidal river smell rose this high, like the smell of mop water. From every side he heard pianos, and the voices of men and women singing scales and opera, all mixed, and the sounds of pigeons on the ledges.

Again Wilhelm took the phone. "Can you locate Doctor Tamkin in the lobby for me?" he asked. And when the operator reported that she could not, Wilhelm gave the number of his father's room, but Dr. Adler was not in either. "Well, please give me the masseur. I say the massage room. Don't you understand me? The men's health club. Yes, Max Schilper's—how am I supposed to know the name of it?"

There a strange voice said, "Toktor Adler?" It was the old Czech prizefighter with the deformed nose and ears who was attendant down there and gave out soap, sheets, and sandals. He went away. A hollow endless silence followed. Wilhelm flickered the receiver with his nails, whistled into it, but could not summon either the attendant or the operator.

The maid saw him examining the bottles of pills on Tamkin's table and seemed suspicious of him. He was running low on Phenaphen pills and was looking for something else. But he swallowed one of his own tablets and went out and rang again for the elevator. He went down to the health club. Through the steamy windows, when he emerged, he saw the reflection of the swimming pool swirling green at the bottom of the lowest stairway. He went through the locker-room curtains. Two men wrapped in towels were playing Ping-Pong. They were awkward and the ball bounded high. The Negro in the toilet was shining shoes. He did not know Dr. Adler by name, and Wilhelm descended to the massage room. On the tables naked men were lying. It was not a brightly lighted place, and it was very hot, and under the white faint moons of the ceiling shone pale skins. Calendar pictures of pretty girls dressed in tiny fringes were pinned on the wall. On the first table, eyes deeply shut in heavy silent luxury lay a man with a full square beard and short legs, stocky and blackhaired. He might have been an orthodox Russian. Wrapped in a sheet, waiting, the man beside him was newly shaved and red from the steambath. He had a big happy face and was dreaming. And after him was an athlete, strikingly muscled, powerful and young, with a strong white curve to his genital and a half-angry smile on his mouth. Dr. Adler was on the fourth table, and Wilhelm stood over his father's pale, slight body. His ribs were narrow and small, his belly round, white, and high. It had its own being, like something separate. His thighs were weak, the muscles of his arms had fallen, his throat was creased.

The masseur in his undershirt bent and whispered in his ear, "It's your son," and Dr. Adler opened his eyes into Wilhelm's face. At once he saw the trouble in it, and by an instantaneous reflex he removed himself from the danger of contagion, and he said serenely, "Well, have you taken my advice, Wilky?"

"Oh, Dad," said Wilhelm.

"To take a swim and get a massage?"

"Did you get my note?" said Wilhelm.

"Yes, but I'm afraid you'll have to ask somebody else, because I can't. I had no idea you were so low on funds. How did you let it happen? Didn't you lay anything aside?"

"Oh, please, Dad," said Wilhelm, almost bringing his hands together in a clasp.

"I'm sorry," said the doctor. "I really am. But I have set up a rule. I've thought about it, I believe it is a good rule, and I don't want to change it. You haven't acted wisely. What's the matter?"

"Everything. Just everything. What isn't? I did have a little, but I haven't been very smart."

"You took some gamble? You lost it? Was it Tamkin? I told you, Wilky, not to build on that Tamkin. Did you? I suspect—"

"Yes, Dad, I'm afraid I trusted him."

Dr. Adler surrendered his arm to the masseur, who was using wintergreen oil.

"Trusted! And got taken?"

"I'm afraid I kind of—" Wilhelm glanced at the masseur but he was absorbed in his work. He probably did not listen to conversations. "I did. I might as well say it. I should have listened to you."

"Well, I won't remind you how often I warned you. It must be very painful."

"Yes, Father, it is."

"I don't know how many times you have to be burned in order to learn something. The same mistakes, over and over."

"I couldn't agree with you more," said Wilhelm with a face of despair. "You're so right, Father. It's the same mistakes, and I get burned again and again. I can't seem to—I'm stupid, Dad, I just can't breathe. My chest is all up—I feel choked. I just simply can't catch my breath."

He stared at his father's nakedness. Presently he became aware that Dr. Adler was making an effort to keep his temper. He was on the verge of an explosion. Wilhelm hung his face and said, "Nobody likes bad luck, eh Dad?"

"So! It's bad luck, now. A minute ago it was stupidity."

"It is stupidity—it's some of both. It's true that I can't learn. But I—"

"I don't want to listen to the details," said his father. "And I want you to understand that I'm too old to take on new burdens. I'm just too old to do it. And people who will just wait for help—must *wait* for help. They have got to stop waiting."

"It isn't all a question of money—there are other things a father can give to a son." He lifted up his gray eyes and his nostrils grew wide with a look of suffering appeal that stirred his father even more deeply against him.

He warningly said to him, "Look out, Wilky, you're tiring my patience very much."

"I try not to. But one word from you, just a word, would go a long way. I've never asked you for very much. But you are not a kind man, Father. You don't give the little bit I beg you for."

He recognized that his father was now furiously angry. Dr. Adler started to say something, and then raised himself and gathered the sheet over him as he did so. His mouth opened, wide, dark, twisted, and he said to Wilhelm, "You want to make yourself into my cross. But I am not going to pick up a cross. I'll see you dead, Wilky, by Christ, before I let you do that to me."

"Father, listen! Listen!"

"Go away from me now. It's torture for me to look at you, you slob!" cried Dr. Adler.

Wilhelm's blood rose up madly, in anger equal to his father's, but then it sank down and left him helplessly captive to misery. He said stiffly, and with a strange sort of formality, "Okay, Dad. That'll be enough. That's about all we should say." And he stalked out heavily by the door adjacent to the swimming pool and the steam room, and labored up two long flights from the basement. Once more he took the elevator to the lobby on the mezzanine.

He inquired at the desk for Dr. Tamkin.

The clerk said, "No, I haven't seen him. But I think there's something in the box for you."

"Me? Give it here," said Wilhelm and opened a telephone message from his wife. It read, "Please phone Mrs. Wilhelm on return. Urgent."

Whenever he received an urgent message from his wife he was always thrown into a great fear for the children. He ran to the phone booth, spilled out the change from his pockets onto the little curved steel shelf under the telephone, and dialed the Digby number.

"Yes?" said his wife. Scissors barked in the parlor.

"Margaret?"

"Yes, hello." They never exchanged any other greeting. She instantly knew his voice.

"The boys all right?"

"They're out on their bicycles. Why shouldn't they be all right? Scissors, quiet!"

"Your message scared me," he said. "I wish you wouldn't make 'urgent' so common."

"I had something to tell you."

Her familiar unbending voice awakened in him a kind of hungry longing, not for Margaret but for the peace he had once known.

"You sent me a postdated check," she said. "I can't allow that. It's already five days past the first. You dated your check for the twelfth."

"Well, I have no money. I haven't got it. You can't send me to prison for that. I'll be lucky if I can raise it by the twelfth."

She answered, "You better get it, Tommy."

"Yes? What for?" he said. "Tell me. For the sake of what? To tell lies about me to everyone? You—"

She cut him off. "You know what for. I've got the boys to bring up."

Wilhelm in the narrow booth broke into a heavy sweat. He dropped his head and shrugged while with his fingers he arranged nickels, dimes, and quarters in rows. "I'm doing my best," he said. "I've had some bad luck. As a matter of fact, it's been so bad that I don't know where I am. I couldn't tell you what day of the week this is. I can't think straight. I'd better not even try. This has been one of those days, Margaret. May I never live to go through another like it. I mean that with all my heart. So I'm not going to try to do any thinking today. Tomorrow I'm going to see some guys. One is a sales manager. The other is in television. But not to act," he hastily added. "On the business end."

"That's just some more of your talk, Tommy," she said. "You ought to patch things up with Rojax Corporation. They'd take you back. You've got to stop thinking like a youngster."

"What do you mean?"

"Well," she said, measured and unbending, remorselessly unbending, "you still think like a youngster. But you can't do that any more. Every other day you want to make a new start. But in eighteen years you'll be eligible for retirement. Nobody wants to hire a new man of your age."

"I know. But listen, you don't have to sound so hard. I can't get on my knees to them. And really you don't have to sound so hard. I haven't done you so much harm."

"Tommy, I have to chase you and ask you for money that you owe us, and I hate it."

She hated also to be told that her voice was hard.

"I'm making an effort to control myself," she told him.

He could picture her, her graying bangs cut with strict fixity above her pretty, decisive face. She prided herself on being fair-minded. We could not bear, he thought, to know what we do. Even though blood is spilled. Even though the breath of life is taken from someone's nostrils. This is the way of the weak; quiet and fair. And then smash! They smash!

"Rojax take me back? I'd have to crawl back. They don't need me. After so many years I should have got stock in the firm. How can I support the three of you, and live myself, on half the territory? And why should I even try when you won't lift a finger to help? I sent you back to school, didn't I? At that time you said—"

His voice was rising. She did not like that and intercepted him. "You misunderstood me," she said.

"You must realize you're killing me. You can't be as blind as all that. Thou shalt not kill! Don't you remember that?"

She said, "You're just raving now. When you calm down it'll be different. I have great confidence in your earning ability."

"Margaret, you don't grasp the situation. You'll have to get a job."

"Absolutely not. I'm not going to have two young children running loose."

"They're not babies," Wilhelm said. "Tommy is fourteen. Paulie is going to be ten."

"Look," Margaret said in her deliberate manner. "We can't continue this conversation if you're going to yell so, Tommy. They're at a dangerous age. There are teen-aged gangs—the parents working, or the families broken up."

Once again she was reminding him that it was he who had left her. She had the bringing up of the children as her burden, while he must expect to pay the price of his freedom.

Freedom! he thought with consuming bitterness. Ashes in his mouth, not freedom. Give me my children. For they are mine too.

Can you be the woman I lived with? he started to say. Have you forgotten that we slept so long together? Must you now deal with me like this, and have no mercy?

He would be better off with Margaret again than he was today. This was what she wanted to make him feel, and she drove it home. "Are you in misery?" she was saying. "But you have deserved it." And he could not return to her any more than he could beg Rojax to take him back. If it cost him his life, he could not. Margaret had ruined him with Olive. She hit him and hit him, beat him, battered him, wanted to beat the very life out of him.

"Margaret, I want you please to reconsider about work. You have that degree now. Why did I pay your tuition?"

"Because it seemed practical. But it isn't. Growing boys need parental authority and a home."

He begged her, "Margaret, go easy on me. You ought to. I'm at the end of my rope and feel that I'm suffocating. You don't want to be responsible for a person's destruction. You've got to let up. I feel I'm about to burst." His face had expanded. He struck a blow upon the tin and wood and nails of the wall of the booth. "You've got to let me breathe. If I should keel over, what then? And it's something I can never understand about you. How you can treat someone like this whom you lived with so long. Who gave you the best of himself. Who tried. Who loved you." Merely to pronounce the word "love" made him tremble.

"Ah," she said with a sharp breath. "Now we're coming to it. How did you imagine it was going to be—big shot? Everything made smooth for you? I thought you were leading up to this."

She had not, perhaps, intended to reply as harshly as she did, but she brooded a great deal and now she could not forbear to punish him and make him feel pains like those she had to undergo.

He struck the wall again, this time with his knuckles, and he had scarcely enough air in his lungs to speak in a whisper, because his heart pushed upward with a frightful pressure. He got up and stamped his feet in the narrow enclosure.

"Haven't I always done my best?" he yelled, though his voice sounded weak and thin to his own ears. "Everything comes from me and nothing back again to me. There's no law that'll punish this, but you are committing a crime against me. Before God—and that's no joke. I mean that. Before God! Sooner or later the boys will know it."

In a firm tone, levelly, Margaret said to him, "I won't stand to be howled at. When you can speak normally and have something sensible to say I'll listen. But not to this." She hung up.

Wilhelm tried to tear the apparatus from the wall. He ground his teeth and seized the black box with insane digging fiingers and made a stifled cry and pulled. Then he saw an elderly lady staring through the glass door, utterly appalled by him, and he ran from the booth, leaving a large amount of change on the shelf. He hurried down the stairs and into the street.

On Broadway it was still bright afternoon and the gassy air was almost motionless under the leaden spokes of sunlight, and sawdust footprints lay about the doorways of butcher shops and fruit stores. And the great, great crowd, the inexhaustible current of millions of every race and kind pouring out, pressing round, of every age, of every genius, possessors of every human secret, antique and future, in every face the refinement of one particular motive or essence—*I labor, I spend, I strive, I design, I love, I cling, I uphold, I give way, I envy, I long, I scorn, I die, I hide, I want.* Faster, much faster than any man could make the tally. The sidewalks were wider than any causeway; the street itself was immense, and it quaked and gleamed and it seemed to Wilhelm to throb at the last limit of endurance. And although the sunlight appeared like a broad tissue, its actual weight made him feel like a drunkard.

"I'll get a divorce if it's the last thing I do," he swore. "As for Dad— As for Dad— I'll have to sell the car for junk and pay the hotel. I'll have to go on my knees to Olive and say, 'Stand by me a while. Don't let her win. Olive!' " And he thought, I'll try to start again with Olive. In fact, I must. Olive loves me. Olive—

Beside a row of limousines near the curb he thought he saw Dr. Tamkin. Of course he had been mistaken before about the hat with the cocoa-colored band and didn't want to make the same mistake twice. But wasn't that Tamkin who was speaking so earnestly, with pointed shoulders, to someone under the canopy of the funeral parlor? For this was a huge funeral. He looked for the singular face under the dark gray, fashionable hatbrim. There were two open cars filled with fllowers, and a policeman tried to keep a path open to pedestrians. Right at the canopy-pole, now wasn't that that damned Tamkin talking away with a solemn face, gesticulating with an open hand?

"Tamkin!" shouted Wilhelm, going forward. But he was pushed to the side by a policeman clutching his nightstick at both ends, like a rolling pin. Wilhelm was even farther from Tamkin now, and swore under his breath at the cop who continued to press him back, back, belly and ribs, saying, "Keep it moving there, please," his face red with impatient sweat, his brow like red fur. Wilhelm said to him haughtily, "You shouldn't push people like this."

The policeman, however, was not really to blame. He had been ordered to keep a way clear. Wilhelm was moved forward by the pressure of the crowd. He cried, "Tamkin!"

But Tamkin was gone. Or rather, it was he himself who was carried from the street into the chapel. The pressure ended inside, where it was dark and cool. The flow of fan-driven air dried his face, which he wiped hard with his handkerchief to stop the slight salt itch. He gave a sigh when he heard the organ notes that stirred and breathed from the pipes and he saw people in the pews. Men in formal clothes and black Homburgs strode softly back and forth on the cork floor, up and down the center aisle. The white of the stained glass was like mother-of-pearl, the blue of the Star of David like velvet ribbon.

Well, thought Wilhelm, if that was Tamkin outside I might as well wait for him here where it's cool. Funny, he never mentioned he had a funeral to go to today. But that's just like the guy.

But within a few minutes he had forgotten Tamkin. He stood along the wall with others and looked toward the coffin and the slow line that was moving past it, gazing at the face of the dead. Presently he too was in this line, and slowly, slowly, foot by foot, the beating of his heart anxious, thick, frightening, but somehow also rich, he neared the coffin and paused for his turn, and gazed down. He caught his breath when he looked at the corpse, and his face swelled, his eyes shone hugely with instant tears.

The dead man was gray-haired. He had two large waves of gray hair at the front. But he was not old. His face was long, and he had a bony nose, slightly, delicately twisted. His brows were raised as though he had sunk into the final thought. Now at last he was with it, after the end of all distractions, and when his flesh was no longer flesh. And by this meditative look Wilhelm was so struck that he could not go away. In spite of the tinge of horror, and then the splash of heartsickness that he felt, he could not go. He stepped out of line and remained beside the coffin; his eyes filled silently and through his still tears he studied the man as the line of visitors moved with veiled looks past the satin coffin toward the standing bank of lilies, lilacs, roses. With great stifling sorrow, almost admiration, Wilhelm nodded and nodded. On the surface, the dead man with his formal shirt and his tie and silk lapels and his powdered skin looked so proper; only a little beneath so—black, Wilhelm thought, so fallen in the eyes.

Standing a little apart, Wilhelm began to cry. He cried at first softly and from sentiment, but soon from deeper feeling. He sobbed loudly and his face grew distorted and hot, and the tears stung his skin. A man—another human creature, was what first went through his thoughts, but other and different things were torn from him. What'll I do? I'm stripped and kicked out. . . . Oh, Father, what do I ask of you? What'll I do about the kids—Tommy, Paul? My children. And Olive? My dear! Why, why, why—you must protect me against that devil who wants my life. If you want it, then kill me. Take, take it, take it from me.

Soon he was past words, past reason, coherence. He could not stop. The source of all tears had suddenly sprung open within him, black, deep, and hot, and they were pouring out and convulsed his body, bending his stubborn head, bowing his shoulders, twisting his face, crippling the very hands with which he held the handkerchief. His efforts to collect himself were useless. The great knot of ill and grief in his throat swelled upward and he gave in utterly and held his face and wept. He cried with all his heart.

He, alone of all the people in the chapel, was sobbing. No one knew who he was.

One woman said, "Is that perhaps the cousin from New Orleans they were expecting?"

"It must be somebody real close to carry on so."

"Oh my, oh my! To be mourned like that," said one man and looked at Wilhelm's heavy shaken shoulders, his clutched face and whitened fair hair, with wide, glinting, jealous eyes.

"The man's brother, maybe?"

"Oh, I doubt that very much," said another bystander. "They're not alike at all. Night and day."

The flowers and lights fused ecstatically in Wilhelm's blind, wet eyes; the heavy sea-like music came up to his ears. It poured into him where he had hidden himself in the center of a crowd by the great and happy oblivion of tears. He heard it and sank deeper than sorrow, through torn sobs and cries toward the consummation of his heart's ultimate need.

Alexander Solzhenitsyn

ONE DAY IN THE LIFE OF IVAN DENISOVICH

Preface

One Day in the Life of Ivan Denisovich (1962) was published exactly 100 years after *The House of the Dead*, the novel Dostoevsky based on his own experiences in a Siberian labor camp. Alexander Solzhenitsyn (b. 1918) was arrested in 1945 while serving with the Russian Army in Germany, and for expressing anti-Stalin sentiments in a letter to a friend was imprisoned for eight years—ultimately in the Kazakhstan penal camp where he conceived *Ivan Denisovich*. Released in 1953, on the day of Stalin's death, Solzhenitsyn like Dostoevsky before him had to endure further exile in the Kazakhstan village of Kok Teren. In 1956 he was allowed to return to European Russia, having served an exile as long as Dostoevsky's. The coincidence and its shared brutality linking the genius of nineteenth-century Russian literature with Solzhenitsyn, who was awarded the Nobel Prize in 1970 (which he was not permitted to receive until 1972), demonstrates that more than historical accident was at work. The force that imprisoned Solzhenitsyn, a dissident critic of Communist totalitarianism, is the same that punished Dostoevsky, originally a utopian socialist in Czarist Russia—the intentional repression of art's message of human freedom by a society built on the power of false domination and unnatural dictatorship, whether of the proletariat or not. And just as that force pursued Dostoevsky with continuing censorship even after his release, so it challenged Solzhenitsyn with new imprisonment and death when he released his ultimate indictment of Soviet penal labor camps, *The Gulag Archipelago*, in 1973. With the free world joining his cause—as in Saul Bellow's public praise of Solzhenitsyn's "courage, power of mind, and strength of spirit" in speaking out for truth—his life was saved. Deprived of his Soviet citizenship, he was deported in 1974, coming to the United States in 1975. The parallel of Dostoevsky's and Solzhenitsyn's mutual persecution is deepened by shared paradox as well. Neither writer was an ardent revolutionary; each, instead, stands for the eternal countervalent force opposing dictatorship—a deep conservative faith in native Russian Christian virtue and peasant wisdom. The works of each reveal a strong harking back to the most fundamental human values, although this is more clearly observed in *Ivan Denisovich* than in either *Notes from the Underground* or *The House of the Dead*, which shows as well that Solzhenitsyn had the harder time in servitude for by his time punishment had become more vicious, systematic, and encompassing than in the nineteenth century. But Solzhenitsyn clearly understood the values of Dostoevsky's final and major novels when he called the modern world the world of Dostoevsky's *The Devils*.

   One Day in the Life of Ivan Denisovich differs from *The House of the Dead* not only in terms of the severity of its persecution, but also in terms of literary form. Solzhenitsyn makes contemporary Russian fiction as valuable as Dostoevsky's because of his rediscovery of the fundamental truth in Dostoevsky's works, but his realism turns to other Russian sources for its ultimate form. Instead of putting an aristocrat in jail, he puts the peasant Ivan Denisovich Shukov; instead of giving centuries of European history, he gives us a day in one man's life—as Tolstoy remarked was the writer's choice. Solzhenitsyn found Shukov in Tolstoy, and also the genius of Tolstoy's realism that invests the full scope of history in the fabric of everyday reality, as in the classic short novel *The Death of Ivan Ilych*, whose servant, Gerasim, is Tolstoy's Shukov. But sharing an identical purpose in their realism, Tolstoy and Solzhenitsyn differ on method, and Solzhenitsyn, keenly aware of his place in the tradition of Russian fiction, ultimately turned to Chekov for his technique—as the relation of Chekov's famous short novel *Ward No. Six* and Solzhenitsyn's third major novel *Cancer Ward* (1968) demonstrates. Tolstoy's realism, no matter how real, is still Romantic realism, not in the belief that a single man can influence history, but in its belief that history can indeed be found in one man. Conrad found a way out of this problem in symbolism, and Faulkner in myth. But if we compare the convict tales *Old Man* and *Ivan Denisovich*—both of which employ primitive prisoners—the realistic technique Solzhenitsyn found in Chekov may be isolated. Cancer in *Cancer Ward* is a disease that is symbolic of an overall political state of affairs, but more important it is a disease that heightens reality for those inflicted with it—as Solzhenitsyn knew from his own experience in a Tashkent cancer ward that he reached during exile nearly dead himself. Seeking a way to enlarge realism from within by concentrating reality to its moments of crisis—as Shukov's one day fuses smaller crises of penal camp life into an epic struggle, however ordinary it may at first appear—Solzhenitsyn shares a technique with Bellow's one day in the life of Tommy Wilhelm called *Seize the Day*. Both writers give us a valid reality that is more than it is, and so becomes meaningful to us, by recognizing that crisis reveals reality's potential to exceed itself in any one moment.

Despite the similarity of technique, the crises of *Seize the Day* and *Ivan Denisovich* are of very different orders. Wilhelm's predicament is the result of displaced family and disappearing religion, sociological problems that Solzhenitsyn in filmed interviews has identified with the historical decline of the West. Shukov's predicament is to be trapped—not by his own selfishness, but by historical forces rejecting a man out of his time, a man belonging to an earlier historical period. Wilhelm is modern selfishness entrapped by historical decline; Shukov is history trapped by a force that wishes to stop history altogether—and to stop time—by locking up human nature and all nature. *Ivan Denisovich* is an epic of human, not just one human's, survival, and not simply the novel of one man's catharsis and release from self-pity. If Shukov cannot survive no man can. That is precisely why *Ivan Denisovich* is an epic, why Shukov is an old-fashioned epic hero in modern guise, and why Solzhenitsyn, who believes in epic heroes, fashioned him that way. Solzhenitsyn's belief is by necessity, not only because his own experiences threatened his life, but because he knew that they threatened every man's right to be a man by knowing the truth. *Ivan Denisovich* was first published in the Soviet literary magazine *Novy Mir*, which sold one hundred thousand copies of that issue the first day it appeared. Russian people wanted to know the truth, but because too many of them knew it first hand, what they wanted was to see the truth of what everyone knew and no one could say in print. *Ivan Denisovich* confirmed that the totalitarian state was more insane than its citizens thought that they themselves might be. But Solzhenitsyn knew from the fact of Premier Khrushchev's personal approval of the publication of *Ivan Denisovich* that his novel had merely been enlisted in the de-Stalinization of the Khrushchev era. With Khrushchev's fall, Solzhenitsyn was to experience loss of the Lenin prize to a lesser writer, an increasing campaign of personal attack (Brezhnev saying in 1971 that writers like Solzhenitsyn deserve only public scorn), expulsion from the Soviet writers union, and the failure to find Russian publication for any of his works despite their obvious merit—as indicated by the West's recognition of that merit with the Nobel Prize. Knowing the very nature of the forces set against him, as his public statements of the time reveal, Solzhenitsyn knew the epic nature of Shukov's struggle. That knowledge powers his epic literary realism in a way that ultimately reminds the Western reader neither of Faulkner, nor of Bellow, but of the tragic realism of Richard Wright's *Down by the Riverside*, despite the destruction of Mann and the survival of Shukov.

Solzhenitsyn's literary purpose lives in Shukov's survival, for the purpose of his epic realism is to demonstrate that man can outlast totalitarianism. Doing so, Solzhenitsyn does away with the fiction of its timelessness, a fiction that inhibits our return to fundamental humanity, which should be the goal of all fiction that is not propaganda. Russian fiction, Solzhenitsyn believed, went off course with the political imposition of the doctrine of socialist realism in literature, a doctrine that had not existed to hinder Dostoevsky, Tolstoy, and Chekov. Socialist realism is a crippling paradox because it demands that the writer tell the truth and lie at the same time, that he represent the reality around him as concretely as possible, while contributing to the socialist ideological indoctrination of his readers. But how could Solzhenitsyn fashion Communist propaganda out of the truth of its prison camps that he knew first hand? What Solzhenitsyn did was to tell the simple truth. But he does so with his particular irony that serves to turn socialist realism back upon itself. His epic realism has this purpose: it inculcates a sense of an earlier socialist ideology, of a primitive and Christian communalism, at the expense of the modern state of socialist ideology—totalitarian Communism. Shukov's struggle can be more easily compared with that of the early Christians than with the imaginary struggles of many Heroes of the Soviet Union. This is the point of the single discussion of the arts that we hear in *Ivan Denisovich*, when Shukov overhears a discussion of Eisenstein's film, *Ivan the Terrible*. In that conversation, Solzhenitsyn strongly opposes an art that "is not *what* but *how*" because he is a realist; and, because he is an epic realist, he stands for an art that is "our daily bread," knowing that "genius doesn't fit its treatment to the taste of tyrants." Knowing the precise epic significance of our daily bread, Shukov's sense of its absolute value for human survival, Solzhenitsyn makes his art of it by giving us not *Ivan* the Terrible, but *Ivan* Shukov, who is no less heroic than his namesake and a lot more humble. And Shukov shares the same artistic concerns that Solzhenitsyn does, for when he wonders how his fellow peasants back home could leave their fields—and leave them to take up rug painting when they don't even know how to paint—Solzhenitsyn tells him that they use stencils, the ultimate tools of totalitarian art that wants outlines, not human beings.

Shukov serves his term in a prison camp built by the prisoners themselves. That simplest irony is compounded by the fact that the camp will eventually be absorbed by the socialist "new town" now being built around it by the same prisoners. A town established on the foundations of a prison camp will certainly be another prison, for all men are prisoners of the totalitarian state that hopes to extend itself indefinitely by building cities out of prisons and then prisons out of cities. And within the new town, and within the prison camp within it, is the ultimate prison that Shukov worked on, the place of solitary confinement known as the "cooler." This final prison demonstrates how the maze of Solzhenitsyn's irony leads to epic realism. The stone prison that can kill a man in fifteen days is the ultimate totalitarian prison that perverts nature by making it serve the forces of death and eternal ice age. Cold is the ultimate antagonist of Shukov's human warmth, and his struggle with a monolithic political "they" is made epic by a false league of inhuman oppression and nature. Solzhenitsyn returns to the earliest of Christian equations, that of sun and Son, when he pits Shukov against the devil who has won control of natural energy and ironically enslaves Shukov to make him work on a power plant. But Shukov's human nature triumphs with a folk wisdom more naturally intelligent than totalitarian lies. Shukov, not his bosses, knows that too much water in the mortar will collapse walls in the spring when nature makes it expand naturally. Shukov and his partner, seeing the frozen rays of the sun as posts, can joke about barbed wire on the sun, sure that it is not there. And Shukov is too simple to comprehend a naval-officer prisoner's irony about the Soviet dictate that the sun is highest at one, rather than at noon. But even the captain's navigation in the anti-natural world of the camp must be guided by simple, natural Shukov, whose folk wisdom knows that there is a new moon every month because people are born every day, and knows where the old moon goes: God breaks it up into stars because the stars keep falling down. And back in Shukov's village they call the moon the wolves' sun, and in the camp they call the disciplinary officer wolf, and no wolf can make the moon into the sun, and so all wolves must fall like the stars because people are born everyday, and that birth is the strongest force opposing totalitarianism. But this holds true only if the sun will last in Shukov, only if he keeps joking about barbed wire on the sun, only if he can look right into the sun; because you couldn't see the wire if you looked into the sun, only if you looked away from it, as he discovers when looking at the camp from the top of the power plant. And this is to discover that the camp is a cold hell: that is its natural and Christian significance, and that significance is restated in the title of Solzhenitsyn's second novel, *First Circle* (1968). The novel's title comes from Dante's *Inferno*, while its hell is Mavrino prison.

The camp is seventeen degrees below zero, and Shukov realizes that he is ninety-nine degrees above, and in that realization his epic struggle is defined: keeping warm means keeping human. The camp opposes his natural humanity with lights so bright that the stars are blotted out, and more fundamentally by keeping time out of the prisoners' hands by allowing them no watches. Time must remain frozen, and Shukov be no more than a mummy wrapped in rags and turned out into the cold. The last trace of his humanity is the only exposed part of him, his eyes, which is one reason why he doesn't eat fish eyes when they are separated from the fish. The morality of his epic struggle is revealed by the folk proverbs that connect conflict with nature and human moral conflict. Shukov is cold because when you are cold you don't expect sympathy from someone who is warm. Selfish totalitarianism doesn't want warm humanity because, as Kafka has shown, its ultimate wish is death. To stay warm and alive and human, Shukov must best the converse proverb: It's only cows who can get warm from the sun in January. Is man to be an animal or a mummy? Solzhenitsyn answers this question by affirming our ability to continue human, and by understanding that the food Shukov struggles for is daily bread in both real and religious terms. Food is warmth, and it puts a sun in Shukov that makes him a Christian son. *One Day in the Life of Ivan Denisovich* is directed toward this climax, beginning with Shukov carrying in his boot a spoon that he has made in his first camp. The boot and spoon are the hammer and sickle of native Russian Christianity, and Solzhenitsyn pointedly reminds us that the Russians in the camp had forgotten which hand to cross themselves with. And his novel ends with Shukov giving a cookie to the Baptist Alyesha, and when we know just how much that food has cost Shukov and what it ultimately signifies, then we know the communion intended. It is this final gesture that explains why Shukov's prayer before the search guards is answered, and why food is more important than freedom: because there is no freedom if you can't go home. Even if they let Shukov out they would never let him go home, because the only home a man has in a totalitarian state is a home of the very spirit that such a state puts you in prison for possessing in the first place. And epic Christian hero Shukov has the spirit: "We'll live through it. We'll live through it all. And if God wills, it will end someday."

What we learn about Shukov's camp, just as what we learn about Shukov, continues to invert its totalitarian purpose, making its jungle law superior to the Soviet code. In the camp "it was every man for himself," but Solzhenitsyn makes Shukov into Everyman of the morality play of early Christianity, so that in his camp men help each other as much as they hurt: a man's gang becomes his family, his gang boss his father, an artist painting numbers becomes a priest, thought is more free inside than out, and the medical orderly can write the kind of poetry not permitted outside. Another message is that sooner or later everyone outside turns up inside because men are human after all. Solzhenitsyn's insistence is that, when one-eighth of a dictatorship's population is in prison, outside and inside become empty distinctions. And indeed when we ask just who is in Shukov's camp, we find left-over people, the legacy of history since the Russian Revolution, people whose imprisonment undermines the Revolution as revolution: the Kulaks and the Baptists, socially and religiously persecuted; and the politically persecuted—the Kirov affair, the Bendera business, and finally the Latvians and Estonians, men of the little nations that fell under the German onslaught and could not revive under the Russians. The central cause is the Revolution's failure to deal with World War Two, a war that in one way or another connects all the prisoners; this tells us why men once imprisoned in Buchenwald—men who survived Buchenwald!—are now inmates of Shukov's camp. They are all there for the same profoundly ironic reason that Shukov is there, and that reason is the meaning of *Ivan Denisovich*. Shukov got caught by the Germans in the Second World War, escaped with a party and made his way back to his own lines, only to see his fellow escapees shot by their own comrades and himself accused of collaboration and so imprisoned. Shukov is in prison because he escaped the Germans, *because he could escape*. That is Solzhenitsyn's point. Anyone who might escape had to be locked up in Stalinist Russia. The penal camp is ultimately a symbol of the paranoid fear that turned revolution in Russia into new repression further driven into insanity by World War Two. And as a symbol of just that fear, the camp itself is proof that totalitarian dictatorship must fall—as Shukov discovers for himself: "He wasn't a jackal, not even after eight years of . . .

camps, and the longer he lived the firmer he became in his resolve not to be one." Because of this resolve, Shukov is becoming the vision revealed to him, his witness of the oldest prisoner of all camps, of the man who has been in camps forever and will forever be in them, the man who sits with the straightest back before a clean-washed rag of a napkin and eats with his own wooden spoon, the man who is a rock, who will never compromise while he is alive because he knows that ultimately only those defined as man can live, men who know their proverbs, for he who eats with the devil must use a wooden spoon, or with its modern counterpart—Shukov's aluminum one.

Solzhenitsyn

ONE DAY
IN THE LIFE OF
IVAN DENISOVICH

Translated by Thomas P. Whitney

At five, as always, reveille was sounded—a hammer pounded on a rail at head-quarters barracks. The clanging crept faintly, sporadically, through the window glass and the inch-thick coating of ice that covered it. It ended soon. That morning was cold and the guard didn't feel like hammering very long.

Outside the window deep darkness lay everywhere, just as it had in the middle of the night when Shukov had waked to go to the latrine barrel. Only the gleam of lamplight fell on the window from two yellow lamps out in the zone and one inside the camp.

For some reason they hadn't come to open the barracks yet. And Shukov didn't hear the usual noises of the orderlies lifting the latrine barrel on poles to carry it out.

Shukov never slept past the rising gong. He always got up when he heard it. Until lineup there was an hour and a half of one's own time, not the government's. Anyone who knew camp life could always earn a bit then. He could sew a mitten-cover out of an old lining. He could run to deliver the dry *valenki* —felt boots—of some rich fellow-member of the work brigade to his bunk so he wouldn't have to hop barefoot around the pile to find them himself. A man could busy himself in the storerooms doing odd chores, sweeping or carrying.

Or he could go to the mess hall to gather bowls from the tables and carry them in piles to the dishwasher. For that job he'd be fed, but many others were playing that game, too. Too many in fact. But the dangerous thing about that job was that if a bowl had something left in it, one couldn't restrain oneself and would lick it clean. Shukhov remembered the warning words of his first-brigade foreman, Kuzyemin. An old camp wolf who had served time for twelve years by 1943. Kuzyemin once said, at a bonfire in a clearing in the woods, to reinforcements brought from the front, "It's the law of the jungle here. But even so, people live. The men who die in camp are the ones who lick bowls, the ones who pin hopes on the medical department, and the ones who play stool-pigeon."

About the stool-pigeon bit—there, of course, he overdid it. That kind took good care of themselves, though it cost the blood of others.

Shukhov always got up at rising gong. But not today. Since the evening before, he'd felt ill: at times he felt feverish, at times he ached all over. And he hadn't been able to get warm. During the night, even in his sleep, he felt as though he had really fallen seriously ill. Then a while later he seemed better. He kept wishing morning wouldn't come.

But the morning came on schedule.

Where could he get warm? There was ice an inch thick on the window, white spiderwebs of frost high up on the walls. What a barracks!

Shukhov didn't get up. He stayed in his bunk, his head covered with blanket and coat. Both feet were pushed down together into one turned-under sleeve of his cotton-padded underjacket. With his head covered he couldn't see, but he knew exactly what was going on by the sounds in the barracks and in the corner of it occupied by his own brigade. There now, moving clumsily along the corridor, came the orderlies carrying one of the eight-bucket latrine barrels. That's considered light work, you invalid! But just try to haul it out without slopping it over! In the section occupied by the 75th brigade, the bundle of valenki returned from the dryer was slammed down on the floor. Now: the same sound in our section. It was our turn, too, to dry out valenki today. The brigade foreman and assistant foreman were pulling on their boots in silence, but their bunks creaked. The assistant foreman would be going off to the bread rationing office: the foreman to headquarters barracks, to the planning-production section.

Yes, and today the foreman was not just going to the work assignment officers as he did every day. Today the brigade's fate was being decided. There were plans afoot to shift the 104th from the construction of workshops to a new project, the "Socialist Life Town." The Socialist Life Town was now just a bare open field, all snow ridges and drifts. Before anything could be built there, the prisoners would have to dig holes, set in posts, and put up barbed wire—fencing themselves in so they couldn't escape. Only when that was done could they start to build. For at least a month there'd be no place to get warm out there. No bonfires either—nothing to build them with. Working like hell would be the only salvation.

another prisoner

The brigade foreman was worried about that project and he'd gone to try to fix things so that some other brigade would get sent there, instead of his own. Of course, he couldn't manage this empty-handed. He had to take a pound of fat bacon for the senior work-assignment officer. Maybe even two pounds. It was worth trying, anyway.

Maybe Shukhov should have a try at the infirmary, see if he could get out of work today. Really, his whole body felt as if it was coming apart.

He tried to recall which of the guards was on duty that day.

He remembered—it was One-and-a-Half Ivan, a thin, tall sergeant with black eyes. The first time you saw him he seemed terrifying. But actually he was the easiest to get along with of all the duty guards. He didn't put people in solitary, didn't drag them off to the chief of discipline. So it was all right for Shukhov to lie there awhile—even till barracks nine went to the mess hall.

His bunk shook and shuddered. Two men were getting out of bed at the same time: the Baptist, Alyesha, who was next to Shukhov in a top bunk, and Buinovsky, who had the bunk under Shukhov. Buinovsky was a navy captain, second rank—that is, he used to be.

Now the orderlies, having carried out the latrine barrel, were squabbling about who would go for the hot water. They sounded like a couple of old women. The electric welder from the 20th brigade yelled at them:

"Hey, you old good-for-nothings!" He threw a boot at them. "I'll shut you up!"

The fat boot whammed hollowly against a post. They shut up.

In the neighboring brigade the assistant foreman growled, just audibly:

"Vasil Fedorych! They cheated again at the ration counter, the bastards: there were four two-pound loaves, and now there are only three. Who gets short rations?"

He said this in a low voice, but, of course, that whole brigade was listening with bated breath. Some of them were going to be missing part of their bread that evening.

Shukhov just kept lying there on the hard-packed sawdust. He wished that he would either come down with a fever or else that the ache would go away. This way he was neither sick nor well.

Meanwhile, the Baptist whispered his prayers and Buinovsky returned from the latrine and announced to no one in particular, but in a gloating tone: "Brace yourselves, Red Navy men! It's twenty below for certain!"

Shukhov decided to go to the infirmary.

And right at that moment an authoritative hand jerked his blanket and underjacket off him. Shukhov pushed his coat off his face and lifted his head. Beneath him, his head level with the upper edge of the bunk, stood the lean Tartar.

So the Tartar was on duty, though it wasn't his turn—and had sneaked up on Shukhov silently.

"S-854!" the Tartar read the numbered label on the back of the black coat. "Three days penalty—with outside work!"

And hardly had his lowered voice sounded, than throughout the still-dim half of the barracks, where not all the bulbs were burning, where on fifty bedbug-infested bunks two hundred men slept, a buzz of activity began and everyone who was not up hurriedly started dressing.

"Why, citizen chief?" Shukhov asked, putting into his voice a more imploring-pitiful tone than he really felt. Because work outside was only semi-solitary. There was hot food and there was no time to brood. Total solitary was when they didn't take you out to work.

"Why didn't you get up at the signal? Let's get going to the commandant," the Tartar explained carelessly, because he and Shukhov and everyone else knew what the penalty was for.

The hairless, worn face of the Tartar was an expressionless blank. He turned to look for another victim, but in half-darkness, under lamps, on lower bunks and upper, everyone was pushing his legs down into the black quilted trousers, or else, already dressed, was bundling up and hurrying off to the exit in order to wait outside till the Tartar left.

If Shukhov had received solitary for something else, something that really rated solitary, he wouldn't have been so put out. He was angry because he was always one of the first to get up. But he knew he couldn't beg off. Not from the Tartar. And though he continued for appearance' sake to ask to be let off, Shukhov pulled on his quilted trousers (on the left knee there was a ragged, dirty patch, with a black number in faded ink—S-854) and then his quilted underjacket (there were two numbers on the jacket—one in front and the other on the back), then went and picked out his valenki from the pile on the floor, put on his cap (with the same kind of patch and number in front) and followed the Tartar.

All the 104th saw Shukhov led out, but no one said a word. It was useless. What was there to say? The foreman might have defended him, but he wasn't in the barracks. And Shukhov didn't say a word to his bunkmates. They'd look after his breakfast without his asking.

The two went outside.

The cold, combined with mist, made one gasp. Two big searchlights swept the zone in a crisscross starting from the two corner watchtowers. Lamps were lit in the zone and inside the camp itself. There were so many of them they shut out the stars with their light.

With valenki crunching in the snow, *zeks*—prisoners—ran quickly about their affairs: some to latrines, some to storerooms, one to the warehouse for a package from home, another to the individual kitchen to turn in cereals to be cooked for him. All of them had their shoulders hunched, heads down, coats buttoned up. All were cold, not so much from the low temperature itself, as from the realization that they were going to be spending the whole day out in that low temperature. But the Tartar, in his old army coat with its bedraggled blue tabs, walked erect as if he didn't feel the cold one bit.

They went past the high board fence that surrounded the BUR—the internal camp punishment prison—then past the barbed wire that protected the camp bakery from the prisoners, past the corner of the headquarters barracks where the frost-covered length of track hung suspended from its post by a thick wire, past another post where the frost-covered thermometer hung in a sheltered corner so it didn't show too low a temperature. Shukhov hopefully sneaked a glance at its milky-white tube. If it were to show 42° below they would not drive the zeks out to work. But today it wasn't anywhere near 40° below.

They went into headquarters barracks and straight into the guards' room. There it quickly became clear (as Shukhov had begun to sense on the way) that he was not going to be given solitary at all, but simply ordered to scrub the dirty floor in the guards' room. At this point the Tartar announced that he had forgiven Shukhov and orded him to wash the floor.

Washing the floor in the guards' room was the assignment of a special zek who was not sent out in the zone to work. He was the barracks orderly and this was his own particular job. But, having made himself at home in the head-quarters barracks, he had access to the offices of the major, the chief of discipline, and the "Godfather" too—the security chief. He waited on them, and now and then heard things even the guards did not know. As a result, he had come to consider it beneath his dignity to wash floors for ordinary guards. These called for him once or twice, then understood what the score was, and began to grab men from among the camp working stiffs to wash their floors.

In the guards' room the stove was vigorously radiating heat. Stripped down to dirty undershirts, two guards were playing checkers. The third slept on a narrow bench in his belted sheepskin and valenki. In a corner stood a bucket with a rag.

Shukhov was pleased to be let off. He said to the Tartar:

"Thank you, citizen chief. I'll never sleep too late again."

The rule here was simple: finish and get out. Now that Shukhov had work to do it seemed his aches had stopped. He took the pail. He had no mittens—in his hurry he had left them under his pillow. He went out to the well.

Several brigade foremen on their way to the planning and production section were gathered around the pole where the thermometer was hung. And one, younger than the rest, a former Hero of the Soviet Union, had climbed up the pole to read the thermometer. From below came words of advice:

"Be careful to breathe to one side—otherwise it will rise."

"Like your prick it will! Rise! Not a chance!"

Tyurin, Shukhov's brigade foreman, was not there. Having put down his bucket and shoved his hands in his sleeves, Shukhov watched, curious.

Then the one up the pole said hoarsely:

"Seventeen below! Oh, the hell with it!"

And taking one more look to be sure, he dropped down.

"Well, it's never right, it's always wrong," someone said. "Unlikely they'd hang an accurate one here!"

The brigade foremen went their ways. Shukhov ran on to the well. Beneath his untied earflags the frost bit at his ears.

The log well-housing was coated with a thick layer of ice. The bucket hardly fit through the opening in it. The rope was as stiff as a stick.

With his full bucket giving off a frosty mist, Shukhov returned to the guard-room. His hands were numb: he shoved them into the cold water. They seemed to get warmer.

The Tartar was no longer there. But there were four guards now. They had given up checkers and sleep and were quarreling about how much millet they were going to be given in January. In the nearby settlement food was short, and the guards, even though rationing had long since come to an end, were being sold certain food products outside the general distribution system for the locals, at cut rate.

As Shukhov came in, one shouted, "Shut that door, you *shit!* There's a draft!"

It was very bad to get valenki wet in the morning. There were no other shoes even had he been able to run back to the barracks. Shukhov had seen various deals with footwear in his eight years of sitting in camps. Once he had gone a whole winter without either valenki or leather shoes, at all, just with *lapty*—sandals of bark—and C-T-Zs—from the initials of the Chelysbinsk Tractor Factory—made out of pieces of tires. Now things had improved: in October Shukhov had trailed along behind the assistant foreman to the store-rooms, and received a pair of tough leather boots. They had hard toes, with room for two warm footcloths. For a week he had gone about as gaily as if he were celebrating his birthday and he kept clapping his heels. And then in December the felt valenki had come. What a good life! No need to die after all! But then some devil in the bookkeeping department had whispered to the chief: let them have the valenki and turn the leather shoes in. It seemed it was out of order for a zek to have two pairs of shoes at once. And so Shukhov had to choose: either go out in leather shoes all winter long, or keep the valenki even for the thaws, when they would get soaked through. He turned in the shoes. He had taken loving care of them, softened their leather with oil, new shoes, oh my! He hadn't been so regretful about anything in all eight years as those shoes. They were thrown on a big pile. There was no chance that he'd find his own again in the spring.

Now Shukhov deftly slipped off his valenki, put them in a corner, and threw his footcloths after them. His spoon fell out of his valenki, and rang out as it hit the floor. No matter how hurriedly he had dressed for solitary, he never forgot his spoon. He retrieved it: then, barefoot, generously sloshing water on the floor with the rag, he went to work right under the feet of the guards.

"You! Bastard! Careful!" one of the guards noticed the water, lifting his feet onto a chair.

"Rice? Rice is in another category," another guard went on. "Don't try to draw comparison with rice!"

"Listen, fool, how much water are you going to slop around? Who washes that way?"

"Citizen chief! You can't wash it off otherwise. The dirt has eaten its way in."

"Haven't you ever seen how your old woman washed floors, pig?"

Shukhov drew himself up straight, holding in his hand the dripping rag. He smiled simple-mindedly, showing where teeth were missing which he'd lost when he had had scurvy at Ust-Izhma[1] in the far north, in 1943. He had nearly been done for then: he had come so close that bleeding diarrhea had just about emptied him of his insides and his exhausted stomach hadn't wanted to hold a thing. But now all he had left of that was missing teeth and a lisp.

"From my old woman, citizen chief, they gave me a discharge in 1941. I can't even remember what kind of an old woman she was."

"That's the way they wash. . . . The bastards don't know how to do anything and don't want to do anything. They aren't worth the bread they are given. They should get shit to eat."

"Fuck it! Why should the floor be washed every day! The damp won't go away. Listen here, 854! You wipe it off easy, so it's a little wet, and then get out."

"Rice! Don't compare millet and rice."

Shukhov quickly dealt with the task.

Work—it's like a stick. It has two ends. If you do it for humans then you give quality. If you do it for idiots then it's just for show.

Otherwise everyone would have dropped dead long since. Everyone knew that.

Shukhov wiped the floor boards just so no dry spots were left. He threw the unwrung rag behind the stove. At the threshold he pulled on his valenki, splashed the pail of water out along the path that the chiefs used, and hurried out past the bath, past the dark, cold club building, taking a short cut to the mess hall.

He still had to get to the infirmary. He was aching all over again. And he had to be careful not to run into guards in front of the mess hall. There was a strict order from the camp chief: catch lone zeks who lagged behind their brigades and put them in solitary.

In front of the mess hall today—it was a miracle—there was no crowd milling about, no line. He could just go in.

Inside there was as much steam as a bath house. Gusts of frost from the door and steam from the thin camp soup. Brigades were sitting at the tables or crowding about in the aisles, waiting for room to sit down. Yelling to each other through the mob, two or three workers from each brigade were carrying wooden trays with bowls of thin soup and *kasha*—cooked porridge: usually oats, buckwheat or grits. They were looking for room on the tables.

That guy blocking the aisle doesn't hear, the stupid ass. There you go, you've bumped a tray! Slip, slop! Give it to him good with your free hand, on the neck! That's right! Get out of the way! Don't stand there looking for a bowl to lick.

At a nearby table, a young chap crossed himself before be began to eat. That meant he was Western Ukrainian, and a newcomer. The Russians have even forgotten what hand to cross themselves with.

It was cold in the mess hall. Most of the men ate with their caps on but

[1] [A labor camp.—Editors' note.]

without hurrying, catching the boiled chunks of disintegrated fish out from under the leaves of black cabbage and spitting the bones on the table. When a whole pile of bones accumulated someone brushed them off the table and they crunched beneath the boots on the floor. But spitting them straight onto the floor was considered to be sort of improper.

In the center of the barracks were two rows of things which weren't quite pillars and not quite supports either. And at one of these posts sat Shukhov's fellow-brigade member, Fetyukov, guarding Shukhov's breakfast. He was one of the lowest-ranking members of the brigade, lower than Shukhov. From outside the brigade everyone seemed alike in their black three-quarter length coats, in their similar numbers, but on the inside it was very unequal—it went by steps. Buinovsky would not be asked to sit guarding a bowl, and even Shukhov would not undertake just any kind of work. There were steps beneath him.

Fetyukov noticed Shukhov and sighed, yielding his seat.

"Everything is cold. I was just about to eat your portion. I thought you were in solitary."

He didn't hang around because he knew Shukhov wouldn't leave a thing that he would clean out both bowls.

Shukhov pulled his spoon from one of his valenki. That spoon was dear to him. It had travelled with him through the whole north country. He had cast it himself out of aluminum wire in sand. On it was etched in dots: "Ust-Izhma, 1944."

Then Shukhov took his cap off his shaved head. He didn't eat with his cap on, no matter what the temperature. He stirred the cooled-off soup and studied it to see what he had in the bowl. What he had received was from the middle. It wasn't from the top of the pot nor from the bottom either. And he knew Fetyukov: it could well be that while guarding the bowl he might have picked out a potato or two.

The one pleasure in that thin camp soup was that it was hot. Shukhov's was quite cold by now. However, he began to eat it as slowly, as attentively, as usual. He wouldn't have hurried if the building were burning. Not taking sleep into account, a camp inmate lives for himself only ten minutes in the morning at breakfast, five at lunch, and another five at dinner.

The camp soup didn't change from day to day. It depended on what vegetable had been procured for the winter. The year before they had had only salted carrots. And so the soup had been made of plain carrots from September to June. This year it was black cabbage. The most nourishing time of the year for the camp inmates was June. All the vegetables were finished and were replaced by grits. The most meagre time was July: the cooks cut up nettles for the pot.

They got mostly the bones of the little fish. The meat boiled off the bones, fell apart, and clung only to the head and tail. Shukhov chewed and sucked away on the brittle network of the fish skeleton, which bore no trace of flesh or scale—then spat it out on the table. In any fish he ate everything, even gills and tail. Even the eyes, when they were still in their place in the head. But when they boiled out and swam about in the bowl separately—big fish eyes—he wouldn't eat them. The other zeks laughed at him for this.

Today Shukhov had saved up a bit of food. Since he hadn't gone back to the barracks and had not received his bread ration he was now eating without bread. Bread—that could be eaten later by itself. Even more satisfying.

For his second course there was kasha made from *magara*. It came in one chunk. Shukhov broke pieces off it. Even when it was hot it was without any taste or feeling of nourishment: grains like grass, only yellow, looking like millet. It was said to come from the Chinese. In boiled weight it ran to maybe ten ounces a portion; kasha which wasn't kasha but given out instead of kasha.

Having licked off his spoon and shoved it down in its former place in one of his valenki, Shukhov put on his cap and went off to the infirmary.

It was still just as dark in the sky. The two searchlights still cut with the same powerful beams across the camp zone. When they had originally set up that camp, a Special Camp, the guards had had a lot of rocket illuminating flares on hand left from the war. Whenever the electricity failed they showered rockets over the zone—white, green, red. Just like a real war. Then they stopped shooting off rockets. Maybe it was too costly?

It was just as dark outside as it had been when the rising gong had rung, but to an experienced eye various small details would easily have indicated that lineup was soon to be called. The assistant to that mess hall orderly named Khromoi—whom Khromoi supported on his own—went to call to breakfast the sixth barracks, which was filled with invalids—those who did not go out to work in the zone. An old artist with a little beard made his way slowly to the cultural and educational section to get paints and a brush to paint prisoner numbers. Then the Tartar strode hurriedly through the lineup ground in the direction of headquarters barracks. There were few people out—that meant nearly everyone had taken shelter to be warm for those last lovely minutes.

Shukhov adroitly hid from the Tartar behind the corner of the barracks. If he caught Shukhov once more he'd come at him again. The fact was, one couldn't even afford to yawn: stay alert! One had to keep from being caught alone by any guard. A guard might be looking for someone for some work, or he might be looking for someone on whom to vent his meanness. For instance, take that order that had been read off in the barracks—remove your cap five steps in front of a guard, and two steps beyond him put it on. Some guards didn't look and didn't care—but for others this was sugar candy. How many zeks had been dragged off to solitary because of that cap deal! Still it was always better to hide around a corner.

The Tartar went by. Shukhov was about to go on to the infirmary when he suddenly remembered that he had planned to go before lineup this morning to the seventh barracks to buy two glassfuls of home-grown tobacco from that tall Latvian. But Shukhov had been so rushed it had completely slipped his mind. The tall Latvian had received a package last night. It was possible that tomorrow he'd have no more of that tobacco left. Then Shukhov would have to wait a whole month before more arrived. The Latvian had good tobacco, just strong and pungent enough. Brownish.

Shukhov tapped a foot in annoyance—should he go to the seventh barracks? But he was very close to the infirmary now so he trotted over to the building. The snow crunched loudly beneath his feet.

In the infirmary, as always, the hallway was so clean he was almost afraid to walk on the floor. The walls painted in white enamel. All the furniture white, too.

But the doors of all the receiving rooms were shut. The doctors, he supposed, weren't up yet. The medical assistant was on duty, a young chap named Kolya Vdovushkin. He was sitting behind a clean table, in a fresh white coat, writing.

No one else was about.

Shukhov took off his cap, as if the young man were a camp official, and with the camp habit of noticing everything he shouldn't, he saw that Kolya was writing level, even lines and every line was indented from the edge and began with a capital letter. Shukhov understood immediately, of course, that this was not official work, but something of his own. But that wasn't Shukhov's affair.

"Listen, Nikolai Semenych," he said to Kolya, "I am kind of . . . sick. . . ." Shukhov spoke guiltily as if he had designs on something that didn't belong to him.

Vdovushkin lifted his calm, big eyes from his work. He had on a white cap, as well as the white coat. His numbers were not visible.

"Why are you so late? And why didn't you come last night? You know that we don't receive patients in the morning. The list of those excused from work today has been sent to the planning and production section already."

Shukhov knew all that. He also knew that it wasn't any easier to get excused from work in the evening.

"Look Kolya. . . . In the evenings, when I need it, it doesn't ache. . . ."

"What is *it*? What aches?"

"Well, if I try to pin it down then nothing aches. But I hurt all over."

Shukhov was not one of the men who made pests of themselves at the infirmary and Vdovushkin knew that. But he only had the right to excuse two men in the morning. He had already given permission to two, and their names were written beneath the greenish glass on the desk.

"Well, you should have done something about it before. What are you thinking of—right before lineup! Here, take this!"

Vdovushkin pulled a thermometer from the jar in which several were stuck through cuts in gauze, wiped off the solution, and gave it to Shukhov to take his temperature.

Shukhov sat on the bench next to the wall, on its farthest edge, so that he almost but not quite tipped over with it. He picked this uncomfortable position not on purpose—but involuntarily showing he was not at home in the infirmary and wasn't there for anything of major importance.

Vdovushkin went on writing.

The infirmary was in the quietest, most distant corner of the zone and no sounds at all reached here. No wall clock ticking away. (The prisoners were not allowed watches or clocks: the administration was supposed to know the time for them.) And not even a mouse scratching. The hospital cat had caught all of them. That was his function.

Shukhov felt delighted to be sitting in such a clean room, in such stillness, under a bright lamp, doing nothing for five whole minutes. He looked over the walls, but there was nothing on them. He inspected his underjacket—the number on his chest was worn and should be touched up; otherwise they might get him for that. He felt his beard with his free hand. It had grown out a lot. Been growing ever since the last visit to the bath house, more than ten days ago. But it didn't matter anyway. In another three days there'd be another visit to the bath house and then he would be shaved. Why stand in the barber shop line for nothing? Shukhov had nobody to pretty up for.

Then, looking at Vdovushkin's white cap, Shukhov remembered the field hospital on the Lovat River, how he had arrived there with a wounded jaw and then—what a stupid jackass he'd been—of his own will he had returned to the front, though he could have spent at least five days in bed.

And now he even had dreams about getting sick for a week or two, not mortally ill, of course, and nothing that required operations, but just sick enough so they'd put him in the hospital, where he could lie still for three weeks, not moving. They would feed him only clear broth. That was all right too.

But then Shukhov remembered that even in the hospital they no longer allowed a stay in bed. A new doctor had appeared among a new load of prisoners. Stepan Grigorich, noisy and active, never kept still himself, and wouldn't allow the patients to rest either. He thought up the idea of forcing all the patients who could move to work around the hospital: to put up a fence around the garden, to make little paths, to carry soil for flower beds, and in the winter to pile snow for soil moisture. He declared work was the best medicine for sickness.

But even horses die from overwork; he ought to know that. If *he* had to work his tail off laying cement blocks, he might quiet down for a change.

Vdovushkin went on writing. It was true that he was busy working for himself, but what he was doing would have been incomprehensible to Shukhov even if Shukhov had known what it was. He was copying out a long new poem he had finished the night before and had promised to show to Stepan Grigorich, that same doctor who was a supporter of work therapy.

It was one of those things that happens only in camps. Stepan Grigorich had advised Vdovushkin to declare himself to be a medical assistant, and had put him to work as a medical assistant. He had begun to teach Vdovushkin to give intravenous injections to unenlightened working stiffs whose decent honest minds would never suspect that a medical assistant might not really be a medical assistant at all. Actually Kolya had been a student in a university literary department and was arrested in his second year. Stepan Grigorevich wanted him to have the chance to write in prison what he would not have been allowed to write in freedom.

Through the double windows covered over with translucent white ice, the lineup gong was barely audible. Shukhov sighed and stood up when he heard it. He felt as feverish as before, but it didn't look as if he had much chance to get out of working. Vdovushkin reached for the thermometer and read it: "Well, it's neither one thing nor the other—just 99. If it were 100.4 then the whole thing would be quite clear. As it is I can't free you from work. If you want, you can wait here at your own risk. If the doctor believes you're ill, you'll be excused from work. If he thinks you're healthy and malingering—off to solitary. You'd be smarter to go out to the zone."

Shukhov didn't answer. Without even nodding he pulled on his cap and went out.

Will a warm man ever understand one who's cold?

The cold pinched. The cold, and a biting little fog, made Shukhov cough. Out in the cold it was 17° below. Inside Shukhov it was 99° above. Now it was a question of who would do in whom.

Shukhov trotted to the barracks. The lineup grounds were completely empty. The whole camp was empty. It was that short minute, relaxed, when though all retreat had 'been cut off people were pretending that there wouldn't be any lineup. The convoy of escort guards sat in their warm barracks, sleepy heads leaning on rifles—it wasn't sweet butter for them either to stamp up and down in guard towers in such a cold. The guards on duty in the main watch house shovelled some coal in the stove. The guards in the guards' room smoked their last hand-rolled cigarette. The zeks, dressed in all their tatters, all belted with ropes, all wrapped from chin to eyes with pieces of cloth to protect them against the cold, were lying on their bunks on top of their blankets, eyes closed, hearts sinking. Waiting for the foreman to shout, "Let's go!"

With the rest of the ninth barracks, the 104th brigade dozed. Only the assistant foreman, Pavlo, with silently moving lips, was adding something with a pencil, yes, and up on the upper bunk the Baptist, Alyesha, Shukhov's neighbor, clean, well-washed, was reading the notebook in which he had copied half of the Gospels.

Shukhov ran in fast but quiet and went straight to the assistant foreman's bunk.

Pavlo raised his head.

"So they didn't put you in solitary, Ivan Denisych? You're alive?"

Those Western Ukrainians, no matter how they tried to teach them better in the camps, addressed people politely and decently.

And taking Shukhov's bread ration from the table he handed it over to him. On the bread there was, in a little white mound, a scoop of sugar.

Shukhov was in a great hurry but nevertheless he replied politely. For the assistant foreman was also a chief and in fact was even more important to Shukhov than the chief of the camp. As he hurried, he licked the sugar off the bread and, with one foot on the bracket—he had to climb up to make his bunk —managed to look over the bread ration and weigh it with his hand to see whether it was really the eighteen ounces it was supposed to be. He had received thousands of these rations in prisons and camps. Though he had never had the chance to check any of them on a scale, and although he, shy as he was, did not dare to make a fuss and yell about his rights, nevertheless to Shukhov (and to every prisoner) it had long been evident that anyone who weighed bread out honestly wouldn't keep his job long in the bread-cutting room. There was something missing in every ration. The only question was how much. A lot? And so every day you look, to ease your soul—maybe today they didn't cheat me badly? Maybe it's close to the correct weight.

"One ounce missing," Shukhov decided. He broke the ration in two. One half he shoved down inside his clothes, beneath his underjacket, where he had sewed a special white pocket—underjackets for zeks were made without pockets. The other half he almost ate right then and there, but food is not food if eaten in a hurry. It goes down for nothing, without satisfying the appetite. He started to push the half-ration into his locker but thought better of that idea too. He remembered that the orderlies had been beaten up twice for stealing. It was a big barracks and accessible to anyone who wanted to come in.

And therefore, without letting go of the bread, Ivan Denisovich pulled his feet out of his valenki, adroitly leaving inside both his footcloths and his spoon, and climbed up barefoot. He then set to widening a little tear in his mattress, and he hid there, in the sawdust, his half-ration. He pulled his cap off, pulled out his needle and thread. They were also hidden deeply. At inspection caps were examined, and once a guard had pricked himself on the needle and almost broke Shukhov's head in fury. Stitch, stitch again, and stitch a third time, and he had sewn shut the little hole behind which the ration was hidden. By this time the sugar in his mouth had melted. Shukhov was tense as he could be. Any second the duty detail guard was going to start shouting at the door. Shukhov's fingers worked nimbly and his brain, running ahead, figured what to do next.

The Baptist was reading the Gospels, not in silence, but softly under his breath. Perhaps this was for Shukhov's benefit. Those Baptists liked to hand out a little propaganda.

"But let none of you suffer as a murderer, or a thief, or a wrongdoer, or as a mischief-maker; yet if one suffers as a Christian, let him not be ashamed, but under that name let him glorify God."

Alyesha had managed to hide his little book in a cranny in the wall so well that they hadn't found it during any search yet. He deserved a pat on the back.

Shukhov, with the same quick movements, hung his coat up on a crossbar, pulled his mittens out from under his mattress, and a second pair of footcloths —thin ones—a piece of rope and a piece of cloth with ribbons on its ends.

He smoothed out the sawdust in the mattress—it was hard and bumpy. He pushed the edges of the blanket under and tossed the pillow to its place. Then he climbed down and began to put on his footwear, first his good footcloths, then the thin ones over those.

Then the foreman coughed, got up and barked emphatically:

"Off the beds, 104th, get outside!"

Immediately the whole brigade, those dozing, those not dozing, got up, yawning, and headed for the door. The foreman had been sitting in camps for nineteen years. He wasn't likely to drive the men out for lineup one minute earlier than necessary. When he said "Get outside!" It meant get out as fast as you can.

And during the brief interval while the brigade members tramped out without a word, in file, into the corridor and then into the covered entry and out to the porch, and the foreman of the 20th, imitating Tyurin, had also declared, "Get outside!" Shukhov had succeeded in pulling on his valenki over two sets of footcloths, pulling on his coat over his underjacket and tightly belting himself with rope. (Leather belts had been taken away from any who had them— no belts in Special Camps.)

So Shukhov succeeded in getting everything done and in the covered entry he caught up with his last fellow brigade members as they hurried through the door onto the porch. Thick with layers of clothing, wearing everything they owned, the brigade members, moving in single file far enough apart to keep off each other's heels, tramped to the lineup ground. The only sound they made was the noise of feet crunching on snow.

It was still dark, though the sky in the east was becoming greenish and light. A thin mean little wind was blowing from the east, too.

There is no moment more bitter than this—to go out to lineup in the morning, in the darkness, in the cold, with hungry stomachs for a whole day. Your tongue is bitten off. You don't want to talk with each other.

Out on the lineup ground a junior work assignment officer was rushing back and forth. He snapped:

"Well, Tyurin, how long are we supposed to wait? You dragging things out again?"

Shukhov was afraid of the junior assignment officer but Tyurin certainly wasn't. He wouldn't even waste one breath on the officer this cold morning, just strode on in silence. And the whole brigade right behind him: tramp-tramp, crunch-crunch.

The two pounds of bacon evidently had worked as a bribe because the 104th was still in its old place. Some poorer and more stupid outfit was being driven out to the Socialist Life Town. Oh, but it would be ferocious out there today —a windy 17° below and no shelter, no fire!

The brigade foreman had to have a great deal of bacon. He had to have some to take to the planning and production section and some to satisfy his own stomach. The foreman, even though he didn't receive any parcels himself, ate bacon all the time. Everyone in the brigade who got any took it to him right away.

Otherwise you wouldn't last.

The senior work assignment officer noted on his board:

"One sick for you today, Tyurin, and twenty-three at work?"

Who is missing? Panteleyev is missing. Is he supposed to be sick? Immediately there were whispers in the brigade. Panteleyev, the dog, had remained in camp again. Not very likely he's sick! The security section had been asking for him. He was probably denouncing someone right now.

During the day the security section could send for him without hindrance. Hold him for three hours or more if they felt like it. No one saw. No one heard. They processed him through the medical department.

The whole lineup ground was dark with black coats. The brigades slowly pushed and shoved forward to body inspection. Shukhov remembered he had wanted to have the number on his underjacket touched up and pushed his way through the lineup ground to the far side. Two or three zeks were standing in line waiting for the artist. Shukhov got in line too. For the zeks, the number was one big pain in the neck. By your number a guard could spot you at a distance and the convoy guard could write it down, but if you let it fade, then solitary for you—why don't you take care of your number?

Three artists in the camp. They painted free pictures for the officers and in addition to that took turns at painting numbers at lineup. Today it was the old man with the little gray beard. When he painted the number on a cap with his brush he seemed like the priest anointing foreheads with oil.

He painted away and painted away and breathed into his glove. He wore thin knit gloves. His hand was stiff, didn't make the numbers clear. The artist touched up the S-854 on his underjacket. Shukhov, without buttoning his coat, because it was only a few minutes to body search, rushed off and caught up with his brigade, the rope belt in his hand. Right away he noticed that his fellow brigade member, Tsezar, was smoking. And smoking not a pipe but a cigarette. That meant he might be able to bum a butt-end. Shukhov didn't ask directly, but he moved right next to Tsezar and his face, half-turned, looked over past him.

He looked past him, pretending to be indifferent, but saw how after every puff—and they were infrequent because Tsezar was buried in thought—the red ember moved along the cigarette, and approached the cigarette holder.

Right then Fetyukov, the jackal, appeared opposite Tsezar and stared right at his mouth, his eyes burning.

Shukhov didn't have a shred of tobacco left and he didn't foresee any chance of getting any till evening. He was strained in expectation, and, it seemed at that moment that he wanted that cigarette butt more than he wanted freedom. But even so, he wouldn't humiliate himself like Fetyukov, by staring at Tsezar's lips.

All nations were mingled in Tsezar. Whether he was a Greek, Jew, or Gypsy was hard to say. He was still young. He had been a motion picture cameraman, but he hadn't even finished his own first film before he was arrested. He had a moustache, black, thick, dense as if sculptured. They were not shaved off because in his official record he had been photographed with them on.

"Tsezar Markovich!" Losing restraint, Fetyukov slobbered. "Let me have a drag!" His face was twisted with hunger and greed.

Tsezar barely raised his eyelids, which half covered his black eyes, and looked at Fetyukov. Lately Tsezar had begun to smoke a pipe so that the zeks wouldn't interrupt him while he was smoking, with a plea for a drag. It wasn't the tobacco he regretted but the interrupted thought. He smoked and gave himself over to contemplation: he got ideas that way. But he was able to hardly light a cigarette before he read in several eyes: "Let me finish it off!"

Now Tsezar turned to Shukhov and said:

"Take it, Ivan Denisych!"

And with his thumb he twisted the burning butt out of his short amber mouthpiece. Shukhov roused himself and hurriedly and gratefully took the butt end, holding a hand on guard underneath so he wouldn't drop it. He had waited for Tsezar himself to offer it. He was not offended that Tsezar was squeamish about giving him the mouthpiece along with the cigarette. After all some people have clean mouths and others have putrid mouths. And his calloused fingers were not burned, even touching the burning end. The main thing was that he had beat out the jackal, Fetyukov, and was now inhaling smoke while his lips began to burn from the fire. Yummmmmm! The smoke went all through his hungry body. He felt it in his feet and in his head.

And hardly had that bliss poured through his body than he heard the roar: "They're taking away our undershirts!"

Trouble was a zek's whole life. Shukhov was used to it. Just watch out or they'll tear out your throats.

Why undershirts? The undershirts had been given out by the chief himself! No, it couldn't be. . . .

There were two brigades ahead of them before body search. The 104th watched as the chief of camp discipline, Lieutenant Volkovoi, came out of headquarters barracks and shouted to the guards. The guards, who without Volkovoi around had been carrying out the body searches haphazardly and inactively, immediately got a real move on, went for the men like beasts. And their supervisor shouted:

"Unnnnnbutttton undershirts!"

Not just the zeks and the guards but, it was said, the chief of the camp feared Volkovoi too. His name meant "wolf." God certainly had marked that rascal well—gave him a name that belonged to him. He even glared like a wolf. Dark, tall, frowning—fast on his feet. Jumped out at people from behind barracks: "What's going on here?" No hiding from him. At first he carried a short whip, made of braided leather. They said he flogged prisoners with it, in solitary. Sometimes when the zeks were too crowded and unruly during the evening count at the barracks, he might sneak up from behind and: whop! Whip on the neck! "Why didn't you fall in, shit?" Then the men would retreat from him in a wave. The burned one grabbed his neck, wiped off the blood, kept his mouth shut—to keep from getting solitary.

Now for some reason Volkovoi had stopped carrying the whip.

In extreme cold the system of body search was relaxed in the mornings, though not in the evenings. Each zek unbuttoned his three-quarter length coat and pulled it open. Then they advanced in rows of five. Five guards stood opposite. The guards slapped the zek up the sides of his belted underjacket, clapped him on his only permitted pocket on his right knee, remaining gloved themselves. And if they felt something unusual, instead of going right after it, they asked lazily:

"What's that?"

In the mornings, what was there to look for on a zek? Knives? They don't get carried out of camp, just into camp. Mornings they just had to discover if a zek might be carrying six pounds or so of food, in order to escape. There was even a time when they were so afraid of a piece of bread, a six-ounce chunk for lunch, that they issued an order that every brigade should make a wooden case and carry in it all the brigade's bread for the midday meal. Just exactly what they expected to accomplish by this it was hard to imagine. Probably they did it just to cause trouble and extra bother. A zek had to take a bite out of his own ration to try to mark it when he put it in the case. But all those pieces were the same, just like each other, all from the same bread. So then all the way to work a zek worried whether someone else was going to get his piece. And there were quarrels between brigade members, sometimes even to the point of fights. But then three zeks ran away from the work zone in an automobile and took with them one of the wooden cases full of bread. At that point the chiefs came to their senses and all the cases were chopped up in the watch house. Everyone carry his own chunk, they said.

Another thing they were supposed to check on in the mornings was whether there might not be civilian clothes on under prison clothes. But, after all, civilian things had long since been taken away from all of them and they had been told they would not be given back till the end of their sentences. And no one had finished a term in this camp yet.

Also the guards were supposed to check to see if letters were being carried out to be passed on through a free person. But if they really looked for letters on everyone then they'd have to mess around until lunch time.

But Volkovoi shouted something, and the guards quickly took off their gloves, ordered that underjackets be opened, where everyone had stored a bit of barracks warmth, shirts be unbuttoned. Then they went on to see if something extra was being worn, against the rules. A zek was supposed to have two shirts—an undershirt and an outer shirt. The rest to be removed! That's how the zeks passed Volkovoi's order from row to row. Whatever brigades had gone through already—they were lucky. Some brigades were already outside the gates. But these men still here—open up. Whoever had something extra on, toss it down, right there in the cold.

That's the way they began, but things got in a mess. The gates had been cleared out and the convoy guards from the watch house were yelling: come on! come on! Volkovoi relaxed his rule for the 104th. He ordered that instead of removing unauthorized garments on the spot, the guards write down the names of any zek who was wearing extra clothing. In the evening the zeks must turn in the extra garments at the storeroom and with a note explaining how and why they hid them.

Everything on Shukhov was government issue. Here I am, so to speak, feel me over body and soul. But Tsezar Markovich had an extra flannelette vest which they listed and Buinovsky, too, some kind of a vest or wrap around.

Buinovsky let out a bellow. On his destroyers he had been used to shouting. And he had only been in camp three months:

"You don't have the right to undress people in the cold! You don't know the ninth clause of the criminal code!"

They have and they know. You're the one, brother, who doesn't know yet.

"You aren't Soviet people!" the captain hammered away. "You aren't Communists!"

Volkovoi let the one about the ninth clause pass, but at the next remark, like lightning, he flashed:

"Ten days of strict solitary!"

And aside to the senior guard:

"Document it for tonight."

They don't like to take men to solitary in the morning. Man-hours lost on the job. So let him break his back during the day and go to solitary in the evening.

The camp punishment prison was right next to the lineup ground. It was made of masonry, in two wings. The second wing had been added that fall. There wasn't enough room in the first. It was a prison of eighteen cells, and those cells had been partitioned off into smaller solitary confinement cells. The whole camp was built of wood: only the prison was built of concrete block.

The cold had crept under Shukhov's shirt and now he couldn't drive it out. The zeks had wrapped themselves up for nothing. Shukhov's back was bothering him again. Oh, how he'd like to be lying on a hospital cot right now—asleep. He didn't want anything more than that. And the heavier the blanket, the better.

The zeks stood in front of the gates, buttoning up, tying themselves together. Outside the gates the convoy guards waited.

"Get a move on! Get a move on!"

The work assignment officer pushed them from the rear:

"Get a move on! Get a move on!"

The first gates. The pre-zone area. The second gates. And a rail on both sides next to the watch house.

"Stop!" shouted the guard on watch. Like a herd of sheep. "Divide into fives."

It was growing light. The convoy's bonfire was burning out beyond the watch house. Before lineup they always lit a bonfire to get warm and to have more light for counting.

One watch guard counted out loudly, sharply:

"One! Two! Three!"

And the groups of five separated out into columns so that from ahead and behind there could be seen five heads, five backs, ten feet.

And a second watch guard—a count checker—stood silently at the other railing. His only job was to verify whether or not the count was correct. In addition a lieutenant was standing, watching.

He was from the camp.

A man was more precious than gold to the guards. If one head was missing behind the barbed wire, a guard would take his place.

Once more the brigade was together again.

And now the sergeant from the convoy was counting:

"One! Two! Three!"

And again the five separated and marched in individual columns.

And the assistant chief of the convoy guard was on the other side, checking. And another lieutenant.

This one was from the convoy.

The guards could not afford to make a mistake. If they signed for an extra head their own heads were forfeit.

The place was full of convoy guards. They surrounded the column of zeks in a semicircle, sub-machineguns at the ready, stuck right in your snout. And the dog-leaders were there with their gray dogs. One of the dogs bared his fangs as if he were laughing at the zeks. The convoy guards were all in short sheepskins, except for six who wore full length sheepskin coats. The long coats were assigned by the day, only to those who had to stay up in the watch towers.

And once more mingling brigades, the convoy counted the whole power station column by fives again.

"It's coldest of all at the dawn!" explained the captain. "Because that's the last point of night-time heat reduction."

The captain loved to explain things. He could tell you what phase of the moon it was, new, old, for any day of any year.

The captain himself was waning right in front of everyone. His cheeks were sunken, but his spirit hadn't collapsed.

The wind bit sharply in the open zone. Even Shukhov's face, which was used to everything, felt frostbitten. Realizing that the wind would be blowing in his teeth all the way to the project, Shukhov decided to put on his head rag. The rag, that he kept for just such cases of head wind, had a long ribbon at each end. Many zeks had such rags: they considered them helpful. He bound the cloth over his face to the very eyes, drew the tapes beneath his ears, tied them behind his head. Then he covered the back of his neck with the flap of his cap and raised the collar of his coat. Then he dropped the front flap of his cap over his forehead. Finally, only his eyes were exposed to the weather. He bound his coat tightly at the waist with his length of rope. Everything was tight by this point, and snug, except that his mittens were thin and his hands were chilled already. He rubbed and clapped them, knowing that he would have to put them behind his back and hold them there the entire march.

Every day the chief of the guard read the prisoners' "prayer." Everyone was sick and tired of it:

"Attention, prisoners! Observe strict column order. Do not stretch out; do not run; do not move from one five to another; do not talk; do not look to the sides; hold your hands behind your backs only. One step to the right or left is considered an attempt to escape and the convoy will open fire without warning! Leader, forward march!"

At that point, the two lead guards stepped forward on the road. The column swayed forward, shoulders rocking, and the convoy guards were arrayed twenty steps to the right and left of the column, ten steps apart from each other, marching, holding sub-machineguns at the ready.

There had been no snow for a week. The road was worn down, packed hard. They passed the camp and the wind hit them obliquely in the face. Hands behind their backs, heads down, the column marched as if to a funeral. And there were visible only the feet of the preceding two or three men, yes and a piece of trampled earth where you were setting down your own feet. From time to time some convoy guard would shout out: "U-47! Hands Back!" "B-502! Catch up!" And then they began to shout less often. The wind was cutting at them, and it hindered them from seeing clearly. They weren't allowed to wear face rags. Their jobs weren't too pleasant either!

When the weather was warmer everyone in the column would talk no matter how much the guards shouted. But today everyone was huddled up. Everyone was burying himself behind the back of the man in front—and deep in his own thoughts.

Even a prisoner's thoughts are not free. Shukhov's thoughts kept coming back to the same thing over and over again. Would they find the ration in the mattress? Would the infirmary let him off work in the evening? Would they put the captain in solitary or not? And how had Tsezar gotten hold of his warm underwear? Probably he had bribed someone in the storeroom for personal belongings. Where else?

Because he had breakfasted without his bread ration and eaten everything cold Shukhov felt unfed today. So that his stomach wouldn't gnaw, so that it would not beg for food, he stopped thinking about the camp and began thinking how he would soon be writing a letter home.

The column moved past the woodworking enterprise built by the zeks, past the apartment block built by the zeks in which free workers lived, past the new club built by the zeks in which only the free workers watched the movies. Then the column moved out onto the open plain, directly against the wind, facing the rosy dawn. Naked white snow lay right and left to the horizon and there wasn't a single tree on the whole steppe.

A new year had begun, '51, and Shukhov would have the right to send and receive two letters sometime during the year. He had sent his last letter off in July, and he had received an answer to it in October. In Ust-Izhma there had been a different system—write every month if you want. But what could you write about? Shukhov hadn't written home any oftener than he did now.

Shukhov had left home on June 23, 1941. That Sunday, the day before people had come from mass at church in Polomnya and said there's a war. The post office in Polomnya had heard, but in Temgenyevo no one had a radio before the war. Now, his wife wrote, there was a radio making a racket in every house—a wired loudspeaker.

Writing letters nowadays was like tossing a pebble into a deep dense pool. It sank and disappeared without a trace. You hardly felt like writing about your brigade, about what sort of a foreman Andrei Prokofyevich Tyurin was for you. Right now you had more in common with that Latvian, Kilgas, than with your family at home.

Yes, and they would write to you twice a year themselves, but you couldn't make head or tails of their lives. There was a new chairman of the collective farm, Shukhov's wife said. But there was a new one every year. The collective farm had been merged and enlarged—well they had enlarged it before and then later made it smaller again. Yes, and those who didn't fulfill their work quota on the collective farm had their garden plots cut down to less than half an acre, some of them to practically nothing.

Shukhov couldn't understand at all what his wife had written about the collective farm. She said that since the war the collective farm had not increased by even one living soul. All the young people, and whoever else could manage it, were departing in crowds for factories in the city or for the peat workings. Half of the men hadn't come back from the war at all. Those who had returned didn't pay any attention to the collective farm. They lived at home and worked on the side. The only men left in the collective farm were the foreman, Zakhar Vasilich, and the 84-year-old carpenter, Tikhon. Tikhon got married not long ago and already has children. The collective farm was still being dragged along by those same women who'd been there since 1930 when it was formed.

Shukhov couldn't understand that at all. "They live at home and work on the side." Shukhov had seen life as an individual peasant farmer as well as life as a member of the collective farm. But he couldn't understand how peasants would not work in their own village—that he couldn't accept. Did they have something like a seasonal trade away from home? And what about the haying season?

Seasonal trades away from home, his wife wrote, had long since disappeared. The men didn't get work as carpenters, though that was a craft for which their district had been famous, nor did they weave baskets because no one wanted them any more. But there was some sort of jolly new trade— painting rugs. Someone had brought stencils back from the war, and ever since then more and more painters had appeared. They weren't attached to anything, didn't work in any one place. They helped the collective farm for a month— at haying or harvest, to get a document from the farm: collective farmer so-and-so has permission to leave on his personal business and owes the farm no back payments. And then they can travel around the whole country. They even travel by plane to save time and they rake in money by the thousands. Everywhere they go they paint those rugs. For fifty rubles they paint a rug on any old wornout sheet or blanket you give them. And it takes no more than an hour. Ivan's wife cherishes the hope that he too will come home and become such a painter. Then they'll rise out of the poverty in which she is struggling, send the children to technical schools, and build a new house instead of the rotting old hut. All the rug painters are building themselves new houses. Homes near the railroad now cost, not 5,000 rubles, as they used to, but 25,000.

So he wrote and asked his wife—how could he become a painter if as long as he could remember he'd never even been able to draw? And what kind of miraculous rugs were they anyway, what do they have on them? His wife answered that only a fool couldn't draw these: put down the stencil and brush through the holes. There were types: One rug was called "Troika"—a beautiful troika in full regalia carrying a Hussar officer. The second was called "Reindeer" and the third was an imitation of a Persian rug. And that was all the designs there were. But everywhere in the country people were glad to get them and would say thank you and practically grab them out of your hands. Because they were only fifty rubles, while a real rug cost several thousand.

Shukhov just wished he could get a look at one of those rugs.

During his many years in camps and prisons Ivan Denisovich had lost the habit of thinking about tomorrow, about what might happen in a year's time, and planning how to feed his family. The camp administration did all his thinking for him, and in a way that was simpler. Besides he still had two full years to serve. But that rug deal really had him bothered.

Earnings there, obviously, as easy as spitting. And one wouldn't want to be behind all one's fellow-villagers. That would hurt. . . . But, really, Ivan Denisovich didn't want to get involved with those rugs. One had to have impertinence, insolence, for that sort of thing. One had to grease someone's extended hand. Shukhov had been tramping the earth for forty years. Half his teeth were gone already. There was a bald spot on his head. But he'd never given a bribe to anyone, never taken one. He hadn't learned that bit even in camp.

Easy money has no weight, no feeling that you've earned it. The old folks were right when they said that what you don't pay for in full you don't take all the way home. Shukhov's hands were still skilled, capable. Was it possible that when he got free he wouldn't find work as a stove-builder, carpenter, tinsmith!

But then, perhaps he wouldn't be allowed to work, because he had been in prison. Maybe they wouldn't let him go home either. Then maybe he'd be ready to try the rug deal.

By this time the column had reached its destination and was standing in front of the watch house of the outer zone of the *project*. Even before that, from the corner of the zone, two convoy guards in long sheepskin coats had separated from the others and made their way across the field to their distant watch towers. Until all the watch towers were manned they wouldn't let the prisoners inside the zone. The chief of convoy guards, sub-machinegun hung over his shoulder, went into the watch house. Smoke kept pouring out of the watch house chimney. They kept a civilian watchman there all night long to prevent pilferage of cement and planks.

Through the wire gates, across the construction zone, and through the wire away over on the far side, a big red sun was rising through a mist. Standing next to Shukhov, Alyesha looked happily at the sun, a smile curving his lips. Sunken cheeks, lives on his ration, doesn't earn an extra penny—what's he so happy about? On Sundays he whispers and mumbles with the other Baptists. Camp life rolls off them like water off a duck's back.

Shukhov's muzzle for the wind, his face rag, had become all wet from his breath. And here and there the frost had caught it, so it had a crust of ice. Shukhov shifted it from face to neck, turned to stand with his back to the wind. The cold hadn't gotten inside his clothes very much, but his hands had grown chilled in his thin mittens, and so had the toes on his left foot. They were numb. That left felt boot of his was worn out. It had been mended twice already.

He ached from the small of his back all the way up to his shoulders. How was he supposed to work?

He looked around and noticed his brigade foreman, Tyurin. He was in the last five. The foreman was wide in the shoulders and broad in the face. With a scowl. He permitted his brigade no nonsense, but he fed them pretty well. He worried about getting them a better bread ration. He was in camp for the second term, a real son of GULAG, the agency that administered concentration camps for the whole country. He knew camp life and customs from beginning to end.

In camp a foreman is everything to the zek. A good foreman can give you a second life. A bad foreman will drive you into a wooden overcoat—underground. Andrei Prokofyevich knew Shukhov from Ust-Izhma, the general camp where they had met. But in that camp Ivan hadn't been in Andrei's brigade. And when they had driven all of those sentenced under the 58th clause of the code—the clause dealing with counter-revolutionary crimes and activities—from Ust-Izhma to this hard-labor camp, Tyurin had picked him up here. Shukhov had nothing to do with the chief of the camp, with the planning and production section, with the work bosses, with the engineers. His foreman stood up for him as if he were made of iron. And in return if Tyurin frowned or raised his finger, Shukhov ran fast, did whatever he wanted. Deceive whoever you feel like deceiving in the camp—but not Andrei Prokofyevich. That way you stay alive.

Shukhov wanted to ask the foreman whether they would work where they had the day before or move on to another place—but he hesitated to interrupt Tyurin's weighty thoughts. He had just settled the business of that Socialist Life Town and now was thinking about the problem of "exceeding the quota." This meant the food for the whole brigade for the next five days.

The foreman's face was marked by big red pits, from smallpox. He stood facing the wind without squinting. The skin on his face was like oak bark.

The zeks slapped their hands together, stamped up and down, throughout the column. A mean wind. Well, it looked as if the birds were now perched in all six of the watch towers. But they still weren't admitting prisoners to the zone. More vigilance.

At last the chief of escort guard and the checking officer came out of the watch house, stopped at the gates and opened them.

"Ssseppparrrattte by fffffivvvves; Onnne! Twooo!"

The prisoners marched as if on parade, almost in step. If only they could get inside the zone! You don't need to teach them what to do there.

Right behind the watch house was the office shed. Next to the office, the project construction supervisor was calling all the brigade foremen to him. They were hurrying over. Der was going, too. He was a junior work supervisor who had been a zek. He was a real swine, who drove his brother zeks worse than any dog.

It was eight o'clock, five minutes after eight—that generator train had just blown its whistle—and the officers were afraid that the zeks might waste time, might scatter around to warm themselves. But the zeks had a long day ahead of them. There was time for everything. The ones already inside the zone were bending over, searching. Here a stick. There a stick. Kindling for the stove. They shoved the pieces of wood into hiding places in their ragged clothes.

Tyurin ordered Pavlo, his assistant, to accompany him to the office. Tsezar headed that way too. Tsezar was rich. He got parcels twice a month and made presents wherever it was necessary. He was employed in the office in a soft job as assistant to the work norms officer.

And the rest of the 104th moved to the side right away—stay out of sight, out of sight.

The sun rose red, foggy, over the empty zone. Over the section where the panels for prefab houses were piled up, covered with snow. Over the place where a foundation had been dug and some cement blocks had been laid. Over the spot where an excavator lay abandoned, along with a scoop and a mass of iron scrap. There were ditches, trenches, and holes all about. There were the auto repair shops ready to be roofed over. And on a ridge stood the power station under construction, with the second floor already started.

All the men had hidden. The only people outside were the six guards up in the towers—and the big to-do going on next to the office. Now this is our chance! The senior work supervisor had threatened many times to give out the brigade assignments the night before, but he never managed to do it because between evening and morning everything had always been turned upside down.

So this moment is ours. While the bosses are settling the assignments, hide. Hide wherever it's warmer. Sit down, sit. Don't break your back. If you're near a stove, it's a good idea to turn your footcloths about and warm them a bit. Then your feet will be warm the rest of the day. And even with no stove handy—not bad then, either!

The 104th went into a big hall in the auto repair shops that had been glassed in since fall, where the 38th brigade was pouring concrete panels. Some panels were lying in their forms and others were set upright. One on side there was reinforcement netting. Earthen floor and high ceiling. It wasn't possible to keep that building very warm, nevertheless they heated the place. They don't mind using coal. Of course they don't use it so that people can get warm, but so that the panels will dry better. There was even a thermometer hanging in there.

And on Sundays, if the zeks didn't go out to work, there was a civilian to keep the stove going.

The 38th, of course, didn't permit anyone from another brigade near the stove. They monopolized it themselves. Well, that's all right! We can sit in the corner. That's not so bad either.

Shukhov rested the backside of his cotton-padded trousers, which had rested on almost everything, on the edge of a wooden form. He leaned back against the wall. As he leaned back, his coat and underjacket stretched out and on the left side of his chest, next to his heart, he felt a sudden pressure. This hard object was the piece of bread, his morning ration which he had taken with him for lunch. He always took half his ration to work with him and didn't touch it till lunch. But other days he ate half at breakfast, and today he hadn't. And Shukhov understood at last that he wasn't really ahead. He wanted to eat that half ration right now, while he was warm. Five hours to lunch. A long time!

The pain in his back had now settled into his legs. They felt very weak. Oh, if only he could get to a stove.

Shukhov put his mittens on his knees, unbuttoned his coat, untied his frozen face rag, bent it across several times to snap off the ice, and dropped it in his pocket. Then he got out his bread, wrapped in a white cloth, and, holding the cloth so that not a crumb could escape, he started to bite slowly into the bread and chew it. Since the bread had been carried beneath two layers of clothing, warmed with his body, it wasn't the least bit frozen.

In camps Shukhov had often remembered how they ate at home in the village; potatoes by the frying-panful, kasha by the cast-iron potful, and long ago, meat in big chunks. And then they had swilled milk till their stomachs were ready to burst. Shukhov had learned in camp that it shouldn't have been that way. One should eat so that one's mind focuses on what one is eating. Like now, these little pieces that you bite off and mill about with your tongue and suck with your cheeks. How tasty that wet black bread is. What has Shukhov been eating for eight-years-going-on-nine? Nothing. But work he's done! Ho-ho! Not so bad!

So Shukhov was occupied with his six ounces, and near him sat the whole 104th.

Two Estonians, who were as close as brothers, sat on a low concrete panel and took turns smoking half a cigarette from one cigarette holder. Both of them were blonds, both tall, both spare, with long noses, big eyes. They stayed so close that it seemed as if one couldn't breathe the blue air without the other. The foreman never separated them. They shared all their food and slept on an upper bunk together. And they talked with each other all the time, softly and slowly when they stood in the column, or waited at lineup, or went to bed at night. But they weren't brothers at all and had met right there in the 104th. One was a sailor who had been raised at the coast; the other, when Soviet power had been established, had been taken to Sweden as a child. He had grown up and on his own had returned to Estonia for his education.

They say nationality doesn't mean anything, that in every nation there are men who are no good. But no matter how many Estonians Shukhov met, he never came across a bad one.

So the prisoners all sat, some on panels, some on casing for panels, some on the ground. The tongue won't wag in the morning; everyone concentrated on his own thoughts, everyone was silent. Fetyukov, the jackal, had somehow collected some cigarette butts. He would even forage butts out of a spittoon— he didn't care. Now he had them out on his knee where he was unrolling them and pouring the unburned tobacco into one paper. Fetyukov had three children on the outside, but when he had been arrested all of them renounced him, and his wife married again. So he got no help from them.

Buinovsky kept looking sideways at Fetyukov and finally barked at him.

"Why are you picking up all kinds of crap? You'll end up with syphilis of the lip! Get rid of that!"

The naval captain was used to giving orders: he spoke to everyone that way. But Buinovsky had no hold on Fetyukov. The captain got no parcels either. Laughing maliciously Fetyukov said:

"Wait a while, captain. You just serve for eight years—and you'll be picking things up, too. Prouder people than you have come to camp. . . ."

Fetyukov was judging by his own standards, but the captain might just make it in his own way. . . .

"What, what?" The deaf Senka Klevshin hadn't heard what was said: he thought the conversation was about Buinovsky's trouble at lineup. He said, "You shouldn't have stuck your neck out!" He shook his head in distress. "Everything would have worked out all right."

Senka Klevshin was a quiet, unfortunate man. One of his eardrums had been broken in 1941. Then he had been taken prisoner, escaped, been recaptured and shoved into Buchenwald. By a miracle he had escaped death in Buchenwald. Now he was serving his sentence quietly. "Stick your neck out," he said, "and you're done for."

That was right. Groan and bend. If you fight back you'll be broken.

Alyesha was silent, his face in his hands. He was praying.

Shukhov ate his bread ration right down to the last crumb, leaving only a round piece of crust from the top of the bread. No spoon in the world is as good at cleaning the last bit of kasha from your bowl as a piece of bread. He rewrapped that piece of crust in the white cloth to save it for lunch, put the cloth in his inside pocket beneath the underjacket, fastened himself up against the cold, and was ready. Let them send him out to work now. Though it would be nicer if they took a while longer.

The 38th got up and separated. Some went to the cement mixer, some for water, some over to the reinforcing rods. Neither Tyurin nor his assistant Pavlo came to the 104th. And even though the brigade had been waiting hardly twenty minutes, and the working day (shortened for winter) lasted until six, this pause seemed to all of them great good luck, as if the hours to evening had really been cut shorter.

The red-faced, well-fed Latvian, Kilgas, sighed. "Well, we haven't had any snowstorms for a long time! The whole winter long—not one snowstorm! What kind of winter is that?"

"Yes—no snowstorms, no snowstorms," the rest of the brigade sighed in turn.

When one of the local snowstorms started blowing in that area, it wasn't just a question of not going out to work. They were not even let out of barracks. Between the barracks and the mess hall you could get lost if you didn't hold on to the guide rope. If a prisoner got frozen in the snow, let a dog eat him—who cared. But if he ran away? There had been cases. During the snowstorms the snow was very fine and if it lodged in a drift it became as hard as if someone had packed it down. A few men had escaped over the barbed wire on such a drift. True, they didn't get far.

If one really considered it, there wasn't any advantage to a snowstorm. The zeks were under lock and key. Coal wasn't sent on time. The warmth was blown out of the barracks. Flour wasn't delivered, so there was no bread. They didn't get things done in the kitchen. And no matter how long the storm lasted —three days or a week—those days were counted as if they were rest days, and afterwards for that many Sundays in a row they marched you out to work.

Just the same the zeks loved snowstorms and prayed for them. If the wind rose a bit, everyone watched the sky. *Come on stuff! Come on stuff!*

They meant snow.

Someone tried to move up close to the stove of the 38th to get warm, but he was pushed away.

Tyurin came in. He was gloomy. The brigade members understood that there was work to be done, quickly.

"Sssooo!" Tyurin looked around. "Everyone here, 104?"

And then without checking and counting them, because no one could have gone anywhere, he handed out assignments swiftly. He sent the two Estonians and Klevshin and Gopchik to get the big mortar mixing box nearby, to bring it into the power station building. It was clear that the brigade was moving over to work on the power station building which was incomplete and which had been untouched since autumn. He sent another two men to the tool room where Pavlo was getting the tools. He ordered four men to clear the snow next to the power station building, at the entrance to the generator room, in the generator room itself, and off the ladders. Two others he told to start a fire in the stove in the generator room with coal and with whatever wood they could swipe. He sent one to take cement to the building on a sled, two to bring water, two to get sand, and one more to help clean the snow off that sand and break it up with a crowbar.

And after all this only Shukhov and Kilgas—the most highly skilled workers in the brigade—remained unassigned. Calling them over, the foreman said:

"Listen here, boys!" Even though he was no older than they were, he called all of them boys. "After lunch you'll lay cement blocks on the second-story wall, up there where the sixth brigade left off last fall. Right now the problem is to heat up the generator room. There are three big windows there. Cover them with something. I'll give you men some others to help; just figure out what we can use to cover the windows. The generator room is going to be used both for mixing and for warming ourselves. And if we don't have a place to warm ourselves we're going to freeze like dogs."

Maybe he would have said something else but Gopchik rushed up to complain. He was a boy of sixteen, rosy as a piglet. The other brigade wouldn't hand over the mixing box, was fighting over it. Tyurin ran right out there.

No matter how hard it was to begin the working day in such cold, the only important thing was to cross over that beginning, just that.

Shukhov and Kilgas looked at one another. They had worked together often and respected each other's skills both as carpenter and mason. To scrounge around and come up with something, out there in the naked snow, something practical to cover the window openings, was not going to be easy. But Kilgas said:

"Vanya, where the prefabricated panels are stored I know there's a big roll of roofing paper. I hid it myself. Shall we go get it?"

Kilgas, though a Latvian, knew Russian as if it were his own tongue. Next to his home was a village of Old Believers,[2] and he'd learned Russian in his childhood. He had only been in camps for two years, but he already understood the important thing: if you don't bite it off yourself you won't get it at all. His name was Johann. Shukhov called him Vanya, as he called Shukhov Vanya.

They decided to go for the roofing. But first Shukhov ran into the auto repair shop, which was under construction, to get his mason's trowel. A well-balanced trowel is important to a mason especially if it's light and fits the hand. But at the construction projects tools were handed out every morning and turned in every evening. Whatever you got the next day was just a matter of luck. But Shukhov once managed to give the tool clerk a short count and thus grab off the best trowel. Every day he hid it again. And every morning if he was laying brick or block he went to get it. Of course, if they had driven the 104th out to the Socialist Life Town today he would have been left without his trowel. But now he moved some stones, stuck his fingers into a cranny, and pulled it out.

Shukhov and Kilgas went out of the auto repair shop toward the prefabricated houses. Their breath formed thick steam. The sun had already risen but it was without rays as if in a fog, and along the sides of the sun there rose streaks almost like poles of light.

"Are they poles?" Shukhov asked, gesturing at the sun with his head.

"Poles don't bother us," Kilgas brushed the remark aside, laughing. "Just so they don't have barbed wire on them. That's the kind to watch out for."

Kilgas could hardly talk without joking. The whole brigade liked him for that. And other Latvians in the camp all esteemed him a great deal. Well, Kilgas

[2] [A sect that refused to accept liturgical reforms introduced into the Russian Orthodox Church in the seventeenth century.—Editors' note.]

ate normally. Got two packages a month. Rosy-cheeked as if he weren't in the camp at all. He could afford to joke.

The zone for their construction project was big. It was a long way across. On the way they ran into the boys from the 82nd. They had been ordered again to try to dig holes in the frozen ground. Not very big holes, a foot and a half wide by a foot and a half long and a foot and a half deep. But the ground was like stone here, even in summer, and now, frozen solid, just try to chew it up. Pound it with a pick and the pick merely slides off. Sparks—but no loosened dirt, not a crumb. Each of the men was standing over his little hole, and looked around as Shukhov and Kilgas went by. No place to get warm, and they were not permitted to leave their posts. Back to the pick—the only warmth there came from using it.

Shukhov saw an acquaintance among them, a fellow from Vyatka, and advised him, "Listen here, you earth-cutters, what you ought to do is build a fire over every hole. That way the earth would thaw out."

"They don't permit it," said the fellow from Vyatka. "They don't give us any firewood."

"You have to find it."

Kilgas just spat.

"Well, now, tell me, Vanya, if the bosses were smart—would they really put men hammering at the ground with picks in such cold?"

Kilgas swore several times indistinctly and shut up. You don't talk much in that kind of cold. They went further and came to the place where the panels of the prefabs were piled beneath the snow.

Shukhov liked working with Kilgas. Just one disappointment about Kilgas. He didn't smoke and got no tobacco in his parcels.

This was really the right spot. Kilgas was an observing sort. Together they raised one plank, then another. Under the planks was a roll of roofing.

They pulled it out. Now, how to carry it? If the guards saw them from the watch towers that didn't matter. The birds perched up there had just one concern—that the zeks did not escape. And the guards inside the working zone? Well, for all they cared you could chop up all the panels for firewood. Even if a camp guard ran smack into you, that was all right, too. He would be looking around himself for something he could use at home. And so far as the ordinary zeks were concerned, they spit on those prefabs. And the brigade foremen, too. The only men who cared about them were, first, the civilian (in other words, free) work supervisor; second, the junior work supervisor, Der (a zek); and then, third, the tall, thin Shkuropatenko. He was a nobody, Shkuropatenko, just another zek. He'd been given a work assignment at time rates for just one thing—to keep the zeks from walking off with the prefabs. That Shkuropatenko was the type who would be most likely to catch them out in the open.

"Here's what, Vanya, we can't carry it lengthwise," said Shukhov. "Let's carry it upright, holding it up from both sides and move along with it quickly, covering it with our bodies. From a distance no one will be able to make it out."

Shukhov's idea was not so bad. It wouldn't be smart to carry the roll length-wise, so they didn't carry it that way, but held it up between them like a third man, and hurried away with it. From the side the only thing that could be seen was two men walking close together.

"But the work supervisor is going to see that roofing on the windows. He'll figure it out," said Shukhov.

"What's that got to do with us?" Kilgas asked, surprised. "So they come to the power station and it's already there. So, it *was* there before. Do you think they're going to tear it down?"

That made sense.

His fingers had grown numb in his thin mittens, he could hardly feel them. But his left felt boot was holding up. The valenki—they were the main thing. Hands would get warm in work.

They made their way on virgin snow. Then they came to a sled track that led from the tool storeroom to the power station. Evidently the cement had been carted along ahead.

The power station stood on a ridge. Behind it the zone came to an end. It had been a long time since anyone had worked on the power station, and all the approaches to it were covered with snow. The sled tracks and the fresh deep trail seemed really clear by contrast. Brigade members had passed that way, clearing off the snow with wooden shovels near the power station and the auto road.

It would be very pleasant if the elevator at the power station were working. But the motor had burned out, and it had not been fixed. Everything would have to be hauled by hand up to the second story. Mortar. Cement blocks.

For two months the power station had stood there like a gray skeleton abandoned in the snow. And then the 104th had come along. And what was there to hold the men of the 104th together? Empty stomachs tied about with canvas belts? Crackling cold? No cover, and no spark of a fire. Nevertheless the 104th arrived, and life began again in the building.

At the very entrance to the generator room the mortar mixing box had fallen apart. The box was rotten. Shukhov hadn't even believed that it would arrive in one piece. The foreman swore a whole series of oaths, just for appearance's sake, but he could see that no one was to blame. And at that moment Shukhov and Kilgas came in with the roofing between them. The foreman was pleased. Immediately he rearranged his men. Shukhov to fix the stovepipe, so that the stove could be lit as soon as possible. Kilgas to fix the mixing box, with the two Estonians to help him. And for Senka Klevshin there's an axe, cut up some long planks so we have something to fasten the roofing to. Two widths of roofing would cover the window. Where should the planks come from? The work supervisor won't allot boards just for shelter. The foreman looked around and so did the rest of them. One way to get planks was to knock off a pair of boards that served as handrails on the ladder to the second floor. What else was there to do? When you climb up don't be careless or you'll fall off.

One might wonder why a zek in for ten years should break his back working hard in a camp. I don't feel like it—and that's that, so to speak. Fool away the time during the day till evening. The night is mine.

Well, it didn't work that way. That was the reason the work brigades were organized. Not the same kind of brigade as in freedom, where Ivan Ivanych receives separate pay and Petr Petrovich separate pay. In camps the brigade is a kind of system to make the zeks watch each other so the administration doesn't have to. Here's the way it goes: either everyone gets *additional* food or everyone goes hungry. If you don't work, you viper, I will be hungry because of you. Get a move on, you shit!

A set-up like this put the screws on. Very unlikely that you could sit around on your ass. Want to or not you jump, hop, get moving. If we haven't built shelter for ourselves in two hours, then we're all screwed. But good.

Pavlo had brought the tools. Just pick out what you need. And some stovepipe. No tinsmith's tools, true, but there's a metal-workers' hammer and a small axe. We'll manage one way or another.

Shukhov was clapping his hands together to warm them, and matching stovepipes and pounding the joints together. Clap again and pound again. He had hidden his trowel close by. Even though they were all from his own brigade they might switch it on him. Even Kilgas.

All thought whisked out of his head. Shukhov didn't recollect anything or concern himself with anything at all. He kept in mind just one thing—how to place and arrange the stovepipe elbows in such a way that the stove wouldn't smoke. Gopchik was sent to look for wire—to fasten the stovepipe at the window where it emerged to the outside.

In the corner there was another stove, a low-slung one with a brick chimney. It had a cast-iron plate atop it which grew hot and on which sand was thawed and dried. The brigade had already built a fire in that stove and the captain and Fetyukov were hauling barrows of sand to it. No intelligence needed to push hand barrows. So the foreman put the former bosses on that job. Fetyukov, they said, had been a big chief in some office or other, and used to go about in a car.

Fetyukov at first had tried to bully the captain, yelled at him. But the captain whacked him in the teeth just once. After that they made peace.

The zeks were pushing their way to that stove to warm themselves, but the foreman warned them.

"I'll warm you—on the head! Do your work first!"

Show the whip to the whipped dog, and that's enough. The cold was fierce but the foreman fiercer! The men moved off to their jobs.

Shukhov heard the foreman say softly to Pavlo:

"You stay here. Hold tight. I have to go and exceed the quota."

More depended on surpassing the quota than on the work itself. A smart foreman was one who worked hard on the paper work involved in reporting plan fulfillment—on "surpassing the quota." That was how one got fed. Whatever hadn't been done—prove that it had been done. Whatever was classified at cheap rates—manipulate it so that it was classified at higher rates. For this maneuvering a foreman needed a quick mind. Plus some pull with the quota-setters. The quota-setters had to be handed gifts, too. And if one thought about it—who were those quotas for? For the camp. The camp raked in thousands of extra rubles from the construction organizations and gave bonuses to its officers. To Volkovoi for his whip. While the zeks got six extra ounces of bread in the evening. Six ounces of bread rules life.

The men carried in two buckets of water which had frozen on the way. Pavlo decided that there was no point to getting any more. Better to melt snow right in the building. They put the buckets on the stove.

Gopchik swiped some new aluminum wire, the kind the electricians were putting up. He said: "Ivan Denisych! Here's good wire to make a spoon. Will you teach me to cast a spoon?"

Ivan Denisych loved that little rogue Gopchik. His own son had died in child-hood and he had two grown daughters at home. Gopchik had been imprisoned because he carried some milk to the woods for the Western Ukrainian Bendera partisans.[3] He had been sentenced as if he were an adult. He was a gentle little calf and played up to all the men. But he'd already acquired some slyness. He ate what was in his food parcels all by himself, alone. Sometimes he was even chewing away at night.

Well, after all, he couldn't feed everyone.

They broke off a piece of wire for the spoon and hid it in a corner. Shukhov used two boards to hammer together a makeshift stepladder and sent Gopchik climbing up to hang the stovepipe. Gopchik was as quick as a squirrel. He made his way up the crosspieces, hammered in a nail, hung the wire on it and slung it around the pipe. Shukhov wasn't idling, either. He made the outlet for the stovepipe, using one extra elbow. Even if there wasn't much wind today there might be some tomorrow, and he didn't want the smoke backing up, not when this stove was for themselves.

Senka Klevshin had already split some long planks. They told Gopchik-Klopchik to nail them in place. The imp clambered about and yelled down at them from above.

The sun rose higher and chased away the mist. There were no more of those sunrays that resembled poles. Crimson sparkled inside the building. Right then they lit the second stove with the stolen firewood. A lot happier!

"In January the sun warms the cow's ass!" announced Shukhov.

Kilgas finished fixing the mixing box, gave it one last whack with the axe and shouted:

"Listen, Pavlo, I won't take less than one hundred rubles from the foreman for that work!"

Pavlo laughed:

"You'll get one hundred grams." That would be about three ounces of vodka.

"The prosecutor will add something to it," shouted Gopchik from up above.

---

[3] [Stepan Bendera, a Western Ukrainian, led a group that for a while collaborated with the Germans.—Editors' note.]

"Don't touch that, don't touch that!" Shukhov yelled to the boy. That wasn't the right way to cut the roofing.

Shukhov showed him how it ought to be done.

The men crowded up to the iron stove; Pavlo chased them away. He gave Kilgas some helpers, and ordered him to make hand barrows for carrying the cement. He set a few more men to hauling sand, and sent some up above to clean the snow off the scaffolding and off the section where new blocks were to be laid. One more man was assigned to move the heated sand from the stove top to the mixing box.

Outside a motor sputtered; the concrete blocks were being delivered. A truck was making its way through the snow. Pavlo went out to wave it in and point out where to dump the blocks.

They nailed up one sheet of roofing, and another. What protection would it be? It's just paper. But it looked as if a real wall was there. Inside it became darker. In the dimness the stove seemed brighter.

Alyesha brought coal. Some shouted at him, "Pour it on!" Others, "Don't pour it on! At least with firewood we can warm up." He just stood there, confused.

Fetyukov got up to the stove and, like an idot, stuck his valenki right in the fire. The captain lifted him by the scruff of his neck, and shoved him at the barrows:

"Go and haul sand, scum!"

The captain regarded camp work like naval service. If you're told to do something, do it! His cheeks had sunken fast in the last month but he pulled his load.

Finally all three windows had been closed in. The only light came from the doors now. And the cold came in that way, too. Pavlo ordered the top parts of the doors shut off and the bottoms left as they were, so a man could walk in if he stooped. They boarded them off as he directed.

By this time three truckloads of blocks had been delivered. The problem now was how to get the blocks up without any elevator.

"Masons! Let's go up!" Pavlo shouted in his customary broad Ukrainian.

That was a matter of honor. Shukhov, Kilgas and Pavlo climbed up. The ladder was narrow enough anyway but now that Senka had knocked the railing off it you had to press close to the wall so you didn't fall. Worse, snow had stuck to the treads and made them rounded. No footing. How would they carry up the mortar?

They looked at the place they were to lay blocks. The snow was being shovelled off. Right here. They'd have to hammer the ice off the top layer of the last rungs and then sweep with a twig broom.

They studied the layout for the best way to get the blocks up to the second story. After looking down they decided that instead of having the men climb up that long ladder carrying blocks, they would put four men on the ground to toss blocks up to the scaffolding stage. From there another two men could pass the blocks up. On the second floor another two could deliver them to the masons. That would be the fastest way.

Up on the second floor the wind wasn't strong, but it cut. As soon as they started to lay blocks it would get hold of them all right. But if they could get behind the rows already done, there'd be some protection; not too bad, much warmer.

Shukhov looked at the sky, surprised. In the clear sky the sun had almost reached lunch time. Miracle of miracles. That's the way time passes at work. Many times Shukhov had noticed that the days in the camp just rolled by. There was no time to look around. But his term didn't seem to change; as if it wasn't getting shorter at all.

They went down and found the rest of the men were sitting around the stove. Only the captain and Fetyukov were carrying sand. Pavlo, furious, sent eight men to fetch blocks, two to pouring cement into the mixing box where they were to mix it dry with the sand. Another for water. Another for coal. Kilgas said to his crew:

"Come on, boys, get those barrows finished."

"Should I help them?" Shukhov asked Pavlo.

"Go ahead," Pavlo nodded.

Then they brought a tank in which to melt snow for the cement. Someone announced it was noon.

"Right," declared Shukhov. "The sun's at its peak."

"If it's at its peak," retorted the captain, "then that means it's not noon but one o'clock."

"Why is that?" Shukhov was surprised. "Every grandfather knows that the sun is highest of all at noon."

"*That* for the grandfathers!" the captain shot back. "Since their time a new decree has been passed. The sun is highest at one o'clock."

"Whose decree?"

"Soviet authority."

The captain went out with the barrows. But Shukhov wouldn't have argued with him anyway. Was it possible that the sun was subject to government decrees, too?

They hammered, pounded, and finished four barrows.

"All right—let's sit down and warm up," Pavlo said to the two masons. "You too, Senka. After lunch you're going to lay blocks with them."

So they had a right to sit by the stove. There wasn't time to begin laying blocks before the meal break and if the cement were mixed too soon it would freeze.

The coal had finally begun to burn and was now throwing off heat steadily. But you could only feel it if you were right beside the stove. The rest of the room was just as cold as ever.

All four took off their mittens and held their hands near the warmth.

But feet in boots or shoes should never be put near a fire. You have to learn that. If you're wearing boots, then the leather will crack in the heat. Valenki grow damp, steam rises from them, and you won't be the slightest bit warmer. And if you try getting even closer to the fire, you'll burn them. That means you wear them with a hole till spring. Don't expect another pair.

"What's it to Shukhov?" Kilgas teased. "Shukhov, brothers, has one foot out of here already."

"That one there—the barefoot one," someone added. They all laughed. Shukhov had taken off his mended felt boot and was warming up the footcloths.

"Shukhov's finishing up his term."

Kilgas was in for twenty-five years. In the good old days, everyone got the same haircut—ten years. But from 1949 a new era had begun—twenty-five years to everyone, no matter what. One might manage to last ten years without kicking the bucket, but just try and stick it for twenty-five.

Shukhov enjoyed having everyone point at him. Actually, he was finishing up his term, but he didn't seriously believe it would end. After all, during the war everyone whose sentence ended was held until a special order was issued in 1946. So the ones who had had a basic sentence of three years got five more. Law—that was something the government turned inside out as it pleased. So your ten is ended. Then they'll say, here you are, take ten more. Or go into exile.

Still, once in a while you'd think about it and it would take your breath away. In spite of everything the term is coming to an end. The spool unwinds . . . good God! To step outside a free man. Free!?

However, it wasn't right for an old camp veteran to talk about that out loud. And so Shukhov said to Kilgas:

"Just don't bother to count your twenty-five. To sit for twenty-five years is like trying to paddle a canoe with a pitchfork. But I have sat out eight full ones—that's the truth."

You live with your head in the sand, like an ostrich, and you don't have time to think how you got into prison and how you'll get out.

According to his record, Shukhov had been sentenced for treason and he had testified to it himself. That he had surrendered to the Germans in order to be a traitor to the motherland, and had returned to the Russian army because he was carrying out assignments for German intelligence. What kind of assignments these were neither Shukhov nor the investigator could invent. So that's the way it was left—just assignments.

Shukhov had simply figured: If you don't sign it means a wooden overcoat. If you sign, you live a little longer. So he signed.

Actually here's what happened. In February '42 on the Northwest front the Russian forces were encircled. No food was dropped to them: there weren't any planes. It got so bad that they were cutting hooves off dead horses, soaking them and eating them. No ammunition. And so the Germans captured them a few at a time. In one such group, Shukhov spent a couple of days as a prisoner, in the woods. Then five men escaped. They slunk through woods, waded through swamps and by a miracle got back to their own lines. But two were shot down by a machine gunner, a third died from wounds. Only two survived. They would have been smarter to have explained that they were lost in the forest. That would have been all right. But they said that they had escaped.

The interrogators shouted, "Escaped from the Germans? Palm that off on your mother!" If all five had been alive maybe they'd have compared the stories and believed the evidence. But they didn't believe two. The interrogators shouted, "You bastards fixed up your 'escape' stories together."

Senka Klevshin heard through his deafness the talk about escape from the Germans and said loudly:

"I escaped from them three times and three times they caught me."

Senka, long-sufferer, was usually silent. He couldn't hear much of what people said, so he didn't talk much. They didn't know a great deal about him except that he had been in Buchenwald, was a member of the underground there, and had smuggled in weapons for the mutiny there. The Germans had hung him up by the arms and beat him with sticks.

"Vanya, you've sat eight years—in what camps?" Kilgas argued. "You were in ordinary camps, living with women. You didn't wear any numbers. Just try and sit eight years in a hard-labor camp! No one yet has sat them out to the end."

"With women? With logs, not with women. . . ."

Shukhov stared into the fire and remembered his seven years in the north. For three years he had hauled logs for crating material and railway ties. And the bonfires had flamed there too—at the timber cuttings at night. The chief had ordered that a brigade which didn't fulfill the day's quota must remain in the forest at night. They didn't get back to the camp till after midnight and were out in the woods in the morning again.

"Nnoo, brothers. . . . It's quieter here, I'd say," he said. "Here whether quotas have been fulfilled or not, it's back to the camp. And the rock-bottom minimum ration is three ounces more than it was there. You can live here. So it's a Special Camp, so what! Do the numbers bother you? They don't weigh anything, those numbers."

"Quieter here," Fetyukov hissed. Everyone was near the stove now, since the lunch break was close. "They knife people in their beds. Quieter."

"Not people but stool-pigeons!" Pavlo pointed his finger threateningly at Fetyukov.

It was true that something new had started in camp. Two well-known stool-pigeons had been knifed in their bunks at the rising gong. Then one innocent working stiff. Had they confused the bunk? One stool-pigeon had run to the officers in the camp punishment prison, and they had hidden him there, in the stone prison. Strange. Nothing like that in ordinary camps. Yes, and it hadn't happened here before this either.

Suddenly the power train whistle blew. Not a full blast at first but a hoarse one as if it were clearing its throat.

Half a day out of the way. Lunch break.

Whew, they'd been slow. They should have gone to the mess-hall long since and taken a place in line. There were eleven brigades at the project and no more than two could get in the mess hall at the same time.

But the foreman still hadn't come. Pavlo looked around quickly.

"Shukhov and Gopchik—with me. Kilgas! When I send Gopchik to you bring the whole brigade."

Their places at the stove were taken immediately. Men surrounded the stove as if it were a woman and they were getting close to embrace her.

"Move off it," some shouted. "Let's have a smoke!"

They all looked at each other to see who would light up. But no one had anything to smoke. Either there was no tobacco or whoever had any was hiding it.

Shukhov and Gopchik went out with Pavlo. Gopchik trailed after them like a little rabbit.

"It's warmer," Shukhov immediately decided. "No more than zero, now. It won't be so bad laying blocks."

They looked back at the blocks. The men had thrown a pile up on the scaffolding. Some blocks were already piled on the second floor.

Shukhov also squinted up at the sun, testing to see if the captain was right about that decree.

Out in the open the wind was still biting. It still smarted as if to say, don't forget it's January.

The work kitchen was just a small shed of planks hammered together around a stove, with rusty sheet metal nailed on to close the cracks. Inside the shed a partition divided it in two, kitchen and mess hall. There were no floorboards, the earth was packed down by feet and that's the way it was left, holes and bumps and all. The entire kitchen equipment consisted of a pot cemented into a square stove.

Two men worked in the kitchen, a cook and a sanitary instructor. In the morning before they left camp, the cook was given the day's ration of grits at the big camp kitchen. Probably not quite two ounces for each working man, two pounds a brigade, less than thirty-six pounds for the whole project. The cook wouldn't haul that bag for nearly two miles. He gave it to a helper. Better to give the helper an extra portion out of the working stiffs' share than to break his own back. Getting water, gathering firewood, or lighting the stove were chores the cook didn't do either. He found other zeks, working stiffs, even some poor fellows on their last legs, to do them and gave them an extra portion. Who cares about what belongs to someone else.

The rule was that they ate without leaving the mess shed. Bowls had to be brought from the camp and couldn't be left out overnight because the free workers made off with them. So they carried fifty to the mess hall, no more, washed them on the spot and put them back into use. The man who carried the bowls got an extra portion. So that the bowls wouldn't be taken out of the mess hall, another helper was put at the door to watch. But no matter how carefully he watched the zeks they still got the bowls out, either by persuading him or distracting his attention. So another helper had to be sent all over the project grounds to collect the dirty bowls and cart them back to the kitchen. One more extra portion, and then another.

The only thing the cook did was to put the meal in the pot, add salt, and divide the fat between himself and the pot. Good fat did not get to the working stiffs, but rancid fat all went into the pot. So when rancid fat was handed out at the warehouse the zeks had a bonus. Then the cook mixed the cereal as it cooked. The sanitary instructor didn't even do that. He just sat and watched. When the kasha was ready, the sanitary instructor tried it first, a bellyful for him. A bellyful for the cook, too. Then the duty foreman came—they changed every day—to try it and see if this kasha could be given to the working stiffs. A double portion for the duty foreman.

Right then the whistle sounded. Then the other foremen came in, and the cook handed the filled bowls out through a window, and only the bottom of those bowls was covered with the thin kasha, and you weren't going to weigh or ask how much there was of your own kasha allotment. You'd get a hundred horseradishes in your mouth if you so much as opened it.

The wind whistled over the naked steppe. In summer the wind was dry and parching; in winter it was cold. Nothing ever grew on that steppe, especially between barbed wire. The only grain that grew around there was in the bread storeroom. Oats ripened only in the food warehouse. And even if you broke your back with work and lay on your stomach, you couldn't suck any food from that earth. You couldn't get more than the chief handed out. And you wouldn't even get the right amount because of the cooks, the helpers, and the zeks in soft jobs. Out here they steal. In the zone they steal. Before that, they steal at the warehouse. And the ones who steal are not usually the ones who swing picks. But as for you, swing away and then take what they give you. And get away from that serving window.

It was every man for himself.

Pavlo, Shukhov and Gopchik went into the mess hall. The men were so crowded in there they couldn't see the tables or the benches. A few ate sitting down but more were standing. The men of the 82nd, who had been digging holes outside without fires for half a day, had grabbed the first places. And now, though they had eaten, they wouldn't leave. Where else could they get warm? Others cursed them but the curses bounced off their backs. It was still better inside than out in the cold.

Pavlo and Shukhov elbowed their way in. They had arrived just at the right time. One brigade was getting its share. Only one group waited in line. Only the assistant foremen at the window. The rest came after us.

"Bowls, bowls!" the cook shouted out of the window, and they shoved them at him. Shukhov himself picked some up and shoved them at him. Not for an extra portion, but so things would move faster.

Helpers were washing the bowls. Extra portions for them too.

The assistant foreman in front of Pavlo began to get his, and Pavlo shouted over his shoulder:

"Gopchik!"

"Me!" from the door. A thin little voice like a small goat.

"Call the brigade!"

Gopchick ran off.

The important thing was that today the cereal was good, the best. Oatmeal. They didn't get it often. Usually it was that *magara* twice a day or waste from the flour mills. In oatmeal the broth between the grains is satisfying—and rich, too.

Shukhov, who in his youth had fed oats so often to his horses, had never thought then that he would long for a handful someday.

"Bowls, bowls!" they shouted from the window.

The turn of the 104th came. The assistant foreman got a double "foreman's portion" and retreated from the window.

That, too, came out of the stomachs of the working stiffs, but no one protested. For every foreman there was one such extra portion, and either he could eat it himself or give it to his assistant. Tyurin gave his to Pavlo.

Shukhov now had the task of pushing his way through to a table. He booted out two men on their last legs, asked one working stiff politely to get out of his way, and cleared part of a table. He would put twelve bowls close together, six on top of them, and another two on top of those. Now he had to take the bowls from Pavlo, repeat his count and watch carefully that no one swiped a bowl. Watch, too, that no one pushed them with their elbows or knocked them over. Close by some were getting up from the benches, others were climbing in, beginning to eat. He had to watch the table boundary. Are you eating from your own bowl or have you gotten into ours?

"Two, four, six!" the cook counted from behind the window. He handed out two at a time. That way he stood less chance of losing count.

"Two, four, six," Pavlo repeated softly in Ukrainian. He gave Shukhov two bowls at once and Shukhov put them on the table. Shukhov said nothing out loud but counted them all the more carefully.

"Eight, ten."

Why wasn't Gopchik bringing in the brigade?

"Twelve, fourteen," went the count.

No bowls in the kitchen. Over Pavlo's head and shoulder Shukhov could see the cook's hands put two bowls in the window and, holding on to them, hesitate. He must have turned about to swear at the dishwasher. Just then another pile of empty bowls was shoved at him through the window. He let go of the two bowls and handed the pile of empties back.

Shukhov left his bowls at the table, and hopped on over a bench, grabbed both bowls in the window, and, as if he were not talking to the cook, but to Pavlo he repeated not very loud:

"Fourteen."

"Stop! Where are you taking them?" hollered the cook.

"He's from ours, ours," Pavlo said.

"Yours, yours, but don't make me miscount."

"Fourteen," Pavlo shrugged his shoulders. He himself would not have gone to the lengths of swiping oatmeal. He, as assistant foreman, had to maintain his dignity, but he had just repeated what Shukhov said. He could blame it on Shukhov.

"I already said 'Fourteen'!" screamed the cook.

"Well, what about it! But you didn't hand them over. You held on to them!" Shukhov yelled. "Go and count them if you don't believe me. They're all on the table over there!"

As Shukhov shouted at the cook, he noticed the two Estonians coming towards him. He quickly shoved the two bowls at them. And then he managed to get back to the table and count to make sure that all the bowls were still there, that no one had swiped any though they could have gotten away with it.

Out of the window peered the cook's red face:

"Where are the bowls?" he asked stiffly.

"Right here, if you please," shouted Shukhov. "Move over, don't block the view!" he pushed someone out of the way. "Here are two!" he lifted the two dishes on top. "And here are three rows of four each, exactly—count them."

"And the brigade hasn't come yet?" the cook looked suspiciously through the small openings of the window which was narrow so that the zeks couldn't peer into the kitchen from the mess hall to see how much was left in the pot.

"The brigade hasn't arrived yet," Pavlo shook his head.

"Then what the hell are you taking bowls for if the brigade isn't here?" the cook raged.

"Here's the brigade, right here!" yelled Pavlo.

And everyone heard the captain shouting as he came through the doorway, just as if he were still on the bridge of his destroyer:

"What are you crowding around for? You've eaten—so get out of here. Give the rest of us some room!"

The cook muttered a bit more, straightened up, and again his hands appeared in the window.

"Sixteen, eighteen...."

And, having poured out the last one, a double portion:

"Twenty-three, that's all! Next!"

The men of the brigade made their way through the room and Pavlo handed out the bowls. He passed the bowls over the heads of those already seated to some at a second table.

In the summer, five men would have sat at each bench, but now when all were dressed in thick clothes four could hardly fit. Even then it was difficult to eat.

Calculating that at least one of the two extra portions would be his, Shukhov quickly set to devouring his rightful one. He raised his right knee to his stomach, removed from the top of his boot his spoon, "Ust-Izhma, 1944," removed his cap and put it in his left armpit. Then he stirred his spoon in his kasha bowl, around the edge.

At that moment one should concentrate entirely on eating, on removing that thin layer of kasha from the bowl, putting it neatly in one's mouth and rolling it over one's tongue. But he had to hurry so that Pavlo could see that he had already finished and would offer him a second portion. Fetyukov, who had come in with the Estonians and watched Shukhov swipe the two bowls for them, ate standing up opposite Pavlo. He kept looking at the extra portions, trying to convince Pavlo that he should be given another portion or at least another half-portion.

The swarthy young Pavlo, however, calmly ate his own double portion and by his face no one could tell whether or not he saw who was next to him, or even if he remembered that there were two extra portions.

Shukhov finished his kasha. Because he had set his heart on two portions, the single bowl left him feeling empty. He reached into his inside pocket, took out the white cloth, unwrapped the piece of bread crust and began to wipe all the remnants of the oatmeal carefully from the bottom and sides of the bowl. He licked the kasha from the crust with his tongue and then wiped the bowl again. Finally it was as clean as if it had been washed, just a little dull on the surface. He handed it back to the bowl-collector and continued to sit for a moment with his cap off.

Even though it was Shukhov who had swiped the two bowls the assistant foreman was their owner. Pavlo kept him in suspense a while longer, till he finished his own bowl. He didn't lick it out; he licked off the spoon, put it away, crossed himself. Then he lightly touched two bowls of the four.

"Ivan Denisovich. Take one for yourself and give one to Tsezar."

Shukhov realized that he was to take one bowl to Tsezar. Tsezar never lowered himself to go to the mess hall, neither here nor in the camp. He remembered that, but when Pavlo had touched two of the bowls at the same time his heart had nearly stopped: was it possible that Pavlo was going to give him both? Then his heart resumed beating as before.

He bent over his lawful prize and began to eat with deliberation, not feeling the new brigades pushing against him. Shukhov was worried only that the other extra kasha might be given to Fetyukov. He was an expert on scavenging, that Fetyukov, though he never had the boldness to swipe anything.

Nearby, across the table, sat Captain Buinovsky. He had long since finished his kasha and didn't even know that there were some extras. He was relaxing, warming himself. He didn't have the strength to get up and go out into the cold or back to the unwarmed shelter. He was unlawfully keeping a place, hindering the newly arrived brigades, just like the people he had hounded out with his metallic voice a few minutes before. He hadn't been long in camp, not long at the common work. Such minutes as these, though he didn't know it, were especially important for him, transforming him from an authoritative brassy naval officer into a slow-moving, quick-eyed zek. Only by virtue of that slow movement would he be able to live through twenty-five years of prison.

People were already shouting at him and pushing him from behind so that he would leave his place.

Pavlo said, "Captain! Hey, captain!"

Buinovsky jumped as if he was just awakening and turned around.

Pavlo handed him another portion of kasha without asking whether he wanted it.

Buinovsky's eyebrows rose. He looked at the kasha as if it were a miracle.

"Take it, take it," Pavlo reassured him and, picking up the last portion for the foreman, left.

A guilty smile crept over the cracked lips of the captain who had often sailed around Europe and over the North Sea route. He bent down, happy, over a half-full scoop of thin oatmeal gruel, no fat in it, just oats and water.

Fetyukov looked hastily at Shukhov and the captain before he went out.

But as far as Shukhov was concerned, he thought it was right to give it to the captain. The time would come when the captain would learn the way to survive, but so far he didn't know how.

Shukhov even had some small hope that Tsezar might give him his portion of kasha. But probably not, because Tsezar hadn't received a parcel from home for two weeks.

After the second kasha, he wiped off the bottom and side of the bowl as carefully as the first time and licked off his crust the same way. Finally he ate the crust. Then he picked up Tsezar's cooled-off kasha and went out.

"To the office!" He elbowed aside the helper at the door who didn't want to let him out with the bowl. The office was a log hut near the watch house. As in the morning, smoke was pouring out of the chimney. An orderly kept the fire going. He was a messenger, too, and was given time rates. And they weren't stingy about kindling and logs for the office fire.

The vestibule door creaked behind Shukhov. There was only one more door, completely covered with rope insulation. Clouds of steam from the frost billowed as Shukhov entered. He pulled the door shut behind himself quickly, hurrying so they wouldn't yell: "Hey, fathead, close the door."

It seemed as hot inside the office as a steam bath. Through the melting ice of the window the sun was playing, not maliciously as it did on top of the power station, but gaily. In its rays the smoke from Tsezar's pipe drifted like incense in a church. The stove was red hot all the way through, they had fired it so fiercely, heartless bastards. The stovepipe was red hot, too. In such heat if you sat down for just a moment you'd fall asleep.

There were two rooms in the office. The second, belonging to the construction supervisor, had a door which wasn't quite shut, and from inside the voice of the construction supervisor rang out.

"We're overspending the wage funds and overspending for construction materials. Valuable boards, to say nothing of panels, are being cut up by your prisoners for firewood and burned in their shelters. And you don't see a thing! Cement was unloaded near the warehouse recently in a strong wind: then the prisoners carried it loose in hand barrows for ten yards. The whole area was ankle deep with cement and the workers went out of there not black but grey. What waste."

Obviously a meeting with the construction supervisor. It must be for the junior work supervisors.

In the corner near the door an orderly sat on a stool, resting. Beyond him stood Shkuropatenko, zek B-219, like a crooked beanpole. He was watching out the window to be sure that no one ran off with his prefabs. You sure missed seeing that roofing walk off, uncle.

Two bookkeepers, also zeks, were toasting bread on the stove. They had made a wire holder so it wouldn't burn.

Tsezar smoked his pipe, sprawled at his desk. His back was to Shukhov; he didn't see him. Opposite Tsezar sat K-123, who had been sentenced to twenty years at hard-labor by a court verdict. He was a sinewy old man. Eating kasha.

"No, old fellow," Tsezar said softly, casually. "Objectivity demands you recognize that Eisenstein is a genius. *Ivan the Terrible*—isn't that a work of genius? The dance of the *oprichniks!*[4] The scene in the cathedral!"

"Affectation!" K-123 grew angry, holding his spoon in front of his mouth. "So much art it isn't art any longer. Pepper and poppy seed instead of our daily bread! And then, too, it's the most repulsive political idea—justification of one-man tyranny. Mockery at the memory of three generations of the Russian intelligentsia."

Eating his kasha absentmindedly—losing all the good of it.

"But what other treatment would they have passed?"

"Ah, *passed?* Then don't talk about genius! Say simply that he's a bootlicker, that he executed a dog's order. Genius doesn't fit its treatment to the taste of tyrants."

"Hmm, hmm," coughed Shukhov, too shy to break into the intellectual conversation. But there wasn't any reason for him just to go on standing there, either.

Tsezar turned around, reached out his hand for his kasha, didn't even look at Shukhov, as if the kasha had floated in through the air on its own.

"But listen to me—art is not *what* but *how.*"

K-123 hit the table with the edge of his hand, once, again. He retorted:

"No sir, to the devil's mother with your 'how' if it doesn't arouse good feelings in me!"

Shukhov stood there just exactly as long as it was dignified for him to stand there after having delivered the kasha. He was waiting to see whether Tsezar might not offer him a smoke. But Tsezar didn't even notice him. So Shukhov turned on his heel and left quietly.

Not too bad, not so very cold outside. They could lay blocks, all right.

Shukhov went along the path. He noticed a piece of steel blade on the snow, a broken piece of a strip. Though he hadn't any particular use for such a piece, you can't foresee all your needs ahead of time. He picked it up, shoved it into his trouser pocket. Hide it at the power station. Thrifty is better than rich.

At the power station first thing he did was get the hidden trowel. He stuck it behind his rope belt. Only then did he duck down into the mortar-mixing room.

In there after being out in the sunlight it seemed dark and not any warmer than outside. Damp too.

4 [The Czar's special soldiers.—Editors' note.]

Everyone was crowded up next to the round stove that Shukhov had installed, or was close to the one where the sand was heating and steaming a little as it dried. Whoever could find no room there was sitting on the edge of the mixing box. The foreman was at the stove, finishing his kasha. Pavlo had warmed it up for him on the stove.

Buzz buzz among the men. They were in a good mood. And they passed the word to Ivan Denisych quietly. The foreman had surpassed the quota well. He had come back pleased.

Where he'd found the work they were supposed to have done and what kind it was—that was his business. So far today, for instance, what had they accomplished? Nothing. There's no pay for installing a stove or for making a shelter. That was for themselves, not for production. But something had to be written in the work sheet. Maybe Tsezar was helping the foreman with the work sheets. The foreman was quite respectful toward Tsezar, and he wouldn't act that way for nothing.

He had surpassed the quota well—that meant five days of good rations. Well, not quite five, only four. The officers would grab one for themselves by putting the whole camp on the guaranteed minimum ration, both the competent and the incompetent workers. Probably it shouldn't cause bad feelings, everyone equal. But they economize on our stomachs. Well, all right, a zek's stomach can stand anything. Somehow or other we'll get through today, and tomorrow we'll eat. The whole camp goes to sleep with that dream on days of the guaranteed minimum.

But then you figure it out—you worked five days and ate four.

The brigade was quiet. Anyone who had anything to smoke was smoking silently. They were gathered close in the dark, looking into the fire. Like a big family. For the zek the brigade is a family. They listened to the foreman telling a story to a few men at the stove. He never talked a lot, so if he had started a story, it meant he was in a good mood.

Andrei Prokofych, too, had never learned to eat with cap on. Without a cap his head looked old. It was shaved short, like all the others, but even in the dim light from the stove you could see how much white was scattered among the gray.

"... I even trembled in front of the battalion commander, and there in front of me was the commander of the regiment. 'Red Army man, Tyurin, awaits your orders.'

"He stared at me from under his wild brows. 'Your patronymic?'

"I told him.

"'Year of birth?' I told him. That was in '30 and I was just 22—just a kid.

"'Well, and how do you serve,[5] Tyurin?'

"'I serve the working people!'[5] How he boiled, banged his two fists on the table—whop!

"'You serve the working people! And who are you, you scoundrel?'

[5] [Standard forms of address in the Soviet army.—Editors' note.]

"I was boiling inside me! But I kept control. 'Infantryman-machine gunner, first class. Distinguished battle and political. . . .'

"And he interrupted: 'What class, you bastard? Your father's a *kulak*.[6] Here's a paper from Kamen. Your father's a kulak and you ran away from there. They've been looking for you for two years!'

"I went pale, kept quiet. I hadn't written letters home for a year so they wouldn't get on the trail. I didn't know whether my folks were alive and they didn't know about me either.

" 'What kind of conscience do you have,' he yelled and all the four bars on his uniform danced, 'to deceive the Soviet authority?'

"I thought he was going to beat me. But he didn't. He signed an order—in six hours out the gate with me. . . . And outside it was November. They tore the winter uniform off my back, handed me a three-year-old summer uniform for raw recruits. I had been given a real screwing. I didn't know that I didn't have to turn in the winter uniform, that I could have told them where to go. And they gave me a fierce document in my hands. 'Dismissed from the ranks . . . as the son of a kulak.' Only try to find work with a reference like that. Four days' train ride to get home and they didn't give me a ticket and not even one day's dry ration. Fed me with lunch the last time and shoved me out of the camp.

"Incidentally in '38 at the Kotlas transit center I met my former squad commander. He'd also been given ten. I found out from him that both the regimental commander and his political commissar were shot in '37. No difference then whether they were proletarians or kulaks, whether they had a conscience or none. . . . When I heard that I crossed myself and I said, 'Nevertheless, Creator, Thou art in heaven. You bide your time but you deal a wicked blow.' "

After two bowls of kasha Shukhov wanted a smoke desperately. Since he counted on buying two mugsful of tobacco from the Latvian in the seventh barracks, he could repay a loan, so he quietly said to the Estonian fisherman, "Listen, Eino, lend me the makings for one smoke till tomorrow. You know I won't cheat you."

Eino looked Shukhov straight in the eyes, then without hurrying he shifted his eyes to his adopted brother. They shared everything fifty-fifty. One of them wouldn't hand out even a bit of tobacco by himself. They muttered something to each other and Eino got out a tobacco pouch decorated with a rose-colored pull string. He took out a pinch of factory-cut tobacco, put it on Shukhov's palm, measured it and added a few more shreds. Just enough for one, that's all.

Shukhov had a piece of newspaper. He tore it off, rolled it, picked up an ember from between Tyurin's feet—and inhaled. He inhaled again. Dizziness flowed through his whole being. It was almost as if he were drunk from head to toe.

He had just started to smoke but already from across the whole mixing room green eyes flashed—Fetyukov. Shukhov might have relented and given the

---

[6] [A rich peasant who opposed collectivization of the land.—Editors' note.]

jackal a puff, but he had scrounged once today already. Shukhov had seen that. Better leave it for Senka Klevshin. Senka couldn't hear what the foreman was saying, just sat there, unlucky guy, in front of the fire, head inclined to one side.

The foreman's pocked face was lighted by the fire. He was talking without any self-pity as if it weren't about himself at all:

"All the trash I had with me I sold to a dealer for a quarter of what it was worth. I bought two loaves of bread from under the counter—there were ration cards. I thought I'd make it on freight trains but there were strict new laws against that. And as anyone can remember you couldn't get tickets even for money, let alone without money—only with travel orders or travel passes. No admission to the station platform either. Militiamen at the doors, guards on the tracks on both sides of the station. The sun cold and sinking. Puddles with coats of ice. Where to spend the night? I managed to get up on top of a smooth brick wall, went right on over with my two loaves. Into the station toilet. Stood there, waited. No one was after me. I went out like a passenger, a soldier. And right there on the track stood the train—Vladivostok-Moscow. A mob was going for hot water, banging each other over the head with their pots. A girl in a dark blue sweater holding a two-quart teapot was wandering about in a circle, afraid to try to get near the hot water heater. Her small feet might get scalded or trampled.

" 'Here,' I said to her, 'take my loaves and I'll get you your hot water.' While I got up to the heater, the train had started to pull out. She was holding my loaves and crying because she didn't know what to do with them. Would have been glad to lose the teapot. 'Run,' I yelled. 'Run, I'll catch up!' She in front and me behind. I caught up. With one hand I lifted her onto the train—the train was gathering speed. I also jumped on the step. The conductor didn't beat me across the knuckles or push against me in the chest. Other soldiers were in the car, he confused me with them."

Shukhov gave Senka a nudge in the side. "Here, take the cigarette, finish it up, unlucky one." Gave it to him with his wooden mouthpiece, let him pull on it, he's all right. Senka was a strange one: like an actor he pressed his hand to his heart and nodded his head. Well, what can you expect from a deaf man.

The foreman went on. "Six girls travelling in a compartment, Leningrad students returning from practice work. On their little table there was nice fresh butter and fancy clutter, raincoats hanging on hooks, pretty little suitcases in covers. They were travelling right past life with green lights. . . . They talked, they joked, we drank tea together. 'And you,' they asked, 'from what car are you?' I sighed and I confessed: 'I'm from the car, girls, that's life for you but death for me. . . .' "

Quiet in the mortar mixing room. The oven crackled.

"They said 'ah' and they said 'oh' and had a conference. . . . They kept me covered with a raincoat on the top shelf. They hid me all the way to Novosibirsk, got me there. . . . Incidentally, I had a chance to thank one of those girls in Pechora. In '35 she got caught in the Kirov round-up,[7] was just about dead of hard labor, and I managed to get her a spot in the tailor shop."

"Maybe we should mix the cement?" Pavlo asked the foreman in a whisper. The foreman didn't hear him.

"I came home at night through the vegetable gardens and left the same night. I took along my little brother and took him down to the warm country, to Frunze. I had nothing to feed him with, or myself either. In Frunze they were melting asphalt in a pot while some young hoodlums sat around and watched. I sat down with them: 'Listen, you gentlemen without britches! Take my little brother on as an apprentice, teach him how to live!' They took him. . . . Sorry I didn't join the thieves myself. . . ."

"And you never saw your brother again?" the captain asked.

Tyurin yawned.

"No, never saw him again." He yawned once more and said: "Well, boys, don't cry! We'll settle in, even here at the power station. Whoever is mixing mortar, get going. Don't wait for the whistle."

And that's what it's like in the brigade. The chiefs up above can't get a working stiff to move, even in working time. But at rest time the foreman says work, and it means work. Because he feeds you, the foreman does. And he doesn't compel you to work for nothing.

While they're mixing mortar what will the masons be doing when work is supposed to begin? Just stand there? Shukhov sighed and got up.

"Going to clear off ice."

He took a small axe and a brush. For laying the blocks he had a mason's hammer, a measuring rod, mason's twine, and a plumb line.

The ruddy Kilgas looked at Shukhov and made a face as if he was asking, why are you jumping for the foreman? But, after all Kilgas didn't care how the brigade got fed: the baldhead could get along on seven ounces a day or less. He lived on his parcels.

Nevertheless he got up, too. He understood. He wasn't going to hold back the brigade.

"Wait, Vanya, I'm coming too!" he called.

No doubt, no doubt, fatface. If you'd been working for yourself you'd have been up at it faster.

Shukhov had hurried for another reason too—in order to grab off the plumb line before Kilgas got it. They'd taken only one plumb from the tool shop.

Pavlo asked the foreman, "Can we make it with three men laying block? What about adding one more? Or don't we have enough mortar?" As usual he spoke in Ukrainian.

The foreman scowled in thought. "I'll be the fourth, Pavlo. You stay here with the mortar. It's a big box—put six on it. Work it so that the ready mortar is taken from one end while new mortar is being mixed in the other half. No interruptions."

---

[7] [The assassination of Sergei Kirov, in 1934, was followed by mass arrests.—Editors' note.]

"Whew," Pavlo jumped up, a young chap, fresh-blooded, not yet worn down by the camps, his face round from eating Ukrainian dumplings. "If you're going to lay blocks yourself—then I'll mix mortar myself. We'll see who gets the most done. Where's the longest shovel?"

Now that's a brigade for you. Pavlo had been a forest partisan, had carried out night raids on provincial towns. Why should he break his back here? But doing it for the foreman, that's something else again.

Shukhov and Kilgas climbed up on the roof and heard Senka creaking up the ladder behind them. The deaf man had guessed what was up without being told.

On the second floor the laying of the walls had barely been started. Three rows all the way around and in a few places, more. They were going to be working with the easiest rows today—from knee to chest and no scaffolding to bother with.

The scaffolding and trestles which had been there previously had been all hauled away by zeks to other buildings, or chopped up for firewood just so another brigade wouldn't get them. Now, they would have to put some trestles together the next day in order to operate efficiently unless they wanted to halt work entirely.

From the top of the power station Shukhov could see a long way. The whole zone was snowy and empty. The zeks were under shelter, warming themselves until the work whistle. Black watch towers and sharpened poles for the barbed wire were sharply outlined. The wire itself could be seen on the sun side— but not in the other direction. The sun was gleaming fiercely. You couldn't keep your eyes wide open.

And then nearby—the power train. Smoking, dirtying up the sky. It puffed heavily, always with a sick hoarse wheeze just before the whistle. There, it blew. They hadn't really gone to work very much ahead of time.

"Hey, you Stakhanovite. Don't waste time with that plumb!" Kilgas hurried him.

"Look at your wall—how much ice there is! Can you get it off before night? You brought your trowel up with you for nothing," Shukhov made fun of him too.

They were about to stand at the respective walls allotted them before lunch, but then and there the foreman shouted from beneath:

"Hey, boys. We're going to work in pairs so the mortar won't freeze on us. Shukhov! You take Klevshin for your wall, and I'll work with Kilgas. And till I get there Gopchik can work at cleaning ice off the wall with Kilgas."

Shukhov and Kilgas exchanged looks. True. That was the most effective way. They took up their axes. Then Shukhov no longer had time to look at the distant view where the sun shone on the snow, or to see how the working stiffs clambered out of their shelters throughout the zone, some to pound away at the little holes which they hadn't managed to complete during that whole morning, some to fasten reinforcement rods in place, some to raise rafters in the plant workshops. Shukhov saw only his own wall, from the joint on the left where the blocks rose higher than his waist to the right where his section met that where Kilgas was working. He showed Senka where to knock ice off and himself whacked zestfully away with both heel and cutting edge of the axe so ice chips flew all about, even right into his face. He worked away recklessly, not a thought in his head. And his imagination and eyes sculptured out from under the ice the wall of the power station, two concrete blocks thick. At this section the wall had been laid by an unknown mason who either didn't know how or didn't gave a damn. But now Shukhov studied the wall as if it was his. Right there, a depression. That can't be leveled off in one row. It will take three rows, each time making the mortar layer a little thicker at that point. Right there the external wall bellies out a bit. That can be straightened two rows later. He divided the wall in his mind's eye into the part he would lay himself from the joint where the blocks rose in steps above the general level on the left, and from Senka's sector between him and Kilgas on the right. There on the corner, he calculated, Kilgas could not help but put down a few blocks for Senka since that would make things easier for himself. And while they were messing around in the corner, he would lay down more than half a run so that his pair didn't fall behind the other two. He made notes where the cement blocks should be set down. And no sooner had the blocks appeared on top than he yelled at Alyesha:

"Bring them over here to me! Put them here. And here."

Senka was still chopping away at the ice. Shukhov gripped the wire brush with two hands and hither-thither, hither-thither, brushed along the wall, cleaning off the top row of cement blocks. Though they were not completely clean, the ice was down to a light touch of gray mainly between the seams.

The foreman clambered up, too, and while Shukhov was still working with his brush, Tyurin put up his measuring rod at the corner. On the edges Shukhov and Kilgas had put theirs up before.

"Hey!" shouted Pavlo from below. "Who's still alive up there? Take the mortar!"

Shukhov started to sweat; his mason's twine hadn't been stretched out yet. He hurried. He decided to stretch the twine for three rows right away leaving space for adjustment. Also to make it easier for Senka he would take another part of the outside row and help him a bit with the inside row, too.

He set up the twine along the top edge and explained to Senka both with words and signs where to lay block. The deaf man understood. He bit his lips, crossed his eyes, nodded in the direction of the foreman's wall as if he were saying, 'let's build a fire under them, what do you say? We won't fall behind.' Shukhov laughed.

Already the mortar was being carried up the ladder. Eight men were to be engaged in mortar hauling. The foreman decided not to put mortar boxes near the masons—the mortar would only freeze. Instead they put the barrows close by so the two masons could take it directly from a barrow and slap it onto the wall, then lay the blocks. During that interval the barrow men were to carry blocks so they wouldn't freeze standing around up there. A soon as the mortar was out of the barrows, new barrow men came to replace them and the first men carried down the empties. Down below they thawed the frozen mortar out of the barrows and warmed themselves a bit, too.

Two barrows at once—one for Kilgas's wall and one for Shukhov's. Mortar steaming out in the cold—smoking, but only the least bit of warmth in it. With trowel slap it onto the wall and if you stop to yawn it will be stiff. Frozen, you have to chip it off with the heel of the axe—the trowel won't chip it. And if you put the block just a little out of line, it freezes into place crooked. You must knock it off with the heel of the axe and then chip off the mortar.

But Shukhov made no mistakes. The blocks were not all exactly the same dimensions. Some had a knocked-off corner, uneven edge, or other defect. Shukhov spotted them right away and spotted the side on which that block wanted to sit, and spotted also the place in the wall that was waiting for that block.

Shukhov scooped up smoking mortar with his trowel and threw it into that place. He remembered where the lower seam went—that seam had to be in the center of the upper block. He laid on mortar evenly, just enough for one block. And then he picked up one block—but carefully so as not to tear his mitten, because cement blocks scratch painfully. And, once more smoothing the mortar with his trowel, plop into place went the block. And right away, right away, even it up, hit it on the side with the trowel if it wasn't quite right. So the outside wall should be exactly straight to the plumb, so the block lay exactly level both length and width.

And then if some of the mortar had been forced out into its sides, that mortar had to be knocked off with the edge of the trowel right away and thrown over the wall. In summer it would have gone under the next block but don't even think of trying that now. Then the lower seams had to be examined. The block might have crumbled. And then you'd put mortar down again, so that it was thicker on the left side. And then you wouldn't just put the block in place but you'd slide it in from the right to the left since otherwise it would press out that excess of mortar between itself and the next on the left. Eye on the plumb line. Eye on the level. It's set. Next.

The work went right along. When two rows are down, the old mistakes will be straightened out. Then it will move along smoothly. But right now—look closely.

And he kept pushing along and pushing along the outside row toward Senka. And Senka there at the corner had moved away from the foreman, and was working toward Shukhov.

Shukhov winked at the barrow men—mortar, mortar, bring it over faster. The work was going so fast there wasn't even time to wipe his nose. When he and Senka met up and took mortar from the same barrow, they quickly scraped bottom.

"Mortar!" yelled Shukhov over the wall.

"Commmming!" Pavlo shouted.

They brought up a barrow and the two finished that off too, all of it that was liquid. On the sides it had frozen. Scratch it off yourselves. If you let a crust form there, you're the ones who haul it up and down. Move along. Next.

Shukhov and the other masons stopped feeling the cold. From the fast and all-absorbing work they felt at first the initial surge of heat—that heat surge that brings dampness underneath the coat, underneath the underjacket, underneath the outer and inner undershirts. But they didn't stop for a minute. They pushed the block-laying further and further. And an hour later came the second heat surge. In this one the sweat dries out. The cold did not get into their feet and that was the main thing. Nothing else, including the biting light wind, could distract their thoughts from the work. Only Klevshin was knocking his feet together. He, poor fellow, a foot size 11, had been given unmatched valenki which were too tight.

The foreman from time to time shouted: "Morrtarr!" And Shukhov too: "Morrrttarr!" Anyone who pushes his work along fast becomes something like a foreman over his fellows. Shukhov wasn't going to fall behind that pair. He would have chased his own blood brother up and down that ladder with barrows.

Buinovsky, from lunch-time on, hauled mortar with Fetyukov. The ladder was both steep and difficult, and at first he wasn't quite pulling his load. Shukhov urged him on quietly. "Captain, faster. Captain, more blocks."

But with every barrow the captain became quicker and Fetyukov slower. Along he went, the bitch's tit, tipping the barrow and slopping mortar out of it so it was lighter to carry.

Shukhov gave him a punch in the back. "Oh, you snake shit. So you were a director, Fetyukov! I'll bet you drove your workers!"

"Foreman," yelled the captain. "Put me with a human being. I'm not going to haul mortar with this piece of shit."

The foreman reshuffled the men. Fetyukov was sent down to throw blocks up to the scaffolding, but his work was set up so that there could be a separate count of how many blocks he had moved. The foreman put Alyesha with the captain. Alyesha was quiet. Anyone at all could order him around.

"Man the pumps, you lubbers," the captain shouted. "Look how fast they're laying blocks there!"

Alyesha smiled submissively:

"If it must be faster then it will be faster—let it be faster. Whatever you say."

And he clumped on down.

A mild man is a treasure for the brigade.

Someone called to the foreman from below. Another truck had arrived with blocks. None for half a year and now a flood. While they were delivering them was the time to work. First day. After that there'd be delays and you couldn't do any rushing along.

The foreman was cursing. Something about the elevator. Shukhov wanted to know what, but there wasn't time. He was levelling the wall. The barrow carriers told him the repairman had come to fix the motor on the elevator and with him came the construction supervisor for electricians, a free worker. The repairman fiddled around and the supervisor watched.

By the book: one works, one watches.

If they could fix the elevator both blocks and mortar could go up on it.

Shukhov had laid his third row and Kilgas had begun his when up the ladder came another one of the snoopers, one more boss; the junior supervisor, Der. A Muscovite they said. Used to work in a ministry.

Shukhov, who was near Kilgas, pointed at Der.

"Bahhh!" Kilgas brushed the warning away. "I don't have anything to do with the bosses. Call me if he falls off the ladder."

Now Der would hover behind the masons and look over their shoulders. These observers were the hardest of all for Shukhov to take. This one acts as if he were an engineer, the pig's ass. Once when he was demonstrating how to lay brick, Shukhov laughed out loud. The way he looked at it was build a house with your own hands and then maybe you'll be a craftsman.

Back in Temgenyevo they didn't have "stone" buildings—brick or block. The huts were of logs. So was the school. Forty-foot tree trunks were brought in from the forest reserve. Here in camp Shukhov had had to become a mason. And so, if you please, he became a mason. Anyone who has two manual skills can pick up another ten.

Der didn't fall. He just stumbled once. He went up the ladder almost at a run. He yelled,

"Tyurin!" His eyes were bulging: "Tyurin!"

On his heels came Pavlo still holding the shovel he'd had in his hand.

Der's coat was camp issue, but new and clean. A nice leather cap, but like everyone else's it had a number on it—B-731.

"Well?" Tyurin went to meet him, trowel in hand, foreman's cap crooked, down over one eye.

Something unusual. Shukhov couldn't ignore it even though the mortar was cooling off in the barrow. Shukhov kept laying blocks, laying and listening.

"What are you up to?" Der shouted, spit flying as he yelled. "That's not just a question of solitary. That smells of a criminal offense. Tyurin, you'll get a third term!"

Only then did Shukhov get what was up. He looked at Kilgas. Kilgas understood too. The roofing. They had seen the roofing on the windows.

Shukhov didn't worry about himself at all. The foreman would never turn him in. He was afraid for the foreman. For us the foreman is a father. For them —he's a pawn. They could really paste another term on to the foreman's sentence.

How the foreman's face had twisted. And how he threw down the trowel. And right toward Der—one step. Der looked behind—Pavlo had his shovel raised high. Pavlo hadn't dragged the shovel along with him for nothing.

And Senka had understood in spite of his deafness. He approached, hands on hips. He was big and rough-looking.

Der blinked, shuddered, looked for a "fifth corner"—a way out.

The foreman bent toward Der and said very, very quietly but distinctly, "Your time to hand out prison terms, you rat, has passed. If you say one word, you bloodsucker, it will be your last day on earth, remember!"

Tyurin's whole body shook. It shook and he couldn't control it. And sharp-faced Pavlo was glaring at Der, really glaring.

"Boys, boys, please!" Der was pale. He edged away from the ladder.

The foreman said nothing more. He adjusted his cap, picked up his trowel, and went to his wall.

And Pavlo, holding his shovel, went slowly down.

Slllllowly. . . .

Der was terrified to stay and terrified to descend. He edged behind Kilgas, and just stood there. Kilgas kept on laying block, the way they weigh out drugs at a pharmacy, a druggist who would not be hurried at all. He stood with his back to Der as if he hadn't noticed him.

Then Der moved toward the foreman. Where had all his arrogance gone?

"What am I going to tell the construction supervisor, Tyurin?"

The foreman continued laying block without turning around.

"You'll tell him that's the way it *was*. We came here and that's the way it *was*."

Der stayed a while longer. He saw they weren't going to finish him off right then. He went about quietly, hands in his pockets.

"Hey, S-854," he muttered. "Why is it you're putting mortar on in such thin layers?"

He had to take it out on someone. He couldn't pick on Shukhov for either his joints or his level.

"Please let me inform you," Shukhov said, with a little laugh, "that if I lay down a thick layer now, the whole power station is going to leak in the spring."

"You are a mason—so listen to what I say," Der frowned and blew out his cheeks, as was his habit.

Well, in places maybe the mortar was thin and could have been thicker. But that was if it were laid under human conditions: not here, in winter. One had to have pity for people. Here there had to be results, work accomplished. But why explain if the man couldn't understand it himself?

Der went down the ladder quietly.

"You get that elevator fixed!" Tyurin hollered after him from the wall. "What do you think we are, donkeys? Moving concrete blocks up to the second story by hand."

"You'll be paid for the lifting work," Der replied from the ladder, submissively.

"At 'wheel barrow' rates? You just take a wheel barrow and try to roll it up the ladder. Pay at 'hand barrow' rates."

"Personally it's all right with me; why not? But the bookkeeping office won't pass it at 'hand barrow' rates."

"The bookkeeping office! And my whole brigade is working to keep four masons busy. How much can we earn that way?"

The foreman kept shouting but didn't stop laying block.

"Mortar!" he shouted down.

"Mortar!" Shukhov caught up the cry. Everything was evened up on the third row and they were ready to get moving on the fourth. The mason's twine had to be raised a row—oh well, he could go for one row without the twine.

Der went out by himself, and through the field, all hunched up. Off to the office to get warm. Not too cosy for him maybe. But he should have thought twice before he attacked a wolf like Tyurin. If he'd managed to get along with such foremen he'd have no trouble. He doesn't have to break his back at work, gets a big bread ration, lives in a separate shack. What more does he want? If he sticks his neck out that way he's just playing the smart aleck.

Some of the zeks came up and said the construction supervisor for electrical repairs had gone and the repairman too. The elevator could not be fixed.

And so donkeys it was.

No matter how much construction work Shukhov had seen, all of the equipment either broke down by itself or else the zeks broke it up. He'd once seen a log conveyor wrecked—the zeks pushed a big stick in the chain and pried till they broke it off. They wanted a rest. The bosses had had them piling on one log after another. They couldn't keep that up.

"Blocks, blocks!" shouted the foreman, annoyed. And he cursed them out with curses and more curses, all of them, the men carrying mortar and the men carrying blocks.

"Pavlo is asking how's it to be with the mortar?" they shouted from below.

"Mix it!"

"There is half a box mixed!"

"So make one more box."

Well they were really cooking now. They were pushing the fifth row. At the beginning they'd had to bend way over to lay the first, and now it was all the way up to chest height, look. Well, and why not push it along—no window nor door spaces to worry about, just two blank walls joining together and plenty of blocks. And he should have put up the mason's twine, but it was too late for that.

"The 82nd went to turn in its tools," Gopchik reported.

The foreman turned on him, eyes snapping.

"You mind your own business, shrimp. More blocks."

Shukhov looked outside. Yes, the sun was sinking. It was going down in a red glow that seemed grayish in the fog. They had really pushed along—you couldn't have asked for more. They had already begun the fifth row. They'd end with the fifth, making it level all the way across.

The mortar carriers were, like overworked horses, short of wind. The captain's face was gray with fatigue. After all, he wasn't so young, that captain second rank. Forty. Not forty, but almost.

Degree by degree the temperature went down. Hands work on but fingers ache through the thin mittens. And the frost had moved into that left felt boot. Tap, tap, went Shukhov with his foot, tap, tap.

They didn't have to bend down over the wall any longer—but they were struggling over every block and every spoonful of mortar.

"Boys, boys." Shukhov fussed. "Just bring the blocks close to the wall. Up to the wall."

The captain was willing but he no longer had the strength. He wasn't used to exhaustion.

But Alyesha said, "Good, Ivan Denisych. Show me where to put them."

That Alyesha was always willing, no matter what he was asked to do. If everyone in the world had been like that then Shukhov would have been like that too. If a man asks for help, why not help him? That was the way it ought to be.

Through the whole zone and sounding clear in the power station came the pounding on the rail. Quitting time. And there they were, caught with fresh mortar on their hands. Ah, they had tried too hard!

"Bring up the mortar! Bring up the mortar!" shouted the foreman. There was a new box of it mixed, so they'd have to keep going—no way out. If the mortar box wasn't emptied they might as well break it up for firewood tomorrow. The mortar would be like rock and even a pickaxe wouldn't get it out.

"Come on, brothers, don't slow down." Shukhov cried.

Kilgas became angry. He hated alarms and emergencies. But he was keeping up the pace too. What else was there to do?

Pavlo came running up the ladder, pulling a barrow, trowel in his belt. And then he set to laying block. Five trowels flying. Now just finish up the joints. Shukhov studied what block to use for the joint. He handed Alyesha a hammer.

"Come on, smooth it off for me, smooth it down!"

Things done fast are not done well. And now, when everyone was hurrying, Shukhov slowed down to examine the wall carefully. He moved Senka toward the left and he himself moved to the right, to the main corner. If they messed up the corner now—that was a catastrophe. It would take a half day's work tomorrow to fix things up.

"Stop!" He pushed Pavlo away from a block and fixed it himself. And in the corner, look. Senka's line was uneven. Shukhov dashed to Senka, corrected the error with two blocks.

Like a good gelding, the captain brought up another barrow of mortar.

"Two more coming," he shouted.

The captain was staggering, but he was pulling his share of the load. Shukhov had once owned a hard-working gelding like the captain. Shukhov had taken good care of him, too. But eventually he had slaughtered the horse. And skinned him.

The sun was sinking to the horizon. Now, even without Gopchik to point things out, one could see that not only had all the brigades turned in their tools, but the men were moving in a wave to the watch house. After the gong sounds no one goes out, no one's fool enough to stand outside and freeze. They were all in their shelters. But then the moment would come when the foremen agreed it was time to leave and all the brigades would pour out at once. If the foremen didn't get together on the time, these convicts were so mean and stubborn they would try to outsit each other, even if it meant staying in their shelters till midnight.

Finally Tyurin came to his senses, saw he had over-stayed. Probably the tool clerk was cursing him out already.

"Hey!" he shouted. "Why worry about that shit. Mortar carriers! Get down and scrape out the big mixing box. Whatever you get out of it bury in that hole in the ground and cover it with snow so it can't be seen. And you, Pavlo, take two men, collect the tools and turn them in. After we've finished the mortar up here, I'll send Gopchik over with these three trowels."

The men scurried. They took Shukhov's hammer and unwound his mason's twine. The mortar carriers and the block haulers, all of them, ran into the mortar-mixing room since there was nothing more for them to do. The three masons remained—Kilgas, Klevshin and Shukhov. The foreman was checking to see how much had been done. Satisfied.

"We laid it out well, eh? In half a day without any elevator, without any other fucking thing, too."

Shukhov saw that Kilgas had very little mortar left. He was worried that the foreman might be cursed out in the tool room because of the trowels.

"Listen, you guys," Shukhov said. "Take the trowels to Gopchik. Because mine isn't on the list, and doesn't have to be turned in, I'll finish up."

The foreman laughed. "How are we ever going to let you go out into freedom? The whole prison will weep for you!"

Shukhov laughed too, and kept laying blocks.

Kilgas took the trowels away. Senka pushed blocks to Shukhov and poured Kilgas's mortar into their barrow.

Gopchik ran all the way to the tool room to catch up with Pavlo. The 104th marched across the field without Tyurin. The foreman was a power, but the convoy was a greater power. The guards wrote down the names of those who were late and into solitary with them.

It was getting too crowded at the watch house. All the men had assembled. It even seemed as if the convoy had arrived and had started to take the count.

They count twice at exit. It's done once inside the closed gates to be sure it's all right to open the gates, and the second count is taken as the men go through the open gates. If the count goes wrong, then they count outside the gates too.

"The hell with the mortar," the foreman waved his arm. "Toss it over the wall."

"Get along with you, foreman. Get along with you—they need you over there!"

Shukhov ordinarily called him Andrei Prokofievich—but right now by virtue of his work he had made himself equal with the foreman. Not that he announced to himself: "Now I have become equal," but he simply had the feeling that this was so. And he tossed a joke in the wake of the foreman who was taking big steps down the ladder. "Why the hell is the working day so short? Just as you get going—it's over."

Shukhov was alone with the deaf man. You couldn't talk much with him and there was nothing to talk to him about, for that matter, since he was smarter than all of them; understood everything without words.

Plop went the mortar. Plop went the block. They pushed it into place. They checked on it. Mortar. Block. Mortar. Block.

The foreman had ordered him not to worry about the mortar—to toss it over the wall. And they had all run off, left him. But Shukhov had such an idiotic character that even eight years in camp hadn't changed him. He couldn't bear to see anything, or any kind of work, go to waste.

Mortar. Block. Mortar. Block.

"We've finished it. Do it to your mother by the leg." Senka shouted. "Let's beat it."

They grabbed the hand barrows. Down the ladder.

But Shukhov ran back to have a look at the work. The guards could have sicked the convoy dogs on him, but even that wouldn't have stopped him. Not so bad! And now he ran up and looked the wall over from right to left. He had an eye like a mason's level. It was straight. His hands had skill in them yet.

He ran down the ladder.

Senka was out of the mortar-mixing room and running along the slope. "Come on, come on." He turned around.

"Go ahead. I'll be there right away!" Shukhov waved him on. Then he went into the mortar-mixing room. He wasn't going to throw away his trowel just like that. Maybe tomorrow he wouldn't be at work. Maybe they'd shove the brigade over to the Socialist Life Town after all, maybe he wouldn't get back here for half a year. Why let that trowel be lost? If you *swipe* something, keep it swiped.

In the mortar-mixing room all the stoves were cold. Dark. Terrifying. Not so terrifying because of the dark but because everyone had left, because only he would be missing at the watch house, because the convoy guards would beat him.

Nevertheless, peek and seek, he noticed a big stone in the corner, rolled it back, shoved the trowel underneath and moved it back again. Everything in order!

Now he had to catch up with Senka. But Senka had only gone a short way, and was waiting for him. Klevshin would never let a man down. If there was trouble then they would face it together.

They ran along side by side, the big man and the little one. Senka was a head and a half taller than Shukhov, and his head was an enormous one.

There are some loafers who willingly run races at a stadium. He'd like to see how they'd run, the devils, after a long day's work, with their backs still bent, and wet mittens, and patched valenki. Yes, and in the cold.

The two ran till they were afire like mad dogs and the only thing they heard was their own panting, in—out, in—out. Anyway, the foreman was at the watch house. He'd explain. Now they were running right into the crowd.

Suddenly hundreds of voices were screaming at them at once. Do that to their mothers, do that to their fathers, do that to them in the mouth, do that to them up their nose and in the ribs. It's terrifying when five hundred men are raging at you at once. But even more important, what about the convoy guards? How about them?

But the convoy guards paid no attention and the foreman was right there in the last row. That meant he had explained, taken the blame himself.

But the zeks yelled and screamed a river of curses. They yelled so loud even Senka could hear. He drew in his breath and whirled on them, big and tall. All his life he had been a quiet man. Now, suddenly, he roared. Lifted his fists and was all set to fight. The zeks quieted down. One of them laughed:

"Hey, 104th! So he isn't deaf after all?" Others shouted, "We found out."

Everyone laughed, even the convoy guards.

"Count off by fives!"

But the guards didn't open the gates. They didn't even trust themselves. They shoved the crowd back from the gate. The crowd had pushed up there, idiotically, as if that would hurry things.

"Count off by fives. One! Two! Three. . . ."

As they called out, each five stepped forward seven yards.

Shukhov was catching his breath, looking around. The moon, the little father, wore a crimson frown and already showed its full face in the sky. But it was starting to wane. Last night at this time it had been higher.

Shukhov was in a gay mood because everything had come out all right. He poked the captain in the ribs.

"Listen, captain second rank, and what does your science have to say—where does the old moon disappear to?"

"What do you mean, where? Ignoramus! It's simply not visible."

Shukhov twisted his head and laughed.

"If it's not visible how do you know that it's there?"

"What's your idea about it?" asked the captain in dismay. "That every month there's a new moon?"

"What's so miraculous about that? Every day in the year people are born, so why can't the moon do it, too; every four weeks?"

"Tfoo!" spat the captain. "I've never even met a sailor who was as ignorant as you. Where do you think the old moon goes?"

"That's what I'm asking you. Where?" Shukhov grinned widely.

"Well, where?"

Shukhov sighed, and reminisced. "They used to say in our village that God crumbles up the old moon for stars."

"That's savages for you." The captain laughed. "I never heard that before! Do you believe in God, Shukhov?"

"Sure, so what?" Shukhov was surprised. "When it thunders try not believing!"

"And why does God do that?"

"What?"

"Crumble up the moon for stars—why?"

"How come you don't understand?" Shukhov shrugged his shoulders. "The stars in time fall down. More have to be made to replace those that fall."

"Turn around!" A convoy guard cursed them with an oath. "Line up!"

The count had already come to them. The twelfth five of the fifth hundred had counted off, and there were two at the end—Buinovsky and Shukhov.

The convoy guards were troubled. They were busily conferring over their count boards. Short count! Again they were missing someone. If only they were able to count right!

They counted 462 and there had to be 463, they said.

Again they pushed everyone back from the gates for the zeks were crowding the gates again. And then once more.

"Count off by fives! One! Two!"

These recounts were unfortunate because the time wasted on them was no longer the government's but the zeks' own time. In addition there was still the march across the steppe to the camp, and then standing in line for body inspection in front of the camp. The groups of zeks from all the different projects usually ran on the double trying to get ahead of each other in order to be first at body inspection and thus sooner into camp. Whichever of the groups got into camp first was king. The mess hall was ready; it would be first in line at the parcels' room, first at the check room and at the kitchen, first at the cultural-educational section to receive letters, or at censorship to hand in letters, or the infirmary, the barber shop, the bath house—first everywhere!

And the convoy guards would hurry to turn them over to the camp, so they could get to their own quarters in camp sooner. Soldiers don't just wander around. They have much to do and little time.

But the count was short.

As the last fives began to count off Shukhov thought for an instant that at the end there would be three. But, no, two again.

The counters went to the chief of convoy guards with their count boards. They talked. The chief of convoy guards shouted:

"Foreman of the 104th!"

Tyurin stepped out half a pace:

"Here."

"No one of yours stayed behind at the power station? Think."

"No."

"Think twice—I'll tear your head off!"

"No, I'm telling the exact truth."

But he glared at Pavlo—had anyone gone to sleep in the mortar-mixing room?

"Count off by brigades!" shouted the chief of convoy guards.

They had been standing by fives as they happened to be, at random. Now they jostled and began to buzz. Shouts rang out: "Seventy-sixth—to me!"

"Thirteenth! Here!" And then somewhere else, "Thirty-second!"

The 104th came after all the others. Shukhov saw that the brigade members were empty-handed. They had been worked so hard they hadn't had time to gather kindling for the stove. Only two of them had bundles.

The same game went on every day. Before the end of the work day the working stiffs gathered up chips, sticks, broken lathes, tied them up with pieces of cloth or thin twine and carried them back to camp. But there were traps. The first was at the watch house. If the construction supervisor or one of the junior supervisors was there he ordered them to drop all bundles. The officials had already sent millions of rubles up in smoke through waste, so they tried mean economies like using the zeks' kindling.

But the working stiffs had their own way of figuring things. If every man in a brigade brought back a few sticks, it would be warmer in the barracks. Otherwise, the barracks orderlies got only ten pounds of coal dust for each stove. Don't expect any warmth from that! That's why the men broke up the sticks, or sawed them shorter, and hid them under their coats, so that the construction supervisor wouldn't see the bundles.

The convoy guard at the construction project would never order the bundles of wood dropped. The convoy guards wanted firewood, too. But they couldn't carry it themselves. For one thing, the prestige of the service didn't permit it. For another their hands were busy holding their sub-machine guns, in order to be able to shoot. However, as soon as they got to the camp the convoy guards would order: "From such and such a row to such and such a row, throw your firewood down over here." But they took with Godlike mercy—after all they had to leave some for the camp guards and for the zeks themselves. Otherwise the zeks wouldn't carry any at all.

And that's the way it worked out: every zek carried wood every day. Didn't know which day he'd get it there or which day they'd grab it from him.

Shukhov looked around to see if he couldn't find some chips underfoot. Meanwhile the foreman had counted the lot of them and reported to the chief of the guard.

"One hundred fourth—all present and accounted for."

And Tsezar had come up to his own brigade from the group of office workers. He puffed away so that a red glow came from his pipe, while his black moustaches were covered with frost.

"Well, how are things, captain?" he asked.

A warm man can't understand a frozen man. Empty question—how are things?

"Well, how?" the captain shrugged his shoulders. "I worked so hard I can hardly straighten my back."

You might at least understand enough to give him a smoke.

Tsezar did give him a smoke. It was only with the captain that he maintained a relationship. There wasn't anyone else with whom he could talk.

"One man missing in the 32nd! In the 32nd! Everyone was buzzing.

The assistant foreman of the 32nd and another chap ran back to the auto repair shop to look for the missing man. And the crowd kept asking: Who? What? They wanted to know. The story got to Shukhov. The missing man was a swarthy little Moldavian. Which Moldavian was that. Not the one who, they said, was a Romanian spy—a real spy?

There were five spies to every brigade but they were made-to-order, artificial spies: their cases had been processed as if they were the real thing, but they were only former P.O.W.s. Shukhov himself was that kind of spy.

But that Moldavian—he was a real spy.

The chief of guard looked at the list and got black in the face. If a spy escaped, what would happen to the chief of convoy guard?

And the crowd, including Shukhov, grew furious. What kind of piece of stinking shit, goddam bastard was that spy? Here it was, getting dark. The only light came from the moon. The stars were out, the cold was working up to its night-time strength. And that wet-behind-the-ears runt was missing. Didn't you have enough work, swine? Is the government's day too short for you, from dawn to dusk, eleven hours? Never mind, the prosecutor will add some.

It seemed queer to Shukhov that someone could work without noticing the stop-work whistle. Shukhov forgot that he had just been working that way himself—and that he had been sorry when he had to start out for the watch house so soon. But now he was frozen like everyone else. Probably there would be a half-hour delay because of that Moldavian. If the convoy could have turned him over to the mob the zeks would have torn him apart the way a wolf tears a calf.

Now the cold really began to gather strength. No one was able to stand still. They either stamped up and down or else moved two steps forward and two steps back.

Could the Moldavian have escaped? The men argued about that. Well, if he got out during the daytime that was one thing. But if he was hidden now and was waiting for the guards to come out of the towers he'd never be able to wait long enough for that. If there was no trail under the barbed wire to show that he had crawled through, then the guards would have to stay in the towers, watching, for as long as it took to find him, if it took three days, four days, even a week. That was the rule, and the old convicts knew it. In general if someone escaped life became hell for the convoy guards, and they were worked day and night without food or sleep. Sometimes the guards were driven so hard they became insane with rage. Then they wouldn't bring the escapee back alive.

Tsezar was trying to persuade the captain:

"For example, that pince-nez hanging on the ship's rigging, do you remember that?"[8]

"Mmmm . . . yes." The captain was smoking his tobacco.

"Or that baby carriage rolling down the long stairway, rolling and rolling down."

"Yes . . . but shipboard life in that film was somehow artificial, doll-like."

[8][The discussion is of Sergei Eisenstein's film *Potemkin* (1925).—Editors' note.]

"We have been spoiled by contemporary techniques of movie photography."

"And the worms in the meat were just like the kind that come out of the ground after a rain. Could it really be the same kind?"

"But you couldn't show any any smaller than that for motion pictures!"

"Well, I think if that meat were brought to us in camp right now instead of the fish we get, and if it were dumped in the pot without being washed or scraped, we would be. . . . "

"Aaaaaaaaah!" roared the zeks. "Ooooooo!"

They had seen three men hurry out of the auto repair shop. That meant they had found the Moldavian.

"Booooooo!" The crowd bellowed from the gates. And then as the three ran up: "Bastard! Stinking son of a bitch! Shithead!" Even Shukhov shouted: "Rat!"

After all, it was a serious matter to take more than half an hour of their time from five hundred men.

With his lowered head, the Moldavian ran like a little mouse.

"Stop!" the guard yelled. He wrote as he talked: "K-460—where were you?" He strode over to the Moldavian and turned the butt of his rifle toward him.

Some in the crowd shouted:

"Swine! Puke! Bastard!"

But the rest fell silent when the sergeant raised his rifle butt.

The Moldavian said nothing. His head bent, he drew back from the guard. The assistant foreman of the 32nd stepped forward:

"This scum climbed up on the scaffolding for plaster work, hid, got warm up there and fell asleep."

And he suddenly cracked him in the face with a fist, then slammed him in the center of his back. And in this way he pushed the Moldavian away from the guard. The Moldavian staggered. Then a Hungarian from the same 32nd kicked him in the rear, and kicked him in the rear again.

This isn't spying for you. Even a fool can be a spy. A spy has a clean, jolly life. But just try to survive ten years in a hard-labor camp.

The guard dropped his rifle.

The chief of guard shouted, "Get back from the gates! Count off by fives!"

The dogs are taking the count again. Why count now when it's all clear? The zeks growled. All their hate for the Moldavian shifted to the convoy guard. They hooted and wouldn't move back from the gate.

"What?" the chief of guard began to roar. "Do you want me to sit you down in the snow? Is that it? I'll do it too! I'll hold you here till morning!"

He would too—wouldn't think twice about it either. He'd do it. Many times the guards sat them down, even made them lie down. "Lie down! Weapons ready to fire!" The zeks knew those things had happened. So they began to move away from the gates.

"Get back! Get back!" the convoy guard pushed at them.

"Well, why are you pushing at the gates, idiots?" The zeks in the rear grew angry at those ahead. They moved back under pressure.

"Count off by fives! One! Two! Three!"

Now the moon was in full glory, it had grown bright and the crimson tinge had disappeared. It had risen a quarter of its way up the sky. The whole evening was lost. That damned Moldavian! That damned convoy guard. This damned life!

The men up front who had been counted turned around and stood on tiptoe to see if the last row had two or three men. Their lives depended on it right now.

For a moment Shukhov imagined he saw four in the last row, and he was numb with fear. An extra man! Another count. But it turned out that Fetyukov, the jackal, had been begging the butt from the captain and hadn't switched back to his own group on time, had been left at the end like an extra.

The assistant to the chief of convoy guard angrily whacked Fetyukov on the neck.

That's right.

There were three in the last line. It tallied, thank the Lord!

"Back from the gates!" Again the convoy pushed them.

But this time the zeks did not growl. They saw soldiers emerging from the watch house and forming a cordon on the other side of the gates.

That meant they would be let out.

The junior construction supervisors were not in sight, nor was the construction supervisor. The zeks still had their firewood. The gates were opened. On the other side, behind timber barriers, waited the chief of convoy guard and the count checker.

"One! Two! Three!"

If the count jibed once more they would call down the watch tower guards.

And it was such a long hike from the distant watch towers along the zone edge. Only when the last zek had been led out of the zone and the count tallied did they telephone the towers: "Come down." If the chief of guard was intelligent he'd move toward camp immediately knowing that there was nowhere for the zeks to escape and that the tower guards would catch up with the columns quickly. But sometimes the chief of guard was a fool, and feared his armed guards were not enough to deal with the zeks. Then the zeks would have to wait.

They had one of those blockheads this evening as chief of guard. He waited.

The zeks had been freezing for a whole day out in the cold. Pure death. And since the end of work they'd been standing outside freezing another hour. But right now the anger hurt even more than the cold. The whole evening gone. No chance to do anything in camp.

"And how is it that you know so much about the English navy?" someone in the next five asked.

"Well, you see, I lived almost a month on an English cruiser, had my own cabin there. I travelled in a naval convoy. I was liaison officer. And then, after the war, can you imagine, the English admiral, the devil take aim, sent me a gift inscribed, 'A token of gratitude.' That did it! So here I am, lumped together with everyone else. Not much satisfaction to sit here with Ukrainian Benderov partisans."

Queer. Queer to look around and see naked steppe, empty zone, snow gleaming beneath the moon. The convoy already in formation, ten steps apart, guns at the ready. A black herd of zeks. And in the midst of all this, in the identical kind of coat was a man to whom life without gold shoulder boards would once have seemed unthinkable, a man who had rubbed elbows with an English admiral, who was now hauling hand barrows with Fetyukov. S-311.

Things can happen one way—or another. . . .

Well, the convoy guard was assuming formation. Take off, without the "prayer." "Forward march! Faster!"

Oh, no, the hell with you. Why faster? We're behind all the other projects, so why hurry now. The zeks, without talking it over, had come to the same conclusion: you kept us there—now we're going to keep you. Probably you want to get warm, too.

"Longer steps!" shouted the chief of guard. "Longer steps, leader!"

The hell with you, "longer steps!" The zeks went along evenly, dragging their heels as if trudging to a funeral. Nothing more for us to lose. We're going to be last into camp anyway. You didn't want to deal with us like humans so now you can shout till you bust.

The chief of guard shouted and shouted: "Longer steps!" Finally he understood the zeks wouldn't move faster. He couldn't shoot, either. They were marching in fives, in a column, in proper order. He didn't have the power to drive the zeks faster. In the morning on the way to work it's their dragging heels that saves the zeks. Whoever runs fast won't finish his term in camp. He'll drop from exhaustion.

So they marched along evenly and neatly. Their boots creaked on the snow. Some talked quietly, some didn't. Shukhov tried to recall what it was he hadn't finished in camp that morning. He remembered—the infirmary! Well, it was practically miraculous, but at work he had completely forgotten about the infirmary.

Right now it was receiving time in the infirmary. He could still get there if he didn't eat. But his aches were gone. And likely they wouldn't even take his temperature, wouldn't take the time for that. He'd gotten over his sickness without the doctors. Those doctors cured their patients right into wooden overcoats.

It wasn't the infirmary that attracted him now, but figuring how he could add a little something to his dinner. His hopes were pinned on Tsezar's receiving a parcel. It was a long time since one had arrived.

Suddenly there was a change in the zeks' column. A flutter. The even step was broken. The column jerked. It buzzed and buzzed. And now the tail-end fives, among them Shukhov, were no longer right on the heels of those ahead but had to run after them. They walked several steps and then ran.

As the tail end of the column came to the crest of the hill, Shukhov saw at their right, far out on the steppe, another column looming black. It was moving diagonally toward his column and it was also hurrying.

That column could only be the zeks from the machine factory. There were three hundred men in it. Evidently they'd had bad luck, too, and had been held up. What for? It happened that now and then they were kept at their work because they hadn't finished repairing some piece of machinery or other. Of course it didn't make much difference to them, since they were inside all day where it was warm.

Now it was a question of who would beat out whom. The zeks were running, really running. And the convoy guards took up the trot.

But the chief of guards shouted, "Don't stretch out! Rear, close ranks! Close ranks!"

We'll rap you in the head, what are you hollering about? Can't you see we're keeping up?

And the men who had been talking or thinking forgot about it. There was just one thought in the whole column, "Beat them out, head them off!"

And now everything was so mixed up, that the convoy guards no longer seemed to be enemies of the zeks, but friends. The enemy was that other column.

The men got cheerful. The anger was gone.

"Get a move on, get a move on!" the ones in the rear called out to those ahead.

The column rushed onto the road while the machine factory men were hidden behind an apartment block. The race was on in the dark. Hurrying was easier for the column in the middle of the road. And things were smoother for the convoy guards on the sides, too.

Shukhov's column had to head them off right there because the machine factory men were submitted to a particularly long body search. Since the first incident of knifing in the camp, the officers suspected that the knives were made at the machine factory and moved from there to camp. Therefore at the camp entrance the machine factory men were searched especially carefully.

In late fall, when the earth was already frozen, the guards shouted at them, "Take off your boots, machine factory. Take your boots in your hands."

And then they searched them barefoot.

And even now, despite the cold, they'd poke a man at random. "Come on there, get off your right felt boot. And you there, take off your left boot."

The zek would take off his felt boots and hop about on one foot, empty out the boot and shake out his foot cloths to show there was no knife there.

Shukhov had heard—he didn't know whether it was true or not—that the machine factory men had brought two volleyball posts into camp in summer and had hidden knives in those posts. Ten long ones in each post. Even now, once in a long while they'd find one of the knives in the camp here, there, another place.

At a half-run they passed the new clubhouse and the block of apartment houses, then the wood-carving factory, and poured out onto the road that crossed to the camp watch house.

"Ho! Ho!" the column roared with one voice.

It was this road crossing on which they were so intent. And now the machine factory men were one hundred fifty yards off to the right—in the rear.

Now all the rows in the column could move along quietly. Like the rabbit in the old story who was glad that at least the frogs were afraid of him, now they too had someone to look down on.

The camp loomed up before them. It was just as light now as it had been when they left in the morning. Night lamps shone in the zone over the solid board fence, and were placed close together in front of the watch house. The entire area for body inspection was so brightly lit it was as though the sun were out.

Then, before they got to the watch house, "Stop!" shouted the assistant chief guard. He handed his sub-machine gun to a soldier, and ran right up to the column. He wasn't permitted to come close to them with his sub-machine gun. "All those standing at the right who have firewood—throw the firewood down to the right."

On the outside row they were carrying the bundles openly—he could see all of them. One . . . two . . . and a third bundle flew. Some tried to hide theirs inside the column but their neighbors objected:

"Because of you they'll take it away from the rest of us! Do what you're told!"

A convict's worst enemy is another convict. If the convicts weren't always at each other's throats, life would be something very different.

"Forward march!" shouted the assistant chief guard.

And they moved on to the watch house.

At the watch house five roads came together. An hour earlier, the groups from the different projects had been milling about. If these roads were made into streets someday then instead of this watch house and yard for body inspection there would be a main square. And in the same way that the columns marching from all the projects converged here now, perhaps holiday demonstration parades would merge here in that future city.

The search guards had already managed to warm themselves at the watch house. They came out and waited across the road.

"Unbutton coats! Unfasten underjackets!"

They extended their arms. During body inspection they'd embrace you. Slap you on the sides. In general, it was just like the morning.

It wasn't so terrifying to unfasten clothes now—the zeks were close to home.

That's the way they all talked—"home." No time to think about any other home during the day.

They had already inspected the head of the column when Shukhov went up to Tsezar and said:

"Tsezar Markovich! From here I'll run to the parcel room and hold a place in line for you."

Tsezar turned to Shukhov, the tips of his sculptured black moustaches now white:

"Why should you take a place in line, Ivan Denisych? Maybe there won't be a parcel."

"Well, if there's none—what have I lost! I'll wait ten minutes and if you don't come, I'll be off to the barracks."

Shukhov figured that even if Tsezar didn't show up, perhaps he could sell his turn in the line to someone else.

It seemed Tsezar was longing for a package.

"Well, all right, Ivan Denisych, run along and hold a spot. Wait ten minutes, no more."

The body inspection was moving closer. Today Shukhov had nothing to hide, and he could move up toward it fearlessly. He unbuttoned his coat, without hurrying, and unfastened the underjacket beneath his canvas sash.

Even though he didn't remember having anything on himself which was forbidden, nevertheless the wariness of eight years of sitting had become a habit. He shoved his hand into his pants knee pocket to prove it was empty— as he knew it was.

But he found the little steel blade, that piece of blade strip! The steel blade he had so thriftily picked up today in the working zone, which he hadn't intended to take into camp at all.

He hadn't intended to take it in, but now when he had it there he just didn't want to throw it away! After all it might be sharpened into a little knife, good enough for shoemaker's work, maybe for tailoring.

If he had planned to take it through body inspection with him, he would have figured out how to hide it well. But now there were only two rows in front of him, and the first had already separated and gone forward to inspection.

He had to decide quicker than the wind. There was a choice. Screened by the five men in front of him, he could throw it down on the snow where it would be found later, but no one would know whose it was. Or, he could try to take it in with him.

They could give him ten days of solitary for that little steel blade if they considered it a knife.

But a shoemaker's knife was earnings, it was bread.

He didn't want to throw it down.

So Shukhov shoved it into his cotton mitten.

Right then the order was issued for the next five to step up for body inspection.

Now, in the glare, just the three of them were left: Senka, Shukhov, and the lad from the 32nd who had run to find the Moldavian.

Because there were three of them and five guards stood facing them, it was possible to play it cleverly—to choose which one of the guards to approach. Shukhov chose not the young, ruddy-faced one, but the old one with the gray moustache. The old one was, of course, experienced and could easily have found it if he had wanted to, but just because he was old it was a sure thing that he was more sick and tired of the service than of hell.

By that time Shukhov had removed both mittens, the one with the blade and the empty one, and was holding them in one hand. The empty mitten was shoved forward. In that same hand he held the rope belt, unfastened his under-jacket completely, obsequiously held up the flaps of both his coat and under-jacket. Never had he been so obsequious at the inspection but now he wanted to show that he was all open, as if to say, 'go ahead, take me!' And at the order he went up to gray-moustaches.

Gray-moustaches clapped Shukhov on sides and back, slapped him on the knee pocket. Nothing there. He pressed the flaps of the underjacket and coat in his hands. Nothing. And, letting him through, for insurance he grasped the mitten Shukhov had shoved forward—the empty one.

The guard pressed the mitten and pincers clamped on Shukhov's insides. One more grasp; on the second mitten, and he would have had it. In solitary on ten ounces a day and warm food every third day. Immediately he imagined how he would weaken there, how he would hunger and how difficult it would be for him to return to that wiry, neither famished nor well-fed state in which he lived now.

At that moment he prayed with real fervor, "God! Save me! Don't give me solitary!"

All those thoughts raced through his mind in the instant that the guard touched the first mitten and moved his hand to grab the second one. He would have pressed them both at once if Shukhov had held them out separately, not together. But right then a voice rang out. The senior noncom who was in com-mand at body search shouted at the convoy:

"Bring up the machine factory men!"

And gray-moustaches, instead of going on to Shukhov's second mitten, waved his hand as if to say: 'Get on with you.' He let him go.

Shukhov ran to catch up with his fellows. They were already lined up by fives between the two long log barriers which were like horse stalls at a market, and formed a kind of pen for the column. He ran quickly, not feeling the ground. He didn't pray to give thanks because there wasn't any time.

The convoy guards who had led their column went to the side now, clearing the road for the guards from the machine factory. They were waiting for the chief. The convoy guards had picked up for themselves the firewood thrown down before inspection. The firewood taken away at inspection time by the camp guards was collected in a pile at the watch house.

The moon rolled up higher. In the white, bright night the cold intensified.

The chief of convoy, going into the watch house to get back his receipt for 463 heads, spoke with Priakha, assistant to Volkovoi, and the latter shouted, "K-460!"

The Moldavian went around. He was ordered to hold his hands behind his and went up to the right barrier. He held his head down and drawn into his shoulders in the same way.

"Come here!" Priakha pointed him around the barrier.

The Moldavian went around. He was ordered to hold his hands behind his back and stand there.

That meant they were going to slap on charges of attempting to escape. Into solitary he would go.

At the gates, right and left, beyond the pen, stood two guards. The gates, three times a man's height, opened slowly and the order was heard:

"Count off by fives!" No necessity to shout "Away from the gates!" at this point, since all the gates opened into the zone. Even if the zeks mobbed them from inside they couldn't break these gates open. "One! Two! Three!"

At that evening count, returning through the camp gates, the zek was exposed to the wind, frozen, hungrier than at any other time during the day. The evening meal, a ladle of scalding hot thin cabbage soup was as welcome as rain on thirsty dry ground. He'd drain the bowl with one gulp. That ladleful was at that moment dearer than freedom, dearer than all his former life and all his life to come.

The zeks poured through the camp gates like soldiers returning from a campaign—loud, tough, rough. Clear the way! That rushing wave of zeks looked frightening to a man with a soft job in headquarters barracks.

After that last count, the zek was a free man for the first time since morning when they rang the six-thirty gong for lineup. He had gone through the big gates of the zone, the smaller gates of the pre-zone sector, and crossed the lineup ground. Now scatter where you please!

Scatter where you please, but the work assignment clerk caught the foremen: "Foremen. Go to the planning production section!"

Shukhov ran past the camp punishment prison, between the barracks, to the parcel room. And Tsezar went at a dignified, leisurely pace in the other direction, to where a crowd was swarming. A plywood board was nailed to a post and on it were written in indelible pencil the names of all those who had received parcels today.

In camp they rarely wrote on paper, more often on plywood. Everything seemed firmer, more reliable, on a board. The assignment clerks and the guards kept count on boards. The next day they would scrape the boards clean—and write on them again. Economy.

Whoever stayed in camp during the day could scavenge a bit. They could see on the board who'd received a package, meet him at lineup ground as he came in and give him the parcel number right then. They couldn't get much for that, but it was worth at least a cigarette.

Shukhov ran to the parcel room, a shed with a big vestibule built onto a barracks. The vestibule had no outside door to close, so the cold entered freely. But it was better than waiting in the open. After all there was a roof overhead.

Inside the vestibule the line stretched along the wall. Shukhov took a place. There were fifteen ahead of him. This meant more than an hour of waiting, right up to curfew. Nevertheless the men from the power station column who went to look at the list first would all be behind Shukhov, as well as all the machine factory men. Likely many would have to come for their parcels a second time, tomorrow morning.

They all stood in line holding bags or sacks. There, behind that door (Shukhov himself had never received a parcel in this camp, but he knew about it from the talk) they opened the packages with a small axe and the guard took everything out and inspected it. Some things he cut open, others he broke open or spilled out. If there was a liquid, the guards would not hand it over in a glass or metal container. They would unbottle it and pour it out for you, hold your hands out for it if that was the best you could do, or wipe it up with a towel or cloth. They would not give out cans. If there was something like a pie, some interesting candy, or sausage, or fish, the guard would eat some. And just try to object. Right away he'd insist that it was a forbidden item. And he wouldn't give it out. Any man who received a package had to give, beginning with that guard, then give some more and keep giving. And when they finished inspecting the package, they wouldn't give the zeks the box the parcel had arrived in. Just pile everything loose into your sack, or even in a fold of your coat. And move along. Next! They were hurried through so fast that now and then a zek would forget something on the counter. Don't go back for it. It isn't there.

Back in Ust-Izhma, Shukhov had received a pair of parcels from home. But after that he wrote to his wife that it was no use. "Don't send them," he told her, "don't take things from the children."

Even though Shukhov had found it easier to feed his whole family when he was free than it was to feed himself in this camp, he knew exactly how much those packages cost. You couldn't squeeze them out of the family for ten years. Better to go without.

But even though he had decided that, still, whenever someone nearby in the barracks or in the brigade received a parcel—just about every day—he felt unhappy that there was none for him. And though he had strictly forbidden his wife to send him anything, even for Easter, and he never went to the post with the list except on behalf of some rich fellow brigade member, he often longed for someone to run up to him and say:

"Shukhov, what are you waiting for? There's a parcel for you."

But no one ever ran up.

And there was ever less and less reason to remember Temgenyvo and his hut. The life here wore him out from waking to sleep, leaving no time for empty recollections.

Now, standing among those who were comfortably anticipating the first bite of bacon, or spreading butter on their bread, or sweetening their mug with sugar, Shukhov kept himself together with one idea and one only, to get to the mess hall with his brigade and eat thin soup that was hot and not cold. Cold soup wasn't half as good as hot soup.

He calculated that if Tsezar's name was not on the list he had long since gone back to barracks to wash. And if the name was there, then he was right now gathering bags, plastic mugs, and other permitted containers. That was why Shukhov had promised to wait ten minutes.

Standing in line, Shukhov heard some news. The zeks would work this Sunday. Again the camp was taking away their Sunday. He had expected that. The others had expected it too. If there were five Sundays in the month then they let the zeks have three, the other two they drove the zeks out to work. But even though he had expected it, when he heard the news his whole soul ached. Who wouldn't grieve for the loss of that dear day? What they were saying in the line was true, of course; the camp bosses could ruin a rest day even when the zeks were allowed to stay inside the camp. They could invent work. Build a bath house. Or build a wall to close a passageway. Or clean up the yard. Or else change your mattresses, shake them out, and catch bedbugs on the bunks. Or there might be verification of identity by identity cards. Or inventory. That meant take all your things outside and sit in the yard half a day.

The bosses couldn't bear it if a zek went to sleep after breakfast.

The line moved along slowly. Several came in and got into line out of turn, silently pushing aside the person in front, one barber, one bookkeeper and one man from the cultural educational section. These people were not just ordinary gray zeks but firmly ensconced camp trusties who had jobs inside the camp. Complete rats. The working stiffs thought them worse than shit. And they looked at the working stiffs in exactly the same way. But it was useless to quarrel with them. The trusties had a gang all their own and were in with the guards, too.

Ahead of Shukhov there were ten men now, behind him seven. At that point Tsezar entered the doorway, ducking down, in his new fur cap sent from freedom. Look at that cap. Tsezar had bribed someone and he was permitted to wear that clean, new, city cap. Most of the others had had even their worn old army caps snatched away, and they'd been handed camp pigskins instead.

Tsezar smiled at Shukhov and greeted a strange fellow in glasses who was reading a newspaper in line, "Ah! Petr Mikhalych."

And they blossomed out at each other like poppies. The stranger said, "I have a new *Evening Moscow* here. Look at it! I got it by mail."

"Well, well." Tsezar stuck his nose in that paper. And beneath the ceiling the lamp was dim. How could they read the small print here?

"Here's a most interesting review of Zavadsky's[9] premiere!"

The Muscovites smell each other out from a long ways away, like dogs. And when they get together they sniff around and sniff around at each other in their own peculiar way. And they mutter quick-quick to see who can say the most words. And when they mutter that way it's rarely that real Russian words are heard. Listening to them talk is like listening to a Latvian or Romanian.

However, Tsezar was holding the sacks he had collected.

"So I . . . Tsezar Markovich. . . ." Shukhov lisped. "Maybe, I can go now?"

---

[9][A Soviet theatrical producer.—Editors' note.]

"Of course, of course," Tsezar raised his black moustaches from his newspaper. "Who's ahead of me? And who is behind me?"

Shukhov explained who came after whom, and without waiting for Tsezar to remember about dinner he asked:

"Shall I bring you your dinner?"

That meant carrying it from the mess hall to the barracks in a mess tin. It was not permitted to take meals out of the mess hall, and there were many rules on the subject. If they caught you they would pour the food on the ground and put you in solitary. But just the same the zeks took meals out and would continue to take them out because when a man had business to do he could not manage to get into mess hall with his own brigade.

Shukhov asked whether to bring dinner but thought to himself, 'Well, can you possibly be stingy and not give me your dinner? After all there's no kasha at dinner, just bare thin soup.'

"No, no," Tsezar smiled. "You eat my dinner yourself, Ivan Denisych!"

Shukhov was waiting for just that. Now he was like a bird uncaged. He rushed out from under the vestibule roof and on through the camp, right through the camp.

The zeks were coming from all directions. At one time the chief of the camp had issued an order that no prisoners were to go about camp alone. Whenever possible the whole brigade must go in formation. And wherever the whole brigade could not go at the same time, say to the infirmary or the latrine, groups of four and five persons should be formed with a man in charge to accompany the group to its destination and then take them back, still in formation.

The chief of camp put much stock in this order. No one dared contradict him. The guards caught men alone and wrote down their numbers and put them in solitary. Yet the order broke down. Quietly, the way many noisy orders break down. Let's say if they called a man by himself to the security section, you wouldn't be likely to send a whole squad with him. Or if you had to go for your food in the parcel check room, why should I go there with you? And if one man wanted to go to the cultural education section to read newspapers, who was going to go along with him? Or if someone else took his felt boots to be repaired, or someone went to the drying room, or someone simply headed from one barracks to another—though going from barracks to barracks was the most strictly forbidden of all. Still, how could you stop them?

With that order the chief of camp—old potbelly—wanted to take their last bit of freedom. But it didn't work.

On the way to the barracks Shukhov met a guard and raised his cap, just in case. He ran on into the barracks. A row was going on. Someone's bread ration had been stolen during the day. Zeks were screaming at the orderlies, and the orderlies were screaming, too. The 104th's corner was empty.

Shukhov had come to think it a lucky evening when he returned to camp and did not find mattresses overturned or the barracks searched.

He dashed to his cot, pulling his coat off on the run. Shoved the coat on top, felt the mattress, his morning piece of bread was still there. He was glad he had sewn it in.

And on the run, outside. To the mess hall.

He dodged to the mess hall without running into a guard. Met only zeks, arguing about rations.

Moonlight lit everything in the courtyard. The lamps were pale, and the barracks cast black shadows. The mess hall was entered through a broad porch with four steps. That porch was in shadow right now, though a hanging lamp bobbed over it, whining in the cold. The lamp bulbs shed rainbows, perhaps from cold, perhaps from dirt.

There used to be another strict order from the camp chief. Brigades were to enter the mess hall in formation, by twos. The order went on: on arriving at the mess hall the brigades were not to go up on the porch but to line up in fives and wait till the mess hall orderly let them in.

The post of mess hall orderly was firmly held in the grip of Khromoi, the "cripple." He had managed to elevate his limp into a formal status as an invalid. He was a big mean son-of-a-bitch. Got himself a birch cane and from the porch he'd lam anyone who tried to get up there against his orders. But not quite everyone. The quick-eyed Khromoi could recognize every man; even in the dark, even by his back. He never hit anyone who was able to give him a crack in the teeth. He beat those who were already beaten. He had nailed Shukhov once.

He was called "orderly." But if you figured it out he was really a prince! A friend of the cook.

Today either all the brigades had piled up at once, or else it had taken a long time to get things organized, but the porch was densely crowded. Khromoi was up there with his helper and the head of mess hall. The fat dogs were running the show without the help of a guard.

The head of mess hall was a well-fed bastard! Head like a pumpkin, shoulders a yard wide. He had so much excess power that when he walked he seemed to be bouncing, as if his legs and arms were made of springs. Wore a white fur cap without a number. No one else—not even any of the free civilians—had a cap like that. And he wore a fur lambskin vest. There was a number on the vest—but only about the size of a postage stamp. That was a concession to Volkovoi. But on his back, no number. The head of mess hall bowed to no one and all the zeks were afraid of him. He held thousands of lives in his hand. Once they started to beat him up, but all the cooks jumped out to his defense, and a real collection of plug-uglies they were too.

It would be bad if the 104th had gone in already. Khromoi knew everyone in the camp, and with the head of mess hall present he would never permit anyone to enter out of turn. He'd be mean just for the fun of it.

Sometimes it was possible to climb the porch railings behind Khromoi's back. Shukhov had done it himself. But not today with the mess hall head standing there. He'd fix you so you'd be carted off to the hospital.

Quick, quick, up on the porch for a look at the black coats, all alike, for those of the 104th.

Right at that minute the brigades moved confusedly ahead, kept moving ahead. Curfew coming soon. As if storming a fortress, they rushed the first, second, third, fourth step and piled onto the porch.

"Stop it, you whores." Khromoi shouted and lifted his cane against those in front. "Get back! I'll smash your heads!"

"Not our fault!" the ones in front shouted at him. "They're pushing from behind."

True enough, they were being pushed from behind. But the men in front were not resisting very energetically, hoping to fly right on into the mess hall.

Then Khromoi held his cane across his chest like a closed railway gate, and with all his weight fell right on those in front. And Khromoi's helper grabbed one end of the long cane. The mess hall head wasn't squeamish about using his hands, either.

They moved fast and they were strong—they ate meat. The zeks fell back. The ones up front fell back on the men behind them, mowed them down like sheaves. "Fuck you, Khromoi . . . in your face, Khromoi!" Voices, well hidden in the crowd, yelled at him. Others fell in silence and silently got up fast before they were trampled.

The steps were cleared. The mess hall head left, and Khromoi stood on the top step.

"Form up by fives, you dumbheads, how many times do I have to tell you? When it's necessary, I'll let you in."

Shukhov spotted someone who looked like Senka Klevshin, was delighted, tried to elbow his way closer. He pushed past a few people but no, not enough strength. You couldn't get through there.

Khromoi shouted: "Twenty-seven! Come on up!"

The 27th jumped up the steps and to the doors. The rest of the crowd started pushing up the steps again. Shukhov pushed with might and main. The porch was shaking. The porch lamp was whining again.

"Again, you shits?" Khromoi became enraged. Whack went his cane on someone's head, on someone's backside. He pushed against the crowd and knocked some down. He cleared the steps again.

Shukhov could see that Pavlo had risen to Khromoi's level. He was taking the brigade in. Tyurin wouldn't come to dirty himself in that mob scene.

"Count off by fives, 104th!" Pavlo shouted from above. "Let them through, friends."

Like hell those friends were going to let them through.

"Let me through. I'm from that brigade!" Shukhov trembled.

The men in front would have been glad to let him through but he was being crushed from every side.

The crowd heaved and suffocated to get its soup. Its rightful soup.

Then Shukhov tried another tack. He grabbed the railings at the left, gripped the porch post with his hands and—hung there. He was off the ground. His legs were kicking someone in the knees. Whoever it was gave it to him in the side, let fly a pair of oaths at him. But he managed to pull himself up. He stood with one foot on the porch cornice at the upper step and waited. His friends saw him, reached out for him.

The head of mess hall looked out of the door. "All right, Khromoi, two more brigades."

"One hundred and fourth!" Khromoi shouted. "And you, bastard, where do you think you're climbing to?" Whack with his stave across the neck of an interloper.

"One hundred and fourth!" Pavlo shouted, letting his own men move past him.

"Phhooo!" Shukhov broke through into the mess hall. And without waiting till Pavlo gave orders, he went to look for empty trays.

In the mess hall as always steam rolled in clouds from the doors. The zeks were sitting at tables, packed as close to each other as seeds in a sunflower. Between tables zeks were wandering, pushing about, some making their way through with full trays. But after so many years Shukhov was used to this. His eyes were sharp and he saw S-208 carrying five bowls on his tray, meaning that was the last tray in his brigade; otherwise there would have been more bowls.

Shukhov caught up with him and whispered in his ear:

"Brother. Let me have the tray after you."

"I promised it to a fellow over there at the window."

"To hell with him. Let him wait. He shouldn't dawdle."

They came to agreement.

That zek unloaded the tray at his table. Shukhov took the tray. The one to whom it had been promised hurried up and grabbed one end. But he was not as big as Shukhov. Shukhov poked him with the tray just as he pulled on it and the zek flew backward as his hands lost their grip. Shukhov tucked the tray under his arm and ran to the window.

Pavlo stood in line at the window, waiting for trays. Happily, "Ivan Denisovich!" And he pushed away the assistant foreman of the 27th.

"Let us through. Don't just stand there. I have a tray."

And look there. Gopchik, the rogue, with another tray.

"They were slow," he was laughing. "And I got it."

Gopchik was going to become a good camp dweller in another three years. He would grow up a bit and then he'd really make good—nothing lower than bread cutter at the very least.

Pavlo ordered the second tray taken by Yermolayev, a husky Siberian who had also received ten as a P.O.W. Pavlo sent Gopchik to look for a table where the men were almost finished. Shukhov leaned his tray on the serving window and waited.

"One hundred and fourth." Pavlo reported into the window.

There were five service windows in all—three for serving, one for those fed a special diet (ten were sick with ulcers, and, because they had influence, the entire bookkeeping office got the same diet), and one more for returning dishes. At that window they fought for the right to lick plates. The windows were low, little more than waist high. Couldn't see the cooks; only their arms and ladles.

This cook had white arms, sleek, hairy, big. More like a boxer, not a cook. He took his pencil and on a list on the wall he wrote:

"One hundred fourth—24!"

Panteleyev had dragged himself along to the mess hall. Of course he wasn't sick, the hound.

The cook took a big ladle that held three quarts and mixed, mixed, mixed it in the tank. The pot in front of him was newly filled, nearly to the top, and steam was rising from it. And then, picking up a ladle less than a quart in size he began, hardly dipping it in, to fill bowls with it:

"One, two, three, four. . . ."

Shukhov noted what bowls were filled before the thick stuff had settled to the bottom, and which were the thinner portions—just liquid. He put ten bowls on his tray, and moved on. Gopchik waved at him from the second row of posts:

"Over here, Ivan Denisych, over here!"

You have to have a steady hand to carry bowls. Shukhov walked smoothly so the tray was steady and he talked as he walked:

"Hey, you, K-920. Look out there, uncle. Get out of the way, fellow."

It wasn't easy to carry even one bowl in this crowd without spilling it—let alone ten. Nevertheless, when he put the tray down carefully at the table end freed by Gopchik there were no fresh splashes on it. And he had even figured out how to put it down so that the two thickest bowls were at the corner of the tray where he would sit.

Yermolayev brought ten. Gopchik ran off and with Pavlo brought the last four by hand.

Kilgas brought bread on a tray. Today they got fed according to their work. Some seven ounces, some ten and Shukhov fourteen. He took his fourteen from the crust, and another seven as Tsezar's share from the center.

Right then the brigade members arrived from all parts of the hall to get their dinner. Just gulp it down wherever you find a place. Shukhov handed out the bowls, remembering who had already eaten, while keeping his eye on his own corner of the tray. He put his spoon into one of the bowls with thick soup. That meant it was taken. Fetyukov took his bowl early and went off. He calculated there'd be nothing to scavenge in his own brigade, so he'd better cover the whole hall. Maybe someone would leave a bit and he could scrounge it. If anyone pushed his bowl away unfinished, several men would grab for it, like vultures.

Shukhov and Pavlo counted the portions. It seemed there were enough. Shukhov put aside one of the bowls with thick soup for Tyurin. Pavlo poured it into a narrow little German mess kit with a top. It would be taken out under his coat, pressed to his chest.

They gave up the trays. Pavlo sat down with his double portion, Shukhov with his two. And no more conversation. The sacred minutes had come.

Shukhov took off his cap, put it on his knees. He examined one bowlful, stirring it with his spoon, and then the other. Not too bad. Even a few little fish. In general the soup was much thinner than in the mornings. Mornings the zeks had to be fed so they'd work, but evenings they'd go to sleep anyway.

He began to eat. First he drank the thin liquid. The warmth poured into him and flooded through his whole body. His innards were palpitating to greet that soup. Goooood. That's it, that fleeting moment for which a zek lives.

Then Shukhov began to eat the cabbage together with the bit of liquid remaining.

At that moment Shukhov was not angry about anything, not even that his term was long, not even that the day was long, not even that Sunday would be a work day. Instead, he was thinking, we'll live through it. We'll live through it all. And if God wills, it will end someday.

Having drunk down the liquid from both the first and second bowls, he poured remains of the second into the first, turned the bowl upside down, and cleaned it out with his spoon. That way it was more relaxed. He didn't have to think about the second bowl, or keep guarding it with his eyes or hand.

Now he could look around at his neighbor's bowls. On his left his neighbor had nothing but water. That's what they do, the vipers, to their own zeks!

Shukhov began to eat the cabbage and the rest of the soup. He'd found one potato in Tsezar's bowl. A middle-sized potato, frozen, of course, but with some firmness and on the sweet side. Hardly any fish, now and then a flesh-less bit of bone. But he had to chew every bit of fish bone and fin, and suck the marrow from them because the marrow was beneficial. To do all this, of course, he needed time. But Shukhov was not in a hurry now. Today was a holiday. At lunch he had managed to snag two portions and now two at dinner. Because of this he could afford to forget about his other affairs.

Except, of course, he must go to the Latvian for tobacco. Maybe there wouldn't be any left by morning.

Shukhov dined without bread. Two portions plus bread would be too much. The bread would hold for the next day. One's stomach was a scoundrel, didn't remember old good turns and would make demands again tomorrow.

Shukhov finished his soup and didn't try very hard to notice who was near him because it wasn't necessary. He wasn't on the lookout for anything extra and was eating what was rightfully his. Yet he did notice that right across the table from him a tall old man—Y-81—sat down when a spot was freed. He was, as Shukhov knew, from the 64th brigade. In line at the parcel room Shukhov had heard that the 64th had gone to the Socialist Life Town instead of the 104th and had been stretching barbed wire a whole day without getting warm, building a new zone for itself.

Shukhov had heard that this old man had been sitting in camps and prisons for years without end, that not one amnesty had touched him. Whenever one ten-year term came to an end they gave him another right away.

Shukhov looked at him closely. Among all the stooped backs in camp, the old man's was notable for its straightness. At the table he sat so tall it seemed he was sitting on something. He hadn't needed a barber in years: his hair had all fallen out from the good life. The old man's eyes did not examine the goings-on in the mess hall, but were fixed on something private, focussed absently over Shukhov's head. He ate his thin soup slowly with a worn-down wooden spoon. He did not bend to the bowl like the others but carried his spoon high up to his mouth. He hadn't a tooth in his head. His bony gums chewed the bread instead of teeth. His face was worn down, not to the weakness of a help-less invalid, but to dark hewn rock. And by his hands, large, wrinkled, work-stained, it was clear that for all his years of sitting he hadn't had much time at soft jobs. There was something in him that refused to compromise. He didn't put his ten ounces of bread on the dirty splotched table as the others did. He put it on a clean-washed piece of cloth.

However, Shukhov didn't have more time to study him. He finished eating, licked off his spoon and shoved it down into his felt boot, pulled his cap down over his forehead, got up, took his bread ration—his own and Tsezar's—and went out. The exit from the mess hall was through another porch. Out there stood two orderlies whose only job was to take off the door hook, let people out, then hang the hook in place.

Shukhov went out with a full stomach, satisfied with himself, and decided that he would run over to see the Latvian though it would be curfew soon. Without taking his bread back to the ninth he marched toward the seventh barracks.

The moon was high, as if sculptured in the heavens, clean, white. The sky was clear. And brilliant stars dotted the darkness. But Shukhov didn't have time to study the heavens. He understood just one thing—the cold was not lessening. Some of the free civilians had heard, and repeated, that by night it would be less than 20° below and toward morning down to 40° below.

A long way off he could hear a tractor humming in the settlement, in the direction of the highway an excavator shrilling. And a crunch and a creak from every pair of valenki walking or running.

But there was no wind.

The homegrown tobacco Shukhov was going to get would cost him one ruble for each small glassful. Outside of camp the same glassful would cost three rubles and maybe more, depending on grade. In a hard-labor camp all the prices were special, not like anywhere else, because there was not supposed to be any money there. Few had any, and it was hard to come by. Zeks were not paid one kopeck in this camp. In Ust-Izhma Shukhov had received thirty rubles or more a month. If relatives sent any here by mail, the officials didn't hand it over but credited it to an account. The money from such an account could be used to buy toilet soap once a month, moldy cake, *Prima* brand cigarettes. You had to order the merchandise from the chief at their prices, and whether you liked it or not, you kept it. If you didn't buy, the money was gone anyway, withdrawn from the account.

Shukhov got money only by doing private work. Slippers made from material given him by the purchaser—two rubles. Patching an underjacket—by agreement.

The seventh barracks was not like the ninth, which had two large halves. In the seventh there was a long corridor, ten doors in it, and a brigade crowded into seven bunks in each room. Yes, and a cabin for the latrine barrel, also a separate room for the barracks' senior orderly. The artists had their own rooms too.

Shukhov went into the room where his Latvian lived. The Latvian was lying on a lower bunk, feet up on the edge, and he was joking with his neighbor in Latvian.

Shukhov sat down beside him. "Hello, so to speak."

"Hello," the Latvian answered and kept his leg up. A small room and everyone would hear everything right away. They both understood that. Therefore, Shukhov sat and waited.

"Well, so to speak, how's everything?"

"All right."

"Cold today?"

"Yes."

Shukhov waited till the men all around had begun to talk again about their own affairs. They were arguing about the war in Korea, whether, because the Chinese had gone into it, there would be a world war or not. Shukhov bent over the Latvian.

"You have some tabacco?"

"I have."

"Show it to me."

The Latvian took his feet off the edge, put them out in the passageway, got up. That Latvian was a skinflint. When he poured out a glassful he was always afraid he'd give one smoke more than he had to.

He showed Shukhov the pouch and opened it.

Shukhov took a pinch of it on his palm, saw that it was the same as the last time, brown and pungent. He lifted it to his nose: smelled. Yes, it was. He said to the Latvian:

"It doesn't seem to be the same."

"The same. The same." The Latvian grew angry. "I don't have any other sort, ever, always the same."

"Well, all right," Shukhov agreed. "You pack down a glassful. I'll have a smoke and maybe buy another, too."

He had said "pack down" because the Latvian liked to fill it loosely.

The Latvian got another pouch from under his pillow, fuller than the first one, and took his small glass out of his locker. Though it was a plastic glass Shukhov had measured it and knew it was equal to a standard one of real glass.

He poured tobacco out.

"Come on, press it down, press it down!" Shukhov poked with his finger himself.

"I know how!" the Latvian angrily grabbed the glass and pressed the tobacco down but more gently. He poured in some more.

Shukhov by that time had unfastened his underjacket and poked the cotton filling until he felt the paper. Using two hands he moved it along the cotton to a small hole that had been torn in another part of the lining and barely sewn with two threads. Having pushed it up to that hole he tore off the threads with his fingernails and folded the paper lengthwise twice. He pulled it out of the hole. Two rubles, so old they didn't even crackle.

And in the room someone shouted, "Just wait for the old boy with the moustaches to take pity on you. He wouldn't believe his own blood brother, let alone you, you jackass."

The good thing about hard-labor camps was that there was plenty of freedom in them. In Ust-Izhma if you whispered that there was a shortage of matches outside they put you in a cell and gave you another ten years. But here—shout whatever you please from the upper bunks—even the stool-pigeons didn't report such stuff, the security section didn't give a damn.

It was free, but there wasn't any time to talk about things.

"Hey, you're putting it in loose," Shukhov complained.

"Well, there, there." The Latvian added a pinch on top.

Shukhov pulled his pouch out of his inner pocket and poured the tobacco into it.

"All right," he decided, not wanting to smoke the first sweet cigarette on the run. "Pat down another."

After some more wrangling the second was poured out. Shukhov handed over two rubles, nodded to the Latvian and left.

Once outside he ran off to his own barracks, not wanting to miss Tsezar when he got back with his package.

But Tsezar was already sitting on a lower bunk and gloating over his package. The things he had were all out on his cot and locker, but the light from the lamp didn't fall there directly, since Shukhov's upper bunk shadowed it.

Shukov walked down the aisle between the captain's bunk and Tsezar's, and bent to hand over the evening bread ration.

"Your bread, Tsezar Markovich."

He didn't say, "So you got it?" because that would be a hint he had taken a place in line and now had a right to a share in the parcel. He knew, without saying it, that he had such right. But he wasn't a jackal, not even after eight years of general work in camps, and the longer he lived the firmer he became in his resolve not to be one.

However, he couldn't control his eyes. His eyes, eagle eyes of an old camp dweller, swiftly glanced over the contents of Tsezar's package as they were spread on the cot and the locker. And even though the things were not entirely unwrapped from their paper and bags, and some of them were still closed, with this swift glance and the confirmation of his sense of smell Shukhov knew that Tsezar had received a sausage, condensed milk, a fat smoked fish, fat bacon, some rusks with a sweet smell, baked goods with a different spicy smell, two pounds of lump sugar, and—besides all that—butter, cigarettes, and pipe tobacco; and that wasn't all.

And he had succeeded in scanning all that during the moment he had said, "Your bread, Tsezar Markovich."

And Tsezar, rumpled, excited, as if he were intoxicated—after receiving a food parcel everyone became that way—waved at the bread with his hand:

"Take it for yourself, Ivan Denisych."

Soup plus seven ounces of bread! That was a full dinner and, obviously, it was to be Shukhov's total share of Tsezar's foodstuffs. Well, there was absolutely nothing worse than to lick your chops in expectation and then get nothing.

Anyway he had fourteen ounces of bread in one ration, seven in another, and at least seven in the mattress. That was enough. Seven ounces right now. Tomorrow morning he could devour another pound or more. Take nearly a pound with him to work, too. To work—what a life! Let the portion in the mattress stay there. Good that he had had the chance to sew it in. Rations had been stolen from a locker in the 75th today. Just complain and see how far it gets you.

Some people think that because a man has a package he's got plenty, so they grab whatever they can get. And yet, if you think about it, easy come, easy go. It often happens that before his next parcel arrives a man is glad to work for an extra kasha, and wait to get a butt. The guard, the foreman, the guy with the soft job in the package room—how can you refuse to give them something? If you refuse, he'll hide your package, so it won't be listed for a week. And what about the man in the checkroom where the packages have to be turned in, where that same Tsezar is going to deliver his bag containing his package, to keep it from thieves, and from inspection. The chief of camp ordered that. If you don't give something to the checkroom man he's going to get his anyway—and more—crumb by crumb. He sits there the whole livelong day, the rat, locked up with other peoples foodstuffs. And just try to catch him stealing! What about services rendered, like the things Shukhov had done? And what about the man at the bath house so that he will give clean linen, not much for him, but something? And for the barber who uses a paper to wipe the razor on instead of wiping it on a zek's naked leg. Not much either, but at least three or four cigarettes. And then something in the cultural educational section so that letters will be saved, so that they don't get lost. And suppose you want to stay in bed for a day or two, something for the doctor too. And what about your next-door neighbor who shares one locker with you—like the captain with Tsezar—can you avoid giving him something? After all he counts every piece you have. Even a man without conscience can't hold out, has to give.

So let someone else be envious of the man with a package, someone who always thinks the turnip in another man's hand is bigger. But Shukhov understood life and didn't expect much from anyone.

By that time he had taken off his boots and climbed to his bunk. He pulled out the piece of blade, looked it over and decided that tomorrow he'd find a good stone to sharpen that blade into a shoemaker's knife. In four days, if he worked on it morning and evenings, he could turn it into a fine little knife with a curved sharp blade.

But for the time being, till morning, he had to hide it. In the wall. And while the captain wasn't in the bunk below—Shukhov didn't want anything to drop on his face—he pulled back his heavy sawdust-filled mattress and proceeded to hide his blade.

His neighbors on other top bunks noticed what he was doing. Alyesha, the Baptist, and, across the passageway on the neighboring bunk, the two brother-Estonians. But Shukhov wasn't worried about them.

Fetyukov came through the barracks, sobbing. Humped over. Blood-smeared lip. He had been beaten up again for plate-licking. Without looking at anyone, not hiding his tears, he went past the entire brigade, climbed up to his bunk, hid his face in his mattress.

If you stopped to think, you felt sorry for him. He wouldn't live through his term. He couldn't adjust.

Then the captain appeared, pleased, carrying a pot of very special tea. In the barracks there were two barrels full of tea—but what kind of tea? Just warm, colored water. Flat tasting. The only fragrance it gave off was the steamy wood and mold smell of the barrels. That was tea fit only for ordinary working stiffs. But the captain must have accepted a handful of real tea from Tsezar, thrown it into a kettle, and run off to the hot water faucet.

"I nearly scalded my fingers at the hot water faucet!" he bragged in satisfaction as he set the tea up at his locker.

Below Shukhov, Tsezar unfolded a sheet of paper and began to write one thing or another. Shukhov moved back on his mattress so as not to see him and not become unhappy. But then Tsezar proved that they couldn't get along without Shukhov. Tsezar stood erect in the aisle, looked up at Shukhov and winked at him:

"Denisych! Give me your *ten days!*"

That meant he wanted the knife, the folding knife, the small one. The one Shukhov owned. He had that hidden in the partition, too. The folding knife was half the size of a finger, but the little so-and-so could easily cut bacon five fingers thick. Shukhov had made that knife; made it and sharpened it, too.

He reached for it, got it out, handed it down. Tsezar nodded and disappeared into his bunk.

So that knife would be income, too. After all, the penalty for owning it was solitary. Only someone totally without conscience could say: 'Lend me the knife. I'm cutting up a sausage, but there's nothing in it for you.'

It was all right if Tsezar borrowed from Shukhov.

Having taken care of bread and blade, Shukhov's next piece of business was the tobacco pouch. He took out a pinch, the same size as the one he had borrowed, and handed it across to the Estonian; well, after all, thank you!

The Estonian opened his lips as if he was trying to smile. He muttered something to his neighbor-brother and they rolled the pinch into a cigarette—'let's try Shukhov's tobacco, so to speak.'

Well it's no worse than yours—try it as much as you like. Shukhov would have tried it himself but a kind of internal wristwatch kept telling him there were only a few seconds till check. Right now was the time the guards wandered around the barracks. To smoke right now meant going out into the corridor, but Shukhov was too cosy on his bunk. It wasn't warm at all in the barracks. Frost was on the ceiling, but for the time being it seemed bearable. It was at night that he shivered.

Now he began to break off small pieces of his seven ounce ration. But unwillingly he overheard the captain talking with Tsezar down below, as they drank tea.

"Come on, captain, eat, don't be shy! Take some smoked fish. Take some sausage."

"Thank you, I will."

"Come on, spread some butter on that bread! It's a real Moscow loaf!"

"Ai, yai, yai! I can't believe that somewhere they are still baking real bread. You know, this sudden abundance reminds me of a situation I was in once, in Archangel. . . ."

There was the racket and din of two hundred voices in that half of the barracks, but despite the noise Shukhov thought he heard the curfew gong hammered out on the rail. No one else heard it. Shukhov also noticed the guard, Pugnose, had entered the barracks. He was a short fellow with a red face. He held a piece of paper in one hand, and because of that, and by his bearing, Shukhov knew he wasn't trying to catch smokers after hours, or chase anyone out for the nightly check. No he was coming for *someone*.

Pugnose looked at his sheet of paper and asked:

"Where is 104?"

"Here," he was answered. The Estonians hid their cigarette and waved away the smoke.

"Where is the foreman?"

"Well?" Tyurin asked, from his cot, hardly moving.

"Have the men written explanatory notes, as ordered?"

"They'll write!" Tyurin answered with conviction.

"It should have been done already."

"My men are illiterates; it's not an easy thing." (That for Tsezar and the captain, second rank. Well, good boy, that foreman, never slow on the uptake.) "No pens. No ink."

"You should have them."

"They take them away."

"Now, look here, foreman, if you keep talking back, I can put you in prison, too!" Pugnose declared, but he wasn't very angry. "I want those explanations to be in the guards' room! And there must be a statement that the illegal items have been turned in to the personal belongings check room. Do you understand?"

"I understand."

(Shukhov thought to himself: 'The captain has had it.' But the captain had heard nothing, was sitting there eating sausage.)

"And now," the guard asked. "Do you have a S-311?"

"I have to look in my list," the foreman began to fumble around. "Should I remember those dogs' numbers?" The foreman was stalling to save Buinovsky for one night, or at least until check time.

"Is there a Buinovsky?"

"What? Me!" the captain replied from beneath Shukhov's bunk where he was sheltered from view.

Well, that's the way it goes. A quick flea always gets caught first on the comb.

"You? Right. S-311, get ready."

"Where?"

"You already know."

The captain just sighed and grunted. And, no doubt, it had been easier for him to lead his squadron of destroyers into the dark and stormy night than to break away from the friendly conversation and go off to icy solitary.

"How many days?" he asked, in a lowered voice.

"Ten. Come on, come on. Faster!"

Right then the orderlies shouted:

"Check! Check! Come on out for check!"

That meant the guard ordered to carry out the check was in the barracks.

The captain looked around. Should he take his coat? But it would be torn off him there anyway, and he'd be left in his underjacket all the same. He concluded he should go as he was. The captain had hoped that Volkovoi would forget—but Volkovoi never forgot anything about anybody. The captain hadn't prepared himself. Hadn't even hidden a bit of tobacco in his underjacket. And to take it now—no good. Probably they'd take it away from him at body inspection anyway. Nevertheless, while he was putting on his cap Tsezar shoved a pair of cigarettes in his hand.

"Well, so long, brothers," the captain absentmindedly called out to the brigade members, and he followed the guard out.

Several voices shouted to him. One—"Buck up." Another—"Don't lose heart." But what was there to say? The brigade had built the camp punishment prison. The 104th knew what it was like. Stone walls, cement floor, no window, stove barely heated, just enough so the ice melted off the wall and formed icy puddles on the floor. Sleep on bare boards. If you didn't shiver the teeth out of your head, you ate ten ounces of bread a day, with hot soup on the third, sixth and ninth days.

Ten days. Ten days of solitary in that place, if sat out strictly to the very end, meant loss of health for life. If it became TB, you'd never get out of hospitals. The men who had gone through fifteen days of strict solitary were in the cold, cold ground.

While you live in the barracks, be happy and grateful and keep your nose clean.

"Come on, get outside, I'm counting to three," the senior barracks orderly yelled. "If anyone isn't out by the count of three, I'll write his number down and give it to the citizen guard."

The senior barracks orderly was also a senior swine. After all, they lock him up in the barracks with us every night, yet he works for the officers, isn't afraid of any zek. On the contrary, everyone is afraid of him. Whenever he betrays a zek to the guards he also hits him in the face. He's classified as an invalid because he lost one of his fingers in a fight. He has the mug of a professional criminal, and he is a criminal, too, sent up on criminal rather than political counts. Though among all the other charges against him they hung a political charge, too—section 58 clause 14 of the code. That's how he got into this camp.

Easy does it—or he writes your number down, passes it to the guard, and there you are with two days in solitary with work outside.

The zeks had been dragging slowly to the doors but when he began to yell they crowded together, immediately piled right on top of each other to get out. The men in upper bunks leaped down like monkeys, and everyone tried to push through the narrow doors at once.

Shukhov, holding the home-rolled, long-desired cigarette, jumped down deftly. He shoved his feet into his felt boots and started out. Then he felt sorry for Tsezar. Not that Shukhov wanted to get anything else from him, but he sincerely pitied him. It was as if he thought too highly of himself, Tsezar, and didn't understand life one little bit. For instance, he got a parcel, but the thing to do was not to gloat over it but to haul it quickly to the checkroom before the check. He could have put part of it aside to eat. And now what could he do with the package? If he took the whole bagful out to the check he'd be the laughingstock of the camp. Five hundred throats roaring. But if he left it inside there was a good chance that whoever ran back into the barracks first would swipe it.

In Ust-Izhma, Shukhov remembered that things had been even rougher. There, when you got back from work, the criminal elements would be in barracks first, and by the time those in the rear had come up their lockers had been cleaned out.

Shukhov saw Tsezar was shoving things here, hiding things there, but he was too late. He was pushing the sausage and bacon down his pocket front—he was going to take them out to check and at least save them.

Shukhov took pity on him and gave him some instructions:

"Sit there, Tsezar Markovich. Sit there hidden in the shadow, and wait till the last second. When the guard and orderlies start around the barracks examining all the corners, then go on out. Act as if you're sick! And I'll go out and hurry back inside first. That's how. . . ."

Then Shukhov ran out.

First he pushed his way swiftly ahead—careful of the home-made cigarette in his hand. In the corridor that was used by both halves of the barracks, and in the entries, no one was going out. Prisoners had animal-cunning. They pressed against the wall in double rows on both sides. That left an empty passageway in the middle, wide enough for one man. Anybody stupid enough can go out into the cold, but as for us, we're going to stay right here. As it is we spend the whole day in the cold, so why should we freeze for an extra ten minutes? No, we're not such fools. You drop dead today—but we'll wait till tomorrow!

Any other night Shukhov would have been huddling against that wall, too. But on this occasion he walked through with long strides and even exposed his teeth in a big grin.

"What are you afraid of, softies? Haven't you seen Siberian cold yet? Go on out and warm yourselves under that wolf's sun up there! How about a light, uncle?"

He lit up out in the entry and went on out on the porch. "Wolf's sun" was what they jokingly called the moon in Shukhov's village.

The moon was high; a little bit more and it would be at its zenith. White sky, touched with green, brilliant stars scattered far apart, glistening white snow. Barracks walls white, too, so that the lamps seemed ineffectual.

Over at another barracks there loomed a black mass—the zeks had come out and were forming up. Over there another group. And from barracks to barracks the buzz of the chatter was not as loud as the creaking of the snow underfoot.

Five men walked down the steps and turned to face the door. Three more came behind them. Shukhov joined the three in the second row. He could stand there and munch bread and hold a cigarette in his teeth. Good tobacco. The Latvian hadn't cheated—it was both biting and pungent.

Other zeks came out slowly and fell in. Soon there were two, three, lines of fives behind Shukhov. Now the men outside got furious at the ones indoors. Why are those snakes jammed in the corridor? Why aren't they out here? We're freezing for their sakes.

None of the zeks ever saw a watch or clock. What was the use of them anyway? A zek only needed to know: When is the rising gong? How long to lineup? To lunch? To curfew?

Despite that, they declared the evening check was held at nine. But it never ended at nine. Often they'd call a second check, even a third one. Prisoners never go to sleep before ten, and the rising gong sounded at five. It wasn't astonishing that the Moldavian fell asleep during work. Wherever a zek got warm he fell asleep in that spot, immediately. During the week so much sleep was lost that on Sunday the entire barracks slept through the whole day. If they were not driven out, that is.

"Hey, get out there. Get down off the porch." The senior barracks orderly and the guard were flushing them out, barking at their backs. Good for them, the sheep!

The first rows shouted at the laggards: "Playing tricks, you vipers? Trying to lick sour cream off shit, is that it? Should have been out here long ago—they'd have counted you off long ago."

The entire barracks piled out. There were four hundred in the barracks;

eighty groups of five. They lined up at the rear, at first strictly by fives, and then farther on—in a mess.

"Line up in fives out there in back!" the senior barracks orderly yelled from the steps.

The pricks aren't separating out; bastards.

Tsezar came out of the door, all huddled up and shivering, pretending to be sick. Two orderlies from that half of the barracks, two from the other half, and one cripple came out too. They made up a first five in front of the rest—making Shukhov's line the third. Tsezar was chased to the end of the line.

And the guard came out on the porch.

"Count off by fives!" He yelled at the tail end. He had a loud voice.

"Count off by fives." The senior barracks orderly yelled. His voice was even louder.

Still hadn't formed up, the pricks!

The senior barracks orderly rushed down from the porch to the back of the crowd. Oaths, and kicks in the ass.

But he looked first: to see whom he kicked. He beat only the ones who wouldn't fight back.

They separated. He returned. Then, together with the guard, "One! Two! Three!"

When they called out a five, it dashed off to the barracks at full speed. For this day they were finally finished with the chief.

That is, they were finished, if there wasn't a second count. Those parasites, those lame brains, counted worse than any herdboy. A herdboy is illiterate, but he drives his herd, and knows without stopping whether all the calves are there. But these types—they train them and what good does it do?

Last winter in this camp there were no dryers: footwear was left in the barracks at night for everyone. So for second, third, fourth count the zeks were driven out of doors. Finally the zeks hadn't even bothered to get dressed, just put on valenki, wrapped themselves in blankets, and went out that way. This year they had built dryers, not for all the shoes at once, but so that after two days every brigade would have a turn to dry its valenki on the third. So now they had begun the practice of conducting second counts inside the barracks: the zeks were chased from one half into the other.

Shukhov ran in. He wasn't exactly first but close enough so he didn't let the first ones in out of his sight. He ran to Tsezar's cot and sat down there. He tore off his valenki, scrambled on the bunk near the stove, and set his valenki on the stove. It was a question of who got his valenki to the stove first. Back to Tsezar's cot. Sat there, legs folded, one eye alert to see that Tsezar's bag didn't get jerked out from under the head of the bed, and another eye peeled to make sure that the men rushing the stove didn't move his valenki.

"Hey!" He had to shout. "You, redhead! How'd you like a boot in the kisser? Put yours down and leave mine alone."

The zeks kept pouring and pouring into the barracks. Over in the 20th a guard yelled:

"Turn in valenki!"

So those zeks would be allowed out of the barracks with their valenki. The barracks would be locked. Then the zeks would return:

"Citizen chief! Let us in the barracks."

And the guards would meet in headquarters barracks and do their book-keeping with their count boards: had someone run away or were all present and accounted for?

Well, Shukhov wasn't concerned with that today. Here came Tsezar diving along between the bunks.

"Thank you, Ivan Denisych!"

Shukhov nodded and climbed up to his bunk as fast as a squirrel. Now he could eat that six-ounce piece, smoke a second cigarette, go to sleep.

Except that he'd had such a good day he didn't feel like sleeping.

Making his bed was a simple matter for Shukhov. Black blanket off the mattress. Lie down on the mattress. (Shukhov had not slept on sheets since 1941 when he had left home. Now it even seemed strange to him that women would bother with sheets and all that extra washing.) His head on his pillow, which was stuffed with shavings. Feet in his underjacket. Coat on top of the blanket. Thank You, good Lord, one more day has passed! Thanks, too, that he was not sleeping in solitary. Here in the barracks, he could manage.

Shukhov lay with his head to the window. Across a ledge from Shukhov Alyesha was nearby on a similar top bunk. Alyesha was leaning back so that light reached him from the lamp bulb. He was reading the Gospels again. The lamp bulb was not far from them. One could read and even sew.

Alyesha heard how Shukhov praised God aloud, and turned.

"You see, Ivan Denisovich, your soul begs to pray to God. Why don't you let it have its way?"

Shukhov looked sideways at Alyesha. The Baptist's eyes were shining like two candles. Shukhov sighed. "Because, Alyesha, those prayers, like official petitions, either don't get there at all or else bear the imprint 'Complaint rejected.'"

In front of headquarters barracks there were four petition boxes, sealed. Once a month a specially empowered officer emptied them. Many zeks slipped declarations and petitions into those boxes. They waited, counting the time, hoping, after two months, for an answer, hoping that in another month a reply would come.

But it doesn't come. Or it does, "Rejected."

"Because, Ivan Denisych, you pray little, poorly, without enthusiasm, that's why things haven't come true from your prayers. Prayer must be incessant. And if you have faith, and you say to that mountain, 'Move!' It will move."

Shukhov laughed and rolled himself one more cigarette. He got a light from the Estonian.

"Stop your chatter, Alyesha! I haven't seen that mountain moved. Well, to be honest, I've never seen any mountains at all. You used to pray in the Caucasus with your Baptist group. Did even one mountain move?"

Those Baptists were unfortunates, too. They prayed to God. Whom did they bother? Yet the whole lot of them got twenty-five years. Because it's that kind of a time now. Twenty-five years, one measure for everything.

"But we didn't pray for that, Denisych," Alyesha said persuasively. He moved closed to Shukhov, close to his face. "Of all that belongs to this earth, all that is transient, the Lord willed only that we would pray for our daily bread, 'Give us this day our daily bread!' "

"The bread ration, you mean?" Shukhov asked.

But Alyesha kept at it. His eyes said more than words, and he took Shukhov's hand in his and stroked it.

"Ivan Denisych! You shouldn't pray to get a package or an extra portion of soup. What people value highly is merely foulness to God. You must pray about spiritual things, ask God to take the scum of evil from your heart. . . ."

"Listen to me instead. In our church in Polomnya the priest. . . ."

"Don't talk to me about your priest!" Alyesha begged, his forehead wrinkled with pain.

"No, you listen to me." Shukov raised himself up on his elbow. "In Polomnya, our parish, no one is richer than the priest. There, let's say they call me to fix a roof—I get thirty-five rubles a day, but get one hundred from the priest. And he doesn't even squawk about it. That Polomnya priest has three women in three towns to whom he pays alimony. He lives with the fourth family. And the provincial bishop is caught on his hook. He shoves a well-greased paw at the bishop. No matter how many other priests are sent to our town, he forces them out; refuses to divide up with anyone. . . ."

"Why do you talk to me about a priest? The Orthodox Church has departed from the Gospels. That's why the government doesn't put them in prison. Because they have no firm faith."

Smoking, Shukhov looked calmly at Alyesha's excitement.

"Alyesha," he took his hand away, blew smoke in the Baptist's face. "I'm not against God, you understand. I willingly believe in God. Only I don't believe in Heaven and Hell. Why do you take us for fools, keep pushing Heaven and Hell at us? That's what I don't like."

Shukhov lay on his back, threw the ash carefully over his head, between bunk and window, in order not to burn the captain's things. Lost in his thoughts, he didn't hear what Alyesha was muttering.

"In general," Shukhov decided, "no matter how much you pray they aren't going to shorten your term. And so you'll keep sitting from gong to gong."

"Don't pray for that either!" Alyesha was horrified. "What's freedom for? In freedom your last particle of faith will be suffocated. Be glad you are in prison. Here you have time to think about your soul. This is what the apostle Paul said: 'What are you doing, weeping and breaking my heart? For I am ready not only to be imprisoned but even to die for the name of the Lord Jesus.' "

In silence Shukhov looked up at the ceiling. He just didn't know whether he still wanted freedom or not. At first he had wanted it very much and each night had counted how many days of his term had passed and how many were left.

Then he got tired of counting. And then it became clear that men in his boots weren't allowed to go home. They were shipped into exile. And he didn't know where he could live better, here or in exile.

He only wanted one thing out of freedom—to go home.

But they don't let people go home.

Alyesha wasn't lying. His voice and his eyes showed that he was glad to sit in prison.

"See here, Alyesha," Shukhov explained to him. "Somehow or other things have worked out for you. Because Christ ordered you to sit, you are sitting for Christ. But what am I sitting for? Because in 1941 they weren't prepared for the war. What's that got to do with me?"

Kilgas muttered from his cot, "Doesn't seem as if there'll be a second check."

"Yesss!" Shukhov replied. "Well, we'll have to write that in the stovepipe with a piece of coal, no second count." He yawned: "Guess I'll sleep."

And at that moment, the men in the quieted-down, pacified barracks heard the rattle of the bolt on the outside door. Two of the zeks who had taken valenki to the dryer ran in and shouted:

"Second check!"

Right then the guard came in after them, commanded, "Go out to the other half."

Some of the men had been asleep. They snarled, began to move, shoved their feet into their valenki. No one took off the padded trousers at night. Without them you'd freeze under the blanket.

"God damn them!" Shukhov swore. But he wasn't very angry, because he hadn't been asleep yet.

Tsezar shoved his hand up, holding out two cookies for him, two pieces of sugar and one round slice of sausage.

"Thank you, Tsezar Markovich," Shukhov bent over the edge of the bunk. "Come on, give me your bag. I'll put it under my mattress head for safety." No one could swipe on the run from an upper, and anyway who would look for anything in Shukhov's bunk?

Tsezar handed up his tied white sack. Shukhov shoved it under his mattress. He waited till the guards had chased more zeks out so he wouldn't have to stand barefoot on the floor too long. But the guard showed his teeth. "Well, how about it, you there in the corner?"

So Shukhov jumped down softly, barefoot, onto the floor. His valenki and footcloths were set so well on the stove that he just didn't want to take them off. And no matter how many slippers he had sewn for others he never left any for himself. Well, after all, he was used to the cold and it wouldn't be for very long.

Anyway they take slippers away when they find them in searches during the day.

As for those brigades that turned their valenki in to the dryer—it's all right for those who have slippers, but the others have to walk on the cold floor either in footcloths or else barefoot.

"Well, well," growled the guard.

"You want me to beat you up, you bastard?" the senior barracks orderly was right there with him.

They pushed the zeks into the other half of the barracks and the last ones into the corridor. Shukhov stood at the partition next to the latrine barrel. Beneath his feet the floor was damp, and there was an icy draft from under the door.

They chased them all out and the guard and the senior barracks orderly went back to see if anyone had hidden, or was in a corner, sleeping. Because if the count was short, it was a catastrophe. And if the count was long, that was a catastrophe. Another recheck either way. They went over the empty half of the barracks, once, twice, and then returned to the doors.

"One, two, three, four. . . ." This time they were readmitting quickly one by one. Shukhov managed to get in as the eighteenth. Ran to his berth, had his foot on the support—whoosh—already up on top.

All right. Feet in the underjacket sleeve, blanket on top of him and on top of that his coat. Sleep. They'd order the other half of the barracks into our half now. No skin off our ass.

Tsezar returned. Shukhov handed down his bag.

Alyesha returned. He was such an incompetent. He helped everyone, but couldn't manage to earn anything extra.

"Here, Alyesha!" Shukhov gave him one cookie.

Alyesha smiled.

"Thank you. You don't have anything yourself."

"Eat."

We don't have any, so we always earn a little something.

Shukhov shoved a little piece of sausage into his mouth. Bite with his teeth. Bite again. Meat fragrance. And real meat juice. It flowed down to his stomach. No more sausage.

He'd eat everything else, Shukhov calculated, in the morning before lineup.

He pulled his thin, unwashed blanket over his head without listening to the zeks from the other half of the barracks who were filling the space between the bunks, waiting till their half was checked.

Shukhov went to sleep, quite content. He had had many successes that day. They hadn't put him in solitary, the brigade had not been driven to the Socialist Life Town, at lunch he had made off with an extra kasha, the foreman had surpassed their quota, Shukhov had had a damn good time laying that wall, he hadn't been caught with that piece of blade at body inspection, he had earned something from Tsezar at evening, and bought himself some tobacco. And he hadn't become really sick. He had managed to recover.

A day had passed that was not darkened by anything. Almost a happy day.

Of such days from gong to gong in his term there were three thousand six hundred and fifty-three.

Three days extra due to leap year.

Carson McCullers

THE BALLAD OF THE SAD CAFÉ

Preface

A year after the publication of her famous first novel, *The Heart Is a Lonely Hunter* (1940), Carson McCullers identified the major influences at work in her fiction in an essay called, "The Russian Realists and Southern Literature." By Russian realist she meant Dostoevsky, and by Southern literature William Faulkner. As Bellow and Solzhenitsyn understand how the past makes the present and do not repeat the past in the present, McCullers too harked back to create, not re-create, her brilliant contemporary short novel *The Ballad of the Sad Café* (1943). What brings Russian and Southern together in that novel, McCullers wrote, is a common technique of realism: "The technique briefly is this: a bold and outwardly callous juxtaposition of the tragic with the humorous, the immense with the trivial, the sacred with the bawdy, the whole soul of man with a materialistic detail." Populating Faulkner's Yoknapatawpha with underground men is no formula for contemporary literature. Instead the writer must understand the common bond of Southern and Russian realism, both of which "have transposed the painful substance of life . . . as accurately as possible," and both of which have understood that in life the painful comes mixed with the ordinary. By callous juxtaposition Southern and Russian realism exaggerate reality without destroying it, and so reveal the irrational and abnormal in the world we think of as everyday. When *The Ballad of the Sad Café* tells us that Marvin Macy carried round with him "the dried and salted ear of a man he had killed in a razor fight," we are being given "the whole soul of man with a materialistic detail."

When Miss Amelia Evans gives her hunchback beloved, Cousin Lymon, a watch chain decorated with her own kidney stones, McCullers is giving us another bold and callous juxtaposition of sacred love with the trivial to again portray a soul with a detail. Celebrating *The Heart Is a Lonely Hunter*, Richard Wright called it "not so much a novel as a projected mood . . . an attitude externalized in naturalistic detail." Wright himself was to unite Southern realism with French existentialism through a technique already at work in *Down by the Riverside*. He was a participant himself in the literary salon McCullers established in an old Brooklyn Heights brownstone in the early 1940's. His understanding of *The Heart Is a Lonely Hunter* is even more suited to *The Ballad of the Sad Café*, for it explains just why that novel is a ballad. McCullers could make naturalistic detail project a mood, could make realistic narrative repeat itself as in refrain, because the realism she built of Faulkner and Dostoevsky comprehends the logic of their juxtapositions. By amassing grotesque details with absolutely realistic precision, McCullers makes her characters images of ourselves, seen in a mirror that accentuates to distort and disfigure what is real on the surface, and so tells the utmost truth about the "whole soul" within.

The purpose of McCullers' freak-show fiction, with its dwarfs, giants, hunchbacks, deaf mutes, deformed, and crippled, is not to scare us. Her grotesque fiction is not Southern gothic. Gothic refers to medieval architecture, but because there is so much pseudo-medieval background in the horror fiction of the late eighteenth century, we call that fiction gothic. Jane Austen called it Nightmare Abbey when she satirized the gothic novel's ridiculous formula of beauty and the beast, of the young, innocent heroine set against experience in the form of a lurking, dark evil from the past that drives deformed villains in the present—as in the novels of Ann Radcliffe, acknowledged master of the genre. Southern gothic adds conflicts of race and family to the earlier formula of skirts and skeletons, but if we call McCullers' fiction Southern gothic we will miss the very point of her grotesques. *The Ballad of the Sad Café* shows us that what may be disregarded as gothic is in fact an intense realism, which knows that what appears to be unreal to us is very often an image of an unadmitted inner reality. The best way to understand the freaks of *The Ballad of the Sad Café* is to take the café-keeper of *The Heart Is a Lonely Hunter* as their interpreter. Biff Brannon of the New York Café in that novel's small southern town finds a freak who is not a freak in Jake Blount, a newly arrived drunken radical: "It was like something was deformed in him—but when you looked at him closely each part of him was normal and as it ought to be." Brannon concludes that Blount's problem "was not in his body, it was probably in his mind," for Blount is a freak who is not a freak—not because a freakish exterior is a simple emblem of an inner condition, but because the division between inner and outer is what makes us all freaks. McCullers' grotesques are as physically different from society as the *normal* members of that society differ internally from their external selves. In turn that difference separates us from one another within society—so that, for McCullers, we are all freaks because we are lonely. In her essay called *Loneliness . . . An American Malady*, she wrote: "Maturity is simply the history of those mutations that reveal to the individual the relation between himself and the world in which he finds himself." Mutations are freaks who measure our progressive alienation, and that alienation is a necessary consequence of growing up. In *The Member of the Wedding* (1946), that metaphor is made explicit when young Frankie Addams, the novel's heroine, looks back on her own physical growth in the past year—four inches—and projects that growth ahead: "According to mathematics and unless she could somehow stop herself, she would grow to be over nine feet tall. And what would be a lady who is over nine feet high? She would be a Freak." Then Frankie remembers her visit to a freak show at last year's fair, where "it seemed to her" that the freaks "had looked at her in a secret way and tried to connect their eyes with hers, as though to say: we know you." Freaks know us by being different from us; our inner isolation is imaged in their external mutation. The last summer of Frankie's adolescence is forcing an awareness of her own isolated self upon her. McCullers, one of the great novelists of growing up, knows that all adults are nine feet high to a child. Her genius is to make her adolescents continue a child's wisdom by understanding its metaphoric significance in an adult world. Adults are as grotesque to the child who does not wish to become one as loneliness is to the adult who has found out that being nine feet high has isolated him from the collective security of childhood. This is the knowledge of Amelia Evans in *The Ballad of the Sad Café*, precisely because she *is* a lady who is over nine feet high, one who exactly answers Frankie's question as McCullers intended.

Carson McCullers wrote *The Ballad of the Sad Café* during a six-week interlude in the middle of the composition of *The Member of the Wedding*, begun in 1941 and finished in 1946. Later, with the help of Tennessee Williams, she rewrote that novel, making it a prize-winning Broadway play produced in 1950. Just as even later playwright Edward Albee, whose early success *Zoo Story* reflects McCullers' O. Henry prize story "A Tree, A Rock, A Cloud," was to dramatize *The Ballad of the Sad Café* for production in 1963. By the time she was thirty, McCullers had written all her major works, and her masterpiece, *The Heart Is a Lonely Hunter*, appeared when she was only twenty-three. Her well-known *Reflections in a Golden Eye* (1941) came out a year later. *Clock without Hands* (1961), her final achievement, does not rank with her earlier successes, but like those novels it again deals with initiation into alienation by teaching its hero, Jester Cane, the meaning of his name. McCullers was a child prodigy, born Lula Carson Smith (1917–1967) in Columbus, Georgia, which she left at seventeen to study music in New York City. By the time she was nineteen, she had written her first published story, *Wunderkind* (1936), about a fifteen-year-old child prodigy like herself. Because McCullers never gave up the theme of *Wunderkind,* and was one herself, the temptation is to find in her giant women and all her grotesques an image of herself land-locked in the South. But it was her Southern upbringing, rather than her prodigy training, that contributed the brilliant understanding of the Southern environment in her fiction. Her grotesque characters do not serve a personal psychological purpose by imaging her own adolescence in Frankie Addams and Mick Kelley of *The Heart Is a Lonely Hunter.* The prodigy of *Wunderkind* realizes during the course of a lesson recital of Beethoven's Variation Sonata that she will never be a brilliant concert pianist, demonstrating McCullers' purpose rather than modeling herself. What hurts is neither the loss of poten-tial fame nor the image of being someone different. The real loss is of the privilege of being treated like an adult while still possessing the security of a child. In *Wunderkind* a freak matures into a normal teenager and inherits the loneliness that comes with just being yourself. In turn that loneliness is shown to be more freakish than the prodigy ever was. And remembering the time when each of us was a prodigy makes the heart a lonely hunter seeking an external companion who will make us whole. But a love that seeks to be what it is not cannot succeed, and that is why McCullers' ballad is about a *sad* café, and why *The Ballad of the Sad Café* is ultimately sung to the music of a chain gang.

Three songs rule *The Ballad of the Sad Café:* the first is "the slow song of a Negro on his way to make love," and it heralds the approach of hunchback Cousin Lymon on his way to Miss Amelia's love. Like that love this song gives way to a woman singing in the darkness "in a high wild voice and the tune had no start and no finish and was made up of only three notes which went on and on." The reappearance of Marvin Macy, Amelia's ex-husband, follows on this song, paralleling the appearance of the hunchback, because McCullers' three characters are three notes interacting endlessly. Endlessness is the point of the novel's last song, heard in the coda McCullers called "The Twelve Mortal Men" after her chain-gang singers: "One dark voice will start a phrase, halfsung, and like a question. And after a moment another voice will join in. . . . The voices are dark in the golden glare, the music intricately blended, both somber and joyful. . . . It is music that causes the heart to broaden and the listener to grow cold with ecstasy and fright. Then slowly the music will sink down until at last there remains one lonely voice, then a great hoarse breath, the sun, the sound of the picks in the silence." This unidentified song is Mc-Cullers' *ballad,* and so as her novel ends it goes on, and we shall always hear its echoes despite the fact that, having gone down to the Forks Falls highway to hear the chain gang, we have also gotten on the Greyhound bus that stops there rather than in town. The construction of the chain gang's ballad out of the individual isolation of the first, questioning, lonely voice seeking a blending of the spirit with another voice in the somber and joyful act of love and of life is the manner of McCullers' novel. Music as love broadens the heart, but ecstacy of love frightens us because we know that loneliness will return after it, with a last hoarse breath giving way to the sound of picks, just as love and life give way as well. Only "mortal men who are together" can make this music because its spirit is of love that gets us together, and the paradox of such love is the meaning of *The Ballad of the Sad Café*.

According to McCullers' narrator there is no such thing as a sad café by definition: What "made the café what it was" was neither appearance nor atmosphere. "There is a deeper reason . . . this deeper reason has to do with a certain pride that had not hitherto been known in these parts. To understand this new pride the cheapness of human life must be kept in mind. . . . There, for a few hours at least, the deep bitter knowing that you are not worth much in this world could be laid low." The café is the house of love that teaches us pride in ourselves—until too much pride drives out love, returning us to a sad, decaying café. The true café is of the spirit—its spirits making us spiritual, turning ballad into spiritual soul music. When McCullers' ballad is over, the café's still is wrecked, and no whiskey survives except the kind that makes men "dream themselves into a dangerous inward world." "Such things . . . happen when a man has drunk Miss Amelia's liquor. He may suffer, or he may be spent with joy—but the experience has shown the truth; he has warmed his soul and seen the message hidden there." Good whiskey brings the inside out and bad does the opposite; these movements are the two notes struck on the soul of Amelia Evans by Marvin Macy and Cousin Lymon. But Amelia herself is the third note, and it was struck long ago when she learned how to make whiskey with "a special quality of its own." The visits to her father's still are the only love Miss Amelia has known; her legacy is the love of parent and child contained in an acorn that she picked up the day Big Papa died and now keeps in a glass case. When Cousin Lymon unlocks that case what he gets is parental love from his kissing cousin. McCullers in all her fiction insists both that "the hearts of small children are delicate organs" and that "a cruel beginning in this world can twist them into curious shapes." When Amelia's love unwinds from child to parent and then from parent to child, the missing love of parents for each other results only in selfish repetition.

The Ballad of the Sad Café is the story of the love between an amazon and a dwarf that analyzes what is grotesque about all human love: "First of all, love is a joint experience between two persons—but the fact that it is a joint experience does not mean that it is a similar experience to the two people involved," and by McCullers' logic dissimilarity is what divides us into lover and beloved, and "the value and quality of any love is determined solely by the lover himself." Knowing this "almost everyone wants to be the lover. And the curt truth is that, in a deep secret way, the state of being beloved is intolerable to many." This contemporary analysis should remind us of the one that modern Thomas Mann, in *Tonio Kröger*, got out of classic Plato, who explained to Mann "that the lover is more divine than the beloved . . . the most derisive thought which has ever been framed, and the one from which spring all the cunning and the profoundest pleasures of desire." Derision and desire interact in *The Ballad of the Sad Café* because McCullers knows that an unselfish mutual experience must be similar. She concentrates on a dissimilar one to analyze our inability to make it similar and thus equal. The lost love of the parent should make adult lovers equal. Because everyone thinks his own loss the greater, competition arises that defines lover and beloved as separate entities, and this definition is false because true lovers are each both lover and beloved in one. McCullers' genius is to understand that selfishness in love means refusing to accept both roles for both partners, and she brilliantly forces us into this understanding by squaring the interrelationships of her three characters. Marvin Macy loves Amelia who rejects him; Amelia loves Lymon who rejects her; and Lymon loves Macy who rejects him. But this system is multiplied to eternity by external similarities reversed in turn by internal similarities reversed in turn by exchanges of sex role that are in turn reversed by exchanges of parent-child role and finally they are reversed by co-existent states of time when past and present merge and divide as the characters mix. Life is an incredible freak show whose wonder ought to teach us to love, because love is the *Square Root of Wonderful* (in McCullers' late play of that name—1958).

McCullers' characters never get to the root of love in eternity because they continually try to escape it. The irony of their failure resides in Amelia's recognition that "everything she tried to do against Marvin Macy rebounded on herself. . . . Miss Amelia would have to stand there helpless, as no one has ever invented a way out of this trap. She could not shout out abuse that would bounce back on herself." Isolation is the name of McCullers' trap, and the true love that teaches equality is the way out, and that love is frustrated precisely by our fear of solitude: "Once you have lived with another, it is a great torture to have to live alone . . . it is better to take in your mortal enemy than face the terror of living alone." But we have all lived with somebody at our earliest point; it is not better to die than to grow up, McCullers intends, by showing us that the enemy we take in is our very fear of being the same as anyone else while knowing that we were born different. The sadness is that fear becomes the pride that routs love in the climactic image of *The Ballad of the Sad Café*, the image of Lymon the hunchback clawing on Amelia's back as she in turn strangles Macy on the café floor. This image proves that "the outward facts of this love are indeed sad and ridiculous," and when McCullers forces us to ask who is who in the brutal and twisted union, she is teaching us the answer to her ultimate question: "So who but God can be the final judge of this or any other love?"

THE BALLAD OF THE SAD CAFÉ

The town itself is dreary; not much is there except the cotton mill, the two-room houses where the workers live, a few peach trees, a church with two colored windows, and a miserable main street only a hundred yards long. On Saturdays the tenants from the near-by farms come in for a day of talk and trade. Otherwise the town is lonesome, sad, and like a place that is far off and estranged from all other places in the world. The nearest train stop is Society City, and the Greyhound and White Bus Lines use the Forks Falls Road which is three miles away. The winters here are short and raw, the summers white with glare and fiery hot.

If you walk along the main street on an August afternoon there is nothing whatsoever to do. The largest building, in the very center of the town, is boarded up completely and leans so far to the right that it seems bound to collapse at any minute. The house is very old. There is about it a curious, cracked look that is very puzzling until you suddenly realize that at one time, and long ago, the right side of the front porch had been painted, and part of the wall—but the painting was left unfinished and one portion of the house is darker and dingier than the other. The building looks completely deserted. Nevertheless, on the second floor there is one window which is not boarded; sometimes in the late afternoon when the heat is at its worst a hand will slowly open the shutter and a face will look down on the town. It is a face like the terrible dim faces known in dreams—sexless and white, with two gray crossed eyes which are turned inward so sharply that they seem to be exchanging with each other one long and secret gaze of grief. The face lingers at the window for an hour or so, then the shutters are closed once more, and as likely as not there will not be another soul to be seen along the main street. These August afternoons—when your shift is finished there is absolutely nothing to do; you might as well walk down to the Forks Falls Road and listen to the chain gang.

However, here in this very town there was once a café. And this old boarded-up house was unlike any other place for many miles around. There were tables with cloths and paper napkins, colored streamers from the electric fans, great gatherings on Saturday nights. The owner of the place was Miss Amelia Evans. But the person most responsible for the success and gaiety of the place was a hunchback called Cousin Lymon. One other person had a part in the story of this café—he was the former husband of Miss Amelia, a terrible character who returned to the town after a long term in the penitentiary, caused ruin, and then went on his way again. The café has long since been closed, but it is still remembered.

The place was not always a café. Miss Amelia inherited the building from her father, and it was a store that carried mostly feed, guano, and staples such as meal and snuff. Miss Amelia was rich. In addition to the store she operated a still three miles back in the swamp, and ran out the best liquor in the county. She was a dark, tall woman with bones and muscles like a man. Her hair was cut short and brushed back from the forehead, and there was about her sun-burned face a tense, haggard quality. She might have been a handsome woman if, even then, she was not slightly cross-eyed. There were those who would have courted her, but Miss Amelia cared nothing for the love of men and was a solitary person. Her marriage had been unlike any other marriage ever con-tracted in the county—it was a strange and dangerous marriage, lasting only for ten days, that left the whole town wondering and shocked. Except for this queer marriage, Miss Amelia had lived her life alone. Often she spent whole nights back in her shed in the swamp, dressed in overalls and gum boots, silently guarding the low fire of the still.

With all things which could be made by the hands Miss Amelia prospered. She sold chitterlins and sausage in the town near-by. On fine autumn days, she ground sorghum, and the syrup from her vats was dark golden and deli-cately flavored. She built the brick privy behind her store in only two weeks and was skilled in carpentering. It was only with people that Miss Amelia was not at ease. People, unless they are nilly-willy or very sick, cannot be taken into the hands and changed overnight to something more worthwhile and profitable. So that the only use that Miss Amelia had for other people was to make money out of them. And in this she succeeded. Mortgages on crops and property, a sawmill, money in the bank—she was the richest woman for miles around. She would have been rich as a congressman if it were not for her one great failing, and that was her passion for lawsuits and the courts.

She would involve herself in long and bitter litigation over just a trifle. It was said that if Miss Amelia so much as stumbled over a rock in the road she would glance around instinctively as though looking for something to sue about it. Aside from these lawsuits she lived a steady life and every day was very much like the day that had gone before. With the exception of her ten-day marriage, nothing happened to change this until the spring of the year that Miss Amelia was thirty years old.

It was toward midnight on a soft quiet evening in April. The sky was the color of a blue swamp iris, the moon clear and bright. The crops that spring promised well and in the past weeks the mill had run a night shift. Down by the creek the square brick factory was yellow with light, and there was the faint, steady hum of the looms. It was such a night when it is good to hear from faraway, across the dark fields, the slow song of a Negro on his way to make love. Or when it is pleasant to sit quietly and pick a guitar, or simply to rest alone and think of nothing at all. The street that evening was deserted, but Miss Amelia's store was lighted and on the porch outside there were five people. One of these was Stumpy MacPhail, a foreman with a red face and dainty, purplish hands. On the top step were two boys in overalls, the Rainey twins—both of them lanky and slow, with white hair and sleepy green eyes. The other man was Henry Macy, a shy and timid person with gentle manners and nervous ways, who sat on the edge of the bottom step. Miss Amelia herself stood leaning against the side of the open door, her feet crossed in their big swamp boots, patiently untying knots in a rope she had come across. They had not talked for a long time.

One of the twins, who had been looking down the empty road, was the first to speak, 'I see something coming,' he said.

'A calf got loose,' said his brother.

The approaching figure was still too distant to be clearly seen. The moon made dim, twisted shadows of the blossoming peach trees along the side of the road. In the air the odor of blossoms and sweet spring grass mingled with the warm, sour smell of the near-by lagoon.

'No. It's somebody's youngun,' said Stumpy MacPhail.

Miss Amelia watched the road in silence. She had put down her rope and was fingering the straps of her overalls with her brown bony hand. She scowled, and a dark lock of hair fell down on her forehead. While they were waiting there, a dog from one of the houses down the road began a wild, hoarse howl that continued until a voice called out and hushed him. It was not until the figure was quite close, within the range of the yellow light from the porch, that they saw clearly what had come.

The man was a stranger, and it is rare that a stranger enters the town on foot at that hour. Besides, the man was a hunchback. He was scarcely more than four feet tall and he wore a ragged, dusty coat that reached only to his knees. His crooked little legs seemed too thin to carry the weight of his great warped chest and the hump that sat on his shoulders. He had a very large head, with deep-set blue eyes and a sharp little mouth. His face was both soft and sassy—at the moment his pale skin was yellowed by dust and there were lavendar shadows beneath his eyes. He carried a lopsided old suitcase which was tied with a rope.

'Evening,' said the hunchback, and he was out of breath.

Miss Amelia and the men on the porch neither answered his greeting nor spoke. They only looked at him.

'I am hunting for Miss Amelia Evans.'

Miss Amelia pushed back her hair from her forehead and raised her chin. 'How come?'

'Because I am kin to her,' the hunchback said.

The twins and Stumpy MacPhail looked up at Miss Amelia.

'That's me,' she said. 'How do you mean "kin"?'

'Because—' the hunchback began. He looked uneasy, almost as though he was about to cry. He rested the suitcase on the bottom step, but did not take his hand from the handle. 'My mother was Fanny Jesup and she come from Cheehaw. She left Cheehaw some thirty years ago when she married her first husband. I remember hearing her tell how she had a half-sister named Martha. And back in Cheehaw today they tell me that was your mother.'

Miss Amelia listened with her head turned slightly aside. She ate her Sunday dinners by herself; her place was never crowded with a flock of relatives, and she claimed kin with no one. She had had a great-aunt who owned the livery stable in Cheehaw, but that aunt was now dead. Aside from her there was only one double first cousin who lived in a town twenty miles away, but this cousin and Miss Amelia did not get on so well, and when they chanced to pass each other they spat on the side of the road. Other people had tried very hard, from time to time, to work out some kind of far-fetched connection with Miss Amelia, but with absolutely no success.

The hunchback went into a long rigmarole, mentioning names and places that were unknown to the listeners on the porch and seemed to have nothing to do with the subject. 'So Fanny and Martha Jesup were half-sisters. And I am the son of Fanny's third husband. So that would make you and I—' He bent down and began to unfasten his suitcase. His hands were like dirty sparrow claws and they were trembling. The bag was full of all manner of junk— ragged clothes and odd rubbish that looked like parts of a sewing machine, or something just as worthless. The hunchback scrambled among these belongings and brought out an old photograph. 'This is a picture of my mother and her half-sister.'

Miss Amelia did not speak. She was moving her jaw slowly from side to side, and you could tell from her face what she was thinking about. Stumpy MacPhail took the photograph and held it out toward the light. It was a picture of two pale, withered-up little children of about two and three years of age. The faces were tiny white blurs, and it might have been an old pictuure in anyone's album.

Stumpy MacPhail handed it back with no comment. 'Where you come from?' he asked.

The hunchback's voice was uncertain. 'I was traveling.'

Still Miss Amelia did not speak. She just stood leaning against the side of the door, and looked down at the hunchback. Henry Macy winked nervously and rubbed his hands together. Then quietly he left the bottom step and disappeared. He is a good soul, and the hunchback's situation had touched his heart. Therefore he did not want to wait and watch Miss Amelia chase this newcomer off her property and run him out of town. The hunchback stood with his bag open on the bottom step; he sniffled his nose, and his mouth quivered. Perhaps he began to feel his dismal predicament. Maybe he realized what a miserable thing it was to be a stranger in the town with a suitcase full of junk, and claiming kin with Miss Amelia. At any rate he sat down on the steps and suddenly began to cry.

It was not a common thing to have an unknown hunchback walk to the store at midnight and then sit down and cry. Miss Amelia rubbed back her hair from her forehead and the men looked at each other uncomfortably. All around the town was very quiet.

At last one of the twins said: 'I'll be damned if he ain't a regular Morris Finestein.'

Everyone nodded and agreed, for that is an expression having a certain special meaning. But the hunchback cried louder because he could not know what they were talking about. Morris Finestein was a person who had lived in the town years before. He was only a quick, skipping little Jew who cried if you called him Christ-killer, and ate light bread and canned salmon every day. A calamity had come over him and he had moved away to Society City. But since then if a man were prissy in any way, or if a man ever wept, he was known as a Morris Finestein.

'Well, he is afflicted,' said Stumpy MacPhail. 'There is some cause.'

Miss Amelia crossed the porch with two slow, gangling strides. She went down the steps and stood looking thoughtfully at the stranger. Gingerly, with one long brown forefinger, she touched the hump on his back. The hunchback still wept, but he was quieter now. The night was silent and the moon still shone with a soft, clear light—it was getting colder. Then Miss Amelia did a rare thing; she pulled out a bottle from her hip pocket and after polishing off the top with the palm of her hand she handed it to the hunchback to drink. Miss Amelia could seldom be persuaded to sell her liquor on credit, and for her to give so much as a drop away free was almost unknown.

'Drink,' she said. 'It will liven your gizzard.'

The hunchback stopped crying, neatly licked the tears from around his mouth, and did as he was told. When he was finished, Miss Amelia took a slow swallow, warmed and washed her mouth with it, and spat. Then she also drank. The twins and the foreman had their own bottle they had paid for.

'It is smooth liquor,' Stumpy MacPhail said. 'Miss Amelia, I have never known you to fail.'

The whisky they drank that evening (two big bottles of it) is important. Otherwise, it would be hard to account for what followed. Perhaps without it there would never have been a café. For the liquor of Miss Amelia has a special quality of its own. It is clean and sharp on the tongue, but once down a man it glows inside him for a long time afterward. And that is not all. It is known that if a message is written with lemon juice on a clean sheet of paper there will be no sign of it. But if the paper is held for a moment to the fire then the letters turn brown and the meaning becomes clear. Imagine that the whisky is the fire and that the message is that which is known only in the soul of a man—then the worth of Miss Amelia's liquor can be understood. Things that have gone unnoticed, thoughts that have been harbored far back in the dark mind, are suddenly recognized and comprehended. A spinner who has thought only of the loom, the dinner pail, the bed, and then the loom again—this spinner might drink some on a Sunday and come across a marsh lily. And in his palm he might hold this flower, examining the golden dainty cup, and in him suddenly might come a sweetness keen as pain. A weaver might look up suddenly and see for the first time the cold, weird radiance of midnight January sky, and a deep fright at his own smallness stop his heart. Such things as these, then, happen when a man has drunk Miss Amelia's liquor. He may suffer, or he may be spent with joy—but the experience has shown the truth; he has warmed his soul and seen the message hidden there.

They drank until it was past midnight, and the moon was clouded over so that the night was cold and dark. The hunchback still sat on the bottom steps, bent over miserably with his forehead resting on his knee. Miss Amelia stood with her hands in her pockets, one foot resting on the second step of the stairs. She had been silent for a long time. Her face had the expression often seen in slightly cross-eyed persons who are thinking deeply, a look that appears to be both very wise and very crazy. At last she said: 'I don't know your name.'

'I'm Lymon Willis,' said the hunchback.

'Well, come on in,' she said. 'Some supper was left in the stove and you can eat.'

Only a few times in her life had Miss Amelia invited anyone to eat with her, unless she were planning to trick them in some way, or make money out of them. So the men on the porch felt there was something wrong. Later, they said among themselves that she must have been drinking back in the swamp the better part of the afternoon. At any rate she left the porch, and Stumpy MacPhail and the twins went on off home. She bolted the front door and looked all around to see that her goods were in order. Then she went to the kitchen, which was at the back of the store. The hunchback followed her, dragging his suitcase, sniffing and wiping his nose on the sleeve of his dirty coat.

'Sit down,' said Miss Amelia. 'I'll just warm up what's here.'

It was a good meal they had together on that night. Miss Amelia was rich and she did not grudge herself food. There was fried chicken (the breast of which the hunchback took on his own plate), mashed rootabeggars, collard greens, and hot, pale golden, sweet potatoes. Miss Amelia ate slowly and with the relish of a farm hand. She sat with both elbows on the table, bent over the plate, her knees spread wide apart and her feet braced on the rungs of the chair. As for the hunchback, he gulped down his supper as though he had not smelled food in months. During the meal one tear crept down his dingy cheek— but it was just a little leftover tear and meant nothing at all. The lamp on the table was well-trimmed, burning blue at the edges of the wick, and casting a cheerful light in the kitchen. When Miss Amelia had eaten her supper she wiped her plate carefully with a slice of light bread, and then poured her own clear, sweet syrup over the bread. The hunchback did likewise—except that he was more finicky and asked for a new plate. Having finished, Miss Amelia tilted back her chair, tightened her fist, and felt the hard, supple muscles of her right arm beneath the clean, blue cloth of her shirtsleeves—an unconscious habit with her, at the close of a meal. Then she took the lamp from the table and jerked her head toward the staircase as an invitation for the hunchback to follow after her.

Above the store there were the three rooms where Miss Amelia had lived during all her life—two bedrooms with a large parlor in between. Few people had even seen these rooms, but it was generally known that they were well-furnished and extremely clean. And now Miss Amelia was taking up with her a dirty little hunchbacked stranger, come from God knows where. Miss Amelia walked slowly, two steps at a time, holding the lamp high. The hunchback hovered so close behind her that the swinging light made on the staircase wall one great, twisted shadow of the two of them. Soon the premises above the store were dark as the rest of the town.

The next morning was serene, with a sunrise of warm purple mixed with rose. In the fields around the town the furrows were newly plowed, and very early the tenants were at work setting out the young, deep green tobacco plants. The wild crows flew down close to the fields, making swift blue shadows on the earth. In town the people set out early with their dinner pails, and the windows of the mill were blinding gold in the sun. The air was fresh and the peach trees light as March clouds with their blossoms.

Miss Amelia came down at about dawn, as usual. She washed her head at the pump and very shortly set about her business. Later in the morning she saddled her mule and went to see about her property, planted with cotton, up near the Forks Falls Road. By noon, of course, everybody had heard about the hunchback who had come to the store in the middle of the night. But no one as yet had seen him. The day soon grew hot and the sky was a rich, mid-day blue. Still no one had laid an eye on this strange guest. A few people remembered that Miss Amelia's mother had had a half-sister—but there was some difference of opinion as to whether she had died or had run off with a tobacco stringer. As for the hunchback's claim, everyone thought it was a trumped-up business. And the town, knowing Miss Amelia, decided that surely she had put him out of the house after feeding him. But toward evening, when the sky had whitened, and the shift was done, a woman claimed to have seen a crooked face at the window of one of the rooms up over the store. Miss Amelia herself said nothing. She clerked in the store for a while, argued for an hour with a farmer over a plow shaft, mended some chicken wire, locked up near sundown, and went to her rooms. The town was left puzzled and talkative.

The next day Miss Amelia did not open the store, but stayed locked up inside her premises and saw no one. Now this was the day that the rumor started—the rumor so terrible that the town and all the country about were stunned by it. The rumor was started by a weaver called Merlie Ryan. He is a man of not much account—sallow, shambling, and with no teeth in his head. He has the three-day malaria, which means that every third day the fever comes on him. So on two days he is dull and cross, but on the third day he livens up and sometimes has an idea or two, most of which are foolish. It was while Merlie Ryan was in his fever that he turned suddenly and said:

'I know what Miss Amelia done. She murdered that man for something in that suitcase.'

He said this in a calm voice, as a statement of fact. And within an hour the news had swept through the town. It was a fierce and sickly tale the town built up that day. In it were all the things which cause the heart to shiver—a hunchback, a midnight burial in the swamp, the dragging of Miss Amelia through the streets of the town on the way to prison, the squabbles over what would happen to her property—all told in hushed voices and repeated with some fresh and weird detail. It rained and women forgot to bring in the washing from the lines. One or two mortals, who were in debt to Miss Amelia, even put on Sunday clothes as though it were a holiday. People clustered together on the main street, talking and watching the store.

It would be untrue to say that all the town took part in this evil festival. There were a few sensible men who reasoned that Miss Amelia, being rich, would not go out of her way to murder a vagabond for a few trifles of junk. In the town there were even three good people, and they did not want this crime, not even for the sake of the interest and the great commotion it would entail; it gave them no pleasure to think of Miss Amelia holding to the bars of the penitentiary and being electrocuted in Atlanta. These good people judged Miss Amelia in a different way from what the others judged her. When a person is as contrary in every single respect as she was and when the sins of a person have amounted to such a point that they can hardly be remembered all at once—then this person plainly requires a special judgment. They remembered that Miss Amelia had been born dark and somewhat queer of face, raised motherless by her father who was a solitary man, that early in youth she had grown to be six feet two inches tall which in itself is not natural for a woman, and that her ways and habits of life were too peculiar ever to reason about. Above all, they remembered her puzzling marriage, which was the most unreasonable scandal ever to happen in this town.

So these good people felt toward her something near to pity. And when she was out on her wild business, such as rushing in a house to drag forth a sewing machine in payment for a debt, or getting herself worked up over some matter concerning the law—they had toward her a feeling which was a mixture of exasperation, a ridiculous little inside tickle, and a deep, unnamable sadness. But enough of the good people, for there were only three of them; the rest of the town was making a holiday of this fancied crime the whole of the afternoon.

Miss Amelia herself, for some strange reason, seemed unaware of all this. She spent most of her day upstairs. When down in the store, she prowled around peacefully, her hands deep in the pockets of her overalls and head bent so low that her chin was tucked inside the collar of her shirt. There was no bloodstain on her anywhere. Often she stopped and just stood somberly looking down at the cracks in the floor, twisting a lock of her short-cropped hair, and whispering something to herself. But most of the day was spent upstairs.

Dark came on. The rain that afternoon had chilled the air, so that the evening was bleak and gloomy as in wintertime. There were no stars in the sky, and a light, icy drizzle had set in. The lamps in the houses made mournful, wavering flickers when watched from the street. A wind had come up, not from the swamp side of the town but from the cold black pinewoods to the north.

The clocks in the town struck eight. Still nothing had happened. The bleak night, after the gruesome talk of the day, put a fear in some people, and they stayed home close to the fire. Others were gathered in groups together. Some eight or ten men had convened on the porch of Miss Amelia's store. They were silent and were indeed just waiting about. They themselves did not know what they were waiting for, but it was this: in times of tension, when some great action is impending, men gather and wait in this way. And after a time there will come a moment when all together they will act in unison, not from thought or from the will of any one man, but as though their instincts had merged together so that the decision belongs to no single one of them, but to the group as a whole. At such a time, no individual hesitates. And whether the matter will be settled peaceably, or whether the joint action will result in ransacking, violence, and crime, depends on destiny. So the men waited soberly on the porch of Miss Amelia's store, not one of them realizing what they would do, but knowing inwardly that they must wait, and that the time had almost come.

Now the door to the store was open. Inside it was bright and natural-looking. To the left was the counter where slabs of white meat, rock candy, and tobacco were kept. Behind this were shelves of salted white meat and meal. The right side of the store was mostly filled with farm implements and such. At the back of the store, to the left, was the door leading up the stairs, and it was open. And at the far right of the store there was another door which led to a little room that Miss Amelia called her office. This door was also open. And at eight o'clock that evening Miss Amelia could be seen there sitting before her rolltop desk, figuring with a fountain pen and some pieces of paper.

The office was cheerfully lighted, and Miss Amelia did not seem to notice the delegation on the porch. Everything around her was in great order, as usual. This office was a room well-known, in a dreadful way, throughout the country.

It was there Miss Amelia transacted all business. On the desk was a carefully covered typewriter which she knew how to run, but used only for the most important documents. In the drawers were literally thousands of papers, all filed according to the alphabet. This office was also the place where Miss Amelia received sick people, for she enjoyed doctoring and did a great deal of it. Two whole shelves were crowded with bottles and various paraphernalia. Against the wall was a bench where the patients sat. She could sew up a wound with a burnt needle so that it would not turn green. For burns she had a cool, sweet syrup. For unlocated sickness there were any number of different medicines which she had brewed herself from unknown recipes. They wrenched loose the bowels very well, but they could not be given to small children, as they caused bad convulsions; for them she had an entirely separate draught, gentler and sweet-flavored. Yes, all in all, she was considered a good doctor. Her hands, though very large and bony, had a light touch about them. She possessed great imagination and used hundreds of different cures. In the face of the most dangerous and extraordinary treatment she did not hesitate, and no disease was so terrible but what she would undertake to cure it. In this there was one exception. If a patient came with a female complaint she could do nothing. Indeed at the mere mention of the words her face would slowly darken with shame, and she would stand there craning her neck against the collar of her shirt, or rubbing her swamp boots together, for all the world like a great, shamed, dumb-tongued child. But in other matters people trusted her. She charged no fees whatsoever and always had a raft of patients.

On this evening, Mis Amelia wrote with her fountain pen a good deal. But even so she could not be forever unaware of the group waiting out there on the dark porch, and watching her. From time to time she looked up and regarded them steadily. But she did not holler out to them to demand why they were loafing around her property like a sorry bunch of gabbies. Her face was proud and stern, as it always was when she sat at the desk of her office. After a time their peering in like that seemed to annoy her. She wiped her cheek with a red handkerchief, got up, and closed the office door.

Now to the group on the porch this gesture acted as a signal. The time had come. They had stood for a long while with the night raw and gloomy in the street behind them. They had waited long and just at that moment the instinct to act came on them. All at once, as though moved by one will, they walked into the store. At that moment the eight men looked very much alike—all wearing blue overalls, most of them with whitish hair, all pale of face, and all with a set, dreaming look in the eye. What they would have done next no one knows. But at that instant there was a noise at the head of the staircase. The men looked up and then stood dumb with shock. It was the hunchback, whom they had already murdered in their minds. Also, the creature was not at all as had been pictured to them—not a pitiful and dirty little chatterer, alone and beggared in this world. Indeed, he was like nothing any man among them had ever beheld until that time. The room was still as death.

The hunchback came down slowly with the proudness of one who owns every plank of the floor beneath his feet. In the past days he had greatly changed. For one thing he was clean beyond words. He still wore his little coat, but it was brushed off and neatly mended. Beneath this was a fresh red and black checkered shirt belonging to Miss Amelia. He did not wear trousers such as ordinary men are meant to wear, but a pair of tight-fitting little knee-length breeches. On his skinny legs he wore black stockings, and his shoes were of a special kind, being queerly shaped, laced up over the ankles, and newly cleaned and polished with wax. Around his neck, so that his large, pale ears were almost completely covered, he wore a shawl of lime-green wool, the fringes of which almost touched the floor.

The hunchback walked down the store with his stiff little strut and then stood in the center of the group that had come inside. They cleared a space about him and stood looking with hands loose at their sides and eyes wide open. The hunchback himself got his bearings in an odd manner. He regarded each person steadily at his own eye-level, which was about belt line for an ordinary man. Then with shrewd deliberation he examined each man's lower regions—from the waist to the sole of the shoe. When he had satisfied himself he closed his eyes for a moment and shook his head, as though in his opinion what he had seen did not amount to much. Then with assurance, only to confirm himself, he tilted back his head and took in the halo of faces around him with one long, circling stare. There was a half-filled sack of guano on the left side of the store, and when he had found his bearings in this way, the hunchback sat down upon it. Cozily settled, with his little legs crossed, he took from his coat pocket a certain object.

Now it took some moments for the men in the store to regain their ease. Merlie Ryan, he of the three-day fever who had started the rumor that day, was the first to speak. He looked at the object which the hunchback was fondling, and said in a hushed voice:

'What is it you have there?'

Each man knew well what it was the hunchback was handling. For it was the snuffbox which had belonged to Miss Amelia's father. The snuffbox was of blue enamel with a dainty embellishment of wrought gold on the lid. The group knew it well and marveled. They glanced warily at the closed office door, and heard the low sound of Miss Amelia whistling to herself.

'Yes, what is it, Peanut?'

The hunchback looked up quickly and sharpened his mouth to speak. 'Why, this is a lay-low to catch meddlers.'

The hunchback reached in the box with his scrambly little fingers and ate something, but he offered no one around him a taste. It was not even proper snuff which he was taking, but a mixture of sugar and cocoa. This he took, though, as snuff, pocketing a little wad of it beneath his lower lip and licking down neatly into this with a flick of his tongue which made a frequent grimace come over his face.

'The very teeth in my head have always tasted sour to me,' he said in explanation. 'That is the reason why I take this kind of sweet snuff.'

The group still clustered around, feeling somewhat gawky and bewildered. This sensation never quite wore off, but it was soon tempered by another feeling—an air of intimacy in the room and a vague festivity. Now the names of the men of the group there on that evening were as follows: Hasty Malone, Robert Calvert Hale, Merlie Ryan, Reverend T. M. Willin, Rosser Cline, Rip Wellborn, Henry Ford Crimp, and Horace Wells. Except for Reverend Willin, they are all alike in many ways as has been said—all having taken pleasure from something or other, all having wept and suffered in some way, most of them tractable unless exasperated. Each of them worked in the mill, and lived with others in a two- or three-room house for which the rent was ten dollars or twelve dollars a month. All had been paid that afternoon, for it was Saturday. So, for the present, think of them as a whole.

The hunchback, however, was already sorting them out in his mind. Once comfortably settled he began to chat with everyone, asking questions such as if a man was married, how old he was, how much his wages came to in an average week, et cetera—picking his way along to inquiries which were downright intimate. Soon the group was joined by others in the town, Henry Macy, idlers who had sensed something extraordinary, women come to fetch their men who lingered on, and even one loose, towhead child who tiptoed into the store, stole a box of animal crackers, and made off very quietly. So the premises of Miss Amelia were soon crowded, and she herself had not yet opened her office door.

There is a type of person who has a quality about him that sets him apart from other and more ordinary human beings. Such a person has an instinct which is usually found only in small children, an instinct to establish immediate and vital contact between himself and all things in the world. Certainly the hunchback was of this type. He had only been in the store half an hour before an immediate contact had been established between him and each other individual. It was as though he had lived in the town for years, was a well-known character, and had been sitting and talking there on that guano sack for countless evenings. This, together with the fact that it was Saturday night, could account for the air of freedom and illicit gladness in the store. There was a tension, also, partly because of the oddity of the situation and because Miss Amelia was still closed off in her office and had not yet made her appearance.

She came out that evening at ten o'clock. And those who were expecting some drama at her entrance were disappointed. She opened the door and walked in with her slow, gangling swagger. There was a streak of ink on one side of her nose, and she had knotted the red handkerchief about her neck. She seemed to notice nothing unusual. Her gray, crossed eyes glanced over to the place where the hunchback was sitting, and for a moment lingered there. The rest of the crowd in her store she regarded with only a peaceable surprise.

'Does anyone want waiting on?' she asked quietly.

There were a number of customers, because it was Saturday night, and they all wanted liquor. Now Miss Amelia had dug up an aged barrel only three days past and had siphoned it into bottles back by the still. This night she took the money from the customers and counted it beneath the bright light. Such was the ordinary procedure. But after this what happened was not ordinary. Always before, it was necessary to go around to the dark back yard, and there she would hand out your bottle through the kitchen door. There was no feeling of joy in the transaction. After getting his liquor the customer walked off into the night. Or, if his wife would not have it in the home, he was allowed to come back around to the front porch of the store and guzzle there or in the street. Now, both the porch and the street before it were the property of Miss Amelia, and no mistake about it—but she did not regard them as her premises; the premises began at the front door and took in the entire inside of the building. There she had never allowed liquor to be opened or drunk by anyone but herself. Now for the first time she broke this rule. She went to the kitchen, with the hunch-back close at her heels, and she brought back the bottles into the warm, bright store. More than that she furnished some glasses and opened two boxes of crackers so that they were there hospitably in a platter on the counter and anyone who wished could take one free.

She spoke to no one but the hunchback, and she only asked him in a some-what harsh and husky voice: 'Cousin Lymon, will you have yours straight, or warmed in a pan with water on the stove?'

'If you please, Amelia,' the hunchback said. (And since what time had any-one presumed to address Miss Amelia by her bare name, without a title of respect?— Certainly not her bridegroom and her husband of ten days. In fact, not since the death of her father, who for some reason had always called her Little, had anyone dared to address her in such a familiar way.) 'If you please, I'll have it warmed.'

Now, this was the beginning of the café. It was as simple as that. Recall that the night was gloomy as in wintertime, and to have sat around the property outside would have made a sorry celebration. But inside there was company and a genial warmth. Someone had rattled up the stove in the rear, and those who bought bottles shared their liquor with friends. Several women were there and they had twists of licorice, a Nehi, or even a swallow of the whisky. The hunchback was still a novelty and his presence amused everyone. The bench in the office was brought in, together with several extra chairs. Other people leaned against the counter or made themselves comfortable on barrels and sacks. Nor did the opening of liquor on the premises cause any rambunctious-ness, indecent giggles, or misbehavior whatsoever. On the contrary the company was polite even to the point of a certain timidness. For people in this town were then unused to gathering together for the sake of pleasure. They met to work in the mill. Or on Sunday there would be an all-day camp meeting—and though that is a pleasure, the intention of the whole affair is to sharpen your view of Hell and put into you a keen fear of the Lord Almighty. But the spirit of a café is altogether different. Even the richest, greediest old rascal will behave himself, insulting no one in a proper café. And poor people look about them gratefully and pinch up the salt in a dainty and modest manner. For the at-mosphere of a proper café implies these qualities: fellowship, the satisfactions of the belly, and a certain gaiety and grace of behavior. This had never been told to the gathering in Miss Amelia's store that night. But they knew it of themselves, although never, of course, until that time had there been a café in the town.

Now, the cause of all this, Miss Amelia, stood most of the evening in the doorway leading to the kitchen. Outwardly she did not seem changed at all. But there were many who noticed her face. She watched all that went on, but most of the time her eyes were fastened lonesomely on the hunchback. He strutted about the store, eating from his snuffbox, and being at once sour and agreeable. Where Miss Amelia stood, the light from the chinks of the stove cast a glow, so that her brown, long face was somewhat brightened. She seemed to be looking inward. There was in her expression pain, perplexity, and uncertain joy. Her lips were not so firmly set as usual, and she swallowed often. Her skin had paled and her large empty hands were sweating. Her look that night, then, was the lonesome look of the lover.

This opening of the café came to an end at midnight. Everyone said good-bye to everyone else in a friendly fashion. Miss Amelia shut the front door of her premises, but forgot to bolt it. Soon everything—the main street with its three stores, the mill, the houses—all the town, in fact—was dark and silent. And so ended three days and nights in which had come an arrival of a stranger, an unholy holiday, and the start of the café.

Now time must pass. For the next four years are much alike. There are great changes, but these changes are brought about bit by bit, in simple steps which in themselves do not appear to be important. The hunchback continued to live with Miss Amelia. The café expanded in a gradual way. Miss Amelia began to sell her liquor by the drink, and some tables were brought into the store. There were customers every evening, and on Saturday a great crowd. Miss Amelia began to serve fried catfish suppers at fifteen cents a plate. The hunchback cajoled her into buying a fine mechanical piano. Within two years the place was a store no longer, but had been converted into a proper café, open every evening from six until twelve o'clock.

Each night the hunchback came down the stairs with the air of one who has a grand opinion of himself. He always smelled slightly of turnip greens, as Miss Amelia rubbed him night and morning with pot liquor to give him strength. She spoiled him to a point beyond reason, but nothing seemed to strengthen him; food only made his hump and his head grow larger while the rest of him remained weakly and deformed. Miss Amelia was the same in appearance. During the week she still wore swamp boots and overalls, but on Sunday she put on a dark red dress that hung on her in a most peculiar fashion. Her manners, however, and her way of life were greatly changed. She still loved a fierce lawsuit, but she was not so quick to cheat her fellow man and to exact cruel payments. Because the hunchback was so extremely sociable, she even went about a little—to revivals, to funerals, and so forth. Her doctoring was as successful as ever, her liquor even finer than before, if that were possible. The café itself proved profitable and was the only place of pleasure for many miles around.

So for the moment regard these years from random and disjointed views. See the hunchback marching in Miss Amelia's footsteps when on a red winter morning they set out for the pinewoods to hunt. See them working on her properties—with Cousin Lymon standing by and doing absolutely nothing, but quick to point out any laziness among the hands. On autumn afternoons they sat on the back steps chopping sugar cane. The glaring summer days they spent back in the swamp where the water cypress is a deep black green, where beneath the tangled swamp trees there is a drowsy gloom. When the path leads through a bog or a stretch of blackened water see Miss Amelia bend down to let Cousin Lymon scramble on her back—and see her wading forward with the hunchback settled on her shoulders, clinging to her ears or to her broad forehead. Occasionally Miss Amelia cranked up the Ford which she had bought and treated Cousin Lymon to a picture-show in Cheehaw, or to some distant fair or cockfight; the hunchback took a passionate delight in spectacles. Of course, they were in their café every morning, they would often sit for hours together by the fireplace in the parlor upstairs. For the hunchback was sickly at night and dreaded to lie looking into the dark. He had a deep fear of death. And Miss Amelia would not leave him by himself to suffer with this fright. It may even be reasoned that the growth of the café came about mainly on this account; it was a thing that brought him company and pleasure and that helped him through the night. So compose from such flashes an image of these years as a whole. And for a moment let it rest.

Now some explanation is due for all this behavior. The time has come to speak about love. For Miss Amelia loved Cousin Lymon. So much was clear to everyone. They lived in the same house together and were never seen apart. Therefore, according to Mrs. MacPhail, a warty-nosed old busybody who is continually moving her sticks of furniture from one part of the front room to another; according to her and to certain others, these two were living in sin. If they were related, they were only a cross between first and second cousins, and even that could in no way be proved. Now, of course, Miss Amelia was a powerful blunderbuss of a person, more than six feet tall—and Cousin Lymon a weakly little hunchback reaching only to her waist. But so much the better for Mrs. Stumpy MacPhail and her cronies, for they and their kind glory in conjunctions which are ill-matched and pitiful. So let them be. The good people thought that if those two had found some satisfaction of the flesh between themselves, then it was a matter concerning them and God alone. All sensible people agreed in their opinion about this conjecture—and their answer was a plain, flat top. What sort of thing, then, was this love?

First of all, love is a joint experience between two persons—but the fact that it is a joint experience does not mean that it is a similar experience to the two people involved. There are the lover and the beloved, but these two come from different countries. Often the beloved is only a stimulus for all the stored-up love which has lain quiet within the lover for a long time hitherto. And somehow every lover knows this. He feels in his soul that his love is a solitary thing. He comes to know a new, strange loneliness and it is this knowledge which makes him suffer. So there is only one thing for the lover to do. He must house his love within himself as best he can; he must create for himself a whole new inward world—a world intense and strange, complete in himself. Let it be added here that this lover about whom we speak need not necessarily be a young man saving for a wedding ring—this lover can be man, woman, child, or indeed any human creature on this earth.

Now, the beloved can also be of any description. The most outlandish people can be the stimulus for love. A man may be a doddering great-grandfather and still love only a strange girl he saw in the streets of Cheehaw one afternoon two decades past. The preacher may love a fallen woman. The beloved may be treacherous, greasy-headed, and given to evil habits. Yes, and the lover may see this as clearly as anyone else—but that does not affect the evolution of his love one whit. A most mediocre person can be the object of a love which is wild, extravagant, and beautiful as the poison lilies of the swamp. A good man may be the stimulus for a love both violent and debased, or a jabbering madman may bring about in the soul of someone a tender and simple idyll. Therefore, the value and quality of any love is determined solely by the lover himself.

It is for this reason that most of us would rather love than be loved. Almost everyone wants to be the lover. And the curt truth is that, in a deep secret way, the state of being beloved is intolerable to many. The beloved fears and hates the lover, and with the best of reasons. For the lover is forever trying to strip bare his beloved. The lover craves any possible relation with the beloved, even if this experience can cause him only pain.

It has been mentioned before that Miss Amelia was once married. And this curious episode might as well be accounted for at this point. Remember that it all happened long ago, and that it was Miss Amelia's only personal contact, before the hunchback came to her, with this phenomenon—love.

The town then was the same as it is now, except there were two stores instead of three and the peach trees along the street were more crooked and smaller than they are now. Miss Amelia was nineteen years old at the time, and her father had been dead many months. There was in the town at that time a loom-fixer named Marvin Macy. He was the brother of Henry Macy, although to know them you would never guess that those two could be kin. For Marvin Macy was the handsomest man in this region—being six feet one inch tall, hard-muscled, and with slow gray eyes and curly hair. He was well off, made good wages, and had a gold watch which opened in the back to a picture of a waterfall. From the outward and worldly point of view Marvin Macy was a fortunate fellow; he needed to bow and scrape to no one and always got just what he wanted. But from a more serious and thoughtful viewpoint Marvin Macy was not a person to be envied, for he was an evil character. His reputation was as bad, if not worse, than that of any young man in the county. For years, when he was a boy, he had carried about with him the dried and salted ear of a man he had killed in a razor fight. He had chopped off the tails of squirrels in the pinewoods just to please his fancy, and in his left hip pocket he carried forbidden marijuana weed to tempt those who were discouraged and drawn toward death. Yet in spite of his well-known reputation he was the beloved of many females in this region—and there were at the time several young girls who were clean-haired and soft-eyed, with tender sweet little buttocks and charming ways. These gentle young girls he degraded and shamed. Then finally, at the age of twenty-two, this Marvin Macy chose Miss Amelia. That solitary, gangling, queer-eyed girl was the one he longed for. Nor did he want her because of her money, but solely out of love.

And love changed Marvin Macy. Before the time when he loved Miss Amelia it could be questioned if such a person had within him a heart and soul. Yet there is some explanation for the ugliness of his character, for Marvin Macy had had a hard beginning in this world. He was one of seven unwanted children whose parents could hardly be called parents at all; these parents were wild younguns who liked to fish and roam around the swamp. Their own children, and there was a new one almost every year, were only a nuisance to them. At night when they came home from the mill they would look at the children as though they did not know wherever they had come from. If the children cried they were beaten, and the first thing they learned in this world was to seek the darkest corner of the room and try to hide themselves as best they could. They were as thin as little whitehaired ghosts, and they did not speak, not even to each other. Finally, they were abandoned by their parents altogether and left to the mercies of the town. It was a hard winter, with the mill closed down almost three months, and much misery everywhere. But this is not a town to let white orphans perish in the road before your eyes. So here is what came about: the eldest child, who was eight years old, walked into Cheehaw and disappeared—perhaps he took a freight train somewhere and went out into the world, nobody knows. Three other children were boarded out amongst the town, being sent around from one kitchen to another, and as they were delicate they died before Easter time. The last two children were Marvin Macy and Henry Macy, and they were taken into a home. There was a good woman in the town named Mrs. Mary Hale, and she took Marvin Macy and Henry Macy and loved them as her own. They were raised in her household and treated well.

But the hearts of small children are delicate organs. A cruel beginning in this world can twist them into curious shapes. The heart of a hurt child can shrink so that forever afterward it is hard and pitted as the seed of a peach. Or again, the heart of such a child may fester and swell until it is a misery to carry within the body, easily chafed and hurt by the most ordinary things. This last is what happened to Henry Macy, who is so opposite to his brother, is the kindest and gentlest man in town. He lends his wages to those who are unfortunate, and in the old days he used to care for the children whose parents were at the café on Saturday night. But he is a shy man, and he has the look of one who has a swollen heart and suffers. Marvin Macy, however, grew to be bold and fearless and cruel. His heart turned tough as the horns of Satan, and until the time when he loved Miss Amelia he brought to his brother and the good woman who raised him nothing but shame and trouble.

But love reversed the character of Marvin Macy. For two years he loved Miss Amelia, but he did not declare himself. He would stand near the door of her premises, his cap in his hand, his eyes meek and longing and misty gray. He reformed himself completely. He was good to his brother and foster mother, and he saved his wages and learned thrift. Moreover, he reached out toward God. No longer did he lie around on the floor of the front porch all day Sunday, singing and playing his guitar; he attended church services and was present at all religious meetings. He learned good manners: he trained himself to rise and give his chair to a lady, and he quit swearing and fighting and using holy names in vain. So for two years he passed through this transformation and improved his character in every way. Then at the end of the two years he went one evening to Miss Amelia, carrying a bunch of swamp flowers, a sack of chitterlins, and a silver ring—that night Marvin Macy declared himself.

And Miss Amelia married him. Later everyone wondered why. Some said it was because she wanted to get herself some wedding presents. Others believed it came about through the nagging of Miss Amelia's great-aunt in Cheehaw, who was a terrible old woman. Anyway, she strode with great steps down the aisle of the church wearing her dead mother's bridal gown, which was of yellow satin and at least twelve inches too short for her. It was a winter afternoon and the clear sun shone through the ruby windows of the church and put a curious glow on the pair before the altar. As the marriage lines were read Miss Amelia kept making an odd gesture—she would rub the palm of her right hand down the side of her satin wedding gown. She was reaching for the pocket of her overalls, and being unable to find it her face became impatient, bored, and exasperated. At last when the lines were spoken and the marriage prayer was done Miss Amelia hurried out of the church, not taking the arm of her husband, but walking at least two paces ahead of him.

The church is no distance from the store so the bride and groom walked home. It is said that on the way Miss Amelia began to talk about some deal she had worked up with a farmer over a load of kindling wood. In fact, she treated her groom in exactly the same manner she would have used with some customer who had come into the store to buy a pint from her. But so far all had gone decently enough; the town was gratified, as people had seen what this love had done to Marvin Macy and hoped that it might also reform his bride. At least, they counted on the marriage to tone down Miss Amelia's temper, to put a bit of bride-fat on her, and to change her at last into a calculable woman.

They were wrong. The young boys who watched through the window on that night said that this is what actually happened: The bride and groom ate a grand supper prepared by Jeff, the old Negro who cooked for Miss Amelia.

The bride took second servings of everything, but the groom picked with his food. Then the bride went about her ordinary business—reading the newspaper, finishing an inventory of the stock in the store, and so forth. The groom hung about in the doorway with a loose, foolish, blissful face and was not noticed. At eleven o'clock the bride took a lamp and went upstairs. The groom followed close behind her. So far all had gone decently enough, but what followed after was unholy.

Within half an hour Miss Amelia had stomped down the stairs in breeches and a khaki jacket. Her face had darkened so that it looked quite black. She slammed the kitchen door and gave it an ugly kick. Then she controlled herself. She poked up the fire, sat down, and put her feet up on the kitchen stove. She read the Farmer's Almanac, drank coffee, and had a smoke with her father's pipe. Her face was hard, stern, and had now whitened to its natural color. Sometimes she paused to jot down some information from the Almanac on a piece of paper. Toward dawn she went into her office and uncovered her typewriter, which she had recently bought and was only just learning how to run. That was the way in which she spent the whole of her wedding night. At daylight she went out to her yard as though nothing whatsoever had occurred and did some carpentering on a rabbit hutch which she had begun the week before and intended to sell somewhere.

A groom is in a sorry fix when he is unable to bring his well-beloved bride to bed with him, and the whole town knows it. Marvin Macy came down that day still in his wedding finery, and with a sick face. God knows how he had spent the night. He moped about the yard, watching Miss Amelia, but keeping some distance away from her. Then toward noon an idea came to him and he went off in the direction of Society City. He returned with presents—an opal ring, a pink enamel doreen of the sort which was then in fashion, a silver bracelet with two hearts on it, and a box of candy which had cost two dollars and a half. Miss Amelia looked over these fine gifts and opened the box of candy, for she was hungry. The rest of the presents she judged shrewdly for a moment to sum up their value—then she put them in the counter out for sale. The night was spent in much the same manner as the preceding one—except that Miss Amelia brought her feather mattress to make a pallet by the kitchen stove, and she slept fairly well.

Things went on like this for three days. Miss Amelia went about her business as usual, and took great interest in some rumor that a bridge was to be built some ten miles down the road. Marvin Macy still followed her about around the premises, and it was plain from his face how he suffered. Then on the fourth day he did an extremely simple-minded thing: he went to Cheehaw and came back with a lawyer. Then in Miss Amelia's office he signed over to her the whole of his worldly goods, which was ten acres of timberland which he had bought with the money he had saved. She studied the paper sternly to make sure there was no possibility of a trick and filed it soberly in the drawer of her desk. That afternoon Marvin Macy took a quart bottle of whisky and went with it alone out in the swamp while the sun was still shining. Toward evening he came in drunk, went up to Miss Amelia with wet wide eyes, and put his hand on her shoulder. He was trying to tell her something, but before he could open his mouth she had swung once with her fist and hit his face so hard that he was thrown back against the wall and one of his front teeth was broken.

The rest of this affair can only be mentioned in bare outline. After this first blow Miss Amelia hit him whenever he came within arm's reach of her, and whenever he was drunk. At last she turned him off the premises altogether, and he was forced to suffer publicly. During the day he hung around just outside the boundary line of Miss Amelia's property and sometimes with a drawn crazy look he would fetch his rifle and sit there cleaning it, peering at Miss Amelia steadily. If she was afraid she did not show it, but her face was sterner than ever, and often she spat on the ground. His last foolish effort was to climb in the window of her store one night and to sit there in the dark, for no purpose whatsoever, until she came down the stairs next morning. For this Miss Amelia set off immediately to the courthouse in Cheehaw with some notion that she could get him locked in the penitentiary for trespassing. Marvin Macy left the town that day, and no one saw him go, or knew just where he went. On leaving he put a long curious letter, partly written in pencil and partly with ink, beneath Miss Amelia's door. It was a wild love letter—but in it were also included threats, and he swore that in his life he would get even with her. His marriage had lasted for ten days. And the town felt the special satisfaction that people feel when someone has been thoroughly done in by some scandalous and terrible means.

Miss Amelia was left with everything that Marvin Macy had ever owned— his timberwood, his gilt watch, every one of his possessions. But she seemed to attach little value to them and that spring she cut up his Klansman's robe to cover her tobacco plants. So all that he had ever done was to make her richer and to bring her love. But, strange to say, she never spoke of him but with a terrible and spiteful bitterness. She never once referred to him by name but always mentioned him scornfully as 'that loom-fixer I was married to.'

And later, when horrifying rumors concerning Marvin Macy reached the town, Miss Amelia was very pleased. For the true character of Marvin Macy finally revealed itself, once he had freed himself of his love. He became a criminal whose picture and whose name were in all the papers in the state. He robbed three filling stations and held up the A & P store of Society City with a sawed-off gun. He was suspected of the murder of Slit-Eye Sam who was a noted highjacker. All these crimes were connected with the name of Marvin Macy, so that his evil became famous through many countries. Then finally the law captured him, drunk, on the floor of a tourist cabin, his guitar by his side, and fifty-seven dollars in his right shoe. He was tried, sentenced, and sent off to the penitentiary near Atlanta. Miss Amelia was deeply gratified.

Well, all this happened a long time ago, and it is the story of Miss Amelia's marriage. The town laughed a long time over this grotesque affair. But though the outward facts of this love are indeed sad and ridiculous, it must be remembered that the real story was that which took place in the soul of the lover himself. So who but God can be the final judge of this or any other love? On the very first night of the café there were several who suddenly thought of this broken bridegroom, locked in the gloomy penitentiary, many miles away. And in the years that followed, Marvin Macy was not altogether forgotten in the town. His name was never mentioned in the presence of Miss Amelia or the hunchback. But the memory of his passion and his crimes, and the thought of him trapped in his cell in the penitentiary, was like a troubling undertone beneath the happy love of Miss Amelia and the gaiety of the café. So do not forget this Marvin Macy, as he is to act a terrible part in the story which is yet to come.

During the four years in which the store became a café the rooms upstairs were not changed. This part of the premises remained exactly as it had been all of Miss Amelia's life, as it was in the time of her father, and most likely his father before him. The three rooms, it is already known, were immaculately clean. The smallest object had its own place, and everything was wiped and dusted by Jeff, the servant of Miss Amelia, each morning. The front room belonged to Cousin Lymon—it was the room where Marvin Macy had stayed during the few nights he was allowed on the premises, and before that it was the bedroom of Miss Amelia's father. The room was furnished with a large chifforobe, a bureau covered with a stiff white linen cloth crocheted at the edges, and a marble-topped table. The bed was immense, an old fourposter made of carved, dark rosewood. On it were two feather mattresses, bolsters, and a number of handmade comforts. The bed was so high that beneath it were two wooden steps—no occupant had ever used these steps before, but Cousin Lymon drew them out each night and walked up in state. Beside the steps, but pushed modestly out of view, there was a china chamber-pot painted with pink roses. No rug covered the dark, polished floor and the curtains were of some white stuff, also crocheted at the edges.

On the other side of the parlor was Miss Amelia's bedroom, and it was smaller and very simple. The bed was narrow and made of pine. There was a bureau for her breeches, shirts, and Sunday dress, and she had hammered two nails in the closet wall on which to hang her swamp boots. There were no curtains, rugs, or ornaments of any kind.

The large middle room, the parlor, was elaborate. The rosewood sofa, upholstered in threadbare green silk, was before the fireplace. Marble-topped tables, two Singer sewing machines, a big vase of pampas grass—everything was rich and grand. The most important piece of furniture in the parlor was a big, glass-doored cabinet in which was kept a number of treasures and curios. Miss Amelia had added two objects to this collection—one was a large acorn from a water oak, the other a little velvet box holding two small, grayish stones. Sometimes when she had nothing much to do, Miss Amelia would take out this velvet box and stand by the window with the stones in the palm of her hand, looking down at them with a mixture of fascination, dubious respect, and fear. They were the kidney stones of Miss Amelia herself, and had been taken from her by the doctor in Cheehaw some years ago. It had been a terrible experience, from the first minute to the last, and all she had got out of it were those two little stones; she was bound to set great store by them, or else admit to a mighty sorry bargain. So she kept them and in the second year of Cousin Lymon's stay with her she had them set as ornaments in a watch chain which she gave to him. The other object she had added to the collection, the large acorn, was precious to her—but when she looked at it her face was always saddened and perplexed.

'Amelia, what does it signify?' Cousin Lymon asked her.

'Why, it's just an acorn,' she answered. 'Just an acorn I picked up on the afternoon Big Papa died.'

'How do you mean?' Cousin Lymon insisted.

'I mean it's just an acorn I spied on the ground that day. I picked it up and put it in my pocket. But I don't know why.'

'What a peculiar reason to keep it,' Cousin Lymon said.

The talks of Miss Amelia and Cousin Lymon in the room upstairs, usually in the first few hours of the morning when the hunchback could not sleep, were many. As a rule, Miss Amelia was a silent woman, not letting her tongue run wild on any subject that happened to pop into her head. There were certain topics of conversation, however, in which she took pleasure. All these subjects had one point in common—they were interminable. She liked to contemplate problems which could be worked over for decades and still remain insoluble. Cousin Lymon, on the other hand, enjoyed talking on any subject whatsoever, as he was a great chatterer. Their approach to any conversation was altogether different. Miss Amelia alway kept to the broad, rambling generalities of the matter, going on endlessly in a low, thoughtful voice and getting nowhere—while Cousin Lymon would interrupt her suddenly to pick up, magpie fashion, some detail which, even if unimportant, was at least concrete and bearing on some practical facet close at hand. Some of the favorite subjects of Miss Amelia were: the stars, the reason why Negroes are black, the best treatment for cancer, and so forth. Her father was also an interminable subject which was dear to her.

'Why, Law,' she would say to Lymon. 'Those days I slept. I'd go to bed just as the lamp was turned on and sleep—why, I'd sleep like I was drowned in warm axle grease. Then come daybreak Big Papa would walk in and put his hand down on my shoulder. "Get stirring, Little," he would say. Then later he would holler up the stairs from the kitchen when the stove was hot. "Fried grits," he would holler. "White meat and gravy. Ham and eggs." And I'd run down the stairs and dress by the hot stove while he was out washing at the pump. Then off we'd go to the still or maybe——'

'The grits we had this morning was poor,' Cousin Lymon said. 'Fried too quick so that the inside never heated.'

'And when Big Papa would run off the liquor in those days——' The conversation would go on endlessly, with Miss Amelia's long legs stretched out before the hearth; for winter or summer there was always a fire in the grate, as Lymon was cold-natured. He sat in a low chair across from her, his feet not quite touching the floor and his torso usually well-wrapped in a blanket or the green wool shawl. Miss Amelia never mentioned her father to anyone else except Cousin Lymon.

That was one of the ways in which she showed her love for him. He had her confidence in the most delicate and vital matters. He alone knew where she kept the chart that showed where certain barrels of whisky were buried on a piece of property near by. He alone had access to her bank-book and the key to the cabinet of curios. He took money from the cash register, whole handfuls of it, and appreciated the loud jingle it made inside his pockets. He owned almost everything on the premises, for when he was cross Miss Amelia would prowl about and find him some present—so that now there was hardly anything left close at hand to give him. The only part of her life that she did not want Cousin Lymon to share with her was the memory of her ten-day marriage. Marvin Macy was the one subject that was never, at any time, discussed between the two of them.

So let the slow years pass and come to a Saturday evening six years after the time when Cousin Lymon came first to the town. It was August and the sky had burned above the town like a sheet of flame all day. Now the green twilight was near and there was a feeling of repose. The street was coated an inch deep with dry golden dust and the little children ran about half-naked, sneezed often, sweated, and were fretful. The mill had closed down at noon. People in the houses along the main street sat resting on their steps and the women had palmetto fans. At Miss Amelia's there was a sign at the front of the premises saying CAFE. The back porch was cool with latticed shadows and there cousin Lymon sat turning the ice-cream freezer—often he unpacked the salt and ice and removed the dasher to lick a bit and see how the work was coming on. Jeff cooked in the kitchen. Early that morning Miss Amelia had put a notice on the wall of the front porch reading: Chicken Dinner—Twenty Cents Tonite. The café was already open and Miss Amelia had just finished a period of work in her office. All the eight tables were occupied and from the mechanical piano came a jingling tune.

In a corner near the door and sitting at a table with a child was Henry Macy. He was drinking a glass of liquor, which was unusual for him, as liquor went easily to his head and made him cry or sing. His face was very pale and his left eye worked constantly in a nervous tic, as it was apt to do when he was agitated. He had come into the café sidewise and silent, and when he was greeted he did not speak. The child next to him belonged to Horace Wells, and he had been left at Miss Amelia's that morning to be doctored.

Miss Amelia came out from her office in good spirits. She attended to a few details in the kitchen and entered the café with the pope's nose of a hen between her fingers, as that was her favorite piece. She looked about the room, saw that in general all was well, and went over to the corner table by Henry

Macy. She turned the chair around and sat straddling the back, as she only wanted to pass the time of day and was not yet ready for her supper. There was a bottle of Kroup Kure in the hip pocket of her overalls—a medicine made from whisky, rock candy, and a secret ingredient. Miss Amelia uncorked the bottle and put it to the mouth of the child. Then she turned to Henry Macy and, seeing the nervous winking of his left eye, she asked:

'What ails you?'

Henry Macy seemed on the point of saying something difficult, but, after a long look into the eyes of Miss Amelia, he swallowed and did not speak.

So Miss Amelia returned to her patient. Only the child's head showed above the table top. His face was very red, with the eyelids half-closed and the mouth partly open. He had a large, hard, swollen boil on his thigh, and had been brought to Miss Amelia so that it could be opened. But Miss Amelia used a special method with children; she did not like to see them hurt, struggling, and terrified. So she had kept the child around the premises all day, giving him licorice and frequent doses of the Kroup Kure, and toward evening she tied a napkin around his neck and let him eat his fill of the dinner. Now as he sat at the table his head wobbled slowly from side to side and sometimes as he breathed there came from him a little worn-out grunt.

There was a stir in the café and Miss Amelia looked around quickly. Cousin Lymon had come in. The hunchback strutted into the café as he did every night, and when he reached the exact center of the room he stopped short and looked shrewdly around him, summing up the people and making a quick pattern of the emotional material at hand that night. The hunchback was a great mischief-maker. He enjoyed any kind of to-do, and without saying a word he could set the people at each other in a way that was miraculous. It was due to him that the Rainey twins had quarreled over a jacknife two years past, and had not spoken one word to each other since. He was present at the big fight between Rip Wellborn and Robert Calvert Hale, and every other fight for that matter since he had come into the town. He nosed around everywhere, knew the intimate business of everybody, and trespassed every waking hour. Yet, queerly enough, in spite of this it was the hunchback who was most responsible for the great popularity of the café. Things were never so gay as when he was around. When he walked into the room there was always a quick feeling of tension, because with this busybody about there was never any telling what might descend on you, or what might suddenly be brought to happen in the room. People are never so free with themselves and so recklessly glad as when there is some possibility of commotion or calamity ahead. So when the hunchback marched into the café everyone looked around at him and there was a quick outburst of talking and a drawing of corks.

Lymon waved his hand to Stumpy MacPhail who was sitting with Merlie Ryan and Henry Ford Crimp. 'I walked to Rotten Lake today to fish,' he said. 'And on the way I stepped over what appeared at first to be a big fallen tree. But then as I stepped over I felt something stir and I taken this second look and there I was straddling this here alligator long as from the front door to the kitchen and thicker than a hog.'

The hunchback chattered on. Everyone looked at him from time to time, and some kept track of his chattering and others did not. There were times when every word he said was nothing but lying and bragging. Nothing he said to-night was true. He had lain in bed with a summer quinsy all day long, and had only got up in the late afternoon in order to turn the ice-cream freezer. Every-body knew this, yet he stood there in the middle of the café and held forth with such lies and boasting that it was enough to shrivel the ears.

Miss Amelia watched him with her hands in her pockets and her head turned to one side. There was a softness about her gray, queer eyes and she was smil-ing gently to herself. Occasionally she glanced from the hunchback to the other people in the café—and then her look was proud, and there was in it the hint of a threat, as though daring anyone to try to hold him to account for all his foolery. Jeff was bringing in the suppers, already served on the plates, and the new electric fans in the café made a pleasant stir of coolness in the air.

'The little youngun is asleep,' said Henry Macy finally.

Miss Amelia looked down at the patient beside her, and composed her face for the matter in hand. The child's chin was resting on the table edge and a trickle of spit or Kroup Kure had bubbled from the corner of his mouth. His eyes were quite closed, and a little family of gnats had clustered peacefully in the corners. Miss Amelia put her hand on his head and shook it roughly, but the patient did not awake. So Miss Amelia lifted the child from the table, being careful not to touch the sore part of his leg, and went into the office. Henry Macy followed after her and they closed the office door.

Cousin Lymon was bored that evening. There was not much going on, and in spite of the heat the customers in the café were good-humored. Henry Ford Crimp and Horace Wells sat at the middle table with their arms around each other, sniggering over some long joke—but when he approached them he could make nothing of it as he had missed the beginning of the story. The moonlight brightened the dusty road, and the dwarfed peach trees were black and motionless: there was no breeze. The drowsy buzz of swamp mosquitoes was like an echo of the silent night. The town seemed dark, except far down the road to the right there was the flicker of a lamp. Somewhere in the dark-ness a woman sang in a high wild voice and the tune had no start and no finish and was made up of only three notes which went on and on and on. The hunch-back stood leaning against the banister of the porch, looking down the empty road as though hoping that someone would come along.

There were footsteps behind him, then a voice: 'Cousin Lymon, your dinner is set out upon the table.'

'My appetite is poor tonight,' said the hunchback, who had been eating sweet snuff all the day. 'There is a sourness in my mouth.'

'Just a pick,' said Miss Amelia. 'The breast, the liver, and the heart.'

Together they went back into the bright café, and sat down with Henry Macy. Their table was the largest one in the café, and on it there was a bouquet of swamp lilies in a Coca Cola bottle. Miss Amelia had finished with her patient and was satisfied with herself. From behind the closed office door there had come only a few sleepy whimpers, and before the patient could wake up and become terrified it was all over. The child was now slung across the shoulder of his father, sleeping deeply, his little arms dangling loose along his father's back, and his puffed-up face very red—they were leaving the café to go home.

Henry Macy was still silent. He ate carefully, making no noise when he swallowed, and was not a third as greedy as Cousin Lymon who had claimed to have no appetite and was now putting down helping after helping of the dinner. Occasionally Henry Macy looked across at Miss Amelia and again held his peace.

It was a typical Saturday night. An old couple who had come in from the country hesitated for a moment at the doorway, holding each other's hand, and finally decided to come inside. They had lived together so long, this old country couple, that they looked as similar as twins. They were brown, shriveled, and like two little walking peanuts. They left early, and by midnight most of the other customers were gone. Rosser Cline and Merlie Ryan still played checkers, and Stumpy MacPhail sat with a liquor bottle on his table (his wife would not allow it in the home) and carried on peaceable conversations with himself. Henry Macy had not yet gone away, and this was unusual, as he almost always went to bed soon after nightfall. Miss Amelia yawned sleepily, but Lymon was restless and she did not suggest that they close up for the night.

Finally, at one o'clock, Henry Macy looked up at the corner of the ceiling and said quietly to Miss Amelia: 'I got a letter today.'

Miss Amelia was not one to be impressed by this, because all sorts of business letters and catalogues came addressed to her.

'I got a letter from my brother,' said Henry Macy.

The hunchback, who had been goose-stepping about the café with his hands clasped behind his head, stopped suddenly. He was quick to sense any change in the atmosphere of a gathering. He glanced at each face in the room and waited.

Miss Amelia scowled and hardened her right fist. 'You are welcome to it,' she said.

'He is on parole. He is out of the penitentiary.'

The face of Miss Amelia was very dark, and she shivered although the night was warm. Stumpy MacPhail and Merlie Ryan pushed aside their checker game. The café was very quiet.

'Who?' asked Cousin Lymon. His large, pale ears seemed to grow on his head and stiffen. 'What?'

Miss Amelia slapped her hands palm down on the table. 'Because Marvin Macy is a ——' But her voice hoarsened and after a few moments she only said: 'He belongs to be in that penitentiary the balance of his life.'

'What did he do?' asked Cousin Lymon.

There was a long pause, as no one knew exactly how to answer this. 'He robbed three filling stations,' said Stumpy MacPhail. But his words did not sound complete and there was a feeling of sins left unmentioned.

The hunchback was impatient. He could not bear to be left out of anything, even a great misery. The name Marvin Macy was unknown to him, but it tantalized him as did any mention of subjects which others knew about and of which he was ignorant—such as any reference to the old sawmill that had been torn down before he came, or a chance word about poor Morris Finestein, or the recollection of any event that had occurred before his time. Aside from this inborn curiosity, the hunchback took a great interest in robbers and crimes of all varieties. As he strutted around the table he was muttering the words 'released on parole' and 'penitentiary' to himself. But although he questioned insistently, he was unable to find anything, as nobody would dare to talk about Marvin Macy before Miss Amelia in the café.

'The letter did not say very much,' said Henry Macy. 'He did not say where he was going.'

'Humph!' said Amelia, and her face was still hardened and very dark. 'He will never set his split hoof on my premises.'

She pushed back her chair from the table, and made ready to close the café. Thinking about Marvin Macy may have set her to brooding, for she hauled the cash register back to the kitchen and put it in a private place. Henry Macy went off down the dark road. But Henry Ford Crimp and Merlie Ryan lingered for a time on the front porch. Later Merlie Ryan was to make certain claims, to swear that on that night he had a vision of what was to come. But the town paid no attention, for that was just the sort of thing that Merlie Ryan would claim. Miss Amelia and Cousin Lymon talked for a time in the parlor. And when at last the hunchback thought that he could sleep she arranged the mosquito netting over his bed and waited until he had finished with his prayers. Then she put on her long nightgown, smoked two pipes, and only after a long time went to sleep.

That autumn was a happy time. The crops around the countryside were good, and over at the Forks Falls market the price of tobacco held firm that year. After the long hot summer the first cool days had a clean bright sweetness. Goldenrod grew along the dusty roads, and the sugar cane was ripe and purple. The bus came each day from Cheehaw to carry off a few of the younger children to the consolidated school to get an education. Boys hunted foxes in the pinewoods, winter quilts were aired out on the wash lines, and sweet potatoes bedded in the ground with straw against the colder months to come. In the evening, delicate shreds of smoke rose from the chimneys, and the moon was round and orange in the autumn sky. There is no stillness like the quiet of the first cold nights in the fall. Sometimes, late in the night when there was no wind, there could be heard in the town the thin wild whistle of the train that goes through Society City on its way far off to the North.

For Miss Amelia Evans this was a time of great activity. She was at work from dawn until sundown. She made a new and bigger condenser for her still, and in one week ran off enough liquor to souse the whole country. Her old mule was dizzy from grinding so much sorghum, and she scalded her Mason jars and put away pear preserves. She was looking forward greatly to the first frost, because she had traded for three tremendous hogs, and intended to make much barbecue; chitterlins, and sausage.

During these weeks there was a quality about Miss Amelia that many people noticed. She laughed often, with a deep ringing laugh, and her whistling had a sassy, tuneful trickery. She was forever trying out her strength, lifting up heavy objects, or poking her tough biceps with her finger. One day she sat down to her typewriter and wrote a story—a story in which there were foreigners, trap doors, and millions of dollars. Cousin Lymon was with her always, traipsing along behind her coat-tails, and when she watched him her face had a bright, soft look, and when she spoke his name there lingered in her voice the undertone of love.

The first cold spell came at last. When Miss Amelia awoke one morning there were frost flowers on the windowpanes, and rime had silvered the patches of grass in the yard. Miss Amelia built a roaring fire in the kitchen stove, then went out of doors to judge the day. The air was cold and sharp, the sky pale green and cloudless. Very shortly people began to come in from the country to find out what Miss Amelia thought of the weather; she decided to kill the biggest hog, and word got round the countryside. The hog was slaughtered and a low oak fire started in the barbecue pit. There was the warm smell of pig blood and smoke in the back yard, the stamp of footsteps, the ring of voices in the winter air. Miss Amelia walked around giving orders and soon most of the work was done.

She had some particular business to do in Cheehaw that day, so after making sure that all was going well, she cranked up her car and got ready to leave. She asked Cousin Lymon to come with her, in fact, she asked him seven times, but he was loath to leave the commotion and wanted to remain. This seemed to trouble Miss Amelia, as she always liked to have him near to her, and was prone to be terribly homesick when she had to go any distance away. But after asking him seven times, she did not urge him any further. Before leaving she found a stick and drew a heavy line all around the barbecue pit, about two feet back from the edge, and told him not to trespass beyond that boundary. She left after dinner and intended to be back before dark.

Now, it is not so rare to have a truck or an automobile pass along the road and through the town on the way from Cheehaw to somewhere else. Every year the tax collector comes to argue with rich people such as Miss Amelia. And if somebody in the town, such as Merlie Ryan, takes a notion that he can connive to get a car on credit, or to pay down three dollars and have a fine electric icebox such as they advertise in the store windows of Cheehaw, then a city man will come out asking meddlesome questions, finding out all his troubles, and ruining his chances of buying anything on the installment plan. Sometimes, especially since they are working on the Forks Falls highway, the cars hauling the chain gang come through the town. And frequently people in automobiles get lost and stop to inquire how they can find the right road again. So, late that afternoon it was nothing unusual to have a truck pass the mill and stop in the middle of the road near the café of Miss Amelia. A man jumped down from the back of the truck, and the truck went on its way.

The man stood in the middle of the road and looked about him. He was a tall man, with brown curly hair, and slow-moving, deep-blue eyes. His lips were red and he smiled the lazy, half-mouthed smile of the braggart. The man wore a red shirt, and a wide belt of tooled leather; he carried a tin suitcase and a guitar. The first person in the town to see this newcomer was Cousin Lymon, who had heard the shifting gears and come around to investigate. The hunchback stuck his head around the corner of the porch, but did not step out altogether into full view. He and the man stared at each other, and it was not the look of two strangers meeting for the first time and swiftly summing up each other. It was a peculiar stare they exchanged between them, like the look of two criminals who recognize each other. Then the man in the red shirt shrugged his left shoulder and turned away. The face of the hunchback was very pale as he watched the man go down the road, and after a few moments he began to follow along carefully, keeping many paces away.

It was immediately known throughout the town that Marvin Macy had come back again. First, he went to the mill, propped his elbows lazily on a window sill and looked inside. He liked to watch others hard at work, as do all born loafers. The mill was thrown into a sort of numb confusion. The dyers left the hot vats, the spinners and weavers forgot about their machines, and even Stumpy MacPhail, who was foreman, did not know exactly what to do. Marvin Macy still smiled his wet half-mouthed smiles, and when he saw his brother, his bragging expression did not change. After looking over the mill Marvin Macy went down the road to the house where he had been raised, and left his suitcase and guitar on the front porch. Then he walked around the millpond, looked over the church, the three stores, and the rest of the town. The hunchback trudged along quietly at some distance behind him; his hands in his pockets, and his little face still very pale.

It had grown late. The red winter sun was setting, and to the west the sky was deep gold and crimson. Ragged chimney swifts flew to their nests; lamps were lighted. Now and then there was the smell of smoke, and the warm rich odor of the barbecue slowly cooking in the pit behind the café. After making the rounds of the town Marvin Macy stopped before Miss Amelia's premises and read the sign above the porch. Then, not hesitating to trespass, he walked through the side yard. The mill whistle blew a thin, lonesome blast, and the day's shift was done. Soon there were others in Miss Amelia's back yard beside Marvin Macy—Henry Ford Crimp, Merlie Ryan, Stumpy MacPhail, and any number of children and people who stood around the edges of the property and looked on. Very little was said. Marvin Macy stood by himself on one side of the pit, and the rest of the people clustered together on the other side. Cousin Lymon stood somewhat apart from everyone, and he did not take his eyes from the face of Marvin Macy.

'Did you have a good time in the penitentiary?' asked Merlie Ryan, with a silly giggle.

Marvin Macy did not answer. He took from his hip pocket a large knife, opened it slowly, and honed the blade on the seat of his pants. Merlie Ryan grew suddenly very quiet and went to stand directly behind the broad back of Stumpy MacPhail.

Miss Amelia did not come home until almost dark. They heard the rattle of her automobile while she was still a long distance away, then the slam of the door and a bumping noise as though she were hauling something up the front steps of her premises. The sun had already set, and in the air there was the blue smoky glow of early winter evenings. Miss Amelia came down the back steps slowly, and the group in her yard waited very quietly. Few people in this world could stand up to Miss Amelia, and against Marvin Macy she had this special and bitter hate. Everyone waited to see her burst into a terrible holler, snatch up some dangerous object, and chase him altogether out of town. At first she did not see Marvin Macy, and her face had the relieved and dreamy expression that was natural to her when she reached home after having gone some distance away.

Miss Amelia must have seen Marvin Macy and Cousin Lymon at the same instant. She looked from one to the other, but it was not the wastrel from the penitentiary on whom she finally fixed her gaze of sick amazement. She, and everyone else, was looking at Cousin Lymon, and he was a sight to see.

The hunchback stood at the end of the pit, his pale face lighted by the soft glow from the smoldering oak fire. Cousin Lymon had a very peculiar accomplishment, which he used whenever he wished to ingratiate himself with someone. He would stand very still, and with just a little concentration, he could wiggle his large pale ears with marvelous quickness and ease. This trick he always used when he wanted to get something special out of Miss Amelia, and to her it was irresistible. Now as he stood there the hunchback's ears were wiggling furiously on his head, but it was not Miss Amelia at whom he was looking this time. The hunchback was smiling at Marvin Macy with an entreaty that was near to desperation. At first Marvin Macy paid no attention to him, and when he did finally glance at the hunchback it was without any appreciation whatsoever.

'What ails this Brokeback?' he asked with a rough jerk of his thumb.

No one answered. And Cousin Lymon, seeing that his accomplishment was getting him nowhere, added new efforts of persuasion. He fluttered his eyelids, so that they were like pale, trapped moths in his sockets. He scraped his feet around on the ground, waved his hands about, and finally began doing a little trotlike dance. In the last gloomy light of the winter afternoon he resembled the child of a swamphaunt.

Marvin Macy, alone of all the people in the yard, was unimpressed.

'Is the runt throwing a fit?' he asked, and when no one answered he stepped forward and gave Cousin Lymon a cuff on the side of his head. The hunchback staggered, then fell back on the ground. He sat where he had fallen, still looking up at Marvin Macy, and with great effort his ears managed one last forlorn little flap.

Now everyone turned to Miss Amelia to see what she would do. In all these years no one had so much as touched a hair of Cousin Lymon's head, although many had had the itch to do so. If anyone even spoke crossly to the hunchback, Miss Amelia would cut off this rash mortal's credit and find ways of making things go hard for him a long time afterward. So now if Miss Amelia had split open Marvin Macy's head with the ax on the back porch no one would have been surprised. But she did nothing of the kind.

There were times when Miss Amelia seemed to go into a sort of trance. And the cause of these trances was usually known and understood. For Miss Amelia was a fine doctor, and did not grind up swamp roots and other untried ingredients and give them to the first patient who came along; whenever she invented a new medicine she always tried it out first on herself. She would swallow an enormous dose and spend the following day walking thoughtfully back and forth from the café to the brick privy. Often, when there was a sudden keen gripe, she would stand quite still, her queer eyes staring down at the ground and her fists clenched; she was trying to decide which organ was being worked upon, and what misery the new medicine might be most likely to cure. And now as she watched the hunchback and Marvin Macy, her face wore this same expression, tense with reckoning some inward pain, although she had taken no new medicine that day.

'That will learn you, Brokeback,' said Marvin Macy.

Henry Macy pushed back his limp whitish hair from his forehead and coughed nervously. Stumpy MacPhail and Merlie Ryan shuffled their feet, and the children and black people on the outskirts of the property made not a sound. Marvin Macy folded the knife he had been honing, and after looking about him fearlessly he swaggered out of the yard. The embers in the pit were turning to gray feathery ashes and it was now quite dark.

That was the way Marvin Macy came back from the penitentiary. Not a living soul in all the town was glad to see him. Even Mrs. Mary Hale, who was a good woman and had raised him with love and care—at the first sight of him even this old foster mother dropped the skillet she was holding and burst into tears. But nothing could faze that Marvin Macy. He sat on the back steps of the Hale house, lazily picking his guitar, and when the supper was ready, he pushed the children of the household out of the way and served himself a big meal, although there had been barely enough hoecakes and white meat to go round. After eating he settled himself in the best and warmest sleeping place in the front room and was untroubled by dreams.

Miss Amelia did not open the café that night. She locked the doors and all the windows very carefully, nothing was seen of her and Cousin Lymon, and a lamp burned in her room all the night long.

Marvin Macy brought with him bad fortune, right from the first, as could be expected. The next day the weather turned suddenly, and it became hot. Even in the early morning there was a sticky sultriness in the atmosphere, the wind carried the rotten smell of the swamp, and delicate shrill mosquitoes webbed the green millpond. It was unseasonable, worse than August, and much damage was done. For nearly everyone in the country who owned a hog had copied Miss Amelia and slaughtered the day before. And what sausage could keep in such weather as this? After a few days there was everywhere the smell of slowly spoiling meat, and an atmosphere of dreary waste. Worse yet, a family reunion near the Forks Falls highway ate pork roast and died, every one of them. It was plain that their hog had been infected—and who could tell whether the rest of the meat was safe or not? People were torn between the longing for the good taste of pork, and the fear of death. It was a time of waste and confusion.

The cause of all this, Marvin Macy, had no shame in him. He was seen everywhere. During work hours he loafed about the mill, looking in at the windows, and on Sundays he dressed in his red shirt and paraded up and down the road with his guitar. He was still handsome—with his brown hair, his red lips, and his broad strong shoulders; but the evil in him was now too famous for his good looks to get him anywhere. And this evil was not measured only by the actual sins he had committed. True, he had robbed those filling stations. And before that he had ruined the tenderest girls in the county, and laughed about it. Any number of wicked things could be listed against him, but quite apart from these crimes there was about him a secret meanness that clung to him almost like a smell. Another thing—he never sweated, not even in August, and that surely is a sign worth pondering over.

Now it seemed to the town that he was more dangerous than he had ever been before, as in the penitentiary in Atlanta he must have learned the method of laying charms. Otherwise how could his effect on Cousin Lymon be explained? For since first setting eyes on Marvin Macy the hunchback was possessed by an unnatural spirit. Every minute he wanted to be following along behind this jailbird, and he was full of silly schemes to attract attention to himself. Still Marvin Macy either treated him hatefully or failed to notice him at all. Sometimes the hunchback would give up, perch himself on the banister of the front porch much as a sick bird huddles on a telephone wire, and grieve publicly.

'But why?' Miss Amelia would ask, staring at him with her crossed, gray eyes, and her fists closed tight.

'Oh, Marvin Macy,' groaned the hunchback, and the sound of the name was enough to upset the rhythm of his sobs so that he hiccuped. 'He has been to Atlanta.'

Miss Amelia would shake her head and her face was dark and hardened. To begin with she had no patience with any traveling; those who had made the trip to Atlanta or traveled fifty miles from home to see the ocean—those restless people she despised. 'Going to Atlanta does no credit to him.'

'He has been to the penitentiary,' said the hunchback, miserable with longing.

How are you going to argue against such envies as these? In her perplexity Miss Amelia did not herself sound any too sure of what she was saying. 'Been to the penitentiary, Cousin Lymon? Why, a trip like that is no travel to brag about.'

During these weeks Miss Amelia was closely watched by everyone. She went about absent-mindedly, her face remote as though she had lapsed into one of her gripe trances. For some reason, after the day of Marvin Macy's arrival, she put aside her overalls and wore always the red dress she had before this time reserved for Sundays, funerals, and sessions of the court. Then as the weeks passed she began to take some steps to clear up the situation. But her efforts were hard to understand. If it hurt her to see Cousin Lymon follow Marvin Macy about the town, why did she not make the issues clear once and for all, and tell the hunchback that if he had dealings with Marvin Macy she would turn him off the premises? That would have been simple, and Cousin Lymon would have had to submit to her, or else face the sorry business of finding himself loose in the world. But Miss Amelia seemed to have lost her will; for the first time in her life she hesitated as to just what course to pursue. And, like most people in such a position of uncertainty, she did the worst thing possible—she began following several courses at once, all of them contrary to each other.

The café was opened every night as usual, and, strangely enough, when Marvin Macy came swaggering through the door, with the hunchback at his heels, she did not turn him out. She even gave him free drinks and smiled at him in a wild, crooked way. At the same time she set a terrible trap for him out in the swamp that surely would have killed him if he had got caught. She let Cousin Lymon invite him to Sunday dinner, and then tried to trip him up as he went down the steps. She began a great campaign of pleasure for Cousin Lymon—making exhausting trips to various spectacles being held in distant places, driving the automobile thirty miles to a Chautauqua, taking him to Forks Falls to watch a parade. All in all it was a distracting time for Miss Amelia. In the opinion of most people she was well on her way in the climb up fools' hill, and everyone waited to see how it would all turn out.

The weather turned cold again, the winter was upon the town, and night came before the last shift in the mill was done. Children kept on all their garments when they slept, and women raised the backs of their skirts to toast themselves dreamily at the fire. After it rained, the mud in the road made hard frozen ruts, there were faint flickers of lamplight from the windows of the houses, the peach trees were scrawny and bare. In the dark, silent nights of winter-time the café was the warm center point of the town, the lights shining so brightly that they could be seen a quarter of a mile away. The great iron stove at the back of the room roared, crackled, and turned red. Miss Amelia had made red curtains for the windows, and from a salesman who passed through the town she bought a great bunch of paper roses that looked very real.

But it was not only the warmth, the decorations, and the brightness, that made the café what it was. There is a deeper reason why the café was so precious to this town. And this deeper reason has to do with a certain pride that had not hitherto been known in these parts. To understand this new pride the cheapness of human life must be kept in mind. There were always plenty of people clustered around a mill—but it was seldom that every family had enough meal, garments, and fat back to go the rounds. Life could become one long dim scramble just to get the things needed to keep alive. And the confusing point is this: All useful things have a price, and are bought only with money, as that is the way the world is run. You know without having to reason about it the price of a bale of cotton, or a quart of molasses. But no value has been put on human life; it is given to us free and taken without being paid for. What is it worth? If you look around, at times the value may seem to be little or nothing at all. Often after you have sweated and tried and things are not better for you, there comes a feeling deep down in the soul that you are not worth much.

But the new pride that the café brought to this town had an effect on almost everyone, even the children. For in order to come to the café you did not have to buy the dinner, or a portion of liquor. There were cold bottled drinks for a nickel. And if you could not even afford that, Miss Amelia had a drink called Cherry Juice which sold for a penny a glass, and was pink-colored and very sweet. Almost everyone, with the exception of Reverend T. M. Willin, came to the café at least once during the week. Children love to sleep in houses other than their own, and to eat at a neighbor's table; on such occasions they behave themselves decently and are proud. The people in the town were likewise proud when sitting at the tables in the café. They washed before coming to Miss Amelia's, and scraped their feet very politely on the threshold as they entered the café. There, for a few hours at least, the deep bitter knowing that you are not worth much in this world could be laid low.

The café was a special benefit to bachelors, unfortunate people, and consumptives. And here it may be mentioned that there was some reason to suspect that Cousin Lymon was consumptive. The brightness of his gray eyes, his insistence, his talkativeness, and his cough—these were all signs. Besides, there is generally supposed to be some connection between a hunched spine and consumption. But whenever this subject had been mentioned to Miss Amelia she had become furious; she denied these symptoms with bitter vehemence, but on the sly she treated Cousin Lymon with hot chest platters, Kroup Kure, and such. Now this winter the hunchback's cough was worse, and sometimes even on cold days he would break out in a heavy sweat. But this did not prevent him from following along after Marvin Macy.

Early every morning he left the premises and went to the back door of Mrs. Hale's house, and waited and waited—as Marvin Macy was a lazy sleeper. He would stand there and call out softly. His voice was just like the voices of children who squat patiently over those tiny little holes in the ground where doodlebugs are thought to live, poking the hole with a broom straw, and calling plaintively: 'Doodlebug, Doodlebug—fly away home. Mrs. Doodlebug, Mrs. Doodlebug. Come out, come out. Your house is on fire and all your children are burning up.' In just such a voice—at once sad, luring, and resigned—would the hunchback call Marvin Macy's name each morning. Then when Marvin Macy came out for the day, he would trail him about the town, and sometimes they would be gone for hours together out in the swamp.

And Miss Amelia continued to do the worst thing possible: that is, to try to follow several courses at once. When Cousin Lymon left the house she did not call him back, but only stood in the middle of the road and watched lonesomely until he was out of sight. Nearly every day Marvin Macy turned up with Cousin Lymon at dinnertime, and ate at her table. Miss Amelia opened the pear preserves, and the table was well-set with ham or chicken, great bowls of hominy grits, and winter peas. It is true that on one occasion Miss Amelia tried to poison Marvin Macy—but there was a mistake, the plates were confused, and it was she herself who got the poisoned dish. This she quickly realized by the slight bitterness of the food, and that day she ate no dinner. She sat tilted back in her chair, feeling her muscle, and looking at Marvin Macy.

Every night Marvin Macy came to the café and settled himself at the best and largest table, the one in the center of the room. Cousin Lymon brought him liquor, for which he did not pay a cent. Marvin Macy brushed the hunchback aside as if he were a swamp mosquito, and not only did he show no gratitude for these favors, but if the hunchback got in his way he would cuff him with the back of his hand, or say: 'Out of my way, Brokeback—I'll snatch you bald-headed.' When this happened Miss Amelia would come out from behind her counter and approach Marvin Macy very slowly, her fists clenched, her peculiar red dress hanging awkwardly around her bony knees. Marvin Macy would also clench his fists and they would walk slowly and meaningfully around each other. But, although everyone watched breathlessly, nothing ever came of it. The time for the fight was not yet ready.

There is one particular reason why this winter is remembered and still talked about. A great thing happened. People woke up on the second of January and found the whole world about them altogether changed. Little ignorant children looked out of the windows, and they were so puzzled that they began to cry. Old people harked back and could remember nothing in these parts to equal the phenomenon. For in the night it had snowed. In the dark hours after midnight the dim flakes started falling softly on the town. By dawn the ground was covered, and the strange snow banked the ruby windows of the church, and whitened the roofs of the houses. The snow gave the town a drawn, bleak look. The two-room houses near the mill were dirty, crooked, and seemed about to collapse, and somehow everything was dark and shrunken. But the snow itself—there was a beauty about it few people around here had ever known before. The snow was not white, as Northerners had pictured it to be; in the snow there were soft colors of blue and silver, the sky was a gentle shining gray. And the dreamy quietness of falling snow—when had the town been so silent?

People reacted to the snowfall in various ways. Miss Amelia, on looking out of her window, thoughtfully wiggled the toes of her bare foot, gathered close to her neck the collar of her nightgown. She stood there for some time, then commenced to draw the shutters and lock every window on the premises. She closed the place completely, lighted the lamps, and sat solemnly over her bowl of grits. The reason for this was not that Miss Amelia feared the snowfall. It was simply that she was unable to form an immediate opinion of this new event, and unless she knew exactly and definitely what she thought of a matter (which was nearly always the case) she preferred to ignore it. Snow had never fallen in this county in her lifetime, and she had never thought about it one way or the other. But if she admitted this snowfall she would have to come to some decision, and in those days there was enough distraction in her life as it was already. So she poked about the gloomy, lamplighted house and pretended that nothing had happened. Cousin Lymon, on the contrary, chased around in the wildest excitement, and when Miss Amelia turned her back to dish him some breakfast he slipped out of the door.

Marvin Macy laid claim to the snowfall. He said that he knew snow, had seen it in Atlanta, and from the way he walked about the town that day it was as though he owned every flake. He sneered at the little children who crept timidly out of the houses and scooped up handfuls of snow to taste. Reverend Willin hurried down the road with a furious face, as he was thinking deeply and trying to weave the snow into his Sunday sermon. Most people were humble and glad about this marvel; they spoke in hushed voices and said 'thank you' and 'please' more than was necessary. A few weak characters, of course, were demoralized and got drunk—but they were not numerous. To everyone this was an occasion and many counted their money and planned to go to the café that night.

Cousin Lymon followed Marvin Macy about all day, seconding his claim to the snow. He marveled that snow did not fall as does rain, and stared up at the dreamy, gently falling flakes until he stumbled from dizziness. And the pride he took on himself, basking in the glory of Marvin Macy—it was such that many people could not resist calling out to him: ' "Oho," said the fly on the chariot wheel. "What a dust we do raise." '

Miss Amelia did not intend to serve dinner. But when, at six o'clock, there was the sound of footsteps on the porch she opened the front door cautiously. It was Henry Ford Crimp, and though there was no food, she let him sit at a table and served him a drink. Others came. The evening was blue, bitter, and though the snow fell no longer there was a wind from the pine trees that swept up delicate flurries from the ground. Cousin Lymon did not come until after dark, with him Marvin Macy, and he carried his tin suitcase and his guitar.

'So you mean to travel?' said Miss Amelia quickly.

Marvin Macy warmed himself at the stove. Then he settled down at his table and carefully sharpened a little stick. He picked his teeth, frequently taking the stick out of his mouth to look at the end and wipe it on the sleeve of his coat. He did not bother to answer.

The hunchback looked at Miss Amelia, who was behind the counter. His face was not in the least beseeching; he seemed quite sure of himself. He folded his hands behind his back and perked up his ears confidently. His cheeks were red, his eyes shining, and his clothes were soggy wet. 'Marvin Macy is going to visit a spell with us,' he said.

Miss Amelia made no protest. She only came out from behind the counter and hovered over the stove, as though the news had made her suddenly cold. She did not warm her backside modestly, lifting her skirt only an inch or so, as do most women when in public. There was not a grain of modesty about Miss Amelia, and she frequently seemed to forget altogether that there were men in the room. Now as she stood warming herself, her red dress was pulled up quite high in the back so that a piece of her strong, hairy thigh could be seen by anyone who cared to look at it. Her head was turned to one side, and she had begun talking with herself, nodding and wrinkling her forehead, and there was the tone of accusation and reproach in her voice although the words were not plain. Meanwhile, the hunchback and Marvin Macy had gone up-stairs—up to the parlor with the pampas grass and the two sewing machines, to the private rooms where Miss Amelia had lived the whole of her life. Down in the café you could hear them bumping around, unpacking Marvin Macy, and getting him settled.

That is the way Marvin Macy crowded into Miss Amelia's home. At first Cousin Lymon, who had given Marvin Macy his own room, slept on the sofa in the parlor. But the snowfall had a bad effect on him; he caught a cold that turned into a winter quinsy, so Miss Amelia gave up her bed to him. The sofa in the parlor was much too short for her, her feet lapped over the edges, and often she rolled off onto the floor. Perhaps it was this lack of sleep that clouded her wits; everything she tried to do against Marvin Macy rebounded on herself. She got caught in her own tricks, and found herself in many pitiful positions. But still she did not put Marvin Macy off the premises, as she was afraid that she would be left alone. Once you have lived with another, it is a great torture to have to live alone. The silence of a firelit room when suddenly the clock stops ticking, the nervous shadows in an empty house—it is better to take in your mortal enemy than face the terror of living alone.

The snow did not last. The sun came out and within two days the town was just as it had always been before. Miss Amelia did not open her house until every flake had melted. Then she had a big house cleaning and aired everything out in the sun. But before that, the very first thing she did on going out again into her yard, was to tie a rope to the largest branch of the chinaberry tree. At the end of the rope she tied a crocus sack tightly stuffed with sand. This was the punching bag she made for herself and from that day on she would box with it out in her yard every morning. Already she was a fine fighter—a little heavy on her feet, but knowing all manner of mean holds and squeezes to make up for this.

Miss Amelia, as has been mentioned, measured six feet two inches in height. Marvin Macy was one inch shorter. In weight they were about even—both of them weighing close to a hundred and sixty pounds. Marvin Macy had the advantage in slyness of movement, and in toughness of chest. In fact from the outward point of view the odds were altogether in his favor. Yet almost everybody in the town was betting on Miss Amelia; scarcely a person would put up money on Marvin Macy. The town remembered the great fight between Miss Amelia and a Forks Falls lawyer who had tried to cheat her. He had been a huge strapping fellow, but he was left three-quarters dead when she had finished with him. And it was not only her talent as a boxer that had impressed everyone —she could demoralize her enemy by making terrifying faces and fierce noises, so that even the spectators were sometimes cowed. She was brave, she practiced faithfully with her punching bag, and in this case she was clearly in the right. So people had confidence in her, and they waited. Of course there was no set date for this fight. There were just the signs that were too plain to be overlooked.

During these times the hunchback strutted around with a pleased little pinched-up face. In many delicate and clever ways he stirred up trouble between them. He was constantly plucking at Marvin Macy's trouser leg to draw attention to himself. Sometimes he followed in Miss Amelia's footsteps—but these days it was only in order to imitate her awkward long-legged walk; he crossed his eyes and aped her gestures in a way that made her appear to be a freak. There was something so terrible about this that even the silliest customers of the café, such as Merlie Ryan, did not laugh. Only Marvin Macy drew up the left corner of his mouth and chuckled. Miss Amelia, when this happened, would be divided between two emotions. She would look at the hunchback with a lost, dismal reproach—then turn toward Marvin Macy with her teeth clamped.

'Bust a gut!' she would say bitterly.

And Marvin Macy, most likely, would pick up the guitar from the floor beside his chair. His voice was wet and slimy, as he always had too much spit in his mouth. And the tunes he sang glided slowly from his throat like eels. His strong fingers picked the strings with dainty skill, and everything he sang both lured and exasperated. This was usually more than Miss Amelia could stand.

'Bust a gut!' she would repeat, in a shout.

But always Marvin Macy had the answer ready for her. He would cover the strings to silence the quivering leftover tones, and reply with slow, sure insolence.

'Everything you holler at me bounces back on yourself. Yah! Yah!'

Miss Amelia would have to stand there helpless, as no one has ever invented a way out of this trap. She could not shout out abuse that would bounce back on herself. He had the best of her, there was nothing she could do.

So things went on like this. What happened between the three of them during the nights in the rooms upstairs nobody knows. But the café became more and more crowded every night. A new table had to be brought in. Even the Hermit, the crazy man named Rainer Smith, who took to the swamps years ago, heard something of the situation and came one night to look in at the window and brood over the gathering in the bright café. And the climax each evening was the time when Miss Amelia and Marvin Macy doubled their fists, squared up, and glared at each other. Usually this did not happen after any especial argument, but it seemed to come about mysteriously, by means of some instinct on the part of both of them. At these times the café would become so quiet that you could hear the bouquet of paper roses rustling in the draft. And each night they held this fighting stance a little longer than the night before.

The fight took place on Ground Hog Day, which is the second of February. The weather was favorable, being neither rainy nor sunny, and with a neutral temperature. There were several signs that this was the appointed day, and by ten o'clock the news spread all over the county. Early in the morning Miss Amelia went out and cut down her punching bag. Marvin Macy sat on the back step with a tin can of hog fat between his knees and carefully greased his arms and his legs. A hawk with a bloody breast flew over the town and circled twice around the property of Miss Amelia. The tables in the café were moved out to the back porch, so that the whole big room was cleared for the fight. There was every sign. Both Miss Amelia and Marvin Macy ate four helpings of half-raw roast for dinner, and then lay down in the afternoon to store up strength. Marvin Macy rested in the big room upstairs, while Miss Amelia stretched herself out on the bench in her office. It was plain from her white stiff face what a torment it was for her to be lying still and doing nothing, but she lay there quiet as a corpse with her eyes closed and her hands crossed on her chest.

Cousin Lymon had a restless day, and his little face was drawn and tightened with excitement. He put himself up a lunch, and set out to find the ground hog —within an hour he returned, the lunch eaten, and said that the ground hog had seen his shadow and there was to be bad weather ahead. Then, as Miss Amelia and Marvin Macy were both resting to gather strength, and he was left to himself, it occurred to him that he might as well paint the front porch. The house had not been painted for years—in fact, God knows if it had ever been painted at all. Cousin Lymon scrambled around, and soon he had painted half the floor of the porch a gay bright green. It was a loblolly job, and he smeared himself all over. Typically enough he did not even finish the floor, but changed over to the walls, painting as high as he could reach and then standing on a crate to get up a foot higher. When the paint ran out, the right side of the floor was bright green and there was a jagged portion of wall that had been painted. Cousin Lymon left it at that.

There was something childish about his satisfaction with his painting. And in this respect a curious fact should be mentioned. No one in the town, not even Miss Amelia, had any idea how old the hunchback was. Some maintained that when he came to town he was about twelve years old, still a child—others were certain that he was well past forty. His eyes were blue and steady as a child's but there were lavender crêpy shadows beneath these blue eyes that hinted of age. It was impossible to guess his age by his hunched queer body. And even his teeth gave no clue—they were all still in his head (two were broken from cracking a pecan), but he had stained them with so much sweet snuff that it was impossible to decide whether they were old teeth or young teeth. When questioned directly about his age the hunchback professed to know absolutely nothing—he had no idea how long he had been on the earth, whether for ten years or a hundred! So his age remained a puzzle.

Cousin Lymon finished his painting at five-thirty o'clock in the afternoon. The day had turned colder and there was a wet taste in the air. The wind came up from the pinewoods, rattling windows, blowing an old newspaper down the road until at last it caught upon a thorn tree. People began to come in from the country; packed automobiles that bristled with the poked-out heads of children, wagons drawn by old mules who seemed to smile in a weary, sour way and plodded along with their tired eyes half-closed. Three young boys came from Society City. All three of them wore yellow rayon shirts and caps put on backward—they were as much alike as triplets, and could always be seen at cock fights and camp meetings. At six o'clock the mill whistle sounded the end of the day's shift and the crowd was complete. Naturally, among the newcomers there were some riffraff, unknown characters, and so forth—but even so the gathering was quiet. A hush was on the town and the faces of people were strange in the fading light. Darkness hovered softly; for a moment the sky was a pale clear yellow against which the gables of the church stood out in dark and bare outline, then the sky died slowly and the darkness gathered into night.

Seven is a popular number, and especially it was a favorite with Miss Amelia. Seven swallows of water for hiccups, seven runs around the millpond for cricks in the neck, seven doses of Amelia Miracle Mover as a worm cure—her treatment nearly always hinged on this number. It is a number of mingled possibilities, and all who love mystery and charms set store by it. So the fight was to take place at seven o'clock. This was known to everyone, not by announcement or words, but understood in the unquestioning way that rain is understood, or an evil odor from the swamp. So before seven o'clock everyone gathered gravely around the property of Miss Amelia. The cleverest got into the café itself and stood lining the walls of the room. Others crowded onto the front porch, or took a stand in the yard.

Miss Amelia and Marvin Macy had not yet shown themselves. Miss Amelia, after resting all afternoon on the office bench, had gone upstairs. On the other hand Cousin Lymon was at your elbow every minute, threading his way through the crowd, snapping his fingers nervously, and batting his eyes. At one minute to seven o'clock he squirmed his way into the café and climbed up on the counter. All was very quiet.

It must have been arranged in some manner beforehand. For just at the stroke of seven Miss Amelia showed herself at the head of the stairs. At the same instant Marvin Macy appeared in front of the café and the crowd made way for him silently. They walked toward each other with no haste, their fists already gripped, and their eyes like the eyes of dreamers. Miss Amelia had changed her red dress for her old overall, and they were rolled up to the knees. She was barefooted and she had an iron strengthband around her right wrist. Marvin Macy had also rolled his trouser legs—he was naked to the waist and heavily greased; he wore the heavy shoes that had been issued him when he left the penitentiary. Stumpy MacPhail stepped forward from the crowd and slapped their hip pockets with the palm of his right hand to make sure there would be no sudden knives. Then they were alone in the cleared center of the bright café.

There was no signal, but they both struck out simultaneously. Both blows landed on the chin, so that the heads of Miss Amelia and Marvin Macy bobbed back and they were left a little groggy. For a few seconds after the first blows they merely shuffled their feet around on the bare floor, experimenting with various positions, and making mock fists. Then, like wildcats, they were suddenly on each other. There was the sound of knocks, panting, and thumpings on the floor. They were so fast that it was hard to take in what was going on— but once Miss Amelia was hurled backward so that she staggered and almost fell, and another time Marvin Macy caught a knock on the shoulder that spun him around like a top. So the fight went on in this wild violent way with no sign of weakening on either side.

During a struggle like this, when the enemies are as quick and strong as these two, it is worth-while to turn from the confusion of the fight itself and observe the spectators. The people had flattened back as close as possible against the walls. Stumpy MacPhail was in a corner, crouched over and with his fists tight in sympathy, making strange noises. Poor Merlie Ryan had his mouth so wide open that a fly buzzed into it, and was swallowed before Merlie realized what had happened. And Cousin Lymon—he was worth watching. The hunchback still stood on the counter, so that he was raised up above everyone else in the café. He had his hands on his hips, his big head thrust forward, and his little legs bent so that the knees jutted outward. The excitement had made him break out in a rash, and his pale mouth shivered.

Perhaps it was half an hour before the course of the fight shifted. Hundreds of blows had been exchanged, and there was still a deadlock. Then suddenly Marvin Macy managed to catch hold of Miss Amelia's left arm and pinion it behind her back. She struggled and got a grasp around his waist; the real fight was now begun. Wrestling is the natural way of fighting in this county—as boxing is too quick and requires much thinking and concentration. And now that Miss Amelia and Marvin were locked in a hold together the crowd came out of its daze and pressed in closer. For a while the fighters grappled muscle to muscle, their hipbones braced against each other. Backward and forward, from side to side, they swayed in this way. Marvin Macy still had not sweated, but Miss Amelia's overalls were drenched and so much sweat had trickled down her legs that she left wet footprints on the floor. Now the test had come, and in these moments of terrible effort, it was Miss Amelia who was the stronger. Marvin Macy was greased and slippery, tricky to grasp, but she was stronger. Gradually she bent him over backward, and inch by inch she forced him to the floor. It was a terrible thing to watch and their deep hoarse breaths were the only sound in the café. At last she had him down, and straddled; her strong big hands were on his throat.

But at that instant, just as the fight was won, a cry sounded in the café that caused a shrill bright shiver to run down the spine. And what took place has been a mystery ever since. The whole town was there to testify what happened, but there were those who doubted their own eyesight. For the counter on which Cousin Lymon stood was at least twelve feet from the fighters in the center of the café. Yet at the instant Miss Amelia grasped the throat of Marvin Macy the hunchback sprang forward and sailed through the air as though he had grown hawk wings. He landed on the broad strong back of Miss Amelia and clutched at her neck with his clawed little fingers.

The rest is confusion. Miss Amelia was beaten before the crowd could come to their senses. Because of the hunchback the fight was won by Marvin Macy, and at the end Miss Amelia lay sprawled on the floor, her arms flung outward and motionless. Marvin Macy stood over her, his face somewhat popeyed, but smiling his old half-mouthed smile. And the hunchback, he had suddenly disappeared. Perhaps he was frightened about what he had done, or maybe he was so delighted that he wanted to glory with himself alone—at any rate he slipped out of the café and crawled under the back steps. Someone poured water on Miss Amelia, and after a time she got up slowly and dragged herself into her office. Through the open door the crowd could see her sitting at her desk, her head in the crook of her arm, and she was sobbing with the last of her grating, winded breath. Once she gathered her right fist together and knocked it three times on the top of her office desk, then her hand opened feebly and lay palm upward and still. Stumpy MacPhail stepped forward and closed the door.

The crowd was quiet, and one by one the people left the café. Mules were waked up and untied, automobiles cranked, and the three boys from Society City roamed off down the road on foot. This was not a fight to hash over and talk about afterward; people went home and pulled the covers up over their heads. The town was dark, except for the premises of Miss Amelia, but every room was lighted there the whole night long.

Marvin Macy and the hunchback must have left the town an hour or so before daylight. And before they went away this is what they did:

They unlocked the private cabinet of curios and took everything in it.

They broke the mechanical piano.

They carved terrible words on the café tables.

They found the watch that opened in the back to show a picture of a waterfall and took that also.

They poured a gallon of sorghum syrup all over the kitchen floor and smashed the jars of preserves.

They went out in the swamp and completely wrecked the still, ruining the big new condenser and the cooler, and setting fire to the shack itself.

They fixed a dish of Miss Amelia's favorite food, grits with sausage, seasoned it with enough poison to kill off the county, and placed this dish temptingly on the café counter.

They did everything ruinous they could think of without actually breaking into the office where Miss Amelia stayed the night. Then they went off together, the two of them.

That was how Miss Amelia was left alone in the town. The people would have helped her if they had known how, as people in this town will as often as not be kindly if they have a chance. Several housewives nosed around with brooms and offered to clear up the wreck. But Miss Amelia only looked at them with lost crossed eyes and shook her head. Stumpy MacPhail came in on the third day to buy a plug of Queenie tobacco, and Miss Amelia said the price was one dollar. Everything in the café had suddenly risen in price to be worth one dollar. And what sort of a café is that? Also, she changed very queerly as a doctor. In all the years before she had been much more popular than the Chee-haw doctor. She had never monkeyed with a patient's soul, taking away from him such real necessities as liquor, tobacco, and so forth. Once in a great while she might carefully warn a patient never to eat fried watermelon or some such dish it had never occurred to a person to want in the first place. Now all this wise doctoring was over. She told one-half of her patients that they were going to die outright, and to the remaining half she recommended cures so far-fetched and agonizing that no one in his right mind would consider them for a moment.

Miss Amelia let her hair grow ragged, and it was turning gray. Her face lengthened, and the great muscles of her body shrank until she was thin as old maids are thin when they go crazy. And those gray eyes—slowly day by day they were more crossed, and it was as though they sought each other out to exchange a little glance of grief and lonely recognition. She was not pleasant to listen to; her tongue had sharpened terribly.

When anyone mentioned the hunchback she would say only this: 'Ho! if I could lay hand to him I would rip out his gizzard and throw it to the cat!' But it was not so much the words that were terrible, but the voice in which they were said. Her voice had lost its old vigor; there was none of the ring of ven-geance it used to have when she would mention 'that loom-fixer I was married to,' or some other enemy. Her voice was broken, soft, and sad as the wheezy whine of the church pump-organ.

For three years she sat out on the front steps every night, alone and silent, looking down the road and waiting. But the hunchback never returned. There were rumors that Marvin Macy used him to climb into windows and steal, and other rumors that Marvin Macy had sold him into a side show. But both these reports were traced back to Merlie Ryan. Nothing true was ever heard of him. It was in the fourth year that Miss Amelia hired a Cheehaw carpenter and had him board up the premises, and there in those closed rooms she has remained ever since.

Yes, the town is dreary. On August afternoons the road is empty, white with dust, and the sky above is bright as glass. Nothing moves—there are no chil-dren's voices, only the hum of the mill. The peach trees seem to grow more crooked every summer, and the leaves are dull gray and of a sickly delicacy.

The house of Miss Amelia leans so much to the right that it is now only a question of time when it will collapse completely, and people are careful not to walk around the yard. There is no good liquor to be bought in the town; the nearest still is eight miles away, and the liquor is such that those who drink it grow warts on their livers the size of goobers, and dream themselves into a dangerous inward world. There is absolutely nothing to do in the town. Walk around the millpond, stand kicking at a rotten stump, figure out what you can do with the old wagon wheel by the side of the road near the church. The soul rots with boredom. You might as well go down to the Forks Falls highway and listen to the chain gang.

THE TWELVE MORTAL MEN

The Forks Falls highway is three miles from the town, and it is here the chain gang has been working. The road is of macadam, and the county decided to patch up the rough places and widen it at a certain dangerous place. The gang is made up of twelve men, all wearing black and white striped prison suits, and chained at the ankles. There is a guard, with a gun, his eyes drawn to red slits by the glare. The gang works all the day long, arriving huddled in the prison cart soon after daybreak, and being driven off again in the gray August twilight. All day there is the sound of the picks striking into the clay earth, hard sunlight, the smell of sweat. And every day there is music. One dark voice will start a phrase, half-sung, and like a question. And after a moment another voice will join in, soon the whole gang will be singing. The voices are dark in the golden glare, the music intricately blended, both somber and joyful. The music will swell until at last it seems that the sound does not come from the twelve men on the gang, but from the earth itself, or the wide sky. It is music that causes the heart to broaden and the listener to grow cold with ecstasy and fright. Then slowly the music will sink down until at last there remains one lonely voice, then a great hoarse breath, the sun, the sound of the picks in the silence.

And what kind of gang is this that can make such music? Just twelve mortal men, seven of them black and five of them white boys from this county. Just twelve mortal men who are together.

Yukio Mishima

THE SOUND OF WAVES

Preface 🔲🔲🔲🔲🔲🔲🔲🔲🔲🔲🔲🔲🔲🔲🔲🔲🔲🔲🔲🔲

The Sound of Waves (*Shiosai*, 1954) seems like a fairy tale because it makes Eden available to adults who in the West have forgotten how to get back to the garden they are so busily paving over. Yukio Mishima's mirror-perfect realism understands that successful love is the true measure of growing up— but we no longer accept happy endings from modern literature because we seem to rarely find them in life. *The Sound of Waves* is a strong and conservative statement to an anxiety-ridden age which insists that happy endings are not inconsistent with life once we have learned to recognize the beauty of what is simply real. Mishima, Japan's most prolific and important postwar novelist, understood that the choice is ultimately our own. Among his thirty-six volume collected works, *The Sailor Who Fell From Grace With the Sea* (1963) is the short novel nightmare that opposes his ultra-realistic fairy tale. The point of Mishima's opposition is not simply to prefer the young fisherman and the diving woman whose love makes them one with their primitive island to the sailor who ends up about to be operated on by a gang of morbid rich kids playing deadly doctor for real in a Tokyo suburb. Rather the difference is in the understanding that nature's grace makes the sound of waves music: any relationship between man and nature that is deaf to that music will end where it started, with a fall that is our own expulsion from paradise. *The Sound of Waves* briefly contrasts the fisherfolk of Uta-jima with Okinawa's American military community, living in prefab housing and driving back and forth endlessly to escape putting down roots. Nature's grace demands that we stay put. Rooting is the only way to grace, a state of unselfish freedom and love understood as fertility by Mishima, who was to call his four-volume final masterpiece (*Spring Snow* 1968, *Runaway Horses* 1969, *The Temple of Dawn* 1970, *The Decay of the Angel* 1970) *The Sea of Fertility.*

Yukio Mishima (Kimitake Hiraoka, 1925–1970) is the most recent of major contemporary writers. Coming after Bellow (1915), Solzhenitsyn (1918), and McCullers (1917), he was a candidate for the Nobel Prize in 1968, the year of its award to his acknowledged literary master and sponsor, Yasunari Kawabata (1899–1972). When we compare *The Sound of Waves* with *Seize the Day, One Day in the Life of Ivan Denisovich,* and *The Ballad of the Sad Café,* not only does it seem a fairy tale of happy adolescent love, contrasting these seemingly more realistic tales of suffering and loss, it also seems somehow closer to the earlier generation of Conrad, Faulkner, and Mann. But, closer to the early moderns, Mishima is the greater contemporary realist. *Confessions of a Mask* (1949), the novel which brought him national recognition in Japan, is auto-biographical. *After the Banquet* (1960), his novel of Japanese politics, is so real that it brought a libel suit against him. His ultimate masterpiece, *The Temple of the Golden Pavilion* (1956), is based directly on a real event—the burning down of Kinkakuji temple by a psychopathic monk in 1950. Mishima characterized the style of *The Temple of the Golden Pavilion* as "Ogai plus Mann." Ogai Mori (1862–1922) means stoic morality and pure, disciplined language; of Thomas Mann, his chief Western influence, Mishima wrote: "It was because he knew the violent quality of beauty that Thomas Mann wrote *Death in Venice.*" Here Mishima is using Mann to explain the workings of Japanese Nō drama, and Mishima was an extremely successful writer of modern Nō plays. The second of his works to be translated in the West was the collection *Five Modern Nō Plays* (1956). By uniting modern realism with classical form, as with a modern play written in a fifteenth-century form, Mishima, like Mann before him, was able to aesthetically shape his realism without violating its surface reality, and in doing so reveal the drama of everyday human experience. Like Mann, Mishima knew who is the ultimate parent of modern literature: The "basic proposition of the modern novel," he wrote, "is, as Dostoevsky said . . . the expression of diametrically opposed attitudes within human beings." The human beings of Mishima's fiction are not underground men, who give us their division instantly, but they are no less divided. Their surface characters are as real as our own to others—more real than Faulkner's mythic primitives who share their connection with nature. But their division is plain in their struggle to come to grips with nature's wholeness, with both the violence and the peace of its beauty, just as Mann's artists must struggle with Life's superiority to their Art. Ultimately Mishima's characters discover that their own reality is a microcosm of nature's totality, and in so doing they enlarge the scope of his fictional reality to make it our own as well. Less mythic and aesthetic, Mishima's reality is closest to Conrad's nature in *Youth,* from which all the fiction that follows must grow and eventually circle back with

The Sound of Waves. Nature teaches Conrad's youth hope in the knowledge of death, in the same way that Mishima's youths learn that fertile love is the outcome of natural roots and the embodiment of natural hope.

The realist is the writer who stays put, but it is a mistake to think that realism is simple-minded writing that can't travel. Mishima, who sold stories to popular magazines, carefully distinguished his serious novels from his pulp fiction. To the credit of his realism, a work as ultimately serious as *The Sound of Waves* was a popular success in Japan, where it was subsequently filmed. From the time of his earliest novels, Mishima had received praise for his ability to tell a realistic story in the most classical Japanese prose, and at the same time replace the Japanese concentration on mood with a Western sense of narrative structure. That structure made Mishima more popular abroad than at home for a time, even though the Western reader of his work in translation is denied the experience of his style and its Japanese significance. But even in translation Western readers have found in Mishima's fiction a realism that achieves classic dimensions. His simple surface is the reflection of a profound inner experience—unexpressed but finally valid. Instead of a complex psychological novel full of uncertain consciousness, we find in *The Sound of Waves* a simple story that is ageless because it reflects many thousand years of human experience, however uncertain. If not for the single sentence telling us late in the novel that "the Korean war had come to an end for the time being," we could not know just when to date the novel's action. In this way Mishima has transferred the ancient Greek pastoral on the love of goatherd and shepherd children, the story of Daphnis and Chloë, to the modern Japanese island of Kamishima—the real world counterpart of fictional Uta-jima.

In this sense the novel is the legacy of Mishima's rare knowledge of Western classics, and even more of his happy trip to Greece in 1952. His trip led Mishima to define Greek classicism as the product of a civilization (like our own) without spirituality but (unlike our own) with equilibrium of mind and body. Maintaining balance helped the Greeks to create beauty, for Greek tragedy—in which the gods rebuke man's arrogance—instructs us to maintain equilibrium. What Mishima found in Greece was what he found with approval in American sociologist Ruth Benedict's analysis of Japanese culture, *The Chrysanthemum and the Sword.* But the idea of balanced duality as the source of beauty, of a Nature that accommodates life and death when people act naturally, is as eternal as Greek harmony, Chinese Yin and Yang theory, or Japanese *bunburyodo*—the samurai dual way of literary and martial arts that modern Mishima followed to his death by hara-kiri on the day he sent the last scene of *The Sea of Fertility* to his publishers.

The Sound of Waves refuses to explain anything, telling its story and nothing more. Looking for something more, we find neither direct or disguised statement of theme, nor gross generality. The story is nothing more than itself, and its simplicity defeats analysis because Mishima wants his story taken for granted—and refuses to permit us to do so. Somewhere along the line, we think, there has got to be a reason for its happy ending, and that elusive reason haunts us at the novel's unanswering end. We are sent back to Mishima's beginning for our answer—just as nature insists we understand that beginning and end were one until modern consciousness forgot our beginning remembering too well our end. But back at Mishima's beginning we find that *The Sound of Waves* appears to be no more than a travel book describing Uta-jima, Song Island, and a guide book that fails to explain the island's very name. Mishima's failure is an intentional invitation to travel Uta-jima with him, finding the island's meaning within not without, to learn how the island itself makes the sound of waves into a song. With this purpose in mind he first isolates the island's two highest points: Yashiro Shrine and the lighthouse near the summit of Mt. Higashi, which offer the island's best views. These points of view tell us that the viewpoint man takes of himself is the novel's main concern. The *torii* pines of the sea god's shrine that once framed a view of the Gulf of Ise—legendary in Japanese culture—have "died some years ago," just as the values of a natural faith are having a hard time in the modern world, whose modern lighthouse can only show Mt. Fuji when the wind is right and the day clear enough to see forever. Finding a natural perspective is both imperiled and imperative, for without it we are unable to hear the sea god's voice in the sound of waves no matter how much we pray at his shrine. This is the secret of the shrine's treasure, "a treasure of some sixty-six bronze mirrors. One is a grape-design mirror from the eighth century. Another is an ancient copy of a Chinese mirror . . . the deer and squirrels carved on its back must have emerged centuries ago from some Persian forest . . . to come finally to rest here on Uta-jima." As the *torii* pines framed one view, the grapes, deer, and squirrels of the singled-out ancient mirrors frame another view *if* we look into them. Doing so we will see man's identity framed by nature as it was in the past and can be in the present of Mishima's lovers—Shinji, a young fisherman, and the diving girl Hatsue. *The Sound of Waves* closes as it begins, with their view from the lighthouse discovering a passing ship. They are rewarded with this view because they are making no honeymoon cruise away from Uta-jima, unlike their modern foils: Yasuo, who "already knew the secret of giving himself importance," and Chiyoko, whose face is a "mask of self-preoccupied virginity." Shinji and Hatsue find their connection with nature and thus with each other by winning their struggle to stay in place. Each might flee the society interfering with their love, Shinji for a sailing career, Hatsue from her captive place in her father's house and her proposed wedding with Yasuo. Instead they seem both to have read *The Sound of Waves* and so learned the meaning of the contrast of the shrine's relation with nature and the lighthouse with its modern function. Winding up his introduction, Mishima drives home his point by passing from points of view to what is seen initially from them. The lighthouse keeper enters the name of a passing ship in his "Record of Shipping Movements" and, again by contrast, Mishima records the delicate soaring and plummeting movements of a hawk whose balancing act upon air currents is Mishima's message.

Each of Mishima's contrasts, *uncalled* to our attention, reinforces his novel's sense of nature's continuity, of its greatest cycle. That cycle is underlined when natural past reappears in modern present to give man the opportunity for harmony if he is willing to take it by being truly natural. Shinji's mother watches a butterfly trying to fly from the island into a breeze and thinks: "What a strange butterfly. . . . It's imitating a sea gull." Escape by unnatural identity gets the butterfly nowhere. And when, that night, Shinji comes to stand exactly in the same place, meditating on elopement and double suicide, he rejects both ways out as selfish. He is surprised to find that his thinking kills time, but we can tell that he has no use for that modern pastime because he has no watch: "His body perceived the turning of the immense wheel of the night, the revolution of the giant wheel of the day. Placed as he was, close to the workings of nature, it was not surprising that he should understand nature's precise system." By contrast, the ticking of Yasuo's proudly worn watch attracts the hornets who foil his attempt to rape Hatsue by stinging him into revealing himself and his hidden character to the girl. But society, even the island society, is less aware than Shinji of nature's precise system, of the necessity for a human ecology revealed by Mishima's contrasts. The island taboos that should guide society into ritual natural behavior were weakened during the war. In that war, Shinji's father was killed while working on a ship bringing a dead woman to Toshi-jima for an autopsy. Seeking the cause of her death causes his death, as much as does a smoking engine that attracts an allied fighter. Rustic fisherfolk ought to know better than to seek causes or machinery, for a taboo had warned: "Never have aboard one woman or one priest"—fertility *as* religion requires more than one.

The religion of fertility is older even than Yashiro Shrine, as old as the island of Uta-jima itself. And when the sea god finally raises his voice it is not at the shrine, but in the island's oldest cavern, whose natural wisdom is testified to by a Sanskrit inscription on its walls. That wisdom resides in the cavern's shaft connecting the island with the bottom of the sea, and the wisdom of that connection is insisted on by waves surging in the shaft, which speak the god's anger to children playing cowboys and Indians in the holy cavern. The sea is angry because of immorality, unrighteousness, *omeko:* Yasuo's attempted rape, the separation of Shinji and Hatsue, the Western movie acted out in its temple, and finally all collected social unnaturalness. Mishima repeats this key scene throughout *The Sound of Waves*, not only to make plain the fact of our separation, but also to insist that natural innocence can teach us to recover what has been lost. A postcard of a Kyoto temple bears a message about a trip to a movie, but the message ends with Shinji's young brother's concern for his mother, reflecting his earlier concern for Shinji in the cavern. Moderns may begin and end with his naturalness of heart if they are properly schooled, as the diving women are schooled by playing with pebbles on the shore to teach them an adult role to come. Hatsue's innocence is manifest as she gives a handbag prize to Shinji's mother when the cavern scene is repeated on the beach before a false shrine erected by a traveling salesman. Hatsue has won a diving contest, sacrificing natural energy for cheap plastic, but she wins more with her innocence. To protect that innocence in the form of a nursing child, one diving woman is "punished for having seen a fearful something at the bottom of the sea, a something that humans are not meant to see." Death is the price of violating fertility taboos by diving too deep, by seeing ourselves as more than human. "Women really are the wise ones," remarks an old fisherman to Shinji, and his mother explains their wisdom: "The interior of a house dark even at noon, the somber pangs of childbirth, the gloom at the bottom of the sea—these were the series of interrelated worlds in which she lived her life." Woman's wisdom is natural because it understands the logic of this interrelationship to be a fertility that must not be violated by selfishness, no matter how harsh nature may be.

To connect surface and depth becomes Shinji's mission, just as it was Mishima's literary goal. Shinji does so by diving, like Hatsue, into the face of a typhoon to join his ship to a buoy. He joins the two with a lifeline to restore an umbilical connection with mother nature. By diving deep, Shinji gets to the top of Yashiro Shrine with Hatsue, whose father's wisdom in testing the lovers shows him to have been a bronze sea god in truth when earlier he bathes. The fan he carries advertising a drug store in Toba is a reminder of Prince Deki's treasure, a nobleman's fan-shaped baton—revealed only to the long united with nature and with their spouses. Prince Deki came to Uta-jima and took an island girl to wife; no stories survive him because his life was uneventful, happy, and natural. But natural happiness—and Mishima insists on this pointedly—is no fairy tale of milk and honey. The fishermen work for a cooperative, and the cooperative works for nature—a hard taskmaster. Shinji and his rope are first seen as he hauls in octopus: "Shinji stood with his legs spread wide, one foot stretched to the prow, and continued his endless tug-of-war against whatever there was in the sea. One hand-pull by one hand-pull, the rope came up. Shinji was winning. But the sea was not surrendering: one after the other, mockingly, it kept sending the pots up—all empty." Shinji is playing no game, but the sea is—to teach him outer strength and inner humility. So nature confirms that the "fisherman's conception of the sea was close to that of the farmer for his land. The sea was the place where he earned his living, a rippling field where, instead of waving heads of rice or wheat, the white and formless harvest of the waves was forever swaying above the unrelieved blueness of a sensitive and yielding soil." Nature makes us truly earn our living; the soil that is sea yields only to those who know its grace, who know the song of the waves' sound, who are no more than the sea itself. *The Sound of Waves* makes it no wonder that Mishima called the final effort of his life *The Sea of Fertility*.

Mishima

THE SOUND
OF WAVES

Translated by Meredith Weatherby

Chapter One

Uta-jima—Song Island—has only about fourteen hundred inhabitants and a coastline of something under three miles.

The island has two spots with surpassingly beautiful views. One is Yashiro Shrine, which faces northwest and stands near the crest of the island. The shrine commands an uninterrupted view of the wide expanse of the Gulf of Ise, and the island lies directly in the straits connecting the gulf with the Pacific Ocean. The Chita Peninsula approaches from the north, and the Atsumi Peninsula stretches away to the northeast. To the west you can catch glimpses of the coastline between the ports of Uji-Yamada and Yokkaichi in Tsu.

By climbing the two hundred stone steps that lead up to the shrine and looking back from the spot where there is a *torii* guarded by a pair of stone temple-dogs, you can see how these distant shores cradle within their arms the storied Gulf of Ise, unchanged through the centuries. Once there were two *"torii"* pines growing here, their branches twisted and trained into the shape of a *torii*, providing a curious frame for the view, but they died some years ago.

Just now the needles of the surrounding pine trees are still dull-green from winter, but already the spring seaweeds are staining the sea red near the shore. The northwest monsoon blows steadily from the direction of Tsu, making it still too cold to enjoy the view.

Yashiro Shrine is dedicated to Watatsumi-no-Mikoto, god of the sea. This is an island of fishermen and it is natural that the inhabitants should be devout worshippers of this god. They are forever praying for calm seas, and the very first thing they do upon being rescued from some peril of the sea is to make a votive offering at the sea-god's shrine.

The shrine possesses a treasure of some sixty-six bronze mirrors. One is a grape-design mirror from the eighth century. Another is an ancient copy of a Chinese mirror of the Six Dynasties period, of which there are not more than fifteen or sixteen in all Japan; the deer and squirrels carved on its back must have emerged centuries ago from some Persian forest and journeyed halfway around the earth, across wide continents and endless seas, to come finally to rest here on Uta-jima.

The other most beautiful view on the island is from the lighthouse near the summit of Mt. Higashi, which falls in a cliff to the sea. At the foot of the cliff the current of the Irako Channel sets up an unceasing roar. On windy days these narrow straits connecting the Gulf of Ise and the Pacific are filled with whirlpools. The tip of the Atsumi Peninsula juts out from across the channel, and on its rocky and desolate shore stands the tiny, unmanned beacon of Cape Irako. Southeast from the Uta-jima lighthouse you can see the Pacific, and to the northeast, across Atsumi Bay and beyond the mountain ranges, you can sometimes see Mt. Fuji, say at dawn when the west wind is blowing strong.

When a steamship sailing to or from Nagoya or Yokkaichi passed through the Irako Channel, threading its way among the countless fishing-boats scattered the length of the channel between the gulf and the open sea, the lighthouse watchman could easily read its name through his telescope. The *Tokachi-maru*, a Mitsui Line freighter of nineteen hundred tons, had just come within telescopic range. The watchman could see two sailors dressed in gray work-clothes, talking and stamping their feet on the deck. Presently an English freighter, the *Talisman*, sailed into the channel, bound for port. The watchman saw the sailors clearly, looking very tiny as they played quoits on the deck.

The watchman turned to the desk in the watchhouse and, in a log marked "Record of Shipping Movements," entered the vessels' names, signal marks, sailing directions, and the time. Then he tapped this information out on a telegraph key, warning cargo owners in the ports of destination to begin their preparations.

It was afternoon and the sinking sun had been cut off by Mt. Higashi, throwing the vicinity of the lighthouse into shadow. A hawk was circling in the bright sky over the sea. High in the heavens, the hawk was dipping now one wing and then the other, as though testing them, and, just when it seemed about to plummet downward, instead it suddenly slipped backward on the air, and then soared upward again on motionless wings.

After the sun had completely set, a young fisherman came hurrying up the mountain path leading from the village past the lighthouse. He was dangling a large fish in one hand.

The boy was only eighteen, having finished high school just last year. He was tall and well-built beyond his years, and only his face revealed his youthfulness. Skin can be burned no darker by the sun than his was burned. He had the well-shaped nose characteristic of the people of his island, and his lips were cracked and chapped. His dark eyes were exceedingly clear, but their clarity was not that of intellectuality—it was a gift that the sea bestows upon those who make their livelihood upon it; as a matter of fact, he had made notably bad grades in school. He was still wearing the same clothes he fished in each day— a pair of trousers inherited from his dead father and a cheap jumper.

The boy passed through the already deserted playground of the elementary school and climbed the hill beside the watermill. Mounting the flight of stone steps, he went on behind Yashiro Shrine. Peach blossoms were blooming in the shrine garden, dim and wrapped in twilight. From this point it was not more than a ten-minute climb on up to the lighthouse.

The path to the lighthouse was dangerously steep and winding, so much so that a person unaccustomed to it would surely have lost his footing even in the daytime. But the boy could have closed his eyes, and his feet would still have picked their way unerringly among the rocks and exposed pine roots. Even now when he was deep in his own thoughts, he did not once stumble.

A little while ago, while a few rays of daylight yet remained, the boat on which the boy worked had returned to its home port of Uta-jima. Today, as every day, the boy had gone out fishing on the *Taihei-maru*, a small, engine-powered boat, together with its owner and one other boy. Returning to port, they transferred their catch to the Co-operative's boat and then pulled their own up onto the beach. Then the boy started for home, carrying the halibut he was going to take shortly to the lighthouse. As he came along the beach the twilight was still noisy with the shouts of fishermen pulling their boats up onto the sand.

There was a girl he had never seen before. She leaned resting against a stack of heavy wooden frames lying on the sand, the kind called "abacuses" because of their shape. The fishing-boats were pulled up onto the beach stern-first by means of a winch, and these frames were placed under the keels so they went sliding smoothly over one after another. Apparently the girl had just finished helping with the work of carrying these frames and had paused here to get her breath.

Her forehead was moist with sweat and her cheeks glowed. A cold west wind was blowing briskly, but the girl seemed to enjoy it, turning her work-flushed face into the wind and letting her hair stream out behind her. She was wearing a sleeveless, cotton-padded jacket, women's work-pants gathered at the ankles, and a pair of soiled work-gloves. The healthy color of her skin was no different from that of the other island girls, but there was something refreshing about the cast of her eyes, something serene about her eyebrows. The girl's eyes were turned intently toward the sky over the sea to the west. There a crimson spot of sun was sinking between piles of blackening clouds.

The boy could not remember ever having seen this girl before. There should not have been a single face on Uta-jima that he could not recognize. At first glance he took her for an outsider. But still, the girl's dress was not that of outsiders. Only in the way she stood apart, gazing at the sea, did she differ from the vivacious island girls.

The boy purposely passed directly in front of the girl. In the same way that children stare at a strange object, he stopped and looked her full in the face.

The girl drew her eyebrows together slightly. But she continued staring fixedly out to sea, never turning her eyes toward the boy.

Finishing his silent scrutiny, he had gone quickly on his way. . . .

At the time he had felt only the vague satisfaction of curiosity gratified, and it was only now, much later, while climbing the path to the lighthouse, that he realized how rude his inspection had been. The thought filled his cheeks with shame.

The boy looked down at the sea between the pine trees along the path. The incoming tide was roaring, and the sea was quite black now before the moon rose. Turning the bend around what was known as Woman's Slope—the ghost of a tall woman was said sometimes to appear here—he caught sight for the first time of the brightly lighted windows of the lighthouse, still high above him. The brightness blinded him for a moment: the village generator had been out of order for a long time and he was accustomed only to the dim light of oil lamps in the village.

The boy often brought fish in this way to the lighthouse, feeling a debt of gratitude toward the lighthouse-keeper. He had flunked his final examinations last year, and it had seemed his graduation would have to be postponed a year. But his mother, on her frequent trips past the lighthouse to gather firewood on the mountain beyond, had struck up an acquaintance with the mistress of the lighthouse, to whom she now appealed. She explained that she simply couldn't support her family any longer if her son's graduation were postponed.

So the lighthouse-keeper's wife spoke to her husband, and he went to see his good friend the school principal. Thanks to this friendly intervention, the boy had finally been able to graduate on schedule.

The boy had become a fisherman as soon as he finished school. And since then he had made it a point to take part of the day's catch to the lighthouse from time to time. He also performed other small errands for them and had become a favorite of both the lighthouse-keeper and his wife.

The residence provided the lighthouse-keeper was just to the side of a flight of concrete steps leading up to the lighthouse itself and had its own small vegetable garden. As the boy approached, he could see the wife's shadow moving about on the glass door of the kitchen. She was evidently preparing supper.

He announced himself by calling from outside and the wife opened the door.

"Oh, it's you, Shinji-san," she said.

The boy held the fish out without a word.

The woman took it from him and called out loudly over her shoulder, this time using the boy's family name:

"Father, Kubo-san has brought us a fish."

From another room the good-natured voice of the lighthouse-keeper answered familiarly:

"Thank you, thank you. Come on in, Shinji boy."

The boy was still standing hesitantly at the kitchen door. The halibut had already been placed on a white enamelware platter, where it lay faintly gasping, blood oozing from its gills, streaking its smooth white skin.

Chapter Two

Next morning Shinji boarded his master's boat as usual and they set out for the day's fishing. The overcast sky of daybreak was mirrored in a calm sea. It would take about an hour to reach the fishing grounds.

Shinji was wearing a black rubber apron reaching from the breast of his jumper to the tops of his knee-length rubber boots, and a pair of long rubber gloves. Standing in the bow of the boat and gazing ahead to their destination in the Pacific, far ahead under the ashen morning sky, Shinji was remembering the night before, the time between his leaving the lighthouse and going to bed.

Shinji's mother and brother had been awaiting his return in the small room lit by a dim lamp hanging over the cookstove. The brother was only twelve. As for the mother, ever since the last year of the war, when her husband had been killed in a strafing attack, until Shinji had become old enough to go to work, she had supported the family all alone on her earnings as a diving woman.

"Was the lighthouse-keeper pleased?"

"Yes. He said: 'Come in, come in,' and then asked me to have something they called cocoa."

"What was it, this cocoa?"

"Some sort of foreign bean soup is what it seemed like."

The mother knew nothing about cooking. She served their fish either in raw slices—sometimes vinegared—or else simply grilled or boiled—head, tail, bones, and all. And as she never washed the fish properly, they often found their teeth chewing on sand and grit as well as fish.

Shinji waited hopefully during their meal for his mother to say something about the strange girl. But if his mother was not one for complaining, neither was she given to idle gossip.

After supper Shinji and his brother went to the public bath. Here again he hoped to hear something about the girl. As the hour was late, the place was almost empty and the water was dirty. The head of the fishermen's Co-operative and the postmaster were arguing politics as they soaked in the pool, their booming voices echoing pompously off the ceiling. The brothers nodded to them silently and then went to a far corner to dip hot water from the pool.

No matter how Shinji waited and strained his ears, the men simply would not move on from their politics to talk of the girl. Meanwhile his brother had finished bathing with unusual haste and had gone outside.

Shinji followed him out and asked the reason for all his hurry. Hiroshi, the brother, explained that he and his friends had been playing at war today, and that he had made the son of the head of the Co-operative cry by hitting him over the head with his wooden sword.

Shinji always went to sleep easily, but last night he had had the strange experience of lying long awake. Unable to remember a day of sickness in his life, the boy had lain wondering, afraid this might be what people meant by being sick.

That strange unrest was still with him this morning. But the vast ocean stretched away from the prow, where he was standing, and gradually the sight of it filled his body with the energy of familiar, day-to-day toil, and without realizing it he felt at peace again. The boat was shaking mincingly with the vibrations of the engine, and the biting morning wind slapped at the boy's cheeks.

High on the cliff to starboard, the beacon of the lighthouse was already extinguished. Along the shore, under the brownish pine branches of early spring, the pounding breakers of Irako Channel showed vivid white in the cloudy morning landscape. Two submerged reefs in the channel kept the water in a constant churning turmoil; an ocean liner would have had to work its way gingerly through the narrow passage between them, but with the skillful sculling of its master the *Taihei-maru* sailed smoothly through the swirling current. The water in the channel was between eighteen and a hundred fathoms deep, but over the reefs it was only thirteen to twenty fathoms. It was here, from this spot where buoys marked the passage, on out to the Pacific, that the numberless octopus pots were sunk.

Eighty per cent of Uta-jima's yearly catch was in octopus. The octopus season, which began in November, was now about to give way to the squid season, which would begin with the spring equinox. It was the end of the season, the time when the pots were lying in wait for their last chance at what were called the "fleeing octopus" as they moved to the depths of the Pacific to escape the cold waters of the Gulf of Ise.

To master fishermen the exact rise and fall of every inch of the bottom of the shallow waters off the Pacific side of the island were as familiar as their own kitchen gardens. They were always saying: "It's only a blind man that can't see the ocean floor." They knew their direction from their mariner's compass, and by watching the changing outline of the mountains on the far distant capes they could always tell their exact position. Once they had their bearings, they unerringly knew the topography of the ocean floor beneath them.

Countless ropes had been methodically laid out over the floor of the ocean, to each of which were tied more than a hundred pots, and the floats attached to the ropes rolled and tossed with the rise and fall of the tides. In their boat it was the master who knew the art of octopus fishing; all Shinji and the other boy, Ryuji, had to do was lend their strong bodies willingly to the heavy labor involved.

Jukichi Oyama, master fisherman, owner of the *Taihei-maru*, had a face like leather well-tanned by sea winds. The grimy wrinkles of his hands were mixed indistinguishably with old fishing scars, all burned by the sun down into their deepest creases. He was a man who seldom laughed, but was always in calm good spirits, and even the loud voice he used when giving commands on the boat was never raised in anger. While fishing he seldom left his place on the sculling platform at the stern, only occasionally taking one hand off the oar to regulate the engine.

Emerging into the fishing grounds, they found already gathered there the many other fishing-boats, unseen until now, and exchanged morning greetings with them. Upon reaching their own fishing area, Jukichi reduced the speed of the engine and signaled Shinji to attach a belt from the engine to the roller-shaft on the gunwale.

This shaft turned a pulley which extended over the gunwale. One of the ropes to which the octopus pots were tied would be placed over the pulley, and the boat would slowly follow the rope along as the pulley drew one end up from the sea and let the other fall back into the sea. The two boys also would take turns at pulling on the rope, because the water-soaked hemp was often too heavy a load for the pulley alone and also because the rope would slip off unless carefully guided.

A hazy sun was hidden behind the clouds on the horizon. Two or three cormorants were swimming on the sea, their long necks thrust out over the surface of the water. Looking back toward Uta-jima, one could see its southern cliffs shining, dead-white, stained by the droppings of countless flocks of cormorants.

The wind was bitterly cold, but while he pulled the first rope toward the pulley Shinji stared out over the dark-indigo sea and felt boiling up within him energy for the toil that would soon have him sweating. The pulley began to turn and heavy, wet rope came rising from the sea. Through his thin gloves Shinji could feel the thick, icy rope he grasped in his hands. As it passed over the pulley the taut rope threw off a sleet-like spray of salt water.

Soon the octopus pots themselves were rising to the surface, showing a red-clay color. Ryuji stood waiting at the pulley. If a pot was empty, he would quickly pour the water out of it and, not letting it strike the pulley, again commit it to the care of the rope, now sinking back into the sea.

Shinji stood with his legs spread wide, one foot stretched to the prow, and continued his endless tug-of-war against whatever there was in the sea. One hand-pull by one hand-pull, the rope came up. Shinji was winning. But the sea was not surrendering: one after the other, mockingly, it kept sending the pots up—all empty.

More than twenty pots had already been pulled up at intervals of from seven to ten yards along the rope. Shinji was pulling the rope. Ryuji was emptying water from the pots. Jukichi, keeping a hand on the sculling oar and never once changing his expression, silently watched the boys at their work.

Sweat gradually spread across Shinji's back and began to glisten on his forehead, exposed to the morning wind. His cheeks became flushed. Finally the sun broke through the clouds, casting pale shadows at the feet of the quickly moving boys.

Ryuji was facing away from the sea, in toward the boat. He upended the pot that had just come up, and Jukichi pulled a lever to disengage the pulley. Now for the first time Shinji looked back toward the pulley.

Ryuji poked around inside the pot with a wooden pole. Like a person awakened from a long nap, an octopus oozed its entire body out of the pot and cowered on the deck. Quickly the cover was jerked off a large bamboo creel standing by the engine room—and the first catch of the day went slithering down into it with a dull thud.

The *Taihei-maru* spent most of the morning octopus fishing. Its meager catch consisted of five octopuses. The wind died and the sun shone gloriously. Passing through the Irako Channel, the *Taihei-maru* sailed back into the Gulf of Ise to do some "drag fishing" on the sly in the prohibited waters there.

To make their drag they tied a number of large hooks and lines on a crossbar, tied it to a stout hawser, and then, putting the boat in motion, dragged this across the floor of the gulf like a rake. After a time they pulled the drag in; with it four flatheads and three soles came flapping up from the water.

Shinji took them off the hooks with his bare hands. The flatheads fell to the blood-smeared deck, their white bellies gleaming. The black, wet bodies of the soles, their little eyes sunk deep in folds of wrinkles, reflected the blue of the sky.

Lunchtime came. Jukichi dressed the flatheads on the engine-room hatch and cut them into slices. They divided the raw slices onto the lids of their aluminum lunchboxes and poured soy sauce over them from a small bottle. Then they took up the boxes, filled with a mixture of boiled rice and barley and, stuffed into one corner, a few slices of pickled radish. The boat they entrusted to the gentle swell.

"Say, what do you think about old Uncle Teru Miyata bringing his girl back?" Jukichi said abruptly.

"I didn't know he had."

"Me neither."

Both boys shook their heads and Jukichi proceeded with his story:

"Uncle Teru had four girls and one boy. Said he had more than enough of girls, so he married three of them off and let the other one be adopted away. Her name was Hatsue and she was adopted into a family of diving women over at Oizaki in Shima. But then, what do you know, that only son of his, Matsu, dies of the lung sickness last year. Being a widower, Uncle Teru starts feeling lonely. So he calls Hatsue back, has her put back in his family register, and decides to adopt a husband into the family for her, to have someone to carry on the name.... Hatsue's grown up to be a real beauty. There'll be a lot of youngsters wanting to marry her.... How about you two—hey?"

Shinji and Ryuji looked at each other and laughed. Each could guess that the other was blushing, but they were too tanned by the sun for the red to show.

Talk of this girl and the image of the girl he had seen on the beach yesterday immediately took fast hold of each other in Shinji's mind. At the same instant he recalled, with a sinking heart, his own poor condition in life. The recollection made the girl whom he had stared at so closely only the day before seem very, very far away from him now. Because now he knew that her father was Terukichi Miyata, the wealthy owner of two coasting freighters chartered to Yamagawa Transport—the hundred-and-eighty-five-ton *Utajima-maru* and the ninety-five-ton *Harukaze-maru*—and a noted crosspatch, whose white hair would wave like lion whiskers in anger.

Shinji had always been very level-headed. He had realized that he was still only eighteen and that it was too soon to be thinking about women. Unlike the environment of city youths, always exploding with thrills, Uta-jima had not a single pin-ball parlor, not a single bar, not a single waitress. And this boy's simple daydream was only to own his own engine-powered boat some day and go into the coastal-shipping business with his younger brother.

Surrounded though he was by the vast ocean, Shinji did not especially burn with impossible dreams of great adventure across the seas. His fisherman's conception of the sea was close to that of the farmer for his land. The sea was the place where he earned his living, a rippling field where, instead of waving heads of rice or wheat, the white and formless harvest of waves was forever swaying above the unrelieved blueness of a sensitive and yielding soil.

Even so, when that day's fishing was almost done, the sight of a white freighter sailing against the evening clouds on the horizon filled the boy's heart with strange emotions. From far away the world came pressing in upon him with a hugeness he had never before apprehended. The realization of this unknown world came to him like distant thunder, now pealing from afar, now dying away to nothingness.

A small starfish had dried to the deck in the prow. The boy sat there in the prow, with a coarse white towel tied round his head. He turned his eyes away from the evening clouds and shook his head slightly.

Chapter Three

That night Shinji attended the regular meeting of the Young Men's Association. This was the name now applied to what in ancient times was called the "sleeping house," then a dormitory system for the young, unmarried men of the island. Even now many young men preferred to sleep in the Association's drab hut on the beach rather than in their own homes. There the youths hotly debated such matters as schooling and health; the ways of salvaging sunken ships and making rescues at sea; and the Lion and Lantern Festival dances, functions belonging to the young men of the village since ancient days. Thus they felt themselves part of the communal life and found pleasure in that agreeable weight that comes from shouldering the burdens and duties of full-grown men.

A wind was blowing from the sea, rattling the closed night-shutters and making the lamp sway back and forth, now dim, now suddenly bright. From outside, the night sea came pressing very near them, and the roar of the tide was constantly revealing the unrest and might of nature as the shadows of the lamp moved over the cheerful faces of the young men.

When Shinji entered the hut one boy was kneeling on all fours under the lamp, having his hair cut by a friend with a pair of slightly rusty hair clippers. Shinji smiled and sat down on the floor against the wall, clasping his knees. He remained silent as usual, listening to what the others were saying.

The youths were bragging to each other of the day's fishing, laughing loudly and heaping each other unstintingly with insults. One boy, who was a great reader, was earnestly reading one of the out-of-date magazines with which the hut was supplied. Another was engrossed, with no less enthusiasm, in a comic book; holding the pages open with fingers whose knuckles were gnarled beyond his years, he would study some pages for two or three minutes at a time before finally understanding the point and breaking into a loud guffaw.

Here, for the second time, Shinji heard talk of the new girl. He caught a snatch of a sentence spoken by a snaggle-toothed boy who opened a big mouth to laugh and then said:

"That Hatsue, she's—"

The rest of the sentence was lost to Shinji in a sudden commotion from another part of the room, mixed with answering laughter from the group around the snaggle-toothed boy.

Shinji was not at all given to brooding about things, but this one name, like a tantalizing puzzle, kept harassing his thoughts. At the mere sound of the name his cheeks flushed and his heart pounded. It was a strange feeling to sit there motionless and feel within himself these physical changes that, until now, he had experienced only during heavy labor.

He put the palm of his hand against his cheek to feel it. The hot flesh felt like that of some complete stranger. It was a blow to his pride to realize the existence of things within himself that he had never so much as suspected, and rising anger made his cheeks even more flaming hot.

The young men were awaiting the arrival of their president, Yasuo Kawamoto. Although only nineteen, Yasuo was the son of a leading family in the village and possessed the power to make others follow him. Young as he was, he already knew the secret of giving himself importance, and he always came late to their meetings.

Opening the door with a bang, Yasuo now entered the room. He was quite fat and had inherited a red complexion from his tippling father. His face was naïve enough in appearance, but there was a crazy look about his thin eyebrows. He spoke glibly, without any trace of the local dialect:

"Sorry to be late. . . . Well, then, let's not waste time. There're definite plans to be made for next month's projects."

So saying, he sat down at the desk and opened a notebook. They could all see that he was in a great hurry about something.

"As decided at the last meeting, there's the business of—er—holding a meeting of the Respect for Old Age Association, and also hauling stones for road repairs. Then there's the matter of cleaning the sewers to get rid of the rats—it's a request of the Village Assembly. We'll do this as usual—er—on a stormy day when the boats can't go out. Fortunately, rat-catching can be done in any weather, and I don't believe the police will get after us even if we kill a few rats outside the sewers."

There was general laughter and shouts of "You tell 'em! You tell 'em!"

Next, proposals were made to ask the school doctor to give them a talk on hygiene, and to hold an oratorical contest. But the old-style, lunar-calendar New Year was just over, and the youths were so fed up with gatherings that they were lukewarm to both proposals.

So they turned themselves into a committee of the whole and sat in critical judgment on the merits of their mimeographed bulletin, *The Orphan Island*. Something called a quatrain by Verlaine had been quoted at the end of an essay in the last issue by the boy who liked books so much, and this now became the universal target for their jibes:

I know not why
My mournful soul
Flies the sea, fitfully, fitfully,
On restless, frantic pinions . . .

"What do you mean by that 'fitfully, fitfully'?"
" 'Fitfully, fitfully' means 'fitfully, fitfully'—that's what!"
"Maybe it's a mistake for 'flitfully, flitfully.' "

"That's it! If you'd said 'it flies flitfully, flitfully'—then that would've made some sense."

"Who's this Verlaine fellow anyhow?"

"One of the most famous French poets—that's who!"

"And what do you know about French poets, hey? You probably got it all out of some popular song somewhere."

Thus the meeting had ended as usual in a give-and-take of insults.

Wondering why Yasuo, the president, had been in such a hurry to leave, Shinji stopped one of his friends and asked him.

"Don't you know?" the friend replied. "He's invited to the party Uncle Teru Miyata's giving to celebrate his daughter's homecoming."

Normally Shinji would have walked home with the others as they talked and laughed, but now, hearing of the party to which in no case would he have been invited, he soon slipped away and walked alone along the beach toward the stone steps leading to Yashiro Shrine.

Looking up at the village houses, built one above the other on a steep rise, he picked out the lights shining from the Miyata house. All the lights in the village came from the same oil lamps, but these looked somehow different, more sparkling. Even if he could not see the actual scene of the banquet, he could clearly imagine how the sensitive flame of the lamps there must be throwing flickering shadows from the girl's tranquil eyebrows and long lashes down onto her cheeks.

Reaching the bottom of the stone steps, Shinji looked up the flight of stairs, dappled with shadows of pine branches. He began to climb, his wooden clogs making a dry, clicking sound. There was not a soul to be seen around the shrine, and the light in the priest's house was out.

Even though he had just bounded up two hundred steps, Shinji's thick chest was not laboring in the least when he reached the shrine. He stopped before it, filled with a feeling of reverence.

He tossed a ten-yen coin into the offertory chest. Thinking a moment, he tossed in ten yen more. The sound of his clapped hands, calling the god's attention, sounded through the shrine garden, and Shinji prayed in his heart:

"God, let the seas be calm, the fish plentiful, and our village more and more prosperous. I am still young, but in time let me become a fisherman among fishermen. Let me have much knowledge in the ways of the sea, in the ways of fish, in the ways of boats, in the ways of the weather . . . in everything. Let me be a man with surpassing skill in everything. . . . Please protect my gentle mother and brother, who is still a child. When my mother enters the sea in the diving season, please protect her body somehow from all the many dangers. . . . Then there's a different sort of request! I'd like to make. . . . Some day let even such a person as me be granted a good-natured, beautiful bride . . . say someone like Terukichi Miyata's returned daughter. . . ."

The wind came blowing, and the pine branches set up a clamor. It was a gust of wind that raised solemn echoes even in the dark interior of the shrine. Perhaps it was the sea-god, accepting the boy's prayer.

Shinji looked up at the star-filled sky and breathed deeply. Then he thought: "But mightn't the gods punish me for such a selfish prayer?"

Chapter Four

It was some four or five days later and the wind was blowing a gale. The waves were breaking high across the breakwater of Uta-jima's harbor. The sea, far and wide, was choppy with whitecaps.

The skies were clear, but because of the high wind not a single fishing-boat had gone out.

Shinji's mother had asked a favor of him. The women of the village gathered firewood on the mountain and left it stored at the top in what had formerly been a military observation tower. His mother had marked hers with a red rag. Since he had finished by noon with the Young Men's Association work of carrying stones for the road building, she asked him to bring her gatherings down from the mountain for her.

Shinji shouldered the wooden frame on which brushwood was carried, and set out. The path led up past the lighthouse. As he rounded Woman's Slope the wind died as completely as though it had been a trick.

The residence of the lighthouse-keeper was as quiet as though in a deep noonday sleep. He could see the back of a watchman seated at the desk in the watchhouse. A radio was blaring music.

Climbing the pine-grove slope behind the lighthouse, Shinji began to sweat.

The mountain was utterly still. Not a single human form was to be seen; there was not even so much as a stray dog prowling about. In fact, because of a taboo of the island's guardian deity, there was not a single stray dog on the entire island, let alone a pet dog. And as the island was all uphill and land was scarce, neither were there any horses or cows for draft animals. The only domestic animals were the cats that came trailing the tips of their tails through the jagged shadows thrown in sharp relief in the lanes leading always downward in cobbled steps between rows of village houses.

The boy climbed to the top of the mountain. This was the highest point on Uta-jima. But it was so overgrown with *sakaki* and silverberry bushes and tall weeds that there was no view. There was nothing but the sound of the sea roaring up through the vegetation. The path leading down the other side to the south had been practically taken over by bushes and weeds, and one had to make quite a detour to reach the observation tower.

Presently, beyond a sand-floored pine thicket, the three-story, reinforced-concrete tower came into view. The white ruins looked uncanny in the deserted, silent scene.

In former days soldiers had stood on the second-floor balcony, binoculars to their eyes, and checked the aim of the guns that were fired for target practice from Mt. Konaka on the far side of Irako Cape. Officers had called out from inside the tower to know where the shells were hitting, and the soldiers had called back the ranges. This way of things had continued until mid-war, and the soldiers had always blamed a phantom badger for any provisions that were mysteriously short.

The boy peeped into the ground floor of the tower. There was a mountain of dried pine needles and twigs tied into bundles. This floor had evidently been used as a storehouse, and its windows were quite small; there were even some with their glass panes still unbroken. The boy entered and, by the faint light of the windows, soon found his mother's mark—red rags tied to several bundles, the name "Tomi Kubo" written on them in childish characters.

Taking the frame off his back, Shinji tied the bundles of dried needles and twigs to it. He had not visited the tower for a long time and now felt reluctant to depart so soon. Leaving the load lying where it was, he was about to start up the concrete steps.

Just then there was a faint sound from overhead as though of stone and wood striking together. The boy listened intently. The sound ceased. It must have been his imagination.

He went on up the stairs, and there on the second floor of the ruins was the sea, framed desolately in wide windows which lacked both glass and casings. Even the iron railing of the balcony was gone. Traces of the soldiers' chalk scribblings could still be seen on the gray walls.

Shinji continued climbing. He paused to look at the broken flagpole out a third-story window—and this time he was certain he heard the sound of someone's sobbing. He gave a start and ran lightly on up to the roof on sneaker-clad feet.

The one who was really startled was the girl on the roof, having a boy suddenly appear before her out of nowhere, without so much as a footfall. She was wearing wooden clogs and was sweeping, but now she ceased her sobbing and stood petrified with fear. It was Hatsue.

As for the boy, he had never dreamed of such a fortunate meeting and could not believe his eyes.

So the two of them simply stood there, startled, like animals that come suddenly face to face in the forest, looking into each other's eyes, their emotions wavering between caution and curiosity.

Finally Shinji spoke:

"You're Hatsue-san, aren't you?"

Hatsue nodded involuntarily and then looked surprised at his knowing her name. But something about the black, serious eyes of this boy who was making such an effort to put up a bold front seemed to remind her of a young face that had gazed at her fixedly on the beach the other day.

"It was you crying, wasn't it?"

"Yes, it was me."

"Why were you crying?" Shinji sounded like a policeman.

Her reply came with unexpected promptness. The mistress of the lighthouse gave lessons in etiquette and homemaking for the girls of the village who were interested, and today Hatsue was going to attend for the first time. But, coming too early, she had decided to climb the mountain behind the lighthouse and had lost her way.

Just then the shadow of a bird swept over their heads. It was a peregrine. Shinji took this for a lucky sign. Thereupon his tangled tongue came unloose and, recovering his usual air of manliness, he told her that he passed the lighthouse on his way home and would go that far with her.

Hatsue smiled, making not the slightest effort to wipe away the tears that had flowed down her cheeks. It was as though the sun had come shining through rain. She was wearing a red sweater, blue-serge slacks, and red-velvet socks—the split-toed kind worn with clogs.

Hatsue leaned over the concrete parapet at the edge of the room and looked down at the sea.

"What's this building?" she asked.

Shinji too went to the parapet, but at a little distance from the girl.

"It used to be a target-observation tower," he answered. "They watched from here to see where the cannon shells landed."

Here on the south side of the island, screened by the mountain, there was no wind. The sunlit expanse of the Pacific stretched away beneath their eyes. The pine-clad cliff dropped abruptly to the sea, its jutting rocks stained white with cormorant droppings, and the water near the base of the cliff was black-brown from the seaweed growing on the ocean floor.

Shinji pointed to a tall rock just offshore where the surging waves were striking, sending up clouds of spray.

"That's called Black Isle," he explained. "It's where Policeman Suzuki was fishing when the waves washed him away and drowned him."

Shinji was thoroughly happy. But the time was drawing near when Hatsue was due at the lighthouse. Straightening up from the concrete parapet, she turned toward Shinji.

"I'll be going now," she said.

Shinji made no answer and a surprised look came over his face. He had caught sight of a black streak that ran straight across the front of her red sweater.

Hatsue followed his gaze and saw the dirty smudge, just in the spot where she had been leaning her breast against the concrete parapet. Bending her head, she started slapping her breast with her open hands. Beneath her sweater, which all but seemed to be concealing some firm supports, two gently swelling mounds were set to trembling ever so slightly by the brisk brushing of her hands.

Shinji stared in wonder. Struck by her hands, the breasts seemed more like two small, playful animals. The boy was deeply stirred by the resilient softness of their movement.

The streak of dirt was finally brushed out.

Shinji went first down the concrete steps and Hatsue followed, her clogs making very clear, light sounds which echoed from the four walls of the ruins. But the sounds behind Shinji's back came to a stop as they were reaching the first floor.

Shinji looked back. The girl was standing there, laughing.

"What is it?" he asked.

"I'm dark too, but you—you're practically *black*."

"What?"

"You've *really* been burnt by the sun, you have."

The boy laughed in meaningless reply and went on down the stairs. They were just about to leave the tower when he stopped abruptly and ran back inside. He had almost forgotten his mother's bundles.

On the way back toward the lighthouse Shinji walked in front, carrying the mountain of pine needles on his back. As they walked along, the girl asked him his name and now, for the first time, he introduced himself. But he went on hurriedly to ask that she not mention his name to anyone or say anything about having met him here: Shinji well knew how sharp the villagers' tongues could be. Hatsue promised not to tell. Thus their well-founded fear of the village's love of gossip changed what was but an innocent meeting into a thing of secrecy between the two of them.

Shinji walked on in silence, having no idea how they could meet again, and soon they reached the spot from which they could look down upon the lighthouse. He pointed out the short cut leading down to the rear of the lighthouse-keeper's residence and told her good-by. Then, purposely, he took the roundabout way on down to the village.

Chapter Five

Until now the boy had been leading a peaceful, contented existence, poor though he was, but from this time on he became tormented with unrest and lost in thought, falling prey to the feeling that there was nothing about him that could possibly appeal to Hatsue. He was so healthy that he had never had any sickness other than the measles. He could swim the circumference of Uta-jima as many as five times without stopping. And he was sure he would have to yield to no one in any test of physical strength. But he could not believe that any of these qualities could possibly touch Hatsue's heart.

Another opportunity to meet Hatsue simply would not come. Whenever he returned from fishing he always looked all along the beach for her, but on the few occasions when he caught sight of her she was busy working and there was no chance to speak.

There was no such thing as that time when she had been alone, leaning against the "abacuses" and staring out to sea. Moreover, whenever the boy resolved that he was sick of it all and that he would put Hatsue completely out of his mind, on that very day he was sure to catch sight of her among the bustling crowd that gathered on the beach when the boats came in.

City youths learn the ways of love early from novels, movies, and the like, but on Uta-jima there were practically no models to follow. Thus, no matter how he wondered about it, Shinji had not the slightest idea what he should have done during those precious minutes between the observation tower and the lighthouse when he had been alone with her. He was left with nothing but a keen sense of regret, a feeling that there was something he had utterly failed to do.

It was the monthly commemoration of the day of his father's death, and the whole family was going to visit the grave, as they did every month. Not to interfere with Shinji's work, they had chosen a time before the boats set out, and before his brother's school.

Shinji and his brother came out of the house with their mother, who was carrying incense sticks and grave flowers. They left the house standing open: there was no such thing as theft on the island.

The graveyard was located some distance from the village, on a low cliff above the beach. At high tide the sea came right up to the foot of the cliff. The uneven slope was covered with gravestones, some of them tilting on the soft sand foundation.

Dawn had not yet broken. The sky was just beginning to become light in the direction of the lighthouse, but the village and its harbor, which faced north-west, still remained in night.

Shinji walked in front carrying a paper lantern. Hiroshi, his brother, was still rubbing the sleep out of his eyes when he pulled on his mother's sleeve and said:

"Can I have four rice dumplings in my lunch today? Can I, huh?"

"Such foolishness! *Two* you'll get. Three'd more than give you the belly-ache."

"Please! I want *four!*"

The rice dumplings they made on the island to celebrate the Day of the Monkey, or on death-memorial days, were almost as large as the small pillows they slept on.

In the graveyard a cold morning breeze was blowing fitfully. The surface of the sea in the lee of the island was black, but the offing was stained with dawn. The mountains enclosing the Gulf of Ise could be seen clearly. In the pale light of daybreak the gravestones looked like so many white sails of boats anchored in a busy harbor. They were sails that would never again be filled with winds, sails that, too long unused and heavily drooping, had been turned into stone just as they were. The boats' anchors had been thrust so deeply into the dark earth that they could never again be raised.

Reaching their father's grave, their mother arranged the flowers she had brought and, after striking many matches only to have them blown out by the wind, finally succeeded in lighting the incense. Then she had her sons bow before the grave, while she herself bowed behind them, weeping.

In their village there was a saying: "Never have aboard one woman or one priest." The boat on which Shinji's father died had broken this taboo. An old woman had died on the island toward the end of the war, and the Co-operative's boat had set out to take her body to Toshi-jima for the autopsy.

When the boat was about three miles out from Uta-jima it was sighted by a plane from an aircraft carrier. The boat's regular engineer was not aboard and his substitute was unaccustomed to the engine. It was the black smoke from his sluggish engine that had given the plane its target.

The plane dropped a bomb on the boat and then strafed it with machine-gun fire. The boat's funnel was split open, and Shinji's father had his head torn apart down to his ears. Another man too was killed instantly, hit in the eye. One was hit in the back by a bullet, which entered his lungs. One was hit in the legs. And one who had a buttock shot away died shortly after of the bleeding.

Both the deck and the bilge became a lake of blood. The fuel tank was hit and kerosene spread on top of the blood. Some hesitated to fling themselves prone in this mess and were hit in the hips. Four persons saved themselves by taking shelter in the icebox in the forward cabin. In his panic, one man squeezed himself through the porthole behind the bridge, but when he tried to repeat the feat back in port he found that, no matter how he tried, he could not wriggle through that tiny opening a second time.

Thus, of eleven persons, three were killed and a number wounded. But the corpse of the old woman, stretched out on the deck under a rush mat, was not so much as touched by a single bullet. . . .

"The old man was really something fierce when fishing for sand launce," Shinji said reminiscently to his mother. "He'd beat me every day. Really, there wasn't time for the welts to go down before he'd raise more."

Sand launce were found in the Yohiro Shallows, and catching them required unusual skill. A flexible bamboo pole with feathers on the tip was used to imitate a sea-bird pursuing a fish under the water, and the operation called for split-second timing.

"Well, I guess so," said his mother. "Sand-launce fishing is real man's work even for a fisherman."

Hiroshi took no interest in the talk between his mother and brother but was dreaming of the school excursion that was to take place in only ten days more. Shinji had been too poor to go on school excursions when he was Hiroshi's age, so he had been saving money out of his own wages for Hiroshi's travel expenses.

When they had finished paying their homage at the graveside, Shinji went on alone directly to the beach to help with the preparations for sailing. It was agreed that his mother would return home and bring him his lunch before the boats put out.

As he hurried toward the *Taihei-maru* along the busy beach, someone's voice from out of the throng came to him on the wind and struck his ears:

"They say Yasuo Kawamoto's to marry Hatsue."

At the sound of those words Shinji's spirits became pitch-black.

Again the *Taihei-maru* spent the day octopus fishing.

During the eleven hours they were out in the boat Shinji threw his whole soul into the fishing and scarcely once opened his mouth. But as he usually had very little to say, his silence was not particularly noticeable.

Returning to harbor, they tied up as usual to the Co-operative's boat and unloaded their octopuses. Then the other fish were sold through a middleman and transferred to the "buyer ship" belonging to a private wholesale fish dealer. The giltheads were flapping about inside the metal baskets used for weighing fish, flashing in the light of the setting sun.

It was the day out of every ten when the fishermen were paid, so Shinji and Ryuji went along with the master to the office of the Co-operative. Their catch for the ten-day period had been over three hundred and thirty pounds and they cleared 27,997 yen after deducting the Co-operative's sales commission, the ten per cent savings deposit, and maintenance costs. Shinji received four thousand yen from the master as his share. It had been a good take considering that the height of the fishing season was already past.

Licking his fingers, the boy carefully counted the bills in his big, rough hands. Then he returned them to the envelope with his name on it and put it deep in the bottom of the inner pocket of his jumper. With a bow toward the master, he left the office. The master had drawn up to the brazier with the head of the Co-operative and was proudly exhibiting a cigarette holder he had carved himself out of a piece of coral.

The boy had intended to go straight home, but somehow his feet took him of their own accord back to the darkening beach.

The last boat was just being pulled up onto the sand. There were only a few men to turn the winch and to help it along by pulling on the rope, so the women, who usually only placed the "abacus" frames under the keel, were pushing from behind. It was obvious that no headway was being made. The beach was growing dark and no trace was to be seen of the grammar-school boys who usually came out to help. Shinji decided to lend a hand.

Just at that moment one of the women pushing the boat raised her head and looked in Shinji's direction. It was Hatsue. He had no wish to see the face of this girl who had put him in such a black mood all day. But his feet carried him on to the boat. Her face was glowing in the semi-darkness; he could see her forehead moist with sweat, her rosy cheeks, her dark, flashing eyes fixed again steadily in the direction the boat was being pushed.

Without a word, Shinji took hold of the rope. The men at the winch called out:

"Much obliged."

Shinji's arms were powerful. In an instant the boat was sliding up over the sand, and the women were running helter-skelter after it with their "abacus" frames.

Once the boat was beached, Shinji turned and walked off toward home, not once looking back. He wanted terribly to turn around, but smothered the impulse.

Opening the sliding door of his house, under the dim lamp Shinji saw the familiar expanse of straw mats, turned reddish-brown with age and use. His brother was lying on his stomach reading, holding a textbook out under the light. His mother was busy at the cookstove. Without taking off his rubber boots, Shinji lay back face up, the upper half of his body on the straw mats and his feet still in the tiny entry.

"Welcome back," said his mother.

Shinji liked to hand his pay envelope to his mother without saying anything. And, being a mother, she understood and always pretended to have forgotten that this was the tenth day, payday. She knew how much her son liked to see her look surprised.

Shinji ran his hand into the inner pocket of his jumper. The money was not there! He searched the pocket on the other side. He searched his trouser pockets. He even ran his hands down inside his trousers.

Surely he must have dropped it on the beach. Without a word, he ran out of the house.

Shortly after Shinji had left, someone came calling in front of the house. Shinji's mother went to the entry and found a young girl standing in the darkness of the alleyway.

"Shinji-san—is he at home?"

"He came home just a bit ago, but then he went out again."

"I found this on the beach. And since Shinji-san's name was written on it . . ."

"Well, now that's truly kind of you. Shinji must have gone to look for it."

"Shall I go tell him?"

"Oh, would you? Much obliged, much obliged."

The beach was now completely dark. The meager lights of Toshi-jima and Sugashi-jima were glinting from across the sea. Fast asleep in the starlight, many fishing boats were lined up, facing domineeringly out to sea.

Hatsue caught a glimpse of Shinji's shadow. But at that instant he disappeared behind a boat. He was stooping over, searching the sand, and apparently had not seen Hatsue. She came upon him face to face in the shadow of a boat, standing stock-still, in a rage.

Hatsue told him what had happened and that she had come to tell him his money was already safely in his mother's hands. She went on to explain that she had had to ask two or three people the way to Shinji's house, but had always satisfied their curiosity by showing them the envelope she had found, with Shinji's name on it.

The boy gave a sigh of relief. He smiled, his white teeth flashing handsomely in the darkness. The girl had come in a hurry and her breasts were rising and falling rapidly. Shinji was reminded of opulent dark-blue waves on the open sea. All the day's torment disappeared, and his spirits revived within him.

"I hear you're going to marry Yasuo Kawamoto. Is it true?" The words rushed out of the boy's mouth.

The girl burst out laughing. Her laughter gradually increased until she was choking with it.

Shinji wanted to stop her but did not know how. He put his hand on her shoulder.

His touch was light, but Hatsue dropped to the sand, still laughing.

"What's the matter? What's the matter?" Shinji squatted down beside her and shook her by the shoulders.

At last the girl's laughter abated and she looked seriously into the boy's face. Then she broke into laughter again.

Shinji stuck out his face toward hers and asked:

"Is it true?"

"Silly! It's a big lie."

"But that's what they're saying all right."

"It's a big lie."

The two had clasped their knees and were sitting in the shadow of the boat.

"Oh, I hurt! I've laughed so much that I hurt—right here," the girl said, putting her hand over her breast.

The stripes of her faded work-clothes were moving and shifting where they crossed her breasts.

"This is where it hurts," Hatsue said again.

"Are you all right?" And without thinking Shinji put his own hand on the spot.

"When you press it, it feels a little better," the girl said.

And suddenly Shinji's breast too was moving fast.

Their cheeks came so close they were almost touching. They could plainly smell each other—it was a fragrance like that of salt water. They could feel each other's warmth.

Their dry, chapped lips touched. There was a slight taste of salt.

"It's like seaweed," Shinji thought.

Then the moment was past. The boy moved away and stood up, propelled by a feeling of guilt at this first experience in his life.

"Tomorrow I'm going to take some fish to the lighthouse-keeper's place when I come back from fishing." Still looking out to sea, Shinji had now recovered his dignity and could make this declaration in a manly voice.

"I'm going there too tomorrow afternoon," the girl replied, likewise looking out to sea.

With that, the two parted and went walking away on opposite sides of the row of boats. Shinji was starting for home, but he noticed that the girl had not appeared from behind the boats. Just then he saw her shadow cast on the sand from behind the last boat and knew she was hiding there.

"Your shadow's giving you away," he called out.

Suddenly the figure of a girl dressed in wide-striped work-clothes came darting out, like some wild animal, and went running at full speed across the beach, never looking back.

Chapter Six

Returning from fishing the next day, Shinji set out for the lighthouse carrying two scorpion-fish, each about five or six inches long, strung by the gills on a straw rope. He had already climbed to the rear of Yashiro Shrine when he remembered that he had not yet offered a prayer of thanks to the god for having showered him with blessings so quickly. He went back to the front of the shrine and prayed devoutly.

His prayer finished, Shinji gazed out over the Gulf of Ise, already shining in the moonlight, and breathed deeply. Clouds were floating above the horizon, looking like ancient gods.

The boy felt a consummate accord between himself and this opulence of nature that surrounded him. He inhaled deeply, and it was as though a part of the unseen something that constitutes nature had permeated the core of his being. He heard the sound of the waves striking the shore, and it was as though the surging of his young blood was keeping time with the movement of the sea's great tides. It was doubtless because nature itself satisfied his need that Shinji felt no particular lack of music in his everyday life.

Shinji lifted the scorpion-fish to the level of his eyes and stuck out his tongue at their ugly, thorny faces. The fish were definitely alive, but they made not the slightest movement. So Shinji poked one in the jaw and watched it flop about in the air.

Thus the boy was loitering along the way, loath to have the happy meeting take place too quickly.

Both the lighthouse-keeper and his wife had taken Hatsue, the newcomer, to their warm hearts. Just when she was so silent that they were thinking maybe she was not so attractive after all, suddenly she would break into her lovely, girlish laughter; and if she sometimes seemed lost in the clouds, she was also most considerate. For instance, at the end of an etiquette lesson Hatsue would immediately begin clearing away the cups they had drunk their tea in—a thoughtful action that never would have occurred to the other girls—and while she was at it she would go on to wash any other dirty dishes she might find in the kitchen.

The couple at the lighthouse had one child, a daughter, who was attending the university in Tokyo. She only came home during vacations and, in her absence, they regarded these village girls who came so often to the house as their own children. They took a deep interest in the girls' futures, and when good fortune came to one of them they were as pleased as though the girl had been their own child.

The lighthouse-keeper, who had been in the service for thirty years, was feared by the village children because of his stern look and the tremendous voice with which he stormed at the young scamps who stole in to explore the lighthouse; but at heart he was actually a gentle person. Solitude had divested him of any feeling that men could have base motives. At a lighthouse there can be no greater treat than to have visitors. Surely no one would go the great distance to call at an isolated lighthouse with hidden ill-will, or at least any such feelings would surely vanish from his heart in the face of the unreserved hospitality he was certain to receive. Actually, it was just as the lighthouse-keeper so often said: "Bad intentions cannot travel as far as good."

The mistress too was truly a good person, and also very well read. Not only had she once been a teacher in a rural girls' school, but her many years of living in lighthouses had fostered her love of reading even more, until she now possessed an almost encyclopedic knowledge about everything. If she knew that La Scala Opera House was in Milan, she also knew that such-and-such a Tokyo film star had recently sprained her right ankle at such-and-such a place. She would argue her husband into a corner, and then, as if to make amends, put her whole soul into darning his socks or fixing his supper. When visitors came she would chatter away incessantly. The villagers listened spellbound to the mistress's eloquence, some of them comparing her unfavorably with their own taciturn women and feeling a meddlesome sort of sympathy for the lighthouse-keeper. But he himself had great respect for his wife's learning.

The living-quarters provided for the lighthouse-keeper was a one-story house of three rooms. Everything about it was kept as neat and polished as the light-house itself. A steamship-company calendar hung on the wall, and the ashes in the sunken hearth of the sitting-room were always neatly shaped up around the charcoal. Even in their daughter's absence, her desk stood in one corner of the parlor, its polished surface reflecting the blue glass of an empty pen-tray and decorated with a French doll. Behind the house there was a caldron-style bath heated by gas made from the dregs of the oil used to lubricate the beacon light. Unlike conditions in the squalid houses of the fishermen, here even the indigo pattern of the new-washed hand towel hanging by the basin at the toilet-room door was always bright and clean.

The lighthouse-keeper spent the greater part of each day beside the sunken hearth, smoking cheap New Life cigarettes, economically cutting them into short lengths and fitting them into a long, slender brass pipe. The lighthouse was dead during the daytime, with only one of the young assistants in the watchhouse to report ship movements.

Toward evening that day, even though no etiquette lesson was scheduled, Hatsue came visiting, bringing a door-gift of some sea-cucumbers wrapped in newspaper. Beneath her blue-serge skirt she was wearing long flesh-colored stockings, and over them red socks. Her sweater was her usual scarlet one.

Hatsue had no sooner entered the house than the mistress began giving advice, not mincing her words:

"When you wear a blue skirt, Hatsue-san, you ought to wear black hose. I know you have some because you were wearing them only the other day."

"Well . . ." Blushing slightly, Hatsue sat down beside the hearth.

At the regular lessons of etiquette and home-making the girls sat listening fairly intently and the mistress spoke in a lecturing tone of voice, but now, seated by the hearth with Hatsue, she began talking in a free and easy way. As her visitor was a young girl, she talked first in a general sort of way about love, and finally got around to asking such direct questions as "Isn't there someone you like very much?" At times, when the lighthouse-keeper saw the girl become rattled, he would ask a teasing question of his own.

When it began to grow late they asked Hatsue several times if she didn't have to get home for supper and if her father wouldn't be waiting for her. It was Hatsue who finally made the suggestion that she help prepare the supper.

Until now Hatsue had simply sat there blushing furiously and looking down at the floor, not so much as touching the refreshments put before her. But, once in the kitchen, she quickly recovered her good spirits. Then, while slicing the sea-cucumbers, she began singing the traditional Ise chorus used on the island for accompanying the Lantern Festival dancing; she had learned it from her aunt the day before:

> Tall chests, long chests, traveling chests—
> Since your dower is so great, my daughter,
> You must never think of coming back.
> But oh, my mother, you ask too much:
> When the east is cloudy, they say the wind will blow;
> When the west is cloudy, they say the rain will fall;
> And when a fair wind changes—
> Yoi! Sora!—
> Even the largest ship returns to port.

"Oh, have you already learned that song, Hatsue-san?" the mistress said. "Here it's already three years since we came here and I don't know it all even yet."

"Well, but it's almost the same as the one we sang at Oizaki," Hatsue answered.

Just then there was the sound of footsteps outside, and from the darkness someone called:

"Good evening."

"That must be Shinji-san," the mistress said, sticking her head out the kitchen door. Then:

"Well, well! More nice fish. Thanks. . . . Father, Kubo-san's brought us more fish."

"Thanks again, thanks again," the lighthouse-keeper called from the hearth. "Come on in, Shinji boy, come on in."

During this confusion of welcome and thanks Shinji and Hatsue exchanged glances. Shinji smiled. Hatsue smiled too. But the mistress happened to turn around suddenly and intercept their smiles.

"Oh, you two already know each other, do you? H'm, it's a small place, this village. But that makes it all the better, so do come on in, Shinji-san—Oh, and by the way, we had a letter from Chiyoko in Tokyo. She particularly asked about Shinji-san. I don't guess there's much doubt about who Chiyoko likes, is there? She'll be coming home soon for spring vacation, so be sure and come to see her."

Shinji had been just on the point of coming into the house for a minute, but these words seemed to wrench his nose. Hatsue turned back to the sink and did not look around again. The boy retreated back into the dusk. They called him several times, but he would not come back. He made his bow from a distance and then took to his heels.

"That Shinji-san—he's really the bashful one, isn't he, Father?" the mistress said, laughing.

The lone sound of her laughter echoed through the house. Neither the lighthouse-keeper nor Hatsue even smiled.

Shinji waited for Hatsue where the path curved around Woman's Slope.

At that point the dusk surrounding the lighthouse gave way to the last faint light that still remained of the sunset. Even though the shadows of the pine trees had become doubly dark, the sea below them was brimming with a last afterglow. All through the day the first easterly winds of spring had been blowing in off the sea, and even now that night was falling the wind did not feel cold on the skin.

As Shinji rounded Woman's Slope even that small wind died away, and there was nothing left in the dusk but calm shafts of radiance pouring down between the clouds.

Looking down, he saw the small promontory that jutted out into the sea to form the far side of Uta-jima's harbor. From time to time its top was shrugging its rocky shoulders swaggeringly, rending asunder the foaming waves. The vicinity of the promontory was especially bright. Standing on the promontory's peak there was a lone red-pine, its trunk bathed in the afterglow and vividly clear to the boy's keen eyes. Suddenly the trunk lost the last beam of light. The clouds overhead turned black and the stars began to glitter above Mt. Higashi.

Shinji laid his ear against a jutting rock and heard the sound of short, quick footsteps approaching along the flagstone path that led down from the stone steps at the entrance to the lighthouse residence. He was planning to hide here as a joke and give Hatsue a scare when she came by. But as those sweet-sounding footsteps came closer and closer he became shy about frightening the girl. Instead, he deliberately let her know where he was by whistling a few lines from the Ise chorus she had been singing earlier:

> When the east is cloudy, they say the wind will blow;
> When the west is cloudy, they say the rain will fall;
> And even the largest ship . . .

Hatsue rounded Woman's Slope, but her footsteps never paused. She walked right on past as though she had no idea Shinji was there.

"Hey! Hey!"

But still the girl did not look back. There was nothing to do but for him to walk silently along after her.

Entering the pine grove, the path became dark and steep. The girl was lighting her way with a small flashlight. Her steps became slower and, before she was aware of it, Shinji had taken the lead.

Suddenly the girl gave a little scream. The beam of the flashlight soared like a startled bird from the base of the pine trees up into the treetops.

The boy whirled around. Then he put his arms around the girl, lying sprawled on the ground, and pulled her to her feet.

As he helped Hatsue up, the boy remembered with shame how he had lain in wait for her a while ago, had given that whistled signal, had followed after her: even though his actions had been prompted by the circumstances, to him they still seemed to smack of evil. Making no move to repeat yesterday's caress, he brushed the dirt off the girl's clothing as gently as though he were her big brother. The soil here was mostly dry sand and the dirt brushed off easily. Luckily there was no sign of damage.

Hatsue stood motionless, like a child, resting her hand on Shinji's strong shoulder while he brushed her. Then she looked around for the flashlight, which she had dropped. It was lying on the ground behind them, still throwing its faint, fan-shaped beam, showing the ground covered with pine needles. The island's heavy twilight pressed in upon this single area of faint light.

"Look where it landed! I must have thrown it behind me when I fell." The girl spoke in a cheerful, laughing voice.

"What made you so mad?" Shinji asked, looking her full in the face.

"All that talk about you and Chiyoko-san."

"Stupid!"

"Then there's nothing to it?"

"There's nothing to it."

The two walked along side by side, Shinji holding the flashlight and guiding Hatsue along the difficult path as though he were a ship's pilot. There was nothing in particular to say, so the usually silent Shinji began to talk stumblingly to fill in the silence:

"As for me, some day I want to buy a coastal freighter with the money I've worked for and saved, and then go into the shipping business with my brother, carrying lumber from Kishu and coal from Kyushu. . . . Then I'll have my mother take it easy, and when I get old I'll come back to the island and take it easy too. . . . No matter where I sail, I'll never forget our island. . . . It has the most beautiful scenery in all Japan"—every person on Uta-jima was firmly convinced of this—"and in the same way I'll do my best to help make life on our island the most peaceful there is anywhere . . . the happiest there is anywhere. . . . Because if we don't do that, everybody will start forgetting the island and quit wanting to come back. No matter how much times change, very bad things—very bad ways—will all always disappear before they get to our island. . . . The sea—it only brings the good and right things that the island needs . . . and keeps the good and right things we already have here. . . . That's why there's not a thief on the whole island—nothing but brave, manly people— people who always have the will to work truly and well and put up with whatever comes—people whose love is never double-faced—people with nothing mean about them anywhere. . . ."

Of course the boy was not so articulate, and his way of speaking was confused and disconnected, but this is roughly what he told Hatsue in this moment of rare fluency.

She did not interrupt, but kept nodding her head in agreement with everything he said. Never once looking bored, her face overflowed with an expression of genuine sympathy and trust, all of which filled Shinji with joy.

Shinji did not want her to think he was being frivolous, and at the end of his serious speech he purposely omitted that last important hope that he had included in his prayer to the sea-god a few nights before.

There was nothing to hinder, and the path continued hiding them in the dense shadows of the trees, but this time Shinji did not even hold Hatsue's hand, much less dream of kissing her again. What had happened yesterday on the dark beach—to them that seemed not to have been an act of their own volition. It had been an undreamed-of event, brought about by some force outside themselves; it was a mystery how such a thing had come about. This time, they barely managed to make a date to meet again at the observation tower on the afternoon of the next time the fishing-boats could not go out.

When they emerged from the back of Yashiro Shrine, Hatsue gave a little gasp of admiration and stopped walking. Shinji stopped too.

The village was suddenly ablaze with brilliant lights. It was exactly like the opening of some spectacular, soundless festival: every window shone with a bright and indomitable light, a light without the slightest resemblance to the smoky light of oil lamps. It was as though the village had been restored to life and come floating up out of the black night. . . . The electric generator, so long out of order, had been repaired.

Outside the village they took different paths, and Hatsue went on alone down the stone steps and into the village, lit again, after such a long time, with street lamps.

Chapter Seven

The day came for Shinji's brother, Hiroshi, to go on the school excursion. They were to tour the Kyoto-Osaka area for six days, spending five nights away from home. This was the way the youths of Uta-jima, who had never before left the island, first saw the wide world outside with their own eyes, learning about it in a single gulp. In the same way, schoolboys of an earlier generation had crossed by boat to the mainland and stared with round eyes at the first horse-drawn omnibus they had ever seen, shouting: "Look! Look! A big dog pulling a privy!"

The children of the island got their first notions of the world outside from the pictures and words in their schoolbooks rather than from the real things. How difficult, then, for them to conceive, by sheer force of imagination, such things as streetcars, tall buildings, movies, subways. But then, once they had seen reality, once the novelty of astonishment was gone, they perceived clearly how useless it had been for them to try to imagine such things, so much so that at the end of long lives spent on the island they would no longer even so much as remember the existence of such things as streetcars clanging back and forth along the streets of a city.

Before each school excursion Yashiro Shrine did a thriving business in talismans. In their everyday lives the island women committed their own bodies, as a matter of course, to the danger and the death that lurked in the sea, but when it came to excursions setting forth for gigantic cities they themselves had never seen, the mothers felt their children were embarking on great, death-defying adventures.

Hiroshi's mother had bought two precious eggs and made him a lunch of terribly salty fried eggs. And deep in his satchel, where he would not quickly find them, she had tucked away some caramels and fruit.

On that day alone the island's ferryboat, the *Kamikaze-maru*, left Uta-jima at the unusual hour of one in the afernoon. Formerly the stubborn old-timer who captained this putt-putt launch of something under twenty tons had refused as an abomination any departure from the established schedule. But then had come the year when his own son went on the excursion. Ever since then he had understood what they meant by saying the children would squander their money if the boat got to Toba too much ahead of time for their train to leave, and had grudgingly agreed to let the school authorities have their own way with the schedule.

The cabin and the deck of the *Kamikaze-maru* were overflowing with schoolboys, satchels and canteens hanging across their breasts. The teachers in charge were terror-stricken by the swarm of mothers on the jetty. On Uta-jima a teacher's position depended upon the disposition of the mothers. One teacher had been branded a Communist by the mothers and driven off the island, while another, who was popular with the mothers, had even gotten one of the women teachers pregnant—and still been promoted to be acting assistant-principal.

It was the early afternoon of a truly springlike day, and as the boat set sail every mother was screaming the name of her own child. The boys, with the straps of their student-caps fixed under their chins, waited until they were sure their faces could no longer be distinguished from the shore and then began to yell back in high-spirited fun:

"Good-by, stupid! . . . Hooray! you old goose! . . . To hell with you! . . ."

The boat, jam-packed with black student-uniforms, kept throwing reflections of metal cap-badges and polished buttons back to shore until it was far out at sea. . . .

Once Hiroshi's mother was back, sitting on the straw mats of her own house, gloomy and deadly quiet even in the daytime, she began weeping, thinking of the day when both her sons would finally leave her for good and take to the sea.

The *Kamikaze-maru* had just discharged its load of students at the Toba pier opposite Mikimoto's "Pearl Island" and, regaining its usual happy-go-lucky, countrified air, was preparing for the return crossing to Uta-jima. There was a bucket atop the ancient smokestack, and water reflections were playing over the underside of the prow and over the great creels hanging from under the pier. A gray godown stood looking out across the sea, with the large white character for "Ice" painted on its side.

Chiyoko, the daughter of the lighthouse-keeper, was standing at the far end of the pier, holding a Boston bag. This unsociable girl, returning to the island after a long absence, disliked having the islanders greet and speak to her.

Chiyoko never wore a trace of make-up and her face was made all the more inconspicuous by the plain, dark-brown suit she was wearing. There was something about the cheerful, slapdash way her dingy features were thrown together that might have appealed to some. But she always wore a gloomy expression and, in her constantly perverse way, insisted upon thinking of herself as unattractive. Until now this was the most noticeable result of the "refinements" she was learning at the university in Tokyo. But probably the way she brooded over her commonplace face as being so unlovely was just as presumptuous as if she had been convinced she was an utter beauty.

Chiyoko's good-natured father had also contributed, unwittingly, to this gloomy conviction of hers. She was always complaining so openly that she had inherited her ugliness from him that, even when she was in the next room, the outspoken lighthouse-keeper would grumble to his guests:

"Well, there's no doubt about this grown-up daughter of mine being homely. It really makes me sad. I'm so ugly myself that I guess I have to take the blame for it. But then, I suppose that's fate."

Someone clapped Chiyoko on the shoulder and she turned around. It was Yasuo Kawamoto, the president of the Young Men's Association. He stood there laughing, his leather jacket glistening in the sun.

"Ho! Welcome home. Spring vacation, isn't it?"

"Yes. Exams were over yesterday."

"So now we've come back to have another drink of mother's milk?"

The day before, Yasuo's father had sent him to attend to some business for the Co-operative with the prefectural authorities at Tsu. He had spent the night at an inn in Toba run by relatives and now was taking the boat back to Uta-jima. He took great pride in showing this girl from a Tokyo university how well he could speak, without any trace of island dialect.

Chiyoko was conscious of the masculine joviality of this young man her own age: his worldly manner seemed to be saying: "There's no doubt but what this girl has a fancy for me." This feeling made her even more bad-tempered.

"Here it is again!" she told herself. Influenced both by her natural disposition and by the movies seen and novels read in Tokyo, she was always wishing that she could have a man look at her at least once with eyes saying "I love you" instead of "You love me." But she had decided she would never have such an experience in all her life.

A loud, rough voice shouted from the *Kamikaze-maru*:

"Hey! Where the blazes is that load of quilts? Somebody find them!"

Soon a man came carrying a great bale of arabesque-patterned quilts on his shoulders. They had been lying on the quay, half hidden in the shadows of the godown.

"The boat's about ready to leave," Yasuo said.

As they jumped from the pier to the deck, Yasuo took Chiyoko's hand and helped her across. Chiyoko thought how different his iron-like hand felt from the hands of men in Tokyo. But in her imagination it was Shinji's hand she was feeling—a hand she had never even so much as shaken.

Peering down through the small hatchway into the murky passenger cabin, all the more darkly stagnant to their daylight-accustomed eyes, they could barely make out, from the white towels tied around their necks or the occasional flickering reflection from a pair of spectacles, the forms of people lolling on the straw matting.

"It's better on deck. Even if it's a bit cold, it's still better."

Yasuo and Chiyoko took shelter from the wind behind the wheelhouse and sat down, leaning against a coil of rope.

The captain's snappish young helper came up and said:

"Hey! How about lifting your asses a minute?"

With that, he pulled a plank out from under them. They had sat down on the hatch used for closing the passenger cabin.

Up in the wheelhouse, where scruffy, peeling paint half revealed the grain of the wood underneath, the captain rang the ship's bell. . . . The *Kamikaze-maru* was under way.

Surrendering their bodies to the shuddering of the ancient engine, Yasuo and Chiyoko gazed back at Toba's receding harbor. Yasuo very much wanted to drop a hint about how he had slipped off and bought himself a piece last night, but decided he had better not. If he had been a boy from an ordinary farming or fishing village, his experience with women would have been cause for boasting, but on strait-laced Uta-jima he had to keep his mouth tightly shut. Young as he was, he had already learned to play the hypocrite.

Chiyoko was betting with herself as to the instant when a sea gull would fly even higher than the steel tower of the cableway that ascended the mountain behind Toba station. This girl who, out of shyness, had never had any sort of adventures in Tokyo, had been hoping that when she returned to the island something wonderful would happen to her, something that would completely change her world.

Once the boat was well away from Toba harbor, it would be an easy matter for even the lowest-flying gulls to seem to rise higher than the receding steel tower. But right now the tower was still soaring high in the air. Chiyoko looked closely at the second-hand of her wrist watch, fastened with its red-leather strap.

"If a sea gull flies higher than that within the next thirty seconds, that'll mean something wonderful really is waiting for me."

Five seconds passed. . . . A sea gull that had come following alongside the boat suddenly flew high into the air, flapping its wings—and rose higher than the tower!

Afraid that the boy at her side might remark on her smile, Chiyoko broke her long silence:

"Is there any news on the island?"

The boat was passing Sakate Island to port. Yasuo's cigarette had become so short it was burning his lips. He crushed the butt out on the deck and answered:

"Nothing in particular. . . . Oh, yes, the generator was broken down until ten days ago and the whole village was using lamps. But it's fixed now."

"Yes, my mother wrote me about that."

"Oh, she did? Well, as for any more news . . ."

Yasuo narrowed his eyes against the glare of the sea, which was overflowing with the light of spring. The Coast Guard cutter *Hiyodori-maru* was passing them at a distance of about ten yards, sailing in the direction of Toba.

". . . Oh, I forgot. Uncle Teru Miyata has brought his daughter back home. Her name's Hatsue, and she's a real beauty."

"So?"

Chiyoko's face had clouded at the word "beauty." Just the word alone seemed an implied criticism of her own looks.

"I'm a great favorite of Uncle Teru's, all right. And there's my older brother to carry on our own family. So everybody in the village is saying I'm sure to be chosen for Hatsue's husband and adopted into her family."

Soon the *Kamikaze-maru* had brought Suga Island into view to starboard, and Toshi Island to port. No matter how calm the weather, once a boat passed beyond the protection of these two islands, high-running waves would always set the boat's timbers to creaking. From this point on they saw numerous cormorants floating in the wave-troughs and, farther out to sea, the many rocks of Oki Shallows projecting up above the water.

Yasuo knitted his brows and averted his eyes from the sight of Oki Shallows, the reminder of Uta-jima's one and only humiliation. Fishing rights in these shallows, where the blood of Uta-jima's youth had been shed in ancient rivalries, had now been restored to Toshi Island.

Chiyoko and Yasuo got to their feet and, looking across the low wheel-house, waited for the shape of an island that would soon appear in the ocean before them. . . .

As always, Uta-jima rose from the level of the sea shaped like some amorphous, mysterious helmet.

The boat tilted—and the helmet seemed to tilt with it.

Chapter Eight

A day of rest from fishing seemed never to come. Finally, two days after Hiroshi left on the school excursion, the island was struck by such a storm that no boats could put out. It seemed that not one of the island's meager cherry blossoms, just then beginning to open, could escape destruction.

On the previous day an unseasonably damp wind had enveloped and clung to the sails, and at sunset a strange light had spread over the sky. A ground swell set in; the beach was aroar with incoming waves; the sea-lice and dango bugs scurried for high ground. During the night a high wind came blowing, mixed with rain, and the heavens and the sea were filled with sounds like human shrieks and shrilling fifes. . . .

Shinji listened to the voice of the storm from his pallet. It was enough to tell him the boats would not put out today. This would be too much even for braiding rope or repairing fishing tackle, perhaps too much even for the Young Men's Association rat-catching project.

Not wanting to waken his mother, whose breathing from the next pallet told him she was still asleep, Shinji thoughtfully kept still, waiting eagerly for the first grayness at the window. The house was shaking violently and the windows were rattling. Somewhere a sheet of tin fell with a great clatter. The houses on Uta-jima, the big rich houses as well as the tiny one-story houses such as Shinji's, were all built alike, with the entrance into a dirt-floored work-room, flanked by the toilet-room on the left and the kitchen on the right; and amid the wind's fury, in the pre-dawn blackness, there was a single odor that dominated the entire house, hanging quietly on the air inside—that darkish, cold, meditative odor of the toilet-room.

The window, which faced the wall of the next-door neighbor's storehouse, slowly turned gray. Shinji looked up at the pouring rain, beating upon the eaves and spreading wetly across the windowpanes. Before, he had hated days when there was no fishing, days that robbed him both of the pleasure of working and of income, but now the prospect of such a day seemed the most wonderful of festival days to him. It was a festival made glorious, not with blue skies and flags waving from poles topped with golden balls, but with a storm, raging seas, and a wind that shrieked as it came tearing through the prostrate tree-tops.

Finding it unbearable to wait, the boy leaped from bed and jerked on a pair of trousers and a black, crew-neck sweater full of holes.

A moment later his mother awakened to see the dark shadow of a man against the window, faintly lit with dawn.

"Hey! Who's there?" she shouted.

"Me."

"Oh . . . don't scare me so! Today, in weather like this, you're going fishing?"

"The boats won't be going out, but . . ."

"Well, then, why not sleep a little longer? Why, I thought it was some stranger at the window!"

The mother was not far wrong in the first thought she had had upon opening her eyes: her son did indeed seem a stranger this morning. Here he was, this Shinji who almost never opened his mouth, singing at the top of his voice and making a show of gymnastics by swinging from the door-lintel.

Not knowing the reason for her son's strange behavior and fearing he would pull the house down, his mother grumbled:

"If it's a storm outside, what else is it we've got right here inside the house?"

Countless times Shinji went to peer up at the sooty clock on the wall. With a heart unaccustomed to doubting he never wondered for an instant whether the girl would brave such a storm to keep their rendezvous. He knew nothing of that melancholy and all-too-effective way of passing time by magnifying and complicating his feelings, whether of happiness or uneasiness, through the exercise of the imagination.

When he could no longer bear the thought of waiting, Shinji flung on a rubber raincoat and went down to meet the sea. It seemed to him that only the sea would be kind enough to answer his wordless conversation.

Raging waves rose high above the breakwater, set up a tremendous roar, and then rushed on down. Because of the previous evening's storm-warning, every last boat had been pulled up much higher on the beach than usual. When the giant waves receded, the surface of the water tilted steeply; it almost seemed as if the bottom of the sea inside the harbor-works would be exposed to view.

Spray from the waves, mixed with the driving rain, struck Shinji full in the face. The sharp, fresh saltiness ran down his flushed cheeks, down the lines of his nose, and Shinji recalled the taste of Hatsue's lips.

The clouds were moving at a gallop, and even in the dark sky there was a restless fluctuation between light and dark. Once in a while, still deeper in the sky, Shinji caught glimpses of clouds charged with an opaque light, like promises of clear skies to come. But these would be effaced almost instantly.

Shinji was so intent upon the sky that a wave came right up to where he stood and wet the toe-thongs of his wooden clogs. At his feet there lay a beautiful small pink shell, apparently just washed up by the same wave.

He picked the shell up and examined it. It was perfectly formed, without even the slightest chip on its paper-thin edge. Deciding it would make a good present, he put it in his pocket.

Immediately after lunch Shinji began getting ready to go out again. Seeing him going out into the storm for a second time, the mother paused in her dish-washing to stare fixedly after him. But she did not venture to ask where he was going: there was something about her son's back that warned her to keep silent. How she regretted she had not had at least one daughter, who would always have been at home to help with the housework. . . .

Men go out fishing. They board their coasting ships and carry cargo to all sorts of ports. Women, not destined for that wide world, cook rice, draw water, gather sea-weed, and when summer comes dive into the water, down to the sea's deep bottom. Even for a mother who was a veteran among diving women this twilight world of the sea's bottom was the world of women. . . .

All this she knew. The interior of a house dark even at noon, the somber pangs of childbirth, the gloom at the bottom of the sea—these were the series of interrelated worlds in which she lived her life.

The mother remembered one of the women of the summer before last, a widow like herself, a frail woman still carrying a nursing child. The woman had come up from diving for abalone, and had suddenly fallen unconscious as she stood before the drying-fire. She had turned up the whites of her eyes, bitten her blue lips, and dropped to the ground. When her remains were cre-mated at twilight in the pine grove, the other diving women had been filled with such grief that they could not stand, but squatted on the ground, weeping.

A strange story had been told about that incident, and some of the women had become afraid to dive any more. It was said that the dead woman had been punished for having seen a fearful something at the bottom of the sea, a some-thing that humans are not meant to see.

Shinji's mother had scoffed at the story and had dived to greater and greater depths to bring up the biggest catches of the season. She had never been one to worry about unknown things. . . .

Even such recollections as these could not dent her natural cheerfulness; she felt boastful about her own good health, and the storm outside quickened her feeling of well-being, just as it had her son's.

Finishing the dishwashing, she opened wide the skirts of her kimono and sat down with her bare legs stretched out in front of her, gazing at them earnestly in the dim light from the creaking windows. There was not a single wrinkle on the sunburnt, well-ripened thighs, their wonderfully rounded flesh all but gleaming with the color of amber.

"Like this, I could still have four or five children more." But at the thought her virtuous heart became filled with contrition.

Quickly tidying her clothing, she bowed before her husband's memorial tablet.

The path the boy followed up to the lighthouse had been turned into a mountain torrent by the rain, washing away his footprints. The tops of the pine trees howled. His rubber boots made walking difficult and, as he carried no umbrella, he could feel the rain running down his close-cropped hair and into his collar. But he kept on climbing, his face to the storm. He was not defying the storm; instead, in exactly the same way that he felt a quiet happiness when surrounded by the quietness of nature, his feelings now were in complete concord with nature's present fury.

He looked down through the pine thicket at the sea, where countless whitecaps were tearing in. From time to time even the high rocks at the tip of the promontory were covered by the waves.

Passing Woman's Slope, Shinji could see the one-storied lighthouse residence kneeling in the storm, all its windows closed, its curtains drawn fast. He climbed on up the stone steps toward the lighthouse.

There was no sign of a watchman within the fast-shut watchhouse. Inside the glass doors, which streamed with driven rain and rattled ceaselessly, there stood the telescope, turned blankly toward the closed windows. There were papers scattered from the desk by the drafts, a pipe, a regulation Coast Guard cap, the calendar of a steamship company showing a gaudy painting of a new ship, and on the same wall with the calendar a pair of drafting triangles hanging nonchalantly from a nail.

Shinji arrived at the observation tower drenched to the skin. The storm was all the more fearful at such a deserted place. Here, almost at the summit of the island, with nothing to intervene between naked sky and earth, the storm could be seen reigning in supreme dominion.

The ruined building, its windows gaping wide in three directions, gave not the slightest protection against the wind. Rather, it seemed as though the tower were inviting the tempest into its rooms, and there abandoning it to the revel. The immense view of the Pacific from the second-floor windows was reduced in sweep by the rain clouds, but the way the waves, raging and ripping out their white linings on every hand, faded off into the encircling black clouds made the turbulent expanse seem instead to be boundless.

The boy went back down the outside staircase and peered into the room on the ground floor where he had come before to get his mother's firewood. It had apparently been used originally as a storehouse, and its windows were so tiny that only one of them had been broken. He saw that it offered ideal shelter. The mountain of pine needles that had been there before had apparently been carried away bale by bale until now only four or five bales remained in a far corner.

"It's like a jail," Shinji thought, noticing the moldy odor.

No sooner had he taken shelter from the storm than he was suddenly conscious of a wet-cold feeling. He sneezed hugely. Taking off his raincoat, he felt in the pockets of his trousers for the matches that life at sea had taught him always to carry with him.

Before he found the matches his fingers touched the shell he had picked up on the beach that morning. He took it out now and held it up toward the light of a window. The pink shell was gleaming lustrously, as though it might have been still wet with sea water. Satisfied, the boy returned the shell to his pocket.

He gathered dried pine needles and brushwood from a broken bale, heaped them on the cement floor, and with much difficulty succeeded in lighting one of the damp matches. Then for a time the room was completely filled with smoke, until at last the dismal smoldering broke into a tiny flame and began to flicker.

The boy took off his sodden trousers and hung them near the fire to dry. Then he sat down before the fire and clasped his knees. Now there was nothing to do but wait. . . .

Shinji waited. Without the slightest uneasiness he whiled away the time by poking his fingers into the holes in his black sweater, making them still larger.

He became lost in the sensations of his body as it gradually became warm, and in the voice of the storm outside; he surrendered himself to the euphoria created by his trusting devotion itself. The fact that he was lacking in the ability to imagine all sorts of things that might keep the girl from coming did not trouble him in the least.

And thus it was that he laid his head on his knees and fell asleep.

When Shinji opened his eyes, the blazing fire was there before him, burning as brightly as ever, as though he had only closed his eyes the moment before. But a strange, indistinct shadow was standing across the fire from him. He wondered if he was dreaming.

It was a naked girl who stood there, her head bent low, holding a white chemise to dry at the fire. Standing as she was, the chemise held down toward the fire with both hands, she was revealing the whole upper half of her body.

When he realized that this was certainly no dream, the idea occurred to Shinji that, by using just a little cunning and pretending to be still asleep, he could watch her through half-closed eyes. And yet, her body was almost too beautiful to be watched without moving at all.

Diving women are accustomed to drying their entire bodies at a fire upon coming out of the water. Hence Hatsue had apparently not given the matter a second thought upon doing so now. When she arrived at the meeting place, there the fire was, and there the boy was—fast asleep. So, making up her mind as quickly as a child, she evidently had decided to waste no time in drying her wet clothes and her wet body while the boy slept. In short, the idea that she was undressing in front of a man had never crossed her mind. She was simply undressing before a fire—because this happened to be the only fire there was, because she was wet.

If Shinji had had more experience with women, as he looked at the naked Hatsue standing there across the fire, in the storm-encircled ruins, he would have seen unmistakably that hers was the body of a virgin. Her skin, far from fair-complexioned, had been constantly bathed in sea-water and stretched smooth; and there, upon the wide expanse of a chest that had served for many long dives, two small, firm breasts turned their faces slightly away from each other, as though abashed, and lifted up two rose-colored buds. Since Shinji, fearful of being discovered, had barely opened his eyes, the girl's form remained a vague outline and, peered at through a fire that reached as high as the concrete ceiling, became almost indistinguishable from the wavering flames themselves.

But then the boy happened to blink his eyes, and for an instant the shadow of his lashes, magnified by the fire-light, moved across his cheeks.

Quick as thought, the girl hid her breasts with the white chemise, not yet completely dry, and cried out:

"Keep your eyes shut!"

The honest boy immediately clamped his eyes tightly shut. Now that he thought about it, it had certainly been wrong of him to pretend to be still sleeping. . . . But then, was it his fault that he had waked up when he did? Taking courage from this just and fair reasoning, for a second time he opened wide his black, beautiful eyes.

Completely at a loss as to what to do, the girl still had not even so much as started putting on her chemise. Again she cried out in a sharp, childlike voice:

"Keep your eyes shut!"

But the boy no longer made the slightest pretense at closing his eyes. Ever since he could remember, he had been used to seeing the women of this fishing village naked, but this was the first time he had ever seen the girl he loved naked. And yet he could not understand why, just because she was naked, a barrier should have risen between them, making difficult the everyday civilities, the matter-of-course familiarities. With the straightforwardness of youth, he rose to his feet.

The boy and girl faced each other then, separated by the flames.

The boy moved slightly to the right. The girl retreated a little to the right also. And there the fire was, between them, forever.

"What are you running away for?"

"Why, because I'm ashamed."

The boy did not say: "Then why don't you put your clothes on?" If only for a little longer, he wanted to look at her. Then, feeling he must say something, he burst out with a childish question:

"What would make you quit being ashamed?"

To this the girl gave a truly naïve answer, though a startling one:

"If you took your clothes off too, then I wouldn't be ashamed."

Now Shinji was at a complete loss. But after an instant's hesitation he began taking off his crew-neck sweater, saying not a word. Struck by the thought that Hatsue might run away while he was undressing, he kept a lookout that was scarcely broken even during the instant when the sweater passed over his face. Then his nimble hands had the sweater off and thrown aside, and there stood the naked figure of a young man—far handsomer than when dressed—wearing only a narrow loincloth, his thoughts turned so ardently upon the girl opposite him that for the moment his body had completely lost its sense of shame.

"Now you're not ashamed any more, are you?" He flung the question at her as though cross-examining a witness.

Without realizing the enormity of what she was saying, the girl gave an amazing explanation:

"Yes . . ."

"Why?"

"You—you still haven't taken everything off."

Now the sense of shame returned, and in the firelight the boy's body flushed crimson. He started to speak—and choked on the words. Then, drawing so near the fire that his fingertips were all but burned, and staring at the girl's chemise, which the flames set swaying with shadows, Shinji finally managed to speak:

"If—if you'll take that away—I will too."

Hatsue broke into a spontaneous smile. But neither she nor Shinji had the slightest idea what the meaning of her smile might be.

The white chemise in the girl's hands had been half covering her body, from breast to thigh. Now she flung it away behind her.

The boy saw her, and then, standing just as he was, like some piece of heroic sculpture, never taking his eyes from the girl's, he untied his loincloth.

At this moment the storm suddenly planted its feet wide and firmly outside the windows. All along, the wind and rain had been raging madly around the ruins with the same force as now, but in this instant the boy and girl realized the certainty of the storm's existence, realized that directly beneath the high windows the wide Pacific was shaking with everlasting frenzy.

The girl took a few steps backward. . . . There was no way out. The sooty concrete wall touched her back.

"Hatsue!" the boy cried.

"Jump across the fire to me. Come on! If you'll jump across the fire to me . . ." The girl was breathing hard, but her voice came clearly, firmly.

The naked boy did not hesitate an instant. He sprang from tiptoe and his body, shining in the flames, came flying at full speed into the fire. In the next instant he was directly in front of the girl. His chest lightly touched her breasts.

"Firm softness—this is the firm softness that I imagined the other day under that red sweater," he thought in a turmoil.

They were in each other's arms. The girl was the first to sink limply to the floor, pulling the boy after her.

"Pine needles—they hurt," the girl said.

The boy reached out for the white chemise and tried to pull it under the girl's body.

She stopped him. Her arms were no longer embracing him. She drew her knees up, crushed the chemise into a ball in her hands, thrust it down below her waist, and exactly like a child who has just thrown cupped hands over an insect in the bushes, doggedly protected her body with it.

The words which Hatsue spoke next were weighted with virtue:

"It's bad. It's bad! . . . It's bad for a girl to do that before she's married."

"You really think it's so bad?" the crestfallen boy asked, without any conviction.

"It's bad." As the girl's eyes were closed, she could speak without hesitation, in a tone of voice that seemed to be both reproving and placating. "It's bad for *now*. Because I've decided it's you I'm going to marry, and until I do, it's really bad."

Shinji had a sort of haphazard respect for moral things. And even more because he had never yet known a woman, he believed he had now penetrated to the moralistic core of woman's being. He insisted no further.

The boy's arms were still embracing the girl. They could hear each other's naked throbbing. A long kiss tortured the unsatisfied boy, but then at a certain instant this pain was transformed into a strange elation.

From time to time the dying fire crackled a little. They heard this sound and the whistling of the storm as it swept past the high windows, all mixed with the beating of their hearts. To Shinji it seemed as though this unceasing feeling of intoxication, and the confused booming of the sea outside, and the noise of the storm among the treetops were all beating with nature's violent rhythm. And as part of his emotion there was the feeling, forever and ever, of pure and holy happiness.

He moved his body away from hers. Then he spoke in a manly, composed tone of voice:

"Today on the beach I found a pretty shell and brought it for you."

"Oh, thanks—let me see it."

Getting up, Shinji went to where his clothes had fallen and began putting them on. At the same time Hatsue softly pulled on her chemise and then put on the rest of her clothes.

After they were both fully dressed, the boy brought the shell to where the girl was sitting.

"My, it *is* pretty." Delighted, the girl mirrored the flames in the smooth face of the shell. Then she held it up against her hair and said:

"It looks like coral, doesn't it? Wonder if it wouldn't even make a pretty hair ornament?"

Shinji sat down on the floor close beside the girl.

Now that they were dressed, they could kiss in comfort. . . .

When they started back, the storm still had not abated, so this time Shinji did not part from her above the lighthouse, did not take a different path out of deference to what the people in the lighthouse might think. Instead, together they followed the slightly easier path that led down past the rear of the lighthouse. Then, arm in arm, they descended the stone stairs leading from the lighthouse past the residence.

Chiyoko had come home, and by the next day was overcome with boredom. Not even Shinji came to see her. Finally a regular meeting of the etiquette class brought the village girls to the house.

There was an unfamiliar face among them. Chiyoko realized this must be the Hatsue of whom Yasuo had spoken, and she found Hatsue's rustic features even more beautiful than the islanders said they were. This was an odd virtue of Chiyoko's: although a woman with the slightest degree of self-confidence will never cease pointing out another woman's defects, Chiyoko was even more honest than a man in always recognizing anything beautiful about any woman except herself.

With nothing better to do, Chiyoko had begun studying her history of English literature. Knowing not a single one of their works, she memorized the names of a group of Victorian lady poets—Christina Georgina Rossetti, Adelaide Anne Procter, Jean Ingelow, Augusta Webster—exactly as though she were memorizing Buddhist scriptures. Rote memorization was Chiyoko's forte; even the professor's sneezes were recorded in her notes.

Her mother was constantly at her side, eager to gain new knowledge from her daughter. Going to the university had been Chiyoko's idea in the first place, but it had been her mother's enthusiastic support that had overcome her father's reluctance.

Her thirst for knowledge whetted by a life of moving from lighthouse to lighthouse, from remote island to remote island, the mother always pictured her daughter's life as an ideal dream. Never once did her eyes perceive her daughter's little inner unhappiness.

On the morning of the storm both mother and daughter slept late. The storm had been building up since the evening before, and they had kept vigil most of the night with the lighthouse-keeper, who took his responsibilities most seriously. Very much contrary to their usual ways, their midday meal was also their breakfast. And after the table had been cleared, the three of them passed the time quietly indoors, shut in by the storm.

Chiyoko began to long for Tokyo. She longed for the Tokyo where, even on such a stormy day, the automobiles went back and forth as usual, the elevators went up and down, and the streetcars bustled along. There in the city almost all nature had been put into uniform, and the little power of nature that remained was an enemy. Here on the island, however, the islanders enthusiastically entered into an alliance with nature and gave it their full support.

Bored with studying, Chiyoko pressed her face against a windowpane and gazed out at the storm that kept her shut up in the house. The storm was a monotone of dullness. The roar of the waves came as persistently as the garrulity of a drunk man.

For some reason Chiyoko recalled the gossip about a classmate who had been seduced by the man she was in love with. The girl had loved the man for his gentleness and refinement, and had even said so openly. After that night, so the story went, she loved him for his violence and willfulness—but this she never breathed to anyone. . . .

At this moment Chiyoko caught sight of Shinji descending the storm-swept stairs—with Hatsue snuggled against him.

Chiyoko was convinced of the advantages of a face as ugly as she believed her own to be: once such a face hardened in its mold, it could hide emotions far more cleverly than could a beautiful one. What she regarded as ugly, however, was actually only the plaster-of-Paris mask of self-preoccupied virginity.

She turned away from the window. Beside the sunken hearth her mother was sewing and her father was silently smoking his New Life. Outdoors was the storm; indoors, domesticity. Nowhere was there anyone to heed Chiyoko's unhappiness.

Chiyoko returned to her desk and opened the English book. The words had no meaning; there was nothing but the lines of type running down the page. Between the lines the vision of birds wheeling high and low flickered in her eyes. They were sea gulls.

"When I returned to the island," Chiyoko told herself "and made that bet about a sea gull flying over Toba's tower—*this* is what the sign meant. . . ."

Chapter Nine

A message came by express delivery from Hiroshi on his trip. It was written on a picture postcard showing Kyoto's famous Shimizu Temple and was impressed with a large, purple souvenir seal. If he had sent it by ordinary mail, he himself would probably have been back on the island before it arrived. Even before reading it, his mother became angry, saying that Hiroshi had been extravagant to pay all that extra postage, that children nowadays didn't know the value of money.

Hiroshi's closely written card was all about seeing his first motion picture, with not so much as a word about the famous scenic spots and historic places he was seeing:

"The first night in Kyoto they let us do as we pleased, so Sochan, Katchan, and I went straight to a big moviehouse in the neighborhood. It was really swell—just like a palace. But the seats seemed awful narrow and hard, and when we tried to sit on them it was just like perching on a chicken roost. Our bottoms hurt so that we couldn't get comfortable at all.

"After a few minutes the man behind us yelled: 'Down in front! Down in front!' We were already sitting down, so we thought this was funny. But then the man very kindly showed us what to do. He said they were folding seats, and that if we'd turn them down, they'd become chairs. We all scratched our heads, knowing we'd made a foolish mistake. And when we put them down, sure enough they were seats soft enough for the Emperor himself to sit on. I told myself that some day I'd like to have Mother sit on these seats too."

As Shinji read the card aloud for his mother, that last sentence brought tears to her eyes. She put the card up on the god-shelf and made Shinji kneel down with her to pray that the storm two days before had not interfered with Hiroshi's excursion and that nothing would happen to him before he came home the day after tomorrow.

After a minute, as though the thought had just occurred to her, she started heaping Shinji with abuse, going on about how terrible his reading and writing were and how much smarter Hiroshi was than he. What she called Hiroshi's smartness was nothing more or less than his ability to make her shed happy tears.

She wasted no time in hurrying off to show the postcard at the homes of Hiroshi's friends Sochan and Katchan. Later that evening, when she and Shinji went to the public bath, she met the postmaster's wife, and she got down on her bare knees in the midst of the steam to bow and thank her because the express delivery had been made in such good order.

Shinji soon finished his bathing and waited before the bathhouse entrance for his mother to come out of the women's side. The carved and painted wood under the eaves of the bathhouse was faded and peeling where the steam came curling out. The night was warm, the sea calm.

Shinji noticed someone standing a few yards farther along the street, his back turned in Shinji's direction, apparently looking up toward the eaves of one of the houses. The man stood with both hands in his pockets and was beating time on the flagstones with his wooden clogs. In the twilight Shinji could see that he was wearing a brown leather jacket. On Uta-jima it was not everyone who could afford a leather jacket, and Shinji was sure this was Yasuo.

Just as Shinji was about to call out to him, Yasuo happened to turn around. Shinji smiled. But Yasuo only stared back at him, the blank expression on his face never changing, and then turned away again.

Shinji did not particularly take this as a slight, but it did seem a bit odd. Just then his mother came out of the bathhouse, and the boy walked along home with her, silent as usual.

The day before, after the boats had returned from a day of fishing in the fine weather that followed the storm, Chiyoko had gone to see Yasuo. She said she had come to the village shopping with her mother and had decided to drop by, and explained her coming to Yasuo's place alone by saying her mother was visiting the home of the head of the Co-operative, which was near by.

Chiyoko's version of how she had seen Shinji and Hatsue coming down together from the deserted mountain, clinging to each other, certainly did nothing to make the event less compromising; and her story was a staggering blow to Yasuo's pride. He brooded about it all night. And the next night, when Shinji happened to see him, what he was actually doing was reading the roster displayed under the eaves of a house beside the steep street that ran through the center of the village.

Uta-jima had a meager water supply, which reached its lowest point about the time of the old-calendar New Year, leading to endless quarrels over water rights. The village's sole source of water was a narrow stream beside the cobbled street that tumbled in flights of steps down through the center of the village. During the wet season or after a heavy rain the stream would become a muddy torrent, on whose banks the village women would do their laundry, chattering together noisily. Here too the children would hold the launching ceremonies for their hand-carved warships. But during the dry season the stream would all but become a dried-up marsh, without strength enough to wash away even the slightest bit of rubbish.

The stream was fed by a spring. Perhaps it was because the rains that fell on the peaks of the island all filtered down to this spring, but whatever the cause, this was the only such spring on the island. Hence the village government had long since been given the power of determining the order in which the villagers should draw their water, the order being rotated each week.

Only the lighthouse filtered rain water and stored it in a tank; all the other houses on the island depended solely upon this spring, and each family in its turn had to put up with the inconvenience of being assigned the midnight hours for water drawing. But after a few weeks even a midnight turn would gradually move up the roster to the convenient hours of early morning. Drawing water was women's work.

So Yasuo was looking up at the water-drawing roster, posted where the most people passed. He found the name Miyata written precisely under the 2 A.M. column. This was Hatsue's turn.

Yasuo clicked his tongue. He wished it were still octopus season, as the boats did not put out quite so early in the morning then. During the squid season, which had now arrived, the boats had to reach the fishing grounds in the Irako Channel by the crack of dawn. So every household was up preparing breakfast by three o'clock at the latest, and impatient houses were sending up smoke from their cooking fires even earlier.

Even so, this was preferable to next week, when Hatsue's turn would come at three o'clock. . . . Yasuo swore to himself that he would have Hatsue before the fishing boats put out the next morning.

Standing looking at the roster, he had just made this firm resolve when he saw Shinji standing before the men's entrance to the bathhouse. The sight of Shinji annoyed him so that he completely forgot his usual punctilious ways and turned his back to hurry home.

Reaching home, Yasuo glanced out of the corner of his eye into the sitting-room, where his father and elder brother were still serving each other their evening saké and listening to a ballad singer on the radio, which was resounding throughout the house. Yasuo went straight on to his own room on the second floor, where he angrily puffed on a cigarette.

Because of his experience and way of thinking, Yasuo saw the matter thus: As Shinji had seduced Hatsue, he had certainly been no virgin. All the time he had been coming to the meetings of the Young Men's Association, sitting there innocently clasping his knees, smiling and listening attentively to the others' talk, putting on his childish airs—all that time he'd been having women on the sly. The damn little fox!

And yet, given the honesty of Shinji's face, even Yasuo simply could not believe him capable of having won the girl by deceit. The inevitable conclusion then—and this was the most unbearable thought of all—was that Shinji had had his way with the girl fairly and squarely, with complete honesty.

In bed that night Yasuo kept pinching his thighs to keep from going to sleep. But this was not really necessary: the animosity he felt toward Shinji and the jealousy he felt at Shinji's having stolen a march on him were enough to keep him awake of themselves.

Yasuo was the proud and always bragging owner of a watch with a luminous dial. Tonight he had left this on his wrist and had slipped into bed still wearing his jacket and trousers. From time to time he put the watch to his ear, looking often at its luminously glowing face. In Yasuo's opinion the mere ownership of such a wonderful watch made him by rights a favorite with the women.

At twenty minutes past one Yasuo stole out of the house. In the dead of night the sound of the waves could be plainly heard, and the moon was shining brightly. The village was silent.

There were only four street lamps on the island—one at the jetty, two along the steep street through the center of the village, and one on the mountain beside the spring. Except for the ferryboat there were nothing but fishing-boats in the harbor, so there were no masthead lights to enliven the night there, and every last light in the houses had been turned off. Moreover, here in a fishing village where the roofs were made of tile or galvanized iron, there were none of those rows of thick, black roofs that seem so imposing at night in a farm village; there was none of the solemn weightiness of thatch to intimidate and hold back the night.

Yasuo quickly mounted the sloping street to the right, his sneakers making not so much as a footfall. He passed through the playground of the elementary school, enclosed in rows of cherry trees, their blossoms half-open. This playground was a recent addition to the school, and the cherry trees had been blown over by the storm; its trunk showed dead-black against a moonlit sand pile.

Yasuo climbed the stone steps beside the stream until he reached a spot where he could hear the sound of the spring. In the light of the solitary street lamp he could see the outlines of the spring.

Clear water flowed out from between moss-covered rocks, into a stone cistern, and then brimmed over one edge of the stone. The stone there was covered with glossy moss, and it seemed, not that water was flowing down over the moss, but that the moss had been thickly coated with some beautiful transparent enamel. From somewhere in the thicket around the spring an owl was hooting.

Yasuo hid himself behind the lamp-post. There was a tiny flutter of wings taking flight. Yasuo leaned against a huge beech tree and waited, trying to outstare the luminous eyes of his watch.

Soon it was two o'clock and Yasuo caught sight of Hatsue coming across the schoolyard, carrying a water bucket on either end of a wooden pole across her shoulders. Her outline was sharply etched in the moonlight.

Although a woman's body is ill-suited for midnight labor, on Uta-jima men and women alike, rich and poor, had to perform their own tasks. Robust Hatsue, hardened by the life of a diving woman, came up the stone steps without the slightest difficulty, swinging the empty pails to and fro and giving rather the merry appearance of actually enjoying her untimely work.

At long last Hatsue had put her buckets down beside the spring. This was the moment when Yasuo had intended to jump out at her, but now he hesitated and decided to hold back until she had finished drawing her water. Preparing to leap out when the moment came, he reached up and caught hold of a high branch with his left hand. Then he stood perfectly still, imagining himself to be a stone statue. He watched the girl's strong hands, red and slightly frostbitten, as she filled the buckets, splashing the water about with lush sounds, and the sight quickened his imagination with delightfully carnal pictures of her healthy young body.

All the time the luminous watch of which Yasuo was so proud, strapped above the hand with which he was holding onto the branch of the beech tree, was giving off its phosphorescent glow, faintly but distinctly ticking away the seconds. This aroused a swarm of hornets in the nest fastened to this same branch and greatly excited their curiosity.

One of the hornets came flying timidly toward the wrist watch, only to find that this strange beetle that emitted a shimmering light and chirruped methodically was protected within slippery, cold armour of glass. Perhaps out of disappointment, the hornet turned its stinger toward the skin at Yasuo's wrist— and drove it in with all its might.

Yasuo gave a shout.

Hatsue straightened up and turned in his direction, but she did not even so much as scream. Instead, in a flash she had the ropes off the carrying pole and, holding the pole slantwise across her body, took up a posture of defense.

Even Yasuo had to admit he must have been a sorry sight in Hatsue's eyes. She retreated a step or two before him, keeping the same defensive posture.

Yasuo decided it would be better to turn it all off as a joke. He broke into foolish laughter and said:

"Hey! I guess I scared you. You thought I was a hobgoblin, didn't you?"

"Why, it's Brother Yasuo!"

"I thought I'd hide here and give you a scare."

"But—at this time of night?"

The girl did not yet realize how very attractive she was. Perhaps she might have if she had thought about it deeply enough, but just now she accepted

Yasuo's explanation that he had actually hidden here for no other reason than to frighten her.

In an instant, taking advantage of her trustfulness, Yasuo snatched the pole away from her and caught her by the right wrist. The leather of Yasuo's jacket was making creaking sounds.

Yasuo had finally recovered his poise. He stood glaring at Hatsue. Now he was quite self-possessed and, intending to win the girl fairly, he fell unconsciously into an imitation of the open and aboveboard manner he imagined Shinji must have used on a similar occasion.

"All right," he said reasonably, "now will you listen to what I've got so say? You'll be sorry if you don't. So you'd better listen—unless you want everybody to know about you and Shinji."

Hatsue's face was flushed and she was breathing hard.

"Let go of my arm! What do you mean—about me and Shinji?"

"Don't act so innocent. As though you haven't been playing around with Shinji! You really put one over on me."

"Don't say such ridiculous things. I haven't done any such thing."

"Me, I know all about it. What was it you did with Shinji up on the mountain the other day in the storm? . . . Hey! just look at her blush! . . . so now you're going to do the same thing with me. Come on! Come on!"

"Get away! Get away from me!" Hatsue struggled, trying to escape.

Yasuo would not let her go. She would be sure to tell her father if she got away now before anything happened. But afterwards—then she wouldn't tell a soul. Yasuo was hopelessly addicted to the pulp magazines, which came from the city, with their frequent confessions of girls who had been "seduced." What a grand feeling it was to be able to do this to a girl and yet be sure that she could never tell anyone about it!

Yasuo finally had Hatsue pinned to the ground beside the spring. One of the buckets had been knocked over and the water was running over the moss-covered earth. The light of the street lamp showed Hatsue's nostrils quivering and her wide-open eyes flashing. Her hair was half in the spilled water.

Suddenly Hatsue pursed her lips and spat full on Yasuo's chin.

This aroused his passion all the more and, feeling her heaving breasts beneath him, he thrust his face against her cheek.

At that moment he gave a shout and jumped to his feet: the hornet had stung him again, this time on the nape of the neck.

Angered beyond endurance, he tried wildly to catch the hornet, and while he was dancing about, Hatsue went running toward the stone steps.

Yasuo was in a panic of confusion. He was fully occupied with the hornet, and yet still managed somehow to satisfy his urge to recapture Hatsue, but from one moment to the next he had no idea which action he was performing, nor in what order. At any rate, catch Hatsue again he did.

No sooner had he forced her ripening body down again onto the moss than the persistent hornet lit, this time on the seat of Yasuo's trousers, and drove its stinger deeply into the flesh of a buttock.

Hatsue was gaining experience in the art of escape and, when Yasuo leaped up, this time she fled to the far side of the spring. As she dived into the grove of trees and ran to hide behind a clump of ferns, she caught sight of a big rock. Holding the rock over her head in both hands, she finally got her breath and looked down across the spring.

As a matter of fact, until that moment Hatsue had not known what god it was who had come to her rescue. But now, as she suspiciously watched Yasuo's mad cavortings on the other side of the spring, she realized it was all the doing of a clever hornet. Yasuo's hands clawed the air and she could see, just at their fingertips, full in the light of the street lamp, the flashing of little, golden-colored wings.

When he at last realized he had driven the hornet away, Yasuo stood looking blank and wiped the sweat off his face with his handcloth. Then he looked around for Hatsue. Seeing no trace of her, he made a trumpet with his hands and nervously called her name in a low voice.

Hatsue deliberately rustled some ferns with her toe.

"Come on down from up there, won't you? I promise not to do anything else."

"No, I won't."

"Come on down—please."

He started to climb up, and Hatsue brandished the stone. Yasuo drew back.

"Hey, what're you doing! Watch out—that's dangerous. . . . What can I do to get you to come down?"

Yasuo would have liked to run away without more ceremony, but his fear that she would tell her father kept him wheedling:

". . . Please! I'll do anything you say, just so you come on down. . . . I suppose you're going to tell your father on me, aren't you?"

There was no answer.

"Come on, please don't tell your father? I'll do anything you say if only you won't tell. . . . What do you want me to do?"

"Well, if you'll draw the water for me and carry it all the way home . . ."

"Really?"

"Really."

"All right, I'll sure do it then. That Uncle Teru is really something to be afraid of!"

Then Yasuo silently set about his task—earnestly, wholeheartedly, making a truly ridiculous sight. He refilled the bucket that had been overturned, put the rope handles of the buckets on the pole, shouldered the pole, and began walking. . . .

After a moment Yasuo glanced back and saw that Hatsue had come down from the grove without his knowing it and was following along about two yards behind him. She did not so much as smile. When she saw him stop walking, she stopped too, and when he started on down the steps again, she started too.

The village was still buried in sleep, its roofs bathed in moonlight. But as they descended the stone stairs toward the village, step by step, they could hear rising up to them the crowing of cocks from all sides, a sign that the dawn was near.

Chapter Ten

Shinji's brother returned home to the island. The mothers were waiting on the jetty to welcome their sons. There was a drizzling rain and the open sea was invisible. The ferryboat was only a hundred yards from the jetty when its shape came into view through the mist.

In the same breath each mother called the name of her own son. Now they could plainly see the caps and handkerchiefs being waved from the deck.

The boat had arrived, but even when they were ashore, face to face with their mothers, these middle-school boys only smiled a little and went right on playing around among themselves. They all disliked showing affection for their mothers in each other's presence.

Even after he was at his own home, Hiroshi was still too excited to settle down. About all he could tell of his trip were incidents such as the morning he had been so sleepy because one of his friends had been afraid to go to the toilet by himself the night before and had pounded Hiroshi awake in the middle of the night to go with him. But not a word did Hiroshi have for all the famous historic spots they had visited.

Certainly Hiroshi had brought back some deep impressions from his trip, but he did not know how to put them into words. He would try to think of something to say, and all he could recall would be something like the time, already a year or so ago, when he had had such fun waxing a spot on the corridor floor at school and seeing one of the women teachers slip on it and fall. Those gleaming streetcars and automobiles that had come upon him so suddenly, flashed by, and disappeared, those towering buildings and neon lights that had so amazed him—where were they now?

Here at home, looking just the same as they had before he had gone away, there were still the same old cupboard, wall clock, Buddhist altar, dining-table, dressing-table—and the same old mother. There were the cookstove and the dirty straw mats. These things could understand him even without words. And yet all of them, including even his mother, were at him to tell them about his travels.

Hiroshi finally calmed down about the time Shinji came home from the day's fishing. After supper he opened his travel diary and gave his mother and brother a perfunctory account of his trip. Satisfied, they ceased questioning him about the excursion.

Everything was back to normal. His became again an existence in which everything was understood without the need for words. The cupboard, the wall clock, his mother, his brother, the old sooty cookstove, the sea's roaring . . . folded in these familiar arms, Hiroshi slept soundly.

Hiroshi's summer vacation was nearing its end. So every day from the moment he got up until he went to bed he was playing with all his might.

The island abounded in places to play. Hiroshi and his friends had finally seen the Western movies that until that time they had only heard about, and the new game of cowboys and Indians had now become a great favorite with them. The sight of smoke rising from a forest fire around Motoura, on Shima Peninsula across the sea, inevitably reminded them of signal fires rising from some Indian stronghold.

The cormorants of Uta-jima were birds of passage, and by this time of year they were vanishing one by one. All over the island the songs of nightingales were now frequently heard. The steep pass leading down to the middle school was known as Red Nose Pass because of its effect on the noses of passers-by in the winter, when it received every blast that blew, but now, no matter how cool the day, the breezes there would not even so much as turn a nose pink.

Benten Promontory, at the southern tip of the island, provided the boys with their Western locale. The western side of the promontory was entirely of limestone, and it led finally to the entrance of a cave, one of the most mysterious spots on Uta-jima.

The entrance to the cave was small, only about a yard and a half wide and two feet high, but the winding passageway leading into the interior gradually widened out into a three-tiered cavern. Until that point the passageway was truly black, but a strange half-light wavered within the cavern proper. This was because the cave actually went completely through the promontory to an invisible opening on the eastern side, where the sea entered, rising and falling at the bottom of a deep shaft in the rock.

Candles in hand, the gang entered the cave. Calling "Watch out!" and "Be careful!" to each other, they went crawling through the dark passageway. They could see each other's faces floating on the darkness, tinted with grimness in the flickering candlelight, and they thought how wonderful they would look in this light if only they had the unshaven beards of young toughs.

The gang was made up of Hiroshi, Sochan, and Katchan. They were on their way to search for Indian treasure deep in the farthest recesses of the cavern. Sochan was in the lead, and when they came out into the cavern, where they could at last stand erect, his head was splendidly covered with thickly woven cobwebs.

"Hey! look at you!" Hiroshi and Katchan chorused. "Your hair's all decorated. You can be the chieftain."

They stood their three candles up beneath a Sanskrit inscription some unknown person had carved long ago on one of the moss-covered walls.

The sea, ebbing and flowing in the shaft at the eastern end of the cave, roared fiercely as it dashed against the rocks. The sound of the surging waves was completely different from that to which they were accustomed outside. It was a seething sound that echoed off the limestone walls of the cavern, the reverberations overlapping each other until the entire cave was aroar and seemed to be pitching and swaying. Shudderingly they recalled the legend that between the sixteenth and eighteenth days of the sixth moon seven pure-white sharks were supposed to appear out of nowhere within that shaft to the sea.

In this game the boys changed their parts at will, shifting between the roles of enemies and friends with the greatest of ease. Sochan had been made an Indian chief because of the cobwebs in his hair, and the other two were frontier guards, implacable enemies of all Indians, but now, wanting to ask the chief why the waves echoed so frighteningly, they suddenly became his two loyal braves.

Sochan understood the change immediately and seated himself with great dignity on a rock beneath the candles.

"O Chief, what terrible sound is this that we hear?"

"This, my children," said Sochan in solemn tones, "this is the god showing his anger."

"And what can we do to appease the god's anger?" Hiroshi asked.

"Well, now, let me see. . . . Yes, the only thing to do is to make him an offering and then pray."

So they took the rice crackers and bean-jam buns that they had either received or filched from their mothers, arranged them on a sheet of newspaper, and ceremonially placed them on a rock overlooking the shaft.

Chief Sochan walked between the two braves, advancing with pomp to the altar, where after prostrating himself on the limestone floor he raised both arms high, chanted a curious, impromptu incantation, and then prayer, bending the upper half of his body back and forth. Behind the chieftain Hiroshi and Katchan went through the same genuflections. The cold surface of the stone pressed through their trousers and touched their kneecaps, and all the while Hiroshi and the others felt themselves in very truth to be characters in a movie.

Fortunately, the god's wrath seemed to have been placated, and the roar of the waves became a little quieter. So they sat in a circle and ate the offerings of rice crackers and bean-jam buns from the altar. The food tasted ten times more delicious than usual.

Just then a still more tremendous roar sounded, and a spray of water flung itself high out of the shaft. In the gloom the sudden spray looked like a white phantom; the waters set the cavern to rumbling and swaying; and it seemed as though the sea were looking for a chance to snatch even these three Indians, seated in a circle within the stone room, and pull them to its depths.

In spite of themselves, Hiroshi, Sochan, and Katchan were afraid, and when a stray gust of wind blew out of nowhere, fluttering the flames of the candles beneath the Sanskrit inscription and finally blowing one out altogether, their fear grew still stronger. But the three of them were always trying to outdo each other in displays of bravery; so, with the cheerful instinct of all boys, they quickly hid their fear under the guise of playing the game.

Hiroshi and Katchan became two cowardly Indian braves, trembling with fear.

"Oh! oh! I'm afraid! I'm afraid! O Chief, the god is terribly angry. What could have made him so angry? Tell us, O Chief."

Sochan sat on a throne of stone, trembling and shaking majestically like the chieftain he was. Pressed for an answer, he recalled the gossip that had been secretly whispered about the island during the past few days and, without any evil purpose, decided to make use of it. He cleared his throat and spoke:

"It is because of an immorality. It is because of an unrighteousness."

"Immorality?" asked Hiroshi. "What do you mean?"

"Don't you know, Hiroshi? I mean what your brother Shinji did to Miyata's daughter Hatsue—I mean *omeko*—that's what. And that's what the god is angry about."

Hearing his brother mentioned and feeling something disgraceful was being said about him, Hiroshi flared out at the chieftain in a rage:

"What's that you say my brother did with Sister Hatsue? What do you mean by *omeko*?"

"Don't you even know that? It means when a boy and a girl sleep together!"

Actually, Sochan himself knew little more about the word than this. But he knew how to smear his explanation thoroughly with insulting colors, and in a fit of rage Hiroshi went flying at Sochan.

Before he realized it, Sochan felt his shoulders grabbed and his cheek slapped. But the scuffle ended disappointingly soon: when Sochan was knocked against the wall the two remaining candles fell to the ground and went out.

In the cavern there remained only the dim light, barely sufficient for them to see each other's faces vaguely. Hiroshi and Sochan were still facing each other, breathing hard, but they gradually realized what danger they were inviting by fighting in such a spot.

Katchan intervened, saying:

"Stop fighting! Can't you see it's dangerous here?"

So they struck matches, found their candles, and went crawling out of the cave, saying practically nothing. . . .

By the time they had scrambled up the cliff, bathed in the bright light of outdoors, and reached the ridge of the promontory, they were again as good friends as ever, seeming to have forgotten all about their fight of a little while before. They walked the narrow path along the ridge of the promontory singing:

> Along the Five League Beach of Benten-Hachijo,
> And all along the Garden Beach . . .

This Five League Beach was the most beautiful stretch of coastline on the island, lying along the western side of Benten Promontory. Halfway along the beach towered a huge rock called Hachijo Isle, as tall as a two-storied house, and, just now, among the rank-growing vines on its summit, there were four or five playful urchins, waving their hands and shouting something.

The three boys waved back in reply and walked on along the path. Here and there in the soft grass among the pine trees there were patches of milk vetch blooming red.

"Look! the seining boats!" Katchan pointed to the sea off the eastern shore of the promontory.

On that shore the Garden Beach embraced a lovely little cove, and at its mouth there were now three seining boats floating motionless, waiting for the tide. These were the boats that manipulated the drag-nets as they were pulled along the ocean floor by larger vessels.

Hiroshi said "Look!" also and, together with his friends, squinted out over the dazzling sea, but the words Sochan had spoken earlier still weighed on his spirit, seeming to become heavier and heavier as time passed.

At suppertime Hiroshi returned home with an empty stomach. Shinji was not yet home and his mother was alone, feeding brushwood into the cookstove. There was the sound of the crackling wood and the windlike sound of the fire inside the stove, and it was only at times like this that delicious smells erased the stench of the toilet.

"Mother," Hiroshi said, lying spread-eagled on the straw matting.

"What?"

"What's *omeko*? Somebody said that's what Shinji did to Hatsue. What'd they mean?"

Before Hiroshi realized it, his mother had left the stove and was sitting straight beside the spot where he lay. Her eyes were flashing strangely, flashing through some fallen strands of hair to give her a frightening look.

"Hiroshi—you—where'd you hear that? Who said such a thing?"

"Sochan."

"Don't you ever say that again! You mustn't even say that to your brother. If you do, it'll be many a day before I give you anything to eat again. Do you hear what I say?"

The mother took a very tolerant view of young people's amorous affairs. And even during the diving season, when everybody stood about the drying-fire gossiping, she held her tongue. But when it came to its being her own son's affair that was the subject of malicious gossip, then there was a motherly duty that she would have to perform.

That night, after Hiroshi was asleep, the mother leaned close to Shinji's ear and spoke in a low, firm voice:

"Do you know people are spreading bad stories about you and Hatsue?"

Shinji shook his head and blushed. His mother too was embarrassed, but she pressed the point with unwavering frankness.

"Did you sleep with her?"

Again Shinji shook his head.

"Then you've not done a thing that people could talk about? Are you telling me the truth?"

"Yes, I've told you the truth."

"All right, then there's nothing for me to say. But do be careful—people are always minding other people's business."

But the situation did not take a turn for the better. The following evening Shinji's mother went to a meeting of the Ape-god Society, the women's one and only club, and, the moment she appeared, everyone stopped talking, looking as though they had just had a wet blanket thrown over them. Obviously they had been gossiping.

The next evening, when Shinji went to the Young Men's Association, flinging the door open as casually as always, he found a group of youths gathered around the desk, eagerly discussing something beneath the glare of the unshaded electric bulb. When they caught sight of Shinji they fell silent for a moment. There was nothing but the sound of the sea floating in to fill the bleak room, seemingly empty of all human life.

As usual, Shinji sat down against the wall, wrapped his arms around his knees, and said not a word. Thereupon everyone began talking again in their usual noisy way, about a different subject, and Yasuo, the president, who had come to the meeting strangely early today, greeted Shinji from across the desk in a hail-fellow-well-met way. Shinji returned the greeting with an unsuspecting smile.

A few days later, while they were eating their lunch on the *Taihei-maru* and resting from fishing, Ryuji spoke up as though unable to contain himself any longer:

"Brother Shin, it really makes my blood boil—the way Yasuo is going around saying such bad things about you—"

"Is he?" Shinji smiled and kept a manly silence.

The boat was gently rolling on the spring waves.

Suddenly Jukichi, usually so taciturn, broke into the conversation:

"I know. I know. That Yasuo is jealous. The scamp's nothing but a big fool, sticking up his nose because of his father. He makes me sick. So now Shinji too has become a great ladies' man and Yasuo's burned up with jealousy. Don't pay any attention to what they say, Shinji. If there's any trouble, I'm on your side."

Thus the rumor which Chiyoko had originated and Yasuo had broadcast came to be whispered persistently at every crossroads in the village. And yet it still had not reached the ears of Hatsue's father. Then one night there occurred the incident that the village would not tire of talking about for months to come. It took place at the public bathhouse.

Even the richest houses in the village did not have their own baths, and on this night Terukichi Miyata went to the public bath as usual. He brushed through the curtain at the entrance with a haughty toss of the head, ripped off his clothes as though plucking a fowl, and flung them toward a wicker basket. His singlet and sash missed the basket and scattered themselves across the floor. Clicking his tongue loudly, he picked the garments up with his toes and threw them in the basket. It was an awesome sight to those who were watching, but this was one of the few opportunities left for Hatsue's father to give public proof that, old though he was, his vigor was undiminished.

Actually, his aged nudity was a marvel to behold. His gold-and-copper-colored limbs showed no sign of slackness, and above his piercing eyes and stubborn forehead his white hair bristled wildly like the mane of a lion. His chest was a ruddy red from many years of heavy drinking, providing an impressive contrast for his white hair. His bulging muscles had become hardened through long disuse, reinforcing the impression of a crag that has become all the more precipitous under the pounding of the waves.

It might be better to say that Terukichi was the personification of all Utajima's toil and determination and ambition and strength. Full of the somewhat uncouth energy of a man who had raised his family from nothing to wealth in a single generation, he was also narrow-minded enough never to have accepted any public office in the village, a fact that made him all the more respected by the leading people of the village. The uncanny accuracy of his weather predictions, his matchless experience in matters of fishing and navigation, and the great pride he took in knowing all the history and traditions of the island were often offset by his uncompromising stubbornness, his ludicrous pretensions, and his pugnacity, which abated not a whit with the years. But in any case he was an old man who, while still living, could act like a bronze statue erected to his own memory—and without appearing ridiculous.

He slid open the glass door leading from the dressingroom into the bath.

The bathroom was fairly crowded, and through the clouds of steam there appeared the vague outlines of people moving about. The ceiling resounded with the sounds of water, the light tapping noises of wooden basins, and laughing conversations; the room was filled with abundant hot water and a feeling of release after the day's labor.

Terukichi never rinsed his body before entering the pool. Now as always he walked in long, dignified strides directly from the door to the pool and, without further ado, thrust his legs into the water. It made no difference to him how hot the water might be. Terukichi had no more interest in such things as the possible effect of heat upon his heart and the blood vessels in his brain than he had in, say, perfume or neckties.

Even though their faces got splashed with water, when the bathers realized it was Terukichi they nodded to him courteously. Terukichi immersed himself up to his arrogant chin.

There were two young fishermen who were washing themselves beside the pool and had not noticed Terukichi's arrival. In loud voices they went right on with their unrestrained gossip about Terukichi.

"Uncle Teru Miyata really must be in his second childhood. He doesn't even know his girl's become a cracked pitcher."

"That Shinji Kubo—didn't he pull a fast one though? While everybody was thinking he was such a kid, there he went and stole her right from under Uncle Teru's nose."

The people in the pool were fidgety and kept their eyes turned away from Terukichi.

Terukichi was boiling red, but his face was outwardly composed as he got out of the pool. Taking a wooden basin in each hand, he went and filled them from the cold-water tank. Then he walked over to the two youths, poured the icy water over their heads without warning, and kicked them in the back.

The boys, their eyes half closed with soap, immediately started to strike back. But then they realized it was Terukichi they were up against and hesitated.

The old man next caught them both by the scruff of the neck, and, even though their soapy skin was slippery under his fingers, dragged them to the edge of the pool. There he gave them a tremendous shove, burying their heads in the hot water. Still grasping their necks tightly in his big hands, the old man shook the two heads in the water and knocked them together, just as though he were rinsing out laundry.

Then, to top it all, without even washing himself, Terukichi stalked from the room with his long strides, not giving so much as a glance at the backsides of the other bathers, who had now risen to their feet and were left staring after him in blank amazement.

Chapter Eleven

While they were eating their lunch the next day on the *Taihei-maru*, the master opened his tobacco pouch and took out a piece of paper folded very small. Grinning broadly, he held it out to Shinji. But when Shinji reached for it, Jukichi said:

"Now listen—if I give you this, will you promise not to start loafing around after you've read it?"

"I'm not that sort of fellow," Shinji replied definitely and to the point.

"All right, it's a man's promise. . . . This morning when I was passing Uncle Teru's house, Hatsue came trotting out and pressed this note tight in my hand. She didn't say a word and went right back inside. I was tickled to think of getting a love letter at my age, but then I opened it, and how should it begin but 'Dear Shinji'! 'You old fool,' I told myself, and I was just about to tear it up and throw it in the ocean. But then I told myself that would be a shame, so I brought it along for you."

Shinji took the note, while both the master and Ryuji laughed.

The thin paper had been folded many times into a small pellet, and Shinji opened it gingerly, careful not to tear it in his thick, knobby fingers. Tobacco dust sifted onto his hands from the folds. She had started writing on the note-paper with ink, but after a few lines her fountain pen had apparently run dry and she had continued with a faint pencil. Written in a childish hand, the note said:

"*. . . Last night at the bath Father heard some very bad gossip about us and became terribly angry and commanded that I must never see Shinji-san again. No matter how much I explained, it was no use, not with Father's being the kind of man he is. He says I must never go out of the house from the time the fishing-boats come back in the afternoon until after they've gone out in the morning. He says he'll get the lady next door to draw water for us when our turn comes. So there's nothing I can do. I'm so miserable, so very miserable I* *can't stand it. And he says that on the days when the boats don't go out he'll be right at my side and never take his eyes off me.*

"How will I ever be able to see Shinji-san again? Please think of some way for us to meet. I'm afraid for us to send letters by mail because the old post-master would know all about it. So every day I'll write a letter and stick it under the lid on the water jar in front of our kitchen. Please put your replies in the same place. But it would be dangerous for you to come here yourself to get the letters, so please get some friend you trust to come for you. I've been on the island such a short time that I don't know anybody I can really trust.

"Oh, Shinji-san, let us go on truly, with strong hearts! Every day I will be praying before the memorial tablets of my mother and brother that no accident will befall Shinji-san. I'm sure that they in heaven will understand how I feel."

As Shinji read the note the expression on his face alternated, like sunshine and shadow, between the sorrow of being separated from Hatsue and the joy of having this proof of her affection for him.

Just as Shinji fiinished reading the note, Jukichi snatched it out of his hands, as though this were only the rightful due of a bearer of love messages, and read it through. Not only did he read it aloud for Ryuji's benefit, but he also read it in his own unique, ballad-chanting style. Shinji knew that Jukichi always read the newspaper aloud to himself in this same chanting tone and that he was using it now without the slightest malice, but still it hurt to have such a travesty made of those earnest words, written by the girl he loved.

As a matter of fact, Jukichi was sincerely moved by the letter and, during the reading, he heaved many a big sigh and threw in many an interjection. When he was done he gave his opinion in the same powerful voice he used to give fishing orders, a voice that now boomed out over the quiet noonday sea to a radius of a hundred yards in all directions:

"Women really are wise ones, aren't they?"

Here in the boat there were none to hear except these two whom he trusted, so at Jukichi's urging Shinji gradually confided in them. His way of telling the story was awkward. Events were often told in the wrong order, and he would leave out important points. It took him quite a time just to give a brief outline. Finally he reached the heart of the matter and told them how on that day of the storm, even though they were naked in each other's arms, he had been unable to win the prize after all.

At this point Jukichi, who almost never smiled, could not stop laughing.

"If it'd been me! Oh, if it'd been me! Really, what a mess you made of things. But then I guess that's what comes of your being such a virgin. And, besides, the girl's so almighty strait-laced that she was too big a handful for you. But still it's a ridiculous story. . . . Oh, well, it'll be all right after she's your wife; then you'll make up for it by giving her the rod ten times a day."

Ryuji, a year younger than Shinji, was listening to this talk as though he only half understood it. As for Shinji, he was not sensitive and easily wounded the way a citybred boy is during the time of his first love, and to Shinji the old man's raillery was actually soothing and comforting rather than upsetting. The gentle waves that rocked their boat also calmed his heart, and now that he had told the whole story he was at peace; this place of toil had become for him a place of matchless rest.

Ryuji, who passed Terukichi's house on his way to the beach, volunteered to pick up Hatsue's letter from under the lid of the water jar each morning.

"So from tomorrow you'll be the new postmaster," said Jukichi, making one of his rare jokes.

The daily letters became the principal subject of conversation during their lunch hours on the boat, and the three of them always shared the anguish and the anger called forth by the contents of the letters. The second letter in particular aroused their indignation. In it Hatsue described at length how Yasuo had attacked her by the spring in the middle of the night and the threats he'd made. She'd kept her promise and not told about it, but Yasuo had avenged himself by spreading that false story about her and Shinji through the village. Then, when her father had forbidden her to see Shinji again, she had explained everything honestly and had also told him of Yasuo's disgraceful behavior, but her father had not done a thing about Yasuo, had, in fact, even remained on as friendly terms as ever with Yasuo's family, with the same visiting back and forth. But she herself detested the very sight of Yasuo's face. She ended the letter by assuring Shinji that she would never, never let her guard down against Yasuo.

Ryuji became excited on Shinji's behalf, and even Shinji's eyes flashed with a rare expression of anger.

"It's all because I'm poor," Shinji said.

He was usually not one to let such querulous words pass his lips. And he felt tears of shame springing in his eyes, not because he was poor, but because he had been weak enough to give voice to such a complaint. But then he tightened his face with all his might, defying those unexpected tears, and managed to avoid the double shame of having the others see him cry.

This time Jukichi did not laugh.

Jukichi took great pleasure in tobacco and had the odd habit of alternating between a pipe one day and cigarettes the next. Today was the turn for cigarettes. On pipe days he was forever knocking his tiny, old-fashioned brass pipe against the side of the boat, a habit that had worn a small trough in a certain spot on the gunwale. It was because he prized his ship so greatly that he had decided to forgo his pipe every other day and smoke New Life cigarettes instead, carving himself a coral holder for the purpose.

Jukichi turned his eyes away from the two youths and, the coral holder clamped between his teeth, gazed out over the misty expanse of the Gulf of Ise. Cape Moro, at the tip of Chita Peninsula, was faintly visible through the mist.

Jukichi Oyama's face was like leather. The sun had burned it almost black down to the very bottom of its deep wrinkles, and it gleamed like polished leather. His eyes were sharp and full of life, but they had lost the clarity of youth and, in its place, seemed to have been glazed with the same tough dirt that coated his skin, making them able to withstand any light, no matter how brilliant.

Because of his age and his great experience as a fisherman he knew how to wait tranquilly. Now he said:

"I know exactly what you two are thinking. You're planning to give Yasuo a beating. But you listen to me—that won't do a bit of good. A fool's a fool, so just leave him alone. Guess it's hard for Shinji, but patience is the main thing. That's what it takes to catch a fish. Everything's going to be all right now for sure. Right's sure to win, even if it doesn't say anything. Uncle Teru's no fool, and don't you ever think he can't tell a fresh fish from a rotten one. Just you leave Yasuo alone. Right's sure to win in the end."

Even though it was always a day late, village gossip reached the lighthouse together with the daily deliveries of mail and food. And the news that Teruki-chi had forbidden Hatsue to see Shinji turned Chiyoko's heart black with feelings of guilt. She comforted herself with the thought that Shinji did not know she was the source of this false gossip. But, even so, she simply could not look Shinji in the eye when he came one day to bring fish, completely cast down in spirits. And on the other hand her good-natured parents, not knowing the reason, were worried over Chiyoko's moroseness.

Chiyoko's spring vacation was drawing to a close and the day came when she was to return to her dormitory in Tokyo. She simply could not bring herself to confess what she had done, and yet she had the feeling that she could not return to Tokyo until she asked Shinji to forgive her. If she did not confess her guilt, there was no particular reason for Shinji to be angry with her, but still she wanted to beg his pardon.

So she got herself invited to spend the night before her departure for Tokyo at the house of the postmaster in the village, and before dawn the next morning she went out alone.

The beach was already busy with preparations for the day's fishing, and people were going about their work in the starlight. The boats, pulled on the "abacus" frames and urged on by many shouting voices, inched reluctantly down toward the water's edge. Nothing could be seen distinctly except the white of the towels and sweat cloths the men had tied around their heads.

Step by step, Chiyoko's wooden clogs sank into the cold sand. And in its turn the sand slithered whisperingly off the arches of her feet.

Everyone was busy and no one looked at Chiyoko. She realized with a pang of shame that here all these people were, caught fast in the monotonous but powerful whirlpool of earning a daily living, burning out the very depths of their bodies and souls, and that not one of them was the sort of person who could become engrossed in sentimental problems such as hers.

Nevertheless Chiyoko peered eagerly through the dawn's darkness, looking for Shinji. All the men were dressed alike and it was difficult to distinguish their faces in the morning twilight.

One boat finally hit the waves and floated on the water as though it had been freed from cramped confinement. Instinctively Chiyoko moved toward it and then called out to a young man with a white towel tied around his head.

The youth had been about to jump aboard, but now he stopped and turned back. His smiling face revealed the whiteness of two clean rows of teeth, and Chiyoko knew for certain it was Shinji.

"I'm leaving today. I wanted to say good-by."

"Oh, you're leaving? . . ." Shinji fell silent, and then in an unnatural tone of voice, as though he were trying to decide what would be best to say, he added: "Well . . . good-by."

Shinji was in a hurry. Realizing this, Chiyoko felt even more hurried than he. No words would come, much less a confession. She closed her eyes, praying that Shinji would stay before her even one second more. In this moment she realized that her wanting to beg his pardon was actually nothing but a mask to conceal her long-felt desire to have him be kind to her.

What was it she was wanting to be forgiven for, this girl who was so convinced of her ugliness? On the spur of the moment, without thought, she let slip the question she had always kept pushed down in the very bottom of her heart, a question she probably could never have asked anyone but this one boy:

"Shinji—am I so ugly?"

"What?" the boy asked, a puzzled look on his face.

"My face—is it so ugly?"

Chiyoko hoped the dawn's darkness would protect her face, making her appear even the slightest bit beautiful. But the sea to the east—didn't it seem to be already turning light?

Shinji's answer was immediate. Being in a hurry, he escaped a situation in which too slow an answer would have cut into the girl's heart.

"What makes you say that? You're pretty," he said, one hand on the stern and one foot already beginning the leap that would carry him into the boat. "You're pretty."

As everyone well knew, Shinji was incapable of flattery. Now, pressed for time, he had simply given a felicitous answer to her urgent question.

The boat began to move. He waved back to her cheerfully from the boat as it pulled away.

And it was a happy girl who was left standing at the water's edge.

Later that morning her parents came down from the lighthouse to see her off, and even while she talked with them Chiyoko's face was full of life. They were surprised to see how happy their daughter was to be returning to Tokyo.

The *Kamikaze-maru* pulled away from the jetty, and Chiyoko was finally alone on the warm deck. In the solitude her feeling of happiness, on which she had been pondering constantly all morning, became complete.

"He said I'm pretty! He said I'm pretty!" Chiyoko repeated yet again the refrain she had said over and over to herself many hundreds of times since that moment.

"That's really what he said. And that's enough for me. I mustn't expect more than that. That's really what he said to me. I must be satisfied with that and not expect him to love me too. He—he has someone else to love. . . . What a wicked thing it was I did to him! What terrible unhappiness my jealousy has caused him! And yet he repaid my wickedness by saying I'm pretty. I must make it up to him . . . somehow I must do whatever I can to return his kindness. . . ."

Chiyoko's reveries were broken by a strange sound of singing that drifted across the waves. When she looked she saw a fleet of boats, covered with red banners, sailing from the direction of the Irako Channel.

"What are those?" Chiyoko asked the captain's young assistant, who was coiling a hawser on the deck.

"They're pilgrim boats bound for the Ise Shrines. The fishermen from around Enshu and Yaizu on Suruga Bay bring their families with them on the bonito boats to Toba. All those red flags have the boats' names on them. They have a great time drinking and singing and gambling all the way."

The red banners became more and more distinct, and as the fast, ocean-going fishing-boats drew near the *Kamikaze-maru*, the singing voices borne on the wind were almost raucous.

Once more Chiyoko repeated to herself:

"He told me I'm pretty."

Chapter Twelve

In this way the spring had neared its end. It was still too early for the clusters of crinum lilies that bloomed in the cliffs on the eastern side of the island, but the fields were colored here and there with various other flowers. The children were back in school again, and some of the women were already diving in the cold water for the seaweed called "soft lace." As a consequence there were now more houses that were empty during the daytime, doors unlocked, windows open. Bees entered these empty houses freely, flew about in them lonesomely, and were often startled upon running headlong into a mirror.

Shinji, not clever at scheming, had been able to discover no way to meet Hatsue. Although their meetings before had been few and far between, still the happy anticipation of their next meeting had made the waiting bearable. But now that he knew there could be no next meeting, his longing to see her became even stronger. And yet the promise he had given Jukichi not to loaf made it impossible for him to take even a day off from fishing. So there was nothing for him to do every night after he returned from fishing but to wait until the streets were empty and then prowl about the neighborhood of Hatsue's house.

Sometimes an upstairs window would be thrown open and Hatsue would look out. Except on those lucky occasions when the moon was shining just right, her face was lost in the shadows. Even so, the boy's sharp eyesight allowed him to see clearly even how her eyes were wet with tears. Out of fear of the neighbors Hatsue never spoke. And Shinji too, from behind the stone wall of the small vegetable garden at the back of her house, would simply stand looking up at the girl's face, not saying a word. Without fail, the letter Ryuji would bring the next day would dwell at great length upon the pain of such an ephemeral meeting, and as Shinji read the words Hatsue's image and voice would finally come into focus together, and in his mind the wordless girl he had seen the night before would come alive with speech and action.

Such meetings were painful for Shinji too, and there were times when he preferred to relieve his pent-up emotions by wandering to those parts of the island where people seldom came. Sometimes he went as far as the ancient burial mound of Prince Deki. The exact boundaries of the tumulus were not clear, but at the highest point there were seven ancient pine trees and, in the midst of them, a small *torii* and shrine.

The legend of Prince Deki was vague. Nothing was known even about the origins of his strange name. In a time-honored ceremony held during the lunar New Year, the strange box that reposed in the shrine was briefly opened each year and old couples of more than sixty years of age were allowed a fleeting glimpse of the object it contained, which looked like an ancient nobleman's fan-shaped baton, but no one knew what relationship there was between this mysterious treasure and Prince Deki. Until about a generation past the children of the island had called their mothers *eya*, and this was said to have arisen from the fact that the prince had called his wife *heya* meaning "room," and that his infant heir had mispronounced the word as *eya* when trying to imitate his father.

Be that as it may, the story goes that long, long ago, in a golden ship, the prince drifted from a far land to this island, took a girl of the island to wife, and when he died was buried in an imperial tumulus. No accounts have been handed down concerning the prince's life, nor are there recounted any of those tragic tales that are apt to grow up and adhere to such a legendary figure. Assuming the legend to be based on fact, this silence suggests that Prince Deki's life on Uta-jima must have been so happy and uneventful that it left no room for the birth of tragic yarns.

Perhaps Prince Deki was a heavenly being who descended to a nameless land. Perhaps he lived out his earthly years without being recognized and, do what he would, will as he could, was never separated from happiness, nor from the blessings of Heaven. Perhaps this is the reason why his remains were interred in a mound overlooking the beautiful Five League Beach and Hachijo Isle, leaving behind not a single story. . . .

But the boy knew only unhappiness as he wandered about the shrine until exhausted. Then he sat down absentmindedly on the grass, hugged his knees, and gazed out at the moonlit sea. There was a halo around the moon, foretelling rain on the morrow. . . .

The next morning when Ryuji stopped by Hatsue's house to pick up the daily letter, he found it sticking out a little from under one corner of the wooden lid on the water jar, covered with a metal basin to keep the rain from wetting it.

The rain continued during the entire day's fishing, but Shinji managed to read the letter during the noon rest by protecting it with his raincoat.

Her handwriting was terribly difficult to read, and she explained that she was writing in her bed early in the morning, groping in the dark to avoid arousing her father's suspicions by turning on the light. Usually she wrote her letters at odd moments during the day and "posted" them before the fishing-boats went out the next morning, but this morning, she wrote, she had something she wanted to tell him at once, so she had torn up the long letter she had written him yesterday and was writing this in its place.

Hatsue's letter went on to say that she had had a lucky dream. In the dream a god had told her that Shinji was a reincarnation of Prince Deki. Then they had been happily married and had had a jewel-like child.

Shinji knew that Hatsue could not have known about his visit to Prince Deki's tomb the night before. He was so struck by this uncanny happening that he decided to write Hatsue at length when he got home that night and tell her this amazing proof of her dream's deep meaning.

Now that Shinji was working to support the family it was no longer necessary for his mother to go diving when the water was still cold. So she had decided to wait until June to start diving. But she had always been a hard worker, and now, as the weather became warmer, she became dissatisfied, with nothing to do but the housework. Whenever she found herself unoccupied she was apt to let herself become upset with all sorts of unnecessary worries.

Her son's unhappiness was always on her mind. Shinji was now completely different from the person he had been three months before. He was as taciturn as ever, but the youthful gaiety that had lighted up his face even when he was silent was now extinguished.

One day she had finished her darning in the morning and was facing a boring afternoon. Idly she began to wonder if there was not something she could do to relieve her son's misery. Theirs was not a sunny house, but over the roof of the next-door neighbor's godown she could see the tranquil sky of late spring. Making up her mind, she left the house.

She went directly to the breakwater and stood there watching the waves as they dashed themselves to pieces. Like her son, she too went to take counsel with the sea whenever she had something to think about.

The breakwater was covered with the ropes of the octopus pots, spread there to dry. The beach too, now almost empty of boats, was spread with drying nets. The mother caught sight of a lone butterfly that came flying capriciously from the outspread nets toward the breakwater. It was a large and beautiful black swallowtail. Perhaps the butterfly had come searching for some new and different flower here among the fishing tackle and sand and concrete. The fishermen's houses had no gardens worthy of the name, but only ragged flowerbeds along the narrow, stone-faced paths, and the butterfly had apparently come to the beach, disgusted with their niggling blossoms.

Beyond the breakwater the waves were always churning up the bottom of the sea, and the water was a muddy yellow-green. And as the waves rolled in, the muddiness was chopped into patterns of tossing bamboo leaves. Presently the mother saw the butterfly take off from the breakwater and fly close to the surface of the muddy water. There it seemed to rest its wings a moment, and then it soared high into the air again.

"What a strange butterfly," she told herself. "It's imitating a sea gull." And at the thought her attention became riveted upon the butterfly.

Soaring high, the butterfly was trying to fly away from the island, directly into the sea-breeze. Mild though it seemed, the breeze tore at the butterfly's tender wings. In spite of it, however, the butterfly, high in the air, finally got clear of the island. The mother stared until it was only a black speck against the dazzling sky.

For a long time the butterfly continued to flutter there in one corner of her field of vision, and then, flying low and hesitantly over the surface of the water, it returned to the breakwater, bewitched by the wideness and glitter of the sea, doubtless driven to despair by the way the next island looked so close and was yet so far. The butterfly added what appeared to be the shadow of a large knot to the shadow made by one of the drying ropes, and rested its wings.

The mother was not one to put faith in signs and superstitions, and yet the butterfly's futile labor cast a shadow over her heart.

"Foolish butterfly! And if it wants to get away, all it has to do is perch on the ferryboat and go in style."

And yet she herself, having no business in the world outside the island, had not been on the ferryboat now for many, many years. ·

At this moment for some reason a reckless courage was born within her heart. With firm steps she strode quickly from the breakwater. A diving woman greeted her along the way and was surprised when Shinji's mother walked steadily on as though deep in thought, not even returning the greeting.

Terukichi Miyata was one of the richest men in the village. Of course, about all that could be said of his house was that it was a bit newer than the other village houses. Otherwise it could not even be said that its tile roof towered in particular above the houses around it. The house had neither an outer gate nor a stone wall. Nor was it different from the other houses in its arrangement: the hole for ladling out night soil was to the left of the main door, and the kitchen window to the right, both insisting majestically upon their equal rank, precisely in the same way that the Ministers of the Left and the Right occupy their seats of honor at either side of a Doll Festival arrangement. And yet, being built on a slope, the house did derive a certain air of stability from a stoutly constructed concrete basement on the lower level, where the slope dropped away; this was used as a storeroom and had windows opening directly on the narrow road.

Beside the kitchen door there was a water jar large enough for a man to crawl into. Its wooden lid, under which Hatsue left her letter each morning, gave the outward appearance of protecting the water from dust and dirt, but when summer came it could not keep out the mosquitoes and other flying insects whose dead bodies would suddenly be found floating on the water in the jar.

Shinji's mother hesitated a moment as she was about to enter the house. Just the fact that she had come calling at the Miyata house, where she was not on intimate terms, would be enough to set the villagers' tongues to wagging. She looked about; there was not a human form to be seen. There was nothing but a few chickens scratching in the alley and the color of the sea below, glimpsed through the scanty azalea blossoms of the next house.

The mother put her hand to her hair and, finding it still disarranged from the sea-breeze, took from her bosom a small, red celluloid comb with several teeth missing and quickly combed her hair. She was wearing her everyday work-clothes. Beneath her face, which was bare of any make-up, there was the beginning of her sunburned chest; then came her kimono-like jacket and bloomer-like work-pants, both with many patches, and the wooden clogs on her bare feet.

Her toes had been toughened by the repeated cuts and bruises they had received from the diving women's customary way of always kicking off against the floor of the sea when ready to surface, and the nails were thick and badly twisted; her feet could in no way have been called beautiful, but when planted on the earth they were firm and unshakable.

She opened the door and entered the central workroom. Several pairs of clogs had been taken off and dropped pellmell on the earthen floor, one lying upside down. A pair with red thongs seemed to have just returned from a trip to the sea; wet sand in the shape of footprints was still clinging to the surface of each clog.

The house was filled with silence, and the odor of the toilet floated on the air. The rooms opening off the earthen floor were dark, but sunlight was streaming in through a window somewhere at the back of the house and had spread a bright patch, like a saffron-colored wrapping cloth, in the middle of the floor of one of the farther rooms.

"Good day," the mother called.

She waited awhile. There was no answer. She called again.

Hatsue came down the ladder-like steps at the side of the earth-floored room.

"Why, Auntie!" she said. She was wearing quiet-colored work-pants, and her hair was tied with a yellow ribbon.

"That's a pretty ribbon," the mother complimented her. As she spoke she made a thorough inspection of this girl for whom her son was so lovesick.

It may have been her imagination, but Hatsue's face seemed a little haggard, her complexion a little pale. And because of this her black eyes, clear and shining, seemed all the more prominent.

Becoming aware of the other's scrutiny, Hatsue blushed.

The mother was firm in her courage. She would meet Terukichi, champion her son's innocence, lay bare her heart, and get the two married. The only solution to the situation was for the two parents to talk it over face to face. . . .

"Is your father at home?"

"Yes, he is."

"I've something to talk over with him. Will you please tell him so?"

"Just a minute."

Hatsue climbed the stairs, an uneasy expression on her face.

The mother took a seat on the step leading up from the earthen room into the house proper. . . .

She waited a long time, wishing she had brought cigarettes with her. And as she waited her courage drooped. She began to realize what folly her imagination had led her into.

The stairs creaked softly as Hatsue started down. But she did not come all the way. She called from mid-stairs, seeming to bend her body slightly. The stairs were dark and her face could not be seen clearly as she looked down.

"Uh . . . Father says he won't see you. . . ."

"He won't see me?"

"That's right, but . . ."

With this reply the mother's courage was utterly crushed, and her feeling of humiliation spurred her to a fit of passion. In a flash she recalled her long life of sweat and toil, all the hardships she had faced as a widow. Then, in a tone of voice that sounded as though she were spitting in someone's face—but not until she was already half out the front door—she bawled out:

"All right then! So you say you don't want to see a poor widow. You mean you don't want me to cross your threshold ever again. Well, let me tell you something—and you tell that father of yours—hear! Tell him I said it first— that never in my life will I ever cross his damned threshold again!"

The mother could not bring herself to tell her son about this fiasco of hers. Looking for a scapegoat, she turned her spite against Hatsue and said such bad things about her that, instead of having helped her son, she had a quarrel with him.

Mother and son did not speak to each other for one whole day, but then the next day they made up. Thereupon the mother, suddenly overcome with the desire for her son's sympathy, told him all about her abortive call on Terukichi. As for Shinji, he had already learned of it from one of Hatsue's letters.

In her confession the mother omitted the final scene, in which she had spewed forth those outrageous parting words of hers, and Hatsue's letter also, out of consideration for Shinji's feelings, had made no mention of this. So for Shinji there was nothing but the smarting thought of how his mother had had to eat the humiliation of being turned away from Terukichi's door. And the soft-hearted boy told himself that even if he could not agree with the bad things his mother said about Hatsue, still he could not blame her for saying them. Until now he had never tried to hide his love for Hatsue from his mother, but he made up his mind that henceforth he must never confide in anyone except the master and Ryuji. It was out of devotion for his mother that he made this decision.

Thus it came about that, because she had tried to do a good deed and had failed, the mother was lonelier than ever.

It was fortunate that there was not a single day of rest from fishing, for if there had been, it would have served only to make him bemoan the tedium of a day in which he could not meet Hatsue. Thus the month of May came, and their meetings were still prohibited. Then one day Ryuji brought a letter which made Shinji wild with joy:

". . . Tomorrow night, for a wonder, Father is having visitors. They're some prefectural officials from Tsu and will spend the night. Whenever Father has guests he always drinks a lot and goes to bed early. So I think it'll be safe for me to slip out of the house about eleven o'clock. Please wait for me in front of Yashiro Shrine. . . ."

When Shinji returned from fishing that day he changed into a new shirt. His mother, given no explanation, sat looking up at him nervously. She felt as though she were once more looking at her son on that day of the storm.

Shinji had now learned well enough the pain of waiting. So he decided it would be better if he let the girl do the waiting this time. But he could not do it. As soon as his mother and Hiroshi were in bed, he went out. It still lacked two hours of eleven o'clock.

He thought maybe he could kill the time by going to the Young Men's Association. Light was shining from the windows of the hut on the beach and he could hear the voices of the boys who were sleeping there. But then he had the feeling that they were gossiping about him, and he went on by.

Going out onto the nighttime breakwater, the boy turned his face to the sea-breeze. As he did so he recalled the white ship he had seen sailing against a background of sunset clouds on the horizon that day when he had first learned Hatsue's identity from Jukichi, recalled the strange feeling he had had as he watched the ship sail away. That had been the "unknown." So long as he had observed the unknown from a distance, his heart had been peaceful, but once he himself had boarded the unknown and set sail, uneasiness and despair, confusion and anguish had joined forces and borne down upon him.

He believed he knew the reason why his heart, which should have been filled with joy at this moment, was instead crushed and unable to move: the Hatsue whom he would meet tonight would probably insist upon some hasty solution or other to their problem. Elopement? But they were living on an isolated island, and if they were to flee by boat, Shinji had no boat of his own nor, even more important, did he have any money. Double suicide then? Even on this island there had been lovers who took that solution. But the boy's good sense repudiated the thought, and he told himself that those others had been selfish persons who thought only of themselves. Never once had he thought about such a thing as dying; and, above all, there was his family to support.

While he had been pondering these matters, time had moved ahead surprisingly fast. This boy who was so inexpert at thinking was surprised to discover that one of the unexpected properties of thought was its efficacy as a time-killer. Nevertheless the strong-willed young man abruptly turned off his thoughts: no matter how efficacious it might be, what he had discovered above all else about this new habit of thinking was that it also comprised point-blank peril.

Shinji did not have a watch. As a matter of fact, he needed none. In its place he was endowed with the marvelous ability of being able to sense what time it was instinctively, day or night.

For instance, the stars moved. And even if he was not an expert at measuring their changes precisely, still his body perceived the turning of the immense wheel of the night, the revolution of the giant wheel of the day. Placed as he was, close to the workings of nature, it was not surprising that he should understand nature's precise system.

But, to tell the truth, as he sat on the stairs at the entrance to the office of Yashiro Shrine he had already heard the clock give the single stroke of the half-hour and so was doubly sure it was past ten thirty. The priest and his family were fast asleep. Now the boy pressed his ear to the night-shutters of the house and counted, at full length, the eleven strokes that sounded lonesomely from the wall clock inside.

The boy stood up and, passing through the dark shadows of the pine trees, came to a stop at the top of the flight of two hundred stone steps leading downward to the village. There was no moon, thin clouds covered the sky, and only an occasional star was to be seen. And yet the limestone steps gathered together every last gleam of the night's faint light and, looking like some immense, majestic cataract, fell away from the spot where Shinji stood.

The vast expanse of the Gulf of Ise was completely hidden by the night, but lights could be seen on the farther shores, sparse along the Chita and Atsumi peninsulas, but beautifully and thickly clustered about the city of Uji-Yamada.

The boy was proud of the brand-new shirt he was wearing. He felt sure that its unparalleled whiteness would immediately catch the eye even from the bottommost of the two hundred steps. About halfway down the stone steps there crouched a black shadow, caused by the pine branches that hung over both sides of the stairway there. . . .

A human figure came into view at the bottom of the steps, looking very small. Shinji's heart pounded with joy. The sound of the wooden clogs running determinedly up the steps echoed with a loudness out of all proportion to the smallness of the figure. The footsteps sounded tireless.

Shinji resisted the desire to run down the steps to meet her. After all, since he had waited so long, he had the right to stay calmly at the top. Probably, however, when she came close enough for him to see her face, the only way he could keep from shouting out her name in a loud voice would be to go running down to her. When would he be able to see her face clearly? At about the hundredth step? What—

At that instant Shinji heard a strange roar of anger from below. The voice seemed for certain to be calling Hatsue's name.

Hatsue came to an abrupt halt on the hundredth step, which was slightly wider than the others. He could see her breast moving.

Her father came out of the shadows where he had been hiding. He caught his daughter by the wrist, and Shinji watched them exchange a few violent words. He stood motionless at the top of the steps as though bound there. Terukichi never once so much as glanced in Shinji's direction. Still holding his daughter's wrist, he started down the steps.

Not knowing what he ought to do and feeling as though even his head was half-paralyzed, the boy continued to stand in the same motionless posture, like a sentinel at the top of the stone steps.

The figures of the father and daughter reached the bottom of the steps, turned to the right, and disappeared from view.

Chapter Thirteen

The young girls of the island faced the arrival of the diving season with precisely the same heart-strangling feeling city youths have when confronted by final school-term examinations. Their games of scrambling for pebbles on the bottom of the sea close to the beach, begun during the early years of grade school, first introduced them to the art of diving, and they naturally became more skillful as their spirit of rivalry increased. But when they finally began diving for a living and their carefree games turned into real work, without exception the young girls became frightened, and the arrival of spring meant only that the dreaded summer was approaching.

There was the cold, the strangling feeling of running out of breath, the inexpressible agony when water forced its way under the water-goggles, the panic and sudden fear of collapsing that invaded the entire body just when an abalone was almost at the fingertips. There were also all kinds of accidents; and the wounds inflicted on the tips of the toes when kicking off against the sea's bottom, with its carpet of sharp-edged shells, to rise to the surface; and the leaden languor that possessed the body after it had been forced to dive almost beyond endurance. . . . All these things had become sharper and sharper in the remembering; the terror had become all the more intense in the repeating. And often sudden nightmares would awaken the girls from sleep so deep as seemingly to leave no room for dreams to creep in. Then, in the dead of night, in the darkness surrounding their peaceful, dangerless beds, they would peer at the flood of sweat clenched within their fists.

It was different with the older divers, with those who had husbands. Coming out of the water from diving, they would sing and laugh and talk in loud voices. It seemed as though work and play had become united in a single whole for them. Watching them enviously, the young girls would tell themselves that they could never become like that, and yet as the years passed they would be surprised to discover that, without their quite realizing it, they themselves had reached the point where they too could be counted among those light-hearted, veteran divers.

The divers of Uta-jima were at their busiest during June and July. Their operations centered about Garden Beach, on the eastern side of Benten Promontory.

One day, before the onset of the rainy season, the beach lay under a strong, noonday sun that could no longer be called that of early summer. A drying-fire had been lit, and a southerly breeze was carrying its smoke in the direction of the ancient grave-mound of Prince Deki. Garden Beach embraced a small cove, directly beyond which there stretched the Pacific. Summer clouds were towering over the distant sea.

As its name suggested, Niwa-hama—Garden Beach—did indeed have the qualities of a landscaped park. Many limestone crags surrounded the beach, seeming to have been arranged purposely in order that children could hide themselves and fire their pistols in games of cowboys and Indians; moreover, the surfaces of the rocks were smooth to the touch, with occasional finger-size holes as dwellings for crabs and sea-lice. The sand held in the arms of these crags was pure white. Atop the cliff facing the sea to the left the flowers called beach-cotton were in full bloom; their blossoms were not those of the season's end, looking like disheveled sleepers, but were vividly white petals, sensuous and leek-like, brandished against the cobalt sky.

It was the noonday rest period and the area around the fire was noisy with laughing banter. The sand was not yet so hot as to scorch the soles of the feet and, though cold, the water was no longer of that freezing temperature that made the divers rush to put on their padded garments and huddle around the fire the minute they emerged from the sea.

Laughing boisterously, all the divers were thrusting out their chests, boastfully exhibiting their breasts. One of them started to lift her breasts in both hands.

"No, no, it's no fair using your hands. There's no telling how much you might cheat if you used your hands."

"Listen to who's talking! Why, with those breasts of yours you couldn't cheat even if you *did* use your hands."

Everybody laughed. They were arguing as to who had the best-shaped breasts.

All of their breasts were well tanned, and if they lacked the quality of mysterious whiteness, still less did they have the transparent skin that reveals a tracery of veins. Judging merely by the skin, there seemed to be no particular indication of any sensitivity. But beneath the sunburned skin the sun had created a lustrous, semi-transparent color like that of honey. The dark areolas of the nipples did not stand out as isolated spots of black, moist mystery, but instead shaded off gradually into this honey color.

Among the many breasts jostling around the fire there were some which already hung slack and others whose last vestiges remained only in the form of dry, hard nipples. But in most cases there were well-developed pectoral muscles, which supported the breasts on firm, wide chests, without letting them droop under their own weight. Their appearance bespoke the fact that these breasts had developed each day beneath the sun, without any knowledge of shame, like ripening fruit.

One of the girls lamented the fact that one of her breasts was smaller than the other, but an outspoken old woman consoled her:

"That's nothing to worry about. Any day now there'll be some handsome young swain to pet them into shape for you."

Everyone laughed again, but the girl still seemed to be worried.

"Are you sure, Grandma Ohara?" she asked.

"I'm sure. I knew a girl like that once before, but once she got herself a man, her breasts evened right up."

Shinji's mother was proud of the fact that her own breasts were still young and fresh, the most youthful among the married women of her age. As though they had never known the hunger of love or the pains of life, all summer long her breasts turned their faces toward the sun, deriving there, first-hand, their inexhaustible strength.

The breasts of the young girls did not particularly arouse her jealousy. There was, however, one beautiful pair that had become the object of everyone's admiration, including that of Shinji's mother. These were the breasts of Hatsue.

This was the first day Shinji's mother had come out to dive. So it was also her first opportunity to have a leisurely look at Hatsue. Even after she had hurled those insulting parting words at Hatsue, they had kept exchanging nods whenever they happened to meet, but Hatsue was by nature not a talkative person. Today again they had been busy with one thing and another and had not had many opportunities for speaking with each other. Even now during the breast-beautiful contest it was mainly the older women who were doing all the talking, and so Shinji's mother, already prejudiced anyway, purposely avoided getting into conversation with Hatsue.

But when she looked at Hatsue's breasts she nodded to herself, understanding why with the passage of time the ugly rumor about the girl and Shinji had died out. No woman who saw those breasts could have any more doubts. Not only were they the breasts of a girl who had never known a man, but they had just begun to bloom, making one think how beautiful they would be once they were in full flower.

Between two small mounds that held on high their rose-colored buds there was a valley that, though darkly burned by the sun, still had not lost the delicacy, the smoothness, the veined coolness of skin—a valley fragrant with thoughts of early spring. Keeping pace with the normal growth of the rest of her body, her breasts were in no way late in their development. Yet their roundness, still tinged with the firmness of childhood, seemed on the verge of awakening from sleep, seemed ready to come awake at the slightest touch of a feather, at the caress of the slightest breeze.

The old grandmother could not resist the impulse to lay her hand against the nipples of these breasts that were so healthily virginal and, at the same time, so exquisitely formed. The touch of her rough palm made Hatsue jump to her feet.

Everyone laughed.

"So now do you understand how men must feel about them, Grandma Ohara?" someone asked.

The old woman rubbed her own wrinkle-covered breasts with both hands and then spoke in a cracking voice:

"What're you talking about? Hers are just green peaches, but mine—mine are well-seasoned pickles. They've soaked up a lot of delicious flavor, let me tell you."

Hatsue laughed and tossed her head. A piece of green, transparent seaweed fell from her hair to the dazzling sand.

While they were all eating their lunches, a favorite man of theirs suddenly appeared from behind some rocks where he had been awaiting what he knew would be the propitious moment.

The women all screamed for the sake of screaming, put their lunches back into the bamboo-leaf wrappers on the ground beside them, and covered their breasts. Actually, they were not in the slightest taken aback. The intruder was an old peddler who made his way to the island every season, and their pretense at bashfulness was nothing but their way of poking fun at his old age.

The old man was wearing a seedy pair of trousers and a white, open-necked shirt. He put down on a rock the big cloth-wrapped bundle he was carrying on his back and wiped the sweat from his face.

"I guess I gave you an awful scare, didn't I? Maybe it was wrong of me to come like this. Shall I go away?"

The peddler said this in full confidence that they would never let him go. He well knew that there was no better way of arousing the divers' desire to buy than by exhibiting his goods here on the beach. The divers always felt bold and open-handed when they were beside the sea. So he would have them choose what they wanted to buy here, and then the same night he would deliver the goods to their homes and collect his money. The women too liked it this way because they could judge colors better in the sunlight.

The old peddler spread his wares out in the shade of some rocks. Still cramming the lunches into their mouths, the women crowded around the display.

There were lengths of stencil-dyed cotton material for summer kimonos. There were light housedresses and children's clothes. There were unlined sashes, underpants, undershirts, and sash strings.

The peddler took the lid off a flat wooden box, and cries of admiration escaped from the women's mouths. The box was filled to overflowing with beautiful notions—coin purses, clog thongs, plastic handbags, ribbons, brooches, and the like, all in assorted colors.

"There's not a thing there I wouldn't like to have," one of the young divers truthfully remarked.

In a flash many sun-blackened fingers reached out; the goods were painstakingly examined and criticized; arguments broke out among the women as to whether something was or was not becoming to so-and-so; and half-joking bargaining grew apace. As a result the peddler sold two lengths of summer-kimono material in tawdry, towel-like patterns at almost a thousand yen each, as well as one unlined sash of a mixed weave, and a large amount of sundry merchandise. Shinji's mother bought a plastic shopping-bag for two hundred yen, and Hatsue bought a length of the better cotton-kimono material, in a youthful pattern of dark-blue morning-glories on a white background.

The old peddler was pleased with all this unexpectedly good business. He was quite gaunt, and his sunburned ribs could be seen through the open collar of his shirt. His pepper-and-salt hair was cut short, and the years had deposited a number of dark splotches on his cheeks and temples. He had only a few straggling tobacco-stained teeth, which made it difficult to understand what he said, and still more so now when he raised his voice loudly. Nevertheless, by the laughter that made his cheeks tremble as though with a twitch and by his exaggerated gestures, the women realized that the peddler was about to render them some magnificent service, "quite apart from any desire for gain."

With scurrying fingers—he had let the nail grow long on the little finger of each hand—the peddler produced three beautiful plastic handbags from the box of notions.

"Look! This blue one is for young ladies, this brown for the middle-aged, and this black for the ladies of advanced years—"

"I'll take the young ladies' one," the same old woman broke in, and everyone laughed, causing the peddler to raise his quavering voice still higher.

"Plastic handbags of the very latest fashion. Fixed price, eight hundred yen—"

"Oh, they're *dear*, aren't they?"

"Of course; he's padded the price."

"No, no, eight hundred yen without any padding at all. And I'm going to present one of these beautiful handbags to one of you ladies as a token of my appreciation for your kind patronage . . . absolutely free!"

Dozens of guileless, open hands were simultaneously stretched forth. But the old man brushed them aside with a flourish.

"One, I said. Just one. It's the Omiya Prize, a sort of sacrificial service rendered by my shop, the Omiya Shop, in celebration of the prosperity of Utajima Village. We'll have a contest, and one of these bags shall go to whoever wins. The blue if the victor is young, the brown if it's a middle-aged lady . . ."

The diving women were holding their breath. Each was thinking that, with just a little luck, she would receive an eight-hundred-yen handbag for nothing.

The peddler had once been a grade-school principal and often brooded over having come to his present humble circumstances because of a mess he had gotten into with a woman, but now the divers' silence gave him new confidence in his ability to win people's hearts, and once again he told himself that he would quit peddling and become an athletic director.

"Well, then, if we're to have a contest, it ought to be something for the good of Uta-jima Village, to which I owe so much. How about it, everyone— what would you say to an abalone contest? And to the person who brings up the biggest catch in the next hour I'll present the prize."

Ceremoniously he spread a cloth in the shade of another rock and gravely decked it with the prizes. To tell the truth, not one of the handbags was worth more than about five hundred yen, but they looked worth fully eight hundred. The youthful prize was sky-blue and box-shaped, and its cobalt color, bright as a new-built boat, made an inexpressibly lovely contrast with its glittering, gold-plated clasp. The brown, middle-aged one was also box-shaped, and its ostrich-skin pattern had been so exceedingly well pressed into the plastic that at first glance one could not tell whether it was genuine ostrich skin or not. Only the black one, for old ladies, was not box-shaped, but with its long and slender golden clasp and its oblong boat shape, it was indeed a tasteful, refined piece of workmanship.

Shinji's mother, who wanted the brown, middle-aged bag, was the first to announce her name for the contest.

The second person who called out her name was Hatsue.

Carrying the eight divers who had entered the contest, the boat pulled away from the shore. A fat, middle-aged woman, who had not entered the contest, stood in the stern and sculled. Of the eight, Hatsue was the only young girl. All the other girls had held back, knowing they could not win anyway; they were cheering for Hatsue. As for the other women left on the beach, each was shouting encouragement to her own favorite.

The boat took a southward course along the beach and moved away to the eastern side of the island.

The divers who were left behind gathered around the old peddler and sang songs.

The water in the cove was clear and blue, and when the waves were still one could plainly see the round rocks on the bottom, covered with red seaweed and looking as though they were floating close to the surface. Actually, however, they were deeply submerged. The waves swelled large at this point, throwing shadows of their patterns and refractions of froth over the rocks on the ocean floor as they passed over them. Then, no sooner had a wave risen full than it smashed itself to pieces on the beach. Thereupon a reverberation like that of a deep sigh would overflow the entire beach and drown out the women's singing.

An hour later the boat returned from the eastern side of the island. Many times more exhausted than usual because of the competition, the eight divers sat silent in the boat, leaning against one another, each staring out toward whatever direction her eyes happened to fancy. Their wet, disheveled hair was so tangled together that it was impossible to tell one diver's hair from that of her neighbors. Two of them were hugging each other to keep warm. All their breasts were covered with goose flesh, and in the too-brilliant sunshine even their naked, sunburned bodies seemed to turn pale, making them look like a group of pallid, drowned corpses.

The noisy reception they received from the beach was out of keeping with the quietness of this boat that moved so soundlessly forward. The moment they were on land the eight women collapsed on the sand around the fire and would not even speak.

The peddler checked the contents of the buckets he had collected from the divers. When he was done, he called out the results in a loud voice:

"Hatsue-san is first—twenty abalone! And the mistress of the Kubo family is second—eighteen!"

The winner and the runner-up, Hatsue and Shinji's mother, exchanged glances out of tired, bloodshot eyes. The island's most expert diver had been bested by a girl who had learned her skill from the divers of another island.

Hatsue got to her feet in silence and went around the rock to receive her prize. And the prize she returned with was the brown, middle-aged handbag, which she pressed into the hands of Shinji's mother.

The mother's cheeks flushed red with delight.

"But . . . why? . . ."

"Because I've always wanted to apologize ever since my father spoke so rudely to Auntie that day."

"She's a fine girl!" the peddler shouted, and when everyone joined in with unanimous praise of Hatsue, urging the older woman to accept the girl's kindness, Shinji's mother took the brown handbag, wrapped it carefully in a piece of paper, clasped it under a bare arm, and spoke quite casually:

"Why, thanks."

The mother's simple, straightforward heart had immediately understood the modesty and respect behind the girl's gesture. Hatsue smiled, and Shinji's mother told herself how wise her son had been in his choice of a bride. . . . And it was in this same fashion that the politics of the island were always conducted.

Chapter Fourteen

For Shinji the rainy season brought only one bitter day after another. Even Hatsue's letters had ceased. Doubtless, after her father had frustrated their meeting at Yashiro Shrine, which he had probably learned about by reading her letter, he had absolutely forbidden Hatsue to write again.

One day before the end of the rains the captain of the *Utajima-maru* came to the island. The *Utajima-maru* was the larger of Terukichi Miyata's two coasting freighters and was now anchored at Toba.

The captain went first to Terukichi's house, and next to Yasuo's. The same night he went to see Shinji's boss, Jukichi, and then at last went to Shinji's house.

The captain was a few years past forty and had three children. He was a man of big stature and proud of his strength, but he had a gentle disposition. He was a zealous member of the Nichiren sect, and if he happened to be on the island at the time of the Lantern Festival, he would always officiate as a sort of lay priest in reading the *sutras* for the repose of the souls of the dead. He had women in various ports, whom his crew referred to as the Yokohama aunt, the Moji aunt, and the like. Whenever the ship called at one of these ports, the captain would take the young crew members along to his woman's place for a drink. The "aunts" all dressed conservatively and always treated the young men with great kindness.

The gossip was that the captain's half-bald head was the result of his debaucheries. This was the reason he always maintained his dignity with a gold-braided uniform cap.

As soon as the captain reached the house he began discussing his business with Shinji's mother. Shinji too was present.

When the boys of the village reached the age of seventeen or eighteen they began their maritime training in the capacity of "rice-rinsers," the local word for apprentice seamen. And Shinji was at the age to be thinking about it. The captain asked if he would like to join the *Utajima-maru* as a "rice-rinser."

The mother was silent, and Shinji replied that he would give his answer after he had a chance to discuss it with Jukichi, his boss. The captain said that if it was a question of Jukichi's approval, he had already secured that.

But still there was something strange about it all. The *Utajima-maru* belonged to Terukichi, and there certainly was no reason for him to employ Shinji, whom he disliked so much, as a crew member on one of his own ships.

"No, Uncle Teru himself sees that you'll make a good sailor. As soon as I mentioned you, Uncle Teru agreed. So come on then, do your best and work hard."

To make sure it was all right, Shinji accompanied the captain to Jukichi's house, and Jukichi also strongly urged Shinji to take the job. He said it would be a bit difficult on the *Taihei-maru* without Shinji, but that he couldn't stand in the way of the boy's future. So Shinji agreed.

The next day Shinji heard the startling news that Yasuo too was going to serve an apprenticeship on the *Utajima-maru*. The story went that Yasuo had not at all relished the idea of becoming a "rice-rinser" and had been forced to agree only when Uncle Teru declared that the apprenticeship had to come before any betrothal to Hatsue.

When Shinji heard this, his heart was filled with anxiety, pain, and then, at the same time, hope.

Together with his mother, Shinji went to Yashiro Shrine to pray for a safe voyage and to obtain a charm.

The day of departure had come. Accompanied by the captain, Shinji and Yasuo boarded the *Kamikaze-maru* for the ferry-crossing to Toba. A number of people came to see Yasuo off, including Hatsue, but there was no sign of Terukichi. Shinji was seen off by no one but his mother and Hiroshi.

Hatsue did not look in Shinji's direction. But just as the boat was about to sail, she whispered something to Shinji's mother and handed her a small package. The mother gave it to her son.

Even after he was on the boat Shinji had no chance to open the package, as the captain and Yasuo were with him. He gazed at the receding outline of Utajima. And as he did so he became aware of his own feelings for the first time.

Here he was, a young man born and bred on that island, loving it more than anything else in the world, and yet he was now eager to leave it. It was his desire to leave the island that had made him accept the captain's offer of a berth on the *Utajima-maru*.

Once the island was out of sight the boy's heart became peaceful. As he had never been on his daily fishing trips, he was now free of that thought that tonight he would have to return to the island again.

"I'm free!" he shouted in his heart. This was the first time he had ever realized there could be such a strange sort of freedom as this.

The *Kamikaze-maru* sailed on through a drizzling rain. Yasuo and the captain stretched out on the straw mats in the passenger cabin and went to sleep. Yasuo had not spoken to Shinji once since they had boarded the ferry.

The boy pressed his face close to one of the round portholes, across which the raindrops were running, and by its light examined the contents of the package from Hatsue. It contained another charm from Yashiro Shrine, a snapshot of Hatsue, and a letter. The letter read:

"Every day from now on I'll be going to Yashiro Shrine to pray for your safety. My heart belongs to you. Please take care of yourself and come back safe and sound. I'm enclosing my picture so I can go voyaging with you. It was taken at Cape Daio. About our voyage—Father hasn't said a word to me, but I think he must have some special reason for putting both you and Yasuo on his ship. And somehow I think I can see a ray of hope for us. Please, please don't give up hope; please keep on fighting."

The letter encouraged the boy. Strength filled his arms and the feeling that life was worth living flooded through his entire body.

Yasuo was still asleep. By the light from the porthole Shinji studied Hatsue's photograph. In it the girl was leaning against one of Cape Daio's huge pines and a seabreeze was blowing her skirts, whirling about inside her thin, white summer dress, caressing her bare skin. And his courage was still further revived by the thought that he too had once done just what the wind in the photograph was doing.

Reluctant to take his eyes off the picture, Shinji had propped it up on the edge of the rain-blurred porthole and had stared at it for a long time, when behind it there slowly moved into view the outline of Toshi Island to port. . . .

Once again the boy's heart lost its peacefulness. But the strange way in which love can torture the heart with desire was no longer a novel thing for him.

It had stopped raining by the time they reached Toba. Dull silver rays of light shone down from between rifts in the clouds.

Among the many small fishing boats in Toba's harbor the one-hundred-and-eighty-five-ton *Utajima-maru* stood out conspicuously. The three jumped down onto its deck, which was sparkling in the sunshine after the rain. Raindrops were still running gleaming down the white-painted masts, and the imposing booms were folded down over the hatches.

The crew had not yet returned from shore leave. The captain led the two boys to their quarters, an eight-mat cabin next to the master's quarters and directly over the kitchen and mess hall. Other than the lockers and a small central space covered with thin straw matting, there was nothing except two sets of two-tiered bunks on the right and, on the left, one set of bunks and a separate bunk for the chief engineer. Several photographs of movie actresses were stuck to the ceiling like charms.

Shinji and Yasuo were assigned to the first tier of bunks on the right. The chief engineer, the first and second mates, the bosum, the seamen, and the firemen all slept in this one small cabin, but as they alternated the watches, there were always bunks enough to go round at any one time.

After showing them the bridge, the master's quarters, the holds, and the mess hall, the captain left them to rest in the crew's cabin.

Left alone in the cabin, the two looked at each other. Yasuo felt downhearted and decided to make peace.

"Well, here we are at last, just the two of us to be friends. A lot of things happened on the island, but let's forget about them and be good friends from now on."

Shinji gave a grunt of agreement and smiled.

Toward evening the crew returned to the ship. Most of them were from Uta-jima and were known by sight to Shinji and Yasuo. Still smelling of liquor, they all teased the newcomers. Then the two of them were instructed in the daily routine and assigned their various duties.

The ship was to sail at nine in the morning. Shinji was given the task of taking the anchor-light off the mast at the first crack of dawn the next morning. The anchor-light was very much like the night-shutters of a house ashore: turning it off meant that the ship was awake, just as opening the night-shutters means a house is awake.

Shinji scarcely closed his eyes all night and was up before the sun the next morning, taking down the anchor-light as things began to turn gray. The morning was wrapped in a misty rain, and the street lamps of Toba ran in two straight lines from the harbor to the railway station. The thick-throated whistle of a freight train sounded from the direction of the station.

The boy scrambled up the naked mast over the furled sails, used for auxiliary power. The wood was wet and cold, and the rocking motion of the faint waves that lapped the ship's sides was transmitted directly to the mast. In the first rays of the morning sun, wet with mist, the anchor-light was a hazy, milk-white color. The boy reached up for the hook. As though it disliked being taken down, the anchor-light gave a big swing, the flame flickered inside the drenched glass, and a few drops of water fell into the boy's upturned face.

Shinji wondered what port they would be in when he next took down this light.

The *Utajima-maru*, on charter to the Yamagawa Transport Company, was to carry lumber to Okinawa and return to Kobe in about six weeks. After sailing through the Kii Channel and calling at Kobe, the ship sailed westward through the Inland Sea and had its quarantine inspection at Moji. It then proceeded southward along the eastern coast of Kyushu and received its sailing clearance at the port of Nichinan in Yamazaki Prefecture, where there was a Customs office.

The ship then called at the harbor of Fukushima, at the southern tip of Kyushu. There it took on a cargo of fourteen thousand cubic feet of lumber.

After leaving Fukushima the *Utajima-maru* became in fact a sea-going vessel and was handled as such. It was due to reach Okinawa in about two or two and a half days. . . .

When there was no work to be done with the cargo, or during their rest periods, the crew would loll about on the thin straw matting that covered the three-mat space in the center of their quarters and listen to a portable phonograph. There were only a few records, and most of them were so worn out that they produced only dingy music through the scratching of a rusty needle. Without exception they were all sentimental ballads concerning ports or sailors, fog or memories of women, the Southern Cross or liquor or sighs. The chief engineer was tone-deaf and never succeeded in his efforts to learn at least one tune during a voyage, always forgetting what little he had memorized before the next voyage. Whenever the ship would pitch or roll suddenly, the needle would go sliding across the record, leaving another scratch in its wake.

Often at night they would sit up late arguing ridiculous points. Such subjects as love and marriage, or whether the human body can take as large an injection of salt as of dextrose, were sufficient to keep them talking for hours. The person who maintained his point with the most stubbornness usually won in the end but the reasoning of Yasuo, who had been president of the Young Men's Association on the island, was so logical that it even won the respect of his elders. As for Shinji, he always sat silent, hugging his knees and smiling as he listened to the others' opinions.

"There's no doubt but what the boy's a fool," the chief engineer once told the captain.

It was a busy life aboard the ship. From the moment the newcomers got up there were always decks for them to clean or some other of their numerous odd jobs to be performed.

It gradually became abundantly clear to the crew that Yasuo was lazy. His attitude was that it was enough just to go through the motions of performing his duties. Shinji, however, covered up for him and even did part of Yasuo's work, so this attitude of his did not become immediately apparent to his superiors.

But one morning the bosun, finding Yasuo loafing in the cabin after having stolen away from his deck-cleaning duties on the pretext of going to the head, lost his temper and berated him roundly.

Yasuo gave a most ill-considered reply:

"Oh well, anyway, when this voyage is over I'm going to become Uncle Teru's son. Then this ship will belong to me."

The bosun was in a rage, but he prudently held his tongue, telling himself it just might turn out the way Yasuo said. He never again scolded Yasuo to his face, but from his whispered words the other men soon learned what the insubordinate youngster had said, and the result was all to Yasuo's disadvantage rather than otherwise.

Shinji was extremely busy, and the only chance he had to look at Hatsue's picture was a brief moment each night before going to bed or when he was on watch. He never let anyone else so much as set eyes on the picture. One day when Yasuo was bragging about being adopted by Terukichi as Hatsue's husband, Shinji took what was for him a most unusually devious means of revenge. He asked Yasuo if he had a photograph of Hatsue.

"Sure I have," Yasuo replied immediately.

Shinji knew without a doubt that this was a lie and his heart was filled with glee.

A few moments later Yasuo spoke very nonchalantly.

"Do you have one too?" he asked.

"Have one what?"

"A picture of Hatsue."

"No, I don't have one."

This was probably the first deliberate lie Shinji had ever told in his life.

The *Utajima-maru* arrived at Naha. After clearing quarantine, it entered the harbor and discharged its cargo. It was forced to lie at anchor two or three days, waiting and waiting for permission to enter the closed port of Unten, where it was to load scrap metal for the return voyage to Japan. Unten was on the northern tip of Okinawa, where the American forces had made their first landing in the war.

Since the crew were not allowed ashore, they spent their time staring from the deck out at the desolate, barren hills. The Americans had burned down every tree on the hills when they landed, fearing unexploded mines.

The Korean war had come to an end for the time being, but in the crew's eyes the island still had a most unusual air. From morning to night there was the droning thunder of fighter planes practicing, and countless vehicles, gleaming in the sun of a tropical summer, were constantly moving back and forth along the broad, paved highway that bordered the harbor—sedans and trucks and various military vehicles. Beside the road, the prefabricated houses for families of American military personnel were aglint with the color of new cement, while the patched tin roofs of the battered native houses were ugly blotches on the landscape.

The only person who went ashore—to get the agent for Yamagawa Transport to send a chandler—was the first mate.

At last the permit to enter Unten was received. The *Utajima-maru* entered the port and took on its cargo of scrap. They had just finished when the report came that Okinawa was in the path of a threatening typhoon. Hoping to escape the typhoon by sailing as quickly as possible, they cleared port early the next morning. Then all the ship had to do was lay its course straight for Japan.

That morning a light rain was falling. The waves were high and the winds southwesterly. The hills quickly vanished from view behind them, and the *Utajima-maru* sailed on by compass for six hours, with very poor visibility. The barometer fell steadily and the waves became still higher. The atmospheric pressure reached an abnormal low.

The captain decided to return to Unten. The rain was blown to mist by the wind, visibility had gone down to absolute zero, and the six-hour run back to port was extremely difficult.

Finally the hills of Unten were sighted. The bosun, who was quite familiar with these waters, stood on lookout in the bow. The harbor was enclosed by about two miles of coral reef, and the channel through the reef, not even marked with buoys, was most difficult to navigate.

"Stop! . . . Go! . . . Stop! . . . Go! . . ."

Checking its headway countless times and then moving ahead very slowly, the ship passed through the channel between the coral reefs. It was then six o'clock in the evening.

One bonito ship had taken shelter within the reefs. Fastening themselves together with several ropes, the two ships proceeded side by side into Unten's harbor.

The waves in the harbor were low, but the wind grew always stronger. Still side by side, the *Utajima-maru* and the bonito ship threw out four lines each—two hawsers and two cables—tying their bows to a buoy the size of a small room, and prepared to ride out the storm.

The *Utajima-maru* had no radio equipment, depending solely upon its compass. So the radio operator on the bonito ship passed on to them every report he received concerning the typhoon's development and course.

When night came the bonito ship put out a deck watch of four men and the *Utajima-maru* put out a three-man watch. Their duty was to watch the hawsers and cables, as one could never be sure they might not snap at any moment.

There was also the uneasy feeling that the buoy itself might not hold. But the danger of snapping lines was much the greater. Fighting the wind and the waves, the watch courted death many times to keep the ropes wet with salt water, fearing they might fray if they became too dry in the wind.

By nine o'clock that night the two ships were beset by a wind with a speed of fifty-six miles an hour.

An hour before midnight Shinji and Yasuo and one of the young seamen took the watch. Their bodies were hurled against the wall as soon as they began crawling out onto the deck. The wind-whipped rain struck their cheeks as though it were needles.

It was impossible to stand upright on the deck, which rose up like a wall before their very eyes. Every timber of the ship was creaking and rumbling. The waves in the harbor were not quite high enough to sweep the decks, but the spray of the waves, blown on the wind, had become a billowing mist, shrouding their vision. Crawling along the deck, the three finally reached the prow and clung to the bitts there. The two hawsers and two cables that secured the ship to the buoy were tied to these bitts.

They could see the buoy dimly about twenty-five yards away in the night, just barely revealing its white-painted existence through the pervading darkness. And when, to the accompaniment of the creaking of the cables, which was like shrieks, a huge mass of wind would strike the ship and lift it high into the air, the buoy would fall far below them into the blackness and seem all the smaller.

The three looked at each other's faces as they clung to the bitts, but they did not speak. And the salt water striking their faces made it all but impossible for them even to keep their eyes open. The neighing of the wind and the roar of the sea, surprisingly enough, gave the infinite night that enveloped them a quality of frenzied serenity.

Their job was to keep their eyes riveted on the lines tying the *Utajima-maru* to the buoy. Stretched taut, the hawsers and cables drew the only indomitably straight lines across a scene in which everything else was pitching and rolling with the gale's madness. The way they stared fixedly at these rigidly drawn lines created in their hearts a feeling akin to confidence, born of their very concentration.

There were times when it seemed as if the wind had suddenly stopped, but instead of reassuring them, such moments made the three young men shiver with terror. Instantly the huge mass of the wind would come crashing again, rattling the yardarms and thrusting the atmosphere aside with a tremendous roar.

The three continued their silent watch over the lines. Even above the sound of the wind they could hear intermittently the shrill and piercing creaking of the lines.

"Look!" Yasuo cried in a thin voice.

One of the cables wrapped around the bitts was rasping ominously; it seemed to be slipping a little. The bitts were directly before their eyes, and they perceived an extremely slight but sinister alternation in the way the lines were wrapped about the bitts.

At that instant a length of cable came recoiling out of the darkness, flashing like a whip, and hit the bitts with a snarling sound.

They had dodged instantly, just in time to escape being slashed by the severed cable, which had force enough to have cut them to the bone. Like some living thing that takes long in dying, the cable writhed about in the darkness of the deck, making a shrill noise. Finally it came to rest in a semicircle.

When they finally grasped the situation, the three young men turned pale. One of the four lines tying the ship to the buoy had given way. And no one could guarantee that the cable and two hawsers that remained might not give way also at any moment.

"Let's tell the captain," Yasuo said, moving away from the bitts.

Searching for handholds as he went creeping along, being thrown off his feet many times, Yasuo groped his way to the bridge and made his report to the captain.

The burly captain remained calm, or at least gave the outward appearance of doing so.

"I see. Well, then, let's just use a lifeline. The typhoon passed its peak at one o'clock, so there's no danger at all in using a lifeline now. Someone can just swim out to the buoy and tie the lifeline to it."

Leaving the second mate in charge of the bridge, the captain and the chief mate followed Yasuo back. Like mice tugging at a rice cake, they rolled and dragged a lifeline and a new marline along with them step by step from the bridge to the bow bitts.

Shinji and the sailor looked up at them inquiringly.

The captain stooped over them and shouted to the three youths in a loud voice:

"Which one of you fellows is going to take this lifeline over there and tie it to that buoy?"

The roaring of the wind covered the youths' silence.

"Don't any of you have any guts?" the captain shouted again.

Yasuo's lips quivered. He pulled his neck down into his shoulders.

Then Shinji shouted out in a cheerful voice, and as he did so the white flash of his teeth shone through the blackness to prove that he was smiling.

"I'll do it," he shouted clearly.

"Good! Go ahead!"

Shinji rose to his feet. He was ashamed of himself for the way he had been squatting on the deck until now, practically cowering. The wind came attacking out of the black reaches of the night, striking him full in the body, but to Shinji, accustomed to rough weather in a small fishing-boat, the heaving deck on which his feet were firmly planted was nothing but a stretch of earth that was frankly a bit out of sorts.

He stood listening.

The typhoon was directly above the boy's gallant head. It was as right for Shinji to be invited to a seat at this banquet of madness as to a quiet and natural afternoon nap.

Inside his raincoat the sweat was running so profusely that both his back and chest were drenched. He took the raincoat off and threw it aside. As he did so his barefoot figure, wearing a white T shirt, loomed through the blackness of the storm.

Under the captain's directions, the men tied one end of the lifeline to the bitts and the other end to the marline. Hindered by the wind, the operation progressed slowly.

When the ropes were finally tied, the captain handed the free end of the marline to Shinji and yelled into his ear:

"Tie this around your waist and swim for it! When you reach the buoy, haul the lifeline over and make it fast!"

Shinji wrapped the marline twice around his waist above his belt. Then, standing in the bow, he stared down at the sea. Down beneath the spray, down beneath the white-caps that beat themselves to pieces against the prow, there were the jet-black, invisible waves, twisting and coiling their bodies. They kept repeating their patternless movements, concealing their incoherent and perilous whims. No sooner would one seem about to come rising into sight than it would drop away to become a whirling, bottomless abyss again.

At this point there flashed across Shinji's mind the thought of Hatsue's photograph in the inside pocket of his coat hanging in the crew's quarters. But this idle thought was blown to bits upon the wind.

He dived from the prow of the ship.

The buoy was about twenty-five yards away. Despite his great physical strength, which he was confident would have to yield to none, and despite too his ability to swim around his home island five times without stopping, still it seemed impossible that these would suffice to get him across the immensity of those twenty-five yards.

A terrible force was upon the boy's arms; something like an invisible bludgeon belabored them as they tried to cut a way through the waves. In spite of himself, his body was tossed on the waves, and when he tried to bring his strength into opposition to the waves and grapple with them, his movements were as useless as though he were trying to run through grease.

He would be certain that the buoy was finally within arm's reach, and when he rose up out of the trough of the next wave he would look for it—and find it just as far away as ever.

The boy swam with all his might. And, inch by inch, step by step, the huge mass of the enemy fell back, opening the way for him. It was as though a drill were boring its way through the hardest of solid rock.

The first time his hand touched the buoy he lost his hold and was pulled away. But then by good luck a wave swept him forward again and, just as it seemed on the point of dashing his chest against the iron rim, lifted him up with a single sweep and deposited him on the buoy.

Shinji took a deep breath, and the wind filled his nostrils and mouth to the choking point. At that instant it seemed to him that he could never breathe again, and for a time he even forgot the task he was supposed to perform.

The buoy rolled and pitched, surrendering its body openheartedly to the black sea. The waves ceaselessly washed over half of it, pouring off with great commotion.

Lying face down so as not to be blown off by the wind, Shinji started untying the line from around his waist. The knot was wet and difficult to loosen. When it was finally untied, he began pulling the marline.

Now for the first time he looked toward the ship. He could see the forms of the four men clustered about the bow bitts. The men on watch in the bow of the bonito ship also were gazing steadily in his direction. Although only a scant twenty-five yards away, everything seemed exceedingly distant. The black shadows of the two moored ships were rising together, side by side, high into the air, and then sinking back into the waves again.

The thin marline offered little resistance to the wind and was comparatively easy to haul in, but soon a heavy weight was added to its end. It was the lifeline, almost five inches thick, which he was now pulling. Shinji was all but thrown forward into the sea.

The wind resistance against the lifeline was very strong, but at last the boy had one end of it in his hands. It was so thick that even one of his big hands would not go entirely around it.

Shinji was at a loss as to how to apply his strength. He wanted to brace himself with his feet to pull, but the wind would not permit that posture. And when he heedlessly applied all his strength to the rope, he was all but dragged into the sea. His drenched body was at fever heat, his face burning hot, and his temples were throbbing violently.

He finally managed to wind the lifeline once around the buoy; then the operation became easier. The line provided him with a fulcrum for his strength, and now for a change he could support his body with the thick line.

He wound the line once more around the buoy and then proceeded methodically to tie it fast. He waved his arms to announce the successful completion of the job.

He could plainly see the four men on the ship waving their arms in reply. The boy forgot how exhausted he was. His instinct for cheerfulness reasserted itself and flagging energy welled up anew. Facing into the storm, he inhaled his fill of air and then dived into the sea for the return trip.

They lowered a net from the deck and hoisted Shinji aboard. Once the boy was back on deck, the captain clapped him on the shoulder with a huge hand. Although Shinji was ready to faint with fatigue, his masculine energy still maintained him.

The captain had Yasuo help Shinji to his quarters and the men who were off duty wiped him dry. The boy fell asleep the moment he was in his bunk. No noise the storm could make could have disturbed that deep sleep. . . .

The next morning Shinji opened his eyes to find brilliant sunshine falling across his pillow. Through the round porthole in his bunk he looked out at the crystal-clear blue sky that followed the typhoon's departure, at the view of bald hills under a tropical sun, at the glitter of a placid, undisturbed sea.

Chapter Fifteen

The *Utajima-maru* returned to Kobe several days behind schedule. So by the time the captain and Shinji and Yasuo reached the island, where they were to have returned before mid-August, in time for the lunar-calendar Lantern Festival, the festivities were already over.

They heard the news of the island while being ferried across on the *Kamikaze-maru*. A huge turtle had come ashore on Five League Beach a few days before the Lantern Festival and had been quickly killed. There were more than a basketful of eggs in it, which had been sold for two yen apiece.

Shinji went to worship at Yashiro Shrine, to give thanks for his safe return, and then on to Jukichi's, where he had been immediately invited for a celebration. Over the protests of the boy, who never drank, his saké cup was filled many times.

Two days later he once again went out fishing on Jukichi's boat. Shinji had not said anything about his voyage, but Jukichi had heard all the details from the captain.

"I hear you did a great thing."

"Oh, no." The boy blushed a little, but had nothing further to say. Anyone unfamiliar with his personality might easily have concluded that he had spent the last month and a half off sleeping somewhere.

Jukichi was silent awhile and then spoke in an offhand way:

"Have you heard anything from Uncle Teru?"

"No."

"Oh."

No one made any mention of Hatsue, and Shinji, feeling no great loneliness, threw himself into the old familiar work, while the boat rocked in the rough seas of the dog days. The work fit both his body and soul perfectly, like a well-tailored suit, leaving no room for the intrusion of other worries.

The strange feeling of self-sufficiency did not leave him all day. At dusk he saw the outline of a white freighter sailing far out at sea, and it was different from that he had seen on that day so long ago, but once again Shinji felt a new emotion.

"I know where that ship is bound for," he thought. "I know what sort of life they live aboard it, what sort of hardships they have. I know everything about that ship."

At least, the white ship was no longer a shadow of the unknown. Instead, there was that about the distant white freighter, trailing its long plume of smoke through the late-summer dusk, that quickened his heart even more than had

the unknown. The boy felt again in his hands the weight of that lifeline he
had pulled with the last ounce of his strength. With these strong hands he had
certainly once actually touched that "unknown" at which he had previously
stared from a great distance. He had the sensation that now, by simply stretching out his hand, he could touch that white ship out at sea.

On a childish impulse, he held his five big-knuckled fingers out toward the
sea to the east, already thick with the shadows of evening clouds....

Summer vacation was half over, and still Chiyoko did not come home. The
lighthouse-keeper and his wife waited day by day for their daughter's return to
the island. The mother wrote an urgent letter. No reply came. She wrote again.
Ten days later there was a grudging answer. Giving no reason, Chiyoko simply
wrote that she would not be able to come back to the island during this vacation.

The mother finally decided to try tears as a means of persuasion and sent a
special-delivery letter of more than ten pages, pouring out her feelings and begging her daughter to come home. A reply came when only a few days remained
of vacation and a week after Shinji's return to the island. It was a reply which
the startled mother had never dreamed of.

In her letter Chiyoko confessed how she had seen Shinji and Hatsue coming
down the stone stairs arm in arm that day of the storm, and how she had then
landed the two of them in great difficulties by the uncalled-for act of running to
Yasuo with the tale. Chiyoko was still tormented with feelings of guilt, and
she went on to say that unless Shinji and Hatsue finally found their happiness,
she herself would be too ashamed ever to come back to the island. If her mother
would act as a go-between and persuade Terukichi to let them get married . . .
This was the condition she set for her return to the island.

This tragic, demandingly badgering letter sent chills up the kind-hearted
mother's spine. She was struck with the thought that, unless she took appropriate steps, her daughter, unable to bear the pangs of conscience, might even
commit suicide. From her wide reading the mistress of the lighthouse recalled
various frightening instances of adolescent girls who had killed themselves
over some equally trivial matter.

She decided not to show the letter to her husband, the lighthouse-keeper,
and told herself that every day counted, that by herself she would have to
manage everything at once in such a way as to bring her daughter home as
quickly as possible.

As she changed into her best clothes, a suit of white cambric, there was reborn within her the mettlesome feelings of years gone by when, as a teacher
in a girls' high school, she was on her way to complain to some parent about
a problem student.

Straw mats were spread out in front of the houses along the roadside leading down into the village, and on them there were sesame and red beans and soy
beans drying in the sun. The tiny green sesame seed, washed by the late-
summer sun, cast their miniature, spindle-shaped shadows one by one across
the coarse straw of the fresh-colored mats.

From here one could look down upon the sea. The waves were not running high today.

As the mother descended the steps that formed the main street of the village, her white shoes made light sounds against the concrete. Then she began to hear lively, laughing voices and the springy sound of wet clothes being beaten.

She drew nearer the sounds and found a half-dozen women in housedresses doing their laundry by the side of the stream bordering the road. Shinji's mother was one of the group.

After the Lantern Festival the diving women had more leisure, going out only occasionally to gather edible seaweed, so they turned then to an energetic washing of the accumulation of dirty clothes. Using almost no soap, they one and all would spread the laundry over flat rocks and trample it with their feet.

"Why, hello, mistress. Where are you on your way to today?"

They all bowed and called out their greetings. Beneath their tucked-up skirts the water reflections were playing over their dark thighs.

"I just thought I'd drop by Terukichi Miyata-san's place a minute."

As she made this reply, it occurred to her that it would be strange to meet Shinji's mother this way and then, without so much as a word to her, proceed on to arrange for her son's engagement. So she turned and started down the precipitous flight of slippery, moss-covered stone steps that led from the road to the stream. Her shoes made the descent perilous, so, turning her back to the water, but stealing many a glance over her shoulder, she backed slowly down the steps on all fours. One of the women, standing in the middle of the stream, reached out and lent her a helping hand.

Reaching the bank, she took off her shoes and began to wade across. The women on the farther bank stood watching her hazardous progress with blank amazement.

She caught hold of Shinji's mother's sleeve and made a clumsy attempt at private conversation, whispering words into her ear that everyone around could plainly hear.

"Maybe this isn't quite the place, but I've been wanting to ask how things have gotten on for Shinji-san and Hatsue-san lately."

The suddenness of the question made the other's eyes grow round, and she said nothing.

"Shinji-san likes Hatsue-san, doesn't he?"

"Well—"

"And still Terukichi-san is standing in the way, isn't he?"

"Well—that's what the trouble is all right, but . . ."

"And how does Hatsue-san feel about it?"

At this point the other divers, who could not have helped overhearing, broke into the private conversation. Where talk of Hatsue was concerned all the divers without exception had become her staunch defenders ever since that day when the peddler had held the contest. They had also heard the whole true story from Hatsue herself and were one and all against Terukichi.

"Hatsue—she's head over heels in love with Shinji too. That's the plain truth of it, mistress. And yet, would you believe it, that Uncle Teru is planning to marry her to that good-for-nothing Yasuo! Have you ever heard of such foolishness?"

"Well, that's that," said the mistress of the lighthouse, as though addressing a classroom of students. "Today I received a threatening letter from my daughter in Tokyo saying she didn't know what she might do if I wouldn't help get the two married. So I'm on my way to have a talk with Terukichi-san, but I thought I ought to stop and find out how Shinji-san's mother felt about it first."

Shinji's mother reached down and picked up her son's sleeping kimono, which she had been treading clean beneath her feet. Slowly she proceeded to wring it out, gaining time for thought. Finally she turned to face the mistress of the lighthouse and bowed her head low.

"I'll greatly appreciate anything you can do," she said.

Moved by a spirit of helpfulness, the other women went into noisy conclave with each other, like a flock of water fowl beside a river, and decided that if they went along too as representatives of the women of the village, the show of strength might help awe Terukichi. The mistress of the lighthouse agreed, so the five of them, not including Shinji's mother, wrung out their washing hurriedly and ran to take it home, arranging to meet at the bend of the road leading to Terukichi's house.

The mistress of the lighthouse stood just inside the gloomy earthen-floored room of the Miyata house.

"Good day!" she called in a voice still youthful and steady.

There was no answer.

The other five women stood just outside the door, their sunburned faces thrusting forward like so many cactus leaves, their eyes glittering with enthusiasm as they peered into the dark interior.

The mistress of the lighthouse called out again, her voice echoing emptily through the house.

Presently the staircase gave a squeak and Terukichi himself came down wearing an undress kimono. Hatsue was apparently not at home.

"Why, it's Mistress Lighthouse-Keeper," Terukichi grumbled, standing imposingly on the threshold leading up from the earthen floor.

Most visitors at this house felt the urge to flee when received by this perpetually inhospitable visage with its bristling mane of white hair. The mistress herself was daunted, but she drummed up courage to continue:

"There's something I'd like to talk with you about for a minute."

"So? All right, please come in."

Terukichi turned his back and promptly went up the stairs. She followed him, with the other five women tip-toeing after her.

Terukichi led the way into the inner sitting-room upstairs and, without further ceremony, took the seat of honor in front of the alcove for himself. His face revealed no great surprise when he noticed the number of visitors in the room had grown to six. Ignoring them all, he looked toward the open windows. His hands were toying with a fan showing a picture of a beautiful woman advertising a drugstore in Toba.

The windows looked out directly over the island's harbor. There was only one vessel inside the breakwater, a boat belonging to the Co-operative. Far in the distance summer clouds were floating over the Gulf of Ise.

The sunshine outdoors was so brilliant that it made the room seem dark. On the alcove wall there hung a calligraphic scroll done by the last-governor-but-one of Mie Prefecture, and beneath it, gleaming with a luster like that of wax, there were an ornamental rooster and its hen, their bodies carved out of a knotty and gnarled root of a tree and their tails and combs formed from the natural growth of the slender shoots.

The mistress of the lighthouse sat at this side of the bare rosewood table. The other five women, having mislaid somewhere their courage of a little while before, now sat primly just in front of the bamboo blind hanging in the entrance to the room, as though they were giving an exhibit of housedresses.

Terukichi continued looking out the window and did not open his mouth.

The sultry silence of a summer afternoon came upon them, broken only by the buzzing of several large blue-bottle flies that were flying about the room.

The mistress of the lighthouse wiped the sweat from her face several times. At long last she began to speak:

"Well, what I want to talk to you about is your Hatsue-san and the Kubo family's Shinji-san, and . . ."

Terukichi was still looking out the window. After a long pause he spoke, seeming to spit out the words:

"Hatsue and Shinji?"

"Yes . . ."

Now for the first time Terukichi turned his face toward her, and then he spoke, without so much as a sign of a smile:

"If that's all you have to talk about, it's all already settled. Shinji's the one I'm adopting for Hatsue's husband."

There was a stir among the women as though a dam had burst. But Terukichi went right on speaking, paying not the slightest heed to his visitors' reaction:

"But in any case they're still too young, so for the time being I've decided to leave it at an engagement, and then, after Shinji comes of age, we'll have a proper ceremony. I hear his old lady isn't having too easy a time of it, so I'll be willing to take both her and the younger brother in, or, depending upon how it's finally decided, help them out with some money each month. I haven't said anything to anybody about all this yet, though.

"I was angry at first, but then, after I made them stop seeing each other, Hatsue became so out of sorts that I decided things couldn't go on that way. So I decided on a plan. I gave Shinji and Yasuo berths on my ship and told the captain to watch and see which one of them made the best showing. I let the captain tell all this to Jukichi as a secret, and I don't suppose Jukichi has told Shinji even yet. Well, anyway, to make a short story of it, the captain really fell in love with Shinji and decided I'd never be able to find a better husband for Hatsue. And then when Shinji did that great thing at Okinawa—well, I changed my mind too and decided he was the one for my girl. The only thing that really counts . . ."

Here Terukichi raised his voice emphatically.

"The only thing that really counts in a man is his get-up-and-go. If he's got get-up-and-go he's a real man, and those are the kind of men we need here on Uta-jima. Family and money are all secondary. Don't you think so, Mistress Lighthouse-Keeper? And that's what he's got—Shinji—get-up-and-go."

Chapter Sixteen

Shinji could now visit the Miyata house openly. One night after returning from fishing he called Hatsue's name from the front door. He was wearing freshly laundered trousers and a clean white sport shirt, and from each hand there dangled a big red-snapper.

Hatsue was ready and waiting. They had made a date to go to Yashiro Shrine and the lighthouse to announce their engagement and express their thanks.

The dusk in the earthen-floored room became lighter when Hatsue entered. She was wearing the light summer kimono with large-patterned morning-glories on a white background that she had bought on that occasion from the peddler, and its whiteness was brilliant even at night.

Shinji had been leaning against the door waiting, but when Hatsue came out he suddenly looked down, waved one clog-shod foot as though to drive away insects, and mumbled:

"The mosquitoes are terrible."

"Aren't they though?"

They went up the stone stairs leading to Yashiro Shrine. They could easily have run up them at a single breath, but instead, their hearts filled to over-flowing with contentment, they ascended slowly, as though savoring the pleasure of each separate step. When they reached the hundredth step, they paused as though reluctant to end this happy climb by going on to the top. The boy wanted to hold her hand, but the red-snappers prevented him.

Nature too again smiled on them. When they reached the top they turned around and looked out over the Gulf of Ise. The night sky was filled with stars and, as for clouds, there was only a low bank stretching across the horizon in the direction of the Chita Peninsula, through which soundless lightning ran from time to time. Nor was the sound of the waves strong, but coming regularly and peacefully, as though the sea were breathing in healthy slumber.

Passing through the pine grove, they reached the unpretentious shrine and stopped to worship. The boy was filled with pride by the loud and clear sound his formal handclap made, ringing out far and wide. So he clapped his hands again.

Hatsue had bowed her head and was praying. Against the white background of her kimono collar, the nape of her suntanned neck did not look particularly white, and yet it charmed Shinji more than the whitest of white necks could have done.

In his heart the boy reminded himself again of his happiness—the gods had indeed given him everything he had prayed for.

They prayed for a long while. And, in the very fact of their never once having doubted the providence of the gods, they could feel that providence around them.

The shrine office was brightly lit. Shinji called out and the priest came to the window.

Shinji's words were rather vague, and for a while the priest could make neither head nor tail of what the two had come about. But at last he understood, and Shinji presented him with one of the red-snappers as their offering to the gods. Receiving this splendid gift from the sea, the priest was reminded that presently he would be officiating at their wedding rites. He congratulated them heartily.

Climbing the path through the pine grove behind the shrine, they again savored the night's coolness. Though the sun was completely set, the cicadas were still singing. The path leading up to the lighthouse was steep. One of his hands was now free, so Shinji held the girl's hand.

"Me," said Shinji, "I'm thinking I'll take the exam and get a first mate's license. You can after you're twenty, you know."

"Oh, that'd be wonderful."

"If I got my license, I guess it'd be all right to have the wedding then."

Hatsue made no reply but only smiled shyly.

They rounded Woman's Slope and approached the residence of the light-house-keeper. The boy called out his greeting as always at the glass door, where they could again see the mistress's shadow moving about as she prepared supper.

The mistress opened the door. There in the darkness she saw the boy and his betrothed standing hesitantly.

"Oh, here you both are, and welcome," the wife called out in a loud voice, finally taking in both hands the large fish that was thrust out to her. Then she called back into the house:

"Father, here's Shinji-san with a fine red-snapper for us."

Taking his ease in one of the inner rooms, the lighthouse-keeper called back without getting up:

"Thanks as always. And this time it's congratulations too. Come in, come in."

"Please do come in," the mistress added. "Tomorrow Chiyoko's coming back, too."

The boy had not the slightest idea of all the emotions he had aroused in

Chiyoko, nor of the mental anguish she had experienced because of him, and he heard the mother's abrupt remark without attaching any significance to it.

Having been almost forcibly made to stay for supper, they stayed on for nearly an hour longer, and then it was decided that the lighthouse-keeper would show them around the lighthouse on their way home. Hatsue, having only recently returned to the island, had never seen the interior of the lighthouse.

First the lighthouse-keeper showed them the watchhouse. To reach it from the residence they walked along the edge of the small vegetable garden, where radishes had been planted just the day before, and climbed a flight of concrete steps. At the top there was the lighthouse, standing back against the mountain, and the watchhouse at the edge of the cliff that fell to the sea.

The beacon of the lighthouse, like a shining column of fog, was sweeping from right to left across the top of the watchhouse gable on the side facing the sea. The lighthouse-keeper opened the door of the watchhouse and, preceding them, turned on a light. They saw the drafting triangles hanging on a window frame, the scrupulously tidy desk with its leg for recording ships' movements, and, on a tripod facing the windows, the telescope.

The lighthouse-keeper opened a window, adjusted the telescope, and lowered it to the right height for Hatsue.

Hatsue took one look through the telescope, stopped and wiped the lens with her kimono sleeve, looked again, and gave a shout of joy:

"Oh, beautiful!"

Then, as Hatsue pointed to the lights in various directions, Shinji picked them out with his phenomenally keen eyes and explained them to her.

Keeping her eye to the telescope, Hatsue pointed first to the scores of lights dotting the sea to the southeast.

"Those? They're the lights of the drag-net boats. They come from over in Aichi Prefecture."

It seemed as though each of the vast number of lights out over the sea found its counterpart somewhere among the vast number of stars in the sky. Directly opposite was the beam from the lighthouse on Cape Irako. Behind it were scattered the lights of the town of Cape Irako, and to the left the lights of Shino Island were faintly visible.

At their extreme left they could see the Cape Noma lighthouse on the Chita Peninsula. To its right were the clustered lights of the port of Toyohama. That red light in the middle—that was the light on the port's breakwater. And, far to the right, there flickered the aircraft beacon on top of Mt. Oyama.

Hatsue gave a second cry of admiration. A large ocean-liner had just come into the field of the telescope. It was scarcely visible to the naked eye, but as the ship made its stately way across the telescope's field of view, its delicate reflection was so splendid and clear that the boy and girl compromised by taking turns at the telescope.

It seemed to be a combined cargo and passenger ship of two or three thousand tons. In a room off the promenade deck they could plainly see several tables spread with white cloths, and a number of chairs. Not a single person was visible. The room was apparently the dining-salon, and as they were examining its walls of white asphalt-tile, suddenly a white-uniformed steward entered from the right and passed in front of the windows. . . .

Presently the vessel, carrying green lights at bow and stern, passed out of the telescope's range and sailed away through the Irako Channel, bound for the Pacific.

The lighthouse-keeper took them next to the lighthouse itself. On the ground floor the electric generator was making a rumbling noise, surrounded by the odor of oil—oil cans, oil lamps, and tins of oil. Ascending the narrow spiral staircase, they found, housed in a small and lonely round room at the top, the source of the lighthouse's light, living its life away in silence.

Looking from the window, they watched the beam of light making its vast sweeps from right to left across the black, clamoring waves of the Irako Channel.

Tactfully, the lighthouse-keeper went back down the spiral staircase, leaving the two of them alone there.

The small round room at the top of the tower was enclosed in walls of polished wood. Its brass fittings gleaming, the thick glass lens revolved leisurely around the five-hundred-watt electric bulb, magnifying this source of light to sixty-five thousand candle power and maintaining a speed that produced a constant series of flashes. Reflections from the lens moved around the circular wooden walls and, to the accompaniment of the squeak-squeak-squeak revolving sound characteristic of lighthouses built before the turn of the century, these same reflections played across the backs of the boy and his betrothed, who had their faces pressed against the window.

They felt their cheeks so close together that they could touch at any moment, felt too the flaming heat of each other's cheeks. . . . Out in front of them stretched the unfathomable darkness, where the beam from the lighthouse was making its vast, regular sweeps. And the reflections of the lens kept circling around inside the little room, their patterns disrupted only at the spot where they crossed the backs of the white shirt and the flower-patterned kimono.

Once again it came to pass that Shinji, little given to thinking as he was, was lost in thought. He was thinking that in spite of all they'd been through, here they were in the end, free within the moral code to which they had been born, never once having been estranged from the providence of the gods . . . that, in short, it was this little island, enfolded in darkness, that had protected their happiness and brought their love to this fulfillment. . . .

Suddenly Hatsue turned to Shinji and laughed. From her sleeve she took out a small, pink shell and showed it to him.

"Remember this?"

"I remember."

The boy flashed his beautiful teeth in a smile. Then, from the breast pocket of his shirt, he took out the snapshot of Hatsue and showed it to her.

Hatsue touched the picture lightly with her own hand and then returned it. Her eyes were full of pride. She was thinking it was her picture that had protected Shinji.

But at this moment Shinji lifted his eyebrows. He knew it had been his own strength that had tided him through that perilous night.

GLOSSARY OF
CRITICAL TERMS

absurd. The "Literature of the Absurd" grew out of the "Theater of the Absurd," but novel or play, the works of Samuel Beckett are typical absurdist literature, which aims to reveal the fundamental absurdity or irrationality of all human life, particularly by deliberately distorting the normal conventions of literature as in *Waiting for Godot*. Kafka and Dostoevsky shared a similar aim in part, but while forcing convention to the limit, they did not turn upon it in their works.

aesthetic. Aesthetics is the branch of philosophy dealing with art and beauty, and a literature of pure aestheticism embodies the doctrine of art for art's sake. When we speak of a writer's aesthetic, the beauty or harmony of the logic of his metaphor-making is our subject.

affective fallacy. See *fallacy*.

allegory. See *metaphor*.

anti-hero. See *protagonist*.

archetype. See *metaphor*.

bildungsroman. From the German for "novel of education" and now meaning the novel of adolescence or growing up. In this collection, Mishima's *Sound of Waves* is a good example, as are *Tonio Kröger* and *Youth*.

black comedy.   See *tragi-comic*

carpe diem.   From the Latin phrase meaning "seize the day," and referring to the theme of short-lived youth and the pursuit of pleasure as typified in the seventeenth-century English poetry of Robert Herrick ("Gather ye rosebuds while ye may") and Andrew Marvel ("The grave's a fine and pleasant place / But none I think do there embrace"). **Ubi sunt** is the Latin phrase that asks "Where are?"—meaning where are the joys of yesterday?—and so suggests the impermanence of life that prompts the idea of *carpe diem.*

catharsis.   Takes its literary meaning from Aristotle's discussion of the effects of tragedy upon an audience purged of its emotions and conflicts and so spiritually renewed. Catharsis is an experience of discharge and growth, and it occurs in readers and characters both. Generally a catharsis involves what James Joyce termed an **epiphany,** meaning a sudden revelation or insight into basic meaning. Epiphany may also refer to that moment in a fiction—as when a work's climax is made from the achievement of awareness on the part of its protagonist. But the epiphany is the perception; the process of realizing it before and after is the catharsis.

classicism.   An idea of formal elegance in literature, derived from Greek and Roman emphasis on clarity, simplicity, dignity, balance, and order achieved through restraint of emotion and passion. **Neoclassicism** refers to the revival of this doctrine, particularly in eighteenth-century literature (Racine, Pope). Neoclassicism also emphasizes the Aristotelian doctrine of the **unities,** calling for unity of time, place, and action in a literary work—in the drama meaning a play with a single plot that takes place in only one place in a single day.

coda.   From the Latin word meaning "tail," a coda refers to an independent passage at the end of a literary or musical work, as in the passage entitled "The Twelve Mortal Men" that concludes Carson McCullers' *The Ballad of the Sad Café.* **Epilogue** also refers to such a passage, but with more of the sense of "afterword"; in both coda and epilogue summation is the central purpose, but as in music we may expect the coda to reenact a work's argument in small scale as it makes its summary.

convention.   See *genre.*

counterpoint.   See *irony.*

criticism.   The act of interpretation, usually taken to mean the act of convincing others that what a work of literature means to the critic is what it should mean to all other readers. Because literature by definition means a different thing to each of its readers, the best criticism recognizes this and takes the form of a debate whose purpose is not to convince but to enlarge, by a process of sharing, the meaning that an individual discovers for himself. Schools of criticism follow from tools—psychological, biographical, political, etc.—favored by individual critics. Readers and writers, however, tend to use more than one tool, suggesting that the critic do so as well.

denouement. From the French for "unraveling" and referring to the final explanation of a plot's complexities by means of the revelation of earlier stages of cause and effect, or of deepest motives. "The butler did it" is a typical denouement in a phrase.

deus ex machina. A Latin phrase meaning "god from a machine," once referring to an actual device employed by Euripides to bring about the solution of his dramas' conflicts, and now meaning a trick ending based on the intervention of outside fate that is not justified by a work's plot. In a western novel the cavalry is a *deus ex machina* when it arrives, uncalled for, at the last minute to rescue us.

dramatic monologue. See *monologue.*

epic. Referring traditionally to such works as Homer's *Iliad* and to *Beowulf,* but more generally referring to a clearly-defined heroic struggle with a force larger than man himself—as in the description of *One Day in the Life of Ivan Denisovich* as the epic story of Shukov's survival.

epilogue. See *coda.*

epiphany. See *catharsis.*

existentialism. A contemporary philosophical movement made popular in France during the 1940's by thinker Jean-Paul Sartre, who declared that "Man is alone in a godless universe," and having its origins in the work of Kierkegaard and Nietzsche in the nineteenth century. Existentialists believe that "existence precedes essence," by which they mean that man has no essential self that transcends individual existence, that he is what he himself has become at any one moment, and that he is responsible to himself alone. The existentialist conception of a purely meaningless existence that follows the abandonment of human illusions underlies absurdist literature.

fallacy. A false argument, but often made with a purpose in literature that displays the erroneous reasoning of its characters for our benefit. The **pathetic fallacy,** the understanding of non-human objects in human terms—"a leaf cries loneliness"—is closely involved with the formation of metaphors, and therefore central to all art. Criticism defines two central fallacies of its own: the **intentional fallacy,** the understanding that a novel, for example, means what its author intended, his expressed purpose in writing; and the **affective fallacy,** that confuses the novel's meaning with its results on the reader. These fallacies in fact account for the motivation of our reading in the first place, but we must not mistake them for the essential debate with another human mind that reading ultimately can be.

form.   The organization of content in literature. Form is the expression of the writer's decision making, his choice of narrative technique, of words and images, of plot, etc., and as such it is ultimately the impress of the writer's self upon experience. This impress is part and parcel of the experience itself, for ultimately the writer can only tell his story in his unique way. **Style** is a component of form, a more easily recognized way of telling peculiar to a particular author and common to all his works. **Structure** refers more specifically to the exact method of construction employed, and to discerned patterns within a composition, both resulting in final shape, or form. **Formalism** refers to a doctrine that elevates form, as opposed to experience or a novel's social content, believing ultimately that the medium is the message, and so more important than what is actually narrated. However, in life shape and substance come united, nor should they be separated in any art, for no matter how great the artist's perspective, he remains a part of the world he writes about.

formalism.   See *form.*

genre.   Genre refers to the categories of literature—novel, short novel, poem, play, epic, etc. The **conventions** of a genre refer to the accepted patterns for composing in these categories at any particular time. Writers may be more or less experimental in their obedience to the conventions of a particular genre, and in their determination of the validity of these conventions occurs the evolution of literature, as from modern to contemporary.

gothic.   Referring to medieval architecture, and in literature to the conventions of late-eighteenth-century horror fiction, as in the novels of Ann Radcliffe. Gothic is discussed at length in the introduction to *The Ballad of the Sad Café.*

grotesque.   Refers to a writer's use of images of deformity and disgust, and of actions that appear subhuman in their conception. This term is discussed at length in the introduction to *The Ballad of the Sad Café.*

hero.   See *protagonist.*

hubris.   The sin of pride, from the Greek word for "insolence," and a frequent flaw of the tragic hero.

image.   Literally a picture: both the word-picture of the author and the picture we find in an author's words. As all literature intends to describe, images are the bedrock of fiction, though we may find them of greater strength and subtlety in the works of different writers. Faulkner's *Old Man* is a short novel of strong imagery, which also employs the technique of **montage,** or the superimposition of image upon image, as well as the joining of image fragments into a new whole.

intentional fallacy. See *fallacy.*

interior monologue. See *monologue.*

irony. Irony occurs when what is said is the opposite of what is meant. It is ever present in literature, for life is an ironic experience, individual man always knowing less than what is intended and believing that he knows it all. When an author has told us more than his individual characters know, we experience a sense of irony in our evaluation of their behavior, which may appear ridiculous to those granted a larger perspective; but irony also suggests that even our enlarged perspective may be superseded, and so it continually teaches humility. **Counterpoint** is frequently a technique of irony, and refers to the juxtaposition of opposites within a single work. **Satire** frequently incorporates irony, but generally describes a work of literature aimed at exposing the inherent fallacy of a particular point of view or cause.

metaphor. All art is metaphor, for art is an unreal communication about the real. Art begins with images, the sun for example, but art must communicate the author's subjective experience of the sun—a ruby setting in the west. That comparison, explicit or inexplicit, is a metaphor. **Sign, simile, allegory,** and **symbol** are terms that measure the degree to which the comparisons of metaphor are made less explicit. A ruby setting in the west is not a ruby but the sun, and the degree to which it can be anything else is the degree to which a metaphor is symbolic—a cross can mean many things. Ambiguity of meaning within the comparison any metaphor makes may be more or less desirable in terms of an author's goals, and in terms of the fixity of a world view within any particular historical period. Allegory prevailed in the middle ages, symbolism today, when any particular meaning seems uncertain and approximate. **Archetypes** refer to original patterns, or the most fundamental of metaphors; the conception of the Hero is an archetype, as is the conception of a Messiah. Both are metaphors comparing man with what he might be.

monologue. Meaning literally "one voice," and a character talking to himself, as in **soliloquy** or **interior monologue;** the latter may include a more specific voicing of the thoughts occuring within the character's head at the particular moment involved. When these thoughts are given to us without being voiced, the writer pretending to transcribe thought as it occurs in the form it occurs, the technique called **stream of consciousness** is being employed. **Dramatic monologue** refers to a literary genre in which a single character talks to us with the fiction that he is talking to another person, present or not, as a silent interlocutor. Drama is created by the tension between the speaker and his fictional audience, and witnessing that drama the reader, the ultimate audience, is taught the essential character of the speaker, as in Dostoevsky's *Notes from the Underground,* whose introduction provides a further discussion of the concept of dramatic monologue.

montage.   See *image.*

myth.   A myth is the oldest story that people believe in, despite the fact that it cannot be proved. The Greek myths refer to the body of legends at the basis of Greek culture. The transmission of these legends over centuries has obscured the particular events or content of their stories, reducing them to narratives in which human behavior is distilled to its most fundamental essence.

naturalism.   See *realism.*

neoclassicism.   See *classicism.*

nihilism.   The belief in nothing without the correspondent belief in everything. Nihilism is the philosophy of total and negative denial of meaning and transcends existentialism. It is the consequence of the deepest skepticism, of a cynicism that is even cynical of itself.

parable.   A story that aims to teach, a fiction designed to illustrate a particular moral principle by making an explicit comparison between that principle as found in the fiction and in actuality.

paradox.   Paradox refers to an argument that appears to contradict itself and which in so doing appeals to our sense of reason for a solution. Literature teaches us to solve paradoxes by increasing our self-knowledge, for often what appears paradoxical may be solved on the human rather than the individual level.

pastoral.   Fiction or poetry of rural life celebrating rural virtues and frequently composed in the most civilized societies with no experience of the rural. Thus a pastoral is a picture of rural life that is aesthetically satisfying because it is in fact a picture of paradise in the country that is longed for but non-existent. *The Sound of Waves* is a modern pastoral, though a realistic one, that celebrates innocence as all pastorals do.

pathetic fallacy.   See *fallacy.*

persona.   Persona is a Latin word meaning mask and referring to a character or narrator who seems to speak directly for the author. See the discussion of persona in the introduction to Conrad's *Youth.*

picaresque.   *Tom Jones* is a picaresque novel because it depicts the wandering adventures of a rogue from the lower classes who triumphs with native shrewdness over the enlightened upper classes.

plot.   The sequence of events in a story as we read it, and progressing from conflict to climax to denouement. **Story** refers to the chronological sequence of events from earliest to latest, plot to the sequence given to us by the author.

primitive. From an earlier, less-sophisticated or civilized culture. Primitive form refers to a greater emphasis on substance and use, rather than on style and structure. Primitive characters may be genuine (American Indians) or modern throwbacks, as in the convict of Faulkner's *Old Man*. Primitivism in the arts is the worship of the Noble Savage and others like him. Mishima's *Sound of Waves* and Faulkner's *Old Man* both embody a degree of primitivism in their preference for the uncivilized and unselfconscious.

protagonist. The main character of a literary work, to whom its action accrues. Protagonist is a simpler conception than **hero** and its opposite **antihero**, or the hero who no longer believes in heroism, for protagonist implies no moral distinction, and indeed the protagonist may be a villain. However, historic emphasis has drawn the terms hero and protagonist together, so that it is difficult to image a hero who is not a protagonist. But the hero is involved in a quest understood as a contest with forces beyond himself, while the protagonist is more the subject of a story. With the shift in fiction from adventure to inner analysis, the term hero becomes less applicable than the more passive protagonist.

realism. The doctrine of faithfulness to life in art—but with the knowledge that no art can ever be real. Realism does not copy life, rather it creates life in the world of art with the intention of making its comparison with the world more explicit. **Verisimilitude** is the measure of accuracy in art's portrayal of the real. **Regionalism** is realism applied to a particular region and generally incorporating the dialect spoken in that place—Richard Wright and William Faulkner are Southern realists, among other things. Surrealism is a style of art that reverses the aims of realism which it attempts to supersede. But reality may supersede art with a surrealism of its own as Carson McCullers understood (see the introduction to *The Ballad of the Sad Café*). **Naturalism** is another term for realism, but the naturalistic novel of Zola and Balzac, writers who read newspapers for their plots, implies as well a downward movement in its characters caused by decay of the social fabric.

regionalism. See *realism*.

romance. Prose fiction originates in the late-Greek romances, tales of abduction, adventure, love, and mistaken identity. By the middle ages the term came to refer to heroic narratives, generally embodying the principles of chivalry and courtly love. Modern usage applies romance to tales of colorful and exotic setting that emphasize passion and the supernatural for the purpose of excitement without enlightenment. Romance is popular fiction, but not all popular fiction is romance.

romanticism.   Romanticism in literature refers to the doctrine of the supreme imagination, of imaginative or subjective reason as opposed to objective reason, and of the imagination's ability to find the universal in the specific—to "see the world in a grain of sand," as William Blake put it. The Romantic period in literature followed the American and French Revolutions, continued into the nineteenth century, and continues in much that we call modern or contemporary. Because of the nature of its heroes, romanticism has been identified with both escapism and existentialism, but these terms refer instead only to elements of romanticism's central doctrine of imagination.

satire.   See *irony.*

sign.   See *metaphor.*

simile.   See *metaphor.*

soliloquy.   See *monologue.*

story.   See *plot.*

stream of consciousness.   See *monologue.*

structure.   See *form.*

style.   See *form.*

surrealism.   See *realism.*

symbol.   See *metaphor.*

tragi-comic.   Applies to works of literature which use the comic to offset the tragic, or find tragic reasons beneath laughter as particularly in **black comedy** or **black humor,** a technique of absurd literature. With the breakdown of literary conventions and genres in modern times that mistrust simple laughter and have lost faith in the tragic hero comes the understanding that life is tragi-comic and that literature must reflect a life so conceived.

ubi sunt.   See *carpe diem.*

unities.   See *classicism.*

verisimilitude.   See *realism.*

1 2 3 4 5 6 7 8 9 0